OFFICIAL GUIDE TO THE ACT ASSESSMENT

BY

American College Testing

A Harvest Test Preparation Book
Harcourt Brace & Company
San Diego New York London

ACT endorses the *Code of Fair Testing Practices in Education,* a statement of the obligations to test takers of those who develop, administer, or use educational tests and data. The *Code* sets forth criteria for fairness in four areas: developing and selecting appropriate tests, interpreting test scores, striving for fairness, and informing test takers. ACT is committed to ensuring that each of its testing programs upholds the *Code's* standards as they apply to test developers.

A copy of the full *Code* may be obtained free of charge from ACT Publications, P.O. Box 168, Iowa City, Iowa 52243, 319/337-1429.

Inquiries concerning this publication should be mailed to:
ACT Publications
P.O. Box 168
Iowa City, Iowa 52243

Printed in the United States of America

Library of Congress Cataloging-in-Publication Data

Official guide to the ACT Assessment / by ACT, American College Testing [Program].—1st ed.
ISBN 0-15-600995-1
1. ACT Assessment—Study guides. I. American College Testing Program.
LB2353.48.035 1990
378.1′664—dc20 90-37774

ISBN 0-15-600995-1

First edition
I H G F E D

CONTENTS

A LETTER TO THE STUDENT

Congratulations!

Since you're reading this book, you must be close to completing an important stage in your life and looking forward to new challenges.

This is a good time to stop and remind yourself how much you've already accomplished. Think about all the classes you've taken, the work you've completed, the skills you've learned, the abilities you've developed, and the friends you've made. High school isn't easy. Even if you've had fun during these years, you've also done a great deal of work, and you should give yourself credit for all that effort.

Because you've accomplished so much, you now have important decisions to make. Will you go to college? Will you begin college immediately after high school, or do you plan to take some time to work or travel first? What kind of college do you prefer: large or small, state or private, liberal arts or practical arts, close to home or across the country? Where will you live: at home, in a dorm, in an apartment? Are you interested in studying abroad? How will you pay for college? Do you hope to receive a scholarship or grant? Do you need or want to have a job while you're in school? If you have a job, will you work during the summer, during the school year, or both?

You may feel overwhelmed by the number of decisions you have to make. We at ACT realize how tough these decisions are, and we want to help. A number of our services are designed to help you as you make important decisions about the years after high school; we encourage you to see your school counselor to learn about ACT services.

The purpose of this book is to help you with what for many students is an important stage in preparing for college—taking college admission exams, especially the ACT Assessment. We hope you find our book helpful. As you read it, remember: Taking the ACT Assessment is one sign you've already accomplished a great deal.

We wish you success as you move on to new accomplishments!

1
PURPOSE OF THIS BOOK

1 PURPOSE OF THIS BOOK

The purpose of this book is to supplement the booklet *Preparing for the ACT Assessment* in making available to as many students as possible information about the ACT Assessment:

- the content of the exam,
- the procedures you'll follow when you're actually taking the exam,
- the types of questions you can expect to find on the exam, and
- suggestions on how you might approach the questions.

You'll find information about the ACT, general test-taking strategies, some suggested specific strategies for each of the four tests in the ACT Assessment (English, Mathematics, Reading, and Science Reasoning), and actual sample ACT exams you can use for practice. With those sample tests, you'll find detailed explanatory answers that can help with your review.

The more you know about what to expect on **any** test you take, the more accurately your performance on that test should reflect your overall preparation for it and your abilities in the areas it measures. Knowing what to expect can help reduce any nervousness you may feel as you approach the test. Not only will this knowledge make you more comfortable, it can also help prevent your performance on the test from being unfairly hampered by outside factors, like worrying about what's going to happen next.

This book is intended to help you **know what to expect** when you take the ACT so you can relax and concentrate on doing your best.

Knowing what to expect on a test can reduce your nervousness.

USING THIS BOOK

You'll find that there are a number of different ways to use this book, whether you use it on your own, in a review class at school, or in an informal study group with friends. Some people may want to use it to do a quick general review just before taking the ACT. Others may want to space their review out over several weeks and cover all or most of the material in the book thoroughly. Still others may want to familiarize themselves with the format of the ACT quickly and then concentrate only on those academic areas in which they feel they need work.

No matter which way you choose, the book has been arranged to make it easy to use:

The **table of contents** serves as a guide to the different sections of the book.

The **colored arrows** running down the outside edge of the book correspond to the sections identified in the table of contents. They allow you to see at a glance where each section is located.

The **headings** at the top of each page, which also refer to the table of contents, provide another way for you to find what you're looking for.

We suggest that you take a little time to familiarize yourself with the layout of the book and to decide what sort of review and practice you're interested in. Regardless of whether you plan to spend a few hours or a few weeks preparing for the ACT, we urge you to read at least two sections of this book carefully:

- the description of how the ACT Assessment is administered (Section 4), and
- the description of the content and format of the four tests in the ACT (Section 6).

Here are some possible **study patterns for this book.** Feel free to choose one of these study plans or create your own.

If you feel pretty confident about your test-taking abilities and just want to know a little more about the ACT, read the first few sections of the book, paying special attention to Section 4 and to Section 6, which includes specific strategies for approaching each of the four tests in the ACT Assessment. If you wish, try taking one of the sample ACT exams included in Section 9 and checking your answers against the answer key or the explanatory answers. If you're satisfied with your performance on that sample exam, you may decide you're ready to take the ACT without any further preparation.

If your score on any of the tests in the first sample exam isn't as high as you wanted, try rereading the suggested strategies for approaching that test in Section 6. Then work through the sample test included in that section. If you still want more practice, turn to the other sample exam in Section 9.

Take advantage of the two-part explanatory answers with the sample ACT exams in Section 9. They're designed to help you understand the process of arriving at the correct answers to the test questions. Read all of the explanatory answers for an entire exam, if you like, or just the ones for the questions you missed. (The purpose and uses of these explanatory answers are discussed in more detail at the beginning of Section 9.)

If you're concerned about the time limits for the ACT, use the practice tests in Sections 6 and 9 to experiment with different strategies for pacing yourself. Through practice, you'll find the strategy that works best for you.

If you feel quite confident in all the areas tested except one, concentrate on just that area, working through all three sample tests for that subject.

You may feel nervous about test taking. Most people do. If you're concerned that your nervousness may prevent you from doing your best on the ACT, you might find it helpful to work through the materials in this book at home, in familiar, relaxing, and comfortable surroundings. On the other hand, you might find it easier to control your nervousness on exam day if you simulate the actual test situation as closely as possible beforehand. If that's the case, ask one of your teachers to arrange for you and a group of your friends to take one of the sample exams in a classroom in your school.

As you can see, there are a number of ways to take advantage of the materials offered in this book. Consider your own abilities and needs, perhaps with the advice of a teacher. Then decide what's best for you.

ABOUT THE ACT ASSESSMENT

The ACT Assessment is a standardized examination designed to measure academic achievement in four major curriculum areas: English, mathematics, reading, and natural sciences. Materials covered in the four tests that make up the ACT Assessment correspond very closely to topics covered in typical high school classes. Each of the four tests—English, Mathematics, Reading, and Science Reasoning—is described in detail in Section 6 of this book.

Because the ACT Assessment isn't an intelligence test, it shouldn't be seen as a measure of your intellectual capability. Instead, it's been carefully designed—using surveys of classroom teachers, reviews of curriculum guides for schools all over the country, and advice from curriculum specialists and college faculty—to be one effective tool for evaluating your readiness for college work.

The tests making up the ACT Assessment consist of tasks that ask you to use your skills and knowledge. You're **not** required to memorize facts or vocabulary to do well on the ACT. Of course, all the terms and formulas and other facts you've learned over the years will be useful to you when you take the tests, but last-minute cramming—for instance, memorizing 5,000 vocabulary words or the entire periodic table of chemical elements or the significance of a long list of dates like April 10, 1849, and May 22, 1931*—while no doubt an exciting way to spend a Saturday night, won't directly improve your performance on the ACT.

What you **can** do to improve your performance—on the ACT or any test—is to find out ahead of time what tasks you'll be expected to perform and to think about how you can use your unique abilities to perform those tasks.

First sale of canned rattlesnake meat, 1931.

*Walter Hunt created and patented the safety pin on April 10, 1849.

The first sale of canned rattlesnake meat was by Floridian Products Corporation on May 22, 1931.

2
PREPARING FOR THE ACT ASSESSMENT

2
PREPARING FOR THE ACT ASSESSMENT

The first thing you should realize is that you've been preparing for the ACT Assessment for **years.** The best possible preparation for a college admission test is active, thoughtful high school course work. If you've been taking challenging courses, paying attention in class, doing your homework, and thinking about the assignments, you've already done most of the preparing you need to do for the ACT.

Of course, it's a good idea to think about how you'll use what you've learned in school when you take the ACT. What kind of approach and preparation for this exam will allow you to demonstrate most fully the abilities and skills you've developed over the years? How can you make sure that you'll do your best on the exam?

It might be helpful to compare taking the ACT (or any other significant exam) to playing an important match in tennis, or meeting a rival school in football, or performing in a music concert, or facing another team in debate, or acting a role in a play. The best way to get ready for a game or performance is to prepare actively: practice the skills required, learn strategies to enable you to demonstrate your strengths, exercise your mind and body, learn how to deal with the stress of the moment and turn it to your advantage.

To get ready for an important test, you need to prepare in much the same way. You need to learn (do your course work), exercise your mind (through discussion, reading, problem-solving), take care of your body (it's difficult for your mind to function well when your body is hungry or tired), and develop strategies (find out in advance as much as you can about the test so you'll know what to expect).

You started preparing for the ACT years ago. This book will help you build on what you've already done and feel confident that you can do your best on the exam.

PHYSICAL PREPARATION

Physical preparation may seem like an odd place to start. After all, taking an exam isn't exactly like playing a game of soccer. So why should you prepare yourself **physically**?

Think of the body as the mind's support system. Being sure that your body is at peak performance the morning you take the ACT will help your mind work at its peak, too.

This is not the time to neglect your usual **exercise.** Be sure you get plenty of physical activity in the days before the exam. Hiking, running, walking, biking, swimming, sports—all the aerobic exercises you regularly enjoy will improve your body's performance.

Diet is also important. You've probably heard the standard advice: "Be sure to eat a **good breakfast** before you take the test." That's sensible advice, but it may be more complicated than it sounds at first.

For one thing, what exactly **is** a "good breakfast"? A two-egg omelet, three strips of bacon, two slices of whole grain toast, fruit, and milk? Cereal, milk, and juice? Pancakes with butter and syrup, plus sausages and hash browns? A couple of donuts and black coffee?

You should probably select the healthiest breakfast **you** are accustomed to. If you routinely eat a very light breakfast, it makes sense to choose your **best** light breakfast, not switch to something entirely new. If you usually have a bowl of cereal and juice, for example, you probably shouldn't have a huge stack of pancakes the morning of an exam. On the other hand, if you're accustomed to a substantial breakfast, it would be a mistake to skip breakfast altogether, or even to eat significantly less than you're used to.

A sugary breakfast will probably work against you. While it may give you an initial charge of energy to start the morning, that energy will most likely burn off before you're halfway through.

What exactly is a "good breakfast"?

Sleep is another need you should keep in mind. The common wisdom says, "Get plenty of sleep the night before the test." But how much sleep is "plenty"? Again, keep in mind **your** typical schedule. If you routinely go to bed at 11:00, this is probably not the time to stay up until 2:30. On the other hand, going to bed at 8:00 may also be a mistake. If you suddenly go to bed much earlier than your body is used to, you may find yourself tossing and turning for three hours, and you'll be more tired than you would have been if you'd watched television or read or shot baskets during that time.

Somebody may suggest to you that you'll do better on the test if you "take something." This simply isn't true. The effect on your body of doing drugs is negative. Period.

The advice you hear often focuses on just **the day before the test.** You'll find, however, that the amount of sleep and exercise you get—not just the day before the test, but for days and even weeks before—will make a difference in how you feel and how you are able to perform. Similarly, it's not just what you eat for breakfast the morning of test day, but what you've eaten for several days before, that gives you the power you need to perform well.

Going to bed much earlier than your body is used to may be a mistake.

MENTAL PREPARATION

Just as good physical preparation can make you feel alert and physically confident, good mental preparation can make you feel calm and mentally confident.

As we've said before, the best mental preparation for the ACT is solid schoolwork. However, there are some things you can do to bolster your confidence as well.

Learn as much as you can about what you're going to be asked to do. That's what this book is for, after all. Surprises may be fine for a birthday party, but they can be very upsetting when they turn up on tests. The more you know about a test in advance, the more confident you can feel.

Surprises may be fine for birthday parties, but they can be very upsetting when they turn up on tests.

For any kind of exam, find out what kinds of information you'll be expected to know. Will you be asked to recall factual material (dates, definitions, mathematical formulas, names)? Will you be asked to discuss the importance of something you've been studying (like the impact of the cotton gin or the pencil or television or baseball on American economic development)? Will you be asked to compare and contrast different theories? Will logical processes be central to the test? Arithmetic procedures?

Once you know **what** to expect, you can concentrate on **how** to do the work. For instance, if a mathematics test will ask you to determine the relative dimensions of parallelograms, you can put all those other fascinating geometric figures out of your mind for a while and focus your attention on the properties of rectangles and squares and rhomboids.

Maybe this seems obvious to you, but focusing attention on the task at hand is often harder than it sounds. Training yourself to concentrate your mental energies on small, manageable jobs instead of letting yourself be distracted by all sorts of other interesting things will have long-term benefits, including making it easier for you to prepare yourself mentally for any test.

Decide what sort of review you need for the particular test. Should you quickly skim your textbook's discussion of the settlement of Plymouth Plantation, concentrating just on key points and headings? Or should you carefully reread the entire chapter? For a test on Spanish verbs, do you need to make a review chart with all those different verb endings, or are you confident enough just to practice reciting them?

An important part of mental preparation is learning to appreciate and use your particular abilities. Maybe your best friend needs to spend several hours memorizing tree classifications for the same science test that you can do well on with only a quick review of pin oaks, red oaks, white oaks, and live oaks. Or maybe you need to spend several hours of careful concentration, while she seems to need only a half-hour review. The important thing is to know your abilities and to make your study decisions based on what **you** need to do.

Plan your study time. If you have three weeks to get ready for an exam, it's pretty easy to let yourself get talked into spending a few hours playing video games. After all, you still have three weeks left. Unfortunately, something else always seems to come up: going on a date, seeing a movie, watching your favorite television show, even cleaning your room may seem more interesting than studying for a test that's still two weeks away. Then there's that paper assignment you'd forgotten about. You've got to go to the library, read a couple of books, and type the paper. Well, you still have a week to study for that test, anyway. But somehow the days disappear and you find yourself frantically cramming the night before the test, overwhelmed by just how much material you have to cover.

If this sounds familiar, try setting up a reasonable schedule for studying—for a classroom test or for the ACT exam. **Set aside small amounts of time** for studying over several days, or even weeks, so that you won't have so much to do at once that you get swamped. For some people, it's much too easy to scrap the whole plan once there's a small change in it, so **make your schedule flexible** enough to allow for a surprise homework assignment or some unexpected fun. And find a way to **reward yourself** as you get the work done, even if it's just a checklist you can mark.

In setting up a schedule to prepare for the ACT exam, refer to the suggestions in Section 1 for some ideas. Figure out how you can best use the materials in this book, estimate the time you want and need to spend, and plan a schedule that will allow you to complete the materials at least several days before your scheduled exam date. If something interferes with your plan, don't discard your schedule; just revise it to a more manageable one. You can still benefit from a scaled-down plan.

Develop a positive mental attitude.

Develop a positive mental attitude. In addition to learning the material you'll be tested on and reviewing to make sure it's fresh in your mind, it's important to go into an exam with a good mental attitude, confident that you can do your best. While confidence obviously isn't enough by itself to produce good performance on a test, a real lack of confidence can hurt your performance.

Some small changes can make a surprising difference. For example, how you imagine yourself taking the exam may affect how well you actually do. Negative thoughts have a way of turning into negative actions. So practice positive thinking: imagine yourself meeting the challenge of the exam with ease, successfully. The day of the test, tell yourself you intend to do your best, and act as if you mean it. You probably won't get a perfect score, but that's not the point. You want to be sure you do as well as you can against the most important measure: your own capabilities. The real satisfaction doesn't lie in meeting somebody else's expectations for you, but in knowing that you've met your own expectations—that you've done your personal best.

3
REGISTERING FOR THE ACT ASSESSMENT

3

REGISTERING FOR THE ACT ASSESSMENT

SELECTING A TEST DATE

Obviously, one of the first decisions you'll need to make is **when** to take the ACT exam. There are several factors to consider:

- When is the ACT being offered nearby?
- When does each college or scholarship agency you're interested in need to have your scores?
- Where do you stand in your high school academic program?
- Will you take the ACT only once, or more than once?

Let's take a look at each of these considerations in turn.

The ACT Assessment is offered nationally five times a year, between October and June. However, it's not offered at every test center on each of those dates. If you need to take the ACT on a day other than Saturday because of religious reasons, you'll want to be especially attentive in selecting a test date because the non-Saturday dates may be less frequent.

One of the first things you should find out, then, is where and when the ACT is being offered in your area. Your high school guidance counselor should be able to give you that information. It's also printed in the booklet *Registering for the ACT Assessment,* which is available free from your school counselor. (See the inside cover of this book for information on requesting a copy if it's not available from your high school.) Select a test date and location that are convenient for you. Often your own or a neighboring school will serve as a test center.

One important decision is whether you should take the ACT during your junior or senior year in high school, and a number of factors will affect your decision. First, you should find out when the colleges you're interested in need to have your test scores. Is there a special program or scholarship you want to apply for? If so, is there a deadline by which you need to have test scores submitted to the college or agency?

It takes between four and seven weeks after your test date for your scores to arrive, so be sure to allow enough time. You may not be certain yet which school or program you'll decide on. That's okay. Just be sure you're doing everything, including taking the ACT, early enough to keep all your options open.

Another consideration is where you stand in your high school course work. If you're in a college-prep program and taking "heavy" courses in your sophomore and junior years, it may be especially important for you to take the ACT in your junior year, while those subjects are fresh in your memory. If, on the other hand, you're taking some of the classes covering content tested by the ACT during your senior year, it's reasonable to assume that your performance on the ACT might be better then.

Perhaps you'll decide to take the ACT more than once, in hopes of improving your score. In that case, it's especially important to take the exam early enough to allow for a second round.

There are several advantages to taking the ACT in your junior year:

- You've probably completed much of the course work corresponding to the material covered by the ACT.
- You'll have your ACT scores and other information in time to help make decisions about your final year of high school course work. (For example, you may decide to take additional classes in an area in which your test score was low.)
- Colleges will know of your interests and have your scores in time to contact you during the summer before your senior year, when many of them like to send information about such things as admissions, advanced placement, and special programs to prospective students.
- You'll have your ACT scores and information from colleges in time to make decisions about visiting campuses or contacting schools.
- You'll still have the opportunity to take the ACT a second time if you feel your scores don't accurately reflect your ability.

Colleges will have your scores in time to contact you during the summer before your senior year.

TEST INFORMATION RELEASE

On certain test dates, you may request (for an additional fee) a copy of the test questions used to determine your score, a copy of your answers, a list of the correct answers, and a copy of the table used to convert raw scores to reported scores. The service isn't offered for all dates, so if you're interested in receiving this information, you'll need to check the dates in *Registering for the ACT Assessment* to be sure you're registering for a date on which the service is available.

REGISTERING

You can usually get an ACT registration packet from your high school counselor. If no registration packets are available, you or your counselor can write or call ACT. The address appears on the inside front cover of this book.

The ACT registration packet includes a copy of the booklet *Registering for the ACT Assessment.* The booklet describes the steps you need to take to register for the ACT exam and lists deadlines for mailing your registration form and payment.

It's important to realize that **you must register in advance for the ACT exam.** Standby or walk-in registration on the day of the test is **not** permitted.

See the registration packet for instructions for special registrations—if, for example, your religious beliefs prevent you from taking the exam on Saturday, or if you have special physical requirements.

4
AT THE TEST CENTER

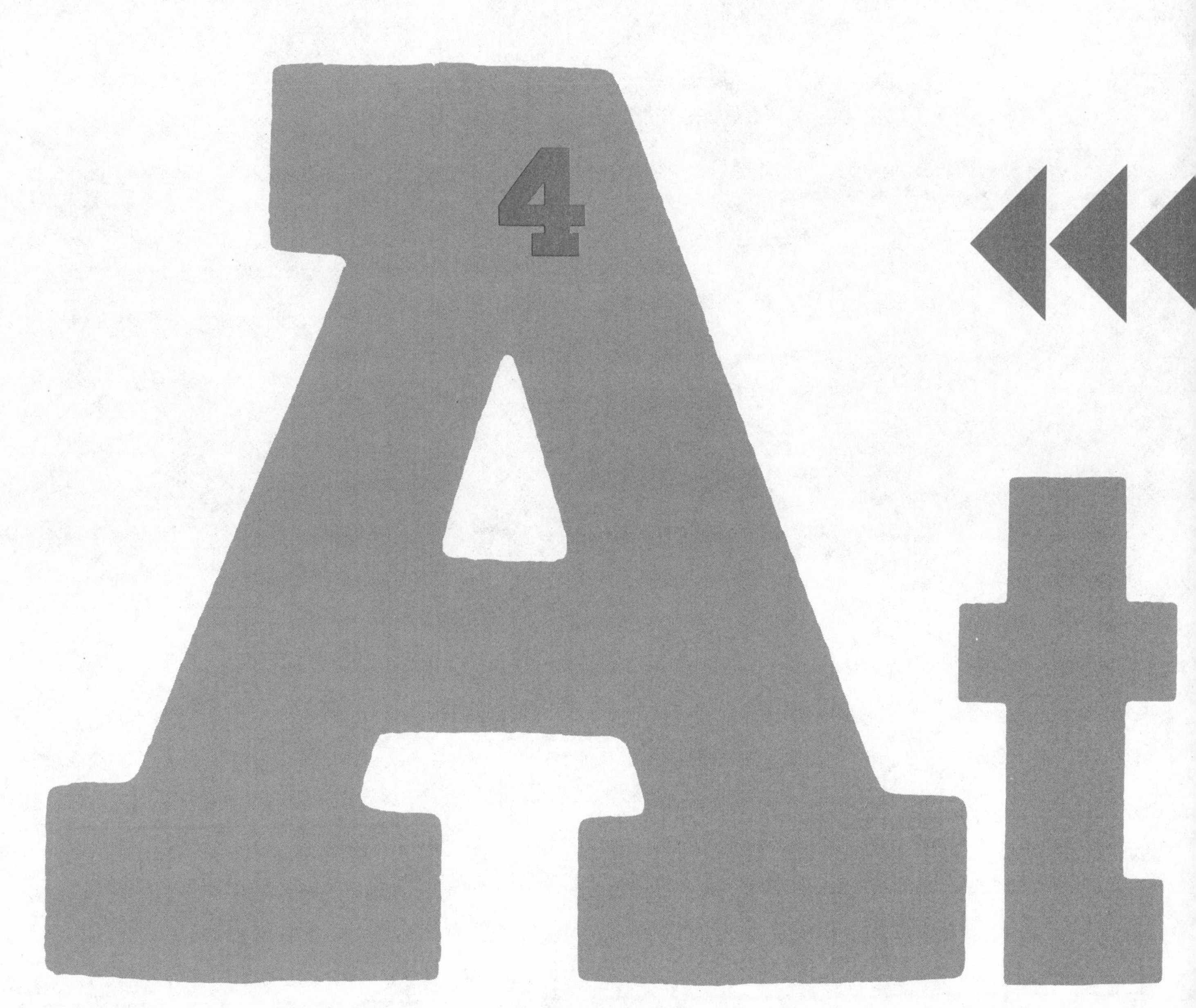

4
AT THE TEST CENTER

ARRIVING AT THE TEST CENTER

You'll be asked to **report at the test center by 8:00 a.m.** The doors may be closed after that, and no one arriving late may be admitted. Under no circumstances will you be admitted after the actual timed test has begun, so be **sure** to arrive on time.

You may need to walk a few blocks to arrive at the test center, or you may need to drive several hours, perhaps to an unfamiliar city. Whatever your situation, be certain to allow plenty of time. If the test is being administered in a place that's new to you, you might consider finding the location the night before the test or even a few days in advance.

Test centers vary considerably. You may be taking the ACT in your own high school, at a local community college, or in a large building on a nearby university campus. Your surroundings may be quite familiar, or they may be uncomfortably new. If they're new, allow yourself a few extra minutes to get used to the place. Then forget about it so you can concentrate on the test.

It's probably best to **bring with you only the things you'll need that morning,** since other materials will just be in your way. Be sure to bring:

- several sharpened **pencils with erasers,**
- your **admission ticket,** and
- your **photo ID** or **letter of identification.**

If you need **glasses or contacts** for reading, bring them, too, of course.

If you wish to pace yourself, bring a **watch.** Not all testing centers have wall clocks.

What to wear? Try making this decision ahead of time so you'll have one less thing to think about on the morning of the test. Keep in mind that the building used for administering the ACT is often one not normally used on a Saturday. As a result, you may find that the heat or air conditioning has been turned off. It's a good idea to dress in layers so that you can adjust to the temperature you find in your room.

Remember, too, that you're going to be sitting in the same place for about four hours. Wearing something you're especially comfortable in may make you better able to relax and concentrate on the test. For many people, what they're wearing can make a difference in how they feel about themselves. Picking something you like and feel good wearing may give you a little extra boost of confidence.

WHAT TO EXPECT AT THE TEST CENTER

The way **check-in procedures** are handled at a particular test center depends on such things as how many students are taking the ACT at that center. You may find that all students are met at a central location and directed from there to different classrooms. You may find signs posted, telling you that everyone whose last name falls between certain letters should report directly to a particular room. However this part of the check-in is handled at your center, you can anticipate that certain things will be done, including **verification of ID.**

You will be asked for your admission ticket and a suitable ID. **Acceptable forms of ID for the ACT Assessment** are:

- **an ID** issued by your school, state/federal government, or employer on which **both** your name and current photo appear; **or**
- **a letter of identification** written on school letterhead. This letter must have been signed by you in the presence of your counselor (or other school official) and signed by that person as well. The letter must include your name and your full physical description. You'll be asked to sign this letter a second time at the test center.

Most students bring a driver's license or laminated school ID. If you don't have either, you can bring a recent yearbook with your individual photo identified by name. To be admitted to take the ACT, you **must** present an acceptable photo ID or letter of identification or you must be personally recognized by one of the test center personnel. Check the ACT test registration materials for more detailed information about acceptable forms of ID.

In the room you'll be directed to a seat by a room supervisor or proctor (a member of the testing staff). If you are left-handed, let the room supervisor know, and an appropriate desk or table should be made available to you. If there is any problem with your desk, let the room supervisor know.

You'll be asked to put away **everything** except your ID, admission ticket, and pencils. Nothing else will be allowed on your desk: no dictionaries, no books, no scratch paper, no calculators, no radios or earphones—nothing except your pencils and identification. If you have a calculator watch, you'll be asked to remove it. If your watch has an alarm, you'll be asked to turn the alarm off so it won't disturb others.

Eating, drinking, and the use of tobacco are not allowed in the testing room, but you can have a snack before the test or during the break.

Even though every room is different, you should expect an environment that is quiet, well lighted, and reasonably comfortable. If you have problems with the testing environment, let your room supervisor know immediately.

While you're waiting for the test to begin, you may find yourself getting anxious or jittery. That's perfectly normal. Most of us get nervous in new situations. People handle this nervousness in different ways.

Some people find it helpful to practice **mental and physical relaxation techniques.** If this appeals to you, try alternately flexing and relaxing your muscles, beginning at your toes and moving up through your shoulders, neck, and arms. Meanwhile, imagine yourself in a quiet, peaceful place: at the beach, in the mountains, or just in your favorite lounge chair. Breathe deeply and smoothly.

Other people like to **control that nervous energy** and turn it to their advantage. For them, concentrating on the task at hand and shutting everything else out of their minds is the most helpful strategy. If this is your style, you may even want to close your eyes and imagine yourself already working on the exam, thinking about how it will feel to move confidently and smoothly through the tests.

If you have the chance, try out the two approaches on some classroom tests and see which one works better for you. The important thing is to keep the exam in perspective. Try not to let it become "larger than life." Remember, it's just one part of a long academic career.

Instructions will be read for each part of the exam, but it's helpful to know the test directions in advance. You'll find them in the sample tests in this book.

Be **sure** to ask about any aspect of the test-taking procedure that is not perfectly clear to you. After all, how can you expect to do your best if you're worrying about a procedural detail? Testing staff members will be available throughout the exam. In fact, they'll be moving quietly around the room while you're working. If you have a question about the administration of the test (not about any of the test questions), raise your hand and quietly ask for information.

During the exam, **you may find yourself getting tired.** If so, check your posture to make sure you're sitting up straight. Remember what your vocal music teacher said: it's difficult to get enough air in your lungs when you're slouching. You'll stay more alert and confident if you have a steady supply of fresh oxygen going to your brain.

You might want to practice those relaxation techniques again, too, since tension contributes to fatigue. During the short breaks between the individual tests, try stretching your neck and shoulder muscles, rotating your shoulders, stretching back in your chair, and taking some long deep breaths.

You can expect a slightly longer break (approximately 10 minutes) at the end of Test 2. **During this break,** it's a good idea to stand up, walk around a little, stretch, and relax. You may wish to get a drink, go to the rest room, have a snack, or chat with friends. It's important to keep in mind, though, that you still have work requiring concentration ahead of you. It's also important to return to the room quickly. Your room supervisor will start the third section of the test promptly, and you'll need to be back at your desk and ready to go on time.

If you become ill during the test, you certainly may turn in your test materials and leave if you need to. Let your room supervisor know that you are ill and whether you wish to have your answer sheet scored. One caution: Once you've decided to leave the test center, you won't be allowed to return and continue—so be **sure** that leaving is what you want to do. You might try simply closing your eyes or putting your head on the desk for a minute first; then if you feel better, you'll be able to continue.

If you decide you don't want your answer sheet scored, ask the room supervisor to return your admission ticket so that you can reregister for another test date later in the same year (the June date is the last of the year).

Mismarking the answer sheet is an annoying mistake, and it's time-consuming to correct. The best strategy, of course, is to prevent it from happening in the first place. It's a good idea to get in the habit of checking periodically to be sure you're marking your answer in the correct column and row and in the spot corresponding to the question you're reading.

If you discover that you've been mismarking your answer sheet, you'll need to correct your error quickly and go on. If that should happen, don't let it panic you. The time required to correct your answer sheet is shorter than it seems—and panicking will only make things worse. Of course, if you have a serious problem, raise your hand and let the room supervisor know.

You will be expected to follow **a few important rules** during the exam:

- You cannot give assistance to or receive assistance from another student during the exam.
- You will not be allowed to use a calculator or a calculator watch during the exam.
- You cannot work ahead or go back to a different section of the exam.
- You cannot continue to mark your answer sheet after time has been called.

Because the rules are designed to give everyone a fair and even chance, they will be enforced firmly. If you violate any of them, you will be asked to leave the test center and your answer sheet will not be scored.

When you have finished Test 4 and checked your answers *on that test,* you'll need to remain quietly in your seat until time has been called, all the test booklets have been gathered, and security procedures have been completed.

On some of the ACT test dates, students are asked to complete five, rather than four, tests. One of the five is included to try out new test questions and won't be counted toward your score.

You may decide, for whatever reason, that you prefer not to have your answer sheet scored. If you decide you don't want your answer sheet scored after you've completed the exam, let your supervisor know before you leave the room. You don't need to give a reason. The room supervisor will mark your answer sheet "void," and it won't be scored.

At the end of the exam, you may have an opportunity to answer some questions about the testing situation. You may be asked, for example, if you had enough writing space or if you had taken the ACT tests before.

5
TEST-TAKING STRATEGIES

5

TEST-TAKING STRATEGIES

You're already an experienced test-taker. Just think about all the quizzes, tests, and exams you've taken in a dozen years of school. Think about all the tests you've taken outside of school, too: swimming tests, driving tests, qualifying tests for team sports, those tests in popular magazines ("What Kind of Man/Woman Is **Your** Dream Date?").

Tests of all kinds have become a major part of our lives. They help us make informed decisions, give us one way to compare ourselves with others and to measure our own progress, show us how various products stack up against each other, and help assure us that people performing important roles in our lives are qualified to do so. There are tests to ensure that physicians, air traffic controllers, real estate agents, barbers, meat cutters, lawyers, and men and women in many other occupations are able to perform the responsibilities of their work skillfully and accurately. (Imagine what would happen if pilots didn't have to take licensing tests. Would you ever get into a plane?)

The important thing to remember is that **none** of these tests alone makes you qualified to do something; it's the work you do and the skills you learn **before** you take the test that make you qualified. Just taking the driving test, for instance, didn't make you a qualified driver. It was all the parallel parking you did, your knowledge of standard road signs, the skill you developed in your driver's education class, all the things you observed in years of watching other people drive, and your desire to become a licensed driver that motivated you enough to learn everything you needed. These are the things that made you a qualified driver, one who could pass that test.

Remembering that the test alone—any test—is only a small part of a long process of education and training will help you keep that test in perspective. So will remembering that tests like the ACT are designed to provide **you** with information. When you complete the ACT, you will receive valuable information you can use to help make decisions about your future educational plans.

Another way to keep a test in perspective is to remind yourself that it's **you** taking the **test,** not the test taking you. **Put yourself in charge** as you go into the test-taking situation. That's the best way to ensure that your performance on the test will be the best you can make it.

So how do you do that? How do you put yourself in charge? The following suggestions are designed to help you build on the test-taking skills you already have. They're taken from advice gathered over years—from education specialists, from testing specialists, and from people who, like you, have taken lots of tests. Read the advice, try it out, and see how it fits with what you already know about the way you take tests. As with most skills, test-taking strategies vary from person to person. Realize that **you can choose how you will take a test.** Then make intelligent choices about what will work for you.

LEARN AS MUCH AS YOU CAN ABOUT THE TEST YOU'RE GOING TO TAKE.

Before you take any test, the first thing you should do is find out as much about it as you can. This advice may seem obvious, but it's surprising how many people just walk into a test and take their chances. If you're taking a classroom test, your instructor should give you a fair indication of what the test will be like. If you're taking a qualifying test based on published materials, there are usually sample tests and suggestions for review in those materials. For example, most states publish driving manuals that give you a very good idea of what to expect on your driver's license test.

If you're taking a standardized test, such as a school achievement test or a college admission test (like the ACT Assessment), you may find that one good place to look for information is right in your school. Talk to **other students** who've taken the test and ask them for their impressions. Talk to **several** students so that you get a good sampling and you're not swayed by one person's experience. Talk to your **teachers and school counselors,** too. Very often they can give you excellent advice based not only on their knowledge of the test but also on what they know about your abilities. Many times teachers and counselors have brochures from the test companies and test-taking advice books, and they may even offer in-class or after-school preparation classes or tutoring sessions.

Another potential source of information is your school or public library. They may have books and other materials about test-taking in general and the test you'll be taking in particular. They may also have a computer test preparation program that will help you learn more about the test.

Another possibility is the test publisher itself. ACT, for example, provides schools with free copies of the booklet *Preparing for the ACT Assessment,* which describes the test and includes a sample exam for you to work through. Ask your school counselor for a copy.

TAKE A SAMPLE TEST.

The best way to anticipate what it will be like to take a test is to take a sample version of that test.

For a classroom test, you can write your own sample questions based on your textbook and your class notes. What kinds of things are emphasized in the book? Do the chapter headings and review questions give you any ideas? What has your teacher emphasized in assignments, lectures, and discussions? Sometimes writing questions for a friend or a small study group can be the best way for all of you to review for a test.

For a standardized test, you can often obtain previously administered versions of the test to practice on. For instance, you'll find a sample ACT exam in the free booklet *Preparing for the ACT Assessment.* You'll also find three ACT Assessment exams in this book. (See Sections 6 and 9 for the exams and suggestions on how to use them.)

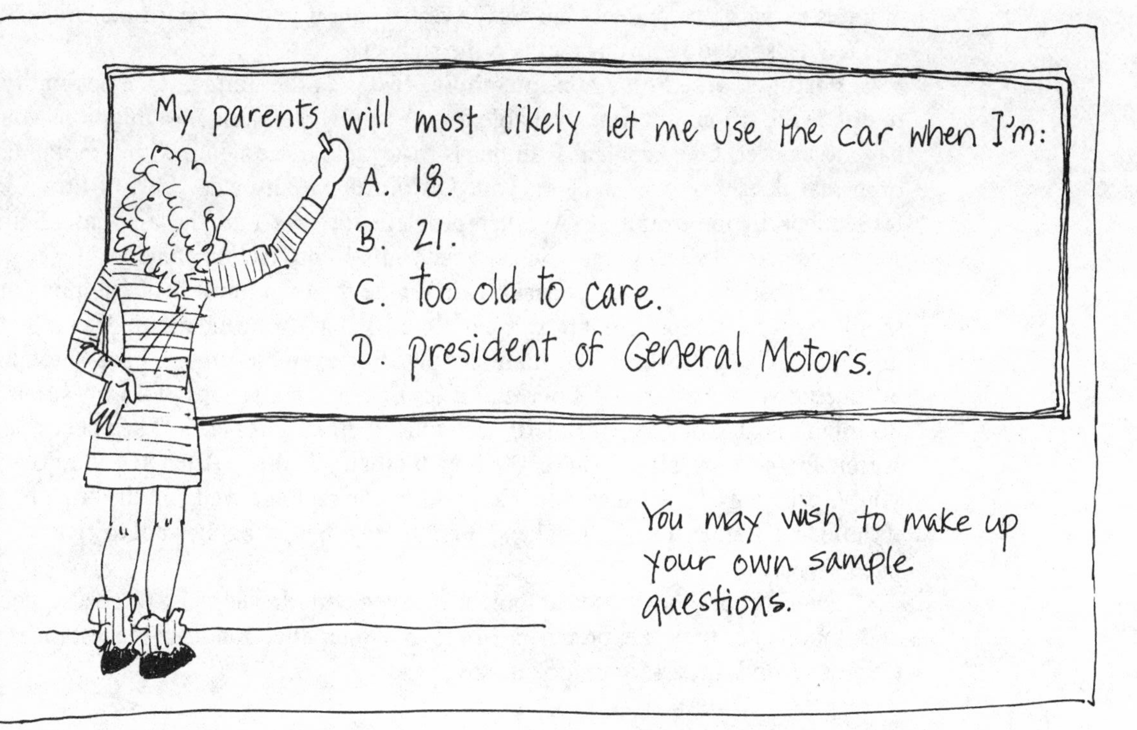

5

LEARN SOME SPECIFIC TEST-TAKING SKILLS.

There are a few basic test-taking skills that apply to nearly every test you take. You've acquired most of these skills already. Recognizing that you have them—and that they are valuable—should help you approach any exam with confidence.

LEARN TO PACE YOURSELF.

Many tests, both classroom and standardized, **must** be completed within a specific and limited amount of time. Classroom tests, for example, usually must be finished within one class period. You'll find this is true in college as well as in high school. Often the final exams for a semester-long college course must be completed in just two or three hours. One of the skills necessary to convey a sense of how much you've learned on the topic being tested, then, is working quickly and efficiently.

Timed essay exams pose particular problems. For these tests, it's wise to use some sort of organizational scheme. One such scheme is to brainstorm for the first few minutes, jotting down as many ideas on your topic as you can think of, and then look for groups of ideas that you can pull together and use as the main points of your essay. Once you've done this, writing the essay is just a matter of stating and developing your main points—all the while keeping your eye on the clock, of course. Your essay won't be perfect—no essay ever is—but if you use your time efficiently, you'll at least get down your ideas on the subject.

Pacing yourself on a multiple-choice test is a little simpler. One possibility is to divide the amount of time available for the test by the number of questions you'll have to answer. One problem with this is that you may come up with a measure of time that doesn't mean much to you. Do you have any clear idea of how long 80 seconds is, for example? Another problem may be that the amount of time sounds so short it's scary, and you can talk yourself into feeling panicky.

Another way to pace yourself is to divide the total number of questions into smaller groups and figure out how much time you have for each group. If you prefer this approach, try to keep the math simple. For example, if you have a total of 30 questions to answer in 1 hour, think of it as either 2 groups of 15 questions at 30 minutes each, or 3 groups of 10 questions at 20 minutes each. Then check your watch to see how close you're keeping to that schedule. After 10 questions, if you've used only 18 minutes, you'll know that you're doing well. On the other hand, if those first 10 questions have taken 23 minutes, you'll probably want to pick up the pace if you can.

Some people choose not to look at the clock at all. They just work as quickly and smoothly as they can, preferring not to take their attention from the test for even the few seconds necessary to look at the clock.

No matter **how you choose to pace yourself,** don't let your concern about time get in the way of your work. Don't try to push yourself to work so fast that you begin to feel out of control or to make careless errors from hurrying. After all, answering 60 questions so quickly that, through carelessness, you miss 20 doesn't give you a better score than answering 50 more slowly and missing only 10.

The ACT Assessment has been designed so that most people taking it are able to finish each test. Many people have time to go back and check their work on each test, too. So, while you won't want to lose time by daydreaming about what you're going to wear to the party that night or wondering which Hollywood marriage will collapse next, or even drifting off into fascinating speculation prompted by one of the test questions (say, "How many isopods **can** you fit on a petri dish, anyway?"), you shouldn't worry unnecessarily about time, either. **The time is yours; use it to your advantage.**

You won't want to drift off into fascinating speculation about how many isopods – whatever they are – you can fit on a petri dish.

We've included the time available for each test of the ACT Assessment in the information in Section 6. Use the sample tests in this book to check your own working pace and see if you, like most people, will have time to finish each test and go back and check your work. Perhaps working through the sample tests will let you know that you need to work quickly in order to finish within the available time. If so, you'll want to keep that in mind when you take the actual exam.

UNDERSTAND THE DIRECTIONS.

It's easy to ignore the directions, no matter what we're doing. Have you ever seen anyone read **all** the directions for installing a new appliance, or putting a child's toy together, or changing the time on a digital watch? Many of us are much more likely to just forge ahead—to do whatever we're doing the way **we** think it ought to to be done, regardless of what the manufacturer had in mind.

Putting the instructions aside and "winging it" is probably all right at home (sometimes the entertainment value may even be worth the frustration), but you're not working under a time deadline at home. If something goes wrong or doesn't make sense, you can always undo what you've done and start over. With an exam, you need to get it right the first time.

No matter how boring those instructions are, then, **pay attention** to them. When you can take a look at them in advance, do. When they're read aloud to you, listen. Okay, it's not MTV, but what you'll learn from the directions **can** make a difference.

For example, the English, Reading, and Science Reasoning tests of the ACT Assessment ask for the "best" answer, while the Mathematics Test asks for the "correct" answer. This simple difference in the instructions signals an important distinction you need to keep in mind as you're working through those tests. Knowing that only one answer is "correct" in the Mathematics Test, you'll want to be sure your understanding of the question and your calculations are precise—so that your answer matches one, and only one, of the possible answers. In the other areas, more than one of the possible answers may arguably be "correct," and you'll need to be careful to select the "best" answer among those potentially "correct" ones.

READ CAREFULLY.

Just as it's important to read and understand the directions for a test, it's also important to read and understand each question on the test. As you've probably discovered somewhere along the line, you can miss even the simplest test question by reading carelessly and overlooking an important word or detail. Some questions on the ACT Assessment, for instance, require more than one step, and the answer to each preliminary step may be included as an answer choice. If you read these questions too quickly, you can easily make the mistake of choosing an attractive but preliminary answer.

DECIDE ON A STRATEGY FOR ANSWERING EASIER AND HARDER QUESTIONS.

Many people work quickly through an entire test (English, Mathematics, Reading, or Science Reasoning), answering only those questions they're pretty sure about the first time and skipping the others. Then they go back and work more slowly through the questions they found difficult at first.

There are several advantages to this approach:

- For one thing, you have the satisfaction of moving along quickly, accomplishing a lot in a short period of time.
- An additional advantage may be that when you return to a tough question, you'll have remembered something important in the meantime. (It's like putting part of your brain "on special assignment" while you go on to the rest of the test.)
- Perhaps the greatest advantage is that you can be sure you'll get to **all** the questions you can answer easily before you run out of time.

The biggest disadvantage to this approach is that you have to be **very** careful about where you're marking your answers on your answer sheet. If you skip a question in your test booklet, be sure to skip the question on your answer sheet, too. You'll probably want to put a check or a star by each of these questions in your test booklet (**not on your answer sheet**) so that you can find them easily later on, when you're ready to return to them. (Remember: Unless you're instructed otherwise, **you can write in the ACT test booklet** as much as you like).

DECIDE ON A STRATEGY FOR GUESSING.

Should you guess or not? The answer depends upon the kind of test you're taking.

In a classroom test, you probably have nothing to lose by guessing. If your answer is completely wrong, you're no worse off than if you'd left the question blank, and if it's partially correct, you may get some credit for it, especially if it shows that you were trying and were headed in the right direction.

On a **standardized test,** it may or may not be wise to guess. The only way to make an informed decision is to find out exactly how the test is scored. On some standardized tests, you're penalized for each incorrect answer. On the ACT Assessment, however, your raw score is based on the number of questions you get right—there's no deduction for wrong answers.

Because **you're not penalized for guessing on the ACT,** it's to your advantage to **answer each question.** Here's a good way to proceed:

- When you come to a question you don't know the answer for, see if you can eliminate at least a couple of the possible choices.
- After you've done that, if you still aren't sure about the answer, take your best guess.

If you can rule out one or two of the possible answers, the odds are in your favor. You don't need an ironclad reason for eliminating one answer and choosing another. Sometimes an intelligent guess is based on a hunch—something you know about the answer but haven't had time to recognize in a timed-test situation.

Maybe you've heard some advice about how to answer questions when you don't know the correct answer, such as "When in doubt, choose C," or "When in doubt, select the longest (or shortest) alternative," or "If NONE OF THE ABOVE is among the answer choices, select it." While each of these bits of advice may hold true for a particular question, you should know that the questions on the ACT Assessment have been carefully written to make these strategies ineffective. The best advice is to rule out any of the possible answers you can on the basis of your knowledge; then, if necessary, make your best guess.

DECIDE ON A STRATEGY FOR CHANGING YOUR MIND.

What do you do with an answer you've changed your mind about? The folk wisdom says, "Always go with your first response." And surely everyone has had the experience of agonizing over a response, trying to decide whether to change it, then doing so only to find out later that the first answer **was** the right one. It was probably those experiences that led to the folk wisdom in the first place.

However, some research by education and testing specialists suggests that you **should** change your answer when you change your mind. If you're like the people tested in that research, your second answer is more likely to be the correct one.

So, how can you decide what you should do? Unfortunately, there's no easy advice that will suit every test-taker and every situation. What you should do depends upon **you** and your test-taking methods. Before you change an answer, think about how you approached the question in the first place. Give some weight to the reasons you now believe another answer is better. Don't mechanically follow an arbitrary rule just because it works for somebody else. Know yourself; then trust yourself to make intelligent, informed decisions.

PLAN TO CHECK YOUR WORK.

When you get to the end of a test, you may feel you've done quite enough. After all, you've just spent half an hour (or 45 minutes or an hour) hassling with questions that didn't seem to want to be answered. You're tired, and you just want to use that extra five minutes for a nap. Maybe when you look around the room you see other people who've closed both their test booklets and their eyes.

Hard as it may be, try to keep your energy going until time is called so you can go back through that test and check your answers. (Remember: You're allowed to work on only one test at a time.)

- Check to be sure you've marked all your answers in the proper places.
- Be certain you've answered **all** the questions, even the ones you weren't sure about. (Of course, you must be very careful to stop marking ovals when time is called.)
- Using the test booklet as scratch paper, check your calculations. Sometimes a simple math error will have led you to select an attractive, but incorrect, answer.
- Check your answer sheet for stray pencil marks that may be misread by the scoring machine.
- Be sure you've marked only one answer for each question.

6
FORMAT & CONTENTS OF THE TESTS IN THE ACT ASSESSMENT

6

FORMAT & CONTENTS OF THE TESTS IN THE ACT ASSESSMENT

The ACT Assessment is made up of four separate tests, each of which is designed to measure academic achievement in a major area of high school study: English, mathematics, reading, and natural sciences. This section of the book discusses each of those four tests in detail and gives examples of the kinds of questions you are likely to find on each of the tests and some suggestions for approaching those questions and each test as a whole.

The discussion of each test is followed immediately by an actual sample of that test, and the questions appearing in the discussion are also drawn from the sample test. Therefore, if you want to use the sample test for practice, you may want to do that before reading the discussion. Or you may prefer to read the description, then work through the sample test with the benefit of the information you've just read.

Either way, before you read the rest of this chapter, you may find it helpful to take a look at the charts shown here to give yourself an idea of the makeup of the ACT Assessment as a whole and of its individual tests.

ACT Assessment English Test

75 items, 45 minutes

Content/Skills	Proportion of Test	Number of Items
Usage/Mechanics	**.53**	**40**
Punctuation	.13	10
Grammar and Usage	.16	12
Sentence Structure	.24	18
Rhetorical Skills	**.47**	**35**
Strategy	.16	12
Organization	.15	11
Style	.16	12
Total	**1.00**	**75**

Scores reported: Usage/Mechanics (40 items)
Rhetorical Skills (35 items)
Total test score (75 items)

ACT Assessment Mathematics Test

60 items, 60 minutes

Content Area	Proportion of Test	Number of Items
Pre-Algebra and Elementary Algebra	.40	24
Intermediate Algebra and Coordinate Geometry	.30	18
Plane Geometry	.23	14
Trigonometry	.07	4
Total	**1.00**	**60**

Scores reported: Pre-Algebra/Elementary Algebra (24 items)
Intermediate Algebra/Coordinate Geometry (18 items)
Plane Geometry/Trigonometry (18 items)
Total test score (60 items)

ACT Assessment Reading Test

40 items, 35 minutes

Reading Context	Proportion of Test	Number of Items
Prose Fiction	.25	10
Humanities	.25	10
Social Studies	.25	10
Natural Sciences	.25	10
Total	**1.00**	**40**

Scores reported: Arts/Literature (Prose Fiction, Humanities: 20 items)
Social Studies/Sciences (Social Studies, Natural Sciences: 20 items)
Total test score (40 items)

ACT Assessment Science Reasoning Test

40 items, 35 minutes

Content Area*	Format	Proportion of Test	Number of Items
Biology Physical Sciences Chemistry Physics	Data Representation	.38	15
	Research Summaries	.45	18
	Conflicting Viewpoints	.17	7
Total		**1.00**	**40**

Scores reported: Total test score (40 items)

*Note: Content areas are distributed over the different formats.

ACT ASSESSMENT ENGLISH TEST

The ACT English Test is designed to measure how well you understand the conventions of standard written English. You might not always use "standard written English" in casual writing (for instance, when you're writing to a friend) or in conversation. In casual writing or conversation, we often use slang expressions that have special meanings with friends of our own age or in our part of the country. Because slang can become outdated (Does anybody say "groovy" anymore?) and regional terms might not be familiar to students everywhere (Do you and your friends say "soda" or "soft drink" or "pop"?), this test emphasizes the standard written English that is taught in schools around the country.

You will have 45 minutes to read 5 prose passages and answer 75 multiple-choice questions about them—an average of 15 questions per passage. The passages cover a variety of subjects, ranging from a writer's personal anecdote about a jogging experience to an essay about prehistoric cave paintings.

The questions fall into two categories:

- **Usage/Mechanics** (punctuation, grammar, sentence structure)
- **Rhetorical Skills** (strategy, organization, style)

You'll receive a total score based on all 75 questions and two subscores—one based on the 40 Usage/Mechanics questions and the other based on the 35 Rhetorical Skills questions.

You will **not** be tested on spelling or on how well you can recall specific rules of grammar. Grammar and usage are tested only within the context of the passage, not by questions like "Must an appositive always be set off by commas?" Likewise, you won't be tested directly on your vocabulary, although the better your vocabulary, the better equipped you'll be to answer questions that involve choosing the most appropriate word. For example, look at this sentence taken from the sample test you'll find following this discussion:

Or, instead, you can rent a small boat and spend a stagnant[6] afternoon on the Thames River.

Question 6 of the sample test asks you about the best choice of words for the underlined portion of the sentence:

---

6. **F.** NO CHANGE
   G. sluggish
   H. slothful
   J. leisurely

Obviously, you'll need to figure out what those words mean before you can answer the question.

Like the other tests in the ACT Assessment, the English Test doesn't require you to memorize what you read. The questions and passages are side by side for easy reference. This is **not** a memorization test.

If you prefer, you may work through the sample test before reading the rest of this discussion. On the other hand, you may read the discussion, then take the sample test if you feel you need the practice.

TYPES OF QUESTIONS ON THE ACT ENGLISH TEST

USAGE/MECHANICS questions always refer to an underlined portion of the passage. You must decide on the best choice of words and punctuation for that underlined portion. Usually, your options include NO CHANGE, which means that the passage is best just as it's written. Sometimes you'll also have the option of removing the underlined portion altogether. For example, question 37 offers you the option of removing the phrase "in all likelihood":

Nearby is a wooden temple also built by local Neolithic communities, perhaps the Rhinelander Beaker Folk, probably in all likelihood [37] around 1800 B.C.

37. A. NO CHANGE
B. very likely
C. by all odds
D. OMIT the underlined portion.

RHETORICAL SKILLS questions may refer to an underlined portion, or they may ask about a section of the passage or an aspect of the passage as a whole. For example, in the following question, you're asked to think about the appropriateness of the use of the first-person pronoun throughout an essay:

30. Considering the tone and subject matter of the essay, is the writer's use of the pronoun "I" appropriate?
F. No, because the writer is speaking for everyone who owns or rents VCRs.
G. No, because the rules of grammar dictate that one should avoid "I" in personal writing.
H. Yes, because the rules of grammar require a writer to use "I" whenever writing about anything he or she has personally experienced.
J. Yes, because this is a personal narrative and using "I" gives the story authenticity and immediacy.

Now let's examine some of the kinds of questions you'll encounter in each category, with an indication of what percentage of the English Test they represent.

USAGE/MECHANICS

USAGE/MECHANICS questions focus on matters of punctuation, grammar, and sentence structure.

Punctuation questions (13% of the English questions) involve misplaced, missing, or unnecessary punctuation marks:

- commas
- colons
- semicolons
- dashes
- parentheses
- apostrophes
- question marks
- exclamation points

These questions focus not on the rules of usage, but on using punctuation to express ideas clearly.

Basic grammar and usage questions (16% of the English questions) involve choosing the best word or words in a sentence based on considerations of appropriate grammar. Aspects of grammar and usage that are covered include the following:

- **Agreement**

  Subject and verb

  "You **is** my best friend"

  should be:

  "You **are** my best friend."

  Adjectives and adverbs with corresponding nouns and verbs

  "Danielle spread frosting **liberal** on the cat"

  should be:

  "Danielle spread frosting **liberally** on the cat."

- **Verb formation**

  "Fritz had just **began** to toast Lydia's marshmallows when the rabbits stampeded through the camp"

  should be:

  "Fritz had just **begun** to toast Lydia's marshmallows when the rabbits stampeded through the camp."

- **Using appropriate pronouns**
  "He is the one man who knows **its** own mind"

  should be:

  "He is the one man who knows **his** own mind."

  "Seymour and Svetlana annoyed **there** parents all the time"

  should be:

  "Seymour and Svetlana annoyed **their** parents all the time."

  "After the embarrassing incident with the peanut butter, the zebra and **me** were never invited back to lunch"

  should be:

  "After the embarrassing incident with the peanut butter, the zebra and **I** were never invited back to lunch."

- **Comparative adjectives and adverbs**
  "My goldfish is **more smarter** than your brother"

  should be:

  "My goldfish is **smarter** than your brother."

- **Superlative adjectives and adverbs**
  "Your brother, however, has the **most cute** aardvark I've ever seen"

  should be:

  "Your brother, however, has the **cutest** aardvark I've ever seen."

- **Idioms**
  "An idiom is an established phrase that follows no logical grammatical rule yet can be looked **down** in the dictionary"

  should be:

  "An idiom is an established phrase that follows no logical grammatical rule yet can be looked **up** in the dictionary."

My goldfish is smarter than your brother.

Sentence structure questions (24% of the English questions) require you to recognize and avoid errors like these:

- **Run-on sentences**
  "We discovered that the entire family had been devoured by **anteaters it** was horrible."

  This one sentence should actually be two:

  "We discovered that the entire family had been devoured by **anteaters. It** was horrible."

- **Comma splices**
  "The anteaters had terrible **manners, they** just ate and ran."

  This sentence could be rewritten as:

  "The anteaters had terrible **manners. They** just ate and ran."

  Or it could appear as:

  "The anteaters had terrible **manners; they** just ate and ran."

- **Sentence fragments**
  "Even when he found scorpions in his socks."

  This needs a subject to let us know who "he" is and what he did:

  "Julio never lost his temper, even when he found scorpions in his socks."

- **Misleading modifiers**
  "**Snarling and snapping, Juanita** struggled to control her pet turtle."

  Unless it was Juanita who was doing the snarling and snapping, the sentence needs to be reordered:

  "**Snarling and snapping, the pet turtle** resisted Juanita's struggle to control it."

- **Shifts in construction**
  "For a long time, the turtle had been the terror of the neighborhood, **and which was named Geoffrey.**"

  Assuming it's the turtle, not the neighborhood, that's named Geoffrey, the sentence should be rephrased as:

  "For a long time, the turtle, **which was named Geoffrey,** had been the terror of the neighborhood."

RHETORICAL SKILLS

RHETORICAL SKILLS questions focus on strategy, organization, and style.

Strategy questions (16% of the English questions) focus on the process of writing and revising. They might ask you to decide if a passage is appropriate for a particular audience, what kind of supporting material could strengthen the passage, or whether the writer has crafted effective introductions, conclusions, and transitions.

Organization questions (15% of the English questions) ask you to consider the most logical order for phrases within a sentence, sentences within a paragraph, and paragraphs within a passage. You'll need to think about which order best explains an idea or supports a point of view clearly and effectively.

Style questions (16% of the English questions) involve writing effective sentences that maintain a consistent tone or voice throughout the passage, using language economically, and using appropriate words. Sometimes a sentence that isn't technically ungrammatical is nevertheless confusing because it's poorly written. Sometimes there's a word or phrase that doesn't fit the tone of the passage. Good writing also involves eliminating trite expressions or clichés, irrelevant information, and redundancies. In other words, good writing involves **revision or editing.** Style questions give you the chance to see the passage from the point of view of an editor as well as a writer.

What you've just read is only an overview of the English Test. Directly or indirectly, a question may test you in more than one of the areas mentioned, so it's important not to become overly concerned with categorizing a question before you answer it. And, while awareness of the types of questions can help you be a more critical reader, just remember: What's important isn't what **type** of question you're answering. The most important thing is to focus on what it's asking, and to do your best to pick out the best answer, given the rest of the passage.

STRATEGIES FOR TAKING THE ACT ENGLISH TEST

PACE YOURSELF.

The ACT English Test contains 75 questions to be completed in 45 minutes. That works out to 36 seconds per item; but, if possible, you should spend less time on each question and use the remaining time allowed for this test to review your work and return to the English questions that were most difficult for you. Spending an average of half a minute on each question, for example, will leave 7 to 8 minutes to review.

Another way to think of it is that you have 45 minutes to read and answer questions on 5 passages, for a maximum of 9 minutes for each passage and its questions.

BE AWARE OF THE WRITING STYLE USED IN THE PASSAGES.

The five passages cover a variety of topics and are written in a variety of styles. It's important that you take into account the writing style used in each passage as you respond to the questions.

Some of the passages will be anecdotes or narratives written from an informal first-person point of view. Others will be more formal essays. Often, questions will ask you to choose the best answer based not only on what is grammatically correct, but also on how consistent it is with the style and tone of the specific passage. An expression that's too breezy for an essay on the life of former President Herbert Hoover might be just right for a personal narrative about a writer's attempt at learning to water ski.

BE SURE TO CONSIDER A QUESTION'S CONTEXT BEFORE YOU CHOOSE AN ANSWER.

Skimming the passage and questions before working through the details of the test is an approach some people find helpful. Particularly when there are questions involving strategy and organization, it can help to have some of the questions in mind before you begin your careful reading. If there are questions about the order of sentences within a paragraph, or of paragraphs within a passage, you might want to answer those questions first to make sure that the major elements of the passage are ordered logically. Understanding the order of the passage may help you answer some of the other questions.

As you're answering each question, be sure to read at least a sentence or two **beyond** the sentence containing the underlined portion that's being questioned. You may need to read even more than that to make sure you understand what the writer is trying to say.

EXAMINE THE UNDERLINED PORTIONS OF THE PASSAGE.

Before responding to a question asking about an underlined portion, carefully examine what is underlined in the text. Consider the features of writing that are included in the underlined portion. The answer choices for each question will contain changes in one or more aspects of standard written English.

NOTE THE DIFFERENCES IN THE ANSWER CHOICES.

Many of the questions that refer to underlined portions will involve more than one aspect of writing. Examine each answer choice and note how it differs from the others. Consider **all** the features of writing that are included in each choice. (Be careful not to select an answer that corrects one error but creates a different error.)

DETERMINE THE BEST ANSWER.

You can take at least two approaches to determining the best answer to a question about an underlined portion. You can reread the question, substituting each of the possible answer choices in turn for the underlined portion, and determine the best choice that way. Or you can decide how the underlined portion might best be phrased in standard written English and look for your phrasing among the choices offered. If the underlined portion is correct as is, select the "NO CHANGE" answer. For questions about a section of the passage or about the passage as a whole, you must decide which alternative response is most appropriate, given the style and tone of the rest of the passage.

If you can't decide which answer is best, you may want to mark the question in your test booklet so that you can return to it later. Remember: You're not penalized for guessing. So, after you've eliminated as many answer choices as you can, take your best guess.

REREAD THE SENTENCE, USING YOUR SELECTED ANSWER.

Once you have selected the answer you feel is best for a question about an underlined portion of text, reread the entire sentence or sentences, substituting the answer you've selected for the underlined portion. Sometimes an answer that sounds fine out of context doesn't "fit" within the sentence or passage. Be sure to keep in mind both punctuation marks and words in each possible response; sometimes just the omission of a comma can make an important difference.

WATCH FOR QUESTIONS ABOUT THE ENTIRE PASSAGE OR PORTIONS OF THE PASSAGE.

Some questions ask about a section of the passage. They are identified by a question number in a box at the appropriate point in the passage and don't refer to an underlined portion. Here's an example:

Either the VCR runs out of tape or the timer clicks off too soon. [4] The story is building to the climax [21] the English countryside turns snowy, and the dialogue becomes a steady buzz. [5] Believe me, thirty-eight steps just won't do. [22]

22. For the sake of unity and coherence, Sentence 2 should be:
   - **F.** placed where it is now.
   - **G.** placed after Sentence 4.
   - **H.** placed after Sentence 5.
   - **J.** OMITTED.

Other questions ask about an aspect of the passage as a whole. These are placed at the end of the passage, following boxed instructions like these:

Items 30 and 31 pose questions about Passage II as a whole.

You may want to read any questions about the passage as a whole first so that you can keep those questions in mind while you're reading the passage.

AVOID MAKING NEW MISTAKES.

Beware of correcting mistakes in the passage and, in your haste, picking a response that creates a new mistake. For example:

I still consider myself a member of the VCR generation, but if I decide to see it [29] again, I intend to see it at the local theater. The evening will be a bargain even after I pay for my ticket and buy popcorn and a cola.

29. A. NO CHANGE
    B. that
    C. that movie;
    D. *The 39 Steps*

This is the last paragraph in a passage devoted mainly to the writer's struggles to watch the movie *The 39 Steps* in its entirety. Stylistically, it would probably be sufficient to refer to it simply as "that movie" (C). However, notice that C is the only answer choice that complicates matters by adding punctuation: a semicolon. Notice that a semicolon here would separate a dependent clause from a following independent clause.

Be observant, especially in questions where the responses have similar wording. One comma or apostrophe can make all the difference:

You might also choose to look at the paintings in the Ashmolean Museum, to browse through the many bookstores and woolen shops, or to wander through Oxford's open markets. Everywhere, at every quarter hour, you will hear chimes pealing out from the <u>cities much</u> spires.
12

12. F. NO CHANGE
    G. city's many
    H. cities many
    J. citys' many

It probably only took you a moment to reject F, the "cities much spires," as not sounding much like standard written English. The word *many,* in responses G, H, and J, is obviously better. But should it be preceded by *city's, cities,* or *citys'*? You could easily fall into the trap of thinking that because *spires* is plural, *city* should be, too. But this is a case of **one** city and its **many** spires, so the correct form is *city's.*

BE AWARE OF THE CONNOTATIONS OF WORDS.

Vocabulary isn't tested in an isolated way on the ACT English Test. Nevertheless, a good vocabulary and an awareness of the connotations as well as the definitions of words will help you do well on the test.

The following question asks you to think about how to downplay the negative aspects of Oxford's traffic and stress the positive aspects of the city's modernization:

Delivery trucks, red double-decker buses, and autos swerve around bicyclists and pedestrians. Fortunately, though, you can escape the crowded streets in the city's large public parks. [5]

5. Paragraph 2 expresses the point of view that traffic, an effect of modernization, is a disruptive and negative feature in Oxford. The writer is revising the whole paragraph to express a more positive attitude toward modernizing the city and a less negative attitude toward the traffic. Which of the following revisions of the preceding sentence would best help to express that new point of view?
   A. If you like, however, you can find an antidote to that hectic rush in the city's large public parks.
   B. After experiencing the bustling excitement of Oxford's lively, crowded streets, you can walk through one of the city's large public parks.
   C. Exhausted, you can escape Oxford's crowded streets in one of its large public parks.
   D. When traffic noise distracts you from the "real" Oxford, you may turn to one of the city's sedate public parks.

6

It helps to look at the adjectives in the various choices and consider their connotations. Does "hectic rush" in A have positive or negative associations? Response C is not as openly critical of Oxford's streets, but it does suggest that the tourist will be "exhausted" and will want to "escape." Response D is also negative in a fairly subtle way, referring to traffic noise as a distraction from "the 'real' Oxford." Only B manages to make the traffic sound appealing by choosing expressions like "bustling excitement" and "lively, crowded streets." Notice that you can't reject any of the responses on the basis of mechanical, grammatical, or stylistic flaws. You have to focus on what the words mean and what associations they'll have for the typical reader.

What are the connotations of the words in the following choices?

Today's machine age does, however, thumb its big nose upon Oxford.[3] Delivery trucks,[4] red double-decker buses, and autos swerve around bicyclists and pedestrians. Fortunately, though, you can escape the crowded streets in the city's large public parks. [5] Or, instead, you can rent a small boat and spend a stagnant[6] afternoon on the Thames River.

6. **F.** NO CHANGE
G. sluggish
H. slothful
J. leisurely

All four words are associated with the idea of something that's slow-moving. But think about what the writer's purpose is in this essay. Is the general tone enthusiastic about Oxford, or does it warn visitors away? Is spending a "stagnant afternoon on the Thames" (F) an appealing prospect for the average reader? *Stagnant* not only refers to water that doesn't move, but also is linked with the idea of staleness (**stagnant** air) or a dead-end situation ("I'm **stagnating** in this job"). *Sluggish* (G) and *slothful* (H) also have negative connotations of laziness. To a workaholic, spending an afternoon floating down the Thames might very well sound **slothful,** but the writer's intent is to promote it as a relaxing pastime. Therefore, *leisurely* (J) is the best choice.

One person's sloth is another person's leisure.

A final thought about connotations: just as one person's sloth is another person's leisure, what provokes belly laughs in one reader may cause only a thin smile in another. Bear that in mind as you read the following question:

At least let me lose ten pounds by virtue of [66] some hard dieting, and the weight is returned to [67] me two weeks later. One good way to avoid that happening is to take up bicycling. [68] The way I figure it's [69] losing weight and losing my car keys or fountain pen are connected: when I'm dieting, I tend to become both crabby and weak. I lose concentration, and then I lose my car keys or pen.

Searching for them is anxious work, it's [70] easy to work up an appetite rooting through drawers. Why wonder, [71] I need a snack or even an extra meal. Never finding the object I'm looking for, I do notice, as I pass the full-length mirror, that my face is fuller than it was a week ago, and that my pants seem just a touch tighter.

75. In relating weight loss to missing personal objects, the writer is:

A. providing real-life situations of memory lapses for a tragic effect.
B. relating unlike problems for an amusing effect.
C. relating physiological and psychological facts for a scientific effect.
D. offering concrete examples of weight loss techniques for a helpful effect.

You may not necessarily feel that the writer has successfully achieved an amusing effect by linking weight loss and fountain pen loss. However, your personal feelings about what's amusing shouldn't lead you to reject this response immediately. Look at all of them. Maybe the essay isn't terribly amusing, but it should be obvious that comedy is closer to the writer's intent than tragedy (A). The scientific effect suggested by C is also off base: the passage is hardly a collection of scientific facts. Nor is it a self-help weight loss guide, as D proposes. Therefore, B is the best answer.

BE CAREFUL WITH TWO-PART QUESTIONS.

Some questions require extra thought because you have to decide not only whether a particular choice is appropriate, but also whether the best supporting reason for that choice is convincing. For instance:

It would cost less than having gone to a [25] movie, in theory that should be a cheap solution, [26] but in practice the result was quite different. You see, I've always had a problem with returning things, from library books to a friend's record. I mean well, but I had tended [27] to procrastinate. With library books I get off lightly—two or three cents per day overdue. With *The 39 Steps,* the bill was a whale, [28] $22.95. It cost me a tidy sum finally to find that last step.

I still consider myself a member of the VCR generation, but if I decide to see it [29] again, I intend to see it at the local theater. The evening will be a bargain even after I pay for my ticket and buy popcorn and a cola.

30. Considering the tone and subject matter of the essay, is the writer's use of the pronoun "I" appropriate?

F. No, because the writer is speaking for everyone who owns or rents VCRs.
G. No, because the rules of grammar dictate that one should avoid "I" in personal writing.
H. Yes, because the rules of grammar require a writer to use "I" whenever writing about anything he or she has personally experienced.
J. Yes, because this is a personal narrative and using "I" gives the story authenticity and immediacy.

Once you decide that the pronoun "I" is or isn't appropriate, you need to decide why. How **do** you feel about the use of "I"? Was it jarring or distracting as you read? Or did it seem to suit the tone and subject matter? If the use of "I" is appropriate, which is the better justification? Response H—which, you'll note, contradicts G although both claim to cite "the rules of grammar"—says that a writer is **required** to use "I" when writing about personal experiences. Can you think of situations in which a writer might wish to discuss personal experiences without using "I"? Do you agree with J that this essay is a personal narrative? Do you feel that the use of "I" gives it immediacy and authenticity—that is, does the use of "I" make the writing seem livelier and more personal?

WATCH FOR INTERDEPENDENT QUESTIONS.

Sometimes you'll find that the best way for you to answer questions about a passage is **not** in their numbered order. Occasionally, you'll find it easier to answer a question after you've answered the one that follows it. Or you might find two questions about different elements of the same sentence, in which case you need to consider them both together.

In general, you may find it helpful to look for questions about the best order for paragraphs within a passage and answer them first. Do the same for questions about sentence order within a paragraph. Otherwise you risk missing crucial relationships that are obvious only when the elements have been ordered properly.

In the following example, you can see that it would be difficult to answer question 63 before determining the best paragraph order, which you're asked to do in question 74.

Neither my keys nor my wallet ever turns up in a friendly lost-and-found; nobody calls to say that she has stumbled across my fountain pen; my stack of catalogs is only a stack of catalogs. [63] I have learned to live, and to search, with resignation.

63. The writer says, "My stack of catalogs is only a stack of catalogs" to mean that the catalogs:

A. are not hiding any missing items.
B. represent resignation.
C. never get returned, unlike the keys or fountain pen.
D. don't usually get lost.

---

74. For the sake of unity and coherence, Paragraph 1 should be placed:

F. where it is now.
G. after Paragraph 2.
H. after Paragraph 3.
J. after Paragraph 5.

"My stack of catalogs is only a stack of catalogs" is a personal remark of the writer's, with little or no meaning for a reader who has yet to envision the stack of catalogs as a hiding place for lost slips of paper.

In the next example, it would probably be desirable to answer question 57 first. Do you think you could logically choose the best transitional phrase—*yet, because, so, although it is true that*—without knowing what will follow in the second part of the sentence? How would you be able to pick the right word to express the relationship between the two ideas?

Up to that time, no other broken record had been similarly <u>treated, yet</u> [56] baseball devotees <u>whose admiration for</u> [57] the ability of both men thought the resolution unfair. They reasoned that all players should receive full credit for their accomplishments, regardless of technicalities.

56. **F.** NO CHANGE
G. treated because
H. treated, so
J. treated, although it is true that

57. **A.** NO CHANGE
B. whom admire
C. who admired
D. whom admired

You must first concentrate on the statement that baseball fans who admired both men thought the resolution unfair. Then go back to the statement that, up to that time, no other broken record had been similarly treated. Does it logically follow that no broken record had been similarly treated **because** fans thought the resolution unfair? **Yet** they thought it was unfair? **Although** they thought it was unfair? Using *so* is the best way to indicate that the reason some baseball fans thought the treatment was unfair was **because** no other broken record had received similar treatment.

Baseball devotees thought the resolution unfair.

REPRESENTATIVE ACT ENGLISH TEST QUESTIONS

Let's take a look now at some of the kinds of questions you're likely to find on the ACT English Test. The examples are taken from the sample test that appears immediately after this discussion. If you want to know what the individual question would look like in an actual test, turn to those pages. You can also use that test for practice if you wish, either before or after reading this discussion.

SENTENCE STRUCTURE

There are various ways in which a sentence in a passage can go wrong. Following are two examples: a comma splice with a confusingly punctuated date in the center and a construction shift in which a wrong answer might seem especially tempting.

Maris's sixty-one home runs broke the record set by the legendary Babe Ruth, in 1927, Ruth [50] slammed sixty home runs.

50. **F.** NO CHANGE
G. Ruth in 1927,
H. Ruth. In 1927,
J. Ruth,

This sentence can be confusing if you become overly concerned with the placement of *1927*. The question is "Which idea should the date *1927* be linked with?" That question can be answered by finding the response with the best punctuation. J creates a comma splice—two sentence-like clauses joined by a comma rather than separated by a semicolon or period. F and G are also comma splices. While G links the date more closely with the sentence about record setting and F sets off the date with commas so that a reader can't tell which idea it belongs with, in this case the date *1927* could make sense with either idea. Only H breaks up the two ideas into two separate and clear sentences; that makes H your best choice.

Here's an example in which the choice of a pronoun can affect the shape of the sentence. You might have heard that in an essay or other formal writing it's better to refer to a reader as *one* rather than as *you.* So you might read the following question and decide that *one* is automatically correct—that all you have to do is choose between *one stands* (F) and *one stood* (G). However, what you should be paying attention to is what happens in the second half of the sentence, which begins after "ancient, empty barrow."

There in the middle of a farmer's field,
as one stands (42) inside the
ancient, empty barrow; (43) you can hear the sounds
of crows cawing and the farmer's tractor as he
works his field nearby.

42. **F.** NO CHANGE
G. one stood
H. he stands
J. you stand

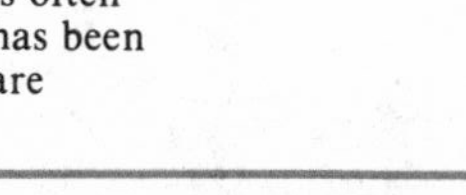

Notice the words *you can hear.* Notice also that the option of changing that *you* isn't offered. **You** can hear the sounds of crows cawing and the farmer's tractor as **who** stands inside the ancient, empty barrow? It can't be *he* (H)—the farmer—because "he's" out on his tractor. And, although you may have a bias toward *one* because you've been told it's preferable to *you,* in this sentence using the pronoun *one* causes a confusing construction shift. The writer could have said, "As **one** stands inside the barrow, **one** can hear crows cawing." But since the *you* in *you can hear* is locked in place, your best bet is the choice that parallels it: *you stand* (J).

SUBJECT/VERB AGREEMENT

Questions dealing with subject/verb agreement can trip you up if you don't read carefully. It's important to look not only at the noun closest to the underlined verb but also at the phrase or sentence as a whole. Take this example:

Oxford. Being (14) a concert by the choir at Christ Church
Cathedral or an organ recital at Merton College
Chapel, where, in spring, bowls of fresh strawberries
and cream is (15) served at intermission.

15. **A.** NO CHANGE
B. is often
C. has been
D. are

If you focused only on the word *cream,* A and B might sound equally good: cream **is** or **is often** served at intermission. However, the writer isn't referring just to cream. The sentence says that guests in the chapel are served "bowls of fresh strawberries and cream." Is the **subject** of that phrase singular or plural? Does the subject require a singular or plural verb? Cream **is** served; bowls **are** served. Since *bowls,* a plural noun, is the subject of the sentence, the plural verb *are served* is called for (D).

COMMAS

Sometimes you might come upon an expression that doesn't have much meaning for you. For instance:

Program the right channel, set the timer, and even the late-late-late movie is within grasp. Neither storm nor sleep will keep a [16] well-running VCR from its appointed task.

16. F. NO CHANGE
    G. Neither, storm nor
    H. Neither storm nor,
    J. Neither storm, nor

You may be unfamiliar with the phrase this writer is referring to here. It comes from an old saying describing mail carriers: "Neither snow, nor rain, nor heat, nor gloom of night stays these couriers from the swift completion of their appointed rounds." Try not to let unfamiliar expressions throw you. Concentrate on the question, which in this case is concerned with commas.

In deciding whether a comma is needed and, if so, where, you may find it helpful to read the choices through, pausing at each comma. Think about whether these pauses clarify the writer's meaning or cause confusion. After trying them all, you should discover that in this case the meaning is clear without a comma, so F is your best answer.

TRANSITIONS

The English Test includes questions about transitions—links between phrases in a sentence, between sentences in a paragraph, and between paragraphs in a passage. A good transition leads a reader smoothly and logically from one idea to the next. It should reflect the proper cause-and-effect relationship, if any, between the elements (**because** rather than **despite,** for instance). Sometimes a transition needs to reflect a certain chronology or sequence of events. Good writing style is not always enough to ensure good transitions. That is, a sentence might be written very well and yet not effectively establish a link between two paragraphs.

As you read the answer choices for the question below, you'll notice that, in this case, none of the sentences can be rejected for being unclear or poorly written. You must read each one and consider how well it would link the two paragraphs.

---

[3]

If you are hungry, you will grow even hungrier if you don't know. The English dining customs—[7] Oxford's eating places close between [8] the traditional meal hours. There is, however, an extra meal hour—teatime, in late afternoon. [9] An order of tea-for-two includes a pot of tea, a plate of big, fluffy, raisin-studded biscuits called "scones" and bowls; of [10] butter, jam, and marmalade.

[4]

There are many interesting and educational places to visit in Oxford center. [11] There you might visit some of the thirty-three colleges that make up Oxford University. You might also choose to look at the paintings in the Ashmolean Museum, to browse through the many bookstores and woolen shops, or to wander through Oxford's open markets. Everywhere, at every quarter hour, you will hear chimes pealing out from the cities much [12] spires.

11. Which of the suggested sentences makes the best introduction to Paragraph 4 and the best transition from Paragraph 3?

A. NO CHANGE
B. Fortified by a teatime snack, you should have plenty of energy for a stroll through the city's center.
C. Most visitors to Oxford enjoy a tea break in the late afternoon.
D. A visit to Oxford is not complete without a stop at Oxford University.

It might help to try summing up the topics of each paragraph in a word or two. Paragraph 3 focuses on teatime. Paragraph 4 is about Oxford center's attractions. Is there a sentence that touches on both topics? It's also important to pay attention to other elements in each paragraph—elements you can't change. Look at the second sentence of Paragraph 4. It begins "There you might visit." Where is "there"? The information in the first sentence should provide a clear answer to that question.

Be sure to read and consider all the choices. Don't just pick the first one that sounds right. For example, take A. It's a clearly written sentence that does a good job of introducing Paragraph 4. "There" in the second sentence unmistakably refers to Oxford center. Response A offers a reasonable **introduction,** but what kind of **transition** does it provide? How smoothly does it get a reader from scones and marmalade to Oxford University? D also makes an awkward transition, and it's a far less effective introduction to Paragraph 4. D might be a way to lead into a discussion of Oxford University, but it's too specific for a paragraph about Oxford center in general. And D sounds awkward when followed by the second sentence, in which the repetition of "Oxford University" would be unnecessary.

C, on the other hand, focuses on teatime without introducing the idea of Oxford center—making the "there" reference in the second sentence completely confusing to a reader.

Notice that B is the only response that incorporates elements of both paragraphs in a single sentence. In this case B is your best choice.

What *is* the best way to get a reader smoothly from scones and marmalade to Oxford University?

The following question tests your ability both to choose a good transitional phrase and to recognize the appropriateness of an idiom:

Searching for them is anxious <u>work, it's</u> [70] easy to work up an appetite rooting through drawers. <u>Why wonder,</u> [71] I need a snack or even an extra meal. Never finding the object I'm looking for, I do notice, as I pass the full-length mirror, that my face is fuller than it was a week ago, and that my pants seem just a touch tighter.

71. **A.** NO CHANGE
B. No wonder
C. Without a doubt
D. No matter what,

The underlined phrase should form a transition between the two sentences. The writer works up an appetite while searching for lost items. Subsequently, the writer needs to satisfy that appetite. Which response offers the best way to connect the two thoughts? Is the relationship between the two thoughts one of cause and effect? Is a contradiction implied? In D, the phrase "no matter what" suggests that the writer needs a snack in spite of other conditions. Yet the writer's just told you the conditions that create the need for the snack. "Without a doubt" in response C doesn't sound incorrect, but it would be better if followed by a comma. Could the writer do better? A is not a good choice because "why wonder" doesn't make a logical transition. "No wonder" is the best choice because it makes the best transition.

REDUNDANCY

You should be alert for redundancies in questions that, like the following one, offer four choices that seem to say almost the same thing:

But, I can hear you murmuring, one can always rent a copy of *The 39 Steps,* one that doesn't fade into oblivion. Before[23] the secret of the man with the missing finger is completely shown and[24] revealed. How much would it cost?

24. **F.** NO CHANGE
G. shown and
H. fully, completely shown and
J. completely

Is there a big difference between *shown* and *revealed* in this context? Does a reader form a clearer image by being told in responses F, G, and H that the secret is both shown **and** revealed? Is there a difference between *fully* and *completely* in this context? Is the effect more emphatic when they're used together as in H? Certain authors may heap similar words on top of one another to create an effect; it's their **style.** In this instance, however, you have to decide whether this repetition fits the style of the rest of the passage or is simply redundant. Something that's "fully, completely shown and revealed" is in truth no more exposed than something that's "completely revealed." J is the best answer. It makes the point concisely.

Shorter isn't always better, though. Don't make the mistake of automatically leaning toward the shortest answer choice without thinking through the whole question:

When Maris broke Ruth's record, in response to[51] protests rather than praise. They argued that Maris had an unfair advantage over Ruth, since the 1961 season included eight extra[52] games than the 1927 season.

51. **A.** NO CHANGE
B. we responded with
C. there was a response of
D. many fans responded with

The issue in this question isn't redundancy. It's sentence structure. The shortest choice—"in response to"—isn't the clearest. The best answer should not only convey the idea that Maris's feat was greeted with protests rather than praise but also provide a reference for the pronoun *they* that begins the next sentence. As it turns out, the longest answer—D—is the best answer in this case.

IRRELEVANT INFORMATION

Simply because a particular statement is **true**, it's not necessarily **relevant** in a given context. When you're offered the option of omitting part of a sentence or paragraph, take a close look at what would be lost. Would the sentence or paragraph be harder to understand? Would important connections between ideas be missing? Would a reader lose vital information? Try not to be swayed by information that you might consider an interesting sidelight, or by observations and insights that you strongly agree with but that don't seem to contribute to the effectiveness of the passage.

The following example offers three ways to phrase a sentence, plus the option of eliminating that sentence.

---

[4]

Not too far from Avebury, if you walk among the cows along a footpath leading away from the highway, you will find a long barrow. <u>It are</u> [39] a kind of man-made cave constructed of huge rocks. This prehistoric burial site is only a few miles from the gigantic circle of stones. It is not too far to <u>walk, however it</u> [40] seems a long way to carry a body for burial if you imagine a funeral procession wending its way from Avebury to the barrow over the expanse of fields known as the Wiltshire Downs. <u>The Salisbury Cathedral could also be visited the same day.</u> [41]

[5]

There in the middle of a farmer's field, as <u>one stands</u> [42] inside the <u>ancient, empty barrow;</u> [43] you can hear the sounds of crows cawing and the farmer's tractor as he works his field nearby.

41. A. NO CHANGE
B. The Salisbury Cathedral can also be visited the same day.
C. On the same day the Salisbury Cathedral could have also been visited.
D. OMIT the underlined portion.

Responses A, B, and C say basically the same thing. The verb tenses differ—*could* versus *can*—but does any one of them seem significantly better here than the others? Do any of them contain flaws that would make you rule them out—aside from the shift to the passive voice they all use?

What is the topic of this paragraph? Does the sentence about Salisbury Cathedral contribute anything to a reader's understanding of prehistoric burial sites? What is the topic of the following paragraph? Could the sentence in question function as a transition to that paragraph? Notice the word *there* in the first sentence of Paragraph 5. When the writer says, "There in the middle of a farmer's field," do you think that's a reference to Salisbury Cathedral? Finally, how does the passage read without that sentence? Is Paragraph 5 actually about something located in Wiltshire Downs?

The writer might be telling the absolute truth about Salisbury Cathedral. And some people might be interested in learning that they could combine visits to ruins and a cathedral in one excursion. However, there's no doubt that the information is misplaced where it is now. Because you don't have the option of moving it to a more suitable place, you should be a ruthless editor and cut it out.

Some people might be interested in combining ruins and a cathedral in one excursion.

Below is another example of information that's true, but irrelevant.

To lose a set of car keys, a fountain pen, or a slip of paper with an important phone number is to know a [64] frustration. That [65] only goes away when what is lost is at last found. For most people, the anxious searching ends when they find their car keys under the sofa, their fountain pen in the pocket of a shirt about to be washed, the slip of paper with an important phone number under a stack of mail or mail-order catalogs—always, as they say, in the last place they look.

At least let me [66] lose ten pounds by virtue of some hard dieting, and the weight is returned [67] to me two weeks later. One good way to avoid that happening is to take up bicycling. [68] The way I figure it's [69] losing weight and losing my car keys or fountain pen are connected: when I'm dieting, I tend to become both crabby and weak. I lose concentration, and then I lose my car keys or pen.

68. F. NO CHANGE
G. My friends and I are dieting together.
H. Dieting is difficult because you must use willpower.
J. OMIT the underlined portion.

You might agree with the writer that bicycling can help keep weight off, but unless diet and exercise are the focus of the narrative, the information hardly seems necessary. The writer's other observations—that he or she and some friends are dieting together, and that dieting is difficult because of the willpower it requires—also veer from the passage's subject—namely, losing **things.**

While "OMIT the underlined portion" is the best answer for both of these examples, remember that won't always be the case.

STYLE

Questions of style can be tricky because often more than one response is grammatically correct. You usually need to consider the tone of the passage as a whole to determine the most appropriate choice of words.

When you first arrive in the English city of Oxford and observe its medieval architecture and narrow cobblestone streets, you may feel you have suddenly traveled back through time. The city's Gothic buildings stand as stoutly as ancient fortresses. Stepping through one of their arched doorways on my visit last spring, I found myself enclosed in a quiet courtyard; a carpeting with freshly mown grass. [1] Luxurious vines climbed the cool walls, and window boxes abounded with yellow roses. [2] I half expected a knight in armor to greet me!

Today's machine age does, however, [3] thumb its big nose upon [4] Oxford. Delivery trucks, red double-decker buses, and autos swerve around bicyclists and pedestrians.

4. F. NO CHANGE
   G. wade into
   H. intrude upon
   J. poke its big nose into

Here, the expression "thumb its big nose upon" Oxford is probably the first response you'd rule out. The idiom for this gesture of ridicule or disrespect is to thumb one's nose **at,** not **upon.** "Poke its big nose into" (J) isn't wrong from a grammatical standpoint. But what does it mean? How does it sound? Given the tone of the rest of the passage, is it an appropriate figure of speech to use to convey the impact of the machine age upon Oxford? "Wade into" (G) isn't ungrammatical either. Like J, it attributes a kind of human-sounding behavior to something nonhuman—today's machine age. The question is whether these uses of the rhetorical device *personification* are effective here or create distracting expressions that mostly call attention to themselves. "Intrude upon" (H) is the best answer because, unlike the other choices, it doesn't strain to inject humor into an essay that's basically serious.

AUDIENCE

The following example is a fairly typical strategy question concerning the appropriateness of an essay for a particular audience and specific purpose.

The story is building to the climax[21] the English countryside turns snowy, and the dialogue becomes a steady buzz. [5] Believe me, thirty-eight steps just won't do. [22]

But, I can hear you murmuring, one can always rent a copy of *The 39 Steps,* one that doesn't fade into oblivion. Before[23] the secret of the man with the missing finger is completely shown and revealed.[24] How much would it cost? It would cost less than having gone to a[25] movie, in[26] theory that should be a cheap solution, but in practice the result was quite different. You see, I've always had a problem with returning things, from library books to a friend's record. I mean well, but I had tended[27] to procrastinate. With library books I get off lightly—two or three cents per day overdue. With *The 39 Steps,* the bill was a whale,[28] $22.95. It cost me a tidy sum finally to find that last step.

I still consider myself a member of the VCR generation, but if I decide to see it[29] again, I intend to see it at the local theater. The evening will be a bargain even after I pay for my ticket and buy popcorn and a cola.

31. If you were putting together a collection of essays for high school seniors, it would be most appropriate to include this passage in a section containing essays on the:

A. pursuit and enjoyment of leisure in modern America.
B. generation gap, or how today's youth differ from their parents and grandparents.
C. changes in the visual arts over the last twenty years.
D. place of small business in modern American capitalism.

In this case, you need to decide which of the four categories offered seems to best fit the essay's topic and style. This is a personal essay—one that's more anecdotal than informational—and the tone is informal rather than scholarly.

Response A talks about the pursuit and enjoyment of leisure. This might seem like a very broad category. Watching movies on the VCR is definitely a leisure activity, but perhaps there's another category that's a closer fit.

Response B discusses the generation gap. It's true that the VCR wasn't available to high school students' parents and grandparents when **they** were high school age. Yet the passage doesn't mention the activities of other generations. The writer isn't trying to draw a contrast in this essay. Of course, it's possible that this essay could be grouped with ones by older writers talking about what people did for fun before VCRs; the editor could, with the proper introduction, make this part of a section on the generation gap. As it stands, however, the essay itself contains no references that would suggest it's about anything besides the pleasures and perils of owning a VCR.

Again, C might sound like a possibility because this essay could certainly be one of several dealing with various aspects of the visual arts. Still, the essay itself doesn't discuss that topic. There's no attempt to make any broad generalizations, identify trends, or otherwise inform a reader about the visual arts scene in the last twenty years. Taken on face value, the essay wouldn't necessarily fit in this category any better than in B.

D gets really distant from the passage. Some video rental stores are small businesses, as are some movie theaters, and the writer does talk about the cost of renting a movie and the cost of going to one. But it would be stretching a point to claim that the writer is attempting to make any statement about small businesses and capitalism. The essay focuses on one person's experiences with a VCR, and there's no reasonable way you can inflate it into a serious political essay.

Response A is the best answer after all, then, even though it doesn't specifically mention VCRs or movies. The essay provides an example of one leisure activity; it doesn't address the issues suggested by the other three responses.

ENGLISH TEST

45 Minutes—75 Questions

DIRECTIONS: In the five passages that follow, certain words and phrases are underlined and numbered. In the right-hand column, you will find alternatives for each underlined part. You are to choose the one that best expresses the idea, makes the statement appropriate for standard written English, or is worded most consistently with the style and tone of the passage as a whole. If you think the original version is best, choose "NO CHANGE."

You will also find questions about a section of the passage, or about the passage as a whole. These questions do not refer to an underlined portion of the passage, but rather are identified by a number or numbers in a box.

For each question, choose the alternative you consider best and blacken the corresponding oval on your answer sheet. Read each passage through once before you begin to answer the questions that accompany it. You cannot determine most answers without reading several sentences beyond the question. Be sure that you have read far enough ahead each time you choose an alternative.

Passage I

[1]

When you first arrive in the English city of Oxford and observe its medieval architecture and narrow cobblestone streets, you may feel you have suddenly traveled back through time. The city's Gothic buildings stand as stoutly as ancient fortresses. Stepping through one of their arched doorways on my visit last spring, I found myself enclosed in a quiet courtyard; a carpeting[1] with freshly mown grass. Luxurious vines climbed the cool walls, and window boxes abounded with yellow roses.[2] I half expected a knight in armor to greet me!

[2]

Today's machine age does, however,[3] thumb its big nose upon[4] Oxford. Delivery trucks, red double-decker buses, and autos swerve around bicyclists and pedestrians. Fortunately, though, you can escape the crowded streets in the city's large

1. **A.** NO CHANGE
   B. courtyard, being carpeted
   C. courtyard, having been carpeted
   D. courtyard carpeted

2. **F.** NO CHANGE
   G. Luxurious cool walls climbed vines, and yellow roses abounded with window boxes.
   H. Yellow roses abounded with luxurious vines, and the cool walls climbed window boxes.
   J. The cool walls climbed with luxurious vines, and yellow roses abounded window boxes.

3. **A.** NO CHANGE
   B. Todays machine age do
   C. Todays' age of machines do
   D. Todays machine age does

4. **F.** NO CHANGE
   G. wade into
   H. intrude upon
   J. poke its big nose into

public parks. [5] Or, instead, you can rent a small boat and spend a stagnant[6] afternoon on the Thames River.

[3]

If you are hungry, you will grow even hungrier if you don't know. The English dining customs—[7] Oxford's eating places close between[8] the traditional meal hours. There is, however, an extra meal hour—teatime, in late afternoon.[9] An order of tea-for-two includes a pot of tea, a plate of big, fluffy, raisin-studded biscuits called "scones" and bowls;[10] of butter, jam, and marmalade.

[4]

There are many interesting and educational places to visit in Oxford center.[11] There you might visit some of the thirty-three colleges that make up Oxford University. You might also choose to look at the paintings in the Ashmolean Museum, to browse through the many bookstores and woolen shops, or to wander through Oxford's open markets. Everywhere, at every quarter

5. Paragraph 2 expresses the point of view that traffic, an effect of modernization, is a disruptive and negative feature in Oxford. The writer is revising the whole paragraph to express a more positive attitude toward modernizing the city and a less negative attitude toward the traffic. Which of the following revisions of the preceding sentence would best help to express that new point of view?
   - **A.** If you like, however, you can find an antidote to that hectic rush in the city's large public parks.
   - **B.** After experiencing the bustling excitement of Oxford's lively, crowded streets, you can walk through one of the city's large public parks.
   - **C.** Exhausted, you can escape Oxford's crowded streets in one of its large public parks.
   - **D.** When traffic noise distracts you from the "real" Oxford, you may turn to one of the city's sedate public parks.

6. **F.** NO CHANGE
   G. sluggish
   H. slothful
   J. leisurely

7. **A.** NO CHANGE
   B. hungrier. If you don't know the English dining customs
   C. hungrier if you don't know the English dining customs.
   D. hungrier if you don't know. The English dining customs:

8. **F.** NO CHANGE
   G. among
   H. to
   J. OMIT the underlined portion.

9. **A.** NO CHANGE
   B. hour. Unlike this, newspapers in America rarely put out "extras" anymore.
   C. hour, unlike America in late afternoon, teatime.
   D. hour, teatime unlike in late afternoon in America.

10. **F.** NO CHANGE
    G. "scones"; and including bowls
    H. "scones," and bowls
    J. "scones," and bowls,

11. Which of the suggested sentences makes the best introduction to Paragraph 4 and the best transition from Paragraph 3?
    - **A.** NO CHANGE
    - **B.** Fortified by a teatime snack, you should have plenty of energy for a stroll through the city's center.
    - **C.** Most visitors to Oxford enjoy a tea break in the late afternoon.
    - **D.** A visit to Oxford is not complete without a stop at Oxford University.

GO ON TO THE NEXT PAGE.

hour, you will hear chimes pealing out from the cities much spires. [12]

[5]

After a refreshing walk, you will be ready for a very perfect conclusion to a day in [13] Oxford. Being [14] a concert by the choir at Christ Church Cathedral or an organ recital at Merton College Chapel, where, in spring, bowls of fresh strawberries and cream is [15] served at intermission.

12. F. NO CHANGE
    G. city's many
    H. cities many
    J. citys' many

13. A. NO CHANGE
    B. very perfect ending
    C. fairly perfect ending
    D. perfect conclusion

14. F. NO CHANGE
    G. Oxford. The ending being
    H. Oxford—
    J. Oxford

15. A. NO CHANGE
    B. is often
    C. has been
    D. are

Passage II

What teases us with the giddy possibilities of freedom better than a videocassette recorder? There are few things that seem to promise so much for so little effort. Program the right channel, set the timer, and even the late-late-late movie is within grasp. Neither storm nor [16] sleep will keep a well-running VCR from its appointed task.

In fact, a VCR can free us from the tyranny of the television schedule altogether. With video stores almost as prevalent as fast-food restaurants. The desire [17] to finally see the conclusion of a movie can be as readily satisfied as the urge [18] for a burger and fries.

[1] Unfortunately, the *us* I've been talking about doesn't including me. [19] [2] For example, I have several versions of Alfred Hitchcock's mystery-comedy *The 39 Steps* [20] none of them includes the last fifteen minutes. [3] Either the VCR runs out of tape or the timer clicks

16. F. NO CHANGE
    G. Neither, storm nor
    H. Neither storm nor,
    J. Neither storm, nor

17. A. NO CHANGE
    B. restaurants, the
    C. restaurants; the
    D. restaurants, and the

18. F. NO CHANGE
    G. the urge by one
    H. you can satisfy the urge
    J. the urge can be satisfied by one

19. A. NO CHANGE
    B. doesn't include I.
    C. didn't include me.
    D. doesn't include me.

20. F. NO CHANGE
    G. *Steps,* but
    H. *Steps* which
    J. *Steps,* where

GO ON TO THE NEXT PAGE.

off too soon. [4] <u>The story is building to the climax</u> [21] the English countryside turns snowy, and the dialogue becomes a steady buzz. [5] Believe me, thirty-eight steps just won't do. [22]

But, I can hear you murmuring, one can always rent a copy of *The 39 Steps,* one that doesn't fade into <u>oblivion. Before</u> [23] the secret of the man with the missing finger is <u>completely shown and</u> [24] revealed. How much would it cost? It would cost less than <u>having gone</u> [25] to a <u>movie, in</u> [26] theory that should be a cheap solution, but in practice the result was quite different. You see, I've always had a problem with returning things, from library books to a friend's record. I mean well, but I <u>had tended</u> [27] to procrastinate. With library books I get off lightly—two or three cents per day overdue. With *The 39 Steps,* <u>the bill was a whale,</u> [28] $22.95. It cost me a tidy sum finally to find that last step.

I still consider myself a member of the VCR generation, but if I decide to see <u>it</u> [29] again, I intend to see it at the local theater. The evening will be a bargain even after I pay for my ticket and buy popcorn and a cola.

21. A. NO CHANGE
B. Just when the story is building to the climax,
C. The story builds to the climax
D. The story builds to the climax thus

22. For the sake of unity and coherence, Sentence 2 should be:
F. placed where it is now.
G. placed after Sentence 4.
H. placed after Sentence 5.
J. OMITTED.

23. A. NO CHANGE
B. oblivion before
C. oblivion! Before
D. oblivion! Before,

24. F. NO CHANGE
G. shown and
H. fully, completely shown and
J. completely

25. A. NO CHANGE
B. being gone
C. going
D. having had gone

26. F. NO CHANGE
G. movie, as a
H. movie in
J. movie. In

27. A. NO CHANGE
B. had this tendency
C. tend
D. tended

28. F. NO CHANGE
G. *Steps,* the bill was elephantine in its spacious size,
H. *Steps* the bill came to
J. *Steps,* the bill came to,

29. A. NO CHANGE
B. that
C. that movie;
D. *The 39 Steps*

GO ON TO THE NEXT PAGE.

Items 30 and 31 pose questions about Passage II as a whole.

30. Considering the tone and subject matter of the essay, is the writer's use of the pronoun "I" appropriate?
    - F. No, because the writer is speaking for everyone who owns or rents VCRs.
    - G. No, because the rules of grammar dictate that one should avoid "I" in personal writing.
    - H. Yes, because the rules of grammar require a writer to use "I" whenever writing about anything he or she has personally experienced.
    - J. Yes, because this is a personal narrative and using "I" gives the story authenticity and immediacy.

31. If you were putting together a collection of essays for high school seniors, it would be most appropriate to include this passage in a section containing essays on the:
    - A. pursuit and enjoyment of leisure in modern America.
    - B. generation gap, or how today's youth differ from their parents and grandparents.
    - C. changes in the visual arts over the last twenty years.
    - D. place of small business in modern American capitalism.

Passage III

[1]

The small village of Avebury in North Wiltshire, England, is set amid large circles of standing stones that date from prehistoric times. Nevertheless tourists [32] come to Avebury specifically to see the stones. Children on school tours touch them and even climb on them. Cows graze in the fields beside them and lie in their cool shadows. The villagers of Avebury feel their presence of them [33] in their daily lives.

[2]

No one knows the original function of these monuments, but both scientific and religious purposes have been suggested. The stones may have been used in some form of worship, including elaborate funeral rituals, or as an astronomical observatory. [34]

[3]

Archaeologists think the stones were gathered in approximately 2500 B.C. and arranged in the same

32. F. NO CHANGE
    - G. Yet tourists
    - H. Since tourists
    - J. Tourists

33. A. NO CHANGE
    - B. the monuments' presence
    - C. it's presence
    - D. its old presence

34. Which of the following strategies would best support the assertion made in Paragraph 2 that scientific and religious purposes have been suggested as the original functions of the monuments?
    - F. Discussing ancient funeral rites in England, because the barrows discussed in Paragraphs 3 and 4 are tombs.
    - G. Discussing other primitive observatories, because the religious functions have already been discussed.
    - H. Discussing primitive man and his religious beliefs, because that is the focus of the passage and should be developed.
    - J. Discussing the various theories concerning religious and scientific use of the monuments, because examples make the point clearer.

GO ON TO THE NEXT PAGE.

pattern seen today. The circles of earth and stone are more[35] formidable in size and appearance, like petrified rocks.[36] The outer bank is twenty feet high and seventy-five feet wide at the base. Inside is a ditch thirty feet deep and forty feet wide. One circle is composed of more than 100 stones, close to fifty tons in weight. Nearby is a wooden temple also built by local Neolithic communities, perhaps the Rhinelander Beaker Folk, probably in all likelihood[37] around 1800 B.C. There are other prehistoric sites in the area around Avebury including;[38] the mounds known as the West and East Kennet long barrows, which also date from 2500 B.C.

[4]

Not too far from Avebury, if you walk among the cows along a footpath leading away from the highway, you will find a long barrow. It are[39] a kind of man-made cave constructed of huge rocks. This prehistoric burial site is only a few miles from the gigantic circle of stones. It is not too far to walk, however it[40] seems a long way to carry a body for burial if you imagine a funeral procession wending its way from Avebury to the barrow over the expanse of fields known as the Wiltshire Downs. The Salisbury Cathedral could also be visited the same day.[41]

[5]

There in the middle of a farmer's field, as one stands[42] inside the

35. **A.** NO CHANGE
B. very much
C. much more
D. OMIT the underlined portion.

36. **F.** NO CHANGE
G. looking like formidable rocks.
H. looking like little monsters from space.
J. OMIT the underlined portion and end the sentence with a period.

37. **A.** NO CHANGE
B. very likely
C. by all odds
D. OMIT the underlined portion.

38. **F.** NO CHANGE
G. Avebury, including
H. Avebury: including
J. Avebury; including

39. **A.** NO CHANGE
B. Its
C. It is
D. It were

40. **F.** NO CHANGE
G. walk, however it,
H. walk; however, it
J. walk, however, it

41. **A.** NO CHANGE
B. The Salisbury Cathedral can also be visited the same day.
C. On the same day the Salisbury Cathedral could have also been visited.
D. OMIT the underlined portion.

42. **F.** NO CHANGE
G. one stood
H. he stands
J. you stand

GO ON TO THE NEXT PAGE.

ancient, empty barrow; you can hear the sounds [43] of crows cawing and the farmer's tractor as he works his field nearby.

43. A. NO CHANGE
B. ancient empty barrow;
C. ancient empty barrow:
D. ancient, empty barrow,

Items 44–46 pose questions about Passage III as a whole.

44. Which of the following sentences, if added at the end of Paragraph 5, would best relate Paragraph 5 to Paragraph 1 in order to tie together the passage as a whole?

- **F.** Ancient burial customs were strange.
- **G.** Avebury lives close to its history.
- **H.** Avebury's farmers find the rocks interfere with their tractors.
- **J.** The circle is a universal symbol.

45. If the writer wanted to strengthen the aspect of the passage relating to the theories about the scientific purpose of the monuments, it would be most logical to put this new material in:

- **A.** Paragraph 1, because all important information has to be introduced immediately.
- **B.** a separate paragraph, because it would be the only one devoted solely to theories about scientific use.
- **C.** Paragraph 3's place, because that paragraph was just description and thus irrelevant.
- **D.** Paragraph 5, because it sums up the points made earlier.

46. Suppose the writer wished to add the following sentences to the passage:

> Several of the burials that are apparently part of the West Kennet long barrows were found to contain beakers and/or bowls. They are thought to be dedication sites.

The new sentences would most logically be placed in which of the following paragraphs?

- **F.** Paragraph 1, because all important information has to be introduced immediately.
- **G.** A separate paragraph following Paragraph 1, because important new material must be placed alone so it stands out.
- **H.** Paragraph 3, because that is where the possible religious use is discussed.
- **J.** Paragraph 5, because every essay should have an important ending.

Passage IV

[1]

[1] Most athletes, who break a record, are [47] honored and praised, even idolized, by fans. [2] Usually, the longer the record has stood, the most acclaims [48] the record-breaker receives. [3] That's usually the case, but not always. [4] Certainly it wasn't with Roger Maris, the Yankee outfielder who, in 1961, broke the record for the most home runs hit in one season. [49]

[2]

Maris's sixty-one home runs broke the record set by the legendary Babe Ruth, in 1927, Ruth [50] slammed sixty home runs. He was remarkable not

47. **A.** NO CHANGE
B. athletes, who break a record
C. athletes who break a record
D. athletes who break a record,

48. **F.** NO CHANGE
G. most acclaim
H. more additional acclaims
J. more acclaim

49. For the sake of unity and coherence, Sentence 3 should be placed:

- **A.** where it is now.
- **B.** after Sentence 1.
- **C.** after Sentence 4.
- **D.** at the end of Paragraph 2.

50. **F.** NO CHANGE
G. Ruth in 1927,
H. Ruth. In 1927,
J. Ruth,

GO ON TO THE NEXT PAGE.

only for his ability to hit homers, but also for the loyalty and affection he inspired. Maris, on the other hand, was not a very popular player.

[3]

When Maris broke Ruth's record, in response to [51] protests rather than praise. They argued that Maris had an unfair advantage over Ruth, since the 1961 season included eight extra [52] games than the 1927 season. In reply, Maris's relatively few supporters indignantly point that; despite [53] the long season, Maris had been at the plate fewer times than Ruth. To Maris's fans it was thrilling that Maris had broken Ruth's record after a considerable period of thirty-four years. [54]

51. **A.** NO CHANGE
B. we responded with
C. there was a response of
D. many fans responded with

52. **F.** NO CHANGE
G. additional
H. excess
J. more

53. **A.** NO CHANGE
B. pointed out that, despite
C. pointed that out. Despite
D. point that out, despite

54. **F.** NO CHANGE
G. a considerable and lengthy period.
H. an endless repetition of thirty-four years.
J. thirty-four years.

[4]

After baseball officials listened carefully to both sides, they determined that, although Maris had broken the record, he should not receive full recognition for his achievement. Nonetheless, [55] when the officials listed the new record, they qualified it by putting an asterisk next to the entry. This indicated that, while Maris had broken the record, he had done so after appearing in more games than had Ruth.

55. **A.** NO CHANGE
B. achievement. Therefore,
C. achievement; however,
D. achievement. Nevertheless,

[5]

Up to that time, no other broken record had been similarly treated, yet [56] baseball devotees whose admiration for [57] the ability of both men thought the resolution unfair. They reasoned that all players should receive full credit for their accomplishments, regardless of technicalities.

56. **F.** NO CHANGE
G. treated because
H. treated, so
J. treated, although it is true that

57. **A.** NO CHANGE
B. whom admire
C. who admired
D. whom admired

GO ON TO THE NEXT PAGE.

Maris, understandably, was bitter about the lack [58] of recognition. [59]

[6]

The Yankees traded Maris after a few seasons. The remainder of his baseball career was unexceptional. He died in 1985, he still felt [60] he had been unjustly denied his rightful place in baseball history.

58. F. NO CHANGE
    G. Maris understandably,
    H. Maris, understandably—
    J. Maris, understandably

59. A. NO CHANGE
    B. recognition, feeling it was his last straw.
    C. recognition of his last last straw.
    D. recognition which was the last straw.

60. F. NO CHANGE
    G. still feeling
    H. and continued to be feeling that
    J. until he felt

Item 61 poses a question about Passage IV as a whole.

61. The writer wants to support the assertion in Paragraph 2 that Maris was not a popular player by explaining why he was unpopular. Which of the following strategies would best accomplish that goal?
    A. Citing some specific examples to illustrate why Maris was not liked
    B. Comparing the number of Maris's fans with the number of Ruth's fans
    C. Explaining why an athlete should not worry about being popular
    D. Citing some specific examples to illustrate why Ruth was popular

---

Passage V

The following paragraphs may or may not be in the most logical order. Each paragraph is numbered in brackets, and item 74 will ask you to choose the best placement of Paragraph 1.

[1]

This, alas, is not my experience. When I lose [62] something, it always stays lost. Neither my keys nor my wallet ever turns up in a friendly lost-and-found; nobody calls to say that she has stumbled across my fountain pen; my stack of catalogs is only a

62. F. NO CHANGE
    G. experience, whenever
    H. experience when
    J. experience, when

GO ON TO THE NEXT PAGE.

stack of catalogs. [63] I have learned to live, and to search, with resignation.

[2]

To lose a set of car keys, a fountain pen, or a slip of paper with an important phone number is <u>to know</u>[64] a <u>frustration. That</u>[65] only goes away when what is lost is at last found. For most people, the anxious searching ends when they find their car keys under the sofa, their fountain pen in the pocket of a shirt about to be washed, the slip of paper with an important phone number under a stack of mail or mail-order catalogs—always, as they say, in the last place they look.

[3]

<u>At least let</u>[66] me lose ten pounds by virtue of some hard dieting, and the weight <u>is returned</u>[67] to me two weeks later. <u>One good way to avoid that happening is to take up bicycling.</u>[68] The way I figure <u>it's</u>[69] losing weight and losing my car keys or fountain pen are connected: when I'm dieting, I tend to become both crabby and weak. I lose concentration, and then I lose my car keys or pen.

[4]

Searching for them is anxious <u>work, it's</u>[70] easy to work up an appetite rooting through drawers.

63. The writer says, "My stack of catalogs is only a stack of catalogs" to mean that the catalogs:
   A. are not hiding any missing items.
   B. represent resignation.
   C. never get returned, unlike the keys or fountain pen.
   D. don't usually get lost.

64. F. NO CHANGE
   G. knowing
   H. known
   J. having known

65. A. NO CHANGE
   B. frustration, that
   C. frustration that
   D. frustration. Which

66. F. NO CHANGE
   G. But, letting
   H. Therefore, let
   J. But let

67. A. NO CHANGE
   B. was returned
   C. is return
   D. having been returned

68. F. NO CHANGE
   G. My friends and I are dieting together.
   H. Dieting is difficult because you must use willpower.
   J. OMIT the underlined portion.

69. A. NO CHANGE
   B. its
   C. it,
   D. it

70. F. NO CHANGE
   G. work it's
   H. work its
   J. work. It's

GO ON TO THE NEXT PAGE.

Why wonder,[71] I need a snack or even an extra meal. Never finding the object I'm looking for, I do notice, as I pass the full-length mirror, that my face is fuller than it was a week ago, and that my pants seem just a touch tighter.

[5]

Luckily, dieting is not the only way I lose weight. For example, I get plenty of exercise walking home when I've lost my car keys and will not be able to find[72] the slip of paper with the locksmith's number. I suppose I could ask Information for it, but, then again, I have never seemed[73] to have my fountain pen handy to write it down.

71. A. NO CHANGE
    B. No wonder
    C. Without a doubt
    D. No matter what,

72. F. NO CHANGE
    G. won't have found
    H. hadn't found
    J. can't find

73. A. NO CHANGE
    B. again. I never seem
    C. again, I never seem
    D. again, never seeming

Items 74 and 75 pose questions about Passage V as a whole.

74. For the sake of unity and coherence, Paragraph 1 should be placed:
    F. where it is now.
    G. after Paragraph 2.
    H. after Paragraph 3.
    J. after Paragraph 5.

75. In relating weight loss to missing personal objects, the writer is:
    A. providing real-life situations of memory lapses for a tragic effect.
    B. relating unlike problems for an amusing effect.
    C. relating physiological and psychological facts for a scientific effect.
    D. offering concrete examples of weight loss techniques for a helpful effect.

END OF TEST 1

STOP! DO NOT TURN THE PAGE UNTIL TOLD TO DO SO.

ACT ASSESSMENT MATHEMATICS TEST

The ACT Mathematics Test asks you to answer 60 multiple-choice questions in 60 minutes. Because the questions are designed to measure your mathematical achievement—the knowledge and skills you have learned over the years and are likely to need in college—they cover a wide variety of topics and techniques. Naturally, you'll have to do some calculating to answer most of the questions; you will also have to recall some basic mathematical principles. However, the test emphasizes quantitative reasoning ability rather than mere computational skills or rote recall of formulas.

The ACT Mathematics Test covers five content areas: pre-algebra (20%), elementary algebra (20%), intermediate algebra and coordinate geometry (30%), plane geometry (23%), and trigonometry (7%). These content areas are grouped into three main categories, represented approximately as follows on the test:

- 24 questions dealing with pre-algebra and elementary algebra
- 18 questions based on intermediate algebra and coordinate geometry
- 14 questions from plane geometry and 4 from trigonometry

You will receive a subscore in each of these three main content categories along with a total score for the entire test.

In the category of pre-algebra and elementary algebra, you can expect questions that require operations with positive and negative integers, fractions, and decimals, as well as operations with simple algebraic expressions, including solving linear equations. The most advanced topic in this category is the solution of quadratic equations by factoring.

In the area of intermediate algebra and coordinate geometry, you can expect questions about graphing in the standard (x,y) coordinate plane and questions on exponents, radicals, rational expressions, inequalities, systems of linear equations, the quadratic formula, and similar topics from a typical intermediate algebra course.

In the category of plane geometry and trigonometry, you can expect questions based on the properties and relations of plane figures and on the six trigonometric ratios, the graphs of trigonometric functions, or basic trigonometric identities.

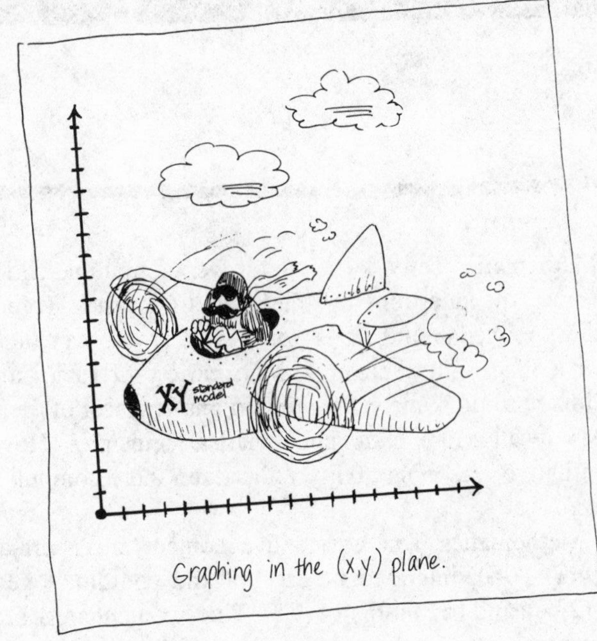

Graphing in the (x,y) plane.

TYPES OF QUESTIONS ON THE ACT MATHEMATICS TEST

At the end of this section, you'll find a sample ACT Mathematics Test. To give you an idea of the wide variety of math problems you're likely to encounter on the ACT, this discussion will focus on a number of questions from that sample test. Before reading the rest of this section, you may want to look through the questions, try some of them out, or even take the whole test. If so, go ahead and do that now. Then you can come back and finish reading this discussion.

In terms of presentation, there is only one type of question on the ACT Mathematics Test—the standard multiple-choice item with five answer choices. Nevertheless, as you may have noticed, the questions on the test differ from one another in many ways. Some of the ways in which they differ are apparent. The differences in content, for instance, are fairly obvious. You've already looked briefly at the three main content categories and will get a better idea of the range of topics in each category as you go along. The other ways in which the questions differ are less obvious, and you'll want to be aware of them just so you'll be prepared for them when you take the ACT.

BASIC MATH PROBLEMS

The sort of question you're most familiar with is the stripped-down, bare-bones, garden-variety math problem—the **"basic" math problem.** Problem 16 from the sample test, which happens to fall into the content category of pre-algebra/elementary algebra, is a perfect example:

---

16. $2\sqrt{28} + 3\sqrt{175} = ?$

F. $12\sqrt{7}$
G. $19\sqrt{7}$
H. 63
J. $5\sqrt{203}$
K. $83\sqrt{7}$

You may not have seen this particular problem before, but you've seen many others like it in your math books. The basic type is notable primarily for its simplicity: it's perfectly straightforward; it tests a readily identifiable skill (in this case the simplification and addition of radicals); it contains no words or extra information that might confuse you; it poses the very question you expect it to pose; and it asks you to find an exact numeric answer. You'll probably have a few questions with these characteristics on the particular version of the ACT Mathematics Test you take. The rest of the questions will be variations on this basic type.

Properly attired math question recoils in horror from stripped-down, bare-bones type.

WORD PROBLEMS

One common variation is the type of **question that uses words** as well as, or occasionally instead of, mathematical symbols. It may use just a few words and be no harder to interpret than the basic type, or it may use a lot of words and be more like the word, or story, problems that you've come to know and love. Problem 36 is an example of a question that includes some, but not many, words:

---

36. What is the sum of the 2 solutions for x in the equation $|2x - 6| = 10$?

F. 12
G. 6
H. -2
J. -6
K. -12

Problem 15 is an example of a more complicated problem:

---

15. The diagram below shows a pasture which is fenced in. All but 1 section of fence run straight north–south or east–west. Consecutive fence posts are 10 feet apart except for the 1 diagonal section. Which of the following statements best describes P, the perimeter of the pasture, in feet?

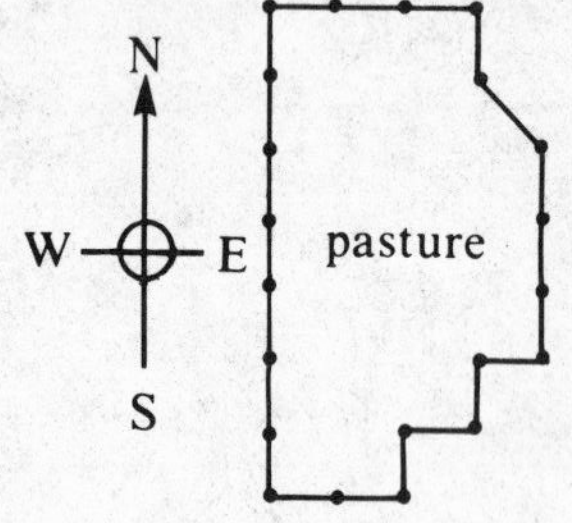

A. $P > 210$
B. $P = 210$
C. $P < 210$
D. $P > 230$
E. $P = 240$

A math question that uses words isn't necessarily harder than one that doesn't, but it's often more challenging. For one thing, a word problem usually doesn't set up the problem for you; you have to set it up for yourself. Also, the words often direct you to do something unexpected. Take a closer look at problems 36 and 15, for instance. Problem 36, which falls into the content category of intermediate algebra/coordinate geometry, doesn't ask you to find one or both of the values of x that satisfy the absolute value equation (something you may have expected); instead, it asks you to find the **sum** of the two solutions (something you may **not** have expected). Problem 15, which falls into the content category of pre-algebra/elementary algebra, doesn't ask you to find the exact perimeter of the pasture; instead, it asks you to pick out the statement that best describes that perimeter. These problems illustrate not just one variation of the basic type but three: the **problem that uses words,** the **problem that poses a question you may not be expecting,** and the **problem that asks for something other than a numeric answer.**

PROBLEMS WITH FIGURES

Problem 15 illustrates a fourth variation—the **problem that includes a figure.** Most of the figures you see will be in the question part of a problem, and they're intended either to aid you in understanding the problem or to convey information that you need to solve it, as in problem 15. Some figures, however, will be in the answer part of a problem; these figures will be images of the solution to the problem, and only one of them will be correct. Problem 21, for instance, which falls into the content category of intermediate algebra/coordinate geometry, asks you to pick out the graph of the solution set of a particular inequality:

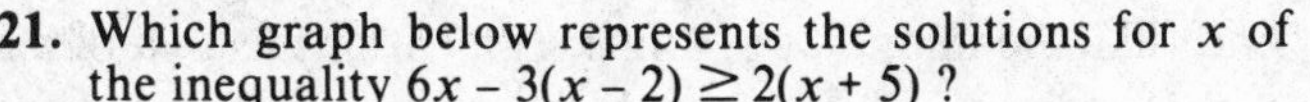

21. Which graph below represents the solutions for x of the inequality $6x - 3(x - 2) \geq 2(x + 5)$?

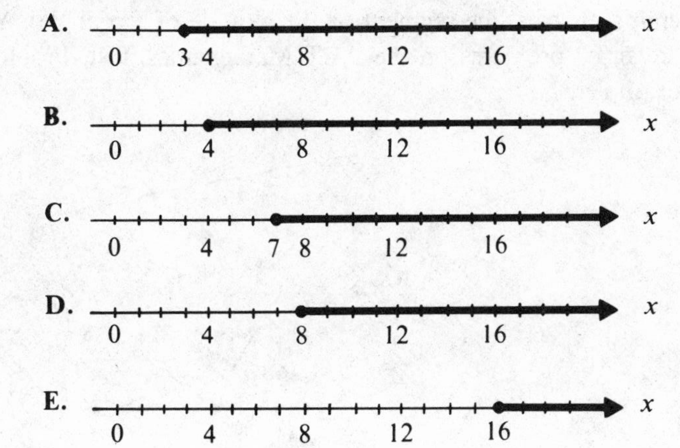

If you'd like to look at another example, problem 54 in the sample test that follows this section is very similar.

REVERSAL OF PROBLEM AND SOLUTION

A fifth variation is the **question that reverses the typical roles of problem and solution.** Problem 57, also a pre-algebra/elementary algebra problem, is an example of this variation:

---

57. The roots of a polynomial are $\frac{2}{5}$ and $-\frac{4}{3}$. Which one of the following could be the polynomial?

A. $(2x + 5)(4x - 3)$
B. $(2x - 5)(3x + 4)$
C. $(2x - 5)(4x + 3)$
D. $(5x + 2)(3x - 4)$
E. $(5x - 2)(3x + 4)$

Here, instead of being given a problem and asked to find the solution, you're given a solution—the zeros of a polynomial—and you're asked to find the problem—the polynomial (in factored form) that has these zeros.

Most "reverse" questions, you'll be happy to know, aren't quite as unusual as this one. These problems give you something you may be accustomed to being asked to find (like the midpoint of a line segment or the area of a triangle) and ask you to find something that you're probably accustomed to being given (like one of the endpoints of a line segment or the altitude of a triangle). You'll likely find several "reverse" problems on the ACT Mathematics Test. Problems 43 and 31 are two examples.

Triangle contemplating its altitude.

SET-UP PROBLEMS

Another variation is the **"set-up" question.** As the name suggests, this variation doesn't ask you to solve a problem; it simply asks you to set it up, usually by translating some of the words in the question into an equation, an inequality, or an algebraic expression. Problem 3, which fits into the content category of pre-algebra/elementary algebra, is an example of this variation:

---

3. When getting into shape by exercising, the subject's maximum recommended number of heartbeats per minute (h) can be determined by subtracting the subject's age (a) from 220 and then taking 75% of that value. This relation is expressed by which of the following formulas?

A. $h = .75(220 - a)$
B. $h = .75(220) - a$
C. $h = 220 - .75a$
D. $.75h = 220 - a$
E. $220 = .75(h - a)$

PROBLEMS WITH EXTRANEOUS OR INSUFFICIENT INFORMATION

A seventh variation is the **question that gives you either less or more information than you need to answer it.** The question that contains insufficient information probably includes as one of the answer choices "Cannot be determined from the given information." Of course "Cannot be determined" isn't the correct answer every time it appears; a question that contains enough, or even more than enough, information may also include "Cannot be determined" as an answer choice. An example of a question that contains extra information is problem 50, a plane geometry/trigonometry problem:

---

50. What is $\tan\theta$ if $\sin\theta = \frac{5}{13}$ and $\cot\theta = \frac{12}{5}$?

F. $\frac{25}{126}$
G. $\frac{5}{12}$
H. $\frac{12}{13}$
J. $\frac{13}{12}$
K. $\frac{12}{5}$

6

In this question, the value of $\sin\theta$ isn't needed. The value of $\tan\theta$ can be determined directly from $\cot\theta$. However, the extra information may cause you to confuse $\cos\theta$ with $\cot\theta$.

In another question, like problem 34, the extra information might cause confusion and make it difficult for you to see what you need to do to solve the problem. You'll find some advice on how to deal with extra information later, in the discussion of problem 34.

STRATEGIES FOR TAKING THE ACT MATHEMATICS TEST

The last section described some of the most common variations on the basic multiple-choice question that you're likely to encounter on the ACT Mathematics Test. It's not important that you remember these variations; it's just important that you be aware of them so that they don't take you by surprise on exam day.

The next section discusses particular problems and some specific strategies you can use to solve them and also introduces a useful four-step problem-solving method. Before that, though, here's some general advice on how to approach the ACT Mathematics Test.

PACE YOURSELF.

You have 60 minutes to answer 60 questions, for an average of 1 minute per question. You may want to check the clock every few minutes to make sure you're maintaining the pace you need to finish the test in an hour. As you're pacing yourself, keep in mind that most people find the first questions on the test easier (and therefore faster to work) than the ones that come later.

DON'T SPEND TOO MUCH TIME ON ANY ONE QUESTION.

If you don't see a way to solve a problem, mark it in your test booklet so you can return to it easily. Then move on to those questions you **can** answer.

DEVELOP A STRATEGY FOR ANSWERING EASIER AND HARDER QUESTIONS.

Many people like to answer the easier questions first, saving the harder ones for last. *Easy* and *hard* are relative terms. You know which math topics are easy for you and which ones are hard for you. Remember that each correctly answered question, no matter how difficult, contributes only 1 point to your raw score; that is, every correct answer counts for the same amount.

READ EACH QUESTION CAREFULLY.

Read carefully enough so that you'll know what you have to find before you start looking for it.

WATCH FOR UNNECESSARY INFORMATION.

Expect at least a few questions to contain extra information—information that you don't need in order to solve the problem.

LOOK FOR INFORMATION IN THE ANSWER CHOICES.

Think of the answer choices as part of the information you're given with each question. Notice the form in which they're expressed and the range of values they represent. These observations may provide a clue as to how you can proceed.

LABEL THE FIGURES.

If a question includes an illustrative figure, you may want to label the figure (with numbers or letters or notes) so that it's a complete picture of everything you're given and everything you must deduce. (Remember: Unless you're instructed otherwise, you're allowed and encouraged to write in your test booklet.)

DRAW A PICTURE.

If it will help you visualize a problem, draw a picture.

THINK BEFORE YOU CALCULATE.

Remember that the test is designed to measure your reasoning ability, not just your computing skill. Your head is a far more powerful and efficient problem-solving tool than your pencil.

RECORD YOUR CALCULATIONS.

Write your calculations in your test booklet so you'll be able to check your work.

CHECK YOUR ANSWER.

When you arrive at an answer, ask yourself whether it makes sense. Then check to make sure that it answers the question.

ANSWER EVERY QUESTION.

If you don't remember how to solve a particular problem, don't panic. Use what you do remember to eliminate as many of the answers as you can. Then choose one of the remaining alternatives.

Answer each question, even if you have to guess. You'll get a point for every correct answer, and you won't lose any points for incorrect answers.

USE ANY TIME YOU HAVE LEFT AT THE END OF THE MATHEMATICS TEST.

If you have time remaining at the end of this test, use it to answer any math questions you may have skipped, check your computations, look over your answer sheet for mismatched answers or stray pencil marks, and be sure you've filled in an answer for **each** question. (Remember: You're allowed to work on only one test at a time.)

FIND A PROBLEM-SOLVING METHOD YOU'RE COMFORTABLE WITH.

The more confident you are about solving math problems, the better you're likely to be at it. One way to build your confidence is through practice, using a systematic method for solving math problems. Here's a simple four-step method, developed by George Polya, that you can try.

STEP 1: UNDERSTANDING THE PROBLEM. The first, and most important, step in the problem-solving process is understanding the problem. The first, and most important, step in understanding the problem is reading it carefully. Sound simple? It is. However, when you're racing against the clock, it's tempting to cut corners by skimming a problem instead of reading it carefully. By all means read as quickly as you can, but don't read so fast that you can't comprehend what you're reading. If you do, you may end up solving the wrong problem—finding the area of a circle, for instance, when you're asked to find the circumference. Then you don't save time; you waste it.

Reading carefully means reading actively—with your mind fully engaged. Your goal in this first step is to find the answers to these two questions:

1. What am I asked to find?
2. What am I given?

Think of the answer to the second question as point A, your starting point. Think of the answer to the first question as point Z, your destination. Before you can figure out a way to get from point A to point Z, you first have to know where the two points are. It's like locating them on a map. As you read, look for the answers to these two questions and, if it helps, circle or underline them as you read the problem, or write them down in the test booklet (in words, symbols, or pictures). Just be sure you know the answers to both questions before you proceed.

STEP 2: DEVISING A PLAN. Once you've read a problem carefully, the next step is to devise a plan for solving it. You've located point A (what you're given) and point Z (what you need to find). Now you want to look at your "map" to see how you might get from A to Z and, if there's more than one way, decide which to try first. Of course, you may know exactly how to proceed. If not, it may help to ask yourself some questions, such as:

What kind of problem is this? Have I seen any problems like this one before? How did I solve those problems? What knowledge and skills did I use? Have I learned any other strategies for solving problems of this type? Can I deduce any additional information from what I've been given? Do the answer choices give me any clues about how I should proceed? Will reasoning or estimating help me figure out what kind of answer to expect?

The answers to one or more of these questions may help you "see" a way to solve a problem that you may not have thought of immediately. So may a knowledge of various problem-solving strategies. The next section discusses some of those strategies. The more strategies you know, the more "routes" you'll be able to use to get from point A to point Z. And the more routes you see, the more likely you'll be to choose the best one—the one that will most efficiently get you to point Z (not point X or Y).

STEP 3: CARRYING OUT THE PLAN. Once you've devised a plan for solving a problem, carrying it out should be fairly easy. You know where you're going and you've mapped out a way to get there. Now all you have to do is follow your map. If you have the knowledge and skills to do that, you should have no trouble—providing, of course, that you pay attention. Proceed as quickly as you can, but proceed cautiously, too. It's often a good idea to write your work down in your test booklet. Then if you make a careless error along the way, you can easily retrace your steps and correct it. And keep going until you reach your destination. If point Q is between point A and point Z, don't stop there. It may be one of the answer choices, but it's not the right one.

STEP 4: LOOKING BACK. When you've finished your work, the first thing you'll want to do, naturally, is look for your answer among the answer choices. If it's there, chances are you've done the problem correctly. **But remember that each of the wrong answers represents a common mistake that you might have made while you were working the problem.** Just to be sure your answer is the right one, it's wise to spend a few seconds checking your work.

Start by asking yourself some questions:

- Did I find what I was asked to find?
- Does my answer make sense?
- Did I use all the information I was given? If not, can I explain why some of the information was unnecessary?

Then quickly look over your work to make sure you haven't made any careless errors—like putting a decimal point in the wrong place or subtracting when you were supposed to add. (You know the kinds of errors you tend to make; look for those.) After you've completed your check, mark your choice on the answer sheet and go on to the next question.

What if your answer isn't among the choices? Well, if your answer resembles the five on the test, chances are you just made a careless error somewhere along the way. First make sure you set up the problem correctly, using the exact information you were given. Then check your work for mistakes (a good general habit to get into, by the way). If you don't find any errors or if your answer doesn't resemble the five on the test, either go back to step 2 and try something else or just mark the question in your test booklet and go on to the next one. While you're working on another problem, something new may occur to you. If so, you can always come back to this problem and try it again. In the meantime, you'll be using your time productively. When you return to the problem, if you still don't find the answer, take your best guess and mark that on your answer sheet.

Here are a couple of problems you can use to see how this four-step method works, starting with a fairly simple one:

---

2. Mr. Brown went grocery shopping to buy meat for his annual office picnic. He bought $7\frac{3}{4}$ pounds of hamburger, 17.85 pounds of chicken, and $6\frac{1}{2}$ pounds of steak. How many pounds of meat did Mr. Brown buy?

F. 21.10
G. 22.10
H. 26.25
J. 31.31
K. 32.10

STEP 1: UNDERSTANDING THE PROBLEM. This is a straightforward problem, so step 1 should be easy. What are you given? You're given the amount of hamburger, chicken, and steak that Mr. Brown bought: $7\frac{3}{4}$ pounds, 17.85 pounds, and $6\frac{1}{2}$ pounds, respectively. What are you asked to find? You're asked to find out how many pounds of meat Mr. Brown bought altogether.

Mr. Brown bought 7¾ pounds of hamburger, 17.86 pounds of chicken, 6½ pounds of steak ... and an unspecified amount of barbecue sauce.

STEP 2: DEVISING A PLAN. You've worked hundreds of problems like this. You know that in order to find the total weight of the meat Mr. Brown bought, you have to add the weights of the hamburger, chicken, and steak together. But you've got two mixed numbers and a decimal, so before you can add them, you first have to express them all in the same form. Which form should you choose? Note that the answer choices are all in decimal form. This suggests that it will be most efficient to convert $7\frac{3}{4}$ and $6\frac{1}{2}$ to decimals before you add the numbers together.

Now you're ready to move on to step 3. Some people like to take a few seconds to get a rough estimate of what the answer ought to be. If you do that and happen to make a careless mistake when doing the addition in step 3, you might catch it faster. Other people save this estimating for step 4.

Here's how you might make your estimate: 7 and 17 is 24, plus 6 is 30; so the total must be a little more than 30 pounds.

STEP 3: CARRYING OUT THE PLAN. It looks as though the correct answer must be J or K. To see which it is, carry out the plan:

$$\begin{aligned} 7\tfrac{3}{4} &= 7.75 \\ 6\tfrac{1}{2} &= 6.50 \\ &\ \underline{+\ 17.85} \\ &32.10 \end{aligned}$$

STEP 4: LOOKING BACK. If you didn't estimate the answer at the end of step 2, now's the time to do that. Did you get an answer you expected? Then go with it, record your answer, and move on to the next question.

Notice that with this particular problem the estimating you did in step 2 allowed you, in effect, to skip step 4 (or at least to combine it with step 3). If you hadn't done the estimate in step 2, you might have done it in step 4 instead—as a quick check to make sure that the answer you got in step 3 made sense. You can see the advantage of estimating at step 2 rather than step 4. When you're taking a multiple-choice test, a good estimate may allow you to eliminate a few answer choices as unreasonable. Then, if you don't have time to work a problem out completely, you can at least make an intelligent guess at the correct answer. Either way, estimating is a very useful aid to problem-solving.

Of course, not every problem lends itself to estimating. Here's an example of one that doesn't.

---

40. If $(x - a)^2 = 4$, which of the following expresses all of the solutions for x in terms of a ?

F. a

G. $a + 2$

H. $a \pm 2$

J. $\pm(2 - a)$

K. $\pm\sqrt{4 - a^2}$

STEP 1: UNDERSTANDING THE PROBLEM. What are you given? You're given an equation in two variables, x and a. What are you asked to find? You're asked to find all of the solutions for x in terms of a.

STEP 2: DEVISING A PLAN. You've had to solve equations before, but usually there's no a in the equation. Can you solve this by treating the a just like a number?

There are a number of ways to solve this problem; let's consider a couple of different ways. One way would be to expand the left side by squaring $(x - a)$. Then you could move the 4 over to the left side (by subtracting 4 from both sides) and try to solve the resulting quadratic equation by factoring, completing the square, or using the quadratic formula. That approach would work. However, since you don't know the value of a, you'd end up with something even worse than you started with: $x^2 - 2ax + a^2 - 4 = 0$.

A second way would be to recognize that $4 = 2^2$, so the equation can be rewritten as $(x - a)^2 = 2^2$. This equation is a lot easier to solve. You can simply take the square root of both sides of the equation, or you can move the 2^2 over to the left side, giving you a difference of squares, which you can then factor. Taking the square root of both sides seems like the simplest way.

STEP 3: CARRYING OUT THE PLAN. The key to carrying out this plan is remembering that there are **two** numbers whose square is 4.

$$x - a = \pm 2$$
$$x = a \pm 2$$

STEP 4: LOOKING BACK. Your answer is among the choices. That's a good sign. Does it make sense? Well, you got two solutions. Did you expect that? How many solutions does a quadratic equation usually have? The only reliable way to check your work on a problem like this is to substitute each of your solutions into the equation and see if it satisfies the equation:

$$(x - a)^2 \rightarrow [(a + 2) - a]^2 = [2]^2 = 4$$
$$(x - a)^2 \rightarrow [(a - 2) - a]^2 = [-2]^2 = 4$$

Since both solutions satisfy the equation, your answer is correct.

In this problem, you used substitution in step 4 to check your answer. Could you have used this method in step 3 to **find** the answer? In other words, could you have substituted each answer choice into the given equation and chosen the correct one? Yes. Generally, however, this strategy works with only a few questions, and here it's more time-consuming than the straightforward approach. In this particular case, it's also risky. If you had not combined it with some reasoning about the number of solutions to expect, you might very well have chosen G as the correct answer. G satisfies the equation in the question, but it's only one solution, and you're asked to find **all** of them.

REPRESENTATIVE ACT MATHEMATICS TEST QUESTIONS

As you've just seen, the four-step method can be very useful when you're solving math problems. The most complex step, of course, is devising a plan. Before you can choose a way to solve a problem, you first have to "see" the way. This section discusses some of the different ways that you might consider when you're devising your plan. You can think of these ways, or strategies, as problem-solving tools. Just as you need different tools to do different jobs, you need different math tools to solve different math problems. Sometimes you may even need several tools for one problem. The more tools you have in your "toolbox," the better equipped you'll be to solve the variety of problems on the ACT Mathematics Test.

You're probably familiar with most of the problem-solving strategies discussed in this section. In fact, you've probably used most of them at one time or another in your math classes. Think now about how you can use them to solve some of the math problems you're likely to find on the ACT. The sample questions are taken from the ACT Mathematics Test that you'll find at the end of this discussion.

The more tools you have in your toolbox, the better equipped you'll be.

USE A FORMULA.

The most obvious, often the simplest, and sometimes the only reasonable strategy for solving certain types of math problems is using a formula. You've learned lots of formulas over the years in your math classes. The key to this strategy is knowing which formula to use in a particular situation—and then recalling that formula, of course. Here are some representative problems to give you an idea of the sorts of formulas you'll be expected to know and the ways in which you'll be expected to apply them. As you'll see, the formulas are very basic ones.

Problems 33 and 48 are typical plane geometry problems. In problem 33, the word *circumference* should bring a formula to mind:

---

33. If the circumference of a circle is 10 units long, how many units long is its radius?

A. $\frac{\sqrt{10}}{\pi}$

B. $\sqrt{\frac{5}{\pi}}$

C. $\frac{5}{\pi}$

D. $\sqrt{\frac{10}{\pi}}$

E. $\frac{10}{\pi}$

To find the radius of the circle, you'll probably use a formula for circumference. You may remember the formula $C = \pi d$ (where d is the diameter) or you might recall the formula $C = 2\pi r$ (where r is the radius). You can see why the second is the better one to use here—the radius is what you're trying to find. Both formulas should work; just remember that it's the radius you're after, not the diameter, because the diameter is also one of the answer choices. (Another incorrect answer choice is the radius you'd get if you used the formula for the area of a circle instead of the circumference.)

In problem 48 an important word is *area*:

48. In the figure below, $\overline{AB}$ and $\overline{CD}$ are parallel, and lengths are given in units. What is the area, in square units, of trapezoid $ABCD$?

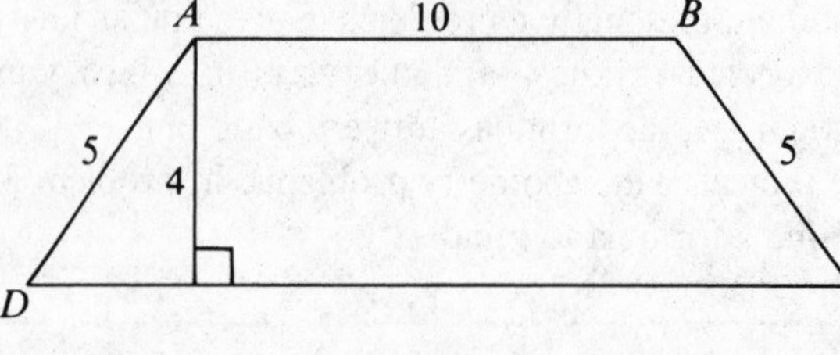

F. 36
G. 52
H. 64
J. 65
K. 104

You might choose to do this problem by recalling a formula for the area of a trapezoid. That's a good method, but you can't possibly memorize every formula in the world. As an example, if you weren't confident you could remember the correct formula for the area of a trapezoid, how else could you approach this question?

Notice that you can divide the trapezoid into a rectangle and two right triangles by using perpendiculars from A and B to $\overline{DC}$.

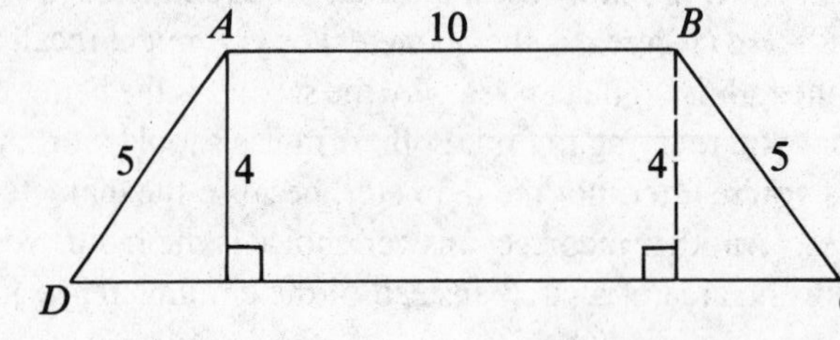

Once you've done that, what you need is not one little-known formula but two well-known ones. The first is the formula for finding the area of a rectangle: $A = lw$, where l is the length and w is the width. The second is the formula for finding the area of a triangle: $A = \frac{1}{2}bh$, where b is the base and h is the height. Either way, you need the Pythagorean theorem: $a^2 + b^2 = c^2$, where a and b are the lengths of the legs of a right triangle and c is the length of the hypotenuse. (You don't have enough information to use the second formula unless you use the third one first.)

The legs of a triangle.

Problems 25 and 43 are typical coordinate geometry problems. In problem 25, the word *slope* might give you some ideas:

---

25. What is the slope of the straight line that passes through (7,–1) and (3,2) in the standard (x,y) coordinate plane?

A. $-\frac{4}{3}$

B. $-\frac{3}{4}$

C. $-\frac{1}{4}$

D. $\frac{1}{10}$

E. $\frac{3}{10}$

When you're given two points on a line and you're asked to find the slope of the line, as you are here, the formula you need is:

$$\text{slope} = \frac{\text{rise}}{\text{run}} = \frac{\text{change in } y}{\text{change in } x} = \frac{y_2 - y_1}{x_2 - x_1}$$

For another slope problem, like number 12 or 28, you may be given the equation of a line instead of being given two points on the line. For that kind of slope problem, it helps to remember the slope-intercept form of a linear equation: $y = mx + b$, where m is the slope and b is the y-intercept.

In problem 43, you're given the midpoint and one endpoint of a line segment and you're asked to find the other endpoint:

---

43. Given point $M(9,6)$ in the standard (x,y) coordinate plane, what are the coordinates of the point N such that $P(2,3)$ is the midpoint of $\overline{MN}$?

A. $(-5, \ 0)$

B. $(-\frac{7}{2}, -\frac{3}{2})$

C. $(\ \frac{7}{2}, \ \frac{3}{2})$

D. $(\frac{11}{2}, \ \frac{9}{2})$

E. $(16, \ 9)$

In another problem, like number 27, you may be given the two endpoints and asked to find the midpoint. You can use the same formula for both types of problems:

$$(x_m, y_m) = \left(\frac{x_1 + x_2}{2}, \frac{y_1 + y_2}{2}\right)$$

You may find it easier to remember this formula (and to solve problem 43) if you look at it as two formulas instead of one:

$$x_m = \frac{x_1 + x_2}{2} \qquad y_m = \frac{y_1 + y_2}{2}$$

As you can see, the x-coordinate of the midpoint, x_m, is just the **average** of the x-coordinates of the two endpoints, x_1 and x_2, and the y-coordinate of the midpoint, y_m, is just the **average** of the y-coordinates of the two endpoints, y_1 and y_2.

Problem 59 is a typical trigonometry problem:

---

59. For all θ, $\frac{\sin^2\theta + \cos^2\theta}{\sin\theta}$ is equivalent to:

A. $\cos\theta$
B. $\tan\theta$
C. $\cot\theta$
D. $\sec\theta$
E. $\csc\theta$

To solve this problem, you need to know a fundamental trigonometric identity: $\sin^2 x + \cos^2 x = 1$. To prepare for trigonometry problems on the ACT Mathematics Test, you should know the six trigonometric ratios. The three principal ones are the sine (sin), cosine (cos), and tangent (tan), which you can remember this way:

$$\sin\theta = \frac{\text{length of side \textbf{opposite} } \theta}{\text{length of \textbf{hypotenuse}}}$$

$$\cos\theta = \frac{\text{length of side \textbf{adjacent} } \theta}{\text{length of \textbf{hypotenuse}}}$$

$$\tan\theta = \frac{\text{length of side \textbf{opposite} } \theta}{\text{length of side \textbf{adjacent} } \theta}$$

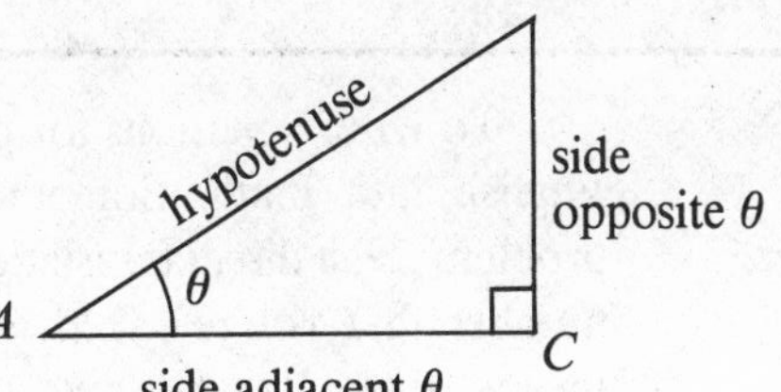

The other three are the reciprocals of these: the cosecant (csc) is the reciprocal of the sine, the secant (sec) is the reciprocal of the cosine, and the cotangent (cot) is the reciprocal of the tangent.

WRITE AN EQUATION.

Many problems will involve the use of simple formulas you'll have memorized—for example, formulas for the area of familiar figures such as circles, rectangles, and triangles. Others will require that you construct an equation in order to solve the problem. Problems 29 and 52 are both examples of ones that writing an equation can help you solve:

---

29. Two more than the product of 4 and a certain number is the same as 12 less than the product of 6 and the number. What is the number?

A. 3
B. 4
C. 5
D. 6
E. 7

---

52. A string that is 8 feet long is cut into 3 parts. If the first part is twice as long as the second, and the second part is twice as long as the third, how many feet long is the first part?

F. $1\frac{1}{7}$
G. $1\frac{3}{5}$
H. $2\frac{2}{7}$
J. $3\frac{1}{5}$
K. $4\frac{4}{7}$

To write equations for problems like these, you have to be able to "translate" English into math. Sometimes you can do that in more than one way. For problem 29, a direct translation is the simplest route to a solution: Let n stand for the number that you're asked to find. Then, since *more than* means "plus," *product* means "times," *is the same as* means "equals," and *less than* means "minus," your equation is $4n + 2 = 6n - 12$.

For problem 52, you can translate either directly or indirectly. A direct translation leads to an indirect solution: Let x stand for the length of the third part of the string, even though that's not what you're asked to find. Then, since *twice* means "two times," the length of the second part is $2x$ and the length of the first part is $2(2x)$, or $4x$. The equation is $x + 2x + 4x = 8$. This equation will give you the length of the third part of the string (x), and from that you can find the length of the first part ($4x$).

You have to be able to translate English into math.

An indirect translation leads to a direct solution: Let y stand for the length of the first part of the string, which is what you're asked to find. Then, since the opposite of *twice* is *half,* the length of the second part is $\frac{y}{2}$ and the length of the third part is $\frac{y}{2} \div 2 = \frac{y}{4}$. The equation is $y + \frac{y}{2} + \frac{y}{4} = 8$. The solution to this equation is the answer to the problem.

When more than one translation is possible, use the one that's easiest for you. Just remember to "look back" when you're finished to make sure that you've found what you were asked to find, and not something else, because frequently the "something else" will also appear as one of the answer choices. (It's good practice, by the way, to write down a short description for any variable that you pick. Here, you could write down that x is the length of the third piece of string. Then, if you were looking back, you'd be able to remember that $x = 1$ is not the length of the **first** piece.)

For problems 29 and 52, writing an equation is the only strategy you need to use. For other problems, you may need to combine this strategy with another one, such as using a formula. Take problem 34, for instance:

---

34. A rectangular box with a base 2 inches by 6 inches is 10 inches tall and holds 12 ounces of breakfast cereal. The manufacturer wants to use a new box with a base 3 inches by 5 inches. How many inches tall should the new box be in order to hold exactly the same volume as the original box? (Note: The volume of a rectangular box may be calculated by multiplying the area of the base by the height of the box.)

F. 8
G. 9
H. 10
J. 11
K. 12

This problem is interesting because it gives you both less and more information than you need to solve it. The "less" part is the formula for finding the volume of a rectangular box, which you can use only if you know how to find the area of the base of the box. That's easy because you know the formula for the area of a rectangle ($A = l \times w$). The "more" part is the number of ounces of cereal that the original box holds, which is more challenging. If you don't see that this information is irrelevant, you may have trouble writing the equation you need to solve the problem.

One way to avoid being confused by unnecessary information when you're writing an equation is to focus closely on the wording of the problem: "How many inches tall should the new box be in order to hold exactly the same volume as the original box?" In this case, *exactly the same . . . as* means "equals." What has to equal what here? The **volume** of the new box has to equal the **volume** of the original box. Using the formula given for volume and letting h stand for the unknown height of the new box, you see that the equation you need is $3 \times 5 \times h = 2 \times 6 \times 10$.

As you can see, the number of ounces of cereal that fit in the original box doesn't figure into this equation. And if you think about it, it shouldn't. Unless the cereal is of a peculiar size or shape, and you're not told that it is, **any** container of the same volume as the original box will hold the same amount of the same cereal as the original box. Remember: Don't be surprised if some problems on the ACT Mathematics Test give you more information than you need to solve them. These problems test an important reasoning skill—the ability to sift through information and decide what's relevant and what isn't.

THINK OF A SIMPLER, SIMILAR PROBLEM.

Often an excellent strategy for getting started on a math problem, especially one that seems complex, is to think of a simpler problem you can solve that's similar to the one you have to solve. Then, by figuring out how you would solve the simpler problem, you might see how you need to proceed with the more complex one.

For problem 11, this strategy works well:

---

11. Joe has taken 4 tests in his algebra class during the current grading period, earning test scores of 86, 66, 78, and 81. A student needs an average score of 80 on 5 tests to earn a "B" for the class. What is the minimum (integer) score Joe can earn on his next test in order to have an average of at least 80 for the 5 tests?

A. 83
B. 85
C. 87
D. 89
E. 91

If you don't see immediately how to set up the equation for this problem, think of a simpler problem first. Suppose Joe took 2 tests and earned 80 on one and 90 on the other. How would you figure out his average? You'd add 80 to 90, divide the sum by 2, and get an average of 85. Your equation for this simpler problem would be

$$\frac{80 + 90}{2} = 85$$

This equation is a pattern for the one you need. To use it, go back to the original problem and replace the numbers in your pattern with the corresponding numbers in the problem. You supposed Joe had taken only 2 tests, but in the problem he'll be taking 5, so replace the 2 with a 5. You found that his average was 85, but his average in the problem will be 80, so replace the 85 with an 80. You supposed that he had 2 scores of 80 and 90, but in the problem he'll have 5 scores of 86, 66, 78, 81, and some unknown number—call it x. Replace the $(80 + 90)$ with $(86 + 66 + 78 + 81 + x)$ and replace the equal sign with $\geq$. Now you should have what you need to be able to solve the problem. "Look back" to be sure.

Notice that when we invented our simpler problem, we chose "nice" numbers—numbers that you could work with in your head. Choosing numbers that are easy to work with can help you use the strategy of simplification successfully. The point is not to waste time thinking up and solving a problem that's **not** on the test; the point is to find a way—a quick way—to solve a problem that **is** on the test.

Another way of employing the concept of simplification is to use a concrete example to help you figure out an abstract problem. This strategy often helps with problems like 20 and 35:

---

20. A person purchased 5 items at c cents each and gave the clerk q quarters, which was enough to pay for the items. How many cents change should this person receive, in terms of c and q ?

F. $25q - 5c$
G. $25q - c$
H. $25q - 5$
J. $q - 5c$
K. $q - 5$

You wouldn't have any trouble solving problem 20 if it used specific numbers, so just pretend that it does. Assign some "nice" values to c and q—say, 2 and 3—and figure out how you'd make change. Then go back and substitute c and q for the easy-to-use values in your figuring.

For problem 35, trying a few examples might help you understand the problem better, and it may allow you to eliminate a few answer choices.

35. The sum of a rational number and an irrational number is always:

A. positive.
B. irrational.
C. rational.
D. the square root of a rational number.
E. rational, unless one of the numbers is zero.

The terms mentioned here are *rational* and *irrational.* What "nice" rational and irrational numbers do you know? If you find a particular rational and a particular irrational number whose sum is negative, then A cannot be **always** true. Since this is multiple choice, it's appropriate to eliminate four answer choices and then the one that's left ought to be correct. For the rational number 0 and the irrational number $\sqrt{2}$, the sum is $\sqrt{2}$. This will eliminate answer choice C. To do this problem, you don't need to work with the terms *rational* and *irrational,* but you can use specific numbers to help. If you were to try to **prove** this result, specific numbers wouldn't be good enough, but that's not what the problem is asking for.

A third way to use a simpler version of a math problem is to choose "nice" numbers that are close to the ones you're given and use them instead. This simpler problem won't usually have exactly the same answer as the original, but the answers should be somewhat close. Since the numbers you select will be ones that are easy to use, you'll be able to calculate the simpler version's answer pretty quickly.

Take problem 8, for example:

8. Mrs. Dorgan's gross monthly income is $1,800. If 15% is withheld for income taxes, 7% for social security, and 2% for insurance, what is her net monthly income (after deducting these expenses)?

F. $ 432
G. $ 630
H. $1,200
J. $1,368
K. $1,530

A little quick arithmetic will tell you that the deductions from Mrs. Dorgan's paycheck amount to 15% + 7% + 2% = 24% of her gross income. That's almost 25%, which is $\frac{1}{4}$. And $\frac{1}{4}$, even though it's a fraction, is a "nice" number. What's $\frac{1}{4}$ of $1,800? $450. So Mrs. Dorgan nets about $1,800 – $450 = $1,350. Your final answer must be reasonably close to $1,350. So, when you work the problem, you'll know something's wrong if you get an answer of, say, $432.

You can often work two "nice" problems to bound the real answer between your estimates. Take problem 53, for instance:

---

53. What is the area, in square inches, of a circle that has a diameter of 9 inches?

A. 20.25π
B. 40.50π
C. 60.50π
D. 80.50π
E. 81.00π

If the diameter of the circle were 8 or 10, instead of 9, then the radius would be 4 or 5, instead of $4\frac{1}{2}$, and you could figure out the area ($A = \pi r^2$) in your head as 16π or 25π. So, by using the fact that the diameter of 9 inches is between 8 and 10, you can arrive quickly at a range (16π to 25π) in which the exact answer **must** fall. Notice that only one answer choice is within this range.

As you can see, choosing "nice" numbers to work with is really just a form of estimating. You can use this strategy either in step 2 of the problem-solving process, to eliminate unreasonable answers, or in step 4, to check the reasonableness of an exact solution that you've worked out. (You should be especially careful when selecting zero and 1 as your nice numbers, by the way. Even though they're easy to work with, both have unique qualities that may cause them to function differently than other numbers would in the same situation.) Practicing this estimating technique until it becomes familiar will let you learn when you can use it to your advantage.

LOOK FOR A PATTERN.

Sometimes when you're not sure how to work a math problem, it's helpful to look for a pattern. This strategy is an especially handy tool if your memory fails you on a problem like this:

---

51. $2^2 + 2^0 + 2^{-2} = ?$

A. 0

B. 1

C. $4\frac{1}{4}$

D. $5\frac{1}{4}$

E. 6

Suppose you get to this problem, or a similar one, such as problem 41, and you simply can't remember how to raise a number to the zero power or to a negative power. You know how to raise a number to a positive power: To square 2, for instance, you multiply it by itself—that is, you take 2 as a factor twice. But what do you get if you take a number as a factor zero times? And how can you multiply a number by itself a negative number of times?

To refresh your memory, you might try working backward from what you remember to what you've forgotten. Write down a few positive powers of 2 and look for a pattern in them.

We've arranged these positive powers in descending order, so that we're climbing down the power ladder, so to speak:

$$2^5 = 32$$
$$2^4 = 16$$
$$2^3 = 8$$
$$2^2 = 4$$

Now to get from 2^5 to 2^4, what do you have to do? There are lots of choices. You could subtract 16, for example. But you need to find a common pattern. Do you see one?

If you divide 2^5 by 2, you get 2^4. Dividing 2^4 by 2 gives you 2^3. And $2^3 \div 2 = 2^2$. Now, keep following the pattern.

$$2^1 = 2$$
$$2^0 = 1$$
$$2^{-1} = 1 \div 2 = \tfrac{1}{2}$$
$$2^{-2} = \tfrac{1}{2} \div 2 = \tfrac{1}{4}$$

Once you see the pattern and figure out the values of 2^0 and 2^{-2}, the problem is simple.

You can use the same pattern, in a slightly different way, to help you with problem 46:

---

46. $8^{-\frac{2}{3}} = ?$

F. $\frac{1}{4}$

G. $\frac{3}{16}$

H. $\frac{1}{12}$

J. $-\frac{1}{12}$

K. $-\frac{3}{16}$

In this case, while the pattern doesn't tell you exactly what a fractional exponent means, it does tell you that the value of 2^0, for instance, is between the value of 2^{-1} and 2^1 (just as 0 is between −1 and 1 on the number line). So the value of $8^{-\frac{2}{3}}$ must be between the value of 8^{-1}, which is $\frac{1}{8}$, and 8^0, which is 1. Knowing that much, you can eliminate choices H, J, and K. Then, even if you can't get any further with the problem than that, you at least have a 50-50 chance of guessing the correct answer. (Just in case you're racking your brain trying to remember, $8^{\frac{2}{3}} = (\sqrt[3]{8})^2$ or, equivalently, $8^{\frac{2}{3}} = \sqrt[3]{8^2}$. And $8^{-\frac{2}{3}}$ is the reciprocal of $8^{\frac{2}{3}}$.)

One useful variation on the strategy of looking for a pattern is **recognizing a pattern.** In this variation, you don't search for a pattern that you've forgotten (or perhaps have never seen before); instead, you search for a pattern that you remember. Sometimes you don't have to search very far at all because the pattern is in plain view; then all you have to do is recognize it. Other times the pattern is hidden, and you may have to look for a while before you see it.

One of the simplest and most useful patterns is the 30°-60°-90° triangle, whose sides are always in the proportions shown in the following figure:

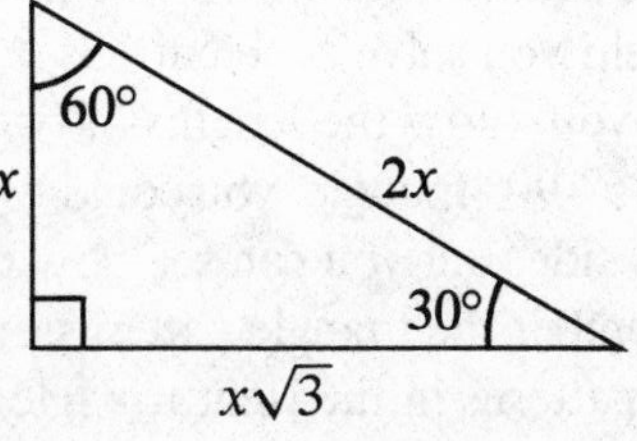

You can use this pattern to solve problem 23, for instance, without using any trigonometry:

---

23. In the right triangle shown below, the length of $\overline{AB}$ is 8 units, $\angle A$ measures 60°, $\sin 60° \approx .866$, $\cos 60° \approx .5$, and $\tan 60° \approx 1.73$. Approximately how many units long is $\overline{BC}$, to the nearest hundredth of a unit?

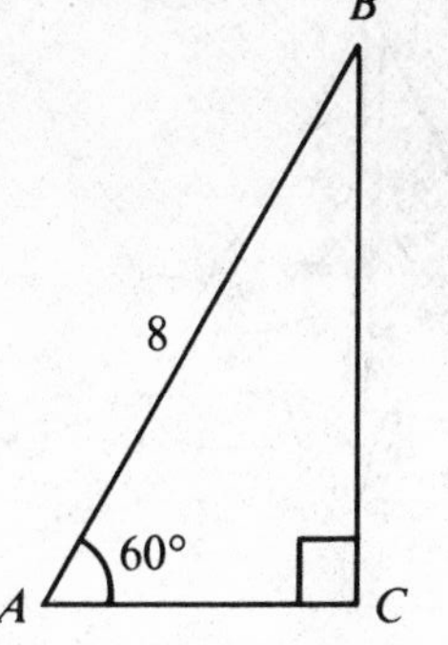

A. 4.00
B. 4.61
C. 4.80
D. 6.93
E. 9.23

The pattern tells you that the length of $\overline{AC}$ is 4 (half the length of $\overline{AB}$, the hypotenuse) and that the length of $\overline{BC}$, which is what you're asked to find, is $4\sqrt{3}$. Since the value of $\sqrt{3}$ is about 1.7, the length of $\overline{BC}$ is about 6.8. The correct answer must be choice D (6.93). Though you may not be able to recognize the pattern quite so easily in problems 18 and 45, you can also use it there.

Another pattern is the isosceles right triangle, or 45°-45°-90° triangle. Its sides are always in the following proportions:

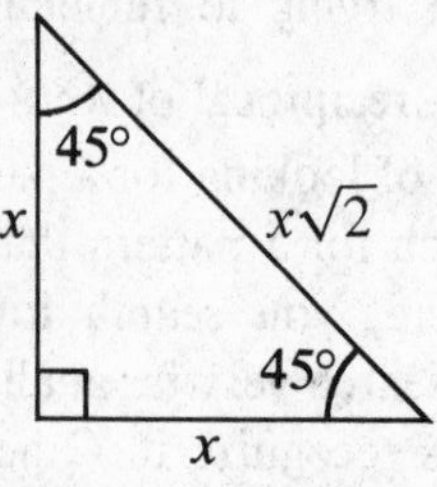

This pattern tells you that if the length of one leg of an isosceles right triangle is, say, 3, then the length of the other leg is also 3 and the length of the hypotenuse is $3\sqrt{2}$. It also tells you that if the length of the side of a square is, say, 10, then the length of the diagonal of the square is $10\sqrt{2}$. If you know that the value of $\sqrt{2}$ is about 1.4, this pattern can help you solve problem 15.

Of course if you know the lengths of two of the sides of either a 30°-60°-90° triangle or a 45°-45°-90° triangle, you could use the Pythagorean theorem to find the length of the third side. But you can see how much faster and easier it is to find the length if you remember the triangle patterns.

Three other patterns in the right triangle family that you might want to learn, too, are the 3-4-5, the 5-12-13, and the 8-15-17. You'll find the 3-4-5 pattern, for instance, in problem 48, which we looked at earlier. These three triangles, and their multiples (such as the 6-8-10 and the 15-36-39), are "nice" right triangles because their sides are all whole numbers. If you recognize one of these triangles when you see it, you can find the length of a missing side simply by recalling the pattern.

The right triangle family.

If you prefer, you can, of course, use the Pythagorean theorem or trigonometry for some of these right triangle problems. Learn all the techniques you can, and use the one you think will work best for you for a given problem. If it doesn't turn out to work, try another. (When you're not taking a timed test, try to figure out why your first choice didn't work.)

REASON WITH YOUR EYES.

Using an accurate drawing of the situation is a good way to estimate the answers. This might be particularly useful in geometry questions. Be very careful, though. The directions for the ACT Mathematics Test caution you that its figures are "NOT necessarily drawn to scale." Some of the figures are reasonably accurate, however, and you might be able to draw a sketch that's accurate enough for your purposes for some of the others. You'll have to compare the information in the question with the way the figure is drawn to decide for yourself whether it is accurate enough.

Remember, this technique only **estimates** the correct answer, so don't spend too much time drawing a super accurate figure, or even deciding whether the current one is good enough. If you are satisfied with your figure, you can use it to estimate lengths and angles. Use this estimate to eliminate unreasonable answers and to look back on the reasonableness of an answer you get in another way. Let's look at a couple of examples to see how this strategy works.

In problem 7, you're asked to find the measure of an angle:

---

7. As shown in the figure below, ΔABC is isosceles with the length of $\overline{AB}$ equal to the length of $\overline{AC}$. The measure of $\angle A$ is 40° and points B, C, and D are collinear. What is the measure of $\angle ACD$?

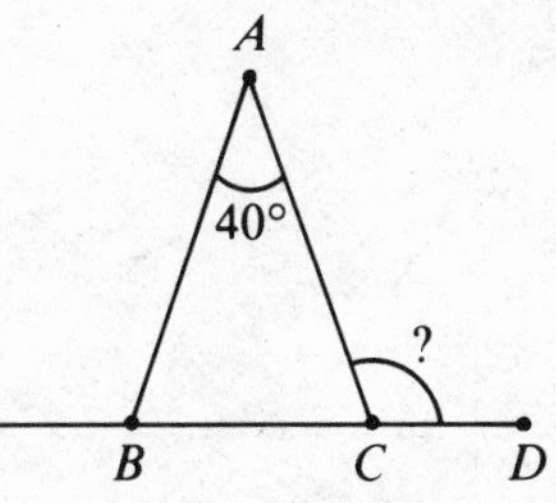

A. 70°
B. 80°
C. 110°
D. 140°
E. 160°

The problem says that ΔABC is isosceles with the length of $\overline{AB}$ equal to the length of $\overline{AC}$. Then ΔABC should also **look** isosceles. The problem says that $\angle A$ measures 40°. Does it look that way? Are B, C, and D collinear? That is, does it look like B, C, and D all lie on the same straight line?

What do you think the measure of $\angle ACD$ is? Remember, you won't be able to use a protractor on the test, so use your eyes. Sketch in a right angle.

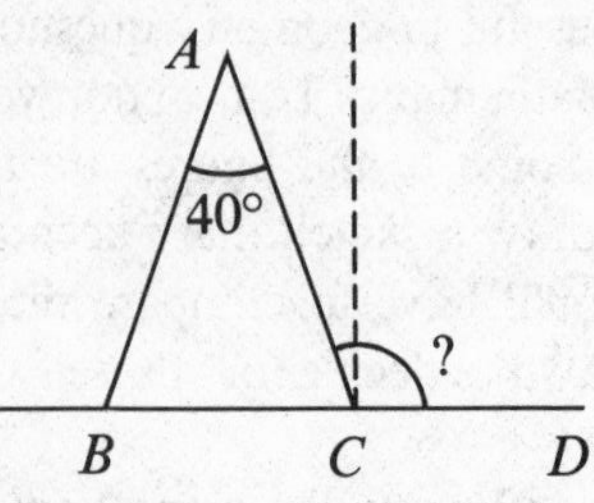

How much bigger than a right angle is $\angle ACD$? It looks like 110° is the most reasonable answer.

You can get an exact answer by applying a few basic principles of plane geometry. But reasoning with your eyes is an easy check. How could you use the strategy of reasoning with your eyes on problem 17, which asks you to find the ratio of the area of one triangle to the area of another triangle:

---

17. In ΔABD shown below, C and E are midpoints of sides $\overline{BD}$ and $\overline{AD}$, respectively. What is the ratio of the area of ΔABC to the area of ΔABE?

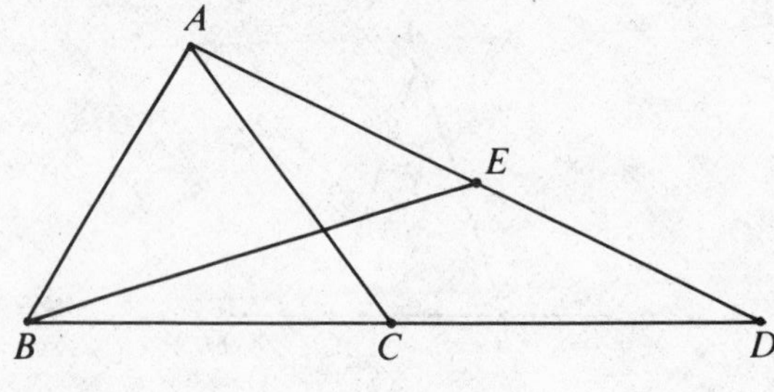

A. 3:1
B. 2:1
C. 1:1
D. 1:2
E. 1:3

In this case, you don't have to bother checking the scale of the figure because scale is not an issue. Triangle ABD could be any size or shape. Because C and E look like they are at the midpoints in the figure, the figure is an accurate image of the words in the problem.

Now, looking at triangles ABC and ABE (be sure you're looking at **these** triangles!), would you say that the ratio of their areas is 3:1 or 1:3 (one is 3 times as big as the other)? Try 2:1 or 1:2 (one is twice as big as the other). Neither looks correct. If you're pressed for time and have to make an educated guess, the ratio 1:1 seems the most reasonable (the areas of the two triangles are equal).

It should be clear from these few examples that the strategy of reasoning with your eyes is a powerful tool for checking problems by using figures that are drawn to scale. Remember you have this tool in your toolbox—but use it carefully.

DRAW A PICTURE.

Many problems on the ACT Mathematics Test that could be accompanied by illustrative figures aren't. For these problems, one good strategy is drawing a picture. This is a good strategy for all sorts of problems—algebra, plane geometry, solid geometry, coordinate geometry, and trigonometry. Because drawing a picture to visualize a problem is such a basic and versatile strategy, you can use it in combination with almost any other strategy. You can use it as a means for understanding a problem, as an aid in devising a plan for solving a problem, and as a device for checking a solution that you arrive at by some other method.

The picture you draw for a problem naturally depends on two things: the nature of the problem and the purpose you want the picture to serve. Often, a rough sketch will do. Here are some problems for which you might be able to use the versatile tool of drawing a picture.

Problem 30 is part plane geometry and part algebra:

---

30. A rectangle 2 units wide by 9 units long has the same area as an isosceles right triangle. If the equal-length sides of the triangle are each x units long, then x = ?

F. $\frac{7}{2}$

G. $\frac{9}{2}$

H. $\frac{11}{2}$

J. 6

K. 7

From reading the problem you should be able to see that you're going to need at least two strategies to solve this problem: write an equation and use a formula (two formulas, in fact). Drawing a picture may help you solve the problem. The equation you'll be writing will say that the area of the rectangle in the problem is equal to the area of the triangle. The rectangle side of the equation is easy: The area is (length × height) = $2 \times 9 = 18$. The triangle side is another matter. As you know, the area of a triangle is $A = \frac{1}{2}bh$, where b equals the length of the base and h equals the height. Does the problem give you any explicit information about either the base or the height of the triangle? No. Instead, it talks about the sides. Unless you draw a rough sketch, you may not see the connection you have to make to write the equation. Here's what a rough sketch of the triangle looks like:

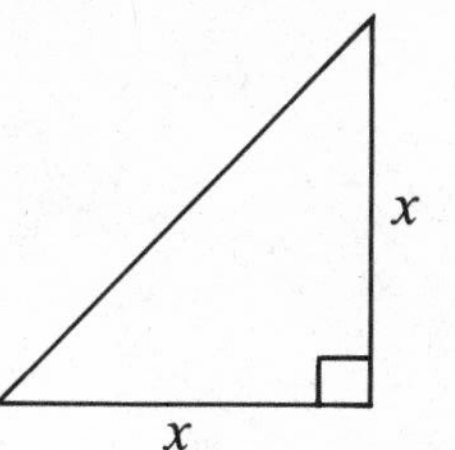

As you can see now, one of the equal-length sides of the triangle is the base and the other one is the height. So the equation you need is $\frac{1}{2}x^2 = 18$. The solution is $x = \pm 6$. Since the second answer, $x = -6$, makes no sense as the length of a side of a triangle, the only answer to the problem is $x = 6$. You can check this by drawing scale sketches of the two figures.

Problem 39 is a trigonometry problem:

---

39. If $0° < x° < 90°$ and $\sin x = \frac{1}{2}$, then $\cos x$ = ?

A. $\frac{1}{2}$

B. $\frac{\sqrt{3}}{2}$

C. 2

D. $\frac{\sqrt{3}}{3}$

E. $\frac{2\sqrt{3}}{3}$

If your knowledge of trigonometry is limited, it may be helpful to draw a picture of the angle described in this problem. The condition $0° < x° < 90°$ tells you that the angle is acute. The condition $\sin x = \frac{1}{2}$ tells you that if you draw this angle as part of a right triangle and the side opposite the angle is 1 unit long, then the hypotenuse is 2 units long. So the angle looks roughly like this:

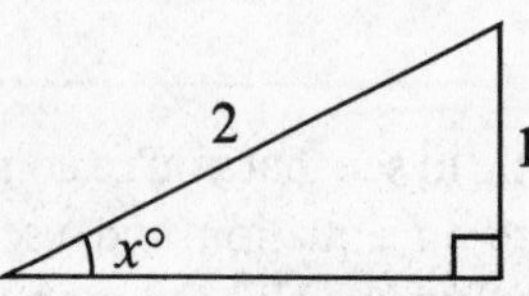

Do you recognize the pattern here? Since the hypotenuse is twice as long as the shortest side, this is a 30°-60°-90° triangle. So the missing side is $\sqrt{3}$ units long, which means that the $\cos x$ is—well, you can do the rest. Using the Pythagorean theorem is, of course, another way to get $\sqrt{3}$.

Problem 27 is a coordinate geometry problem:

---

27. Points A and B in the standard (x,y) plane have coordinates (3,5) and (−2,1), respectively. What are the (x,y) coordinates of the midpoint of $\overline{AB}$?

A. $(\frac{1}{2},2)$

B. $(\frac{1}{2},3)$

C. (1,6)

D. $(\frac{5}{2},2)$

E. (5,4)

This particular problem asks you to find the midpoint of a line segment; other coordinate geometry problems may ask you to find the endpoint of a line segment (like problem 43), the distance between two points in a coordinate plane (like problem 6), or the slope of a line (like problem 25). You can solve these problems by using graphing as an aid to reasoning.

For problem 27, you should be able to sketch a fairly accurate graph quickly because the two points you're given aren't far apart:

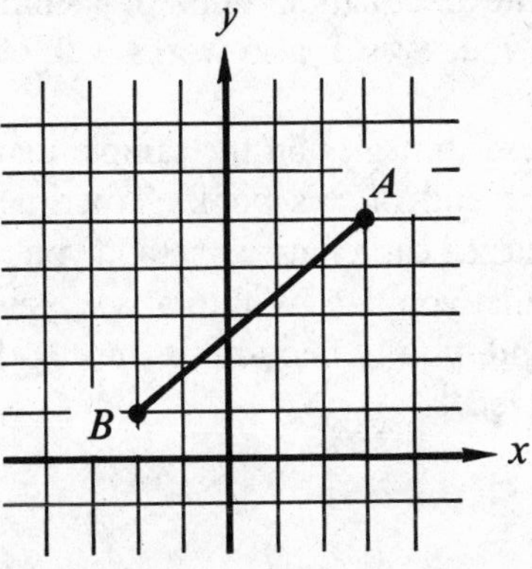

Once you've plotted the two points and connected them, the rest is simple: count coordinate units to find the midpoint.

Problem 56 is a solid geometry problem:

---

56. A rectangular box has a length of 10 feet, a width of 6 feet, and a height of 4 feet. The longest straight rod that could fit in this box would have to go along the diagonal between opposite corners. How many feet long is this distance?

F. $2\sqrt{13}$
G. $2\sqrt{29}$
H. $2\sqrt{34}$
J. $2\sqrt{38}$
K. $4\sqrt{15}$

Drawing a picture in three dimensions is a lot harder than drawing in two dimensions, but if you sketch the box in this problem, you may be able to see the tool you need to find the required distance.

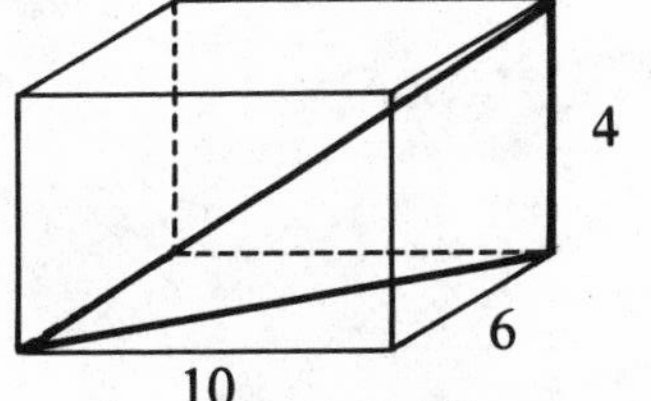

Notice that the distance you're asked to find is the length of the hypotenuse of a right triangle. Notice, too, that one side of that right triangle is 4 feet long and the other side is the hypotenuse of a second right triangle with sides of 6 feet and 10 feet. These two observations should tell you that the tool you need to solve the problem is the Pythagorean theorem. Use it twice and you've got your answer: $x^2 = 4^2 + y^2$, and since $y^2 = 6^2 + 10^2$, then $x^2 = 4^2 + 6^2 + 10^2$. Without the picture, you might have missed the right-triangle connection.

These are just a few of the ways in which you might be able to use the strategy of drawing (or visualizing) a picture. As the sample problems illustrate, the strategy works well both by itself and with the five other strategies we've discussed: use a formula; write an equation; think of a simpler, similar problem; look for a pattern; reason with your eyes. It also works with other problem-solving strategies you may know.

Try these strategies on the sample math test that follows and the two sample exams at the end of this book. Experiment with the four-step problem-solving method discussed earlier, use a method you're already familiar with, or come up with a variation that you like. With practice, you'll find the combinations that work best for you, and you'll become a more efficient, as well as more confident, problem-solver.

MATHEMATICS TEST

60 Minutes—60 Questions

DIRECTIONS: Solve each problem, choose the correct answer, and then blacken the corresponding oval on your answer sheet.

Do not linger over problems that take too much time. Solve as many as you can; then return to the others in the time you have left for this test.

Note: Unless otherwise stated, all of the following should be assumed.

1. Illustrative figures are NOT necessarily drawn to scale.
2. Geometric figures lie in a plane.
3. The word *line* indicates a straight line.
4. The word *average* indicates arithmetic mean.

---

1. Angle C is a right angle in ΔABC. Which of the following statements most precisely characterizes the nature of $\angle A$ and $\angle B$?

A. One, but only one, could be an obtuse angle.
B. One, but only one, could be an acute angle.
C. One could be a right angle.
D. Both could be obtuse angles.
E. Both must be acute angles.

2. Mr. Brown went grocery shopping to buy meat for his annual office picnic. He bought $7\frac{3}{4}$ pounds of hamburger, 17.85 pounds of chicken, and $6\frac{1}{2}$ pounds of steak. How many pounds of meat did Mr. Brown buy?

F. 21.10
G. 22.10
H. 26.25
J. 31.31
K. 32.10

3. When getting into shape by exercising, the subject's maximum recommended number of heartbeats per minute (h) can be determined by subtracting the subject's age (a) from 220 and then taking 75% of that value. This relation is expressed by which of the following formulas?

A. $h = .75(220 - a)$
B. $h = .75(220) - a$
C. $h = 220 - .75a$
D. $.75h = 220 - a$
E. $220 = .75(h - a)$

4. Which of the following is equivalent to $3a + 4b - (-6a - 3b)$?

F. $16ab$
G. $-3a + b$
H. $-3a + 7b$
J. $9a + b$
K. $9a + 7b$

5. Which of the following expresses 60 as a product of prime numbers?

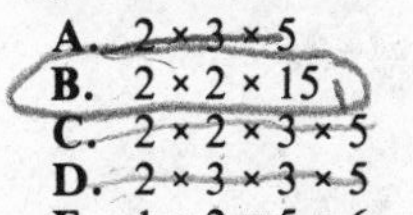

A. $2 \times 3 \times 5$
B. $2 \times 2 \times 15$
C. $2 \times 2 \times 3 \times 5$
D. $2 \times 3 \times 3 \times 5$
E. $1 \times 2 \times 5 \times 6$

6. How many units apart are the points $P(-3,4)$ and $Q(-3,-5)$ in the standard (x,y) coordinate plane?

F. -7
G. -1
H. 1
J. $\sqrt{37}$
K. 9

7. As shown in the figure below, ΔABC is isosceles with the length of $\overline{AB}$ equal to the length of $\overline{AC}$. The measure of $\angle A$ is 40° and points B, C, and D are collinear. What is the measure of $\angle ACD$?

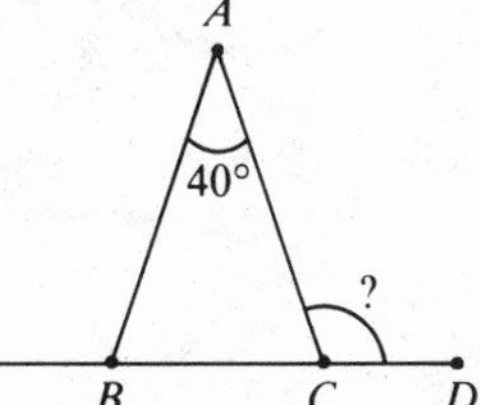

A. 70°
B. 80°
C. 110°
D. 140°
E. 160°

8939B

GO ON TO THE NEXT PAGE.

8. Mrs. Dorgan's gross monthly income is $1,800. If 15% is withheld for income taxes, 7% for social security, and 2% for insurance, what is her net monthly income (after deducting these expenses)?

F. $ 432
G. $ 630
H. $1,200
J. $1,368
K. $1,530

9. Simplify $3\frac{1}{8} - 2\frac{7}{12}$ to a single fraction in lowest terms with a positive denominator. What is the numerator?

A. −11
B. −7
C. 3
D. 13
E. 52

10. For all y and all N, $(y^2 - Ny + 4) + (y^2 - 2) = ?$

F. $-Ny + 6$
G. $2y^2 + 2$
H. $2y^2 - Ny - 2$
J. $y^2 - Ny + 2$
K. $2y^2 - Ny + 2$

11. Joe has taken 4 tests in his algebra class during the current grading period, earning test scores of 86, 66, 78, and 81. A student needs an average score of 80 on 5 tests to earn a "B" for the class. What is the minimum (integer) score Joe can earn on his next test in order to have an average of at least 80 for the 5 tests?

A. 83
B. 85
C. 87
D. 89
E. 91

12. What is the slope of the line with the equation $2x + 3y + 6 = 0$?

F. −6
G. −3
H. −2
J. $-\frac{2}{3}$
K. $\frac{2}{3}$

13. Which of the following pairs CANNOT intersect to form a circle? (Note: A single point is not considered a circle for the purposes of this question.)

A. Surface of a sphere and surface of some cylinder
B. Surface of a sphere and some plane
C. Surface of a cone and some plane
D. Surface of a cylinder and some line
E. Surface of a cylinder and some plane

14. For all x, $(x - 1)^2 + (x - 2)^2 = ?$

F. $2x - 3$
G. $2x^2 - 5$
H. $2x^2 + 5$
J. $2x^2 - 6x - 5$
K. $2x^2 - 6x + 5$

15. The diagram below shows a pasture which is fenced in. All but 1 section of fence run straight north–south or east–west. Consecutive fence posts are 10 feet apart except for the 1 diagonal section. Which of the following statements best describes P, the perimeter of the pasture, in feet?

A. $P > 210$
B. $P = 210$
C. $P < 210$
D. $P > 230$
E. $P = 240$

16. $2\sqrt{28} + 3\sqrt{175} = ?$

F. $12\sqrt{7}$
G. $19\sqrt{7}$
H. 63
J. $5\sqrt{203}$
K. $83\sqrt{7}$

GO ON TO THE NEXT PAGE.

17. In ΔABD shown below, C and E are midpoints of sides $\overline{BD}$ and $\overline{AD}$, respectively. What is the ratio of the area of ΔABC to the area of ΔABE ?

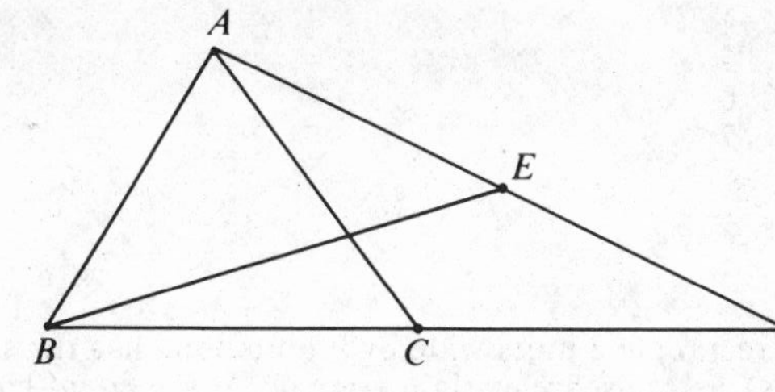

A. 3:1
B. 2:1
C. 1:1
D. 1:2
E. 1:3

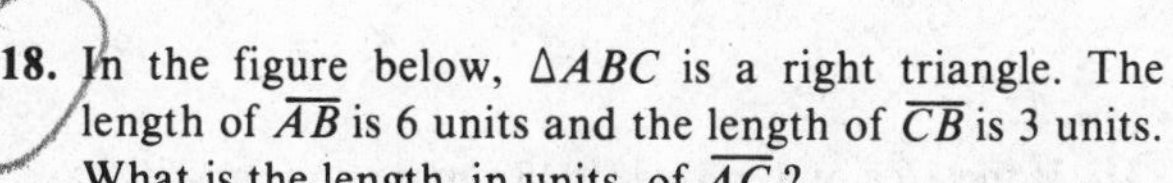

18. In the figure below, ΔABC is a right triangle. The length of $\overline{AB}$ is 6 units and the length of $\overline{CB}$ is 3 units. What is the length, in units, of $\overline{AC}$?

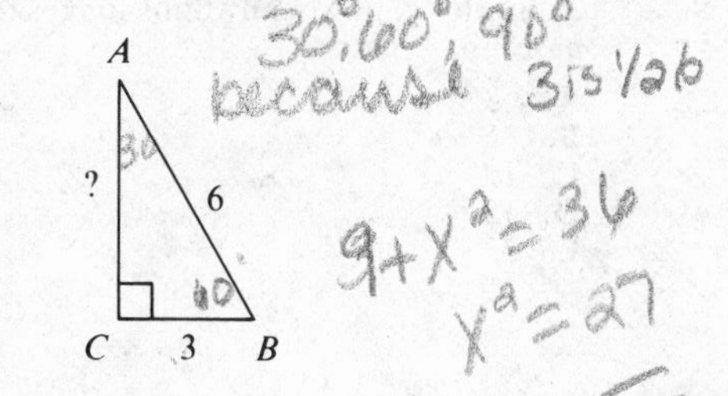

F. 5
G. $3\sqrt{3}$
H. $3+\sqrt{5}$
J. $3\sqrt{5}$
K. $3\sqrt{6}$

19. Which of the following shows the complete factorization of $12a^3b + 26a^2b^2 + 10ab^3$?

A. $2(6ab + 5b^2)(a^2 + ab)$
B. $2(3ab + 5b^2)(2a^2 + ab)$
C. $2ab(2a + 5b)(3a + b)$
D. $2ab(6a + 5b)(a + b)$
E. $2ab(3a + 5b)(2a + b)$

20. A person purchased 5 items at c cents each and gave the clerk q quarters, which was enough to pay for the items. How many cents change should this person receive, in terms of c and q ?

F. $25q - 5c$
G. $25q - c$
H. $25q - 5$
J. $q - 5c$
K. $q - 5$

21. Which graph below represents the solutions for x of the inequality $6x - 3(x - 2) \geq 2(x + 5)$?

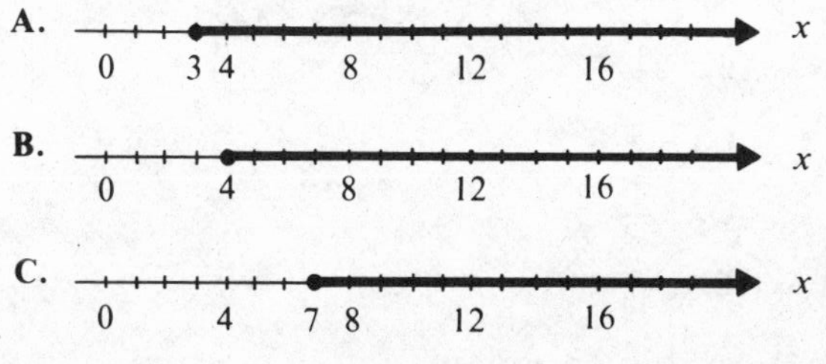

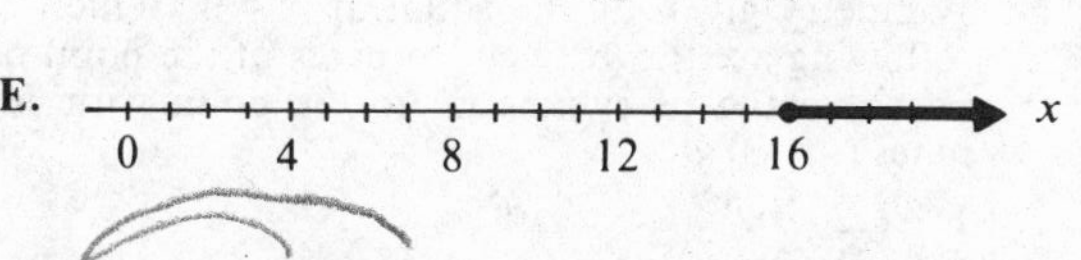

22. $(\sqrt{3} - \sqrt{2})(\sqrt{2} - \sqrt{3}) = ?$

F. -5
G. $2\sqrt{6} - 5$
H. 1
J. $\sqrt{6} - 1$
K. 5

23. In the right triangle shown below, the length of $\overline{AB}$ is 8 units, $\angle A$ measures 60°, $\sin 60° \approx .866$, $\cos 60° \approx .5$, and $\tan 60° \approx 1.73$. Approximately how many units long is $\overline{BC}$, to the nearest hundredth of a unit?

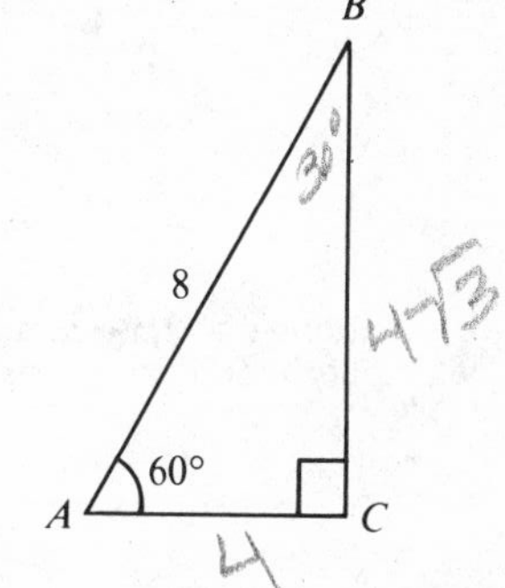

A. 4.00
B. 4.61
C. 4.80
D. 6.93
E. 9.23

GO ON TO THE NEXT PAGE.

24. If $\frac{4}{5} + (-\frac{3}{10}) = x + 1\frac{1}{2}$, then x = ?

F. 2
G. 1
H. –1
J. –2
K. –10

25. What is the slope of the straight line that passes through (7,–1) and (3,2) in the standard (x,y) coordinate plane?

A. $-\frac{4}{3}$
B. $-\frac{3}{4}$
C. $-\frac{1}{4}$
D. $\frac{1}{10}$
E. $\frac{3}{10}$

26. The graph of $y = x^2 - 4$ is a parabola with axis of symmetry given by the equation $x = 0$. Which of the following are the (x,y) coordinates of the point on the parabola that is symmetric to the point with coordinates (–1,–3) ?

F. (2, 0)
G. (1,–3)
H. (0,–4)
J. (–2, 0)
K. (–3, 5)

27. Points A and B in the standard (x,y) plane have coordinates (3,5) and (–2,1), respectively. What are the (x,y) coordinates of the midpoint of $\overline{AB}$?

A. $(\frac{1}{2},2)$
B. $(\frac{1}{2},3)$
C. (1,6)
D. $(\frac{5}{2},2)$
E. (5,4)

28. If 2 lines with equations $y = m_1x + b_1$ and $y = m_2x + b_2$ are parallel, which of the following must be true?

F. $m_1 = m_2$
G. $b_1 = b_2$
H. $m_1 = -\frac{1}{m_2}$
J. $m_1 \neq m_2$ and $b_1 = -\frac{1}{b_2}$
K. $m_1 \neq m_2$ and $b_1 \neq b_2$

29. Two more than the product of 4 and a certain number is the same as 12 less than the product of 6 and the number. What is the number?

A. 3
B. 4
C. 5
D. 6
E. 7

30. A rectangle 2 units wide by 9 units long has the same area as an isosceles right triangle. If the equal-length sides of the triangle are each x units long, then x = ?

F. $\frac{7}{2}$
G. $\frac{9}{2}$
H. $\frac{11}{2}$
J. 6
K. 7

31. If the area of a triangle is 18 square units and its base is 3 units long, how many units long is the altitude to that base?

A. 3
B. 6
C. 12
D. 15
E. 33

32. If a central angle of measure 30° is subtended by a circular arc of length 6 meters, as is illustrated below, how many meters in length is the radius of the circle?

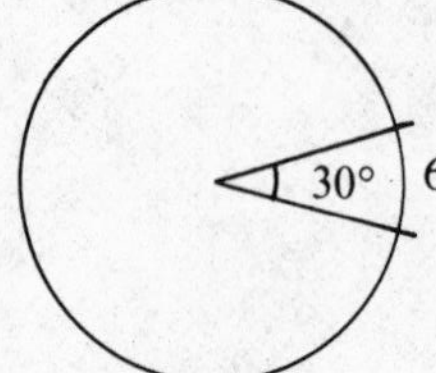

F. $\frac{\pi}{36}$
G. $\frac{1}{5}$
H. π
J. $\frac{36}{\pi}$
K. 180

GO ON TO THE NEXT PAGE.

33. If the circumference of a circle is 10 units long, how many units long is its radius?

A. $\frac{\sqrt{10}}{\pi}$

B. $\sqrt{\frac{5}{\pi}}$

C. $\frac{5}{\pi}$

D. $\sqrt{\frac{10}{\pi}}$

E. $\frac{10}{\pi}$

34. A rectangular box with a base 2 inches by 6 inches is 10 inches tall and holds 12 ounces of breakfast cereal. The manufacturer wants to use a new box with a base 3 inches by 5 inches. How many inches tall should the new box be in order to hold exactly the same volume as the original box? (Note: The volume of a rectangular box may be calculated by multiplying the area of the base by the height of the box.)

F. 8
G. 9
H. 10
J. 11
K. 12

35. The sum of a rational number and an irrational number is always:

A. positive.
B. irrational.
C. rational.
D. the square root of a rational number.
E. rational, unless one of the numbers is zero.

36. What is the sum of the 2 solutions for x in the equation $|2x - 6| = 10$?

F. 12
G. 6
H. −2
J. −6
K. −12

37. $\frac{1}{\sqrt{2} - 1} = ?$

A. $\frac{\sqrt{2} - 2}{2}$

B. $-\sqrt{2} + 1$

C. $-\sqrt{2} - 1$

D. $\sqrt{2} + 1$

E. $\frac{\sqrt{2} + 1}{3}$

38. Let $d = st$ be the formula for distance, where d represents distance traveled in miles; s, speed in miles per hour; and t, time elapsed in hours. If the distance traveled is 15 miles and the time elapsed is 45 minutes, what is the speed, in miles per hour?

F. 11.25
G. 12
H. 18.75
J. 20
K. 30

39. If $0° < x° < 90°$ and $\sin x = \frac{1}{2}$, then $\cos x = ?$

A. $\frac{1}{2}$

B. $\frac{\sqrt{3}}{2}$

C. 2

D. $\frac{\sqrt{3}}{3}$

E. $\frac{2\sqrt{3}}{3}$

40. If $(x - a)^2 = 4$, which of the following expresses all of the solutions for x in terms of a ?

F. a

G. $a + 2$

H. $a \pm 2$

J. $\pm(2 - a)$

K. $\pm\sqrt{4 - a^2}$

41. $(-3)^2 + 3^{(-2)} = ?$

A. 0

B. 1

C. $8\frac{8}{9}$

D. $9\frac{1}{9}$

E. 18

42. What are the values of x for which $\frac{x(x-2)}{(x-1)(x-2)}$ is undefined?

F. 1 only
G. 0 and 1 only
H. 0 and 2 only
J. 1 and 2 only
K. 0, 1, and 2 only

GO ON TO THE NEXT PAGE.

43. Given point $M(9,6)$ in the standard (x,y) coordinate plane, what are the coordinates of the point N such that $P(2,3)$ is the midpoint of $\overline{MN}$?

A. (−5, 0)

B. $\left(-\frac{7}{2}, -\frac{3}{2}\right)$

C. $\left(\frac{7}{2}, \frac{3}{2}\right)$

D. $\left(\frac{11}{2}, \frac{9}{2}\right)$

E. (16, 9)

44. Which of the following is equivalent to $\frac{(2.1 \times 10^5)(1.4 \times 10^7)}{.7 \times 10^{15}}$?

F. .00006
G. .00042
H. .0042
J. 4,200
K. 4.2×10^{20}

45. Trapezoid $ABCD$ has lengths, in units, and angle measures as marked in the figure below. How many units long is $\overline{CD}$?

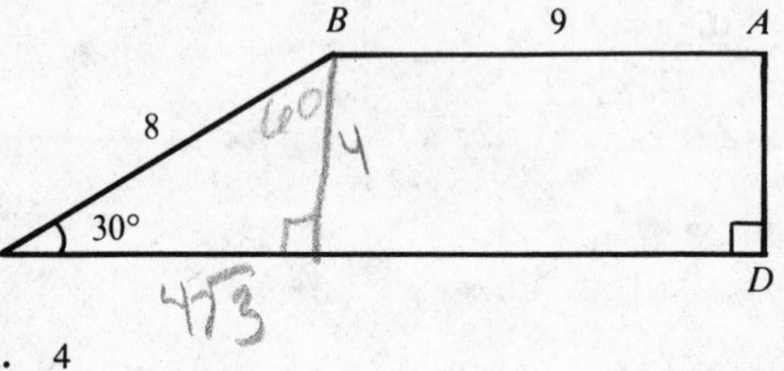

A. 4

B. $4\sqrt{3}$

C. 13

D. $9 + 4\sqrt{2}$

E. $9 + 4\sqrt{3}$

46. $8^{-\frac{2}{3}} = ?$

F. $\frac{1}{4}$

G. $\frac{3}{16}$

H. $\frac{1}{12}$

J. $-\frac{1}{12}$

K. $-\frac{3}{16}$

47. For all $x > 0$ and $y > 0$, the radical expression $\frac{\sqrt{x}}{3\sqrt{x} - \sqrt{y}}$ is equivalent to:

A. $\frac{3x - \sqrt{xy}}{9x + y}$

B. $\frac{3x - \sqrt{xy}}{3x + y}$

C. $\frac{3x + \sqrt{xy}}{9x - y}$

D. $\frac{3x + \sqrt{xy}}{3x - y}$

E. $\frac{x}{3x - y}$

48. In the figure below, $\overline{AB}$ and $\overline{CD}$ are parallel, and lengths are given in units. What is the area, in square units, of trapezoid $ABCD$?

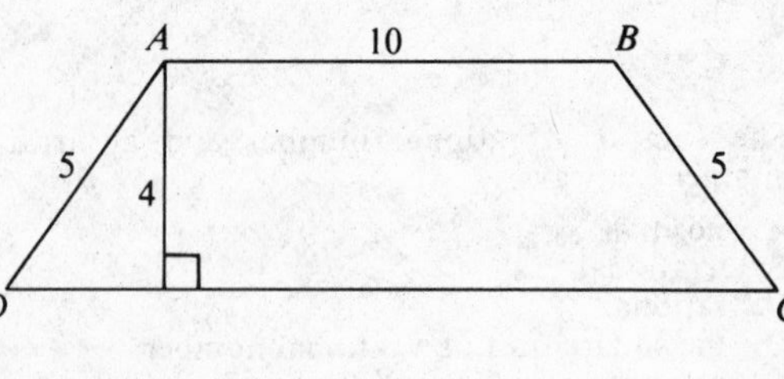

F. 36
G. 52
H. 64
J. 65
K. 104

49. For all $y > 1$, $\frac{1 - \frac{1}{y^2}}{1 - \frac{1}{y}} = ?$

A. $\frac{1}{y}$

B. $\frac{y}{y+1}$

C. $\frac{y}{y-1}$

D. $\frac{y+1}{y}$

E. $\frac{y-1}{y}$

GO ON TO THE NEXT PAGE.

50. What is $\tan\theta$ if $\sin\theta = \frac{5}{13}$ and $\cot\theta = \frac{12}{5}$?

F. $\frac{25}{126}$
G. $\frac{5}{12}$
H. $\frac{12}{13}$
J. $\frac{13}{12}$
K. $\frac{12}{5}$

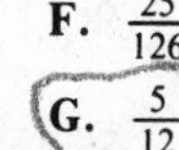
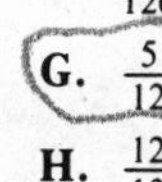

51. $2^2 + 2^0 + 2^{-2} = ?$

A. 0
B. 1
C. $4\frac{1}{4}$
D. $5\frac{1}{4}$
E. 6

52. A string that is 8 feet long is cut into 3 parts. If the first part is twice as long as the second, and the second part is twice as long as the third, how many feet long is the first part?

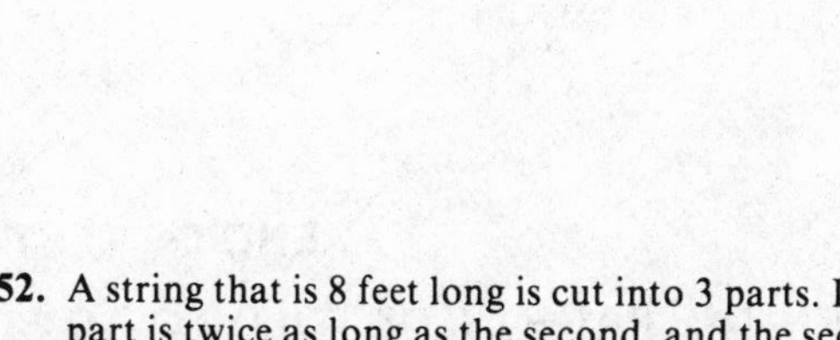

F. $1\frac{1}{7}$
G. $1\frac{3}{5}$
H. $2\frac{2}{7}$
J. $3\frac{1}{5}$
K. $4\frac{4}{7}$

53. What is the area, in square inches, of a circle that has a diameter of 9 inches?

A. 20.25π
B. 40.50π
C. 60.50π
D. 80.50π
E. 81.00π

54. Which of the following graphs in the standard (x,y) coordinate plane correctly shows the points on the graph of $y = |x^2 - 4|$ for $x = -2, -1$, and 0 ?

F.

G.

H.

J.

K.

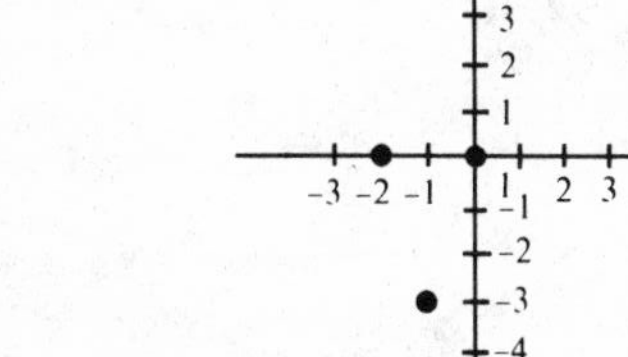

GO ON TO THE NEXT PAGE.

55. The sides of a triangle are 8, 9, and 13 units long, respectively. The shortest side of a second, similar triangle is 12 units long. How many units long is the perimeter of the second triangle?

A. 34
B. 42
C. 45
D. 46
E. 52

56. A rectangular box has a length of 10 feet, a width of 6 feet, and a height of 4 feet. The longest straight rod that could fit in this box would have to go along the diagonal between opposite corners. How many feet long is this distance?

F. $2\sqrt{13}$
G. $2\sqrt{29}$
H. $2\sqrt{34}$
J. $2\sqrt{38}$
K. $4\sqrt{15}$

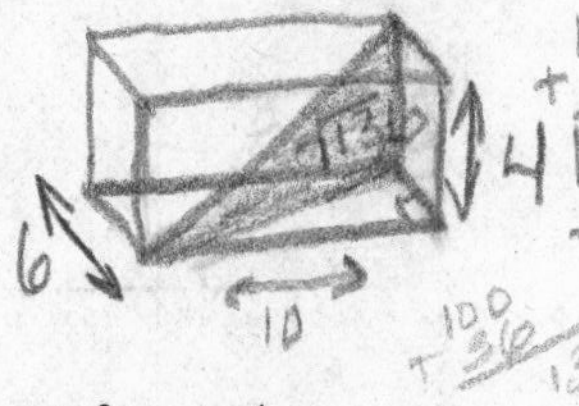

57. The roots of a polynomial are $\frac{2}{5}$ and $-\frac{4}{3}$. Which one of the following could be the polynomial?

A. $(2x + 5)(4x - 3)$
B. $(2x - 5)(3x + 4)$
C. $(2x - 5)(4x + 3)$
D. $(5x + 2)(3x - 4)$
E. $(5x - 2)(3x + 4)$

58. A total of 50 juniors and seniors were given a mathematics test. The 35 juniors attained an average score of 80 while the 15 seniors attained an average of 70. What was the average score for all 50 students who took the test?

F. 73
G. 75
H. 76
J. 77
K. 78

59. For all θ, $\frac{\sin^2\theta + \cos^2\theta}{\sin\theta}$ is equivalent to:

A. $\cos\theta$
B. $\tan\theta$
C. $\cot\theta$
D. $\sec\theta$
E. $\csc\theta$

60. What is the maximum value of $2y$ for x and y satisfying the system of inequalities below?

$$x \geq 0$$
$$y \geq 0$$
$$x + y \leq 6$$

F. −6
G. 0
H. 3
J. 6
K. 12

END OF TEST 2

STOP! DO NOT TURN THE PAGE UNTIL TOLD TO DO SO.

ACT ASSESSMENT READING TEST

The passages in the ACT Reading Test are typical of what a college freshman might be required to read and have been selected from published materials such as books and magazines. There's one passage in each of the following categories:

- **Social Studies** (history, political science, economics, anthropology, psychology, sociology)
- **Natural Sciences** (biology, chemistry, physics, physical sciences)
- **Prose Fiction** (complete short stories or excerpts from short stories or novels)
- **Humanities** (art, music, philosophy, theater, architecture, dance)

Each passage includes 10 questions. You will receive a total Reading Test score that reflects your performance on all 40 questions. You'll also receive a Social Studies/Natural Science subscore based on how you do with those two passages and an Arts/Literature subscore based on the other two.

For the Reading Test, you'll have 35 minutes to read 4 passages and answer a total of 40 multiple-choice questions about them. This is about 8 to 9 minutes for reading each passage and answering the questions that follow it.

The Reading Test evaluates your ability to understand passages written about those four areas, **not** how well you remember facts from outside the passage. For example, you don't need to be an A student in natural sciences to do well on the natural sciences part of the reading test. You **do** need to be an attentive reader and to be able to think carefully about what you've read.

This isn't a vocabulary test, although good readers tend to have good vocabularies. You will be tested indirectly on your vocabulary—for instance, how well you can figure out the meaning of a new word by studying its context, or how well you recognize the synonym of a word. (The passage might state "Mrs. Anderson was overjoyed," while a question about the statement might ask, "Why was Mrs. Anderson ecstatic?")

It's not a memorization test, either. You may consult the passage as often as you need to.

TYPES OF QUESTIONS ON THE ACT READING TEST

No matter what the focus of the passage is, the questions about it will fall into one of two basic categories: **referring** and **reasoning.**

Referring, in this case, means picking out and interpreting information stated explicitly (directly) in the passage.

Reasoning, here, means making inferences—drawing your own conclusions, generalizations, and comparisons—based on what the passage suggests or implies.

While you're actually taking the Reading Test, you won't need to think about which of these categories a question falls into, of course. Whether the question asks you to identify something that's directly stated in the passage or to make a decision about an idea that's indirectly presented or implied, what you'll need to focus on is the question itself and what it asks, not what type of question it is. Among the things that reading questions—either referring or reasoning—will ask you to deal with are:

- details and explicit statements in a passage
- the ways in which elements of a passage are related to each other
- main ideas in paragraphs and passages
- the difference between fact and opinion
- a writer's—or character's—point of view
- logical fallacies—flawed logic

Here's a closer look at some of the things that reading questions often ask you to deal with, using examples drawn from the sample test that follows this discussion.

6

Details. Some questions will ask you to pick out significant details mentioned in the passage. Details can be characteristics of a person, place, or thing:

---

11. A characteristic shared by the predominant shapes of ice crystals is a:

A. hollow interior.
B. hexagonal cross section.
C. length greater than its width.
D. width greater than its length.

Details also include concepts and theories spelled out in the passage:

---

40. The author clearly indicates that he believes genius is:

F. the heritage of each person.
G. a prerequisite for creativity.
H. the product of mental health.
J. not yet explained by psychology.

You can find the answers to these questions by referring to a specific point in the passage.

Cause and effect. Some of these questions are looking for the explanation of a particular event or physical phenomenon:

---

13. The region enclosed by a halo appears dark because:

A. the nearby sun is relatively bright.
B. the light cannot be deflected through smaller angles necessary to reach the center of the halo.
C. raindrops absorb the light in the center.
D. the light is effectively scattered by air molecules.

Sometimes the explanation is stated in the passage; sometimes you must put together the information you've been given and formulate the explanation on your own. For instance, the following question requires you to think about the relationship between the various characters in the passage as a whole in order to interpret one character's actions.

---

3. Peggy most likely leans forward "apprehensively" (line 7) because:

A. the mailbox is open.
B. there is poison ivy growing in the area.
C. she is nervous about meeting her mother-in-law.
D. she is concerned about her husband's driving.

Main idea. You'll need to be able to identify the focus of the passage or a paragraph within the passage. You shouldn't rely on finding this information summed up in the first paragraph of a passage or in the first sentence of a paragraph. You may have been advised to make the first sentence of each paragraph the "topic sentence" in your own writing, but that pattern won't be found in everything you read. You should look at what the writer's main point is in the paragraph or passage **as a whole** and remember that the main idea may be either implied or stated directly.

Conclusions and generalizations. These questions require you to draw a conclusion and make appropriate generalizations from information in the passage. A question could involve interpreting words or actions (in a sense, question 3 above asks you to come to a conclusion about Peggy's behavior). It could involve using hard scientific data to draw a conclusion:

16. Which of the following ratios of ice-crystal length to width does NOT indicate a pencil crystal?

F. 4 to 1
G. 4 to 3
H. 7 to 2
J. 10 to 1

You might also be asked to generalize about the passage as a whole, or about certain arguments put forth by the writer. Note the word *implies* in the following example. It lets you know that the information can't be taken directly from the passage. You'll have to reason out the answer on your own.

37. In the third and fourth paragraphs (lines 39–71), the author implies that he believes a creative activity or product must be one that is:

A. ignored by the public.
B. valued by the public.
C. understood only by the creator.
D. done well by the creator.

Fact versus opinion. An important part of reading comprehension is learning to differentiate between fact (information that can be substantiated) and opinion (the writer's beliefs or judgments).

---

23. Which of the following claims is the writer's opinion, not a historical fact?

A. The major figures of classic Greek tragedy were the culture's great heroes.
B. The population of Athens in the fifth century B.C. was greater than 16,000.
C. Even the early choral singing and chanting was a form of competition.
D. Eisenhower winning a Pulitzer Prize for drama is comparable to Aeschylus's accomplishment.

Logical fallacies. Some questions directly or indirectly test your ability to spot errors in reasoning—to decide whether an idea or conclusion logically follows from information you've been given.

---

25. Which of the following conclusions is(are) suggested by the second paragraph (lines 19–27)?

I. The drama competition's prestige attracted Athens's most distinguished citizens.
II. Dwight Eisenhower equaled Aeschylus as a general and playwright.
III. Aeschylus successfully based his tragedies on his own military experiences.

A. I only
B. II only
C. III only
D. I and II only

Option II is a logical fallacy because the passage says **only** that Aeschylus was an honored general who also repeatedly won first prize for his tragedies, an accomplishment "roughly comparable to having General Dwight Eisenhower win the Pulitzer Prize for drama" (lines 25–27). It doesn't necessarily follow, however, that Eisenhower and Aeschylus were equals any more than it follows that they both would have looked good in togas.

Stereotypes. You may be asked to pick out attitudes that are stereotypical—trite, oversimplified generalizations based on clichés or commonly held beliefs rather than on fact or objective observation. A fiction writer might create a stereotypical character—one whose looks or behavior is determined by type (the temperamental artist or the absent-minded professor, for example). In real life, of course, there are musicians who are difficult to get along with and college instructors who misplace their keys. In general, however, stereotyping is a simpleminded way to group people based on superficial characteristics.

---

34. Which of the following assertions does NOT reflect a stereotyped attitude about creativity?

F. An athletic activity can be creative.
G. Poor, uneducated housewives cannot be creative.
H. A person must be a professional to be creative.
J. Poetry, music, and painting are the most creative activities.

Vocabulary. Some questions ask you to determine the meanings of words or short phrases in the context of a passage.

---

1. The statement that "my first wife, Joan, had never criticized me at all, which itself seemed a deadly kind of criticism" (lines 63–64) can be interpreted to mean that:

A. silence can be just as judgmental as harsh words.
B. silence is preferable to an argument.
C. disagreements are inevitable in any relationship.
D. complaints are always a sign of dissatisfaction.

6

In other questions, your vocabulary is tested indirectly. For instance, although the words *defensive, indifferent, unforgiving,* and *perplexed* don't appear in the passage, you need to know what they mean before you can answer the following question:

---

6. The narrator's response (lines 94–95) to Peggy's comment suggests that the narrator's attitude toward his mother is:

F. defensive.
G. indifferent.
H. unforgiving.
J. perplexed.

As you can see, there is some overlap in these categories. Directly or indirectly, a question might test your abilities in more than one area. The preceding examples are intended only as illustrations of the ideas and relationships you should be watching for as you read. You shouldn't waste time trying to categorize a question before answering it. Focus on what the question is asking, not on the type of question it might be.

STRATEGIES FOR TAKING THE ACT READING TEST

For a moment, think about yourself as a reader and as a test-taker. You've probably read material similar to these passages, and you've also taken tests before. You don't need outside information to do well on this test. Your experience as a reader has already given you the resources you need. Be sure you understand the directions for the test, read the passages carefully, answer the questions **based on the information in the passages,** and do your best.

Remember that the overall structure of the ACT Reading Test is four passages of prose, usually passages taken from longer published works, and ten questions for each of those passages. There are no introductions or headings for the individual passages—you just move from one to the next. It might be helpful, then, to develop some sort of plan for how you'll approach reading them.

READING STUDY STRATEGIES

You may or may not be familiar with some of the **reading study strategies** taught in school to help you with reading and studying textbook information. One often-used study method is **SQ3R** or a variation. The steps in SQ3R, developed by Francis P. Robinson, include:

- **1–S Survey**
  Preview the chapter's title, introductory paragraph, subheadings, graphics, summary, and questions. Look for major points and try to get an overall picture in your head.
- **2–Q Question**
  If the author provides purpose questions at the beginning or end of the chapter, use those. Otherwise, turn each section heading into a "who, what, where, why, or how" type of question.

- **3–R Read**
  Read actively to find the answers to your purpose questions. You may need to add or revise questions to cover all important material. You might want to take notes at this time.
- **4–R Recite**
  Try to answer from memory questions asked in the second step. Check text or notes if you don't remember. Master one section of the chapter before moving on to the next. Repeat steps 2, 3, and 4 for each section.
- **5–R Review**
  When finished with the chapter, go back to the text or notes to verify the answers given in step 4. You will remember the materials better if you do this step now. Occasional reviews later help to refresh your memory of the materials.

Another strategy you may have learned is to look for the **organization** of a textbook chapter or other passage. Knowledge or awareness of the text's structure can help you better understand the material. Bonnie J. F. Meyer and Roy O. Freedle have identified five common organizational patterns of a passage:

- **Description**—tells about a feature or attribute of a topic
- **Collection**—lists several features or attributes associated with a topic
- **Causation**—groups details or features in a time sequence (before and after) and specifies a cause-effect relationship
- **Problem/solution**—includes causation structure but adds a solution
- **Comparison**—organizes features or details on the basis of similarities and differences

Sometimes these patterns are mixed or a text will follow some other organizational pattern.

These reading strategies are obviously designed for passages that are longer than the ones you'll find on the Reading Test. If you've used a reading strategy (one of these or another one) so much that it's become automatic for you, though, you might be able to use part of it or adapt it in some way to help you on the ACT Reading Test. Because your time will be limited, it's probably not a good idea to try a strategy for the first time on the test. Instead, you might want to try out part of a strategy (or adapt or improve your own method) on one of the sample tests in this book, especially the sample ACT Reading Test at the end of this section. You might discover an approach that would be helpful during the actual test.

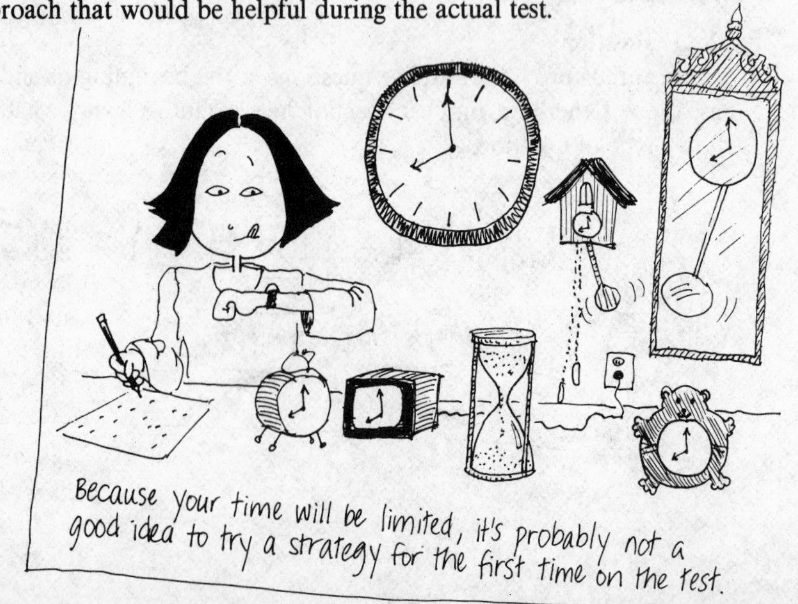

Because your time will be limited, it's probably not a good idea to try a strategy for the first time on the test.

STRATEGIES FOR THE ACT READING TEST

When you take the ACT Reading Test, here are some general things you might do before reading the first passage. First, **make a quick overview of the entire Reading Test.** Flip through the pages and note that there are four passages. Each comes from a different subject area; each has ten multiple-choice questions.

The more you know about a passage before you read it, the easier it is to read it and answer the questions. But you need to **remember that during the test a clock is ticking.** Make a **quick overview of each passage as you come to it** to get an idea of the overall meaning of the passage and of what the questions will ask you to look for.

Some readers find making a **quick overview of the questions** gives them a much better idea of what to look for as they're reading the passage. If you're a very slow reader, though, this may not be such a good idea for you. If you decide to preview the questions, don't spend too much time on them—just scan for a few key words or ideas that you can watch for as you're reading the passage. If you're not certain whether previewing the questions would be a good idea for you, try alternating between the two approaches—previewing the questions and not previewing the questions—as you work through the sample tests in this book to see which is more successful for you.

Before you begin your careful reading of each passage, here are some questions to consider:

- **Why am I reading this?**
  Try to think along the lines of: "I need to understand this passage well enough to answer the questions about it at the end." You are **not** reading it and studying it as you would a passage on which you'd be tested a week or two later. Read quickly but carefully, for comprehension, but don't try to memorize information.

- **How much time do I have?**
  You have 35 minutes to read 4 passages and answer 40 questions. The Reading Test contains a lot of print. You need to pace yourself so you don't spend too much time on one passage or one question. If you take 2 to 3 minutes to read each passage, then you have about 35 to 40 seconds to answer each question. (If that doesn't sound like much time, try holding your breath for 35 or 40 seconds. Longer than you thought, isn't it?)

  Because time is limited, you may want to be especially careful in making decisions about skipping more difficult questions. For example, if you leave the difficult questions from the first passage until you work through the entire Reading Test, you may find you've forgotten the passage when you return to it. Perhaps you'll find it more useful to think of the test as four 9-minute units and try to complete all the questions for each passage within its allotted 9 minutes.

Try holding your breath for 40 seconds.

- **What kind of worker am I?**
"Know thyself." Are you the kind of person who likes to get the big picture in a hurry, then carefully go over your work? Do you like to answer the questions you're sure of quickly, then go back and puzzle out the tougher ones? Or are you something of a perfectionist? Do you find it hard to concentrate on a question until the one before it is answered to your satisfaction? There's no right way or wrong way—just the one that works best for you.

- **How does what I need to know affect the way I read?**
Your overview should give you a framework from which to approach each passage. Notice that there are no titles, subheads, or introductions for these passages. Read thoughtfully and attentively to make sense of what's going on. Remember that, just as a writer makes several drafts, you as a reader will create "drafts" of meaning that you monitor and change as you go along. Also try to remember that the Reading Test asks you to refer and reason **on the basis of the passage.** Be careful not to let other information or opinions you may have distract you from the passage itself.

Read carefully enough to understand the passage well, yet keep in mind that you'll be going back to the passage again and again to answer questions. You should read for both details and main ideas. You'll want to watch for relationships among things, conditions, ideas, and people.

If you come across something in the reading that seems particularly important, you might want to **mark it in the passage** so that you can easily find it when you're answering the questions. Don't waste time actually taking notes, though. Bear in mind, too, that questions often include line numbers to help you locate the specific information that's being questioned.

- **How do I approach each topic?**
Just as going to see the latest movie sequel is different from watching a National Geographic wildlife special, reading a novel or short story is a different experience from reading a scientific essay. As you approach the different kinds of passages in this test, you may find it helpful to keep their essential differences in mind.

Prose Fiction. This type of passage generally includes a narration of events and revelation of character. Think about how you read fiction. What kinds of things do you look for? Do you read fiction hoping to find information or to be entertained? Although we learn a great deal and can certainly pick up interesting facts when we read fiction, most of us read for the story—to "find out what happens"—or because we're interested in the characters or because we just want to "get away." The questions about fiction passages ask about many of the things you pay attention to when you read a short story or novel—plot, characterization, and mood, among other things.

For example, a question about a fiction passage might ask about the underlying meaning of a character's words or actions:

---

7. As he is revealed in the passage, the narrator can best be described as:

   A. indifferent to the feelings of Richard and Peggy.
   B. too concerned with his own thoughts.
   C. dismissive of his past.
   D. nervous about his mother meeting his new family.

As you read, don't just note the events of the narration. Try to be aware of the passage's mood or tone, the relationships of the characters, and the emotion implied by **what** the characters say as well as **how** they say it. A writer often uses dialogue not only to explain a situation to a reader, but also to reveal character.

Natural Sciences. This kind of passage usually presents a science topic and an explanation of its significance. A science passage requires a different sort of analysis than a prose fiction passage does. For instance, the writer is typically concerned with the relationships between natural phenomena—not the relationships between characters. Be alert for words that discuss relationships. Watch for terms signifying:

- **cause and effect** (is related to, depends upon, varies with, is responsible for, results from, causes);
- **sequence** (first, last, before, after); and
- **comparison** (most, least, all, none, only, part of, type of).

Note any specific laws, rules, and theories that are mentioned. At the same time, don't try to memorize them.

Any of the nonfiction passages are likely to include specialized or technical language. Don't let new words throw you. If an unfamiliar word is vital to answering a question, the passage should provide clues to its meaning. Do your best to figure it out from the context and then go on. Don't devote extra time to it unless it comes up later in one of the questions.

Occasionally, a passage will include graphs or drawings. Think of them as tools. For instance, as you read Passage II about ice crystals, you may be unsure of the meaning of *refract.* Figure 3, however, shows refraction, so you can deduce or figure out the meaning from the picture.

Humanities and Social Studies. Humanities passages tend to describe or analyze ideas or works of art. Social Studies passages present information gathered by research (rather than scientific experimentation). Like the Natural Science passages, however, they require a slightly different kind of critical reading than the Prose Fiction passages do.

Humanities passages are informative pieces, not narrative ones, although at times you will be very much aware of the writer's presence and point of view. Sometimes a question will ask you to project the writer's likely response to a hypothetical argument or situation, based on what the passage tells you about the writer's opinions.

These passages might have characters, but not in the same sense that Prose Fiction passages do. They are historical figures or prominent contemporary people—people who have actually lived. You won't be making the same kind of inferences about them as you did about fictional characters. In these passages, the kinds of relationships you'll be asked to infer or identify are those between events, ideas, people, trends, or modes of thought.

What is the basic idea or concept the writer wants to convey? Look for principles. Watch for cause-and-effect relationships, comparisons, and sequences. Try to be alert for dates, names, and titles that could show up in questions. Notice that certain key terms might be placed in italics. Pay careful attention to the specifics—particularly as they help you shape an idea of the passage's subject as a whole.

Characters in humanities passages are people who have actually lived.

- **How do I approach the questions?**
First, you should read the question carefully so you know what it asks. Look for the "best answer"; read and consider **all** the choices, even if you think you have identified the best one. Keep asking yourself if, based on the passage, you can justify your decision.

  An approach that works for some people is to **answer the easy questions first** and skip the difficult ones (being careful, of course, to mark your answer sheet in the right place). Then go back and consider those difficult ones. Try first to eliminate the obviously incorrect answers. Compare the responses to each other and note how they differ. Keep referring to the passage for information. Eliminate as many responses as you can. Then, from the remaining answers, you may have to choose your "best guess."

REPRESENTATIVE ACT READING TEST QUESTIONS

INFERENCES

What is meant by *inference?* What are the kinds of things you'll be expected to conclude on your own? There's quite a range of possibilities. Consider the following question, which asks you to identify a detail from the Prose Fiction passage.

---

5. The character named Richard is the narrator's:

A. son.
B. nephew.
C. stepson.
D. grandson.

You'll notice that although the answer to the question is "stepson," that word doesn't appear anywhere in the passage. You have to come to the conclusion on your own by noting the references to "my wife" in line 6 and "her son's elbow" in lines 7–8. The writer says **her** son, not **my** son or **our** son. Therefore, you must infer that Richard is the writer's stepson.

Here's another example of inference:

---

22. Combined with the passage's additional information on Greek theater, the fact that performances began at dawn and concluded by early afternoon suggests that:

F. no actors performed in more than one play.
G. admission fees were collected after every play.
H. long intermissions occurred during and between each play.
J. the performances were lighted mainly by natural light.

Before you can begin to answer this question, you need to think about what "additional information on Greek theater" is being referred to. There's a **lot** of information it could be. You notice, however, that the question mentions dawn and early afternoon—times of day. What additional information seems relevant to a question about the time of day when performances took place? You have to infer that the additional information is the fact that sunrise was incorporated into a play as a kind of naturally occurring special effect. The question is further complicated by the word *suggests.* You're asked to draw a conclusion that goes beyond what's stated in the passage. Picking the best answer requires extremely careful reading. F and G should be fairly easy to eliminate because the subjects of casting and admission charges seem to have no relation to the time of day performances occurred. Next, look at H, which suggests that long intermissions took place during and between plays. It's certainly a long time from dawn to early afternoon, and it seems perfectly reasonable to think that some of that time might be taken up by long intermissions. However, lines 57–59 of the passage indicate the plays were presented "without serious interruption." Based on that statement, you should rule out the idea of long intermissions and conclude that J is probably the best answer—even though lighting, natural or otherwise, is mentioned only with regard to the "special effect" of the dawn's early light.

If question 22 required a lot of inferring, keep in mind that it's also possible to infer too much. Look at the following question:

---

25. Which of the following conclusions is(are) suggested by the second paragraph (lines 19–27)?

I. The drama competition's prestige attracted Athens's most distinguished citizens.
II. Dwight Eisenhower equaled Aeschylus as a general and playwright.
III. Aeschylus successfully based his tragedies on his own military experiences.

A. I only
B. II only
C. III only
D. I and II only

To begin with, you're forced to do a little mental paraphrasing as you look at the choices. If you make the connection that "Athens's most distinguished citizens" (option I) are probably "the cream of the nation's leadership" mentioned in lines 20–21, you might conclude that I is supported by the passage. What about II and III? In the second paragraph, the writer compares Aeschylus and Eisenhower. Both were generals. The writer likens Aeschylus's awards to Eisenhower's winning a Pulitzer Prize for drama. But is the writer saying that Eisenhower did **in fact** win such a prize? Is any reason given to lead you to believe he wrote any plays at all? The comparison is between an actual situation and a hypothetical one; the writer is making a point by comparing an unfamiliar person and tradition with one a reader is more likely to be familiar with.

Option III might seem reasonable, too. The passage says that Aeschylus wrote tragedies and that he had military experiences. You've probably studied writers whose books and plays **are** based on personal experiences. However, you shouldn't infer that the passage says that Aeschylus is one of them. To take this one step further, let's talk about bringing in outside knowledge. Suppose you've done extensive reading about Greek drama. Let's say that somewhere you uncovered a piece of information suggesting Aeschylus did try his hand at writing a tragedy based on his military experiences. If that information isn't stated or implied in the second paragraph, as the question asks, **it is not part of the answer.** It doesn't fulfill the terms of the question.

You've probably studied writers whose books and plays are based on personal experience.

In the following question, you might agree with response G that "all human beings are creative."

---

36. The main idea of the second paragraph (lines 29–38) is that:

F. creativity depends upon a large reservoir of unconscious attitudes.
G. all human beings are creative.
H. only certain professionals can be creative.
J. the author had held mistaken and preconceived ideas about creativity.

The writer himself says something similar. But that doesn't make it the best answer here. If it doesn't fulfill the conditions of the question—if it isn't, in fact, the main idea of the second paragraph—it's **not** the best answer.

Here's one more example of how you might be asked to put together information on your own:

---

8. At the end of the passage, the narrator most likely displays a "guilty quickness" (line 105) because he is:

F. uncomfortable showing affection to his wife in his mother's presence.
G. happy to be back on the farm.
H. bored with the conversation in the car.
J. eager to greet his mother.

At first, this might seem like a vocabulary question because it focuses on only two words, which you must be able to decipher before answering the question. However, you could define *guilty* and define *quickness* and still not have a clear idea of what *guilty quickness* is. It's a rather unusual combination of two words. There are all kinds of situations that make people act "with quickness." Unless you read the passage carefully and think about it, you might find it perfectly plausible that the writer's quickness might come from eagerness (J), happiness (G), or a desire to escape a boring conversation (H). To really understand the question, you have to address the reason **why** the writer feels guilty and untangle the complex web of emotion that exists between the writer and his wife, the writer and his mother, and the writer's mother and his wife.

PARAPHRASING

You might think of **paraphrasing**—something that was touched on in the preceding section—as a sort of translating. Instead of translating from one language to another, though, you're "translating" from one English word or phrase to another. Sometimes you can't expect to find the information you're looking for spelled out word for word in the passage.

In the following question, for instance, you'll waste a lot of time if you get panicky about searching the passage for the word *insight* before trying to answer the question.

---

35. In the fifth paragraph (lines 72–80), the author's insight about the cellist is that:

A. performers are never truly creative.
B. performing is a creative activity.
C. creativity is more likely to exist in the area of the fine arts.
D. an individual judgment of creativity has to be made about each person.

The line numbers in parentheses (lines 72–80) help you find the reference quickly. You'll notice, though, that the author doesn't refer to his "insight" specifically. His words are "It dawned on me." If you don't make that critical piece of paraphrasing or "translation," you'll have trouble choosing an answer. Don't get caught up in looking for the same words in both the question and the passage. (Notice also that the passage talks about judging creativity individually "in each instance" although the best answer refers to "each person.")

You aren't always given line numbers to help you out:

24. The passage suggests that one guideline affecting a playwright's manner of composition was a need to:

F. allow a limited number of actors to play several parts.
G. encourage audience attendance at repeat performances of the same play.
H. provide roles for many actors in each play.
J. follow the traditions established by Thespis exactly.

The information this question refers to appears in lines 74–78. Notice the amount of "translating" you're expected to do. The question asks about the playwright's "manner of composition." You won't find those words in the passage. You **will** find a sentence beginning "It was up to the playwright to write works." You have to recognize that *writing* and *composing* are roughly equivalent here. F refers to a "limited number of actors." The passage says "the number of speaking characters on stage never exceeded three." F also refers to actors who would "play several parts." The passage says "an exiting actor would have time to change mask and costume before reentering as someone else." Obviously, an actor who's changing clothes and reentering as someone else is playing more than one part. As you can see, it's not enough to be a careful reader with an eye for detail. You have to be a thoughtful reader, too.

It's worth noting here one more thing that could confuse you. J might seem appealing because the passage tells us that Thespis was the inventor of acting. You might assume that the inventor of acting could have had an impact on the playwriting tradition—and maybe he did. But the passage doesn't say so. It **does** say that playwrights had to limit the number of speaking actors on stage to three and that an actor might play more than one part. This makes F the best answer.

The following science question is another example of "translation."

17. What keeps ice crystals in the air?

A. They are lighter than air and thus float.
B. Constant collisions with air molecules support them.
C. Light passing through them pushes them upward.
D. Rising cold air pushes them upward.

Here you're being asked about what keeps ice crystals in the air. The passage doesn't say directly what keeps them in the air; it explains why some ice crystals **aren't** kept in the air. Lines 47–50 refer to ice crystals that are "too heavy to be supported by the random buffeting of air molecules." So you need to infer that random buffeting is what keeps the lighter ice crystals afloat. But look at the responses. "Random buffeting" isn't among them. You have to do some "translating" to equate "random buffeting" and "constant collisions."

Here's one more science question—the one that we discussed earlier as an example of how to use graphs and drawings as tools.

19. Snell's law is used to determine the angle at which light is:

A. reflected from a surface.
B. scattered on an irregular surface.
C. reflected from multiple surfaces.
D. bent when passing through a medium.

If you go back to the passage and read about Snell's law, you'll find that it has to do with measuring the refraction of light. However, the word *refraction* isn't mentioned in any of the responses. Here's where the "translating" comes in. What does *refraction* mean? If you're not sure, try to figure it out from the context. If you're still not sure, take a look at Figure 3. The caption tells you that the drawing shows crystals refracting light. Look at the line that represents a beam of light. Does the line appear to be "reflected" (A and C), "scattered" (B), or "bent" (D)?

Don't let yourself get thrown off by surprising questions. Instead, try to take advantage of all the resources you can find in the passage.

READING CAREFULLY

Reading carefully is an important part of doing well on the entire test. But this section will give you a few examples of questions where it's **especially** important—questions where a quick, superficial reading could lead you astray. For example:

4. The people in the passage are traveling to:

F. a farm in Alton.
G. a farm in Olinger.
H. the narrator's farm near Alton.
J. the narrator's mother's farm near Alton.

Alton and Olinger are both mentioned in the passage. If you noticed that the narrator's grandfather moved to Olinger, you might be tempted to pick G as the answer. Or, because the narrator talks about "our" barn, "our" meadows, and "our" woods, you might think that the farm is **his,** and be led to pick H. In fact, the farm is his mother's and it's **near** Alton (line 25).

Here's another question where hasty reading could lead you to the wrong conclusion:

---

30. Based on the information in the third paragraph (lines 28–38), which of the following phrases best describes a tetralogy?

F. A group of three tragedies and one comic trilogy
G. The total number of plays performed during the Festival of Dionysus
H. Any performance including a burlesque of a serious topic
J. A group of four plays dealing with similar topics, themes, or characters

---

What is a tetralogy, according to lines 28–38? It's a group of three tragedies and one comedy. That's what F says—almost. If it said three tragedies and one comic play, it would be a good answer. But it says "one comic **trilogy.**" Since a trilogy is a group of three, F really describes three tragedies **and** three comedies. H might look appealing because it mentions burlesque. The passage says that a tetralogy did include a burlesque, also known as a satyr play. Burlesque was, however, only one element of a tetralogy. G mentions the Festival of Dionysus. The passage does discuss a festival, which happened to take place in the Theatre of Dionysus, but nowhere is the **Festival** of Dionysus mentioned. Furthermore, a tetralogy includes a specific number of plays, but is not in itself an expression of any total. Even though J doesn't focus on whether the plays were comedies or tragedies, it's the best response because it captures the idea of four **related** plays, as stated in lines 29–34.

Once again, a question from the passage on Greek theater illustrates the pitfalls of careless reading:

---

21. What was the "special effect" (line 57) to which the passage refers?

A. The Theater of Dionysus
B. The sunrise
C. The sunset
D. Agamemnon's entrance

What was the "special effect"? Some of the responses seem related to the question without really answering it. The special effect took place in the Theatre of Dionysus (A) during the opening scene of *Agamemnon,* which you might misconstrue as Agamemnon's entrance (D). Nevertheless, the passage doesn't suggest that either Agamemnon's entrance or the theater itself was a special effect. It's not enough simply to recognize a relevant detail; it must be the detail that answers the question.

Here's a case where the question—not the responses—might confuse you:

---

33. As a result of his study of various types of people, the author's previous understanding of creativity has been:

A. confirmed.
B. changed.
C. limited.
D. stereotyped.

The writer did say that his notions about creativity were stereotyped. Does that mean D is the best answer? Look again at the question and at the words "as a result of his study." The focus is on the writer's feelings **after** the study compared to what those feelings had been **before.** D would be a good answer to a question like "The author's previous understanding of creativity was. . . ." But the passage tells us that his understanding is different now. The best answer is B: "changed."

"REVERSE" QUESTIONS

Sometimes you'll find a question phrased in such a way that the best answer is a statement that's untrue or illogical. The question will ask you to pick the response that's **not** a factor or **not** a logical conclusion based on what you've read. For instance:

---

38. Which of the following opinions about genius would the author most likely reject?

F. Genius is difficult to study.
G. Genius is an interesting phenomenon.
H. Genius is directly related to state of mental health.
J. Genius is much less common than creativity.

The key word here is *reject.* Genius is undoubtedly an interesting phenomenon (G), and the writer has said that genius is difficult to study (F) and is less common than creativity (J). Your natural tendency might be to pick a response you agree with or one substantiated by the passage. Instead, you should pick the one that **doesn't** fit.

You might work out some sort of quick system for dealing with "reverse" questions. For example, on this one you might jot "reject" or just "r" next to the answer choices you think the writer would reject and "accept" or just "a" next to those you believe the writer would accept.

Only a small percentage of the test questions will be phrased negatively, but it's important to be aware of them and consider them carefully when they appear.

OUTSIDE KNOWLEDGE

By now, you've read repeatedly that your outside knowledge of a subject isn't going to be tested. So what happens when you run across a question like the following one?

---

26. Aeschylus wrote the *Agamemnon,* the *Choephori,* and the *Eumenides.* Which of the following statements suggests that they may be from the same tetralogy?

F. Each of the three plays includes a chorus.
G. All three plays focus on members of a single royal family.
H. All three plays are based on Greek myths.
J. None of the three plays is a satyr play.

You do not need prior knowledge of Choephori and the Eumenides.

How can you answer a question about whether three plays are part of a tetralogy when two of them aren't mentioned in the passage? Are you supposed to have prior knowledge of the *Choephori* and the *Eumenides?* No. All you need to do is look at what the question is really asking. Ignore the titles of the specific plays. The question really is: What do any plays in a tetralogy have in common? For that, you turn to the passage.

Line 37 suggests that plays in a tetralogy had choruses. However, is the presence of a chorus enough evidence to link plays in the **same** tetralogy (F)? The last paragraph says that many of the themes in classical Greek drama came from Greek myths. Would you automatically assume, then, that **any** three plays based on Greek myths must come from the same tetralogy (H)? A tetralogy includes three tragedies and a satyr play. So how would it logically follow that the absence of a satyr play would link three plays in a tetralogy (J)? Lines 29–31 state that the tragedies in a tetralogy had to be related somehow—by theme or characters—so if it were true that the same royal family appeared in all three of the Aeschylus plays mentioned, that would indeed suggest that those plays were from the same tetralogy. Notice that the question doesn't ask you whether it **is** true. You don't have to know what the plays are about. The question says: Suppose the three plays involved one royal family. Would that make it likely that they're from the same tetralogy?

All the information you need to answer the question can be found right in the passage.

READING TEST

35 Minutes—40 Questions

DIRECTIONS: There are four passages in this test. Each passage is followed by several questions. After reading a passage, choose the best answer to each question and blacken the corresponding oval on your answer sheet. You may refer to the passages as often as necessary.

Passage I

We turned off the Turnpike onto a macadam highway, then off the macadam onto a pink dirt road. We went up a sharp little rise and there, on the level crest where Schoelkopf's weathered mailbox stood knee-deep in honeysuckle and poison ivy, its flopped lid like a hat being tipped, my wife first saw the farm. Apprehensively she leaned forward beside me and her son's elbow heavily touched my shoulder from behind. The familiar buildings waited on the far rise, across the concave green meadow. "That's our barn," I said. "My mother finally had them tear down a big overhang for hay she always thought was ugly. The house is beyond. The meadow is ours. His land ends with this line of sumacs." We rattled down the slope of road, eroded to its bones of sandstone, that ushered in our land.

"You own on both sides of the road?" Richard asked. He was eleven, and rather precise and aggressive in speech.

"Oh, sure," I said. "Originally Schoelkopf's farm was part of ours, but my grandfather sold it off before moving to Olinger. Something like forty acres."

"How many did that leave?"

"Eighty. As far as you can see now, it belongs to the farm. It's probably the biggest piece of open land left this close to Alton."

"You have no livestock," Richard said. Though I had told him there was none, his tone was accusatory.

"Just some dogs," I said, "and a barn full of swallows, and lots of woodchucks. My mother used to keep chickens before my father died."

"What's the point," Richard asked, "of a farm nobody farms?"

"You'll have to ask my mother." He was silent a moment, as if I had rebuked him—I had not meant to. I added, "I never understood it myself. I was your age when we moved here. No, I was older. I was fourteen. I've always felt young for my age."

Then he asked, "Whose woods are all these?" and I knew he knew my answer and meant me to give it proudly.

"Ours," I said. "Except for the right-of-way we sold the power line twenty years ago. They cut down everything and never used it. There, you can see the cut, that strip of younger trees. It's all grown up again. They cut down oaks and it came up maples and sassafras."

"What's the point," he asked, "of a right-of-way nobody uses right away?" He laughed clumsily and I was touched, for he was making a joke on himself, trying to imitate, perhaps, my manner, and to unlearn the precocious solemnity his fatherless years had forced on him.

"That's how things are down here," I said. "Sloppy. You're lucky to live in New York, where space is tight."

Peggy spoke. "It *does* seem like a lot of everything," she said. . . .

It was true, whenever I returned, after no matter how great a gap of time, to this land, the acres flowed outward from me like a foam of boasting. My wife had sensed this and was so newly my wife she thought it worth correcting. This instinct of correction in her was precious to me (my first wife, Joan, had never criticized me at all, which itself seemed a deadly kind of criticism) but I dreaded its encounter with my mother. Joan in her innocence had once gently suggested that my mother needed a washing machine. She had never been forgiven. My instinct, now, in these last moments before my mother was upon us, was to talk about her aloud, as if to expel what later must be left unsaid.

"Richard," I said, "there *is* a tractor. It drags a rotating cutter bar behind it that cuts the hay. It's the law in Pennsylvania that if your farm is in soil bank you must cut your weeds twice a summer."

"What's soil bank?"

"I don't know exactly. Farms that aren't farmed."

"Who drives the tractor?"

"My mother."

"It'll kill her," Peggy said harshly.

"She knows it," I said, as harshly.

Richard asked, "Can I drive it?"

"I wouldn't think so. Children do it around here, but they get"—I rejected the word "mangled"; a contemporary of mine had had his pelvis broken, and I envisioned his strange swirling limp—"hurt once in a while." . . .

"What's *that?*" The pink ruin had flashed by in the smothering greenery.

"That's the foundation of the old tobacco shed."

"You could put a roof on it and have a garage."

"It burned down forty years ago, when somebody else owned the farm."

Peggy said, "Before your mother bought it back?"

"Don't put it like that. She thinks now that my father wanted to buy it back too."

"Joey, I'm frightened!" . . .

"Don't be. I don't expect you and she to get along. I thought she would with Joan but she didn't."

"And she has less reason to like me."

"Don't think that. Just be yourself. I love you."

But the declaration was given hastily, with a jerky pat of her thigh, for already my mother's shape, a solid blur, had emerged from the house and was moving through the blue shadow of the hemlock that guarded the walk. . . . With a guilty quickness I opened the car door and waved and hailed my mother.

From John Updike, *Of the Farm.* © 1965 by John Updike.

1. The statement that "my first wife, Joan, had never criticized me at all, which itself seemed a deadly kind of criticism" (lines 63–64) can be interpreted to mean that:
   A. silence can be just as judgmental as harsh words.
   B. silence is preferable to an argument.
   C. disagreements are inevitable in any relationship.
   D. complaints are always a sign of dissatisfaction.

2. According to the passage, the intent of Richard's question in line 38 is most likely to:
   F. discover to whom the woods belong.
   G. find something more pleasant to talk about than the narrator's mother.
   H. prove he is not really interested in the farm.
   J. stimulate the narrator's sense of pride.

3. Peggy most likely leans forward "apprehensively" (line 7) because:
   A. the mailbox is open.
   B. there is poison ivy growing in the area.
   C. she is nervous about meeting her mother-in-law.
   D. she is concerned about her husband's driving.

4. The people in the passage are traveling to:
   F. a farm in Alton.
   G. a farm in Olinger.
   H. the narrator's farm near Alton.
   J. the narrator's mother's farm near Alton.

5. The character named Richard is the narrator's:
   A. son.
   B. nephew.
   C. stepson.
   D. grandson.

6. The narrator's response (lines 94–95) to Peggy's comment suggests that the narrator's attitude toward his mother is:
   F. defensive.
   G. indifferent.
   H. unforgiving.
   J. perplexed.

7. As he is revealed in the passage, the narrator can best be described as:
   A. indifferent to the feelings of Richard and Peggy.
   B. too concerned with his own thoughts.
   C. dismissive of his past.
   D. nervous about his mother meeting his new family.

8. At the end of the passage, the narrator most likely displays a "guilty quickness" (line 105) because he is:
   F. uncomfortable showing affection to his wife in his mother's presence.
   G. happy to be back on the farm.
   H. bored with the conversation in the car.
   J. eager to greet his mother.

9. The main point of the narrator's memory of a contemporary's broken pelvis (lines 83–85) is that:
   A. the narrator doesn't want Richard to drive the tractor.
   B. children should drive tractors only when doing farmwork.
   C. a broken pelvis is a serious injury, but not as serious as being mangled.
   D. children find the idea of driving a tractor fascinating.

10. Which of the following would NOT be consistent with the author's portrayal of the characters' attitudes toward the trip?
    I. A discussion between Peggy and the narrator about the beautiful wedding gift they received from his mother
    II. A discussion of the mother's letter warmly inviting them to the farm for a visit
    III. A discussion of the mother's bad temper
    F. I only
    G. III only
    H. I and II only
    J. I and III only

GO ON TO THE NEXT PAGE.

Passage II

Anyone who looks carefully at the sky has occasionally seen a circular luminous ring around the sun or moon when a thin, high cloud intervenes. This is called the *halo.* Tradition says that it is a forerunner of rainy weather. Because the halo is caused by refraction from ice crystals, its connection with impending bad weather can be explained simply. The warm air associated with an oncoming, rainy region will rise over the preceding cooler air because its lower density gives it buoyancy. As it pushes upward, it reaches altitudes in excess of 10 kilometers where the temperature is sufficiently low to freeze the moisture it contains and form clouds of ice crystals. When such a cloud in front of the sun or moon is sufficiently thin to transmit appreciable light, a halo forms in the cloud. The most common halo is merely white, but others are brightly colored, with red on the inside and blue on the outside. The inner edge whose radius subtends an angle of 22° is rather sharp, but the outer edge is diffuse, and the sky has somewhat greater luminance outside the halo.

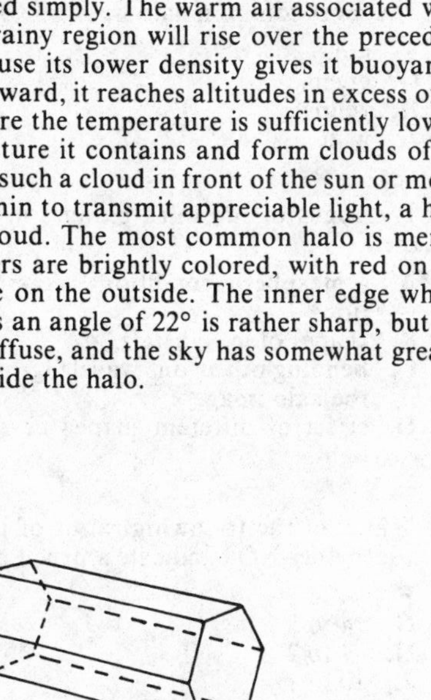

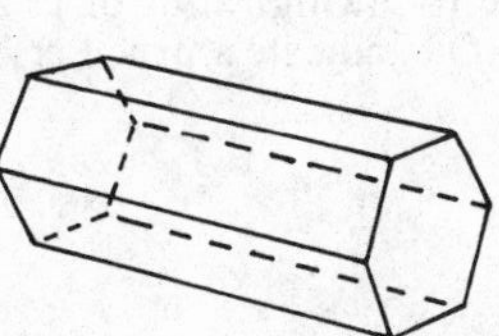

Figure 1: Pencil crystal

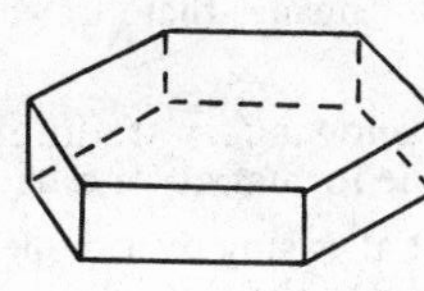

Figure 2: Plate crystal

The shape of ice crystals is responsible for these features of a halo. Although ice crystals may form in a variety of shapes depending on how they begin to grow and the nature of air currents, only a few shapes predominate. All share a common feature: a hexagonal (six-sided) cross section. Figure 1 shows one type whose length greatly exceeds its width; it is known as a *pencil crystal* because of its resemblance to the common wood pencil. Another type has the opposite extreme shape where the length is much shorter than its width; it is called a *plate crystal* (shown in Figure 2). The 22° halo comes from light refracted from pencil crystals. If a crystal should be oriented so that a ray of sunlight passes through alternate sides of the hexagon, as shown in the top illustration in Figure 3, its path is refracted once on entering the crystal and again on leaving. It is a simple matter of using Snell's law to show that because these two sides make an angle of 60°, the least possible total deflection is 22°, for ice whose refractive index is 1.31. This minimum deflection is found when light enters and leaves at the same angle to the surfaces. Other incident angles, either smaller or larger, as illustrated in the bottom two illustrations of Figure 3, result in greater deflection. The consequence of this minimum deflection is simply that when crystals are randomly oriented, as in a cloud, there is a bunching of rays at the angle of 22°. In a cloud, pencil crystals whose lengths exceed approximately 20 micrometers are too heavy to be supported by the random buffeting of air molecules. In still air, they fall slowly and tend to become oriented with their long axes all horizontal, and this helps to intensify the effect.

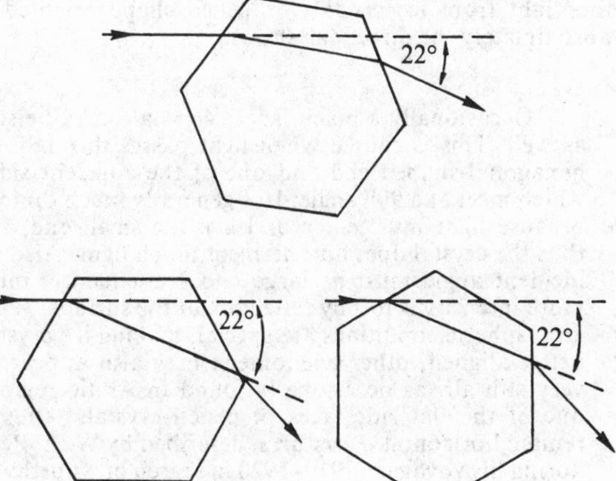

Figure 3: Crystals with differing orientations refract light by varying amounts but never less than 22°.

Figure 4 shows how the 22° deflection angle produces a luminous circle of the same angular radius when we view an appropriate cloud in front of the sun. This region enclosed by the halo appears dark because light cannot be deflected by smaller angles. The region outside has greater luminance because of the haphazard orientations of the ice crystals and the larger deflection angles that are possible. Since dispersion causes long wavelength light to be refracted less than short, the inner edge of the halo is red. The colors are less saturated toward the outer edge because some of the red through green portion of the spectrum is also refracted by these greater angles.

GO ON TO THE NEXT PAGE.

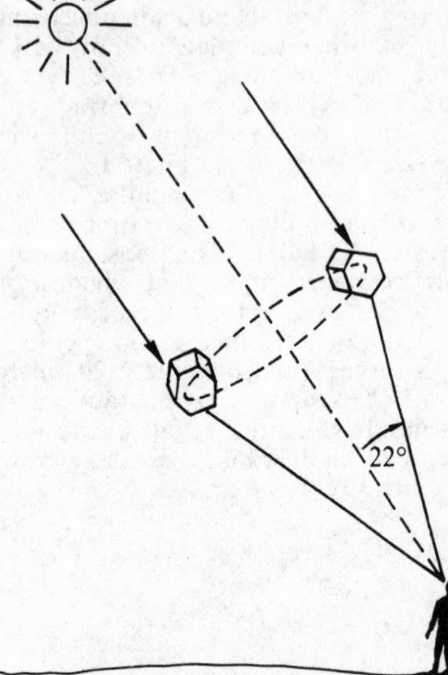

Figure 4: The 22° halo is caused by refraction of sunlight or moonlight from ice crystals of pencil shape oriented in approximately the directions shown.

Occasionally a much larger 46° halo may be seen as well. This is caused when light passes through one hexagonal-shaped end and one of the adjacent sides, which meet at a 90° angle. It is generally much dimmer because light must enter or leave the small end, and thus the crystal does not intercept much light. Also the incident angle must be large and consequently much more intensity is lost by reflection at the surface. When atmospheric conditions are special, making ice crystals better aligned, other phenomena may also appear. In very still air, as occasionally found in Arctic regions, one of the flat side faces of pencil crystals tends to remain horizontal. *Perry arcs,* described by W. E. Perry during his voyage in 1919–1920 in search of a northwest passage, are caused by rays that are only 3° from the horizontal.

11. A characteristic shared by the predominant shapes of ice crystals is a:

A. hollow interior.
B. hexagonal cross section.
C. length greater than its width.
D. width greater than its length.

12. The following is a list of the lengths of four pencil crystals: 8 micrometers, 12 micrometers, 28 micrometers, 40 micrometers. How many of these crystals are too heavy to be supported by the random buffeting of air molecules?

F. 0
G. 1
H. 2
J. 3

13. The region enclosed by a halo appears dark because:

A. the nearby sun is relatively bright.
B. the light cannot be deflected through smaller angles necessary to reach the center of the halo.
C. raindrops absorb the light in the center.
D. the light is effectively scattered by air molecules.

14. The most common halo is:

F. red.
G. green.
H. yellow.
J. white.

15. The focus of the third paragraph (lines 53–65) is on the:

A. atmospheric conditions necessary for halo formation.
B. shapes of ice crystals.
C. bending of various wavelengths of light in forming the halo image.
D. effect of different-shaped crystals on bending of light.

16. Which of the following ratios of ice-crystal length to width does NOT indicate a pencil crystal?

F. 4 to 1
G. 4 to 3
H. 7 to 2
J. 10 to 1

17. What keeps ice crystals in the air?

A. They are lighter than air and thus float.
B. Constant collisions with air molecules support them.
C. Light passing through them pushes them upward.
D. Rising cold air pushes them upward.

18. Which of the following is traditionally considered likely to follow the formation of a halo?

F. Warm, moist air rising over cooler air
G. Rain falling from the sky
H. Moisture in the air freezing into ice crystals
J. A thin ice cloud drifting in front of the sun or moon

19. Snell's law is used to determine the angle at which light is:

A. reflected from a surface.
B. scattered on an irregular surface.
C. reflected from multiple surfaces.
D. bent when passing through a medium.

20. According to the second paragraph (lines 21–52), ice crystals in nonstill air would most likely tend to orient their long axes:

F. horizontally.
G. vertically.
H. in an irregular fashion.
J. in hexagonal patterns.

GO ON TO THE NEXT PAGE.

Passage III

Theatre historians know surprisingly little about the details of theatrical production in fifth century B.C. Athens, and even less about what preceded it. We do know, however, that the Athenians themselves credited a man named Thespis as the inventor of acting, and gave the date of this innovation as less than 100 years earlier. Historians now believe that Thespis became the "first actor" by adding an element of enactment to a form of choral singing and chanting conducted at places sacred to local culture heroes. The practice must have already been old when Thespis first stepped out of the chorus to portray the heroic figure in question. One thing for certain, these early performances were already a competition; the basis for the word "tragedy" in Greek is "goat song," and seems to refer to the goat which was presented as a prize to the winning chorus. This element of competition lasted throughout the fifth century B.C.

To be chosen to compete in the drama competition was itself a great honor, and the cream of the nation's leadership vied for the right. For example, Aeschylus, one of the most revered and successful playwrights, was also one of Athens's most honored generals; for Aeschylus to win the first prize for tragedy, a feat he accomplished repeatedly, was roughly comparable to having General Dwight Eisenhower win the Pulitzer Prize for drama.

Each writer was expected to submit a tetralogy: three tragedies and a satyr play. The tragedies were supposed to relate in some way, because they dealt either with the same heroes or the same themes; the satyr play was a very broad burlesque—usually of the topic that was treated reverently in the trilogy of tragedies. Three of the tetralogies were selected for production and each was assigned to a wealthy citizen who was then expected to pay the cost of the production, excepting the hire of actors and chorus, which was paid for by state funds.

. . . Four comedies were also selected for presentation, the costs of production also assigned to wealthy patrons. In all, some sixteen plays would be presented during the festival: a trilogy of tragedies and the accompanying satyr play on each of the first three days, and four comedies on the final day.

On the day of production, the Theatre of Dionysus would be filled. Although the population of Athens was much larger than the estimated 16,000 people the theatre could hold, it was expected that all the leading citizens would be in attendance. A small admission fee was charged; if a citizen . . . could not afford the admission fee, public funds were provided. It is also said that prisoners were released for the day in order to attend.

The performances began at dawn and at least one play, the *Agamemnon* by Aeschylus, builds the sunrise into the opening scene, thus taking advantage of a special effect provided gratis by nature. It seems that the plays were presented without serious interruption until early afternoon. This suggests that there must have been a steady coming and going in the audience with picnicking and socializing between the plays—or during slow passages.

There is considerable controversy about how the plays themselves were produced. The consensus supports the idea that the actors—if not the choruses—were heavily masked and costumed. The traditional argument is that the exaggerated masks and costumes allowed the audience to see the characters better in the very large theatre; also, megaphonelike structures built into the masks may have made the actors' voices more audible. There is even uncertainty as to the number of actors and chorus members; however, by the end of the century, it is thought that there were only three actors available. It was up to the playwright to write works in which the number of speaking characters on stage never exceeded three and in which an exiting actor would have time to change mask and costume before reentering as someone else. Chorus members numbered twelve or fifteen and were required to sing and chant as well as dance and perhaps play instruments. All performers were male.

Classic Greek tragedy turned for its thematic material to the history of the Greek people themselves, including the many unsubstantiated stories we call myths. The major figures are almost always their great culture heroes, the monumental figures who had consorted with gods, who had fought in the Trojan War, and who had founded their cities and major dynasties. As we read those plays today, we must remind ourselves that the characters are not empty names from a history book, but the godlike ancestors of the people who were watching the plays.

21. What was the "special effect" (line 57) to which the passage refers?

A. The Theater of Dionysus
B. The sunrise
C. The sunset
D. Agamemnon's entrance

22. Combined with the passage's additional information on Greek theater, the fact that performances began at dawn and concluded by early afternoon suggests that:

F. no actors performed in more than one play.
G. admission fees were collected after every play.
H. long intermissions occurred during and between each play.
J. the performances were lighted mainly by natural light.

GO ON TO THE NEXT PAGE.

23. Which of the following claims is the writer's opinion, not a historical fact?

A. The major figures of classic Greek tragedy were the culture's great heroes.
B. The population of Athens in the fifth century B.C. was greater than 16,000.
C. Even the early choral singing and chanting was a form of competition.
D. Eisenhower winning a Pulitzer Prize for drama is comparable to Aeschylus's accomplishment.

24. The passage suggests that one guideline affecting a playwright's manner of composition was a need to:

F. allow a limited number of actors to play several parts.
G. encourage audience attendance at repeat performances of the same play.
H. provide roles for many actors in each play.
J. follow the traditions established by Thespis exactly.

25. Which of the following conclusions is(are) suggested by the second paragraph (lines 19–27)?

I. The drama competition's prestige attracted Athens's most distinguished citizens.
II. Dwight Eisenhower equaled Aeschylus as a general and playwright.
III. Aeschylus successfully based his tragedies on his own military experiences.

A. I only
B. II only
C. III only
D. I and II only

26. Aeschylus wrote the *Agamemnon,* the *Choephori,* and the *Eumenides.* Which of the following statements suggests that they may be from the same tetralogy?

F. Each of the three plays includes a chorus.
G. All three plays focus on members of a single royal family.
H. All three plays are based on Greek myths.
J. None of the three plays is a satyr play.

27. The first paragraph (lines 1–18) suggests that Thespis's way of adding "an element of enactment" to the early "theatrical" performances was to:

A. sing his lines rather than speak them.
B. assign individual parts to chorus members and dress them in costume.
C. stand apart and assume the character of a heroic figure.
D. offer a goat as a prize for the chorus winning the competition.

28. Which of the following statements best describes Athens's drama festivals?

F. During the four days of the festival, sixteen plays were performed.
G. During a typical festival, more comedies than tragedies were performed.
H. During each week of the festival, an entire tetralogy was performed.
J. During each festival, the works of sixteen Athenian playwrights were performed.

29. According to the passage, the major themes of classic Greek tragedy were based on the:

A. plots of the satyr plays.
B. lives of gods, not humans.
C. everyday concerns of the Athenians.
D. history of the Greek people.

30. Based on the information in the third paragraph (lines 28–38), which of the following phrases best describes a tetralogy?

F. A group of three tragedies and one comic trilogy
G. The total number of plays performed during the Festival of Dionysus
H. Any performance including a burlesque of a serious topic
J. A group of four plays dealing with similar topics, themes, or characters

GO ON TO THE NEXT PAGE.

Passage IV

I first had to change my ideas about creativity as soon as I began studying people who were positively healthy, highly evolved and matured, self-actualizing. I had first to give up my stereotyped notion that health, genius, talent and productivity were synonymous. A fair proportion of my subjects, though healthy and creative in a special sense that I am going to describe, were *not* productive in the ordinary sense, nor did they have great talent or genius, nor were they poets, composers, inventors, artists or creative intellectuals. It was also obvious that some of the greatest talents of mankind were certainly not psychologically healthy people, Wagner, for example, or Van Gogh or Byron. Some were and some weren't, it was clear. I very soon had to come to the conclusion that great talent was not only more or less independent of goodness or health of character but also that we know little about it. For instance, there is some evidence that great musical talent and mathematical talent are more inherited than acquired. It seemed clear then that health and special talent were separate variables, maybe only slightly correlated, maybe not. We may as well admit at the beginning that psychology knows very little about special talent of the genius type. I shall say nothing more about it, confining myself instead to that more widespread kind of creativeness which is the universal heritage of every human being that is born, and which seems to co-vary with psychological health.

Furthermore, I soon discovered that I had, like most other people, been thinking of creativeness in terms of products, and secondly, I had unconsciously confined creativeness to certain conventional areas only of human endeavor, unconsciously assuming that *any* painter, *any* poet, *any* composer was leading a creative life. Theorists, artists, scientists, inventors, writers could be creative. Nobody else could be. Unconsciously I had assumed that creativeness was the prerogative solely of certain professionals.

But these expectations were broken up by various of my subjects. For instance, one woman, uneducated, poor, a full-time housewife and mother, did none of these conventionally creative things and yet was a marvellous cook, mother, wife and homemaker. With little money, her home was somehow always beautiful. She was a perfect hostess. Her meals were banquets. Her taste in linens, silver, glass, crockery and furniture was impeccable. She was in all these areas original, novel, ingenious, unexpected, inventive. I just *had* to call her creative. I learned from her and others like her that a first-rate soup is more creative than a second-rate painting, and that, generally, cooking or parenthood or making a home could be creative while poetry need not be; it could be uncreative. . . .

Another was a psychiatrist, a "pure" clinician who never wrote anything or created any theories or researches but who delighted in his everyday job of helping people to create themselves. This man approached each patient as if he were the only one in the world, without jargon, expectations or presuppositions, with innocence and naivete and yet with great wisdom, in a Taoistic fashion. Each patient was a unique human being and therefore a completely new problem to be understood and solved in a completely novel way. His great success even with very difficult cases validated his "creative" (rather than stereotyped or orthodox) way of doing things. From another man I learned that constructing a business organization could be a creative activity. From a young athlete, I learned that a perfect tackle could be as esthetic a product as a sonnet and could be approached in the same creative spirit.

It dawned on me once that a competent cellist I had reflexly thought of as "creative" (because I associated her with creative music? with creative composers?) was actually playing well what someone else had written. She was a mouthpiece. A good cabinetmaker or gardener or dressmaker *could* be more truly creative. I had to make an individual judgment in each instance, since almost any role or job could be either creative or uncreative.

In other words, I learned to apply the word "creative" (and also the word "esthetic") not only to products but also to people in a characterological way, and to activities, processes, and attitudes. And furthermore, I had come to apply the word "creative" to many products other than the standard and conventionally accepted poems, theories, novels, experiments or paintings.

From Abraham H. Maslow, *Toward a Psychology of Being.*

31. Which of the following would the author think the most creative?

A. A new rock group whose style is very similar to that of a famous rock group
B. A physician who deals with each patient in a personal and intuitive manner
C. A composer whose music sounds almost identical to J. S. Bach's
D. A teacher with an extremely well organized syllabus that is carefully followed each year

32. According to the passage, Wagner, Van Gogh, and Byron have in common that they were:

F. psychologically unhealthy.
G. musicians.
H. poets.
J. painters.

GO ON TO THE NEXT PAGE.

33. As a result of his study of various types of people, the author's previous understanding of creativity has been:

A. confirmed.
B. changed.
C. limited.
D. stereotyped.

34. Which of the following assertions does NOT reflect a stereotyped attitude about creativity?

F. An athletic activity can be creative.
G. Poor, uneducated housewives cannot be creative.
H. A person must be a professional to be creative.
J. Poetry, music, and painting are the most creative activities.

35. In the fifth paragraph (lines 72–80), the author's insight about the cellist is that:

A. performers are never truly creative.
B. performing is a creative activity.
C. creativity is more likely to exist in the area of the fine arts.
D. an individual judgment of creativity has to be made about each person.

36. The main idea of the second paragraph (lines 29–38) is that:

F. creativity depends upon a large reservoir of unconscious attitudes.
G. all human beings are creative.
H. only certain professionals can be creative.
J. the author had held mistaken and preconceived ideas about creativity.

37. In the third and fourth paragraphs (lines 39–71), the author implies that he believes a creative activity or product must be one that is:

A. ignored by the public.
B. valued by the public.
C. understood only by the creator.
D. done well by the creator.

38. Which of the following opinions about genius would the author most likely reject?

F. Genius is difficult to study.
G. Genius is an interesting phenomenon.
H. Genius is directly related to state of mental health.
J. Genius is much less common than creativity.

39. After the first paragraph, how does the author treat the subject of "special talent of the genius type" (line 24)?

A. He considers it the highest type of creativity.
B. He excludes it from his consideration of creativity.
C. He calls all types of creativity indicators of genius.
D. He includes it in his consideration of creativity.

40. The author clearly indicates that he believes genius is:

F. the heritage of each person.
G. a prerequisite for creativity.
H. the product of mental health.
J. not yet explained by psychology.

END OF TEST 3

STOP! DO NOT TURN THE PAGE UNTIL TOLD TO DO SO.

ACT ASSESSMENT SCIENCE REASONING TEST

The fourth test in the ACT Assessment is the Science Reasoning Test. If science hasn't been your academic "strong suit," don't worry. You don't have to be a nuclear physicist to do well on this test. You don't even need to know how many hydrogen atoms are in a water molecule or how many chambers are in a cow's stomach. You **do** need to be able to read scientific information thoughtfully and to reason carefully about what you've read. (Of course, if you happen to know that there are two hydrogen atoms and one oxygen atom in a molecule of water and that a cow has four "stomachs," that's great!)

A sample Science Reasoning Test appears at the end of this discussion. You may prefer to use it as a practice test before reading the discussion or to refer to it while you're reading and then work through the test with the benefit of what you've learned from the discussion. The choice is yours.

The contents of the reading passages in the Science Reasoning Test are drawn from biology, chemistry, physics, and the physical sciences of geology, astronomy, and meteorology. You're not required to have advanced knowledge in these subjects, however. The kinds of skills you will need to answer the questions are those taught in most high school general science courses. Advanced math skills aren't required, either, but basic arithmetic will be necessary to answer some questions.

You'll have 35 minutes for the Science Reasoning Test. You may find it easier to think of that as 5 minutes for each of 7 sets of passages and accompanying questions (called "units"), or as a little less than 1 minute for each of 40 questions. You will receive one score for all 40 Science Reasoning questions.

The 7 units of the ACT Science Reasoning Test each consist of a science information passage and a set of multiple-choice questions. Some of the science information passages present just a few paragraphs for you to read. Others combine some text for you to read with diagrams of experiments and/or data presented in charts, tables, graphs, or figures. Each passage falls into one of three general categories: data representation, research summaries, or conflicting viewpoints.

Here are some examples of the kinds of units you're likely to find in each of the three categories.

DATA REPRESENTATION

The information in Data Representation passages may be provided in charts, graphs, tables, or diagrams that convey experimental results or scientific observations. The illustrations may include keys or footnotes and will be accompanied by an introduction or short explanation to help you make sense of the information. For example, you might expect to see three block diagrams, one for each of three countries, showing the proportion of an adult's daily diet that is accounted for by various types of foods in each of those places. Perhaps you will see something like a table of information (mass, speed, time of flight) about several objects propelled into a target.

In Data Representation passages you may be asked to do such things as:

- interpret data
- read and use graphs, tables, and charts
- select answers that best explain, describe, or identify some of the basic scientific concepts or assumptions that underlie the information provided

For example, you may be asked to think about how well sets of given information and/or experimental results support or agree with a point of view, a hypothesis, or a conclusion. Notice that you aren't asked to come up with the hypothesis. Instead, you're asked to think about how reasonable that hypothesis is, given the other information available to you.

Another question might ask you to generalize from given information to determine new information, to generate a model that summarizes the given information, or to make predictions about new situations. For example, you may be asked to use the block diagrams of food consumption to hypothesize about the relationship between the amount of food available and amount of food consumed. In each case, you will be asked to make your decisions on the basis of the information provided—always selecting from four possible answers.

If you'd like to see an example of a Data Representation passage, turn to Passage IV in the sample test following this discussion.

RESEARCH SUMMARIES

Research Summaries provide you with descriptions of experiments and may include charts, graphs, tables, diagrams, or figures, along with an explanation. Research Summaries may include the design of experiments and the interpretation of the results of experiments. For example, you may be asked to consider a series of experiments testing Archimedes' principle: a body immersed in a liquid is buoyed up with a force equal to the weight of the displaced liquid. Or you might be asked to think about a set of experiments that investigate the impact of environmental pollutants by looking at soil composition.

For example, you may be asked to consider a series of experiments testing Archimedes' principle regarding a body immersed in a liquid.

Some questions may ask you to select the best answer to explain, describe, identify, or compare the ideas, procedures, and apparatus that are essential to an experimental design or process. You may be asked to select the answer that best explains or describes the basic scientific concepts or assumptions behind the research discussed. For example, you could be asked: "If the Archimedes' principle experiments were repeated and different results were obtained, what experimental condition could have contributed to this effect?" Or you could be asked to choose the best among a number of suggested ways of illustrating the information provided. The choices you're given may include graphs, figures, or diagrams.

Sometimes you'll be asked to think about the relation between two ideas or between experimental data and ideas, or to think about the nature of that relationship. Another possibility is that scientific testing procedures will be evaluated, and you'll be asked to consider alternative ways of testing a hypothesis or of producing the same results. For example, in the soil composition experiment, you might be asked to identify other methods of determining and confirming environmental impact of pollutants.

Sometimes you'll be asked to think about how the knowledge gained from the experiment that's described might be applied to new situations. You may be asked to think about how experimental information might be used to gain additional knowledge, generate a descriptive model, or create a model to predict outcomes of future experiments. The experimental data on pollutants could be used, for example, as a basis for asking you to determine a trend. From there, you could be asked to predict how soil composition would be affected by pollutants five years from now, assuming that the present circumstances remain constant.

Passage V in the sample test is a Research Summaries unit.

CONFLICTING VIEWPOINTS

The third type of passage included in the ACT Science Reasoning Test is called Conflicting Viewpoints. These passages ask you to read, analyze, and compare alternative viewpoints or hypotheses. Each Conflicting Viewpoints passage contains two or more hypotheses or views that are mutually inconsistent. Perhaps they begin from differing assumptions or premises; maybe the data is incomplete or disputed; or perhaps they offer different interpretations of the data. For example, you may be asked to compare two points of view regarding the disappearance of dinosaurs or to consider two ideas about the origin of the solar system. Like the other kinds of passages, Conflicting Viewpoints passages sometimes include charts, graphs, tables, or diagrams. Conflicting Viewpoints passages emphasize the comparison of opinions. You may even recognize some of the ideas discussed as ones that are generally known to be incorrect. For example, the idea that the earth is at the center of the solar system was proven wrong long ago, but that idea may be used in a Conflicting Viewpoints passage together with the sun-centered solar system hypothesis to allow discussion of the differing ideas and of the strengths and weaknesses of the hypotheses. Remember, you won't be asked to determine which of the ideas presented are **right.** What you will be asked to do is to evaluate and compare them on the basis of the information presented in the passage.

For example, you may be asked to choose between answers that explain, describe, or identify the basic scientific concepts or assumptions behind the information provided in the passage. You may be asked to choose the graph, figure, or diagram that best illustrates the information presented.

Some questions will ask you to determine whether the information or results support or are consistent with a given point of view, hypothesis, or conclusion. You may need to examine relationships between observations and conclusions drawn or hypotheses developed from the observations. You may be asked to use the observations to evaluate the strengths and weaknesses of the opposing points of view ("Which of the following characteristics is most inconsistent with the theory that dinosaurs were warm-blooded?"). Or you may be asked to pay particular attention to the similarities and differences between the two points of view presented in the passage. Sometimes you may be asked to select the best of several alternative procedures for testing the conflicting hypotheses.

Sometimes you'll be asked to think about which descriptive model best accounts for the observations you're given. You may also be asked to use a model to predict outcomes of future experiments on the basis of the information provided ("A general rule on which the two scientists would agree is that the motion of the planets as described in either theory is: . . .").

An example of a Conflicting Viewpoints passage appears as Passage VI in the sample test.

TYPES OF QUESTIONS ON THE ACT SCIENCE REASONING TEST

Different types of questions can be found within each of the three categories of ACT Science Reasoning passages. The different kinds of questions are designed to test science reasoning skills at different levels of reasoning: understanding, analysis, and generalization.

UNDERSTANDING

These questions deal with only small parts of the passage at a time, testing basic ideas about the passage. Among the things that understanding questions might ask you to do are: figure out how the information in a graph is organized, recognize the control group in an experiment, identify an unstated experimental assumption, comprehend the ideas behind a stated theory, and determine which of several graphs best represents some data. Examples of understanding questions are questions 15, 26, and 32 from the sample test.

Question 15 asks you to identify the assumption underlying the experiment.

---

15. Which of the following was assumed in designing the experiment?

A. The length of the string will not influence the period of a simple pendulum.
B. The starting angle will not influence the period of a simple pendulum.
C. The location of a simple pendulum will not influence its period.
D. All variables could be measured to an acceptable degree of accuracy.

Question 26 asks you to consider the data presented in the table from Experiment 1 and to determine which graph best represents those data.

---

26. Which of the following graphs would best represent the results of Experiment 1 ?

F.

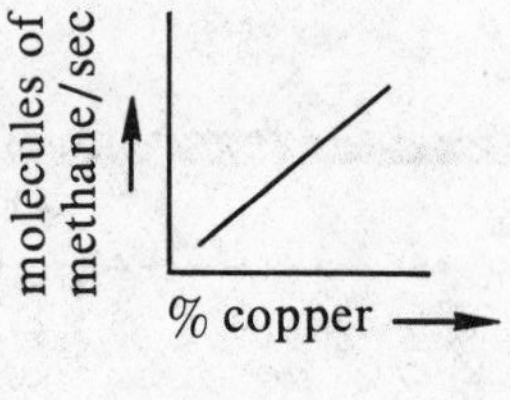

molecules of methane/sec
% copper

G.

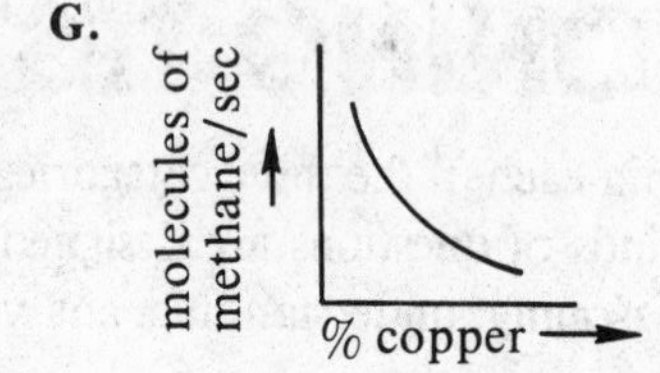

H.

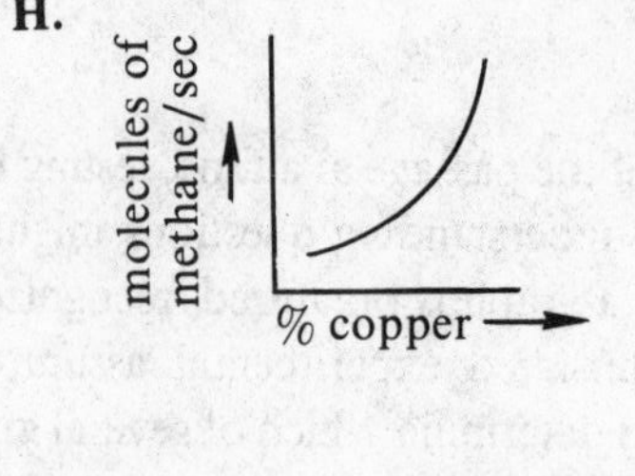

J.

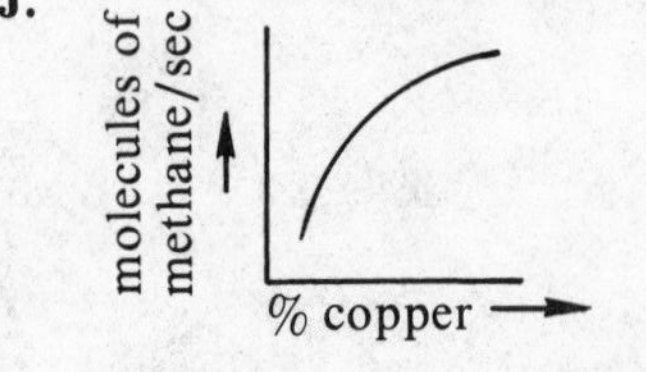

Question 32 asks you to determine which important concept is common to two presented theories about the characteristics of dinosaurs.

---

32. An important concept that underlies both paleontologists' hypotheses is that:
    - **F.** endotherms always have a higher body temperature than ectotherms.
    - **G.** tropical plants can be artificially grown in cold climates.
    - **H.** some characteristics of extinct animals can be determined from their fossil remains.
    - **J.** the fossil bone shapes of dinosaurs were similar to those of modern reptiles.

ANALYSIS

The style of analysis questions is often hypothetical, going beyond the demands of understanding questions. One of these questions might ask you to relate several pieces of information to each other, determine if some data support a particular hypothesis, propose a hypothesis that might explain some observations, or similarly figure out how some information relates to the rest of the passage. Here are some examples of analysis questions that appear in the sample test: 23, 30, and 34.

Question 23 asks you to look at the yield of a particular experiment as it relates to the variation in composition of the catalysts used. You'll need to determine the trend in the data presented in Table 1 to answer the question.

---

23. Concerning the relationship between the yield and the composition of the metal particles in Experiment 1, it appears that:
    - **A.** as the percentage of nickel decreased, the yield of product increased.
    - **B.** as the percentage of copper increased, the yield of product increased.
    - **C.** the yield was greatly improved when the percentage of copper approached zero.
    - **D.** the yields were similar over the range of copper percentages.

In question 30, you are asked to identify which kind of animal would provide the best evidence to support Paleontologist 2's theory.

---

30. Which of the following would most effectively support the theory of Paleontologist 2 ?

F. Large, modern reptiles that live year-round in northern Alaska
G. Large, modern reptiles that exhibit seasonal migration
H. Modern endotherms that are capable of lowering their body temperature during periods of hibernation
J. Modern endotherms that have evolved insulating structures

For question 34, you need to recognize the key points of the theory that dinosaurs were warm-blooded, then decide which of the described characteristics is not consistent with those key points.

---

34. Which of the following characteristics is most inconsistent with the theory that dinosaurs were endotherms?

F. Large numbers of blood vessels in dinosaur bones
G. Their ability to live in cold regions
H. The presence of featherlike structures on some dinosaurs
J. Their reptilian appearance

GENERALIZATION

As the name suggests, generalization questions will ask you to look at the information in the passage and figure out how it relates to the "big picture." You might be asked to relate the information to a new situation, to form a model that explains a set of results, or to make a prediction based on the data provided. The following examples are generalization questions appearing in the sample test: questions 16, 17, and 35.

Getting the "big picture."

For question 16, you need to pull together the data about the period needed (1.5 seconds) and the location (Earth) of the pendulum in order to find the necessary data in the table for a new situation that's not presented in the table.

---

16. A clock is being built for which a pendulum with a period (on Earth) of approximately 1.5 seconds is needed. What would be acceptable values for the length and mass of the pendulum? (Note: Assume that the mass of the pendulum is predominantly at the bottom.)

F. $L = 0.50$ meter, $M = 1.0$ kilogram
G. $L = 1.00$ meter, $M = 2.5$ kilograms
H. $L = 1.50$ meters, $M = 4.0$ kilograms
J. $L = 2.00$ meters, $M = 5.0$ kilograms

Question 17 also asks you to think beyond the presented data, this time in using the same data to determine answers to a different experimental question.

---

17. In order to determine the effect of change in string length on the period of a simple pendulum, which of the following pairs of trials can be used?

A. Trials 1 and 11
B. Trials 1 and 13
C. Trials 6 and 11
D. Trials 12 and 16

Question 35 offers new information for you to consider, asking you to think about its impact on the two theories presented.

---

35. How would the discovery of many dinosaur bone beds in which very few skeletons of prey occurred affect the two hypotheses?

A. It would support Paleontologist 2, because ectotherms generally require more food than endotherms.
B. It would support Paleontologist 2, because ectotherms generally require less food than endotherms.
C. It would support Paleontologist 1, because endotherms generally require more food than ectotherms.
D. It would refute Paleontologist 1, because ectotherms generally require more food than endotherms.

STRATEGIES FOR TAKING THE ACT SCIENCE REASONING TEST

It's important to read carefully and thoughtfully so that you'll understand clearly what you're being asked. Then you can determine the information you need to solve the problem and the information you are given in the passage that will help you find the answer. You may find it helpful to underline important information or to make notes in the margins of your test booklet. Unless you're instructed otherwise, it's okay to write in the booklet, and that may help you find key information more quickly as you respond to the questions.

PACE YOURSELF.

Remember, you have 35 minutes to read 7 units of information and their accompanying questions. That's about 5 minutes per unit. You can also think of it as 40 questions in 35 minutes, or a little less than a minute per question. If you're like most people, you'll find some of the units more familiar and probably easier than some of the others, so it's a good idea to try to work fast enough to allow time for coming back to any questions you have trouble answering the first time.

THINK ABOUT HOW YOU CAN USE THE INFORMATION IN GRAPHS, DIAGRAMS, AND CHARTS.

GRAPHS AND DIAGRAMS

Graphs and diagrams illustrate data in ways that can be very useful if you follow a few rules. First, it's important to **identify what is being displayed** in the graph or diagram (pig iron, nuclear missiles, concentration of cytoplasm, etc.). What **unit(s) of measurement** are used (meters, pounds, kilometers per hour, etc.)? Graphs usually have **captions or labels** that provide this information; diagrams generally have a **key or legend** or other short explanation of the information presented. Many graphs consist of two **axes** (horizontal and vertical), both of which will be labeled. Remember, the first thing to find out about any graph or diagram is exactly what the numbers represent.

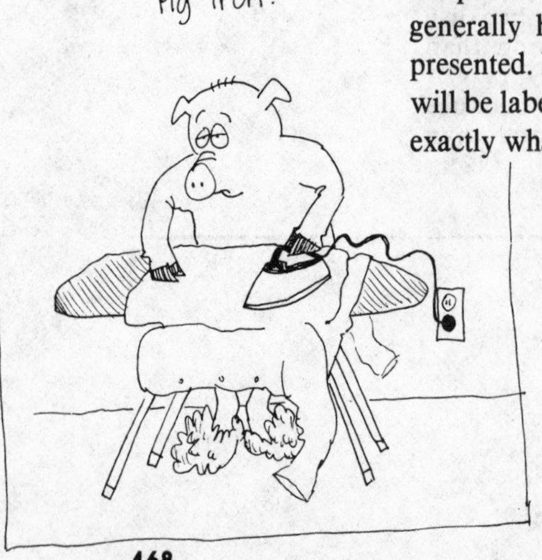

Once you've identified what is being presented in the graph or diagram, you can begin to look for trends in the data. The main reason for using a graph or diagram to present information is to show how one characteristic of the data tends to influence one or more other characteristics.

For a **coordinate graph,** notice how a change on the horizontal (or x) axis relates to the position of the variable on the vertical (or y) axis. If the curve shown angles upward from lower left to upper right (as in Figure 1a), then as the variable shown on the x-axis increases, so does the variable on the y-axis (a direct relationship). An example of a direct relationship is that a girl's weight increases as her height increases. If the curve goes from upper left to lower right (as in Figure 1b), then as the variable on the x-axis increases, the variable on the y-axis decreases (an inverse relationship). An example of an inverse relationship is that the more players there are on a soccer team, the less time each of them gets to play (assuming everyone gets equal playing time). If the graph shows a vertical or horizontal line (as in Figure 1c), the characteristics are probably unrelated.

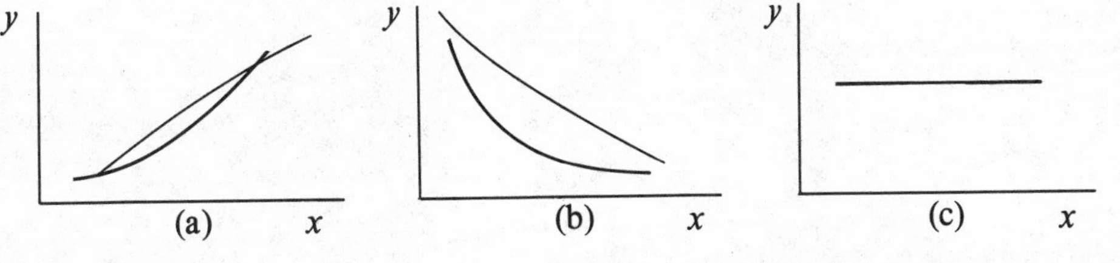

Figure 1

Sometimes, a question will ask you to estimate a value for one characteristic, based on a given value of the other characteristic, that is beyond the limits of the curve shown on the graph. In this case, the solution will require you to **extrapolate,** or extend, the graph. If the curve is a relatively straight line, just use your pencil to extend that line far enough for the value called for to be included. If the graphed line is a curve, use your best judgment to extend the line to follow the apparent pattern. Figure 2 shows how to extend both types of graphs.

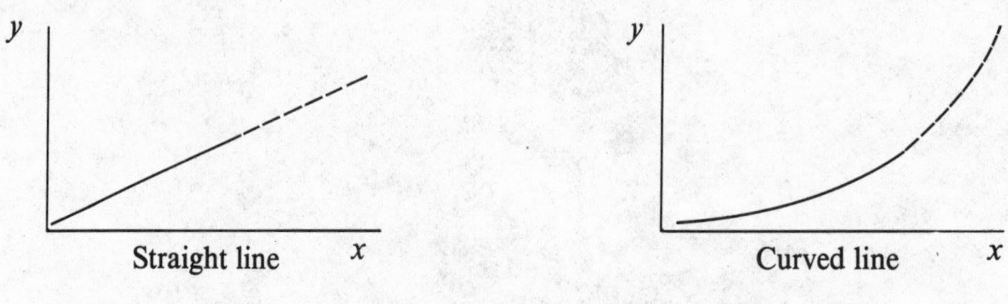

Figure 2

Another type of graph problem asks you to estimate a value that falls between two known values on a curve. This process is called **interpolation** and, if the curve is shown, amounts to finding a point on the curve that corresponds to a given value for one characteristic and reading the value for the other characteristic. (For example, "For a given *x*, find *y*.") If only scattered points are shown on the graph, draw a "best-fit line," or a line that comes close to all of the points. Use this line to estimate the middle value. Figure 3 shows how to construct a best-fit line.

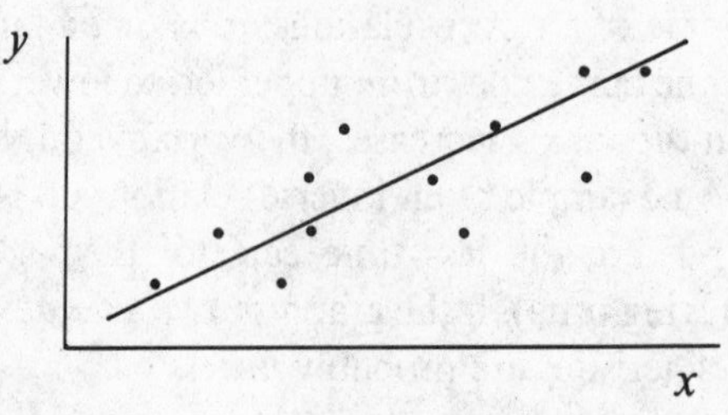

Figure 3

One very useful kind of graph shows more than one curve on the same pair of axes. Such a graph might be used when the results of a number of experiments are compared or when an experiment involves more than two variables. Analysis of this sort of graph requires, first, that you determine the relationship shown by each curve. Then determine how the curves are related to one another. Figure 4 shows a graph with multiple curves.

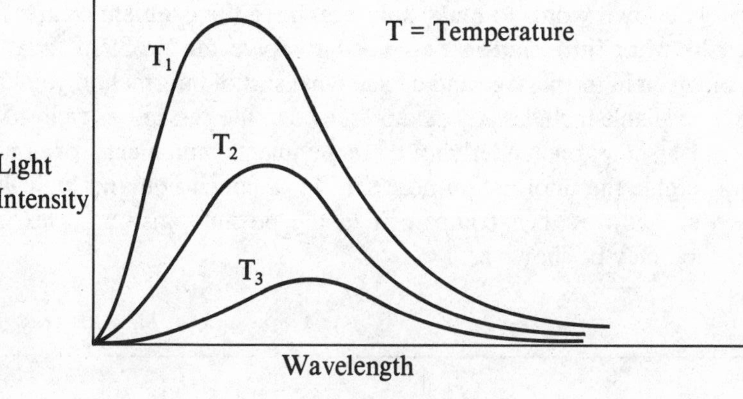

Figure 4

TABLES

While graphs and diagrams offer ways of illustrating data, sometimes you will have to work from raw data presented in a table. To understand what a table is showing you, you need to identify the information or data presented. You need to know two things: how the quantity has been measured (in grams, quarts, hectares, etc.) and what purpose the information or data serve in the experiment. Generally, experiments intentionally vary one characteristic (the independent variable) to see how it affects another (the dependent variable). Tables may report results for either or both.

Once you have identified the variables, it might be helpful to sketch a graph to illustrate the relationship between them. You might sketch an x-axis and a y-axis next to the table and decide which variable to represent by each axis. Mark off the axes with evenly spaced intervals that allow all of the numbers for a category to fit along each axis. Plot some points—ordered pairs of dependent and independent variables. Again, draw a best-fit line and characterize the relationship shown.

As with graphs and diagrams, you may be asked to **look for trends in the data.** For example, do the numbers representing the dependent variable increase or decrease as the numbers representing the independent variable increase or decrease? If no pattern is clear, you may want to refer to a rough graph as discussed above. You may also need to make predictions about values of quantities between the data points shown (interpolation), or beyond the limits of those shown on the table (extrapolation). Another type of problem may require you to compare data from multiple columns of a table. A simple examination of the numbers may be enough to see a relationship, but you may find it helpful to sketch a graph containing a curve for each category. The curves may be compared as described earlier.

DEVELOP A PROBLEM-SOLVING METHOD.

Because you have only a limited time in which to take the Science Reasoning Test, you might find it helpful to work out a general problem-solving method that you can use for all or most of the questions. The method described here is certainly not the only way to solve the problems, but it is one that works—and it works for most science problems. If you can see a way to adapt this method, or if you can work out your own approach, use the method that works best for you.

One approach to solving problems is to break the process into a series of smaller steps. After you have read the passage, take a careful look at the question and restate it in your own words to **make sure you have the problem clearly in mind.** Next, **decide what information you need** to solve the problem. Examine the information given in the passage and decide what sort of information you have. The information available includes any data presented in the passage, as well as scientific concepts and assumptions underlying the experiments, arguments, or conclusions. Sort and assemble the information necessary for a conclusion and **logically think through your answer,** then compare it to the possible answers. This problem-solving method may be shown as:

Problem-solving Method

1. **Restate the problem.**
2. **Decide what information is needed.**
3. **Think through your answer.**

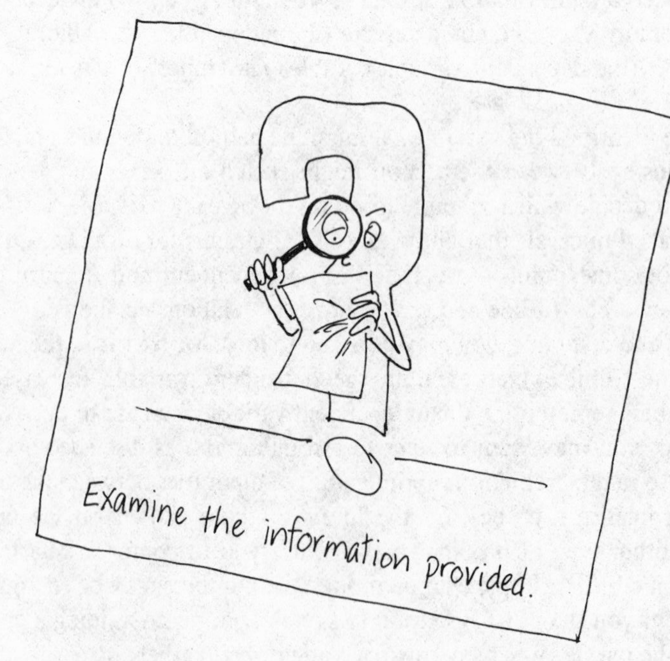

REPRESENTATIVE ACT SCIENCE REASONING TEST QUESTIONS

Earlier, the science reasoning skills assessed by the various types of questions were discussed, using representative questions from the sample test that accompanies this chapter. In this section, the problem-solving method will be applied to additional questions on a step-by-step basis to help you learn to apply the procedure.

Question 13 is an analysis question, based on a physics Data Representation passage that describes experiments with a simple pendulum.

---

13. From Trials 1 through 5, it can be concluded that the period of a simple pendulum depends on the:

A. mass of the ball.
B. length of the string.
C. starting angle.
D. place where the pendulum is located.

In applying the problem-solving procedure to this question, you could first restate the problem (step 1). The question asks you to look at Trials 1 through 5 in the table and to determine what affects the period of a pendulum—that is, what causes the way it swings to change. When you decide what information is needed (step 2), you can determine the key phrases from the question and discover that you need to look at only the data from Trials 1 through 5. When you look at the numbers recorded in the column labeled "period" for Trials 1 through 5, you'll see that the values tend to increase. In looking at the values/information in the other columns (step 3,) you'll find that they are constant except for the length of the string, which increases. Then you can draw the conclusion that there is a relationship between the length of the string and the period of the pendulum and select B as your answer.

Question 14 is also an analysis question.

---

14. From the given data, it can be concluded that when a certain pendulum is taken from Earth to the Moon, the:

F. period will increase.
G. period will decrease.
H. starting angle will increase.
J. starting angle will decrease.

You'll need to compare information about what happens to a pendulum on Earth with what happens to it on the Moon (step 1). To find the information you need

A pendulum on the moon

(step 2), consult the column in the table labeled "Surface where the experiment was performed." The possible answers to the question refer to the period and the starting angle, so data in those columns need to be considered, too. The question describes "a certain pendulum," so you need to have a pendulum with the same mass and length on Earth and on the Moon. In examining the data, you discover that a pendulum with mass of 1.0 kilogram and length 1.00 meter appears in Trials 4 and 15 and meets the requirement that the pendulum be the "same" but experimented with on the Earth and on the Moon, respectively. Reading across the rows for Trials 4 and 15, you find that the starting angles for both pendulums are 5.0°, but that the period for the pendulum on Earth is 2.01 seconds and the period for the pendulum on the Moon is 4.93 seconds. From this you can come to the conclusion (step 3) that the period has clearly increased, and mark F as your answer.

Passage IV describes the environmental impact on a river of the water returned to it from a power plant. Question 18 is an understanding question.

---

18. Which of the following statements best represents the changes observed in the same sampling sites from January to July?

F. The biomass of bass remained constant.
G. The biomass of bass decreased.
H. The population density of crayfish remained constant.
J. The population density of crayfish decreased.

It asks you to compare the data from the same sample sites—for example, site 1 with site 1, site 2 with site 2, and so forth, from January to July (step 1). Thinking about the question in your own words helps you to determine where to find the information you need to answer the question, as well as what information you will need (step 2): you compare the data from each of the January samples with the data from the corresponding July samples. The four answer choices given restrict the

To answer this question, you must compare water temperatures measured during January and July.

columns under which you need to look, however, because they describe only the January-July changes in the biomass of bass and the population density of crayfish. To think through your answer (step 3), take a look at how the biomass of bass and the population density of crayfish change from January to July. You'll discover that the biomass of bass tends to decrease from January to July across all sampling sites and that the population density of crayfish tends to increase. So the only possible answer is G.

Rephrased in simpler terms (step 1), question 20 is a generalization question asking you to summarize what seems to be the impact of the hot water coming out of the power plant on the population densities of the river organisms studied.

---

20. Based on the passage, what might one conclude about the effects of the effluent discharge on the population densities of river organisms?

F. Some may be unaffected, others may be decreased, and others will thrive.
G. Some may be unaffected, others will thrive, but none will be decreased.
H. All organisms will be increased.
J. All organisms will be decreased.

This guides you to consider (step 2) the data presented in the columns of the table describing population density (the last two columns). In order to determine the effects of the effluent on the population densities, focus specifically on the population densities in the river above the power plant (site 1) and how they compare to the population densities in the river below the power plant (sites 2-4). The population densities of water striders don't show a clear pattern of increase or decrease from the first site to the others, and the population densities of crayfish tend to increase in July but decrease in January (step 3). Response F most adequately describes your findings.

Water strider out for a stroll.

6

Passage V is a Research Summaries unit about bimetallic catalysts and their effect on chemical reactions involving gases. Question 26, an understanding question discussed earlier in this section, asks you to determine which graph best represents the results of Experiment 1.

---

26. Which of the following graphs would best represent the results of Experiment 1 ?

F.

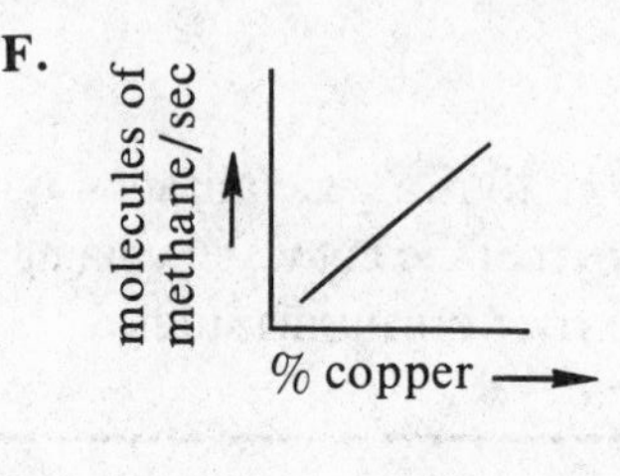

G.

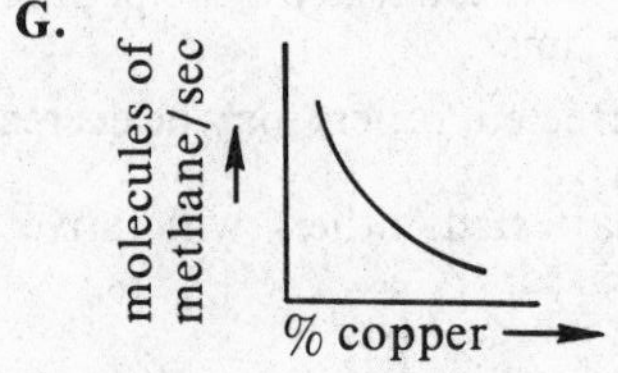

H.

J.

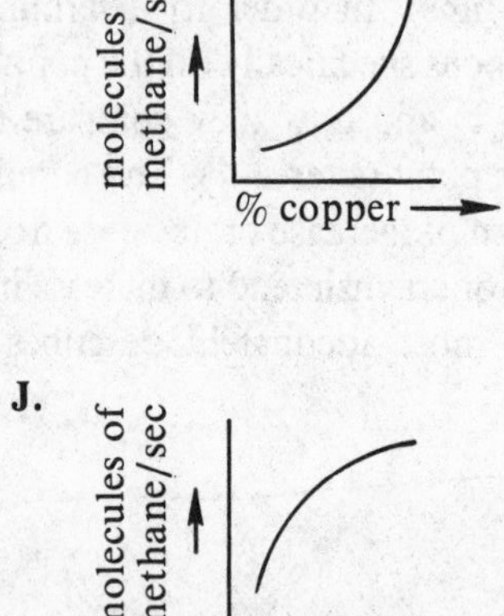

An ethane-hydrogen mixture was passed over a series of beds containing metal particles with varying amounts of copper in them (step 1). To answer the question, review the four choices, all of which compare the change in number of molecules of methane with the change in percent of copper in the metal particles (step 2). This review leads you to look at Table 1 and to compare the results of the successive trials. The percent of copper increases over the trials and the number of molecules of methane decreases over the trials (step 3). This is an **inverse** relationship, as described earlier in this chapter, and is represented by response G.

Question 28, a generalization question, asks you to apply the results of Experiment 1 in Passage V to a new situation.

---

28. Suppose that another set of experiments were done investigating the reaction between ethane and hydrogen using a different bimetallic catalyst, a mixture of ruthenium and copper. If it were then found that as the percent of ruthenium decreased, the product yield decreased, would these results be consistent with Experiment 1 ?

F. No, because ruthenium does not act like nickel.
G. No, because no experiments using pure ruthenium were done.
H. Yes, because for both the new experiment and Experiment 1 an increased percent of copper resulted in an increased product yield.
J. Yes, because for both the new experiment and Experiment 1 an increased percent of copper resulted in a decreased product yield.

To rephrase the question (step 1), you would think about performing Experiment 1 again, this time with a copper-ruthenium mixture as the catalyst. Would the results of this new experiment be consistent with those of Experiment 1 if, as the percent of ruthenium decreased, the number of methane molecules formed per second (the "product yield") decreased? To think about what information you need to answer this question (step 2), you need to remember how you thought about Experiment 1 and its results, and to recall that, as the percent of copper increased, the number of molecules of methane per second decreased. It is also important to consider that, as the percent of copper in the mixture increased, the percent of nickel decreased. For example, if the percent of copper in the catalyst was 0%, the percent of nickel was 100%. If the percent of copper was 60%, the percent of nickel was 40%. So, for Experiment 1, as the percent of nickel decreased, the number of methane molecules per second also decreased. In the new experiment, the mixture is of copper and ruthenium and, as the percent of ruthenium decreases, so does the product yield. Therefore (step 3), in the new experiment and in Experiment 1, because the quantity of the second metal (either ruthenium or nickel) decreases, the quantity of copper must increase. In these circumstances, the number of methane molecules per second increases (the product yield); the answer is J.

6

Passage VI presents a Conflicting Viewpoints unit about dinosaurs and their characteristics. Question 31 is an analysis question.

---

31. When one observes low numbers of predators and high numbers of their prey in a stable community, it can be inferred that the predators are endotherms because endotherms:

A. require more energy to maintain their constant body temperature than do ectotherms of the same size.
B. look for prey only at night when the temperature is lower.
C. store energy as fat for use during hibernation.
D. must run faster than ectotherms to catch their prey.

This question can be rephrased (step 1) as asking what characteristic of endotherms leads to a conclusion that the predators are endothermic in a stable community of few predators and a lot of prey. To answer the question (step 2), you need to look again at Paleontologist 1's theories about endotherms to identify what characteristics they have and, more specificially, which ones apply to the question. The question asks you to consider specifically the circumstance of the predator-to-prey ratio. In paragraph 3, that ratio is described as it applies to certain dinosaur communities. The presence of low numbers of predators and high numbers of prey species suggests that these dinosaurs might have been endotherms. Additional information will be needed to answer the question. The first two paragraphs of Paleontologist 1's theory describe general characteristics of endotherms. The most important characteristic for your purposes is that energy is required to keep endotherms warm, and this energy must come from food. Ectotherms do not have similar needs; endotherms need more food per unit of body weight than ectotherms do. Therefore, (step 3) the endotherms require more prey than ectotherms, and any given area will support fewer endotherms than ectotherms. Response A coincides with this conclusion.

Question 33, also an analysis question, asks you (step 1) to determine what the dinosaurs, had they been ectotherms, might have done to keep their body temperatures nearly constant.

---

33. Assuming that dinosaurs were ectotherms, which of the following adaptations might have allowed them to maintain a near-constant body temperature?

A. Regulating their body temperatures by moving back and forth between sunny areas and shady areas
B. Decreasing blood circulation through their bones
C. Having bones that grow only part of the year
D. Increasing blood circulation through their bones

For information to answer this question (step 2), you need to look at what Paleontologist 2 theorizes about how dinosaurs regulated their body temperatures. Paleontologist 2 believes that dinosaurs moved to warmer climates when winter came. This is parallel (step 3) to response A, which describes a temperature regulation strategy commonly used by modern reptiles.

As you work through the sample Science Reasoning Tests in this book, keep in mind the main points we've discussed. Remember that the questions are not intended to test your knowledge of facts but your problem-solving and reasoning abilities. Even if the topic is unfamiliar to you, you should be able to evaluate the material presented and come to some conclusions. Don't be intimidated by long words or technical terms; simply use your thinking skills to get a clear idea of the topic being presented.

Find a plan that you can use for solving the problems. Try the method demonstrated in this chapter or, if you have a different strategy that you're comfortable with, use that. Remember that you'll be presented with the information you need to answer the questions. What you need to do is assemble and organize the information in a way that you can use.

Remember, too, that the different types of passages and questions on the Science Reasoning Test evaluate different skills that you have. While you're actually taking the test, of course, you don't need to worry about what type of question it is that you're answering. But remind yourself that, as you've seen in this section, a wide variety of questions are presented to allow students to demonstrate a wide variety of abilities. The most important thing is to read carefully and to think about how you can use the information given and the skills you already have.

SCIENCE REASONING TEST

35 Minutes—40 Questions

DIRECTIONS: There are seven passages in this test. Each passage is followed by several questions. After reading a passage, choose the best answer to each question and blacken the corresponding oval on your answer sheet. You may refer to the passages as often as necessary.

Passage I

The *immune system* provides a defense against foreign materials (*antigens*, usually proteins) that enter the mammalian body. An important part of this defense system are lymphocytes that have differentiated into *B cells* and *T cells.* Most *B cells* are found in the spleen, but they are also found elsewhere in the body. B cells function in the production of *antibodies.* These antibodies combine with antigens to form an antibody-antigen complex. *T cells,* which are amoeba-like, migrate throughout the body but congregate especially in lymph nodes and the spleen. These cells engulf and destroy antibody-antigen aggregations. They also attack viruses, bacteria, and transplanted tissues.

The following experiments were designed to study the effect of the thymus gland on the development of the immune system in mice.

Experiment 1

The thymus was removed (a *thymectomy*) from both newborn and adult mice. The newborn mice never produced functional T cells; antibodies were produced, but only against certain antigens. When foreign tissue was transplanted into the newborn thymectomized mice, they did not reject the tissue. However, the mice thymectomized as adults continued to produce functional T cells, to produce antibodies against all antigens, and to reject transplanted tissue.

Experiment 2

Cells were removed from the thymuses of 10-day-old and 12-day-old mice. The cells were then grown in a tissue culture plate. T cells did not develop in cultures of the 10-day-old thymus, but did develop in cultures of the 12-day-old thymus.

Experiment 3

The thymuses of newborn mice were tagged with a radioactive material. They were then transplanted into other nonirradiated newborn mice whose thymuses had been removed. Within 5 days, most of the radioactive material was located in the lymph nodes and spleens of the nonirradiated mice. Most areas in the transplanted thymuses now contained new populations of normal, but nonradioactive cells.

1. According to the experimental data, by what day after the birth of a mouse does the thymus begin to produce T cells?
   - **A.** 1
   - **B.** 8
   - **C.** 10
   - **D.** 12

2. A thymectomy would most influence the immune system development of:
   - **F.** a newborn mouse.
   - **G.** a 14-day-old mouse.
   - **H.** an adolescent mouse.
   - **J.** an adult mouse.

3. Which of the above experiments directly support(s) the conclusion that adult mice can undergo thymectomies with little effect on their immune systems?
   - **A.** 1 only
   - **B.** 3 only
   - **C.** 1 and 3 only
   - **D.** 2 and 3 only

4. The results of Experiment 1 could be used to support which of the following hypotheses?
   - **F.** Newborn mice can produce functional T cells as soon as they are born.
   - **G.** The thymus glands of adult mice function differently from those of newborn mice.
   - **H.** The immune system functions in embryonic mice much as it does in adult mice.
   - **J.** The thymus has no role in the function of the immune system.

5. Which of the following results would be expected if an accident destroyed the thymus of an adult mouse?
   - **A.** The mouse would no longer be able to fight off infections.
   - **B.** The mouse would be unable to reject transplanted tissue.
   - **C.** The mouse would continue to exhibit normal immune responses.
   - **D.** Antibodies would no longer be produced by the mouse.

GO ON TO THE NEXT PAGE.

6. When reporting the data obtained in Experiment 3, the experimenter is assuming that the function of the thymus was NOT affected by:

I. transplantation.
II. being tagged with radiation.
III. the age of the mouse receiving the transplant.

F. III only
G. I and II only
H. II and III only
J. I, II, and III

GO ON TO THE NEXT PAGE.

Passage II

Due to a lack of understanding about rock *porosity* (spaces between mineral grains in rocks), rock *permeability* (connections between those pores) and subsurface water movement, hazardous wastes were often disposed of in unsafe sites. As a result, many *aquifers* (water-yielding rock formations) and soils have become contaminated by leaking wastes.

To determine the safest locations for waste disposal, geologists studied subsurface groundwater movement with the aid of a water-soluble tracer chemical.

Experiment 1

Storage ponds were constructed in 4 types of geological locations:

Pond A in a permeable sandstone
Pond B in an impermeable shale that was fractured
Pond C in an impermeable shale that was not fractured
Pond D in a fractured limestone

Tracer was introduced into each pond. The following data were obtained from 3 test wells, 50 feet deep, at increasing distances from each storage pond. (Note: N.A. means no arrival.)

Table 1

Pond	Hours until arrival of tracer			% tracer arriving at Well 3
	Well 1	Well 2	Well 3	
A	2	5	9	90
B	3	6	8	50
C	N.A.	N.A.	N.A.	0
D	1	3	5	100

Experiment 2

Tracer was injected into several rock formations to observe the effects of porosity, permeability, and water pressure differences on fluid movement. Test wells were located at quarter-mile increments from the injection site. The locations of injection and test wells are shown in Figure 1. Data are shown in Table 2. Arrows indicate direction of flow.

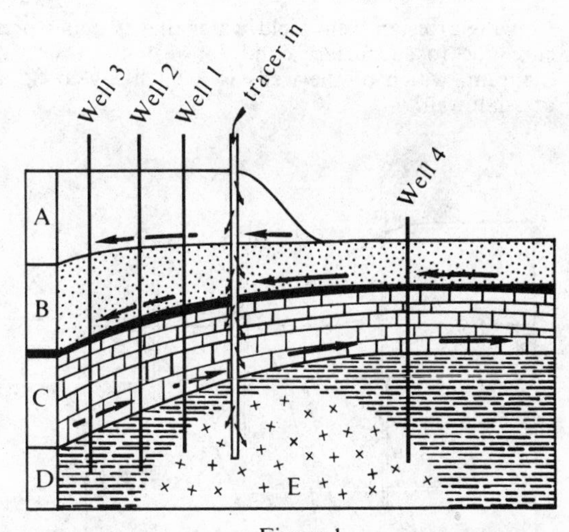

Figure 1

Table 2

Formation	Hours until arrival of tracer			
	Well 1	Well 2	Well 3	Well 4
A	5	13	31	—
B	17	27	51	N.A.
C	N.A.	N.A.	N.A.	55
D	N.A.	N.A.	N.A.	N.A.
E	24	—	—	62

7. If a near-surface or surface site were to be considered for a waste disposal facility, which of the following methods would most likely ensure that no wastes could leak into the surrounding groundwater?

A. Covering the site with a layer of sand
B. Planting trees on and around the site
C. Lining the site with an impermeable material
D. Lining the site with a porous material

8. Which of the formations studied in Experiment 2 was impermeable?

F. Formation A
G. Formation B
H. Formation C
J. Formation D

GO ON TO THE NEXT PAGE.

4 ○ ○ ○ ○ ○ ○ ○ ○ ○ 4

9. Flowing artesian wells yield water that is under pressure due to subsurface conditions. In the following diagram, which of the wells is most likely to be an artesian well?

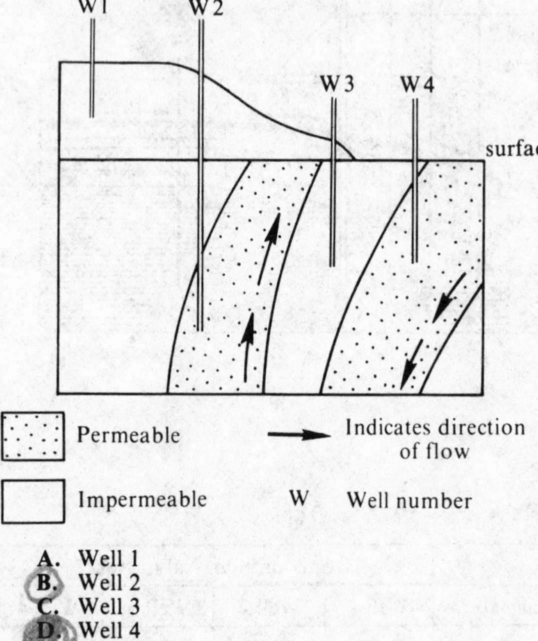
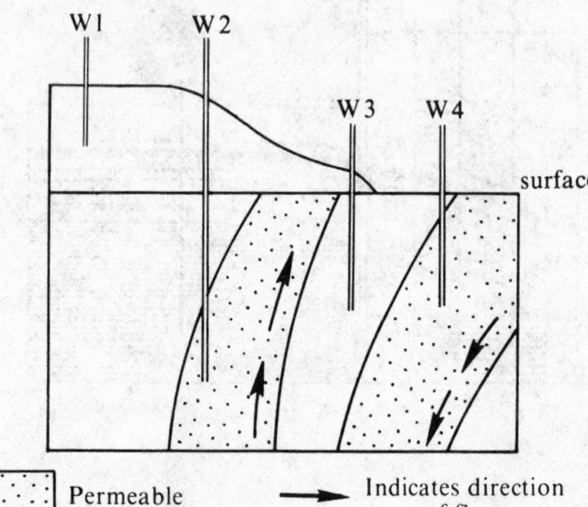

A. Well 1
B. Well 2
C. Well 3
D. Well 4

10. Oil company geologists have drilled in the formations shown below.

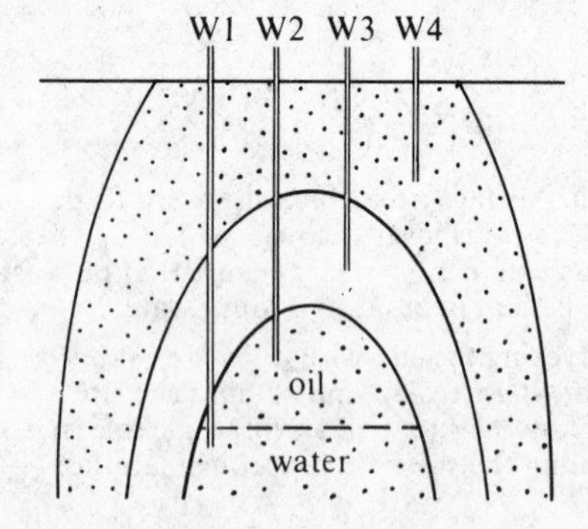

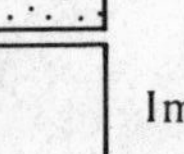

If they want to increase the rate of flow from Well 2, they should pump water:

F. into Well 1.
G. into Well 3.
H. out of Well 1.
J. out of Well 4.

11. Which of the following considerations would be most useful in determining geologically safe sites for hazardous waste disposal?

A. Examination of the surface topography (lay of the land)
B. Determination of local and regional groundwater movement patterns
C. Examination of the amount and type of vegetation in the area
D. Determination of the age of the rock formation

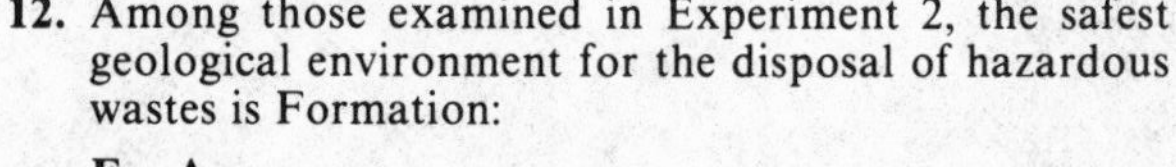

12. Among those examined in Experiment 2, the safest geological environment for the disposal of hazardous wastes is Formation:

F. A.
G. B.
H. C.
J. D.

GO ON TO THE NEXT PAGE.

Passage III

A simple pendulum can be made by hanging a ball from a string that is attached to a stationary support, as illustrated in the figure below.

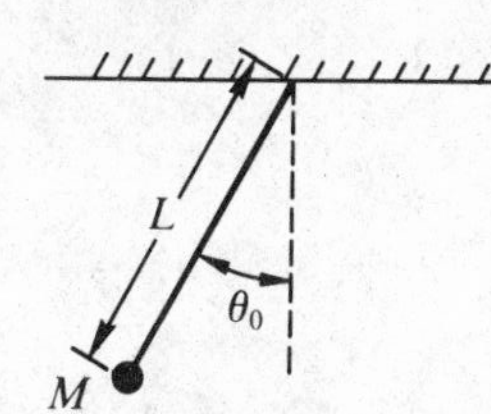

Pendulums with various string lengths (L) and masses (M) of balls were constructed and released from various starting angles (θ_0). Eleven trials were done on Earth, and 5 of these were repeated on the Moon. For each of the trials, the period of the pendulum was measured (time from initial release to return of ball to starting position).

Trial	M Mass of the ball (kilograms) (±0.05)	L Length of the string (meters) (±0.02)	θ_0 Starting angle between the string and vertical (±0.01°)	Surface where the experiment was performed	Period of the pendulum (seconds) (±0.02)
1	1.0	0.10	5.0°	Earth	0.63
2	1.0	0.40	5.0°	Earth	1.27
3	1.0	0.70	5.0°	Earth	1.68
4	1.0	1.00	5.0°	Earth	2.01
5	1.0	1.30	5.0°	Earth	2.29
6	1.0	1.00	5.0°	Earth	2.01
7	2.0	1.00	5.0°	Earth	2.00
8	3.0	1.00	5.0°	Earth	2.01
9	4.0	1.00	5.0°	Earth	1.99
10	5.0	1.00	5.0°	Earth	2.02
11	1.0	1.00	10.0°	Earth	2.01
12	1.0	0.10	5.0°	Moon	1.56
13	1.0	0.40	5.0°	Moon	3.12
14	1.0	0.70	5.0°	Moon	4.13
15	1.0	1.00	5.0°	Moon	4.93
16	1.0	1.30	5.0°	Moon	5.62

13. From Trials 1 through 5, it can be concluded that the period of a simple pendulum depends on the:

A. mass of the ball.
B. length of the string.
C. starting angle.
D. place where the pendulum is located.

14. From the given data, it can be concluded that when a certain pendulum is taken from Earth to the Moon, the:

F. period will increase.
G. period will decrease.
H. starting angle will increase.
J. starting angle will decrease.

15. Which of the following was assumed in designing the experiment?

A. The length of the string will not influence the period of a simple pendulum.
B. The starting angle will not influence the period of a simple pendulum.
C. The location of a simple pendulum will not influence its period.
D. All variables could be measured to an acceptable degree of accuracy.

GO ON TO THE NEXT PAGE.

16. A clock is being built for which a pendulum with a period (on Earth) of approximately 1.5 seconds is needed. What would be acceptable values for the length and mass of the pendulum? (Note: Assume that the mass of the pendulum is predominantly at the bottom.)

F. $L = 0.50$ meter, $M = 1.0$ kilogram
G. $L = 1.00$ meter, $M = 2.5$ kilograms
H. $L = 1.50$ meters, $M = 4.0$ kilograms
J. $L = 2.00$ meters, $M = 5.0$ kilograms

17. In order to determine the effect of change in string length on the period of a simple pendulum, which of the following pairs of trials can be used?

A. Trials 1 and 11
B. Trials 1 and 13
C. Trials 6 and 11
D. Trials 12 and 16

GO ON TO THE NEXT PAGE.

Passage IV

The used, heated water from a power plant passes through a cooling basin and is returned to the river as effluent. To determine the environmental impact of the effluent, biologists compared the water temperatures and studied samples taken from 5 sites along the river in January and July. The organisms studied were: blue-green algae (anchored near the surface), water striders (surface dwellers), smallmouth bass (near-surface to near-bottom dwellers), and crayfish (bottom burrowers).

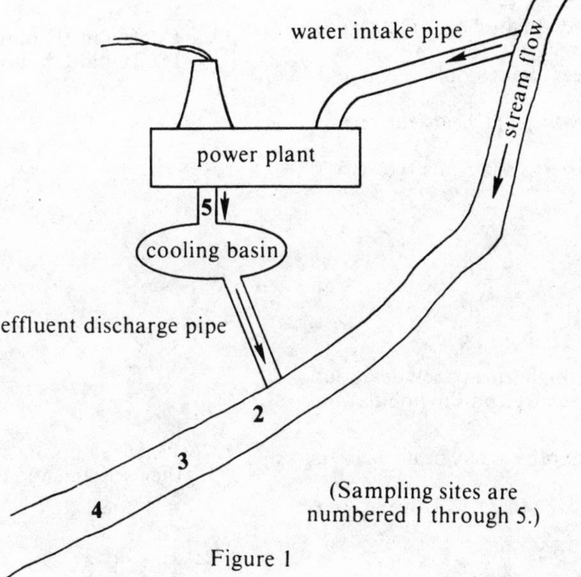

Figure 1

Table 1

Site	Water temperature (°C)	Biomass of algae (grams/meter^2)	Biomass of bass (grams/1,000 liters)	Population density of water striders (# per meter^2)	Population density of crayfish (# per trap per night)
January samples:					
1	2	5	4	1.0	10
2	12	12	10	0.8	1
3	6	7	7	1.1	5
4	3	6	5	1.2	8
5	30	no data	no data	no data	no data
July samples:					
1	20	15	3.0	0.9	11
2	30	24	0.1	1.1	30
3	25	21	0.5	1.0	20
4	23	18	1.0	1.1	15
5	48	no data	no data	no data	no data

GO ON TO THE NEXT PAGE.

18. Which of the following statements best represents the changes observed in the same sampling sites from January to July?

F. The biomass of bass remained constant.
G. The biomass of bass decreased.
H. The population density of crayfish remained constant.
J. The population density of crayfish decreased.

19. Which of the following conclusions about the power plant's effect on the river is(are) supported by the data?

I. In winter, the power plant heats the river's water.
II. In winter, the power plant cools the river's water.
III. In summer, the power plant heats the river's water.
IV. In summer, the power plant cools the river's water.

A. II only
B. III only
C. I and III only
D. II and IV only

20. Based on the passage, what might one conclude about the effects of the effluent discharge on the population densities of river organisms?

F. Some may be unaffected, others may be decreased, and others will thrive.
G. Some may be unaffected, others will thrive, but none will be decreased.
H. All organisms will be increased.
J. All organisms will be decreased.

21. Which of the following statements best describe(s) the relationship between water temperature and crayfish population density?

I. In January, the lower the temperature, the higher their population density.
II. In January, the higher the temperature, the higher their population density.
III. In July, the lower the temperature, the higher their population density.
IV. In July, the higher the temperature, the higher their population density.

A. III only
B. I and IV only
C. II and III only
D. II and IV only

22. Which sampling site (as shown in Figure 1) represents the experimental control?

F. Site 1
G. Site 2
H. Site 3
J. Site 5

GO ON TO THE NEXT PAGE.

Passage V

Catalysts are known to speed up chemical reactions without being used up during the reactions. Bimetallic catalysts are composed of 2 metals and are used to speed up particular reactions involving gases. Researchers interested in investigating the yield of products conducted the following sets of experiments using catalysts that were mixtures of copper and nickel.

Experiment 1

Ethane (C_2H_6) combines with hydrogen gas (H_2) to produce methane (CH_4) in the presence of small particles of copper, nickel, or a mixture of copper and nickel. A mixture with constant composition of ethane and hydrogen gases at 316° C was passed over a series of beds containing metal particles of varying composition. Molecules of methane formed per second for a given bed area were recorded as shown in Table 1.

Table 1

Copper (%)	Methane (molecules/sec)
0	300,000
10	200
20	50
30	30
40	9
60	4
80	2

Experiment 2

In another reaction, cyclohexane (C_6H_{12}) decomposes to give benzene (C_6H_6) and hydrogen gas (H_2) with copper, nickel, or a mixture of both acting as a catalyst. Cyclohexane gas at 316° C was passed over a series of beds containing metal particles of varying composition; the results are shown in Table 2.

Table 2

Copper (%)	Benzene (molecules/sec)
0	20,000
10	70,000
20	70,000
30	70,000
40	70,000
60	70,000
80	70,000
90	30,000
100	600

23. Concerning the relationship between the yield and the composition of the metal particles in Experiment 1, it appears that:

A. as the percentage of nickel decreased, the yield of product increased.
B. as the percentage of copper increased, the yield of product increased.
C. the yield was greatly improved when the percentage of copper approached zero.
D. the yields were similar over the range of copper percentages.

24. What change in procedure would allow a researcher to best determine the effects of temperature on the function of the catalysts in both of these reactions?

F. Running Experiment 1 at several temperatures
G. Running both experiments with the same procedures, using only nickel at several temperatures
H. Running both experiments with the same procedures, using only copper at several temperatures
J. Running both experiments with the same procedures, using the same mixtures of copper and nickel at several temperatures

25. If Experiment 1 were repeated with metal particles of pure copper, the yield of methane in molecules per second would be predicted to be:

A. greater than 300,000.
B. between 300,000 and 200.
C. 50.
D. less than 2.

26. Which of the following graphs would best represent the results of Experiment 1 ?

F.

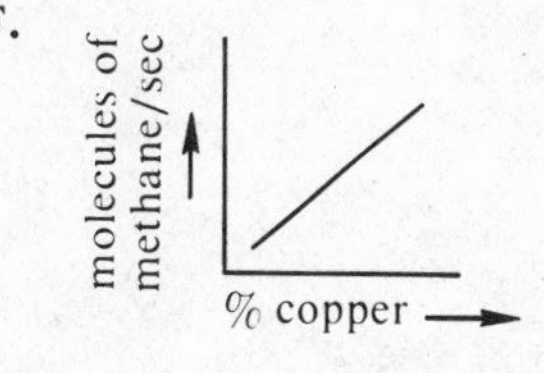

G.

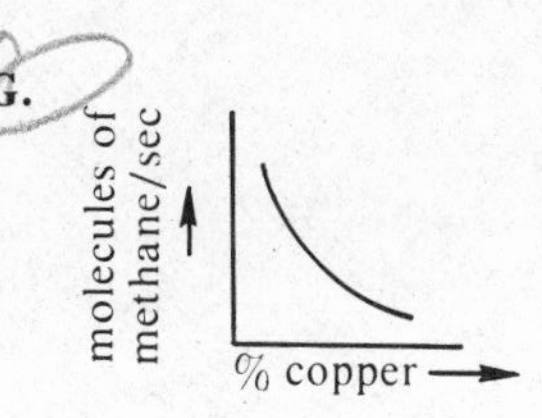

H.

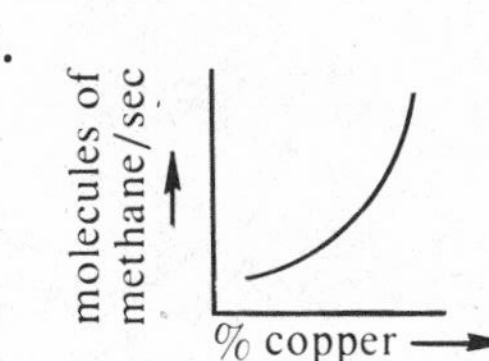

J.

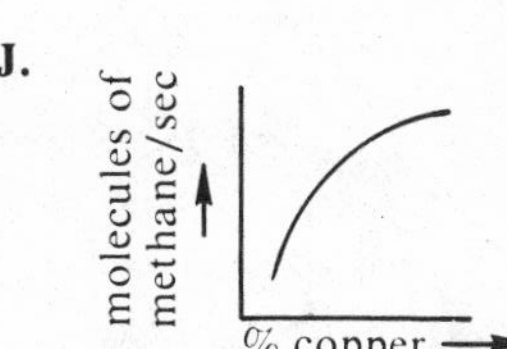

GO ON TO THE NEXT PAGE.

27. Do the results of Experiment 2 support the conclusion that pure copper is the best catalyst for the reaction in Experiment 2 ?

A. No, because the highest percent of copper gave the lowest yield.
B. No, because at the highest percent of nickel, the yields are the best.
C. Yes, because increasing the percent of copper from 0% to 100% increases the yield.
D. Yes, because the product is obtained in the absence of nickel.

28. Suppose that another set of experiments were done investigating the reaction between ethane and hydrogen using a different bimetallic catalyst, a mixture of ruthenium and copper. If it were then found that as the percent of ruthenium decreased, the product yield decreased, would these results be consistent with Experiment 1 ?

F. No, because ruthenium does not act like nickel.
G. No, because no experiments using pure ruthenium were done.
H. Yes, because for both the new experiment and Experiment 1 an increased percent of copper resulted in an increased product yield.
J. Yes, because for both the new experiment and Experiment 1 an increased percent of copper resulted in a decreased product yield.

GO ON TO THE NEXT PAGE.

Passage VI

Two paleontologists discuss their theories about various characteristics of dinosaurs.

Paleontologist 1

Dinosaurs were large endothermic (warm-blooded) creatures that were physiologically more advanced than the ectothermic (cold-blooded) reptiles. Rather than depending on sunlight or ambient air temperature to warm themselves, as would reptiles, dinosaurs were able to metabolically regulate their body temperatures. Endothermy allowed them to survive in temperatures that would have been lethal to most ectotherms.

Evidence for endothermy includes the discovery of many dinosaur bones in regions of Earth that were arctic during the dinosaur's time. Had the dinosaurs been ectotherms, they would have been forced to constantly sun themselves in order to maintain a stable, warm body temperature. Because this would have been impossible during the dark arctic winter, it seems likely that the dinosaurs were endotherms. Like birds (also endotherms), certain dinosaurs evolved featherlike structures that may have served to insulate them from cold temperatures.

The ratio of predators to prey in some dinosaur communities matches that of fossil mammal communities (low number of predators to high number of prey), indicating that the dinosaurs may have had dietary requirements similar to those of the mammals. Additionally, the bone structure of dinosaurs, with its many blood vessels (highly vascularized), seems virtually identical to that of mammals.

Paleontologist 2

Dinosaurs were large ectothermic reptiles that relied on their enormous mass to act as a heat reservoir and stabilize their body temperature. This forced dinosaurs living in seasonally cold regions to migrate to warmer, sunnier regions for the winter. Likewise, the featherlike structures found on some dinosaurs may have helped shield them from the intense summer sun.

Recent investigations of modern ectothermic communities reveal predator-prey ratios similar to those observed in endotherm communities. In addition, although dinosaur bones exhibit a high degree of vascularization (similar to that of mammals), such a pattern has been observed in the bones of numerous modern reptiles. Also, many small birds and mammals have been found to produce bones that are low in vascularization.

29. If the theory of Paleontologist 1 is correct, and dinosaurs were alive in Earth's present climate, what geographical distribution on land could be expected for them?

A. They could live only in arctic and antarctic regions.
B. They could live only in temperate to tropical regions.
C. They could live almost anywhere on Earth.
D. They could not survive anywhere on Earth.

30. Which of the following would most effectively support the theory of Paleontologist 2 ?

F. Large, modern reptiles that live year-round in northern Alaska
G. Large, modern reptiles that exhibit seasonal migration
H. Modern endotherms that are capable of lowering their body temperature during periods of hibernation
J. Modern endotherms that have evolved insulating structures

31. When one observes low numbers of predators and high numbers of their prey in a stable community, it can be inferred that the predators are endotherms because endotherms:

A. require more energy to maintain their constant body temperature than do ectotherms of the same size.
B. look for prey only at night when the temperature is lower.
C. store energy as fat for use during hibernation.
D. must run faster than ectotherms to catch their prey.

32. An important concept that underlies both paleontologists' hypotheses is that:

F. endotherms always have a higher body temperature than ectotherms.
G. tropical plants can be artificially grown in cold climates.
H. some characteristics of extinct animals can be determined from their fossil remains.
J. the fossil bone shapes of dinosaurs were similar to those of modern reptiles.

33. Assuming that dinosaurs were ectotherms, which of the following adaptations might have allowed them to maintain a near-constant body temperature?

A. Regulating their body temperatures by moving back and forth between sunny areas and shady areas
B. Decreasing blood circulation through their bones
C. Having bones that grow only part of the year
D. Increasing blood circulation through their bones

34. Which of the following characteristics is most inconsistent with the theory that dinosaurs were endotherms?

F. Large numbers of blood vessels in dinosaur bones
G. Their ability to live in cold regions
H. The presence of featherlike structures on some dinosaurs
J. Their reptilian appearance

GO ON TO THE NEXT PAGE.

35. How would the discovery of many dinosaur bone beds in which very few skeletons of prey occurred affect the two hypotheses?

A. It would support Paleontologist 2, because ectotherms generally require more food than endotherms.

B. It would support Paleontologist 2, because ectotherms generally require less food than endotherms.

C. It would support Paleontologist 1, because endotherms generally require more food than ectotherms.

D. It would refute Paleontologist 1, because ectotherms generally require more food than endotherms.

GO ON TO THE NEXT PAGE.

Passage VII

Each living cell is enclosed in a cell membrane. In some organisms, a rigid cell wall surrounds this membrane. Osmosis is the movement of water across a cell (or other semipermeable) membrane from an area of higher water concentration (low solute level) to an area of lower water concentration (high solute level). The following table and figures illustrate the basic principles of osmosis and describe the osmotic characteristics of 3 categories of organisms.

Table 1

	Osmoregulators	Osmoconformers	Organisms with cell walls
Description	maintain constant cytoplasmic concentration in changing environment	adjust cytoplasmic solute concentration to match that of the environment	osmoregulate or osmoconform, depending on the organism and environment
Example	salmon	shark	freshwater or marine alga
Response to low solute concentration in environment	avoids retention of excess water by excreting very dilute urine	dilutes cytoplasm in response to low environmental solute concentrations	osmoregulation by absorption of water until cell membrane is pushed against the rigid cell wall
Response to high solute concentration in environment	replaces water by intake and filtering of environmental water; salts excreted through gills	raises cytoplasmic solute concentration by retention of urea	raises cytoplasmic solute concentrations by synthesis of proteins

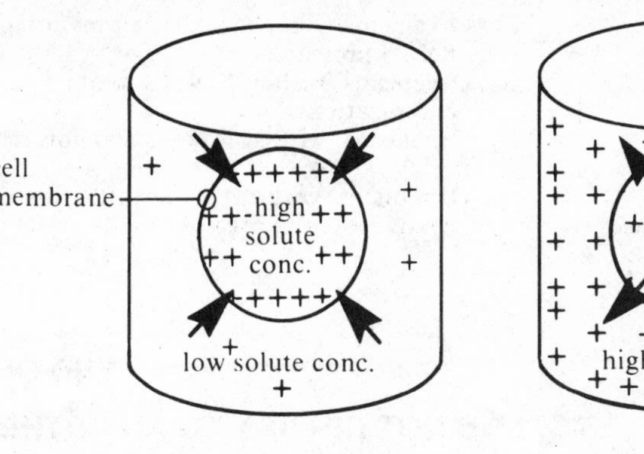

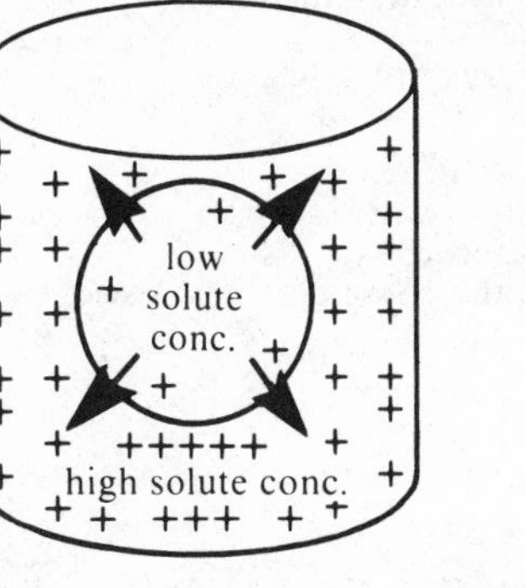

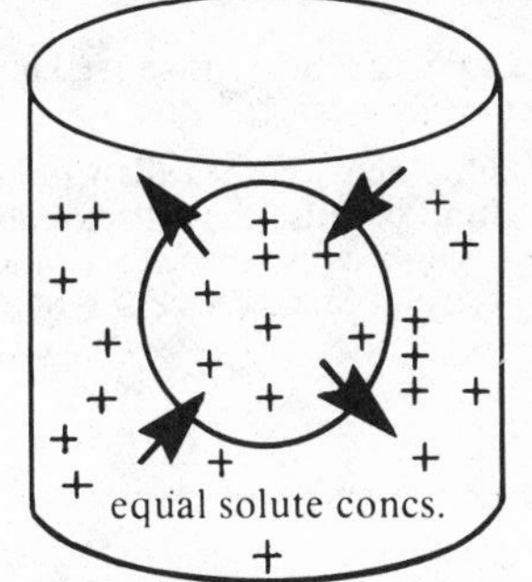

Figure 1
Water movement characteristics in relation to solute concentrations

GO ON TO THE NEXT PAGE.

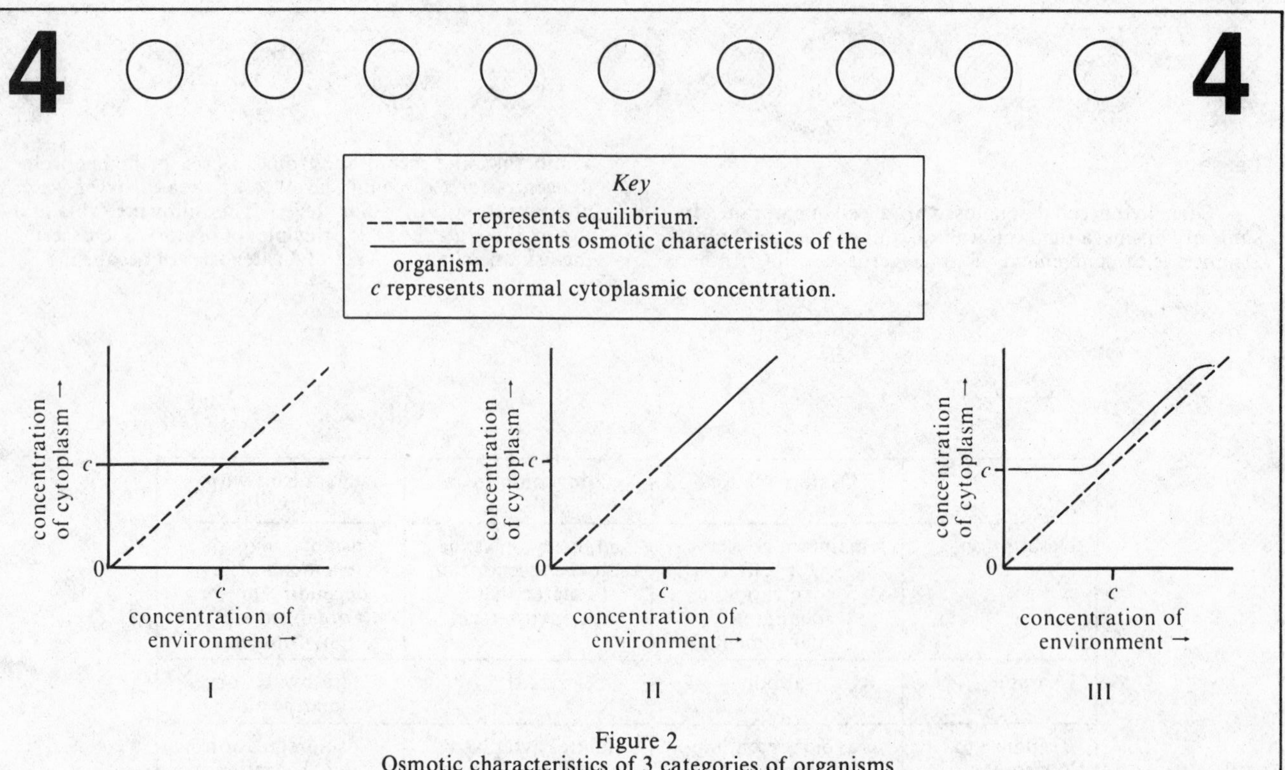

Figure 2
Osmotic characteristics of 3 categories of organisms

36. According to Figure 1-III, when solute concentrations are the same on both sides of a cell membrane, water:

F. moves primarily into the cell.
G. moves primarily out of the cell.
H. movement in the 2 directions across the membrane is approximately equal.
J. movement produces a slightly higher solute concentration outside of the cell.

37. According to the information presented in Figure 2-II, as environmental solute concentration:

A. increases, internal solute concentration decreases.
B. increases, internal solute concentration increases.
C. increases, internal solute concentration remains constant.
D. decreases, internal solute concentration increases.

38. The stem of a plant immersed in very salty water would become:

F. limp because the cells would absorb salt.
G. limp because the cells would lose water.
H. crisp because the cells would absorb salt.
J. crisp because the cells would absorb water.

39. Bacterial cells were placed in 4 salt solutions of varying concentrations. In which of the following solutions would the pressure of the cell membranes against the bacterial cell walls be the greatest?

A. 0% salt solution
B. 5% salt solution
C. 37% salt solution
D. 50% salt solution

40. Which of the following statements explains why Figures 2-II and 2-III in the passage differ when environmental concentrations are greater than *c* ?

F. Organisms with cell walls can maintain a positive internal pressure.
G. Organisms with cell walls require lower solute concentrations.
H. Organisms with cell walls cannot release urine rapidly.
J. Organisms without cell walls can maintain a negative internal pressure.

END OF TEST 4

STOP! DO NOT RETURN TO ANY OTHER TEST.

INTERPRETING YOUR ACT SCORES

7

INTERPRETING YOUR ACT SCORES

DETERMINING RAW SCORES FOR THE PRACTICE TESTS

It's easy enough to figure out raw scores for the sample tests in this book: Just count up all your correct answers for each test, using the answer keys at the back of the book. However, while it's simple to find your raw scores for the sample tests, it may be more difficult to figure out what those numbers mean.

As you're working with your scores, remember everything else you know about your abilities. If, for example, your test score in mathematics isn't as high as you would like, this doesn't mean you're "no good at math." What it can mean is that you need a little more practice in arithmetic calculations, that you could benefit from reviewing some mathematical concepts, that you should work a little faster when you're taking a timed test, or that you simply weren't doing your best work at that particular time. You know your strengths and weaknesses—keep them in mind as you evaluate your scores on these sample tests.

One way of understanding your raw scores on the sample tests is to convert them to scale scores (the form in which ACT reports your results). You'll find the information you need to convert your raw scores to scale scores in the charts at the back of this book. Once you have standard scale scores, you can compare your performance on the different tests and make decisions about how much additional review you wish to make.

INTERPRETING YOUR ACT RESULTS

How does ACT determine the scores it reports for students taking the ACT Assessment? The first step is to do exactly what you've done for the sample tests: count the number of questions you answered correctly to determine your raw score. There's no deduction for incorrect answers.

Next, these raw scores are converted to scale scores—scores that have the same meaning for all versions of each test. Converting raw scores to scale scores makes it possible to compare the performance of students taking different versions of the ACT Assessment on different days. The scale scores range from 1 (low) to 36 (high) for each of the four tests and for the composite score, which is the average of the four test scores.

You'll also receive subscores on areas within three of the tests: English, Reading, and Mathematics. These subscores range from 1 (low) to 18 (high). Because the scores and subscores are determined independently, the total of the subscores doesn't necessarily equal the total score for each area; in other words, the subscores for, say, the Reading Test won't necessarily add up to the score for the Reading Test.

Since no test, including the ACT Assessment, is completely free from measurement error, a system has been devised for estimating the amount of that error. One estimate for the amount of error in test scores is called the "standard error of measurement." On the ACT Assessment, the standard error of measurement is about 2 points for each of the test scores and subscores and about 1 point for the composite score.

One way of using the standard error would be to add and subtract it from each of the test scores. For example, if your score on the English Test were 22, you could think of your score as really falling within the range of 20 to 24 (22 minus 2 or 22 plus 2) rather than at a point (22). To encourage you to keep this range of standard error in mind as you interpret your scores, ACT shows your ranks within bands on the Student Report. Here's a sample of the way your ACT results may be represented:

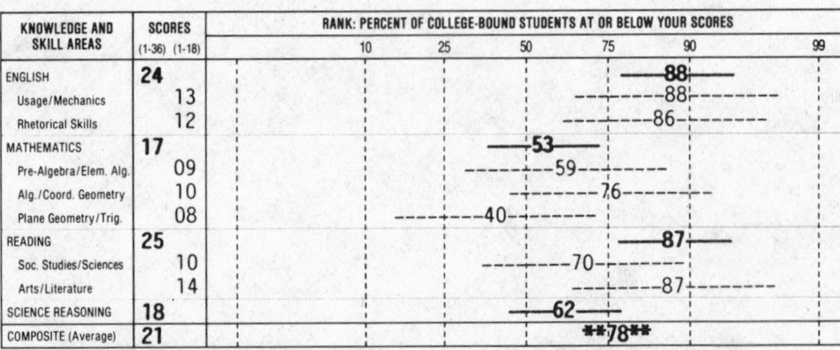

TRACY ARTHUR C
7852 W 46TH ST
WHEAT RIDGE CO 80033

KNOWLEDGE AND SKILL AREAS	SCORES (1-36)	SCORES (1-18)	RANK: PERCENT OF COLLEGE-BOUND STUDENTS AT OR BELOW YOUR SCORES (10, 25, 50, 75, 90, 99)
ENGLISH	24		88
Usage/Mechanics		13	88
Rhetorical Skills		12	86
MATHEMATICS	17		53
Pre-Algebra/Elem. Alg.		09	59
Alg./Coord. Geometry		10	76
Plane Geometry/Trig.		08	40
READING	25		87
Soc. Studies/Sciences		10	70
Arts/Literature		14	87
SCIENCE REASONING	18		62
COMPOSITE (Average)	21		**78**

YOUR COMPOSITE SCORE CAN BE COMPARED TO DIFFERENT GROUPS OF STUDENTS WHO TOOK THE ACT. LISTED BELOW IS THE PERCENT OF EACH GROUP AT OR BELOW YOUR COMPOSITE SCORE:
78% OF STUDENTS IN ACT NATL STUDY
59% OF H.S. GRADUATES NATIONWIDE
52% OF H.S. GRADUATES IN COLORADO

H.S. grades you reported: English=A, Math=C, Social Studies=A, Natural Sciences=B.

In the example, Arthur's scale score of 24 for English means his performance in that area was better than or equal to that of 88 percent of the examinees. The band around 88, which indicates the range of standard error, is used to emphasize that test scores are only estimates.

Notice that you're given two different expressions of your performance in the different areas: scores and ranks. Many people find ranks easier to interpret. A rank is the expression of the percentage of college-bound students whose scores were at the same or a lower level than your score. In the sample report of ACT results, 53 percent of college-bound students had mathematics scores at or below the same level as the imaginary Arthur C. Tracy.

Notice, too, that the average high school grades Arthur reported are listed below his scores. You'll want to compare your score ranks to your own high school grades. Arthur's ranks for the English and Mathematics Tests correspond very closely to his high school grades in those areas. His rank for the Science Reasoning Test, on the other hand, looks a little low compared to the average grade of B that he reported for natural sciences. If Arthur feels he didn't do the kind of work he is capable of on the Science Reasoning Test, the comparison of his rank to his grades in school course work may convince him to take the ACT exam a second time to try to improve his performance on the Science Reasoning Test.

One way to interpret and use your ACT scores, then, is to compare them to your high school grades in the same subjects. This may also give you a better estimate of your educational development in comparison to students in other parts of the country.

Another way to interpret your ACT scores is in comparison to each other. You may find it interesting, for example, to see how your ranks in science and mathematics compare to those in reading and English. Perhaps you've felt more comfortable and successful in one subject area than in others. If your scores in that area are high, too, then you have one more indicator of potential success in that field. Making comparisons among your ACT ranks can be especially helpful as you make decisions about the courses you will take in high school and college. You'll want to build on your strengths, of course, but you may also want to take some courses designed to bolster your abilities in areas in which you may not feel quite so confident.

Another way to understand your ACT scores is in comparison to the scores of students now enrolled at postsecondary schools you're interested in attending. This information can be very useful as you make decisions about applying for college. Keep in mind that admissions offices use a number of measures—including high school grades, recommendations, and extracurricular activities—to determine how students are likely to perform at their schools. Still, knowing that your ACT scores are similar to those of students already enrolled at a school you're considering may make you more comfortable in applying for admission there. A chart in the ACT Student Report helps you compare your ACT scores to those of freshmen at schools you indicated when you registered for the ACT Assessment.

COLLEGE CODE AND NAME	ADMISSIONS POLICY	ESTIMATED RANK OF YOUR ACT COMPOSITE SCORE (ENROLLED FRESHMEN)
0521 UNIVERSITY OF OMEGA	Trad	Middle Half
7111 ALPHA UNIVERSITY	Sel	Middle Half
7222 BETA COMMUNITY COLL	Open	Upper Quarter

The information in the third column provides you with that comparison.

The ACT Student Report provides you with a good deal of additional information to help you understand your ACT results and to use them in making difficult decisions about college and exploring possible future careers. You'll also receive a booklet, *Using Your ACT Assessment Results,* that will help you figure out and use all this information. For example, the booklet provides a list of activities designed to help you identify and explore career options.

As you're approaching decisions about schools and careers, be sure to take advantage of all the assistance you can find. Talk to your parents, counselors, and teachers; visit your local library; and write directly to colleges you're interested in. The more you can find out about your own abilities (including such information as ACT results) and about all the options available to you, the better able you will be to make informed choices.

8
"WHAT'S NEXT?"

8

"WHAT'S NEXT?"

Now that you've taken a look at the ACT Assessment and worked through some sample tests, you should feel ready to take the exam "for real." What happens next? How will your scores be used? What are your options?

HOW HIGH SCHOOLS AND COLLEGES USE ACT ASSESSMENT SCORES

High schools use ACT scores in academic advising and counseling for students. They also look at ACT scores as one tool for evaluating their instruction and curricula.

Colleges use ACT results in a variety of ways.

- **Admissions.** College and university admission staffs use ACT scores, along with high school grades, course work, extracurricular activities, recommendations from teachers, and other important information, to identify students who are likely to do well in their programs.
- **Placement.** College placement officials often use ACT scores as well as high school records to help them place students in appropriate freshman classes or programs.
- **Advising.** College and university academic advisors use ACT scores as one tool among many to assist students in making important decisions about courses of study, academic majors, part-time employment, and career goals.
- **Scholarships, Grants, and Loans.** Some schools and scholarship agencies use ACT scores in addition to other measures of academic progress—course work, grades, out-of-school activities—to help make decisions about scholarships, grants, and loans. ACT reports not only test scores but other information you provide about your high school achievement as well. This additional information can be very valuable in supporting an application for various kinds of financial assistance.

HOW YOU CAN USE YOUR ACT ASSESSMENT SCORES

After you've made sure you understand your ACT scores (see Section 7 and the Student Report form you receive with your scores for more information), what can you do with them? How can you evaluate your performance? How can you determine if you should take the ACT a second time?

One way of assessing your performance on the ACT is to compare your scores in different areas. The Student Report form gives the ranks of your scores in bands or dashed lines. You can use those ranks to get a general sense of your strengths and weaknesses in the four broad areas represented by the test scores and in the seven specific areas represented by the subscores. A high rank in one of the areas may suggest that you have strengths there that you can build on. Maybe you would like to take some college courses in that area. On the other hand, a lower rank in an area may suggest that you need to develop your skills there.

You'll also want to compare your ACT scores with your high school grades. Do your ACT scores follow pretty much the same pattern as your high school grades? If so, you have one more indication of where your relative strengths and weaknesses lie. If not, you may wonder if your performance on the ACT is an accurate reflection of your capabilities. Perhaps some distraction (fatigue, illness, nervousness) got in the way of your doing your best work the day you took the exam.

Maybe you think you should have done better on the ACT. What should you do now? Should you take the exam again? Recall your own impression of your performance. Did you feel you were doing your best? Talk to your teachers and counselors. Do they think the scores reflect your abilities? Do they think you would benefit from some extra review before trying the exam again?

If you decide to take the ACT again in the hope of improving your scores, take advantage of all the help available to you. Find out if there are review classes or computer review programs at your school. Ask your teachers and counselors for extra help. Read carefully the sections of this book that describe the four tests, paying special attention to any that concern you. Work through the sample tests, taking advantage of the built-in explanatory answers.

When you take the ACT again, remind yourself that you're doing it to improve. Tell yourself that you know what to expect and that you're going to give it your best.

9
SAMPLE ACT TESTS AND EXPLANATORY ANSWERS

9

SAMPLE ACT TESTS AND EXPLANATORY ANSWERS

In this section, you'll find two complete ACT exams and two-part explanatory answers for all the questions on those exams. You may want to take a minute to familiarize yourself with the format of this large section before you continue so that you'll be able to take the greatest possible advantage from the materials offered here.

First, you'll find a sample ACT exam—English, Mathematics, Reading, and Science Reasoning Tests. (By the way, the sample tests appear just a little smaller here than they will when you take the actual exam.) That sample exam is followed by Part A explanatory answers for each test, then Part B explanatory answers for the same tests. After that you'll find a second sample ACT exam and the accompanying explanatory answers, Part A and Part B.

Why are the explanatory answers in two parts? They're designed to give you different kinds of help in working through the questions. You might think of the Part A explanatory answers as a sort of written tutor. Part A explanatory answers ask questions, point out details you might have missed, and suggest ways for reasoning your way through to the solutions. Part B explanatory answers give you those solutions, then go on to explain why the listed answer is the best one for each question or problem.

How can you use this information? You can tailor your use of the materials to fit your own interests and abilities. Here are some possibilities:

- If you feel confident about your test-taking abilities and just want some quick practice, you might work through one complete set of ACT tests, timing yourself to simulate actual test conditions. After you've completed the four tests, you can check your answers against the answer key at the back of this book or against the Part B explanatory answers. The advantage of using the explanatory answers for this step is that you can check both your reasoning and the answers. You can then refer to Part A for an explanation of any questions you missed.

- If you feel more confident in some content areas than others, you may want to follow the procedure described above for most of the tests but use the Part A explanatory answers to help you work through the test(s) you feel less confident about. For example, if you feel comfortable in every content area except English, you may want to use the Part A explanatory answers for English alone.

- Another possibility is to work through one complete set of ACT tests, referring to the Part B explanatory answers for explanation and confirmation. If you decide you need more practice on one or more of the tests, you can then use the second ACT exam for review, perhaps working more slowly and referring often to the Part A explanatory answers.
- You may want as much help as possible as you are preparing for the ACT Assessment. In that case, you may decide to work through both sample ACT exams slowly, making full use of the suggestions in Part A and the explanations in Part B.
- Perhaps you'll be working through some of the tests in a test-preparation group or class. In that case, the group may decide to use the explanatory answers, especially Part A, as the basis for discussion.

The sample tests and explanatory answers are here to help you. Think about your own abilities and the time you have available for practice; then decide how you can best use the materials in this section.

SAMPLE TEST 1

YOUR SIGNATURE (do not print): ____________________

YOUR SOCIAL SECURITY NUMBER OR ACT ID NUMBER: ___-__-____

THE ACT ASSESSMENT

DIRECTIONS

This booklet contains tests in English, Mathematics, Reading, and Science Reasoning. These tests measure skills and abilities highly related to high school course work and success in college.

The questions in each test are numbered, and the suggested answers for each question are lettered. On the answer sheet, the rows of ovals are numbered to match the questions, and the ovals in each row are lettered to correspond to the suggested answers.

For each question, first decide which answer is best. Next, locate on the answer sheet the row of ovals numbered the same as the question. Then, locate the oval in that row lettered the same as your answer. Finally, blacken the oval completely. Use a soft lead pencil and make your marks heavy and black. *DO NOT USE A BALLPOINT PEN.*

If you change your mind about an answer, erase your first mark thoroughly before marking your new answer. For each question, make certain that you mark in the row of ovals with the same number as the question.

Your score on each test will be based only on the number of questions you answer correctly. You will NOT be penalized for guessing. *HENCE IT IS TO YOUR ADVANTAGE TO ANSWER EVERY QUESTION.*

You may work on each test ONLY when your test supervisor tells you to do so. If you finish a test before time is called for that test, you should use the time remaining to reconsider questions you are uncertain about in that test. You may NOT look back to a test on which time has already been called, and you may NOT go ahead to another test. To do so will disqualify you from the examination.

Lay your pencil down immediately when time is called at the end of each test. You may NOT for any reason blacken ovals for a test after time is called for that test. To do so will disqualify you from the examination.

Do not fold or tear the pages of your test booklet.

DO NOT OPEN THIS BOOKLET UNTIL TOLD TO DO SO.

1 ■ ■ ■ ■ ■ ■ ■ ■ ■ 1

ENGLISH TEST

45 Minutes—75 Questions

DIRECTIONS: In the five passages that follow, certain words and phrases are underlined and numbered. In the right-hand column, you will find alternatives for each underlined part. You are to choose the one that best expresses the idea, makes the statement appropriate for standard written English, or is worded most consistently with the style and tone of the passage as a whole. If you think the original version is best, choose "NO CHANGE."

You will also find questions about a section of the passage, or about the passage as a whole. These questions do not refer to an underlined portion of the passage, but rather are identified by a number or numbers in a box.

For each question, choose the alternative you consider best and blacken the corresponding oval on your answer sheet. Read each passage through once before you begin to answer the questions that accompany it. You cannot determine most answers without reading several sentences beyond the question. Be sure that you have read far enough ahead each time you choose an alternative.

Passage I

> The following paragraphs may or may not be in the most logical order. Each paragraph is numbered in brackets, and item 15 will ask you to choose the sequence of paragraphs that will make the essay most logical.

[1]

Have you ever found a ten-dollar bill while you were going through the pockets of a jacket you were planning to discard or discovered [1] a great restaurant by taking a wrong turn on the way to somewhere else? There's a word for that kind of lucky accident: *serendipity,* although not all accidents are lucky. [2] The word owes its derivation to a Persian fairy tale, *The Three Princes of Serendip,* in which the princes often made lucky, unexpected discoveries.

[2]

Surprisingly, more than a few scientific discoveries were the result not of careful, systematic theorizing and experimentation, but of serendipity. However, [3] many

1. A. NO CHANGE
   B. discovering
   C. discover
   D. had discovered

2. F. NO CHANGE
   G. *serendipity,* other accidents are not so lucky.
   H. *serendipity,* other accidents lack that luck.
   J. *serendipity.*

3. A. NO CHANGE
   B. For example,
   C. Thus,
   D. Rather,

8939F

GO ON TO THE NEXT PAGE.

of the sugar substitutes so currently popular today[4] were discovered when chemists just happened to taste the solution they were working with. The discovery of penicillin was also serendipitous. When a scientist accidentally caused the contamination of a bacterial parasite with a mold, the parasite started to dissolve. After testing the mold (*Penicillium*), scientists discovered that it produced a substance that destroys many common bacteria that cause disease. [5]

[3]

The scientist who[6] probably benefited the best[7] from serendipity was Joseph Priestley, an eighteenth-century English chemist. One day Priestley was idly dissolving carbon dioxide in some water and[8] began to bubble. He put his finger in the solution and licked it. It tasted good, and[9] that's how Priestley discovered seltzer or soda water.

Another[10] serendipitous discovery occurred while Priestley was trying to identify the properties of oil of vitriol.

4. **F.** NO CHANGE
G. so popular today
H. currently so popular today
J. currently popular now

5. The emphasis on accidental discoveries would best be reinforced by a sentence doing which of the following?
A. Relating an anecdote about a lucky discovery
B. Listing the most common bacterial parasites
C. Outlining the scientific method
D. Describing laboratory procedures for medical research

6. **F.** NO CHANGE
G. scientist, who
H. scientist whom
J. scientist, whom

7. **A.** NO CHANGE
B. most
C. best
D. the more

8. **F.** NO CHANGE
G. water, and which
H. water, which
J. water, it

9. **A.** NO CHANGE
B. good,
C. well, and
D. well,

10. **F.** NO CHANGE
G. Thus, a
H. Consequently, a
J. This

GO ON TO THE NEXT PAGE.

1 ■ ■ ■ ■ ■ ■ ■ ■ ■ 1

When he accidentally dropped some mercury into the oil, he created sulfur dioxide, a preservative and refrigerant. [11]

[4]

Another of Priestley's accidental discoveries <u>have been</u> (12) especially useful to students. While he was studying the sap of a South American tree called the caoutchouc, he found that if he allowed the sap to harden and then rubbed <u>them on</u> (13) paper, he could remove the marks made by his pencil. Thus was born the eraser. It's fitting that one of Priestley's accidental discoveries <u>he didn't intend to make</u> (14) can be used to erase other accidents that are not so fruitful.

11. The writer introduces the scientist Joseph Priestley in Paragraph 3. Which of the statements below follows most logically from the discussion of Priestley in this paragraph?

- **A.** Joseph Priestley finally became the inventor of seltzer.
- **B.** Joseph Priestley based his life on luck, not believing in logical cause and effect.
- **C.** The scientist Joseph Priestley never used systematic theorizing and experimentation.
- **D.** Joseph Priestley thus took advantage of several serendipitous occurrences during his career as a research scientist.

12.
- **F.** NO CHANGE
- **G.** has been
- **H.** are
- **J.** had been

13.
- **A.** NO CHANGE
- **B.** them against
- **C.** them by
- **D.** it on

14.
- **F.** NO CHANGE
- **G.** that he didn't intend on making
- **H.** that he didn't intend to make
- **J.** OMIT the underlined portion.

Item 15 poses a question about Passage I as a whole.

15. Which of the following sequences of paragraphs will make the essay most logical?

- **A.** NO CHANGE
- **B.** 2, 1, 4, 3
- **C.** 3, 2, 1, 4
- **D.** 3, 2, 4, 1

GO ON TO THE NEXT PAGE.

1 ■ ■ ■ ■ ■ ■ ■ ■ ■ 1

Passage II

Five years ago, while visiting Japan, I went to a teahouse to learn about the Japanese tea ceremony. This ceremony is deeply expressive of Japanese culture, and I was eager and anxious awaiting the prospect of watching [16] a tea master demonstrate this art.

[1] The teahouse I visited had been built by the tea master himself whom [17] was eighty years old. [2] The group whom with I was, [18] sat, Japanese style, in a circle in the outer room. [3] It consisted of two rooms: the outer one was a place to learn the ceremony; the inner one was a place for accomplished [19] practitioners to engage in it. [4] The old tea master had a brown wooden box of powdered green tea, ground by his own personal [20] hand. [5] He sent the box around for everyone to see. [6] Each member of the group carefully passed the box to the next person, who firmly embraced it, looked at its contents, and passed it on. [21]

The person sitting to my right turned to pass the box to me. As I reached to take it from her, solemnly [22] an accident happened. The box slipped from my grasp and shot into the air. Powdered green tea spilled everywhere. It covered my blue suit, as well as the floor around me, where it was also spilled. [23] No one knew how to react. All eyes fell on the tea master. He slowly smiled. Then everyone relaxed, and laughter filled the room. The laughter I believe [24] was not aimed at me;

16. F. NO CHANGE
    G. eager, literally champing at the bit, to watch
    H. eager to watch
    J. eager to await the prospect of watching

17. A. NO CHANGE
    B. himself, who
    C. himself, he
    D. himself, whom

18. F. NO CHANGE
    G. with whom I was with
    H. with who I was with
    J. I was with

19. A. NO CHANGE
    B. practiced
    C. accomplishing
    D. well-practiced

20. F. NO CHANGE
    G. personal own
    H. own
    J. own individual

21. For the sake of unity and coherence, Sentence 2 should be placed:
    A. where it is now.
    B. before Sentence 1.
    C. before Sentence 4.
    D. before Sentence 6.

22. F. NO CHANGE
    G. (Place after *I*)
    H. (Place after *take*)
    J. (Place after *happened* and end sentence with a period)

23. A. NO CHANGE
    B. me, where it was spilled as well.
    C. me having spilled.
    D. me.

24. F. NO CHANGE
    G. laughter, I believe
    H. laughter I believe,
    J. laughter, I believe,

GO ON TO THE NEXT PAGE.

1 ■ ■ ■ ■ ■ ■ ■ ■ ■ 1

and,[25] it served to relieve everyone's tension. Two Japanese students rushed over and invited me outside, where they carefully brushed the tea from my suit. The ceremony went on, and I soon returned to take my place in the circle.

Why did the tea master smile? I suppose he was trying to soothe my embarrassment and the nervousness of my American friends. Thus, he imparted not only knowledge of the tea ceremony but to us[26] also offered an example of profound kindness. Indeed it is just this kind of polite consideration of those of others'[27] that is ritualized in the traditional ritual of the[28] tea ceremony.

25. A. NO CHANGE
B. because
C. despite that
D. rather,

26. F. NO CHANGE
G. (Place after *imparted*)
H. (Place after *only*)
J. (Place after *knowledge*)

27. A. NO CHANGE
B. other's
C. others'
D. others

28. F. NO CHANGE
G. ritualized in the traditional
H. ritualized in the ritual of the
J. traditionalized in the tradition of the

Item 29 poses a question about Passage II as a whole.

29. Is the writer's use of the pronoun "I" appropriate in the essay?
A. Yes, because "I" is important to use in all writing about travel.
B. Yes, because the essay is a personal account.
C. No, because it detracts from the description of the tea ceremony.
D. No, because the essay is a factual account.

GO ON TO THE NEXT PAGE.

1 ■ ■ ■ ■ ■ ■ ■ ■ ■ 1

Passage III

[1]

Oxford University students speak of "reading" a subject for a degree instead of talking about "majoring" in a subject, as American students do. To read at the Bodleian Library, Oxford University, students[30] must have ID cards with pictures. To get these cards the students would[31] swear before a librarian wearing an intimidating academic robe never to remove or damage a book, never to deface any property, and never to kindle flames in the library. [32]

[2]

[1] The Bodleian Library is the second largest library in Britain. [2] It is a copyright library, which means copies of all new books and most periodicals that are published in Great Britain are sent to it. [3] The Bodleian acquires 140,000 new books every year in this manner. [4] In addition, the library purchases or is given 108,000 other books, pamphlets, and periodicals annually. [33]

[3]

Seven different buildings are needed to house this vast collection due to the fact that there are so many books.[34] Three of these buildings are among the most famous landmarks in Oxford. The Old[35] Library, which was

30. F. NO CHANGE
G. student's
H. students'
J. students,

31. A. NO CHANGE
B. were to
C. must
D. should

32. Would it advance the orderliness and flow of the essay if the writer added a paragraph at this point arguing against the American tradition of "majoring" in a subject?
F. No, because that argument belongs at the end of the essay.
G. No, because that argument is already made in the essay as a whole.
H. No, because this is an informative, not a persuasive, essay.
J. Yes, because adding argument to an essay always makes it more lively.

33. Which of the following sequences of sentences will make Paragraph 2 most logical?
A. NO CHANGE
B. 1, 4, 3, 2
C. 3, 2, 1, 4
D. 3, 2, 4, 1

34. F. NO CHANGE
G. on account of there are so many books.
H. on account of the fact that there are so many books.
J. OMIT the underlined portion and end the sentence with a period.

35. A. NO CHANGE
B. Oxford. The Old,
C. Oxford: the Old
D. Oxford, the Old

GO ON TO THE NEXT PAGE.

finished in 1489; the Radcliffe Camera, a round, domed building, which was finished in 1749; and the New Library, which was completed in 1946. There is another famous round, domed building, St. Paul's Cathedral, in nearby London. [36] Books requested by a student studying in the Old Library, but shelved in the New Library, can be sent on mechanical conveyor belts through a tunnel under Broad Street to the waiting reader who awaits them. [37] [38]

[4]

The Bodleian is not a lending library; notwithstanding, [39] to use any of the 4.5 million books housed there, students must sit and read at one of the long, oak desks in one of the twenty-four reading rooms, just as their predecessors have done for 500 years.

[5]

With 2,000 people reading in the Bodleian, readers have never felt lonely. In addition to a sense that the ghosts of past students move through the air [40]

36. F. NO CHANGE
G. St. Paul's Cathedral is also a domed landmark.
H. The domed St. Paul's Cathedral is also famous.
J. OMIT the underlined portion.

37. A. NO CHANGE
B. awaiting them.
C. awaiting, them.
D. OMIT the underlined portion and end the sentence with a period.

38. The writer has been told that this paragraph has a lot of loosely connected facts in it and that a topic sentence would help to tie the paragraph together into a more coherent whole. Which of the following sentences would be the most effective, coherent, and accurate one to begin Paragraph 3?
F. As Oxford's book collection grew, so did its Bodleian Library, and the result is a complex of old and very old library buildings linked together by mechanics as well as tradition.
G. Radcliffe Camera was designed by Christopher Wren, and it is just one of the many buildings and tunnels that house the famous Oxford Library.
H. Book storage and retrieval is a complex system at the Bodleian Library, and many of the buildings and books are old and pretty famous.
J. Not all the books are in the Bodleian.

39. A. NO CHANGE
B. contrarily,
C. on the other hand,
D. therefore,

40. F. NO CHANGE
G. are moving through
H. moving through
J. are moving through,

GO ON TO THE NEXT PAGE.

1 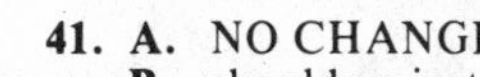 1

and hovering over <u>shoulders, just</u> [41] out of sight, there are the sounds of current students turning pages, shuffling notecards, sighing, <u>or chuckling occurs.</u> [42] Scholarship is definitely not a solitary activity at Oxford.

41. A. NO CHANGE
    B. shoulders just,
    C. shoulder's just
    D. shoulders' just

42. F. NO CHANGE
    G. and chuckling occurs.
    H. chuckling occurs.
    J. or chuckling.

Item 43 poses a question about Passage III as a whole.

43. If the writer wished to add a small amount of material about the manuscripts held by the Bodleian, in which paragraph would it be most logical to place the addition?
    A. Paragraph 1, because all important information should be at least mentioned in the first paragraph.
    B. Paragraph 2, because that is where the types of material collected are mentioned.
    C. Paragraph 3, because the vastness of the collection is mentioned there.
    D. A new paragraph, because new information should always go in a new paragraph.

Passage IV

When Americans hear fox hunting <u>mentioned, you usually imagine</u> [44] movie scenes of mounted, red-coated English gentry galloping after hounds to the cry of "Tallyho!" I, <u>moreover,</u> [45] see overall-clad farmers grouped around a bonfire atop a hill on an autumn night. I hear stories told in tones that hush as distant yelps become melodious bays. This scene emerges from my childhood experience of fox <u>hunting. In</u> [46] the hill country of the southern United States.

The form of fox hunting I remember, <u>it being different, from</u> [47] the English version,

44. F. NO CHANGE
    G. mentioned, they usually imagine
    H. being mentioned, usually you are imagining
    J. mentioned, the person usually is imagining

45. A. NO CHANGE
    B. furthermore,
    C. by the same token,
    D. however,

46. F. NO CHANGE
    G. hunting in,
    H. hunting in
    J. hunting; in,

47. A. NO CHANGE
    B. in contrast to
    C. being different to
    D. it being different than

GO ON TO THE NEXT PAGE.

1 ■ ■ ■ ■ ■ ■ ■ ■ ■ 1

was neither a strenuous activity nor a blood <u>sport, in fact,</u>[48] the main purpose of the hunt was to sit still and enjoy the music of the hounds by identifying the voice of each and determining the hound's location and its proximity to the fox. A cunning fox made the sport <u>exciting,</u>[49] therefore, the hunters wanted it alive to run another night. The hunt ended when the fox "went to earth," that is, escaped underground, and the hunters blew their horns to call in their hounds.

The traditions of the <u>huntsman's horn was</u>[50] different in England and America. American hunters, probably unable at first to purchase the copper horns customary in England, crafted their own from <u>horns' of cows.</u>[51] Furthermore, each farmer with dogs in a <u>hunt, not</u>[52] just the leader, blew a horn; a hill-country hound obeyed only <u>there</u>[53] owner's call.

[1] American hunters prize their dogs more highly. [2] Perhaps the most deeply felt difference in the two styles of hunting, however, <u>layed</u>[54] in the relationship between hunter and hound. [3] My grandfather's favorite was Belle, who helped put meat on the table by instinctively switching prey when the deer season opened. [4] Eating choice leftovers, <u>a family's porch and hearth was enjoyed by such a hound.</u>[55]

48. **F.** NO CHANGE
G. sport. In fact,
H. sport, in fact
J. sport in fact

49. **A.** NO CHANGE
B. exciting
C. exciting;
D. exciting: so

50. **F.** NO CHANGE
G. huntsman's horn, was
H. huntsmans horn, was
J. huntsman's horn were

51. **A.** NO CHANGE
B. horns of cows'.
C. cows horns.
D. cows' horns.

52. **F.** NO CHANGE
G. hunt not
H. hunt; never
J. hunt; not

53. **A.** NO CHANGE
B. its
C. their
D. it's

54. **F.** NO CHANGE
G. laid
H. lain
J. lay

55. **A.** NO CHANGE
B. a family's porch, and hearth was enjoyed by such a hound.
C. such a hound enjoyed a family's porch and hearth.
D. the porch and hearth of the family, were enjoyed by such a hound.

GO ON TO THE NEXT PAGE.

1 ■ ■ ■ ■ ■ ■ ■ ■ ■ 1

[5] They had favorite hounds whose deeds <u>had became</u> [56] legends. [57]

This peculiarly American form of fox hunting has almost disappeared. More sophisticated sports have taken its place. Yet, for me, the plaintive bawl of a distant hound remains music, rousing warm and vivid memories.

56. F. NO CHANGE
   G. had, became
   H. became
   J. was becoming

57. Which of the following sequences of sentences will make the structure of the preceding paragraph most logical?
   A. NO CHANGE
   B. 1, 3, 4, 5, 2
   C. 1, 3, 5, 2, 4
   D. 2, 1, 5, 3, 4

Items 58 and 59 pose questions about Passage IV as a whole.

58. Are the word *tallyho* and the phrase *went to earth* appropriate in this essay?
   F. No, because this essay describes action, not speech patterns.
   G. No, because such expressions are irrelevant in this essay and call too much attention to themselves.
   H. Yes, because typical expressions used in fox hunting add color and vitality to the writing.
   J. Yes, because writers should employ the vocabulary of fox hunting whenever possible.

59. Which of the following sentences would most effectively summarize the essay as a whole?
   A. American night fox hunting has recently been replaced by more sophisticated sports.
   B. American fox hunters, unlike their British counterparts, made their own horns.
   C. Unlike British fox hunting, American night fox hunting was not a blood sport.
   D. American night fox hunting, which is distinctly different from British fox hunting, was a pleasurable and memorable activity.

Passage V

For most people, the word *vacation* evokes images of mountains <u>and beaches, there being</u> [60] a small boat bobbing on a lake, a hammock swaying in the shade of a tree. <u>For me, too,</u> [61] the word has become synonymous with *overhaul.*

Each year the same thing happens. Within hours after I've closed the office door, anticipating a restful two weeks at home free of ringing phones and impatient <u>customers, and</u> [62] "overhaul syndrome" begins with at least one major appliance or machine breaking down. This year, miraculously, it took a full day to start. I began my vacation on <u>Friday,</u> [63] on Saturday, the lawn mower abruptly decided to throw itself out of

60. F. NO CHANGE
   G. and beaches,
   H. and beaches images evoked,
   J. as well as there being beaches,

61. A. NO CHANGE
   B. For me, however,
   C. Therefore, for me,
   D. Besides, for me,

62. F. NO CHANGE
   G. customers,
   H. customers, and so
   J. customers. Until

63. A. NO CHANGE
   B. Friday;
   C. Friday, or
   D. Friday, unfortunately,

GO ON TO THE NEXT PAGE.

1 ■ ■ ■ ■ ■ ■ ■ ■ ■ 1

gear. No <u>amount of adjusting and coaxing,</u> [64] could <u>change it's</u> [65] mind. Not to be outdone by the outdoor equipment, the refrigerator chose the next day to warm its contents to a balmy sixty-five degrees. The net loss in vacation time was two days: one to haul the mower thirty miles to the nearest authorized repair shop and one to wait for the refrigerator repair person, <u>having been expected at ten but who arrived at four.</u> [66]

Appliances aren't the only things that need to be overhauled. By vacation time, the <u>house itself</u> [67] is also begging for attention. Routine maintenance like washing windows, repainting wood trim, and killing crabgrass can be put off for only so long. When the neighbors begin making none-too-subtle comments <u>for</u> [68] "blights on the neighborhood," I <u>know</u> [69] it's time to dig out the stepladder and work gloves. Five days later, the yard and the exterior of the house <u>are</u> [70] once again presentable. Next, I tick off interior jobs left to perform: wash woodwork, clean cupboards, shampoo carpet, straighten attic. As fast as you can say "household cleanser," twelve of my fourteen vacation days have flown by.

My two-week overhaul at an end, <u>and</u> [71] I return to the office exhausted. Ignoring coworkers

64. F. NO CHANGE
G. amount, of adjusting and coaxing
H. amount of adjusting and coaxing
J. amount of adjusting, and coaxing

65. A. NO CHANGE
B. change its
C. have changed it's
D. change its'

66. F. NO CHANGE
G. because this person was expected at ten but arriving at four.
H. who was expected at ten but who arrived at four.
J. who arriving at four, having been expected at ten.

67. A. NO CHANGE
B. house, itself
C. house itself,
D. house by itself

68. F. NO CHANGE
G. about
H. from
J. about;

69. A. NO CHANGE
B. know that,
C. know,
D. know, that

70. F. NO CHANGE
G. was
H. is
J. has been

71. A. NO CHANGE
B. so
C. therefore
D. OMIT the underlined portion.

GO ON TO THE NEXT PAGE.

1 ■ ■ ■ ■ ■ ■ ■ ■ ■ 1

clamoring to see my vacation photos,

<u>my desk chair is awaiting my weary body</u>.[72] What

a relief to find a <u>place, where I can relax,</u>[73]

before I need an overhaul myself.

72. **F.** NO CHANGE
G. with a deep breath my desk chair greets my weary body.
H. my desk chair provides a welcome haven for a deep breath.
J. I sink into my desk chair and breathe deeply.

73. **A.** NO CHANGE
B. place, where I can relax
C. place where I can relax
D. place, where I, can relax,

Items 74 and 75 pose questions about Passage V as a whole.

74. The writer refers to possibly needing a personal overhaul at the end of the essay because the word *overhaul:*

F. might be confused with the word *vacation.*
G. logically comes to mind in relation to work.
H. ties the conclusion to the rest of the essay.
J. suggests that the vacation is over.

75. Which of the following assignments would this essay most likely fulfill?

A. Write a personal article on the stresses of vacation time.
B. Write a helpful article on avoiding the pitfalls of vacation stress.
C. Write a factual article on home improvement.
D. Write a persuasive article on the benefits of staying home over vacation.

END OF TEST 1

STOP! DO NOT TURN THE PAGE UNTIL TOLD TO DO SO.

MATHEMATICS TEST

60 Minutes—60 Questions

DIRECTIONS: Solve each problem, choose the correct answer, and then blacken the corresponding oval on your answer sheet.

Do not linger over problems that take too much time. Solve as many as you can; then return to the others in the time you have left for this test.

Note: Unless otherwise stated, all of the following should be assumed.

1. Illustrative figures are NOT necessarily drawn to scale.
2. Geometric figures lie in a plane.
3. The word *line* indicates a straight line.
4. The word *average* indicates arithmetic mean.

DO YOUR FIGURING HERE.

1. In ΔRST below, the measure of $\angle S$ is 40°, and the measure of $\angle T$ is twice the measure of $\angle S$. What is the measure of $\angle R$?

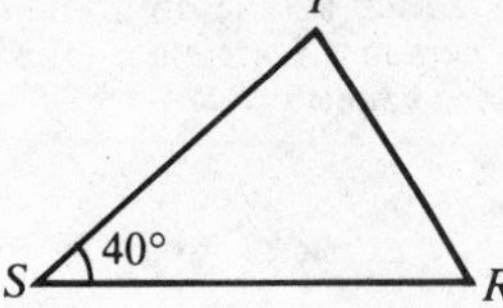

A. 40°
B. 60°
C. 80°
D. 100°
E. 120°

2. Nineteen (19) students agreed to share equally the expenses for printing the announcements for Parents Appreciation Day. If a total of \$133.20 was collected from 12 students who each paid exactly their shares, what was the total printing bill?

F. \$ 84.13
G. \$ 210.90
H. \$ 701.05
J. \$ 777.00
K. \$4,129.20

3. The basic fine for speeding is \$15, to which is added \$3 for each mile per hour (mph) over the speed limit of 55 mph. Sally had to pay a \$72 fine for speeding. For what speed, in miles per hour, was Sally charged?

A. 59
B. 64
C. 74
D. 79
E. 84

8939F

GO ON TO THE NEXT PAGE.

2 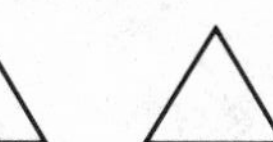     **2**

DO YOUR FIGURING HERE.

4. In a circuit, $E = IR$, where E = number of volts, I = number of amperes, and R = number of ohms. How much current, in amperes, flows through a circuit if the number of volts is 12 and the resistance is 4 ohms?

F. 3
G. 4
H. 8
J. 12
K. 16

5. In the figure below, line m is parallel to line n, and line t is a transversal crossing both m and n. Which of the following lists has 3 angles that are all equal in measure?

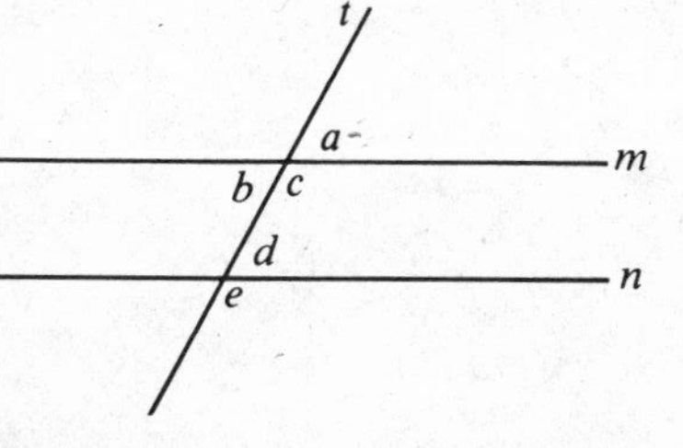

A. $\angle a, \angle b, \angle d$
B. $\angle a, \angle c, \angle d$
C. $\angle a, \angle c, \angle e$
D. $\angle b, \angle c, \angle d$
E. $\angle b, \angle c, \angle e$

6. In scientific notation, 20,000 + 3,400,000 = ?

F. 3.60×10^{12}
G. 3.60×10^{7}
H. 3.42×10^{7}
J. 3.60×10^{6}
K. 3.42×10^{6}

7. $2.542 \div 0.02 = ?$

A. 0.1271
B. 1.271
C. 12.71
D. 127.1
E. 1,271.0

8. For all $x \neq -4$, which of the following is equivalent to the expression below?

$$\frac{x^2 + 12x + 32}{x + 4}$$

F. $x + 3$
G. $x + 8$
H. $x + 11$
J. $x + 16$
K. $x + 28$

9. If $x = -2$, then $12 - x^2 + 1 = ?$

A. 7
B. 9
C. 11
D. 15
E. 17

GO ON TO THE NEXT PAGE.

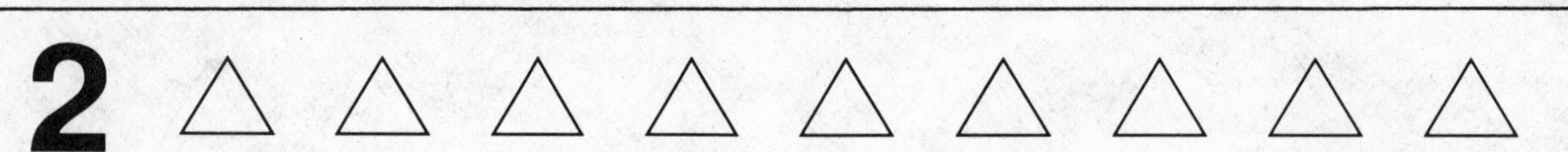

DO YOUR FIGURING HERE.

10. A shirt that originally cost \$35 is on sale at 20% off. If the sales tax on shirts is 5% of the purchase price, how much would it cost to buy the shirt at its sale price?

F. \$ 7.35
G. \$20.00
H. \$26.60
J. \$29.40
K. \$29.75

11. Which of the following graphs represents $x \leq 2$?

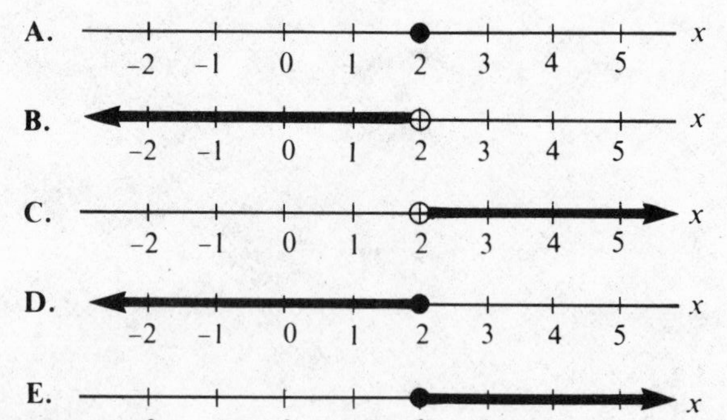

12. If the ratio of $3a$ to $7b$ is 1 to 7, what is the ratio of $6a$ to $7b$?

F. 1 to 14
G. 1 to 35
H. 2 to 7
J. 2 to 21
K. 3 to 7

13. In the figure below, $\overline{CA}$ is perpendicular to $\overline{AB}$, and $\overline{CB}$ is perpendicular to $\overline{BD}$; $\overline{AB}$ is 3 units long, $\overline{AC}$ is 4 units long, and $\overline{BD}$ is 12 units long. How many units long is $\overline{CD}$?

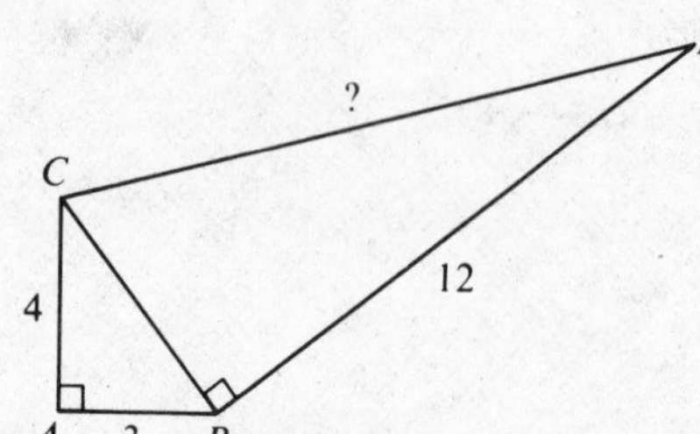

A. 13
B. 17
C. 19
D. 24
E. 25

GO ON TO THE NEXT PAGE.

2 △ △ △ △ △ △ △ △ △ 2

DO YOUR FIGURING HERE.

14. A rectangular tabletop has an area of 54 square feet. It has a length that is 3 feet more than its width. Which of the following equations could be used to find w, the width, in feet, of the table?

F. $w^2 = 54 - 3^2$
G. $2(w + 3) + 2w = 54$
H. $w(3w) = 54$
J. $w(w - 3) = 54$
K. $w(w + 3) = 54$

15. A speedboat traveling in still water at a rate of 30 miles per hour takes $\frac{1}{2}$ hour to reach an island. If the boat traveled at a rate of 3 miles per hour over the same route, how many hours would the trip take?

A. 0.05
B. 5
C. 10
D. 15
E. 45

16. A person had a rectangular-shaped garden with sides of lengths 16 feet and 9 feet. The garden was changed into a square design with the same area as the original rectangular-shaped garden. How many feet in length are each of the sides of the new square-shaped garden?

F. 7
G. 9
H. 12
J. $5\sqrt{7}$
K. 16

17. A hotel has a total of 225 rooms that rent for $50 a day per room. If 80% of the rooms are rented for 2 days, how much rent will be charged for those rooms?

A. $ 9,000
B. $11,250
C. $18,000
D. $22,500
E. $28,125

18. In the figure below, A, C, and D are collinear. If the measure of $\angle A$ is 30° and the measure of $\angle BCD$ is 120°, what is the measure of $\angle B$?

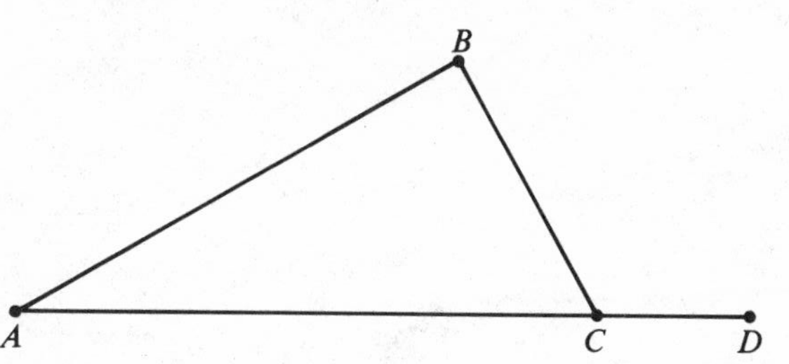

F. 30°
G. 60°
H. 90°
J. 120°
K. 150°

GO ON TO THE NEXT PAGE.

2  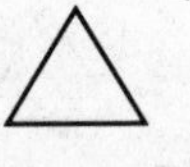  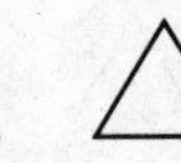  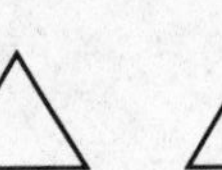 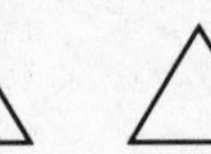   **2**

DO YOUR FIGURING HERE.

19. What is the value of x in the solution for the system of equations below?

$$2x + 5y = 20$$

$$6x - \frac{1}{2}y = 29$$

A. 4
B. 5
C. 6
D. 15
E. 20

20. $\frac{1}{2} + \left(\frac{2}{3} \div \frac{3}{4}\right) - \left(\frac{4}{5} \times \frac{5}{6}\right) = ?$

F. $\frac{1}{6}$
G. $\frac{17}{27}$
H. $\frac{13}{18}$
J. $\frac{7}{9}$
K. $\frac{5}{6}$

21. For all y, $26y - (-10y) - 3y(-y + 3) = ?$

A. $10y$
B. $-3y^2 + 25y$
C. $3y^2 + 7y$
D. $3y^2 + 25y$
E. $3y^2 + 27y$

22. For all $a \neq -2$, $\frac{a^2 - 4}{2a + 4} = ?$

F. a
G. $\frac{a-1}{3}$
H. $a - 1$
J. $\frac{a}{2}$
K. $\frac{a-2}{2}$

23. If $x = -3$ is one solution of the equation $x^2 - kx - 24 = 0$, what is the value of k?

A. 5
B. 8
C. –5
D. –21
E. –27

GO ON TO THE NEXT PAGE.

2 △ △ △ △ △ △ △ △ △ 2

DO YOUR FIGURING HERE.

24. In $\triangle ABC$ shown below, $\overline{BD}$ bisects $\angle ABC$. The measure of $\angle ABC$ is 100°, and $\angle A$ measures 30°. What is the measure of $\angle BDC$?

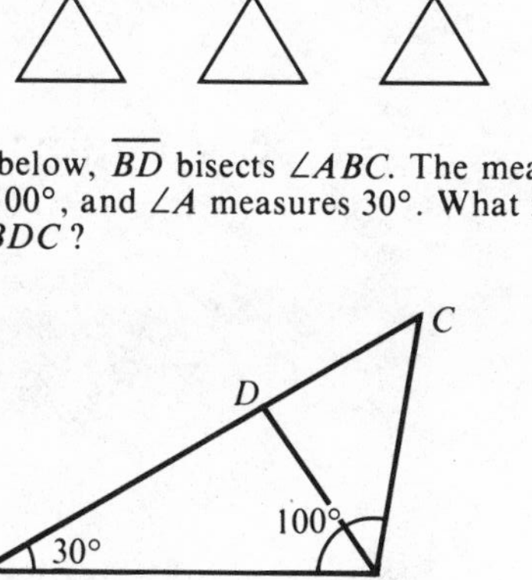

F. 65°
G. 70°
H. 75°
J. 80°
K. 85°

25. A gardener has 78 yards of fencing and wishes to enclose a rectangular plot whose length is to be between 20 and 25 yards. If all the fencing is to be used, then what are the possible choices for the width of the garden, in yards?

A. Between 14 and 19
B. Between 26.5 and 29
C. Between 28 and 38
D. Between 53 and 58
E. All the fencing cannot be used.

26. For all positive values of a, b, and c with $a < b$ and $a > c$, which of the following MUST be true?

I. $a + b > c$
II. $2a > c$
III. $a + c > b$

F. I only
G. II only
H. I and II only
J. II and III only
K. I, II, and III

27. In the figure below, $\angle S$ is a right angle, $\overline{RS}$ is 3 units long, and $\overline{ST}$ is 4 units long. If the measure of $\angle R$ is x, then $\sin x = ?$

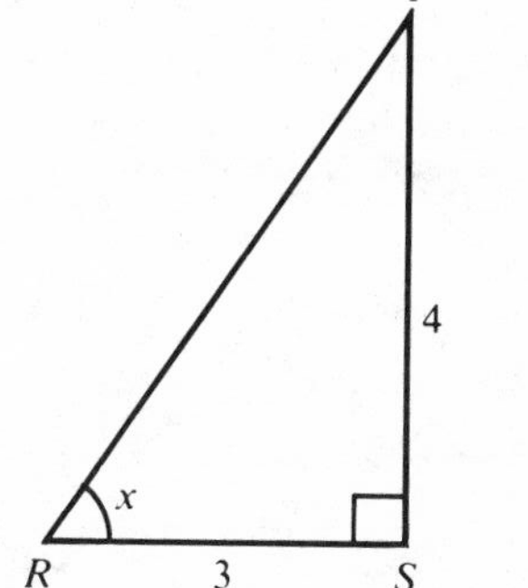

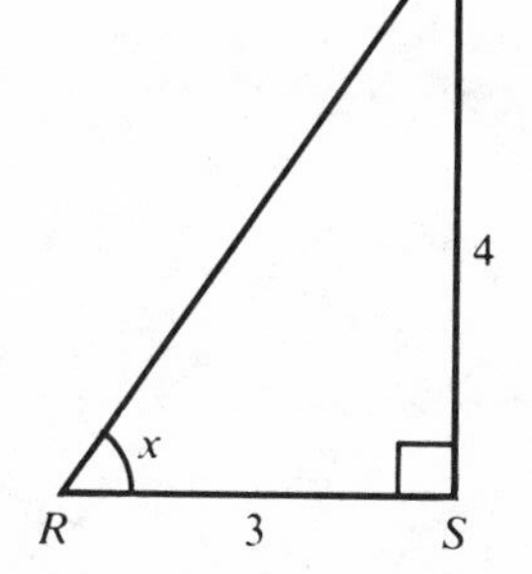

A. $\frac{3}{5}$
B. $\frac{3}{4}$
C. $\frac{4}{5}$
D. $\frac{5}{4}$
E. $\frac{5}{3}$

GO ON TO THE NEXT PAGE.

2    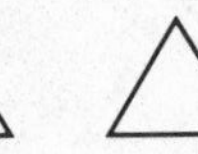    2

DO YOUR FIGURING HERE.

28. What is the sum of all the solutions of the equation $\frac{x}{2+x} = \frac{3x}{4x+3}$?

F. −3
G. 0
H. 2
J. 3
K. 6

29. $-2|-3| - |-5| = ?$

A. −11
B. −1
C. 1
D. 4
E. 11

30. In the figure below, $\overline{BE}$ is parallel to $\overline{CF}$; points A, B, C, and D are collinear; and $\overline{BE}$ is the same length as $\overline{CE}$. If the measure of $\angle FCD$ is 50°, what is the measure of $\angle E$?

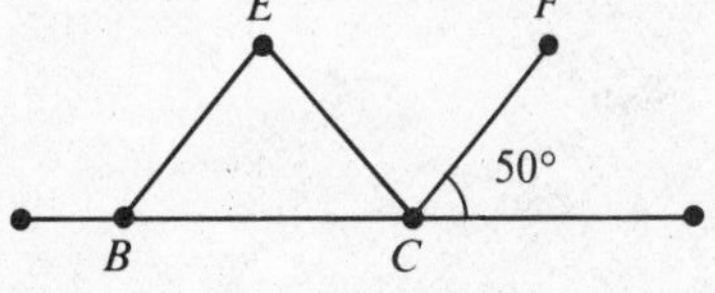

F. 30°
G. 40°
H. 50°
J. 70°
K. 80°

31. If $x^2 - 1 \leq 8$, what is the smallest real value x can have?

A. −9
B. −7
C. −3
D. 0
E. There is no smallest value for x.

32. The diagonal of a square has a length of 10 units. What is the length, in units, of 1 of the sides of the square?

F. 5
G. $5\sqrt{2}$
H. $5\sqrt{3}$
J. 10
K. $10\sqrt{2}$

33. What is the equation of the circle in the standard (x,y) coordinate plane with center at (−3,−4) and radius 6 units long?

A. $x + y = -1$

B. $x + y = 13$

C. $(x-3)^2 + (y-4)^2 = 36$

D. $(x+3)^2 + (y+4)^2 = 36$

E. $\frac{(x+3)^2}{6} + \frac{(y+4)^2}{6} = 1$

GO ON TO THE NEXT PAGE.

2 △ △ △ △ △ △ △ △ △ 2

DO YOUR FIGURING HERE.

34. What is the slope of the line determined by the equation $5x - 2y = 7$?

F. $\frac{5}{2}$
G. $\frac{2}{5}$
H. $-\frac{2}{5}$
J. $-\frac{5}{2}$
K. $-\frac{7}{2}$

35. One hundred (100) cars drove through a certain intersection. The number of persons in each car varied as shown in the chart below. What was the average number of persons per car for those 100 cars?

Number of persons in car	1	2	3	4
Number of cars	50	30	10	10

A. 1.0
B. 1.4
C. 1.6
D. 1.8
E. 2.5

36. In the figure below, the circle centered at B is internally tangent to the circle centered at A. The smaller circle passes through the center of the larger circle and the length of $\overline{AB}$ is 5 units. If the smaller circle is cut out of the larger circle, how much of the area, in square units, of the larger circle will remain?

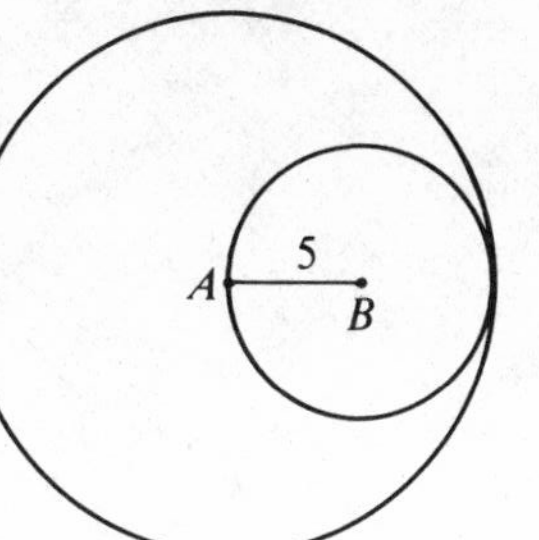

F. 10π
G. 25π
H. 75π
J. 100π
K. 300π

37. What is the equation of the line with the same slope as the line $y = 3x - 4$ but with the same y-intercept as the line $x + y + 2 = 0$?

A. $y = -4x + 2$
B. $y = -4x - 2$
C. $y = -x - 4$
D. $y = 3x + 2$
E. $y = 3x - 2$

GO ON TO THE NEXT PAGE.

2 △ △ △ △ △ △ △ △ △ 2

38. Which of the following represents the solution set of the inequality $2x + 3 < 4x + 7$?

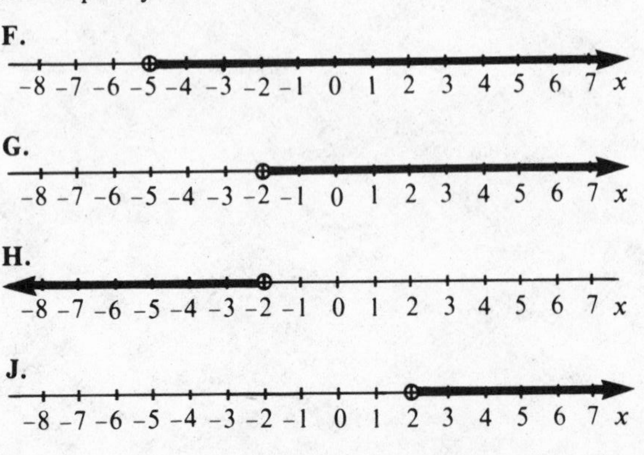

DO YOUR FIGURING HERE.

39. What is the value of c if the line in the standard (x,y) coordinate plane that passes through the points $(5,c)$ and $(2,-c)$ has slope $\frac{4}{3}$?

A. -2

B. $-\frac{9}{8}$

C. 0

D. $\frac{9}{8}$

E. 2

40. A formula for calculating simple interest is $I = Pr$, where I is the number of dollars of interest earned, P is the initial amount invested (principal), and r is the fixed interest rate, all for the period of time that the principal was invested. If $500 was invested and earned $40, what was the interest rate, expressed as a percentage?

F. .80%
G. 1.25%
H. 8.00%
J. 12.50%
K. 80.00%

41. Three vertices of a square in the standard (x,y) coordinate plane have coordinates $(2,-4)$, $(7,1)$, and $(2,6)$. What are the coordinates of the fourth vertex?

A. $(-7,1)$
B. $(-3,1)$
C. $(-3,5)$
D. $(3,-3)$
E. $(7,-3)$

GO ON TO THE NEXT PAGE.

2     **2**

DO YOUR FIGURING HERE.

42. For all $x \neq 0$, $\frac{x^4 + x^4 + x^4}{x^2} = ?$

F. $3x^2$
G. x^6
H. x^{10}
J. x^{32}
K. x^{62}

43. Using a calculator, Heather tried to divide a number, N, by 7, but she pushed the "8" button instead of the "7" button and her result was 12 less than the correct answer. Which of the following equations would determine N?

A. $7N + 12 = 8N$
B. $\frac{N}{8} = \frac{(N - 12)}{7}$
C. $\frac{N}{8} - 12 = \frac{N}{7}$
D. $\frac{(N - 12)}{8} = \frac{N}{7}$
E. $\frac{N}{8} + 12 = \frac{N}{7}$

44. What is the sum of all the values of x that satisfy the equation $2x^2 - 4x - 6 = 0$?

F. -4
G. -2
H. 1
J. 2
K. 4

45. What is the value of $(\cos\frac{\pi}{3})(\cos\frac{\pi}{3}) + (\sin\frac{\pi}{3})(\sin\frac{\pi}{3})$?

A. $\frac{1}{3}$
B. $\frac{1}{2}$
C. $\frac{\sqrt{3}}{3}$
D. $\frac{\sqrt{3}}{2}$
E. 1

46. For a class play, student tickets cost \$1 and nonstudent tickets cost \$2. A total of 35 tickets were sold. If S represents the number of student tickets sold, which of the following is a general formula for the total number of dollars collected in ticket sales?

F. $68S$
G. $69S$
H. 70
J. $70 - S$
K. $70 - 2S$

GO ON TO THE NEXT PAGE.

2 △ △ △ △ △ △ △ △ △ 2

47. Which of the following represents the values of x that are solutions for the inequality $(3 - x)(x + 2) > 0$?

A. $-3 < x < 2$

B. $-2 < x < 3$

C. $-\frac{1}{2} < x < \frac{1}{3}$

D. $x < -3$ or $x > 2$

E. $x < -2$ or $x > 3$

48. In the figure below, $\angle B$ is a right angle, and the measure of $\angle C$ is 30°. What is the ratio of the length of $\overline{CB}$ to the length of $\overline{AC}$?

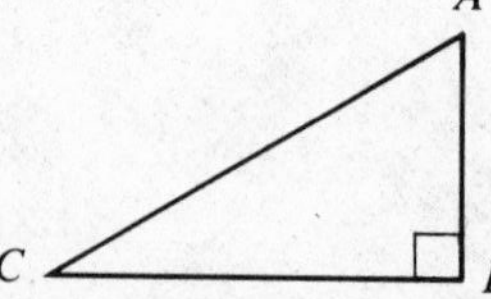

F. $\frac{1}{2}$

G. $\frac{\sqrt{3}}{3}$

H. $\frac{\sqrt{3}}{2}$

J. $\frac{2\sqrt{3}}{3}$

K. $\frac{\sqrt{3}}{1}$

49. If $\cos\theta = \frac{5}{13}$ and $0° \leq \theta° \leq 180°$, then $\sin\theta = ?$

A. $\frac{12}{13}$

B. $\frac{5}{12}$

C. $\frac{5}{13}$

D. $-\frac{5}{12}$

E. $-\frac{12}{13}$

50. For all $x < y < 4$, $\frac{x - y}{4(x - y) - x(x - y)} = ?$

F. $\frac{1}{4 - x}$

G. $\frac{1}{4x(x - y)}$

H. $\frac{1}{5x - 4y}$

J. $\frac{1}{3x - 4y}$

K. $\frac{1}{(4 - x)(x - y)}$

DO YOUR FIGURING HERE.

GO ON TO THE NEXT PAGE.

2 △ △ △ △ △ △ △ △ △ 2

DO YOUR FIGURING HERE.

51. In the figure below, square $ABCD$ has sides of length 4 units, and M and N are midpoints of $\overline{AB}$ and $\overline{CD}$, respectively. What is the perimeter, in units, of quadrilateral $AMCN$?

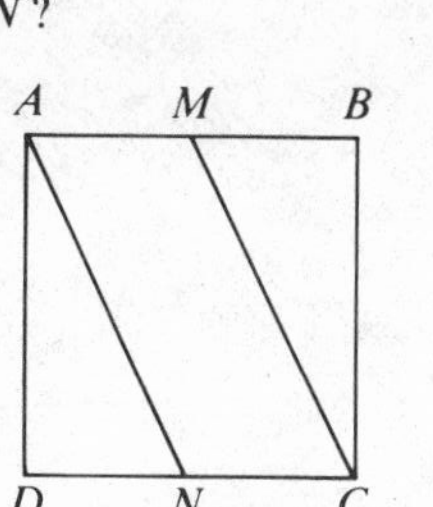

A. 8
B. $8\sqrt{5}$
C. $4+4\sqrt{3}$
D. $4+4\sqrt{5}$
E. $4+8\sqrt{3}$

52. A line in the standard (x,y) coordinate plane has slope -3 and goes through the point $(1,-1)$. If the point with coordinates $(-1,t)$ is on the line, then $t=$?

F. -5
G. -1
H. 1
J. 5
K. 7

53. A 6-foot spruce tree is planted 15 feet from a lighted streetlight whose lamp is 18 feet above the ground. How many feet long is the shadow of that tree?

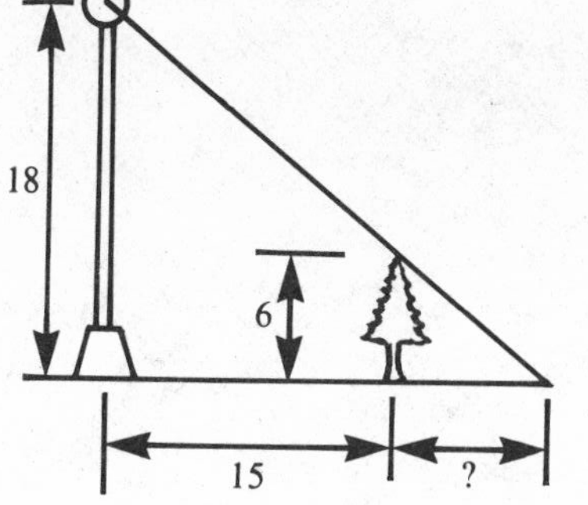

A. 5.0
B. 7.5
C. 7.8
D. 9.6
E. 10.0

54. Which of the following inequalities characterizes the values of x for which the inequality $-4x+5>2x+17$ is true?

F. $x>-2$
G. $x>-6$
H. $x<-6$
J. $x<-2$
K. $x<2$

GO ON TO THE NEXT PAGE.

2 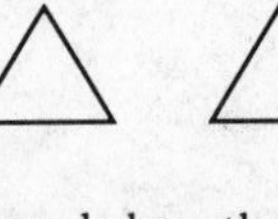   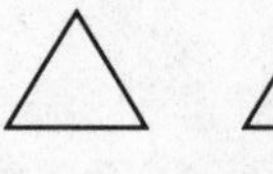   2

DO YOUR FIGURING HERE.

55. In the figure below, the lengths of $\overline{DE}$, $\overline{EF}$, and $\overline{FG}$ are given, in units. What is the area, in square units, of ΔDEG?

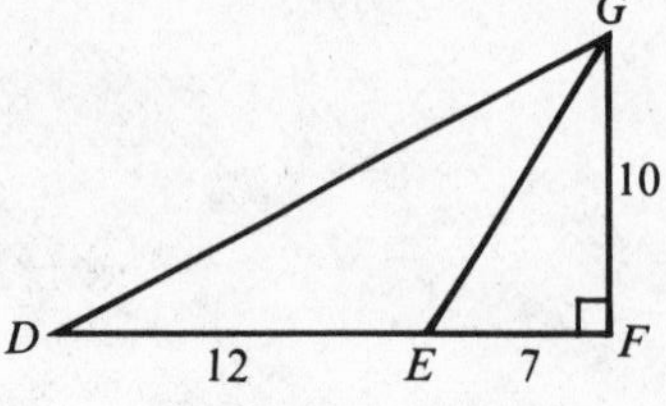

A. 29
B. 47.5
C. 60
D. $6\sqrt{149}$
E. 120

56. Which of the following intervals contains the solution to the equation $\frac{x-7}{4} = x - 10$?

F. $-12 \le x < -5$
G. $5 \le x < 6$
H. $6 \le x < 7$
J. $10 \le x < 12$
K. $15 \le x < 16$

57. In the figure below, A and B lie on the circle centered at O, $\overline{OA}$ is 6 units long, and the measure of $\angle AOB$ is 60°. How many units long is minor arc AB?

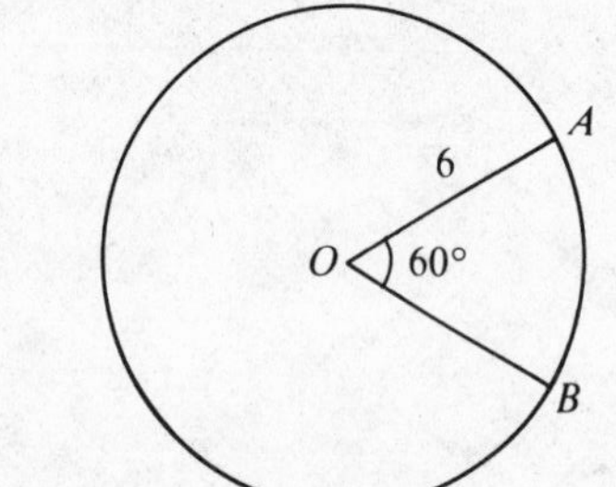

A. π
B. 2π
C. 6π
D. 12π
E. 36π

58. Given the graph in the standard (x,y) coordinate plane below, which of the following statements is true about the slopes m_1 and m_2 of line 1 and line 2, respectively?

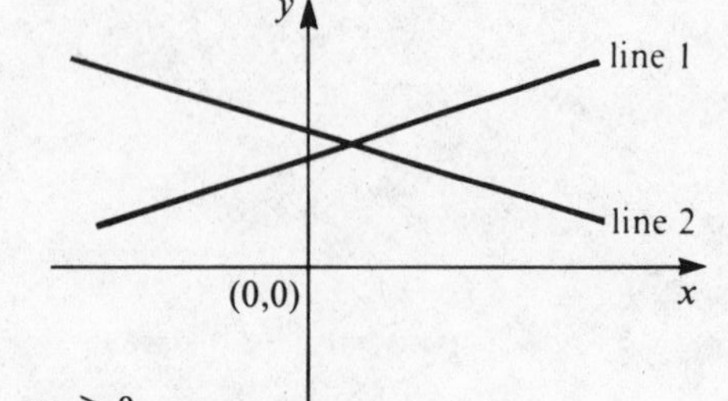

F. $m_2 - m_1 > 0$
G. $m_2 = \frac{1}{2}m_1$
H. $m_1 \cdot m_2 > 0$
J. $m_1 \cdot m_2 = 0$
K. $m_1 \cdot m_2 < 0$

GO ON TO THE NEXT PAGE.

2 △ △ △ △ △ △ △ △ △ 2

DO YOUR FIGURING HERE.

59. In the right triangle below, the length of $\overline{AB}$ is 13 units and the length of $\overline{CB}$ is 12 units. What is the tangent of $\angle A$?

A. $\frac{12}{5}$

B. $\frac{13}{12}$

C. $\frac{12}{13}$

D. $\frac{5}{12}$

E. $\frac{5}{13}$

60. Point $A(-4,1)$ is in the standard (x,y) coordinate plane. What must be the coordinates of point B so that the line $x = 2$ is the perpendicular bisector of $\overline{AB}$?

F. (−6, 1)
G. (−4, −1)
H. (−4, 3)
J. (−2, 1)
K. (8, 1)

END OF TEST 2

STOP! DO NOT TURN THE PAGE UNTIL TOLD TO DO SO.

READING TEST

35 Minutes—40 Questions

DIRECTIONS: There are four passages in this test. Each passage is followed by several questions. After reading a passage, choose the best answer to each question and blacken the corresponding oval on your answer sheet. You may refer to the passages as often as necessary.

Passage I

Julie Hempel and Selina Peake, both finished products of Miss Fister's school, were of an age—nineteen. Selina, on this September day, had been spending the afternoon with Julie, and now, adjusting her hat preparatory to leaving, she clapped her hands over her ears to shut out the sounds of Julie's importunings that she stay to supper. Certainly the prospect of the usual Monday evening meal in Mrs. Tebbitt's boarding house (the Peake luck was momentarily low) did not present sufficient excuse for Selina's refusal. Indeed, the Hempel supper as sketched dish for dish by the urgent Julie brought little greedy groans from Selina.

"It's prairie chickens—three of them—that a farmer west of town brought Father. Mother fixes them with stuffing, and there's currant jelly. Creamed onions and baked tomatoes. And for dessert, apple roll."

Selina snapped the elastic holding her high-crowned hat under her chignon of hair in the back. She uttered a final and quavering groan. "On Monday nights we have cold mutton and cabbage at Mrs. Tebbitt's. This is Monday."

"Well then, silly, why not stay?"

"Father comes home at six. If I'm not there he's disappointed."

Julie, plump, blonde, placid, forsook her soft white blandishments and tried steel against the steel of Selina's decision.

"He leaves you right after supper. And you're alone every night until twelve and after."

"I don't see what that has to do with it," Selina said stiffly.

Julie's steel, being low-grade, melted at once and ran off her in rivulets. "Of course it hasn't, Selie dear. Only I thought you might leave him just this once."

"If I'm not there he's disappointed. And that terrible Mrs. Tebbitt makes eyes at him. He hates it there."

"Then I don't see why you stay. I never could see. You've been there four months now, and I think it's horrid and stuffy; and oilcloth on the stairs."

"Father has had some temporary business setbacks."

Selina's costume testified to that. True, it was modish, and bustled, and basqued, and flounced; and her high-crowned, short-brimmed hat, with its trimming of feathers and flowers and ribbons had come from New York. But both were of last spring's purchasing, and this was September.

In the course of the afternoon they had been looking over the pages of Godey's *Ladies' Book* for that month. The disparity between Selina's costume and the creations pictured there was much as the difference between the Tebbitt meal and that outlined by Julie. Now Julie, fond though defeated, kissed her friend good-bye.

Selina walked quickly the short distance from the Hempel house to Tebbitt's, on Dearborn Avenue. Up in her second-floor room she took off her hat and called to her father, but he had not yet come in. She was glad of that. She had been fearful of being late. She regarded her hat now with some distaste, decided to rip off the faded spring roses, did rip a stitch or two, only to discover that the hat material was more faded than the roses, and that the uncovered surface showed up a dark splotch like a wallspot when a picture, long hung, is removed. So she got a needle and prepared to tack the offending rose in its accustomed place.

Perched on the arm of a chair near the window, taking quick deft stitches, she heard a sound. She had never heard that sound before—that peculiar sound—the slow, ominous tread of men laden with a heavy inert burden; bearing with infinite care that which was well beyond hurting. Selina had never heard that sound before, and yet, hearing it, she recognized it by one of those pangs, centuries old, called woman's instinct. Thud—shuffle—thud—shuffle—up the narrow stairway, along the passage. She stood up, the needle poised in her hand. The hat fell to the floor. Her eyes were wide, fixed. Her lips slightly parted. The listening look. She knew.

8939F

GO ON TO THE NEXT PAGE.

3 3

She knew even before she heard the hoarse man's voice saying, "Lift 'er up there a little on the corner, now. Easy—e-e-easy." And Mrs. Tebbitt's high shrill clamour: "You can't bring it in there! You hadn't ought to bring it in here like this!"

Selina's suspended breath came back. She was panting now. She had flung open the door. A flat still burden partially covered with an overcoat carelessly flung over the face. The feet, in their square-toed boots, wobbled listlessly. Selina noticed how shiny the boots were. He was always very finicking about such things.

From Edna Ferber, *So Big*. ©1924 by Doubleday & Company.

1. Julie says of Selina's father, "He leaves you right after supper. And you're alone" (lines 29–30), in order to:

- **A.** urge Selina to confess where her father goes at night.
- **B.** offer an argument for Selina to stay to supper.
- **C.** make Selina feel guilty about staying for dinner.
- **D.** humiliate Selina by criticizing her father.

2. If the comparison between the meals at Mrs. Tebbitt's and at the Hempels' is an indicator of the general difference between Selina's and Julie's status, it can be inferred that:

- **F.** Selina is wealthier than her father.
- **G.** Julie was once wealthier than Selina.
- **H.** Selina is wealthier than Julie.
- **J.** Selina is poorer than Julie.

3. The statement that Julie "tried steel against the steel of Selina's decision" (lines 27–28) means that Julie was trying to:

- **A.** cut Selina down to size.
- **B.** start a fight with Selina.
- **C.** help Selina make a decision.
- **D.** persuade Selina to stay for supper.

4. Selina utters "a final and quavering groan" (line 20) after Julie mentions the apple roll because Selina:

- **F.** would like to have apple roll for dessert.
- **G.** knows she should not eat desserts.
- **H.** hurts her scalp while putting on her hat.
- **J.** knows Mrs. Hempel's cooking is really awful.

5. Julie first invited Selina to supper after Julie:

- **A.** had been told by her mother that there would be enough food for Selina.
- **B.** heard what Selina would eat at the boarding house.
- **C.** heard of the tragedy at the boarding house.
- **D.** had spent the day with Selina.

6. The "heavy inert burden" (lines 72–73) the men carried into the boarding house is described as "well beyond hurting" (lines 73–74), meaning that it:

- **F.** has been severely damaged.
- **G.** is so healthy it cannot be hurt.
- **H.** is so tough no damage is noticeable.
- **J.** is dead and cannot be harmed further.

7. What is it that Selina "knew" (line 81)?

- **A.** That Mrs. Tebbitt would be angry with her
- **B.** That her father hated the boarding house
- **C.** That she would never see Julie again
- **D.** That her father was dead

8. Julie Hempel lives with:

- **F.** Mrs. Tebbitt.
- **G.** only her father.
- **H.** her mother and father.
- **J.** her mother, father, and Selina.

9. Selina had to sew her hat because:

- **A.** she ripped the hat purposely.
- **B.** she ripped the hat accidentally.
- **C.** the hat did not fit her properly.
- **D.** she wanted to add new flowers to the hat.

10. In the context of the passage, *modish* (line 45) means:

- **F.** modest.
- **G.** old-fashioned.
- **H.** somewhat stylish.
- **J.** flamboyant, yet cheap.

GO ON TO THE NEXT PAGE.

Passage II

Before we decide to dismiss the electoral college as insignificant and look only at the popular vote cast on election day, we should note that there have been instances in which a candidate got more popular votes than his opponent, but not enough electoral votes to become president. In the 1976 election, Jimmy Carter had a popular vote plurality (margin) of 1,680,974 votes over Gerald Ford, and an electoral vote margin of 297 to 241. . . . Even so, the election was so close that a shift of only about 5000 votes in Ohio and Hawaii would have given Ford the majority of electoral votes and a new term as president. Carter, with some 1,675,000 more votes than Ford, would not have become president.

Furthermore, nothing guarantees that all the electors chosen in November will vote as they are pledged in December. In 1976 only one elector bolted, voting for Ronald Reagan instead of Ford. But if twenty-nine Democratic electors had for some reason bolted from Carter to Ford, Ford would again have been president.

So the electoral college is important in its potential impact on the outcome of an election after the people vote. And because it can be important afterward, it is also important before the election. It influences the strategies employed by the major parties because, in effect, some votes . . . are more important to the outcome than others. This is true even though we usually think that in our system of "one person, one vote," all votes are equal. . . .

The founders did not trust the people to elect their own president. They provided instead that each state would choose distinguished representatives (as many as it had members of Congress) who would meet as the electoral college to elect the best candidate president and the runner-up vice-president. . . .

In 1800 there was a tie in the electoral college between Thomas Jefferson and Aaron Burr. The election had to be decided, as the Constitution provides in such cases, in the House of Representatives, where each state's delegation is allowed only one vote, regardless of how many representatives it has. Jefferson finally won. In 1824 in a similar situation, the House elected John Quincy Adams president, even though Andrew Jackson had outpolled him. The controversy this caused abated somewhat when, in the next election, Jackson won a landslide victory. But electoral trouble arose once more in 1876 and again in 1888, when presidents who had not won the popular vote were elected by the electoral college. . . .

To this day, every time there is a close election, such as that of 1976, there is fear that a candidate will win the electoral vote but not the popular vote. That fear is compounded by the fact that electors in most states are not legally bound to vote for the candidate they are pledged to. In others, they face no legal penalty for bolting. . . .

In almost every session of Congress an effort is made to abolish the electoral college by constitutional amendment. . . . Thus far, all efforts have failed, primarily because many believe that the electoral college favors two different interest groups. One is the *small states* like Alaska. Such states get "extra representation" in the electoral college because each state gets two electors for its two senators, regardless of its size. This is in addition to the number of electors the state gets to match its House membership (a number determined by the size of its population). But the more important special interest that many believe is favored by the electoral college is *big urban states* that have the most electoral votes. In these states, the swing vote is usually concentrated in the major cities, which therefore get extra attention—and promises—from the candidates. So the small rural states and the large urban states tend to unite against the middle to preserve the electoral college. . . .

One study of the effects in the 1960s and 1970s concluded that "the electoral college has countervailing biases, which result in a net advantage to large states, and a disadvantage to states with 4 to 14 electoral votes. The electoral college also favors inhabitants of the Far West and East, as well as central city and urban citizen-voters. In contrast, it discriminates against inhabitants of the Midwest, South, and Mountain States, as well as blacks and rural residents. . . ."

What, then, would be the alternative? Some suggest a simple popular vote election, in which all votes count equally, wherever they are cast. In that case, candidates would probably tend to use even more national television and reduce personal appearances, even in areas of heavy voter concentration where most such efforts are now focused. *Direct popular election,* as this proposal is called, would be much more democratic than our present system, in which all of a state's electoral votes go to the winner, even if he or she receives only one more popular vote than the loser.

From David V. Edwards, *The American Political Experience.* © 1985 by Prentice-Hall, Inc.

11. About electors' loyalties, the passage suggests that:
    - **A.** electors must vote for the candidate to whom they are pledged at the time of the November election.
    - **B.** there is no guarantee that electors will vote for the candidate to whom they are pledged.
    - **C.** Jimmy Carter nearly lost the election in 1976 because 29 electors pledged to him voted for Ford instead.
    - **D.** many electors bolt from their candidate after each election.

12. Elections in which the House of Representatives had to resolve a tie in the electoral vote occurred in:
    - **F.** 1800 and 1824.
    - **G.** 1800 and 1876.
    - **H.** 1800 and 1888.
    - **J.** 1888 and 1976.

GO ON TO THE NEXT PAGE.

3 3

13. According to the passage, the most important groups of voters in large, urban states are found in:

A. suburbs.
B. rural areas.
C. major cities.
D. special interest groups.

14. According to the passage, Congress can eliminate the electoral college by:

F. amending the Constitution.
G. issuing a congressional statute.
H. requesting an executive order.
J. holding a referendum on the issue.

15. According to the passage, concerns that the electoral college will not reflect the popular vote are usually voiced whenever:

A. campaigns appeal to special interests.
B. an election is held.
C. the popular vote is close.
D. candidates win in states with 4 to 14 electoral votes.

16. Which of the following statements would the author most likely believe is contradicted by the electoral college system?

F. All votes carry an equal amount of weight in deciding an election.
G. A limited number of people should be responsible for choosing the nation's leaders.
H. Some votes are more important to an election's outcome than others.
J. Electors face no legal penalty for switching candidates.

17. According to the passage, which of the following statements best represents the result of the 1976 presidential election?

A. A small shift in electoral votes would have caused the popular choice to lose in the electoral college.
B. The electoral vote overturned the popular vote.
C. The electoral college could not operate properly in a close election.
D. The election was decided in the House of Representatives due to the closeness of the popular vote.

18. According to the passage, the statement "the electoral college has countervailing biases" (lines 77–78) refers to the fact that:

I. large states have a net advantage.
II. states with between 4 and 14 electoral votes are at a disadvantage.
III. inhabitants of the Midwest, South, and Mountain States are favored over those in the Far West and East.

F. I only
G. II only
H. I and II only
J. I and III only

19. The main reason the author cites for his claim that the electoral college is undemocratic is that:

A. certain voters are prevented from voting.
B. votes for the losing candidate in each state are "lost" because of the winner-take-all provision.
C. the House of Representatives maintains complete control over the choice of candidates.
D. voters are more trustworthy than electors.

20. According to the passage, which group is most likely to be discriminated against by the electoral college system?

F. Big city residents
G. Suburban voters near large cities
H. Farmers
J. Youth

GO ON TO THE NEXT PAGE.

Passage III

Post-Impressionism refers to the several styles that followed Impressionism after 1885. Many painters who tried Impressionism early in their careers felt that solidity of form and composition had been sacrificed for the sake of fleeting impressions of light and color. Post-Impressionism is a confusing term because it refers to various reactions to Impressionism, rather than to a single style. The two dominant tendencies during the period were expressionistic and formalistic. Four painters whose works best exemplify Post-Impressionist attitudes were Paul Gauguin, Vincent van Gogh, Georges Seurat, and Paul Cézanne.

Gauguin and van Gogh brought to their work emotional intensity and a desire to make their inner thoughts and feelings visible. They used bold color contrasts, shapes with abruptly changing contours, and, in van Gogh's case, vigorous brushwork. . . .

Seurat and Cézanne were more interested in developing significant formal structure in their paintings. Both organized visual form in order to achieve a structured clarity of design. . . .

Seurat set out to systematize the optical color mixing of Impressionism and to create a more rigid organization with simplified forms. He called his method *divisionism,* but it is more popularly known as *pointillism.* With it, Seurat tried to develop and apply a "scientific" technique that would make the intuitive approach obsolete. He arrived at his method by studying the principles of color optics that were being discovered at the time. He applied his paint in tiny dots of color to achieve a richly colored surface through optical mixture. . . .

Of the many great painters working in France during the last 20 years of the nineteenth century, Cézanne had the most lasting effect on the course of painting. Because of this, he is referred to as the "father of modern art."

Cézanne, like Seurat, was more interested in the structural or formal aspects of painting than in its ability to convey emotions. He shared the Impressionists' practice of working directly from nature. But in his later works he achieved strong formal images. "My aim," he said, "was to make Impressionism into something solid and enduring like the art of the museums."

Cézanne and Seurat based their work on direct observation of nature, and both used visibly separate strokes of color to build their richly woven surfaces. Cézanne saw the planar surfaces of his subjects in terms of color modulation. He did not use light and shadow in a conventional way, but carefully developed relationships between adjoining strokes of color in order to show the solidity of form and receding space. His paintings are free of atmospheric color effects. Seurat's slow, highly demanding method was not popular among younger artists. Cézanne's looser strokes and his concept of a geometric substructure in nature and art offered a whole range of possibilities to those who studied his later paintings.

Cézanne also gave new importance to the compositional problems that the Impressionists had tended to ignore. Landscape was one of his main interests. He went beyond the reality of nature, organizing it in his own way to create a new reality on the picture surface. . . . He flattened space. . . . He simplified . . . houses and tree masses into almost geometric planes. . . .

Out of [younger painters'] research of Cézanne's analytical approach to painting would grow the new twentieth-century style of Cubism. . . .

With van Gogh, late nineteenth-century painting moved from an outer *impression* of what the eyes see to an inner *expression* of what the heart feels and the mind knows. . . .

From Impressionism, van Gogh learned the expressive potential of divided brushwork and pure color, but the style did not provide enough freedom to satisfy his desire to express his emotions. Without departing from "natural color," van Gogh intensified the surface of his paintings with textural brushwork that recorded each gesture of his hand and gave an overall rhythmic movement to the surface. . . .

[Gauguin's] memories of his childhood in Peru persuaded him that the art of ancient and non-Western cultures had spiritual strength lacking in the European art of his time. . . . Inspiration came from medieval European art and from the arts of ancient and non-European cultures that were little known and generally rejected as crude by European society. . . .

Gauguin's use of color had an important influence on twentieth-century painting. His views on color were prophetic. The subject, as he said, was only a pretext for symphonies of line and color.

21. According to the passage, van Gogh and Gauguin were alike in that both:

A. accepted the emotionalism of most artists.
B. attempted to express inner thoughts and feelings on canvas.
C. were, unlike most artists, rational and scientific in their approach.
D. were, like most artists, highly emotional people.

GO ON TO THE NEXT PAGE.

3 3

22. Which of the following characterizations is made by the passage?

F. Cézanne and Seurat wished to achieve a structural clarity of design.
G. Gauguin and Cézanne were interested in the structural or formal aspects of painting.
H. Van Gogh and Seurat were interested in recording inner feelings with broad, bold shapes.
J. Cézanne and van Gogh wished to systematize optical color mixing.

23. The details in the passage support which of the following statements?

A. The works of Gauguin and Seurat share similar tendencies.
B. The works of Gauguin and van Gogh on the one hand and Seurat and Cézanne on the other represent two major attitudes toward Impressionism.
C. The works of Gauguin and Seurat represent a reaction to the ancient and non-Western values of European art.
D. The works of Gauguin, van Gogh, Seurat, and Cézanne represent one characteristic of Post-Impressionism.

24. Of the following, who does the passage suggest was most interested in the geometric aspects of painting?

F. Impressionists
G. Expressionists
H. Gauguin
J. Cézanne

25. According to the passage, van Gogh was interested in using:

A. bold, simple shapes and brushwork to reflect the physical world.
B. pure color and rhythmic movements to depict accurately the outer world.
C. impressionistic techniques of textural surfaces to reflect reality.
D. textural brushwork and color to reflect his emotions.

26. *Pointillism* (line 26) refers to:

F. Cézanne's attempts to develop a "scientific" technique based on the principles of color optics.
G. Seurat's application of paint in tiny dots of color.
H. Seurat's attempts to build his work on the observation of nature.
J. the attempts of Cézanne and Seurat to use separate shades of color.

27. According to the passage, both Cézanne and Seurat used:

A. color for atmospheric effects.
B. direct observation of nature.
C. planar surfaces.
D. loose brush strokes.

28. According to the passage, both Seurat and Cézanne were particularly interested in:

F. formal aspects of painting.
G. expressing inner feelings.
H. Cubism.
J. pointillism.

29. The seventh paragraph (lines 46–59) implies that while both Cézanne and Seurat:

A. expressed inner emotions, they used demanding techniques.
B. used color conventionally, they had an equally lasting impact on painting.
C. used unconventional methods, Cézanne's technique was more popular with younger painters.
D. avoided showing the relationship between strokes of color, Cézanne's technique was more popular with younger painters.

30. Cézanne and Seurat were similar in that they both:

F. rejected the intuitive approach.
G. rejected divisionism.
H. applied paint in tiny dots of color.
J. used the intuitive approach.

GO ON TO THE NEXT PAGE.

Passage IV

Few ideas in modern science have proved as robust as the theory of the big bang. The theory holds that the universe exploded into being some 15 to 20 billion years ago and that as it expanded, gravity caused relatively dense regions of matter to coalesce into stars and galaxies. The faint microwave radiation that pervades the universe, theorists say, is the afterglow of the cataclysm, and the red shifts (displacements toward the red end of the spectrum) seen in light emanating from distant objects testify to the continuing expansion of the universe. Like the theory of evolution, the big-bang model has undergone modification and refinement, but it has resisted all serious challenges.

Nevertheless, ever since the theory won general acceptance about 20 years ago a few scientists have persistently attacked some of its fundamental assumptions. One group of critics argues that electromagnetic forces generated by plasma have been more important than gravity in shaping the universe; another asserts that red shifts are not necessarily a relic of the big bang's continuing outward thrust. These groups, although long relegated to "fringe" status by mainstream astrophysicists, have been invigorated of late by new converts and new findings.

The elder statesman of the plasma dissidents is Hannes Alfvén. . . . [Alfvén,] who won the Nobel prize for physics in 1970, believes interstellar space is filled with long filaments and other structures of plasma, that is, electrons and positively charged ions. The same electromagnetic forces that push plasmas into distinctive shapes in the laboratory, Alfvén says, caused this cosmic plasma to coalesce into galaxies, stars and planetary systems.

Alfvén believes the universe is expanding, but he speculates that the expansion is driven by the energy released when matter and antimatter meet and annihilate each other. He also believes the expansion is less dramatic than the big-bang theory proposes: a universe dominated by electromagnetic forces, he contends, could never have been less than one-tenth of its present diameter.

Critics have charged that Alfvén's cosmological ideas are vague and unsupported by observations. But Timothy E. Eastman of . . . the National Aeronautics and Space Administration [NASA] points out that laboratory experiments with ever more powerful plasma generators and measurements by space probes have confirmed many of Alfvén's predictions concerning plasmas within the solar system, at least. "There is a revolution brewing," Eastman remarks, "in applying this knowledge to astrophysics."

Workers at Los Alamos National Laboratory are already doing just that. . . . A team led by Anthony L. Peratt has created cosmological models based on recent findings about plasmas and on Alfvén's theories. One simulation shows how plasma filaments like those hypothesized by Alfvén could generate the uniform microwave background, the discovery of which was the clinching evidence for the big-bang model. Other simulations show how electromagnetic forces would help gravity to shape clouds of plasma into galaxies. . . .

Although some plasma dissidents are also red-shift dissidents, . . . Halton C. Arp of the Mount Wilson and Las Campanas Observatories . . . says he does not share Alfvén's "plasma approach." Arp is concerned less with proposing alternative models of the cosmos than with undermining the Hubble relation between red shift and distance, which Arp has called the "single, frail assumption on which so much of modern astronomy and cosmology is built." Named for the American astronomer Edwin P. Hubble, . . . the Hubble relation implies that objects outside our galaxy are receding from the earth at speeds proportional to their distance.

Arp says he has observed many objects with red shifts that do not conform to the Hubble relation. He maintains that quasars, for example, whose large red shifts suggest they are the most distant objects in the universe, are actually no more distant than galaxies and are probably offshoots of them. The images of most quasars, Arp points out, appear near galaxies with much smaller red shifts; moreover, luminous material appears to connect certain quasars with galaxies. Arp contends that because it is unlikely these supposedly connected objects are moving at greatly different speeds, their red shifts—and possibly all red shifts—probably result from something other than recessional velocity.

Most astronomers have dismissed Arp's observations as coincidences that statistically are not really surprising.

31. According to the passage, questions have been raised concerning the:

A. existence of electromagnetic fields.
B. decision to award a Nobel prize for physics to Hannes Alfvén.
C. dimensions of positively charged ions.
D. validity of the basic astrophysical theories.

32. The passage asserts that the big-bang theory "has resisted all serious challenges" (line 13) but also states that "a few scientists have persistently attacked some of its fundamental assumptions" (lines 15–17). Is the passage logically consistent?

F. Yes, because alternatives to the big-bang theory still lack the conclusive evidence to win wide acceptance.
G. Yes, because professional writers invariably know how to avoid inconsistency in logic.
H. No, because none of the theories mentioned in the passage offers a serious challenge to the big-bang theory.
J. No, because persistent criticism of any theory must obviously invalidate its fundamental assumptions.

GO ON TO THE NEXT PAGE.

3 3

33. According to the big-bang theory, the universe's expansion was a result of:

A. a coalescence of cosmic plasmas into galaxies.
B. an attraction of cosmic objects outside of the known galaxies.
C. an enormously powerful explosion.
D. an increased occurrence of red shift.

34. What does the passage suggest about Alfvén's view of the universe?

F. He thinks that it expands because of the big bang.
G. He considers expansion a result of matter-antimatter annihilation.
H. He believes that the expansion is more rapid than previously thought.
J. He believes that unidentified forces influence the expansion.

35. The expression *red shift* means that:

A. the light reaching an observer has moved away from the red end of the spectrum.
B. a star moves from its yellow to its red phase.
C. the light reaching an observer has moved toward the red end of the spectrum.
D. a star motion is detected with the help of a red filter.

36. The main idea of the third paragraph (lines 25–33) is that electromagnetic forces:

F. may have shaped the galaxies.
G. can be formed into distinctive shapes in the laboratory.
H. contain positive ions and lengthy filaments.
J. cannot be generated by cosmic plasmas.

37. The passage includes a statement that quasars "are actually no more distant than galaxies" (line 78). Based on the details in the passage, this information is best described as:

A. a universally accepted fact based on the obvious link between quasars and galaxies.
B. an outdated theory proven false by Arp's research on red shift.
C. a recent theory proven false by the discovery of the Hubble relation.
D. a disputed theory based on an apparent connection between quasars and galaxies.

38. Arp doubts the correctness of the Hubble relation because:

F. some plasma dissidents are also red-shift dissidents.
G. Arp's observational evidence does not conform with this relation.
H. it contradicts the plasma approach.
J. it does not conform with the big-bang theory.

39. Eastman remarked that "there is a revolution brewing in applying [a new] knowledge to astrophysics" (lines 49–51) because:

A. the big-bang theory has become obsolete.
B. laboratory experiments confirmed many of Alfvén's predictions.
C. astrophysics is a more speculative science than astronomy.
D. more powerful plasma generators had been constructed.

40. Who originally proposed the relation between distance and red shift?

F. Alfvén
G. Peratt
H. Arp
J. Hubble

END OF TEST 3

STOP! DO NOT TURN THE PAGE UNTIL TOLD TO DO SO.

4 ○ ○ ○ ○ ○ ○ ○ ○ ○ 4

SCIENCE REASONING TEST

35 Minutes—40 Questions

DIRECTIONS: There are seven passages in this test. Each passage is followed by several questions. After reading a passage, choose the best answer to each question and blacken the corresponding oval on your answer sheet. You may refer to the passages as often as necessary.

Passage I

Food can be sterilized by exposure to intense gamma radiation. The graphs below show the storage period, or shelf life, of normal foods (dark bars) and the storage period of irradiated foods (clear bars). Storage was at 25° C to 30° C unless otherwise noted. The radiation dosage needed to produce the extended storage period is shown as a number of kilorads (kr). Onions and potatoes are vegetables; mangoes and bananas are fruits; and shrimp, Bombay duck, and pomfret are seafood.

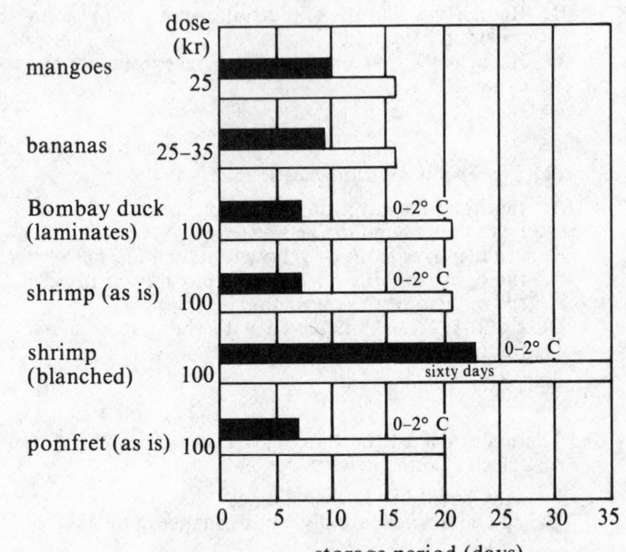

Graphs adapted from D. Allen Bromley, "Neutrons in Science and Technology." © 1983 by the American Institute of Physics.

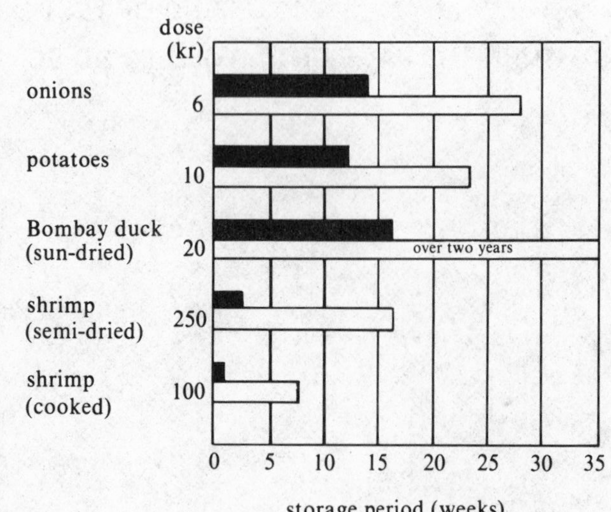

1. According to the graphs, which food shows the greatest absolute increase in storage period due to irradiation?
   A. Onions
   B. Bombay duck (sun-dried)
   C. Shrimp (semi-dried)
   D. Bananas

2. Based only on the information presented in the graphs, a pomfret has storage properties most like:
   F. onions.
   G. shrimp (cooked).
   H. bananas.
   J. shrimp (as is).

8939F

GO ON TO THE NEXT PAGE.

4 ○ ○ ○ ○ ○ ○ ○ ○ ○ 4

3. Based on the graphs, the storage time of a peach irradiated at 30 kr and stored at 25°–30° C would be predicted to be:
   - **A.** less than 10 days.
   - **B.** between 10 and 20 days.
   - **C.** between 20 and 40 days.
   - **D.** between 40 and 60 days.

4. When comparing vegetables (onions, potatoes) with fruits (mangoes, bananas), which of the following conclusions can be drawn about storage time and dosage? (Note: Assume that neither the fruits nor vegetables have been dried.)
   - **F.** Storage time for vegetables is greater, even at reduced dosage.
   - **G.** Fruits have shorter storage times, due to higher dosage.
   - **H.** As the dosage to fruits and vegetables increases, the storage time increases.
   - **J.** As the dosage to fruits and vegetables increases, the storage time decreases.

5. Which of the following sequences of foods listed in the graphs correctly orders the unirradiated food, from shortest storage period to longest storage period?
   - **A.** Fruits, vegetables, seafood (as is)
   - **B.** Vegetables, fruits, seafood (as is)
   - **C.** Seafood (as is), vegetables, fruits
   - **D.** Seafood (as is), fruits, vegetables

Passage II

Cosmic radiation (electromagnetic) of all wavelengths falls on Earth's atmosphere. Radiation at some wavelengths is absorbed by thin gases 100 kilometers or more above Earth's surface. At other wavelengths, radiation penetrates deeper into the atmosphere before being totally absorbed. At still other wavelengths, radiation passes completely through the atmosphere to the ground. The figure below shows the height above Earth's surface to which cosmic radiation of different wavelengths can penetrate before being totally absorbed. The figure also shows the heights at which balloons, rockets, and satellites can be used.

Figure adapted from Hannes Alfvén, "The Plasma Universe." ©1986 by the American Institute of Physics.

6. At about what height is radiation of wavelength 10^{-9} centimeter completely absorbed?
   - **F.** 22 kilometers
   - **G.** 38 kilometers
   - **H.** 80 kilometers
   - **J.** 100 kilometers

7. Which of the following types of cosmic radiation are completely absorbed in the atmosphere at the highest altitude?
   - **A.** γ rays and X rays
   - **B.** X rays and uv
   - **C.** Visible and radio
   - **D.** Visible and infrared

8. Which of the following types of cosmic radiation can each be measured fully from a satellite, but not from a rocket?
   - **F.** X rays and uv
   - **G.** X rays, uv, and infrared
   - **H.** Visible and infrared
   - **J.** Visible, infrared, and radio

9. Which of the following types of electromagnetic radiation is LEAST absorbed by Earth's atmosphere?
   - **A.** γ rays
   - **B.** X rays
   - **C.** Visible
   - **D.** uv

10. To observe the full radio spectrum of cosmic radiation, one could locate a receiver at:
    - **F.** ground level.
    - **G.** an altitude of 25 kilometers.
    - **H.** an altitude of 35 kilometers.
    - **J.** an altitude of 45 kilometers.

GO ON TO THE NEXT PAGE.

4 ○ ○ ○ ○ ○ ○ ○ ○ 4

Passage III

Many aquatic organisms are able to survive only within a narrow range of environmental conditions. By examining fossil assemblages, with knowledge of the conditions required by the various organisms present, geologists can deduce ancient environmental conditions.

Study 1

Geologists compared distributions of modern aquatic organisms relative to 4 environmental factors: salinity, water clarity, substrate (bottom) firmness, and water depth. Their observations are summarized in Table 1. Organisms not listed under an environmental factor in the table were not tested for tolerance of that factor.

Study 2

Geologists examined the fossils in 3 ancient sedimentary rock formations. Formation A contained green algae, corals, and snails. Formation B contained barnacles, clams, oysters, and snails. Formation C contained snails, clams, and hyalosponges.

Study 3

Geologists discovered a sequence of rock units that appeared to represent a drop in sea level. They looked for evidence to support this in the fossil assemblages in the rocks. The lowest rock unit (Formation D) was a moderately deep, clear, "normal marine" water deposit. Over this was a shallow, brackish water deposit (Formation E). Topping the sequence was a shallow, muddy, freshwater deposit (Formation F).

Table 1

Salinity	"normal marine"	brackish	freshwater
Type of organism	corals, snails	barnacles, snails	snails

Water clarity	clear	mildly turbid	muddy
Type of organism	corals, snails, clams, green algae	oysters, clams, snails	clams

Substrate firmness	hard	intermediate	soft
Type of organism	green algae, corals	green algae	clams

Water depth	shallow	moderate	deep
Type of organism	green algae, corals, snails	corals, snails, clams	hyalosponges, snails, clams

11. According to the observations of Studies 1 and 2, Formation A could represent a:

A. freshwater lake deposit.
B. mudflat deposit.
C. shallow, muddy ocean deposit.
D. shallow, clear ocean deposit.

12. On the basis of the observations in Study 1, which of the following organisms probably burrows into the bottom sediments?

F. Barnacles
G. Oysters
H. Snails
J. Clams

13. Which of the following generalizations about aquatic organisms is supported by the results of the studies?

A. Water clarity has little effect on their distribution.
B. Some are more tolerant of environmental variations than others.
C. They generally require similar environments in order to survive.
D. Environmental conditions have little to do with their distribution.

GO ON TO THE NEXT PAGE.

4 ○ ○ ○ ○ ○ ○ ○ ○ 4

14. Which of the following graphs best represents the differences in water clarity between Formations A, B, and C ?

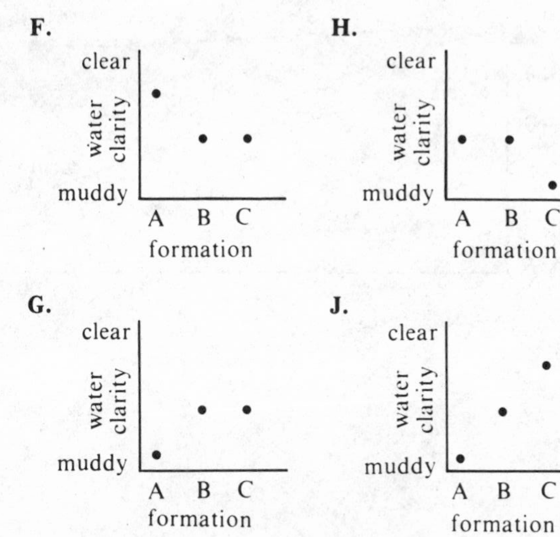

15. On the basis of the results of Study 1, which of the following organisms is the most tolerant of variations in water clarity?

A. Corals
B. Green algae
C. Clams
D. Snails

16. When the geologists examined the fossil assemblage in Formation E of Study 3, they found NO corals. Which of the following statements might account for this?

F. The water was of "normal marine" salinity.
G. The water was fairly shallow at that time.
H. The water was too muddy for their survival.
J. The substrate was too firm in the area of deposition.

GO ON TO THE NEXT PAGE.

4 ○ ○ ○ ○ ○ ○ ○ ○ ○ 4

Passage IV

Beef cattle are susceptible to bacterial infections that can significantly affect their value at the slaughterhouse. Cattle farmers routinely administer antibiotics in the feed to prevent these infections. Since the antibiotic is excreted in the feces, investigators studied the effects of a common antibiotic on the local environment.

Sixty (60) cattle were randomly assigned to 2 groups of 30 cattle each. Group T was treated with an antibiotic while Group C received a placebo. After 7 days of treatment, the feces of each group were collected, homogenized, and shaped into uniform "pats." The pats were placed at regular intervals in a field. Individual pats were then collected, and corresponding soil samples were taken at 20-day intervals for the first 100 days. The weight of each pat was measured to determine the rate of decomposition of Group T and Group C feces (Figure 1). The number and types of organisms present were determined in the pats and the soil samples (Table 1).

At the end of the experiment, the grass around the Group T pats was sparse and brown. The grass around the Group C pats was lush and green.

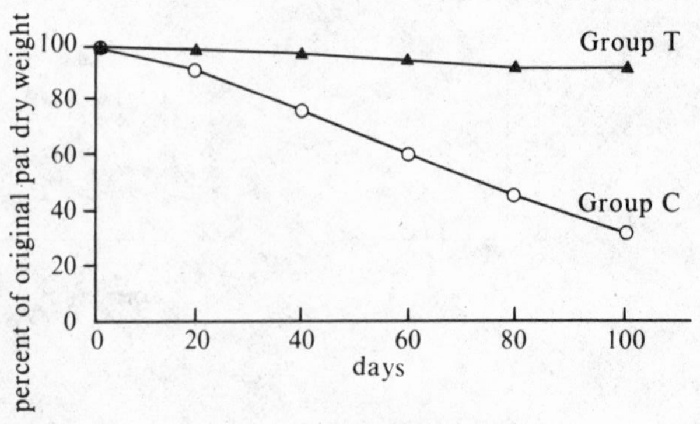

Figure 1

Table 1

Time (days)	Group	Bacteria C	Bacteria T	Fungi C	Fungi T	Insects C	Insects T	Earthworms C	Earthworms T
20		5,600	395	4,866	3,999	513	93	1	1
40		5,300	417	4,915	4,100	461	89	9	8
60		5,300	367	4,898	3,879	297	112	8	8
80		5,400	299	4,851	3,734	156	96	15	40
100		5,550	359	4,955	3,245	780	89	58	60

Number of organisms (per 1,000 cm^3 of soil)

17. Which of the following generalizations best fits the pat decomposition data in Figure 1?
   - **A.** Group T pats decomposed faster than Group C pats.
   - **B.** Group C pats decomposed faster than Group T pats.
   - **C.** Group T and Group C pats decomposed at the same rate.
   - **D.** Group T pats decomposed rapidly, but Group C pats did not decompose appreciably.

18. In order to best determine the cause of grass death in this experiment, one should examine the effects of:
   - **F.** an antibiotic on grass.
   - **G.** an insecticide on grass.
   - **H.** a bactericide on fungi.
   - **J.** a fungicide on earthworms.

19. Bacteria are consumed during normal feeding activity by aquatic insects. Some bacteria live in the digestive tract and aid in digestive processes. On the basis of the experimental results, runoff from the Group T pats would be likely to cause the insect population density in a nearby stream to:
   - **A.** decrease, because the antibiotic decreases the survival of bacteria.
   - **B.** decrease, because the antibiotic increases the survival of bacteria.
   - **C.** increase, because the antibiotic decreases the survival of bacteria.
   - **D.** increase, because the antibiotic increases the survival of bacteria.

20. What conclusion could be appropriately drawn from the decomposition data in Figure 1?
   - **F.** Without soil bacteria, fecal pats do not decompose.
   - **G.** Without earthworms, fecal pats do not decompose.
   - **H.** Without soil bacteria, insects cannot disrupt the fecal pats.
   - **J.** The presence of the antibiotic reduces the decomposition of fecal pats.

GO ON TO THE NEXT PAGE.

4 ○ ○ ○ ○ ○ ○ ○ ○ ○ 4

21. Suppose the investigators treated a group of cattle with a lower level of antibiotic than used in the original test group. As compared to the original test group, this new group's rate of pat decomposition would probably be:

A. greater, because less antibiotic will increase bacterial survival.
B. greater, because less antibiotic will decrease bacterial survival.
C. less, because less antibiotic will increase bacterial survival.
D. less, because less antibiotic will decrease bacterial survival.

22. The Group T pats had the greatest effect on the numbers of:

F. bacteria.
G. fungi.
H. insects.
J. earthworms.

GO ON TO THE NEXT PAGE.

4 ○ ○ ○ ○ ○ ○ ○ ○ ○ 4

Passage V

The following hypotheses present two views about how life first originated.

Hypothesis 1

Stanley Miller showed that organic molecules form spontaneously when energy is applied to a gas mixture thought to comprise the early atmosphere. These organic molecules could have then randomly collided and reacted over time in the primitive ocean "soup" to form macromolecules. These macromolecules could have then served as the building blocks to form such structures as proteins and DNA.

Other experiments have shown that protein-coated droplets can form in solutions containing protein. These droplets have been shown to be capable of absorbing other organic molecules, growing, and even dividing. Many of these early droplets probably formed in the "soup"; some undoubtedly contained DNA. Since DNA can replicate itself, the DNA could have been replicated and reproduced when the protein droplet divided. Since DNA is the basic unit of life today, the DNA in these early "cells" must have somehow provided these droplets with some form of advantage over the droplets without the DNA. Gradually, these droplets evolved into the cells we know today.

Hypothesis 2

The first organic molecules probably did form as shown by Stanley Miller; however, not enough time has elapsed since these molecules first appeared for life to have randomly formed in the "soup." Experiments have shown that organic molecules concentrate on the surfaces of clay particles like those found in the early oceans. This concentration would increase the chances that these molecules would align in such a way as to produce proteins and DNA. Furthermore, clay crystals have also been shown to be able to replicate themselves and to capture solar energy and transmit it to organic molecules attached to their surfaces. The clay could have thus performed the roles of replication and photosynthesis in an early form of life.

This hypothesis is further supported by the fact that when amino acids form in a "soup," mirror images of amino acids—called D and L amino acids—form. However, only L amino acids are found on clay surfaces, and only L amino acids are found in the proteins of modern organisms.

23. Hypothesis 2 indicates that there was NOT enough of which of the following essential ingredients in order for life to have appeared as described by Hypothesis 1 ?

A. Energy
B. Water
C. Organic matter
D. Time

24. Which of the following diagrams best illustrates the early "cells" described in Hypothesis 1 ?

F.

DNA
|
amino acid – amino acid – amino acid
|
water

G.

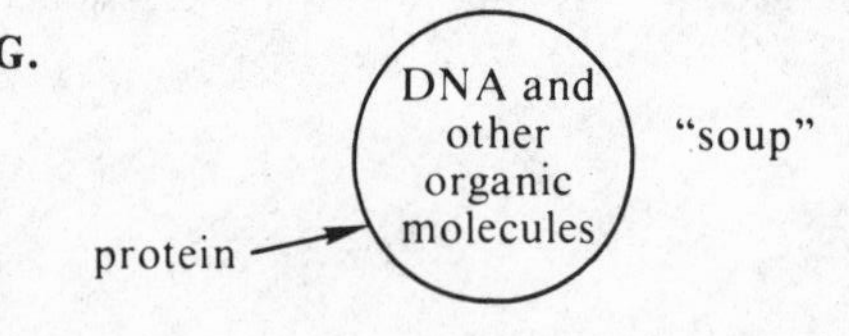

H.

J.

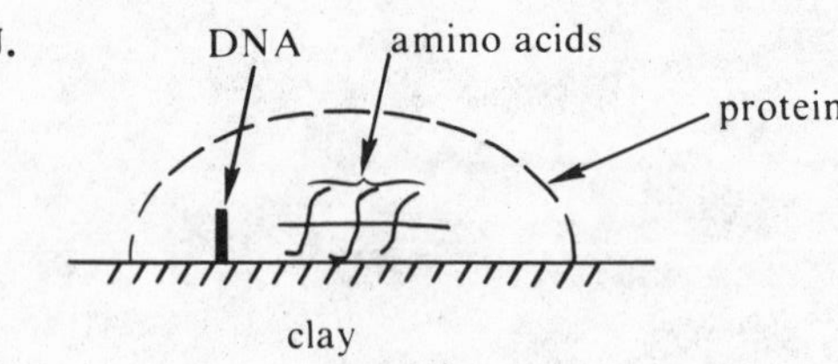

25. In Hypothesis 1, the talk about droplets containing DNA having "some form of advantage" over droplets without DNA is describing a primitive form of:

A. photosynthesis.
B. diffusion.
C. osmosis.
D. evolution.

GO ON TO THE NEXT PAGE.

4 ○ ○ ○ ○ ○ ○ ○ ○ ○ 4

26. In defending Hypothesis 1, which of the following arguments might a supporter of that hypothesis present as an explanation for the fact that only L amino acids are found in modern organisms?

F. Clay crystals contain structures that prevent D amino acids from attaching to them.
G. Organisms containing L amino acids were somehow better adapted to life in the primitive oceans.
H. Cells containing D amino acids evolved faster than those containing L amino acids.
J. Organisms containing D amino acids exist but simply have not been discovered by scientists yet.

27. A supporter of Hypothesis 2 would view the occasional imperfect replication of clay crystals as being analogous to:

A. photosynthesis.
B. mutation.
C. protein synthesis.
D. digestion.

28. Which of the following discoveries would best support Hypothesis 1 ?

F. Bacteria found in oceans
G. Cell membranes found to be crystalline in nature
H. Cells found in clay deposits of ocean trenches
J. Cells created from a solution of organic molecules

29. A supporter of Hypothesis 2 assumes that Hypothesis 2 accurately describes the ability of clay to capture solar energy. To provide supporting evidence for the hypothesis that clay was an early forerunner of chloroplasts, the supporter would need to verify that:

A. chloroplasts can photosynthesize inside of protein droplets.
B. chloroplasts replicate at the same temperature as clay crystals do.
C. the mechanisms used to absorb solar energy and the wavelengths absorbed by chloroplasts are similar to those used and absorbed by clay.
D. the DNA in the chloroplasts has the same crystalline structure as clay.

GO ON TO THE NEXT PAGE.

4 ○ ○ ○ ○ ○ ○ ○ ○ ○ 4

Passage VI

The law of conservation of mass states that, for a chemical reaction, the sum of the masses of the reactants must equal the sum of the masses of the products.

The precise measurements of mass necessary to verify this law may be affected by several experimental difficulties. If the sample is hot, rising air currents will push up on it, making the measurements inaccurate. Also, water in a sample can affect the measurements of its mass. Water is often used to dissolve chemicals before use, so after a reaction is completed, this water must be removed. To do so, the sample is alternately heated and weighed until a constant mass is obtained (all water is evaporated).

The following experiment was performed in an attempt to verify the law of conservation of mass. An aqueous (water) solution containing 5 grams of potassium chromate was added to a beaker containing an aqueous solution of 10 grams of lead(II) nitrate. A yellow precipitate (solid) formed and settled to the bottom of the beaker. Next, the liquid was filtered off into another beaker. Finally, the contents of both beakers were heated gently until all moisture had evaporated and a constant mass was achieved. A mass of 8.3 grams was obtained for the yellow solid.

30. After the liquid was separated from the yellow precipitate, all of the water was removed from each sample. The yellow precipitate had a mass of 8.3 grams. What was the mass of the substance that remained from the liquid portion? (Note: Assume that no experimental error occurred.)

F. 5 grams
G. 6.7 grams
H. 8.3 grams
J. 10 grams

31. In a further attempt to demonstrate the law of conservation of mass, a different reaction was used. In this reaction, one of the products was gaseous. Would the procedure described in the passage need to be modified?

A. Yes, because the gas would have to be driven off before weighing the products.
B. Yes, because the gas would have to be captured and the mass of the gas found.
C. No, since the gas's lack of mass would not cause its production to affect the demonstration.
D. No, since the gas would completely dissolve in the water and the final mass would demonstrate conservation of mass.

32. Which of the following would be expected of all experiments designed to verify the law of conservation of mass?

F. The total mass of the products minus the total mass of the reactants must equal zero.
G. A yellow precipitate must form during the reaction.
H. Any water produced by the reaction must be removed before final weights are determined.
J. The chemical reactions must take place in aqueous solutions.

33. The beaker containing the yellow precipitate was heated, cooled, and weighed. After a second heating and cooling to room temperature, the mass of the beaker and the yellow precipitate was smaller than that found in the first weighing. The reason for this is most likely that:

A. steam was given off in the heating process.
B. more lead(II) nitrate precipitated out of the solution.
C. the beaker did not get as hot the second time, so the air currents had less of an impact.
D. the lead(II) ions evaporated from the solution.

GO ON TO THE NEXT PAGE.

34. Suppose a chemist has heated, cooled, and weighed 3 times a beaker containing a product. The first time the chemist weighed the beaker and product, it had a mass of 84.1 grams. The second time, it had a mass of 83.9 grams. The third time, it had a mass of 83.6 grams. In order to ensure that an accurate mass value for the product is obtained, the chemist should:

F. find the arithmetic average of the 3 weighings and record that as the mass of the beaker and product.
G. record 83.6 grams as the mass of the beaker and 83.9 grams as the mass of the product.
H. continue to reheat, cool, and weigh the beaker until a constant weight results.
J. record the mass of the beaker and product as 83.6 grams.

35. While attempting to filter off the liquid, an experimenter allowed some of the yellow precipitate to be transferred to the second beaker. When the experiment was completed, could the results still be used to demonstrate the law of conservation of mass?

A. Yes, because the remaining solids after drying would still total the weight of the original reactants.
B. Yes, because further heating would cause the yellow precipitate to dissolve in the liquid.
C. No, because there would be too much water present to get an accurate weight for the products.
D. No, because the yellow precipitate would continue to react if it were not separated from the liquid.

GO ON TO THE NEXT PAGE.

4 ○ ○ ○ ○ ○ ○ ○ ○ ○ 4

Passage VII

A minimum amount of energy must be available to the reactants of a chemical reaction before that reaction can occur. This minimum energy is known as the *activation energy* of the reaction. A reaction is accompanied by either the net absorption or the net release of energy because the bonds found in the reactants and products differ in potential energy. The diagrams below illustrate the changes in potential energy of 2 different reactions.

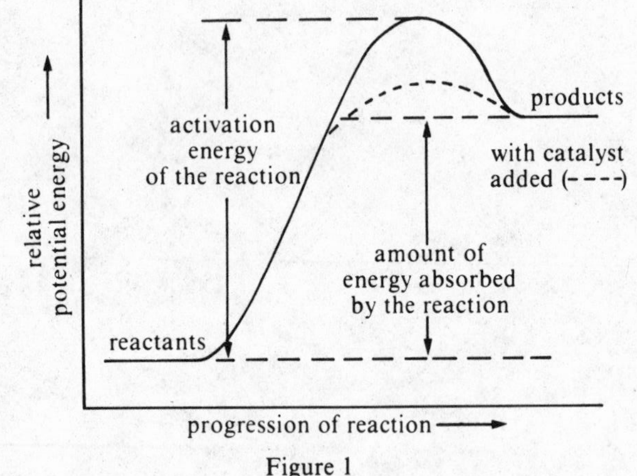

Figure 1

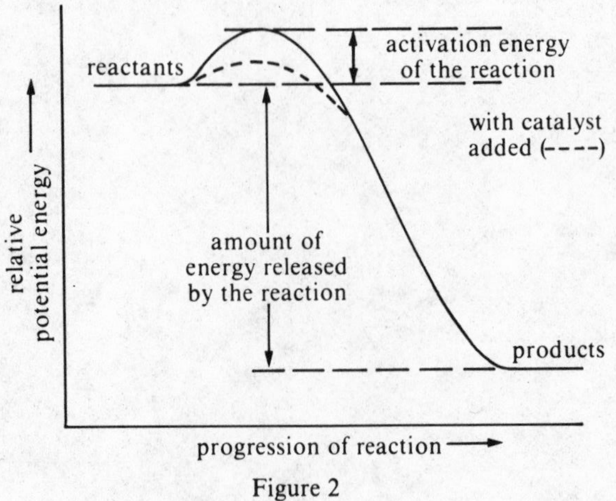

Figure 2

36. The following potential energy diagram is hypothesized for a third reaction.

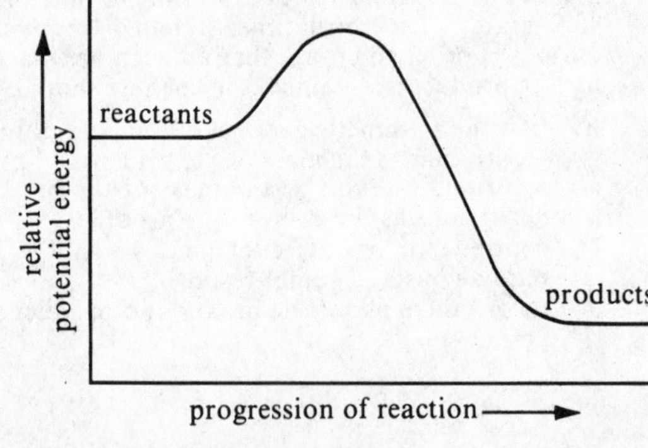

On the basis of this diagram, which of the following predictions can one make about this reaction?

F. The reaction will occur spontaneously.
G. Energy will be released as products are formed.
H. The reaction will not occur without a catalyst being present.
J. Once this reaction starts, it will occur very quickly.

37. On the basis of the information presented in Figures 1 and 2, one can conclude that a catalyst changes a reaction by:

A. increasing the potential energy of the reactants of the reaction.
B. enabling the reaction to occur at a lower energy of activation.
C. lengthening the amount of time needed before the reaction will occur.
D. increasing the amount of product produced by the reaction at equilibrium.

38. Which of the following factors is used to predict whether a chemical reaction absorbs energy or releases energy?

F. The amount of reaction time needed to form products from reactants
G. The presence of a catalyst in the chemical system
H. The amount of product formed during the reaction
J. The relative potential energies of the reactants and products

GO ON TO THE NEXT PAGE.

4 ○ ○ ○ ○ ○ ○ ○ ○ ○ 4

39. In order to calculate the difference between the potential energy of the reactants and the potential energy of the products, a researcher would subtract the:

A. lowest potential energy point on the diagram from the highest potential energy point.
B. potential energy of the product from the lowest potential energy point on the diagram.
C. potential energy of the reactant from the potential energy of the product.
D. potential energy of the reactant from a higher potential energy point on the diagram.

40. In the reaction illustrated in Figure 2, how is the change in the net energy of the reaction mixture related to the potential energies of the products and the reactants?

F. The amount of energy absorbed is twice the potential energy of the products and half of the potential energy of the reactants.
G. The amount of energy absorbed is greater than the potential energies of either the products or the reactants.
H. The amount of energy released is equal to the total potential energies of both the products and the reactants.
J. The amount of energy released is equal to the difference between the potential energies of the products and the reactants.

END OF TEST 4

STOP! DO NOT RETURN TO ANY OTHER TEST.

1. The opening sentence of this essay asks the reader two questions. Looking at the questions, which are joined in one sentence using the conjunction *or,* should help you pick the verb form that works best here. The first question begins with "have you ever found." The verb phrase in the second question should be consistent with the first. To focus on the second question, try adding the words *have you ever* after *or.* Which response agrees best with that addition:

Have you ever **discovered** a great restaurant (A)?

Have you ever **discovering** a great restaurant (B)?

Have you ever **discover** a great restaurant (C)?

Have you ever **had discovered** a great restaurant (D)?

If you're still not sure, turn the question into a statement. Switch the order of the subject and verb from *have you* to *you have.* Try the choices again. (You have *discovered,* you have *discovering,* etc.)

2. The key to solving the problem in this sentence is the colon. What does a colon tell you? What kind of relationship does it imply between the information that comes before and after it?

If you've ever watched the Academy Awards ceremonies on TV, you've undoubtedly seen that climactic moment when an actor or actress opens the envelope to reveal the winner in a certain category.

Think of the colon as the star making the presentation. Think of what comes after the colon as that envelope. What should it contain? The slip of paper inside won't list the contenders who didn't win. It won't include other information about the movie. It **will** have the information that the presenter promised to deliver: the winner.

In this passage, the writer is saying, "And now, the word for that kind of lucky accident," and handing the envelope to the colon. What should be inside?

3. What is the function of the first word in this sentence? What kind of transition does each answer choice provide from the first sentence of this paragraph to the second? What's the gist of those two sentences? What is the relationship between them? Which word or phrase expresses that relationship best?

In the first sentence, the writer tells us that a number of scientific discoveries were the result of serendipity. In the second sentence, we learn that sugar substitutes were discovered as a result of serendipity. How should the writer lead the reader smoothly from the first idea to the second?

What does *however* (A) imply about the relationship between the two sentences? What does *rather* (D) imply? Is there a contradiction between what the two sentences are saying? Is there a cause-and-effect relationship, as *thus* (C) suggests? What does *for example* (B) indicate? Is the writer giving an example of something mentioned in the first sentence of the paragraph?

4. What is the writer saying about the popularity of sugar substitutes? What is the clearest, most concise way to say it, given the choices here?

What does it mean to say that sugar substitutes are **currently** popular? That they're popular **today?** That they're popular **now?** F, H, and J combine two of these words to describe the popularity of sugar substitutes. Is the expression **currently popular** unclear or confusing to a reader without a word like *today* or *now?* Could the writer make the meaning clear simply by saying *popular today,* as G suggests?

5. What is the best way to stress serendipitous scientific discoveries?

Response A suggests "relating an anecdote about a lucky discovery." What does *lucky* imply here? Are there currently any such anecdotes in the essay? Is an anecdote an effective way to reinforce a discussion of accidental discoveries?

The writer tells us that penicillin was discovered when a bacterial parasite was accidentally contaminated. Would a list of "the most common bacterial parasites" (B) strengthen the discussion of accidental discoveries in general?

What is the relationship of the scientific method to accidental discoveries? How would outlining that method (C) emphasize those discoveries? What bearing do medical laboratory procedures (D) have on accidental discoveries?

Remember: You're being asked to **emphasize** accidental discoveries, not contrast them with systematic scientific methods.

6. They're back: *who* and its evil twin, *whom.*

What's the difference between the two? Which one is used as a subject? In other words, which one can act? Which is the object, or the one that's acted upon?

Which one is called for in this sentence?

G and J propose putting a comma after *scientist.* Notice the other comma in this sentence. If you read the sentence aloud, what is the effect of pausing after both *scientist* and *Priestley?* Does it clarify the writer's meaning? Does it make the sentence more difficult to understand?

7. What's the difference between expressions like *best* and *the best* and *most* and *the more?* The first two are generally associated with superior quality; the second two with greater quantity or degree. Which kind of expression fits the writer's purpose better?

Is the passage talking about the **number** of benefits Priestley got from serendipity, compared to other scientists, or making an evaluation of quality? How many examples of Priestley's lucky accidents are we given? How many examples of similar discoveries by other individual scientists?

Is benefiting an action that can be done poorly or well, like playing the bagpipes? Or is it a word like *need?* Can you **need** best—can you be the best at **needing?** You might be the best when it comes to expressing that need (the best at begging, wheedling, clamoring, etc.), but that's not the same thing. Neither is it the same thing as needing the most. Even if the writer were trying to get at some idea of quality here, would it make sense to say that Priestley benefited "best" with his discoveries of soda water and pencil erasers after discussing the discovery of an important substance like penicillin?

8. What's happening in this sentence—and in the mysterious laboratory of that happy-go-lucky bumbler, Joseph Priestley?

The passage states that Priestley was dissolving carbon dioxide in water "and began to bubble." What began to bubble? Find the answer choice that makes it clearest.

In response F, exactly what, or who, is bubbling? G and H suggest using *which.* What is the difference between *and which* (G) and *which* (H) in this sentence? Does one of them seem clearer than the other? Does the word *and* suggest to a reader that the writer is talking about more than one property of the water?

What began to bubble? "It," says J. But look at the comma before *it.* What kind of clause is "it began to bubble"? Can it be a complete sentence by itself? Look at the clause before the comma. Can it be a complete sentence by itself? Did you answer "no" to either of the last two questions? Is the comma appropriate here?

9. Should the two parts of this sentence be joined by *and?* Did the water taste "good"—or "well"?

What's the difference between *good* and *well?* If a friend asks you how you feel, you might say either "I feel good" or "I feel well." However, the two words are far from interchangeable.

Good is an adjective. It describes or limits a noun or a pronoun. (She is a *good* dancer.)

Well is a trickier animal to pin down. It can be an adverb—a word that describes or limits a verb, another adverb, an adjective, or a sentence. "She dances well" uses *well* as an adverb to describe **how** she dances. It can also be an adjective when, for instance, it means the opposite of *ill* ("I feel well"). However, the writer who is boasting about her sensitive fingers might say "I feel well" and use it as an adverb. We will ignore her for the moment.

If you're complimenting a friend on his new snakeskin cowboy boots, you should say, "Those boots look **good** on you." If you say, "Those boots look **well** on you," you're either commenting on the boots' healthful appearance or on their ability to look.

So. Did Priestley's bubbly brew taste **good** or **well?**

Should the two parts of this sentence be connected by *and?* Look at the clause before the comma, then the one after. Are they both independent, or is one dependent? Can both stand alone as sentences, or only one of them? In which case is it appropriate to connect the clauses with a comma? In which case do you need a conjunction like *and* with the comma?

10. Before answering this question, read the sentence following this one, if you haven't already. In Paragraph 3, the writer explains two of Priestley's serendipitous discoveries. The underlined word or phrase should provide a clear, logical transition between the two.

What do *thus* (G) and *consequently* (H) suggest about the relationship between the two discoveries? Is either word an accurate reflection of that relationship? Remember that *consequently* doesn't mean the same as *subsequently. Consequently* means roughly "as a consequence" or "as a result." Does the passage support the idea that Priestley's discovery during the oil of vitriol experiment **resulted** from discovering soda water?

Is it clear to the reader exactly which serendipitous discovery *this* (J) refers to? Does *another* (F) make it clear which discovery is referred to? Is the writer introducing an additional example of a serendipitous discovery or adding information about Priestley's first discovery?

11. After reading this paragraph, would you say that Priestley "finally became the inventor of seltzer" (A)? What does *finally* imply? How **did** Priestley become the inventor of seltzer? Was it something he set out to do and eventually accomplished after a period of time?

We know that Priestley benefited from some lucky accidents, but where does the writer say that Priestley "based his life on luck" (B)? From what you've learned about Priestley's experiments, would you conclude that he didn't believe in cause and effect? If a scientist didn't believe in cause and effect, do you think he'd bother to conduct experiments at all? Since the writer focuses on Priestley's serendipitous accidents, should the reader assume that Priestley was **never** systematic (C)? Is that what the writer is trying to convey? Is that spelled out in this paragraph?

Did Priestley have more than one serendipitous occurrence in his career (D)? Did he take advantage of (that is, did he make use of) the results of his accidents?

12. Choosing the best verb form here can seem like a knotty problem. First, you must decide whether it should agree with the singular *another* or the plural *discoveries.* Then you need to pick the tense that best expresses the writer's point about the usefulness of Priestley's invention.

How many discoveries is the writer talking about in this sentence? One? More than one? Is the key word here *discoveries?* Or *another?*

What is the writer saying about the usefulness of the eraser? Is the eraser still in use today? Or is it a thing of the past, like pet rocks and hoop skirts? Which answer choice suggests that the eraser is obsolete? Which suggests that it continues to be used?

13. According to the passage, what did Priestley apply to the paper? Was it one item, or more than one? Is it a singular noun that should be replaced by a singular pronoun such as *it* (D)? Or is it a plural noun that should be replaced by a plural pronoun such as *them* (A, B, C)? Since only one of the responses offers a singular pronoun, you might solve the pronoun problem before worrying about which preposition best describes the interaction of hardened sap and paper: *on* (A, D), *against* (B), or *by* (C).

14. Responses F, G, and H offer different ways to express Priestley's lack of intentions. J proposes that no expression is necessary.

What does the underlined phrase refer to? What is it that Priestley didn't plan to make?

Look at the phrase *accidental discoveries.* Think about it in relation to the underlined phrase. What does *accidental* mean? Is it reasonable to talk about planning to have an accident? Can an accident be intentional?

Is this a question of choosing the best wording? Does the phrase *accidental discoveries* need any further explanation? Is the sentence clear to a reader without the underlined phrase?

15. Are the paragraphs in the passage ordered in a way that leads a reader smoothly from one idea to the next? Are the transitions easy to follow? Are there any places where a reader could be confused or misled because of poor organization?

Responses B, C, and D propose, among other changes, that Paragraph 1 be placed later in the essay. Is there information in this paragraph that dictates where its best position would be? Is there information in Paragraphs 3 and 4 that suggest where they should be placed with respect to each other?

What sorts of logical connections would help you fit the paragraphs together?

Do any paragraphs begin with a transitional word or phrase that could limit their placement?

16. The underlined phrase describes the writer's feelings about seeing a Japanese tea ceremony. Is the writer looking forward to the ceremony? Which option most clearly and concisely expresses that anticipation?

As you study the choices, think about what the words mean. Each response includes the word *eager.* Look for additional words that mean about the same thing as *eager,* which might indicate that that particular phrasing isn't the most economical.

In F, the writer is both "eager" and "anxious." Also, the phrase *anxious awaiting* is used. Is that phrase an acceptable way to describe anticipation? Are *eager* and *anxious* both necessary here to convey the writer's anticipation, or is F unnecessarily repetitious? Both F and J refer to the awaiting of "the prospect." What is a "prospect"? Is it effective here to talk about **awaiting** one?

In G, the writer is "literally champing at the bit." In this context, is the expression *champing at the bit* appropriate? Does it fit the tone of the passage as a whole? What does it mean to be "**literally** champing at the bit"? Is it likely—or even physically possible—for the writer to be doing it?

H describes the writer simply as "eager to watch" the tea ceremony. It's by far the shortest of the four options. Has the writer sacrificed anything by eliminating so many words? Is the meaning clear?

17. *Who, whom,* or *he*—which one was eighty years old?

It's important to pay attention to the punctuation as well as the pronouns in these choices. Can a reader tell who is being referred to by the pronoun *he* in C? Is the comma between *himself* and *he* appropriate? Look at the clause that begins, after the comma, with *he:* Is it dependent or independent? What kind of clause comes **before** the comma? Is a comma the preferred way to punctuate these two clauses?

A and D offer the word *whom,* while B offers *who.* Think about the difference between the two words. Which one can act? Which one can only be acted upon? Which one is a subject? Which one is an object? Which one is a better choice to precede the phrase "was eighty years old"?

18. Uh oh. Could this be another showdown between *who* and *whom?* Before you get too deep into the question of whether a group of people should be referred to as *who* or *whom*—or, in a different sentence, even *which*—take a look at the other differences among the answer choices. It doesn't matter if the pronoun is correct if the phrase is redundant or worded in a confusing way.

What do you think about the way F is worded? Is the meaning clear? Are the words placed in an order that sounds like standard English?

G offers *whom.* H offers *who.* They do have something in common, however. What is it? Which word appears twice in each answer choice? Does that repetition make the phrase clearer? Or is it repeated unnecessarily?

J avoids *who* and *whom* altogether. Does this phrase make the sentence clear and easy to understand? Do any crucial words seem to be missing? Does it sound like standard English?

19. Which word works best to describe *practitioners* in this sentence?

First, it might be helpful to think about what a practitioner is in this case. Would it be accurate to say that the writer is talking about people who engage in the art of the tea ceremony? What does the writer intend the underlined adjective to say about these practitioners?

Responses A and C have the same root: *accomplish.* B and D share the root *practice.* What is the difference between *accomplished* and *accomplishing?* What does *accomplished* mean as an adjective? What does *accomplishing* mean? *Accomplished,* like *practiced,* is a verb form that can double as an adjective. Can *accomplishing* serve as an adjective, too?

What does *practiced* (B) mean? What does *well-practiced* (D) mean? Is that a word you've heard before? Does adding the word *well* change the meaning of *practiced?* Does it make a stronger expression—or a redundant one?

By now, you might be concluding that your choice has narrowed to *accomplished* or *practiced.* Bearing in mind that the word modifies *practitioners,* which sounds better?

20. The question is, did the tea master do the grinding with his "own personal" hand (F), his "personal own" hand (G), his "own" hand (H), or his "own individual" hand (J)?

One or more of these expressions might sound acceptable to you as a way to emphasize that the tea master did the grinding himself. When speaking or writing informally, we sometimes use repetition or redundancy to make a statement more emphatic. In more formal usage, however, it's usually better to be concise.

As you look at the answer choices, consider whether they contain any redundant phrasing. Keeping in mind the tone of this passage, would the redundancy add emphasis—or would it make the writing seem sloppy and imprecise? Is there a response that doesn't include redundant terms? Does it manage to convey the writer's meaning clearly and economically?

21. What is Sentence 2 about? Does it contain any information that dictates where it should be placed? You might also look for pronouns, transitional phrases, and other elements in this sentence and in the rest of the paragraph that would affect the order.

Sentence 2 explains where the writer's group sat. In its current position (A), Sentence 2 is followed by a sentence that begins, "It consisted of two rooms." What does that phrase refer to? Are the two sentences now in the best position to make the reference clear to a reader? Does one of the answer choices offer a better position? If Sentence 2 is moved elsewhere, does Sentence 3 logically follow after Sentence 1?

Would Sentence 2 be a logical way to begin this paragraph (B)? Does it contain information that belongs between the two sentences about the process of passing tea around the room (D)?

22. Where is the best place for *solemnly?* What does it describe?

What are the two actions in this sentence? Which one might be described as "solemn"? How could the writer convey this to a reader most clearly?

One way to summarize the two actions is:

1. I reached to take it.
2. An accident happened.

Now try inserting the word *solemnly* as indicated by the various answer choices. Which sounds best:

Solemnly an accident happened (F)?

I **solemnly** reached to take it (G)?

I reached to take **solemnly** it (H)?

An accident happened **solemnly** (J)?

23. This question asks you to consider not only the best way to describe where the tea spilled (A, B, C) but also whether a description is necessary at all (D).

According to the passage, where did the tea end up? What did it cover?

Can we make certain assumptions about where it was spilled? The sentence just before this one says, "Powdered green tea spilled everywhere." The writer elaborates by mentioning that it covered both the suit and the floor. Is it helpful to a reader if the writer adds that the floor was another place where the tea was spilled? Would the meaning of the sentence be clear without that addition?

---

24. What's the best way to punctuate this clause so that the writer's statement about the tea-induced laughter is expressed most clearly?

Can you see any phrase that should be set off with commas—a parenthetical expression that interrupts the flow of the sentence?

Try reading the clause aloud, with a pause for each comma suggested by the different answers. What's the effect of pausing only after *laughter* (G)? Only after *believe* (H)? Before and after *I believe* (J)? Is the meaning clearest without any pauses at all (F)? Remember the test of replacing a pair of commas with parentheses and imagining the sentence or clause without them. Does J pass that test?

---

25. A semicolon divides this sentence into two ideas. Which answer choice provides the best transition from one idea to the next? What is the relationship between the ideas?

First, try thinking about what the two ideas are:

1. The writer believes the laughter was not aimed at him.
2. The laughter served to relieve everyone's tension.

As you study the responses, think not only about the word that best expresses the relationship between these two ideas, but also the one that best suits the sentence's punctuation. You have some choice as to whether or not a comma will follow the transitional word. What you can't change is the semicolon that divides this sentence. What kind of clauses can be joined by a semicolon?

You might consider trying each possible answer, then deciding whether the transitional word or phrase creates a clause that's dependent or independent. At the same time, think about what that word or phrase suggests. For instance, is it logical to say that the writer believes the laughter was not aimed at him **because** it served to relieve everyone's tension (B)? Could tension have been relieved just as effectively if the laughter had been aimed at him? Is he including himself among the "everyone" whose tension was allegedly relieved? Is the clause beginning with *because* appropriate after a semicolon—that is, is it an independent clause? You can apply these kinds of tests to the other three answer choices as well.

26. How does the placement of *to us* affect the sentence's meaning? Try the phrase in each position offered. Ask yourself questions like: Is this an accurate reflection of what the writer is trying to say? Is the sentence clear and easy to understand? Does the wording sound natural?

What is implied if the writer says "imparted not only to us" (H)? Does the passage support this implication? Does the sentence support it?

How does it sound to say "imparted not only knowledge to us of the tea ceremony" (J)? How does "imparted to us not only knowledge" (G) sound? Is the phrase *to us* positioned so that the writer's meaning comes through without ambiguity? Does the word order seem fitting? Does the sentence sound smooth and logical?

27. Is the writer talking about polite consideration of other **people?** Or of something **belonging** to other people?

What does the apostrophe indicate in A, B, and C? Is there reason to believe that the writer wants to make *other* or *others* possessive? Does this sentence talk about anything that others possess? Is an apostrophe necessary?

Response A is the only one to include the word *those.* If you read the sentence carefully, can you tell what's being referred to? What kind of consideration is ritualized in the tea ceremony? (Who or what receives the consideration?)

Suppose the writer wants to discuss polite consideration of other people. Would an apostrophe be needed after *others?*

---

28. By now, you're probably developing a sixth sense about questions like this—something like redundancy radar. It should help you to pick the answer choice that presents the writer's point about tea ceremonies most clearly and economically.

What does it mean when we speak of certain behavior as "ritualized"? What does the writer mean by saying that polite consideration of others is "ritualized" in the tea ceremony? Is the meaning clearer if the writer includes the information that the ceremony itself is a ritual, as in F and H? Or is the word *ritual* unnecessary?

What is the meaning of *traditionalized?* Is the word *tradition* in J a helpful clarification, or is it redundant?

G doesn't mention either the ritual or the tradition of the tea ceremony. Is any important information missing from the phrase "ritualized in the traditional tea ceremony"? Is the meaning clear to a reader? Is it an accurate reflection of the point the writer wants to make?

---

29. Is the use of *I* appropriate in this essay? Remember that whether you decide yes or no, the answer you select should also give the best reason for that answer.

Do you agree that it's important to use *I* in all travel writing (A)? Why would it be important? Should all travel writing be firsthand accounts? Is that a reasonable limitation to impose on a travel writer?

Is the essay a personal account (B)?

Does the use of *I* detract from the description of the tea ceremony (C)?

Is the essay a factual account (D)? Do you think the use of *I* is necessarily inappropriate for a factual account? Can you think of instances where *I* **would** be appropriate?

As you read the passage, did you find the pronoun *I* intrusive? Or did it fit the essay's tone and subject matter?

30. All four answer choices here depend on the word *student.* How do they vary? What does an apostrophe signify? Is that what the writer intends here? Is the possessive form of *student* or *students* appropriate? Does the sentence mention something that belongs to a student or students? It talks about something they "must have," of course, but that's not the same.

J puts a comma after *students.* How does the sentence sound if you read it with a pause between *students* and *must have?* How does the noun *students* function as a part of this sentence? What part of the sentence is the phrase *must have?* Should the two parts be separated by a comma?

31. This sentence describes the oath Oxford students take to obtain library cards. Look at the preceding sentence. Is *must have* present, past, or future tense? What does that verb suggest about the appropriate verb for the sentence in question? Is the writer saying that the Bodleian Library used to require ID cards? That it requires them today?

Does the writer go on to explain how students used to get their cards? Or how students qualify for the cards now? Do any of the phrasings suggest action taken in the past? Do any suggest actions that could be going on currently?

What's the difference between *should* (D) and *must* (C)? Is one a stronger indicator of something that's required? According to the passage, can a student get a card without swearing before a librarian? Is the swearing a procedure that the library recommends? Or is it obligatory?

---

32. When does the writer first mention the American tradition of "majoring"? Is it a topic that appears again in this passage?

How would you sum up what the essay is about? What is Paragraph 1 about? What is Paragraph 2 about? Would a paragraph condemning the majoring system be appropriate between them (J)? How would it affect the logical flow of ideas in the essay? Does argument **always** enliven an essay? Could it detract from an essay's main point?

Does an anti-majoring argument belong anywhere else here? Would it be a suitable way to end the passage (F)?

Again, think about the essay as a whole. Is the essay's main concern to provide information, rather than to persuade (H)? Do you agree with G that the passage as a whole already argues against the majoring system? Are there arguments or other persuasive elements throughout the passage?

---

33. What information in each sentence determines where it should be placed in relation to the other sentences? Are there transitional words or phrases that should be taken into consideration? Pay attention to pronouns. Is it clear what they refer to? Look at the following phrases in particular and think about how sentence order could affect their meaning:

Sentence 2: It is a copyright library (**what** is?)

Sentence 3: in this manner (**which** manner?)

Sentence 4: In addition (to **what**?)
other books (besides **which** ones?)

Is there anything in the current sentence order that strikes you as confusing, unclear, or illogical? Is there a response that offers a distinct improvement? Beware of fixing one flaw only to create a new one.

---

34. Is the choice here between *due to the fact that* and *on account of?* Between *the fact that there are* and *there are?* Is this a question of correcting a grammatical error, or of eliminating redundancy?

Look at the phrase *vast collection.* What does *vast* mean? What is the collection that's being referred to—a collection of what?

F, G, and H all include the phrase *so many books.* Does that phrase clarify for a reader what the "vast collection" is? Would you understand the nature of the vast collection with the deletion of the information that it contained "so many books" (J)?

---

35. Be sure to read all the way from "Three of these" to "in 1946" before you pick your answer. Think about the kind of clause (dependent or independent, remembering that only an independent clause can stand alone) that comes before and after the punctuation mark. Think about the relationship between the ideas expressed in those clauses.

The first sentence—as it's written now—mentions three buildings that are among Oxford's most famous landmarks, and the second sentence gives information about the three buildings. Look at the clause that starts with *the Old Library* and think about what it says and how it works. Is it an independent clause—a complete sentence? If so, a period after *Oxford* would be appropriate here (A and B). If not, would a comma (D) be preferable?

36. What kinds of options do F, G, and H offer for discussing St. Paul's Cathedral and its dome? Can you spot grammatical, mechanical, or stylistic flaws that would lead you to eliminate any of the choices? Is one sentence clearly better than the others? Is one more concise? More suited to the tone of the essay? What would be the effect of eliminating the sentence entirely (J)?

What is the topic of this paragraph? How does the underlined sentence fit in? Does it contain information crucial to understanding other elements in the paragraph?

Does the sentence provide a transition between two other sentences? Without it, is the paragraph choppy or awkward to read? Is it confusing? Is it improved?

37. This question concerns a waiting reader who awaits. Do A, B, and C offer different ways to word the idea of awaiting?

How does the sentence sound to you with both *waiting* and *awaiting?* Think about what each word means. Does it clarify what the writer is trying to say if the sentence contains both words? Or does it detract? Does it add new information, or just more words? Is it more emphatic to say "the waiting reader who awaits" than simply "the waiting reader"? Or is it just repetitious?

If you read the sentence without the underlined phrase, is the meaning still clear? Does removing the phrase leave a complete and logical sentence? Has any vital information been sacrificed?

---

38. What criteria does the question suggest for choosing the best topic sentence? Notice the words *effective, coherent,* and *accurate.* Keep them in mind as you read each answer choice.

As you look at F, ask yourself: Is it accurate? Is the Bodleian "a complex of old and very old" buildings? Are they linked by "mechanics"? (You might need to reread the paragraph to puzzle out the answer to that one.) Are they linked by tradition? Is the sentence coherent? Does it effectively introduce the elements discussed in the paragraph?

Is G accurate? Is it correct to refer to the Oxford Library when throughout the passage the writer has been discussing the Bodleian Library? Is focusing on Radcliffe Camera an effective way to introduce the paragraph?

Is H a coherent sentence? Does the second part of the sentence flow logically from the first? Does the sentence offer an effective way to introduce the paragraph? Is it written in a style consistent with the rest of the passage?

Is J accurate? Does the paragraph discuss locations outside the Bodleian where books are kept? Make sure you've read the paragraph very carefully so that you have a clear picture of exactly what the Bodleian is.

---

39. Which response offers the best transition between the parts of this sentence? First, try to sum up the two ideas to be connected by the possible answers. Then think about the relationship between these ideas. Is it a relation of cause and effect?

One way to sum up the two ideas is:

1. The Bodleian is not a lending library.
2. To use the Bodleian's books, students must read in one of its reading rooms.

What is a lending library? Why must students read the Bodleian's books at the Bodleian rather than at home?

Try substituting the various transitions between the two ideas summarized above. Which seems the most accurate reflection of the bearing that the first idea has upon the second?

The Bodleian is not a lending library . . .

- **notwithstanding,** students must read in one of its reading rooms?
- **contrarily,** students must read in one of its reading rooms?
- **on the other hand,** students must read in one of its reading rooms?
- **therefore,** students must read in one of its reading rooms?

40. Brace yourself for a triple whammy: three questions about one sentence. Be sure you read the complete sentence before answering any of the questions.

What's the best way to discuss the ghostly motion that the writer imagines taking place in the Bodleian? After reading the whole sentence, you should have a picture of two actions that the alleged ghosts are engaging in; the word *and* connects them. Focus on those actions as they're described in the passage. The ghosts "move through the air and hovering over shoulders." How does that sound? You don't have the option of changing the verb form of the second action—hovering—so what strategy can you use for making the sentence consistent? Try substituting each optional phrase for the underlined portion and reading the sentence through. Also, notice that although G and J contain the same words, J includes a comma after *through.* When you read the sentence with a pause between *through* and *the air,* what effect does the pause have on what the writer is trying to say?

41. This question may be confusing at first because the phrase *just out of sight* is placed at a point in the sentence where a reader can't easily tell whether it's the ghosts or the sounds of students turning pages that are out of sight—and sounds are always "out of sight," anyway. Turn your attention to the punctuation questions here. Where, if anywhere, should a comma be placed? Does *shoulders* need an apostrophe?

Does the sentence mention anything belonging to a shoulder or shoulders so that the possessive *shoulder's* (C) or *shoulders'* (D) would be appropriate? *Shoulder's* can also be a contraction. Does anything in the sentence suggest that the writer wants to say that a "shoulder is" something?

The two choices with apostrophes are also the only two without a comma. Try reading the sentence without a comma, then read it with a pause for a comma between *shoulders* and *just* (A), and between *just* and *out* (B).

Which response offers the best way to punctuate this sentence for the greatest clarity **and** includes the most appropriate form of the word *shoulders?*

42. While keeping in mind the sentence as a whole, you might want now to focus on the portion of this sentence that begins with "there are the sounds of." Notice that the writer is listing the different sounds that might be heard in a Bodleian reading room. Looking at the answer choices as possible last elements in that list should help you pick the choice that conforms most closely to the other elements.

We hear the sounds of current students doing things:

- turning pages
- shuffling notecards
- sighing

Is the best choice for the last element in the list of sounds *or chuckling occurs* (F)? *and chuckling occurs* (G)? *chuckling occurs* (H)? or *or chuckling* (J)?

43. In two-part questions like this one, it's important to consider both components of each answer choice. Be sure that you're not only picking the best place to add the new information, but also agreeing with the reason for putting it there.

For instance, you might feel that a new paragraph would be appropriate for the information about the Bodleian's manuscripts, as suggested by D, even though the question tells you rather vaguely that the amount of information is "small" (it could be a short paragraph, after all). However, do you feel the second part of D is an accurate statement? Should new information **always** go in a new paragraph? Be cautious when you read statements like this that include absolutes like *always, never, all, none,* etc.

As you review each response, it will probably help you to glance back at the paragraph each one refers to. Look at the focus of each paragraph and think about the information in it. Where would information about the Bodleian's manuscripts fit best, and why?

44. The answer choices offer different verb tenses (*mentioned, being mentioned*) and nouns or pronouns (*they, you, the person*). In this context, the difference between *mentioned* (F, G, J) and *being mentioned* (H) is a small one, so you may want to focus on choosing the noun or pronoun. How do you know which one fits best in the underlined phrase? Look at the beginning of this sentence: "When Americans hear fox hunting mentioned." Is *Americans* a singular or plural noun? Which of the responses offer a singular noun or pronoun? Which offer plural?

Also, try asking yourself: When Americans hear, **who** imagines—you (F and H), the person (J), or they (G)?

45. Although the underlined word isn't the first word in this sentence, it is designed to provide a transition from the sentence before. To choose the best transitional word or phrase, you might start by summing up the main ideas of the two sentences. Think about their relationship to one another. Looking at the answer choices, which one best expresses that relationship and leads the reader smoothly into the main idea of the second sentence?

You could sum up the sentences this way:

Sentence 1. Americans usually imagine fox hunting as mounted, red-coated English gentry crying "Tallyho!"

Sentence 2. I see fox hunting as overall-clad farmers around a bonfire.

Try connecting the sentences, as summarized above, with each of the responses. Think about whether the second sentence supports the premise of the first. Which word or words in the options suggest that kind of relationship? Does Sentence 2 build on Sentence 1, or is a contradiction implied? Is there a word or words that could suggest **that** relationship?

46. Should these two sentences remain separate, as they appear in F? Can each stand alone as a complete sentence? Or should they appear as a single sentence? If so, would the new sentence need any additional punctuation, such as a semicolon or comma?

Is "This scene emerges from my childhood experience of fox hunting" an independent clause? Is "In the hill country of the southern United States"? Look for a subject/verb combination in each. If both constructions are independent, they can be separated by a period (F) or a semicolon (J). Otherwise, joining them with a comma (G) or without (H) would be possibilities.

How does the second expression relate to the first? If you read this as one long sentence without a pause (H), is the sentence clear and easy to understand? How does a pause between *in* and *the* (G) affect the sentence's clarity?

47. The writer remembers a form of fox hunting unlike the English version most people think of. What's the best way to express the relationship between the two versions?

When you think about the best choice, consider whether each phrase sounds like standard English. Is it clear? Is it concise? Is it wordy?

Is there a difference in what B, C, and D mean? Or are they simply different ways of saying the same thing? Do any of them strike you as clumsy or awkward sounding? Do any of them sound smoother and more precise?

Only A adds a comma. How does this sentence sound if you read it through with pauses after *remember, different,* and *version?*

48. Here's another choice between one sentence (F, H, J) or two (G). How can you decide? You might start by reading the sentence through, trying each of the possible answers. Do some of the versions sound confusing? Is one version clearer and easier to understand than the others?

Another tactic might be to take the sentence apart. There is a clause on either side of *in fact.* Identify the main idea in each clause. Look at the subject/verb construction in each. Read them separately. Are both independent? Is only one independent? Does one of the responses provide a good way to combine them in a single sentence? Or should they be split?

49. The construction of this sentence probably reminds you of the one you just examined in question 48. Here, however, you don't have the option of breaking it into two sentences. As you did before, think of this sentence in terms of its main ideas and subject/verb constructions, this time connected by the word *therefore:*

1. A cunning fox made the sport exciting
2. The hunters wanted it alive to run another night

Are both clauses independent? Is only one independent? What kind of punctuation is needed to link them? What kind of clauses can be joined by a semicolon (C) as opposed to a comma (A)?

Notice that D is the only response to propose adding a word: *so.* What does *therefore* mean? What does *so* mean? Is *so* an effective word to use before *therefore?* Does it make *therefore* clearer or more emphatic? Or is it redundant?

50. In this question, you're asked to choose not only the best verb form (*was* or *were*) but also the best punctuation for the phrase and for the word *huntsmans.*

F, G, and H include the verb *was.* Only J suggests *were.* Which verb agrees with the subject of this sentence? Is the subject *traditions?* Is that a singular or plural noun? Is the subject *horn?* Is that a singular or plural noun? Is *was* singular or plural? Is *were* singular or plural?

Also, take a moment to think about the comma that G and H place between *horn* and *was.* Is a comma appropriate between this subject and verb? Is the apostrophe in *huntsman's* appropriate? Is the horn something that belongs to or is characterized as being used by a huntsman?

51. Is there a difference between *cows' horns* and *horns of cows',* except for a matter of economy and style? You have to look closely to be aware of the differences in the phrases offered by the possible answers. Pay particular attention to the apostrophes.

What does an apostrophe signify? As you read the sentence, do you think the writer is talking about something belonging to **cows** or belonging to **horns?** Which word needs an apostrophe to show that it's possessive?

How does *of* function in A and B? Is it necessary to use both *of* and an apostrophe to show possession?

52. How does the phrase *not just the leader* fit with the rest of the sentence? What does it refer to? Is the issue here choosing between *not* and *never* or selecting the best punctuation or both? Should the phrase *not just the leader* be preceded by a comma, a semicolon, or no punctuation at all?

Try reading the sentence through, pausing at the commas and semicolons in each response. Think about how the pauses affect the clarity of the sentence. Is the sentence easier to understand with a pause between *hunt* and *not* (F) or without (G)? A semicolon creates a bigger pause than a comma. It's almost as big a break as a period. Notice that there's already one semicolon in this sentence: after *horn.* Should that affect your choice of punctuation? What are the circumstances that call for a semicolon? Is one appropriate here?

53. What does the underlined word in this sentence refer to? Try asking yourself: A hill-country hound obeyed only **whose** owner's call? Its own owner's call? If so, the answer you choose should agree with *a hill-country hound.* Is that a plural or singular noun? Which of the choices are singular? Which are plural?

You may have noticed that the optional answers consist of two pairs of homonyms—words that sound the same but look different. They are: *there* (A) and *their* (C), and *its* (B) and *it's* (D). They also mean different things. *There* and *their* sound alike, but are they interchangeable? *Its* and *it's* sound alike, but one is a possessive and one is a contraction. Which is which? Should the underlined word be possessive?

54. As you try to puzzle out the best word for the underlined portion of this sentence, it may cross your mind that *lie* and *lay* can be as hard to tell apart as the Doublemint Twins. Remember what you've learned about each verb and how it should be used.

Lay is a transitive verb. It takes an object:

I broke my pencil in half and **laid** it on my desk.

The hens are **laying** eggs faster than we can scramble them.

Lie is an intransitive verb. It can't take an object. You can't "lie" your pencil on your desk.

Ludwig **lay** in the hammock for hours, pondering whether to let sleeping dogmas **lie.**

When you think about the underlined word in this question, it may help you to think about the action of the sentence. Try to identify the subject so you can pick the best verb. Consider putting the sentence in the present tense: the difference **lies** or the difference **lays.** Is *difference* taking an object? Is it **laying** anything?

If you're still not quite sure which word is best, can you at least eliminate one or two possibilities before taking a guess? Be alert for errors in verb tense. Look for a verb that might need another word—an auxiliary verb—to make its meaning clear.

55. Before you get too involved in evaluating the different wordings and punctuation offered by each of the choices, you might notice one crucial difference between response C and responses A, B, and D. Only C begins with the phrase *such a hound.* The other three begin with references to the porch or the family's porch. Is the problem here one of wording and punctuation? Is it a problem of choosing the best conclusion to the opening phrase *eating choice leftovers?* The relationship between the modifying phrase *eating choice leftovers* and the word it modifies should be as clear as possible. What is the word modified? Who's eating the leftovers? Which response expresses most clearly the relationship between *eating choice leftovers* and the leftovers-eater?

56. Which response offers the best verb tense and punctuation for the underlined part of the sentence? Think about what the writer is trying to express about deeds and legends. You might also look at the paragraph as a whole and think about when the actions in it took place. The verbs in the other sentences can provide clues to help you choose the best verb for this sentence.

F and G suggest *had became.* Does it sound like standard English? Is *became* the past participle of *become?* Does it belong with the auxiliary (or helping) verb *had?* How does the verb phrase sound with a pause in the middle, as suggested by the comma in G?

Take a look at J. Is *was* a singular or plural verb? What is the noun this verb should agree with? Is the noun singular or plural? Is *was becoming* the best verb tense to express what the writer wants to say about the hounds' deeds turning into legends?

H suggests simply *became.* Does that convey the writer's meaning? Does it agree with the noun that's the subject of this clause?

57. Before you study each possible answer and try out the sentence order each suggests, think about the sentence that would begin the paragraph. You have only two choices. Should it be Sentence 1, as A, B, and C propose? Or Sentence 2, as D suggests? If Sentence 2 should turn out to be the best answer, you'll have saved a great deal of time by not trying out every possible sentence combination.

Look at Sentence 1. What kind of transition does it provide from the preceding paragraph? Is it clear what—or whom—American hunters prize their dogs more highly than? What kind of introduction does it give to the paragraph?

Look at Sentence 2. What kind of transition does it provide? Is it an effective introductory sentence? Does it tie the topic of the preceding paragraph to the topic of the next one? Does the rest of the sentence order suggested by D seem logical? Is the reference in Sentence 1 clear? Is it obvious who *such a hound* refers to in Sentence 4? Is it clear who "they" are in Sentence 5?

58. After you decide whether the answer is yes or no, be careful to choose the response with the reason that best supports your answer.

Are *tallyho* and *went to earth* appropriate in this essay? Would a reader find them confusing or distracting? What is the topic of the essay? Do the words in question bear any relationship to the topic? Why do you think the writer used them?

Think about whether you agree with the reasoning in each answer choice. Do you agree with F that *tallyho* and *went to earth* belong in an essay describing speech patterns? Do you agree with G that they're distracting and irrelevant? Do you agree with H that they add to the writing? Should writers, as J suggests, use fox hunting terms "whenever possible"—no matter what they're writing about?

59. As you read these sentences, it's important to keep in mind that you're looking for one that sums up the idea of the entire passage. If you were asked to describe to another person what you've just read, which sentence would do it best? As you read each possibility, you may find more than one that makes a statement you consider to be true, based on the passage. Remember that it isn't enough for the statement to be accurate, or for it to sum up the main idea of one of the paragraphs. Does it reflect the point the writer was trying to make by writing this essay?

What should a good summary contain? Think about whether it's more likely to express a generalization or include specific details. If the writer wanted to leave a reader with one thought in mind after finishing the essay, what do you think it would be?

60. The writer is listing some of the images people commonly see when they hear the word *vacation.* As you read the choices, think about which one is the most clear and concise and will make each element in the list consistent with the others.

Try to avoid wordiness. Be alert for options that could cause a shift in construction by inserting a phrase that changes the voice of the sentence.

What are the three images in the list? Do the words *there being* (F) and *as well as there being* (J) help to clarify or emphasize any of the images? How does *there being* fit with the rest of the sentence? Is it consistent with the rest of the sentence?

The writer begins this sentence by saying that, for most people, the word *vacation* evokes images. H suggests adding the words *images evoked* after *beaches.* How does this repetition affect the clarity of this sentence? Do the words add emphasis? Would the sentence lose meaning if they were omitted (G)?

61. Notice that the responses give you different choices of word orders. Also notice that each includes a different transitional word to lead a reader from the first sentence to the second.

What is the main idea of the first sentence? Of the second sentence? What is their relationship to each other? The first sentence talks about what most people imagine when they hear the word *vacation.* The second sentence talks about what the writer imagines: *for most people* versus *for me.* What does *synonymous* mean? How does the writer's mention of *overhaul* fit with the popular concept of relaxing in scenic places? From the information you're given, do you think the writer has the same thoughts as most people? Are those thoughts different from most people's? Do other people's images determine the writer's idea of what a vacation is?

Which of the following sounds most logical?

Most people think of mountains and beaches.

I, **too,** think of the word *overhaul.*

I, **however,** think of the word *overhaul.*

Therefore, I think of the word *overhaul.*

Besides, I think of the word *overhaul.*

62. This is a rather long sentence, with one or two twists and turns. Your job is to determine the best way to straighten it out.

Because the sentence is so long, you might be tempted to break it into two shorter ones (J). Take the time to read both of the new sentences that would be created by putting a period after *customers* and beginning the next sentence with *until.* Are both sentences logical? Are they complete sentences?

Does either *and* (F) or *and so* (H) provide an effective way to link the parts of this sentence? Take a look at what kind of clause comes before and after the *and.* Is the first clause dependent or independent? What about the second? Only if both are independent can they be joined by a comma and a conjunction (such as *and*). If only one is independent, they can be joined by a comma without a conjunction (G).

63. This sentence is talking about two things: what happened Friday and what happened Saturday. How should the two ideas be joined to give a reader a clear idea of what happened each day?

Are the two parts of the sentence independent clauses? Is one dependent? What kind of clauses should be linked by a comma? By a semicolon?

What happens if you add the word *or,* as in C? Is the sentence easier to understand? What about *unfortunately,* in D? Is it easy for a reader to tell exactly what the writer considers unfortunate?

64. The words are the same; it's only the comma that wanders from place to place in these answer choices. Where does a comma belong here—if it belongs at all?

Try reading the sentence through with each response, pausing for every comma. Listen for the version that conveys the writer's meaning without distracting a reader. Is the sentence clear and logical with a pause between *coaxing* and *could* (F)? Between *amount* and *of* (G)? Between *adjusting* and *and* (J)? Without any pauses (H)?

65. Here you must choose from two different verb tenses and three different forms of the pronoun *it* to decide on the best way to discuss changing what the writer calls the lawn mower's "mind."

Since you have more pronoun choices, your best bet might be to tackle that part of the question first. Think about the noun that the pronoun you pick will replace: the lawn mower. The sentence talks about something the lawn mower is said to possess: a mind. Which choice offers you the possessive form of *it?*

What's the usual way to make a noun possessive? Is adding an apostrophe and an *s* the way to make the pronoun *it* possessive? (Don't forget that *it's* is a contraction for *it is.*)

Think about the verb phrases *could change* (A, B, D) and *could have changed* (C). Is there a difference between what the two imply? Read the entire sentence. Does the writer mean to say that an effort was made to adjust and coax, but those methods couldn't change the lawn mower's mind? Or that no effort was even made to adjust and coax because those methods couldn't have worked?

66. The options you're given all offer different ways of saying the same thing—that the refrigerator repair person didn't show up on time—and they are all fairly long. You need to read them with an eye for awkwardness, wordiness, and grammatical errors. Pay particular attention to the verb tenses. Think about how the two actions—of being expected and of arriving—could be expressed with parallel verb constructions.

What do we mean by *parallel?* Basically, it's using the same form of different verbs. Usually, they're verbs that accompany the same subject.

In each of these examples, the verb in parentheses is not parallel with the other verb(s) in the same sentence:

> We sang and danced and (eating) tofu all night long.
>
> Francine, hoping for Prince Charming but (expected) a frog, waited grimly for the doorbell to ring.

Look at F. Are *having been expected* and *who arrived* parallel phrases? Notice that only one of the verbs ends in *-ing.* This also occurs in G: "this person was expected at ten but arriving at four." Do you notice anything awkward about the *-ing* verb in this case? Also, do you think it's effective to repeat the word *person,* after referring to "the refrigerator repair person" earlier in the sentence?

Arriving is used in a similar way in J: *who arriving at four.* Is it standard English to use an *-ing* verb this way, without an auxiliary verb? Is it clear what the subject of the verb is (that is, **who** was arriving)?

By contrast, look at the verb phrases in H: *who was expected* and *who arrived.* Are they parallel? Are the verbs used correctly?

67. What's the action in this sentence? It might help you to identify the subject and verb before you consider what kind of punctuation might be necessary. For instance, you want to avoid breaking up a subject and verb with a punctuation mark (My dog [,] has fleas). A modifying clause can come between a subject and its verb (My dog, who recently spent a week in Florida, has fleas); a comma, semicolon, or other punctuation mark shouldn't.

How does this sentence sound with a pause between *house* and *itself* (B)? Between *itself* and *is* (C)? Without any pause (A)?

Take a look at D. Is the *house by itself* clearer or more emphatic than *the house itself?* Does it sound like standard English?

68. This question asks you to identify an idiom—one of those phrases that you learn through usage, not by memorizing a rule of grammar. Here you're asked to pick the best preposition based on whether the phrase sounds like standard English. For instance, we say:

Her tap dancing resulted **in** the deaths of several mice.

We don't say "resulted with" or "resulted on." For some reason, the idiom has evolved as "resulted in."

You might start by eliminating the adjective *none-too-subtle* and concentrating on the verb and its object. Which preposition sounds best in this context?

If you pare the sentence down to the verb *making* and its object *comments,* it might be easier to picture the idiom as a whole. The neighbors' comments have a topic: "blights on the neighborhood." Which sounds best:

- making comments **for** (F) a topic?
- making comments **about** (G and J) a topic?
- making comments **from** (H) a topic?

Response J is the only one to add a semicolon. What kind of clauses can be connected by a semicolon? If you break the sentence in two at the semicolon, do you see two of those clauses? If you see only one, a semicolon isn't the best punctuation mark.

69. From the neighbors' grumbling, the writer knows when it's time to dig out the stepladder. Is either "I know it's time" or "I know that it's time" preferable? Should *I know* or *I know that* be set off with commas to separate it from the rest of the sentence?

Read the sentence through, pausing at each comma suggested by the choices. What is the effect of pausing between *know* and *it's* (C)? Between *know* and *that* (D)? Between *that* and *it's* (B)? Of no pause at all (A)?

Notice how adding a comma can turn *I know* into a parenthetical expression—as if the writer is confiding something to the reader, indicated by the aside "I know." Is that the effect wanted here? Can you remove that phrase from the sentence without changing the meaning? Or is *I know* vital to the sentence? Think about what the writer is saying. Is it logical to insert a parenthetical *I know* in this sentence?

What is the relationship between the first part of the sentence and the second part (beginning with *I know*)?

70. Don't be too hasty in picking the best verb for this sentence. Make sure you know the subject of this sentence—the noun or nouns that the verb must agree with.

Is the subject singular or plural? What is the noun that comes immediately before the verb? Is it the subject of the sentence?

Ask yourself exactly what is presentable about the house, according to the writer. Is it one thing, or two? Once you've decided whether the subject is singular or plural, look at the verbs offered in the answer choices and think about which of them are singular and which plural. Think, too, about whether the verb should be in the past or present tense. What is the tense of the verb in the preceding sentence?

71. Look at the first part of the sentence: "My two-week overhaul at an end." Is it an independent clause? Does it express a complete thought? Does it have a subject and a verb? Now take a look at the second part: "I return to the office exhausted." Is it an independent clause—a complete sentence? What is the relationship between the two parts? Is the word *therefore* (C) an appropriate way to join them? Is there a cause-and-effect relationship expressed in this sentence that would suggest that the second part results from the first? As readers, we know why the writer returns to the office exhausted. But looking at the sentence by itself, is it logical to use *so* (B) or *therefore* (C) to introduce that idea?

72. Does the arrangement of the elements of this sentence show as clearly as possible the relation between the modifying phrase that opens the sentence and whatever it's describing? What do the answer choices suggest is being described? Is it the desk chair? Or "I"—the writer?

Think about the subject of the clause in each response. Is it the desk chair or the writer? Who's doing the action? How logical is the sentence created by each choice? An inanimate object like a desk chair can, in a sense, "await" (F) or "provide a haven" (H). Can it take "a deep breath" (G)?

73. Where do the commas belong in this sentence—if they're necessary at all? Is the sentence confusing without any added punctuation?

Try reading the sentence through. Does it sound natural to read it without a pause (C)? In this context, *where I can relax* is a modifying phrase; it describes the kind of place the writer finds. But is it a restrictive modifier (one that contains information essential to the sentence's meaning) or a nonrestrictive modifier (one that can be removed without changing the essence of a sentence)?

If it sounds natural to read a sentence without a pause between the modifier (*where I can relax*) and what it modifies (*place*), that's a good indication that the phrase is restrictive. It's vital to the meaning of the sentence. If it sounds natural to pause—if the phrase should be set off with commas—it's probably a nonrestrictive modifier. If you imagine that the commas are parentheses and try removing the enclosed phrase, the sentence's essence should be the same. Think about the phrase *where I can relax*. Is it a parenthetical phrase (A)? Try reading the sentence without it. Does the sentence's meaning change?

How does the sentence sound if you read it aloud, pausing at the commas suggested by B and D?

Which version makes the sentence sound clearest and most natural?

74. Why does the word *overhaul* crop up again at the end of this essay? Where have you seen it before? What effect does it have on you as a reader to find the word repeated at this point in the essay? Is it redundant, or does it give the essay a certain symmetrical shape?

As you read through the answer choices, think about whether they propose logical reasons for the writer's repetition of *overhaul.* How would you define the word? Do you agree that it could be confused with *vacation* (F)?

Can you find a point in the essay where the two words are compared? When the writer says in the first paragraph, "For me, however, the word has become synonymous with *overhaul,*" does that mean a reader would find them synonymous, too?

Is it that *overhaul* "logically comes to mind in relation to work" (G)? Are the two concepts linked in your mind? Are they linked in the essay?

Is it that the repetition "ties the conclusion to the rest of the essay" (H)? Is the rest of the essay concerned with various kinds of overhauls? (Be thankful the writer didn't wear **overalls** for these **overhauls,** or this question could be truly mind-boggling.) Does the repetition of the word give you a sense that the essay has come full circle—beginning and ending with the concept of "overhaul"?

Overhaul contains the word *over.* But does that mean it's related to the concept of something being over, or finished, as J proposes?

75. It might help you to think about two things: What **kind** of essay is this? What does it **do?** What is it **about?**

Each of these options has two parts. The first part tries to characterize the essay: personal, helpful, factual, or persuasive. The second part mentions the focus of the hypothetical assigned article: the stresses of vacation time, avoiding vacation stress, home improvement, or the benefits of vacationing at home. Before you make your choice, be sure you agree with **both** elements of the answer you select.

Is this a personal essay (A)? (Notice the writer's use of the first-person *I.*) Is it about the stresses of vacation time? Is the writer sharing some personal experiences with vacation stress?

Is the essay helpful (B)? Does it give a reader any points on avoiding vacation stress? Or does it merely delineate some of the pitfalls?

Does the essay include facts on home improvement (C)? What home improvements did the writer make? (Note: *Repair* and *improvement* are not synonymous.) Does the essay take a how-to approach and provide useful information about making home improvements?

Is the essay persuasive (D)? Did it persuade **you** that staying home is a good way to spend a vacation?

1. As you read this problem, do any facts concerning the number of degrees in a triangle come to mind?

The sum of the measures of the interior angles of a triangle equals 180°.

So we know that $m(\angle R) + m(\angle S) + m(\angle T) = 180°$. Let's see how this information makes it possible to find the measure of $\angle R$.

We are given that $m(\angle S) = 40°$. We are also told that the measure of $\angle T$ is twice the measure of $\angle S$. So what is the measure of $\angle T$? It is 80°, since twice 40° is 80°.

Since $m(\angle S) = 40°$ and $m(\angle T) = 80°$, the sum of the measures of these two angles is 120°. Remembering that the sum of the measures of all three angles of a triangle is 180°, how many degrees are left for the third angle, $\angle R$?

Based on the figure, does your answer look approximately correct?

2. It is important to sort through the facts of this problem before looking for the answer to the question. Nineteen students agreed to pay for the total cost of printing the announcements for Parents Appreciation Day. The total amount of money collected from 12 students who paid exactly their share was $133.20. To determine the amount of each person's share, divide the total amount of $133.20 by 12. The result is $11.10. This means that each of the 19 students would have to pay $11.10. How much is that?

If you had tried to predict the answer in advance, how close would you have been?

3. To answer the question this problem is asking, it's important to understand exactly what the $72 represents.

If you're not sure what to do, here's a place where trying out a specific example might help. How much would the fine be if Sally had been charged with driving 60 mph in the 55-mph zone?

The $72 represents the basic fine of $15 plus the additional fine. The amount of the additional fine is obtained by multiplying the additional $3 rate by the number of mph **over** 55 that Sally was traveling. So, to answer the question asked, it makes sense to separate the basic fine from the total.

By subtracting $15 from $72, you will get the portion that came from the additional fine. $72 – $15 = $57, so $57 of the total fine came from the additional part of the fine.

At the rate of $3 for each mph over 55 mph, how many miles per hour over the speed limit was Sally traveling if the additional fine totaled $57?

Now that you know how many mph over the speed limit Sally was driving, how fast was she driving?

---

4. The "basic type" problem that presents you with a formula usually can be worked by substituting the given information into the formula and then solving for the one variable that remains. Is this problem the "basic type" or some variation?

In this problem, we have the basic formula for circuitry, $E = IR$, where E = number of volts, I = number of amperes, and R = number of ohms. We are told that $E = 12$ and $R = 4$. By substitution,

$$E = IR$$

becomes $12 = I \cdot 4$

or $\frac{12}{4} = I$

Is this one of the answer choices?

---

5. This problem can be solved if we recall some facts regarding angle measurements when two parallel lines are cut by a transversal.

> When two parallel lines are cut by a transversal, the corresponding angles are congruent, the alternate interior angles are congruent, and the pairs of interior angles on the same side of the transversal are supplementary. (Note: $\cong$ is the symbol for **congruence.**)

What pairs of angles are congruent? By the properties in the box above, $\angle a \cong \angle d$ and $\angle c \cong \angle e$ (corresponding angles); $\angle b \cong \angle d$ (alternate interior angles); and $\angle c$ is supplementary to $\angle d$ (pair of interior angles on same side of transversal).

Using this information, circle all of the angles that you know are congruent to $\angle a$:

a *b* *c* *d* *e*

You should have circled 3 angles. Is there a relation between the other 2 angles?

Could all 5 angles be congruent? Which ones **must** be congruent?

6. Even if you don't remember much about scientific notation, you can add the two numbers together. Then what's left is to change the result to scientific notation. The answer choices are examples of scientific notation. Here's a more general description.

> A positive number is in scientific notation if it is represented as a product of
> 1. A decimal number between 1 and 10 and
> 2. 10 raised to an integer power.

Now, what about converting to scientific notation? You might know how, but what if you've forgotten? Is there a way to figure it out? What if you start with 1.42×10^3?

10^3 is 1,000. Then $1.42 \times 10^3 = 1.42 \times 1{,}000 = 1{,}420$. Do you see the pattern of where the decimal point goes? Try 3.99×10^1, or—if you want a more complicated example—1.07×10^{-2}.

Now, put into scientific notation the result you got when you added 20,000 and 3,400,000.

What would happen if you changed 20,000 and 3,400,000 to scientific notation **before** you added them together?

7. To set this problem up in long division form, which number is divided by which?

The expression 2.542 ÷ 0.02 is read as 2.542 divided by 0.02. This means that 2.542 is the number being divided (the dividend) and it's being divided by 0.02 (the divisor).

Using the traditional format, 2.542 ÷ 0.02 can be rewritten as

$$0.02\,\overline{)\,2.542}$$

Do you recall how to do long division with decimals?

People are usually taught to first change the problem to an equivalent one where the divisor (in this case 0.02) is a whole number. This is done by first moving the decimal point in the divisor the appropriate number of places, then moving the decimal point in the dividend a corresponding number of places in the same direction.

So, $0.02\,\overline{)\,2.542}$ becomes $2\,\overline{)\,254.2}$

You can see that these should give the same answer since

$$\frac{2.542}{0.02} = \frac{254.2}{2}$$ (both the top and bottom were multiplied by the same number, 100)

Now, locate the decimal point in the answer and finish the long division.

How would a calculator have helped make this problem go faster? What would you have done wrong if your calculator gave you 0.00786782 as an answer?

8. Here's another division problem, like #7, but this time polynomials instead of decimals are being divided. Most of us learn three methods for dealing with this kind of problem: long division, short division, and cancelling common factors. (You may have learned different names for these methods.) Each method has its own advantages and disadvantages; which would **you** try first?

Long division

$$\begin{array}{r|l} & x + 8 \\ \hline x + 4 & x^2 + 12x + 32 \\ & \underline{x^2 + 4x} \\ & \quad\;\; 8x + 32 \\ & \quad\;\; \underline{8x + 32} \\ & \qquad\quad 0 \end{array}$$

Short division

$$\begin{array}{r|rrr} -4 & 1 & 12 & 32 \\ & & -4 & -32 \\ \hline & 1 & 8 & 0 \end{array}$$

Cancelling common factors

Factoring is a process of trial and error. You need to find factors of $x^2 + 12x + 32$. Your experience with polynomials should tell you that the factors will have the form $(x + \_\_\_)(x + \_\_\_)$, where you fill in the blanks with positive numbers that multiply together to give 32. So, try all the "nice" possibilities:

$(x + 1)\,(x + 32) = \_\_\_\_\_\_$

$(x + 2)\,(x + 16) = \_\_\_\_\_\_$

$(x + 4)\,(x + 8) = \_\_\_\_\_\_$

In this case, one of these works.

Now write out the original problem and use this factoring information.

$$\frac{x^2 + 12x + 32}{x + 4} = \frac{(x + 4)(x + 8)}{x + 4} = x + 8$$

Which method to use?

Long division is the most universal. Short division is quicker (if you remember it) but only works when the denominator is of the form $(x + a)$ for some number a (which needn't be positive). Cancelling factors helps when the numerator can be factored easily, and when there is a common factor.

Other things to think about

What part does the $x \neq -4$ play?

If you substitute $x = 0$ into the problem and into all the answer choices, what happens? Is this a valid method? What would happen if $2x + 8$ were an answer choice?

9. This problem asks for the value of a polynomial at a specific value of x. This type of problem can usually be solved using substitution.

First, substitute -2 for x in the expression:

$$12 - x^2 + 1$$

becomes $12 - (-2)^2 + 1$.

Notice how we put parentheses around the -2. Many people get into trouble by trying to do too much at once. You can always simplify later, so write down enough steps to be sure you're on the right track.

To evaluate this expression correctly, what do you have to consider? Remember the rules for order of operations that are used when any simplification takes place. What will you do first in this problem?

10. Let's formulate a plan for solving this problem. You might have a simpler one, but let's discuss the following:

1. Find the discount.
2. Find the sale price of the shirt.
3. Find how much tax is due.
4. Find the total cost to buy the shirt.

Do you agree that this plan breaks the problem into simpler steps? If you do all of these steps, have you solved the problem?

The first part of the plan calls for solving a typical percentage problem. Some people have trouble with applied percentage problems because they don't take time to understand where the percentages fit in with the other parts of the problem. A percentage always has to be a percentage **of something.** The first task is to find out what that "something" is. Here, the discount is 20% of the original cost of the shirt. So you need to find 20% of \$35 = $\frac{1}{5}$(\$35) = \$7. (You might use decimals: 20% of \$35 = .20 × \$35 = \$7.00)

For part 2 of the plan, if the shirt is \$7 cheaper than the original price of \$35, how much is the discounted price? Now, what is the sales tax on the shirt? Is it 5% of the original price of \$35? 5% of the discounted price of \$28? 5% of the discount of \$7?

This problem states the relation pretty explicitly; not all problems are this direct. The tax is to be 5% of the purchase price, and the purchase price is the discounted price of \$28. Makes sense, right? That's how it's usually done in stores. Now that you know the "something" the percentage is based on,

$$5\% \text{ of } \$28 = \frac{1}{20}(\$28) = \$\,\frac{28}{20} = \$\,\frac{14}{10} = \$1.40$$

If you like decimals, or if you didn't think about 5% being equivalent to $\frac{1}{20}$, you might do it as follows:

$$5\% \text{ of } \$28 = .05 \times \$28 = \$1.40$$

So, what would be your cost for the shirt, including the purchase price and the tax?

Alternative

You could combine steps 1 and 2: if the discount is 20% of \$35, the discounted price is 80% of \$35. Similarly, if the tax is 5% of \$28, then the total cost is 105% of \$28. You could even write the whole problem as \$35 × .80 × 1.05.

11. A graph of a mathematical relation such as $x \leq 2$ is a picture showing which values of x make the relation true and which don't. The **heavy** lines and **solid circles** on a graph represent values of x where the relation is true, and the **open circles** and absence of heavy lines represent values of x where the relation is **not** true. The heavy arrows on these graphs symbolize that the heavy line continues indefinitely in the direction shown.

The mathematical notation "$x \leq 2$" is translated into English as "x is less than or equal to 2." The graph of all places where this relation holds should have a solid circle at the point corresponding to 2 and a heavy line for all values of x less than 2.

12. Ratios can be expressed in several ways. One way to express this ratio is $3a{:}7b$, but it's often more convenient to express a ratio as a fraction, $\frac{3a}{7b}$.

In this problem, it might be helpful to write down your starting point and your goal. With these two ends of the problem written down, it should be easier to imagine a solution path between them.

Start	Goal
$\frac{3a}{7b} = \frac{1}{7}$	$\frac{6a}{7b} = ?$

How can you get from one end of the path to the other?

One possibility is to solve the starting equation for either a or b and substitute that solution into the goal. Go ahead and try that. It may look like you will always have a variable left in your answer (but there are no variables in the answer choices). Don't worry; if you do it correctly, the variables will all cancel at the end.

There's a faster way to reach the goal, too, but it takes a different kind of insight. What mathematical operation could you perform on $\frac{3a}{7b}$ in order to get $\frac{6a}{7b}$? If you perform this operation on **both** sides of the starting equation (so the equation is still true), you should reach the goal.

Can you do this problem by finding values of a and b that make $\frac{3a}{7b} = \frac{1}{7}$, say $a = 1$ and $b = 3$? This might make a good check. What happens when you substitute these values into the answer choices? What if one answer choice were $\frac{3a+b}{7b}$?

13. As you look at this figure, what do you notice?

You need to find the length of a side of a right triangle. What relations do you know that involve the lengths of the sides of right triangles? The trigonometric quantities sine, cosine, and tangent probably occur to you. But these involve an angle measure, and none is given in the problem. You may already have thought of the Pythagorean theorem.

> Pythagorean theorem: In a right triangle $a^2 + b^2 = c^2$, where c is the length of the hypotenuse and a and b are the lengths of the other two sides.

But this doesn't help much either, because you only know the length of one of the sides of ΔBCD. To use the Pythagorean theorem, you also have to know the length of BC. Does the problem give enough information to find this length? $\overline{BC}$ is the hypotenuse of another right triangle, ΔABC.

So, using the information for ΔABC,

$$4^2 + 3^2 = c^2$$

or $$16 + 9 = c^2$$

or $$25 = c^2$$

and $$\pm\sqrt{25} = c$$

or $$\pm 5 = c.$$

Does this mean that we have two possible values for c, the length of the hypotenuse? Actually, it doesn't. Since the length of the side of a triangle cannot be negative, "–5" is a solution to the equation but not to the problem. So $CB = 5$. Knowing this, in ΔCBD, $CB = 5$ and $BD = 12$.

You can use the Pythagorean theorem a second time to find CD.

Does this answer look reasonable according to the figure? (Does the figure look "to scale"?)

Did you recognize ΔABC as a 3-4-5 triangle? How about ΔBCD as a 5-12-13 triangle? Recognizing these special triangles would save quite a bit of time on this question. (You should know the Pythagorean theorem anyway, in case the triangle isn't one of the "special" ones that you recognize.)

14. The three important quantities in this problem are the width of the table, the length, and the area. Is there a relation between these quantities? Since the table is a rectangle, there is a relation. Can you recall the relation?

> The area of a rectangle with width w and length l is
>
> $$A = lw.$$

Now for a plan: Find expressions for the length, width, and area of the tabletop and substitute into the formula for the area of a rectangle.

You're told that the length is 3 feet more than the width. If w represents the width, what expression represents the length?

Now substitute.

---

15. Let's work on a plan for this problem. Which order for the following steps would make the most sensible plan?

- Find out how far the boat goes to get to the island.
- Find out how big the island is.
- Find out how time, speed, and distance are related in this situation.
- Find out how long it would take to get to the island at 3 mph.

> You can keep the relationship between distance, speed, and time straight by remembering that the speed is expressed in miles per hour.
>
> That is, $$\text{speed} = \frac{\text{miles}}{\text{hour}} \iff s = \frac{d}{t} \iff d = st$$

Now, you can finish carrying out the plan. Which step in the proposed plan isn't necessary? Could you do that step if you wanted?

---

16. Though you might be able to do this one in your head, it doesn't take much extra time to write down some of your thought process, and writing down a few steps may make it easier or help you avoid a mistake.

Do you understand the problem? Did you note that the essential relation is the equality of the two areas? In order to write down this relation, you need to be able to express the area of the rectangle and the area of the square. The rectangle's pretty easy, but for the square you need a symbol. Choosing s to represent the length of one side of the square would be a good choice here. This choice makes it possible to express the area of the square, and the value of s is also the answer to the question.

So, you can write down an equation that expresses the equality of these two areas and solve it for s.

What can you say about this length in advance? Is there any relation between s and the 16 and 9 dimensions of the rectangle?

---

17. What does the 80% mean? 80% **of what**? Formulate a plan and carry it out.

Is your answer reasonable? You could do a quick check to see how much the rent would be if all the rooms were rented out. Here, the hotel gets $100 per room for the two-day period. Ordinarily the number wouldn't be as "nice" as $100, but you can always approximate.

Which of the answer choices represents the total rent if all the rooms are rented out for two days?

---

18. From the picture, can you guess at the measure of $\angle B$? The figure might not be drawn to scale, but the rest of the information that you are given seems to "look" right. How sure are you that you could pick out the correct answer just by using your eyes?

Did you write down the 30° angle measure and the 120° angle measure on the figure? Which angle's measure can you find next?

Is it a coincidence that $120° - 30° = 90°$?

---

19. What the "solution for the system of equations" means is a pair of values (x,y) that satisfies both equations. The pair $x = 0$ and $y = 4$ satisfies the first equation but not the second, so it isn't a solution to the system.

The algebraic techniques for solving this system of equations generally focus on combining the two equations into one equation that has only one variable. You can solve equations like that, and after you solve that simpler equation, you can use the answer to find the answer for the system of equations.

In the "substitution" method, you solve one equation for one of the variables. Here, solving the second equation for y will give the simplest looking expression. Substitute this expression for y in the other equation wherever there is a y. Now you have an equation with no y's and only x's. Solve it.

For this problem, the solution for x will be your answer. But it's good to check it out, since the check is pretty simple. Find the value of y that goes with this value of x to solve the original first equation. Then see whether this pair of (x,y) values satisfies the second original equation. If it doesn't, go back and check your work.

In the "addition" method, you multiply all terms in the top equation by one number, all terms in the bottom equation by another number, and add the equations together. If you pick the two multipliers carefully, you will end up eliminating one of the variables in the sum equation.

20. This problem tests your knowledge of arithmetic fractions. Notice that all four operations are used here.

Notice, too, that the parentheses are significant. Parentheses direct our attention to the mathematical expression inside and indicate that these expressions are the ones to be simplified first.

Simplify within the parentheses. Do you need a common denominator to do this? Where does "invert and multiply" apply? Now what?

With a calculator, you could check the answer, but that would be pretty complicated with all the fractions and parentheses. (And you can't use a calculator during the actual test, anyway.) Probably the best approach here is to look back over your written record of your solution and check for mistakes.

21. Here you need to simplify.

Before determining which terms can be combined, deal with the parentheses first. What kinds of operations are involved?

Usually, the simplification process includes two operations—removing parentheses and combining like terms.

You can eliminate the parentheses by following two rules. The first one comes from the definition of subtraction.

$$a - b = a + (-b)$$

In English it takes a little more space to state: "To subtract a number, add its negative." So subtracting $(-10y)$ is the same as adding $10y$.

The other rule is called the distributive property. Using this property, you can multiply a number outside the parentheses by each of the numbers inside the parentheses and still keep the equality:

$$a(b + c) = ab + ac$$

Using this property,

$$-3y(-y + 3) = (-3y)(-y) + (-3y)(3) = 3y^2 - 9y$$

Now you can simplify.

As a check, what should happen when you substitute a particular value for y? The simplified version should have the same overall value as the original expression. Would this help you eliminate any of the answer choices? What if you tried $y = 0$? (Zero is usually an easy place to evaluate an expression.)

22. This looks like the "basic" simplification problem for one polynomial divided by another. Usually, the top and the bottom will have a common factor that will cancel. So try factoring the numerator and denominator. Is there a common factor?

If you're having trouble factoring the numerator, it might be because you didn't notice that it was a difference of two squares. For the denominator, try looking for a common factor between the two terms, $2a$ and 4.

Here's another place where substituting a particular value for a into the original expression and the simplified version can help you check your answer. Trying two or three values for a can help you make extra sure. Can you tell which answer choice is correct just by trying values for a?

What part does the $a \neq -2$ play? It's really just a technicality. The goal of simplifying is to come up with an expression that is equivalent to the original version for **all** values of the variables. What is the value of your simplified expression when $a = -2$? The original expression is undefined when $a = -2$. Could you have used that as a clue for factoring the denominator in this problem?

23. Before beginning this problem, let's review the concept of a solution set and the relationship between an equation and its solution set.

> The solution set of an equation is the set of all and only those value(s) that, when substituted into the equation, will make the equation true.

So, if we know that $x = -3$ is a solution of the equation $x^2 - kx - 24 = 0$, then substituting -3 for x will make the equation true.

What happens when you substitute $x = -3$ into the equation? You should get a true equation with only the unknown k. What must be the value of k to make the equation true? You can check this answer by substituting the value for k back into the original equation to see if $x = -3$ is a solution; since this might take some time, you might want to save the check until you've finished looking at all the problems.

24. You are asked to find the measure of an angle. What techniques might apply? Trigonometry? Geometry? Algebra? All three?

Trigonometry relates the measure of an angle to the lengths of the sides in a triangle. In this problem, no side lengths are given. It's probably possible to assign some variables to represent side lengths and use trigonometry to solve this problem, but that would be pretty difficult. Perhaps you should try something else; if that doesn't work, you can always come back to this strategy.

Can you use geometry? This **looks** like a typical geometry problem. Can you make any progress? Since $\overline{BD}$ bisects a 100° angle ($\angle ABC$), what are the measures of $\angle ABD$ and $\angle DBC$? Write these measures on the figure, just to keep track of them. Now you have three triangles. If you use the fact that the sum of the measures of the angles in a triangle is 180°, you can find the measure of $\angle BDC$. Make a plan for the order you'll use to find the various angle measures. Several different orders will work.

---

25. In this problem, you are asked to observe how two different pieces of information relate to each other. You are told that a gardener has 78 yards of fencing and wants to enclose a rectangular plot whose length is to be between 20 and 25 yards. You're not given the exact length of the garden.

Since the total length of fencing is a specified quantity (78 yards), the width of the garden depends on the length of the garden.

A good technique here might be to construct a chart, starting with some possible lengths and determining the corresponding widths. For example, what is the width if the length is 20 yards? 25 yards? 22 yards? Draw a picture of the garden if you have trouble with this step.

Now that you have your chart, which of the answers makes sense? Is it always true that the width will be **between** the widths at the extreme values (20 and 25 yards) for the length?

You might choose an alternative strategy for solving this. Assign variables for the length and width and set up relations to describe the problem. Then try to bound the width by working algebraically. Perhaps you'd choose l to represent the length of the garden, in yards, and w to represent the width, in yards. Then you have bounds for l: $20 < l < 25$ (some people might interpret *between* to mean $20 \leq l \leq 25$, and here it wouldn't matter which you pick). You also know that the perimeter is 78, so $2l + 2w = 78$. How can you combine these to bound w?

---

26. If a is less than b and a is greater than c, which of the three numbers is in the middle? Are you sure of the order, or do you think there could be two possible arrangements? You might use a number line to help you think this through.

In a problem like this, where you are asked whether a statement is true, one approach is to look for a counterexample. If you can find one, the statement is not **always** true. Here, if you can find three positive numbers for a, b, and c that fit what's given in the problem—$a < b$ and $a > c$—and that **don't** satisfy $a + b > c$, then $a + b > c$ isn't **always** true. Try some examples to see if you can find which, if any, of these three options is false.

If all of the examples you try make the statement true, then you might **suspect** that it's always true, but you still wouldn't know for sure. How can you know for sure? You might try to combine algebraically the relations you were given in the problem statement to arrive at, for example, $a + b > c$. If you do that by the rules of algebra, you'll **know** that the statement is always true.

This strategy takes a little insight. It will be much easier if you are familiar with the rules of algebra, but that isn't enough. Unless you can imagine where these rules will take you, you'll have to try out rules randomly until you end up where you want to be—and you may get lost.

But don't be discouraged. Even if you can't see exactly how to show that $a + b > c$, perhaps you know the right direction to head. And you'll probably be able to tell when you're getting close.

Which relations from the problem seem relevant to showing that $a + b > c$ (option I)? $a < b$ doesn't have a c, and the a and b are on opposite sides of the relation, but the goal relation has them on the same side.

$a > c$ at least has the a and c in the proper relation. How can you introduce a b? Here's one way, and you can remember how this works for other occasions. $b > 0$ is given, and if $a > c$ and $b > 0$, one of the rules of inequalities says that $a + b > c + 0 \Longrightarrow a + b > c$. So statement I is always true. Do you see how this all fits together?

Now try II and III. If you can't show that these are always true, go back and try to find a counterexample again. The statements are either always true or not; you just have to find out which it is.

27. What do you know about $\sin x$?

Trigonometric functions are defined as ratios of lengths in a right triangle. For $\sin x$, the ratio is the length of the side opposite the angle over the length of the hypotenuse: $\sin x = \frac{\text{opposite}}{\text{hypotenuse}}$.

Which side is opposite? Which side is the hypotenuse? Now what?

28. Solving equations can usually be thought of as just manipulating them to make them look simpler until you get down to one that looks like (x = a number). Here, what qualities of $\frac{x}{2+x} = \frac{3x}{4x+3}$ make it complicated?

If you said that all the x's aren't on the same side, you're right. And if you said that these denominators complicate things, you're right, too.

If you don't like the denominators, you can get rid of them—but you have to do it without disturbing the equality. Multiply **both** sides by $(2 + x)$ and you won't have a denominator on the left side. Then multiply **both** sides to get rid of the right side denominator.

Think a second about what you've done. The rules of equations say that you keep things equal by multiplying both sides by the same thing, but you just **might** be introducing extra "phantom solutions." For example, what if $x = -2$ turns out to be a "solution"? Then, if you multiply by $(2 + x)$ to eliminate a denominator, you've really multiplied both sides by **zero.** The original equation might not have been true, but multiplying by zero made it true. For example, $-1 = 5$ isn't true but $(-1)\,0 = (5)\,0$ **is** true. To eliminate this problem, you'll have to go back and check your answers at the end to catch this kind of phantom solution.

If you wanted to get all the x's on the same side of the equation, you'd then want to find a common denominator and add those fractions together. Now, what should you do to simplify the equation?

Either way you choose to go, you should now have the same quadratic equation to solve. Solve it, and remember to check the answers by substituting them back into the **original** equation, $\frac{x}{2+x} = \frac{3x}{4x+3}$. It isn't good enough, in general, to substitute back into the quadratic equation. Don't forget to add the real solutions together.

29. There's nothing too difficult about absolute values, but you may make mistakes in solving this problem if you're not careful with the absolute value and negative signs. To avoid these mistakes, you should have a good method for writing down your steps, and you shouldn't try to do too much at once.

Again, ask yourself: What is the complicating part of the expression? What would you like to get rid of first? Most people would like to get the absolute value out of the way. Can you do that step?

> If you don't remember much about absolute values, here's all you need to know:
>
> First, an example:
>
> $|2| = 2$ and $|-2| = 2$
>
> Second, the general statement:
>
> The absolute value of a positive number is that number, the absolute value of a negative number is found by dropping the negative sign, and the absolute value of zero is zero.

How can you write this problem down so that you don't skip a step? Well, you're going to find $|-3|$ and $|-5|$ and put them in their proper places, so $-2(\quad) - (\quad) = ?$

Put $|-3|$ and $|-5|$ in place, and finish simplifying. Be sure to keep track of your steps.

If you had tried to do too much at once and thought that $-|-5| = +5$, you'd have chosen response B because absolute values are always positive. Why is this reasoning wrong?

Some students might decide that, since the problem has absolute values, they can just throw away **all** the negative signs. And they'd choose E. Why is this reasoning wrong?

30. Let's begin by looking at the given facts and finding out what other facts can be deduced from them. We are told that $\overline{BE}$ is parallel to $\overline{CF}$ and that A, B, C, and D are collinear.

What is the significance of the fact that A, B, C, and D are collinear? This is important information, since it implies that $\overline{AD}$ is a straight line. We know that when a straight line intersects a pair of parallel lines, certain pairs of equal and supplementary angles are formed.

Since it is given that the measure of $\angle FCD$ is 50°, it would be good to determine if any other angle in the figure is equal in measure to $\angle FCD$ because of the parallel lines. In fact, $\angle EBC$ and $\angle FCD$ are corresponding angles and are, therefore, equal in measure; that is, the measure of $\angle EBC$ is 50°.

Is there any other information that we can use? Yes. It is given that $\overline{BE}$ is the same length as $\overline{CE}$. What implications for ΔBEC does that piece of information provide?

If a triangle has two sides of equal length, then the angles opposite those sides are equal in measure. Since we know that $\angle EBC$ (opposite side $\overline{CE}$) is equal in measure to $\angle ECB$ (opposite side $\overline{BE}$), we also know that $m(\angle EBC) = m(\angle FCD) = 50°$. Then by substitution $m(\angle ECB) = 50°$.

At this point we need to recall a well-known fact about triangles:

> The sum of the measures of the three angles in a triangle is equal to 180°.

So, if the sum of the measures of two angles in ΔEBC is 100°, what is the measure of the third angle, $\angle E$?

31. $x^2 - 1 \leq 8$ is a quadratic inequality, which can be solved in much the same way as a quadratic equation. Do you recall how to solve a quadratic equation? A quadratic equation can often be solved by factoring. Let's use factoring to solve this expression.

The first step is to collect all the terms on one side of the inequality. So,

$$x^2 - 1 \leq 8$$

becomes $\quad x^2 - 9 \leq 0.$

Now let's factor the expression on the left, $(x^2 - 9)$.

$(x^2 - 9)$ is the difference of squares and can be factored as $(x - 3)(x + 3)$. So

$$x^2 - 9 \leq 0$$

becomes $\quad (x - 3)(x + 3) \leq 0.$

For the purposes of discussion, let $(x - 3)$ be represented by a and $(x + 3)$ be represented by b. Under what conditions is the statement $ab \leq 0$ true?

If $ab \leq 0$, then one of the following must be true:

Case I	or	Case II
$a \geq 0$ and $b \leq 0$		$a \leq 0$ and $b \geq 0$

Let's consider each case.

Case I: $a \geq 0$ and $b \leq 0$

This means we are looking for the intersection of $x - 3 \geq 0$ and $x + 3 \leq 0$.

$x - 3 \geq 0$ is equivalent to $x \geq 3$,

and $\quad x + 3 \leq 0$ is equivalent to $x \leq -3$.

There is no intersection between $x \geq 3$ and $x \leq -3$, so Case I yields an empty solution set.

Case II: $a \leq 0$ and $b \geq 0$

This means we are looking for the intersection of $x - 3 \leq 0$ and $x + 3 \geq 0$.

$x - 3 \leq 0$ is equivalent to $x \leq 3$,

and $\quad x - 3 \geq 0$ is equivalent to $x \geq -3$.

The intersection of $x \leq 3$ and $x \geq -3$ can be represented pictorially. Let's put each solution set on a graph. The solution to $x \leq 3$ is graphed below:

Notice that we use a solid circle over "3," the boundary number, to show that 3 is included.

The solution to $x \geq -3$ is graphed below:

If we put these two number lines together, we can see the intersection (the place where the number lines match):

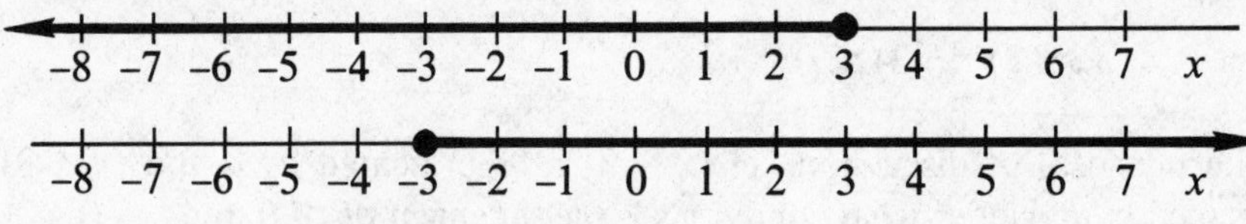

You can see that the intersection is the region bounded on the left by the value of –3 and on the right by the value of 3.

It's now easy to see the smallest real value that x can have:

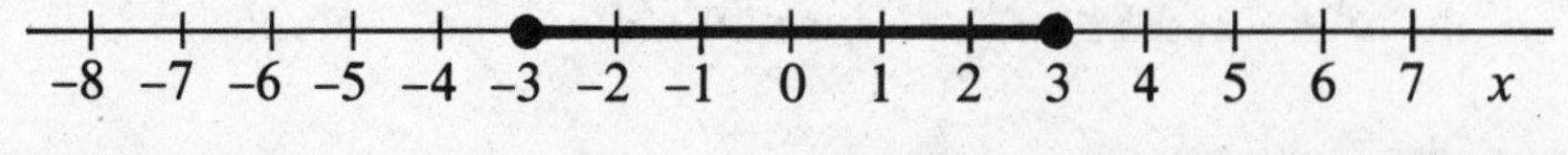

32. It might be helpful to draw a sketch to help identify a plan of attack to solve this problem.

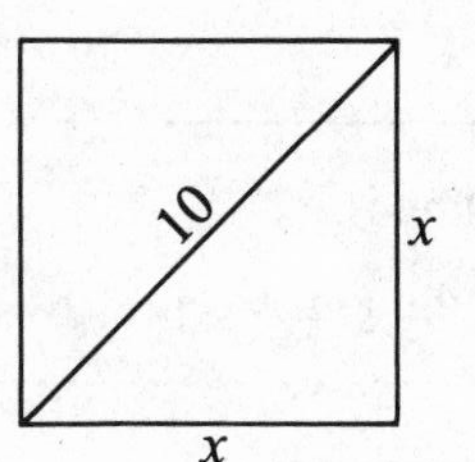

Label the square according to the given information. Let x represent the length of each side of the square.

In a square all sides are of equal length. What other fact do you know about a square that will help here? A square has four right angles. This means that the diagonal in the square creates two right triangles.

What facts can you recall regarding a right triangle and the length of its sides? In a right triangle, the relationship between the three sides is given by the Pythagorean theorem, $a^2 + b^2 = c^2$, where a and b are the lengths of the perpendicular sides of the triangle and c is the length of the hypotenuse. Now substitute and solve.

Does your answer make sense? The side of the square should be shorter than the 10-unit diagonal.

33. In general, any equation that can be written in the form

$$(x - h)^2 + (y - k)^2 = r^2, \text{ where } r > 0$$

is an equation of a circle with radius r and center (h,k) (where $r > 0$).

How can you use this information to generate the correct equation?

34. Do you remember how to find the slope of a line, given its equation?

You can start by putting the equation in slope-intercept form.

> The slope-intercept form for the equation of a line is:
>
> $y = mx + b$, where m is the slope and b is the y-intercept.

To find the slope of the given line, all you need to do is take the given equation, solve it for y, and find the coefficient of x.

You could also find two points that satisfy the equation of the line and calculate the slope as $\frac{y_2 - y_1}{x_2 - x_1}$. This method probably takes a little longer than the first, but there's nothing wrong with it.

---

35. In order to find the average number of persons per car for the 100 cars, you need to remember how to find an average.

> The average of n numbers is the sum of the numbers divided by n.

How many numbers are there? You want to know the average for 100 cars. Could you write out the numbers for all 100 cars? Without actually writing out all 100 numbers, can you imagine how you would do it? That list of 100 numbers is what the chart in the problem was made from—it summarizes those 100 numbers.

Now that you've imagined the list of 100 numbers, how do you figure out their sum? Once you have the sum, what's the average?

9

36. You're asked to find the area shaded below.

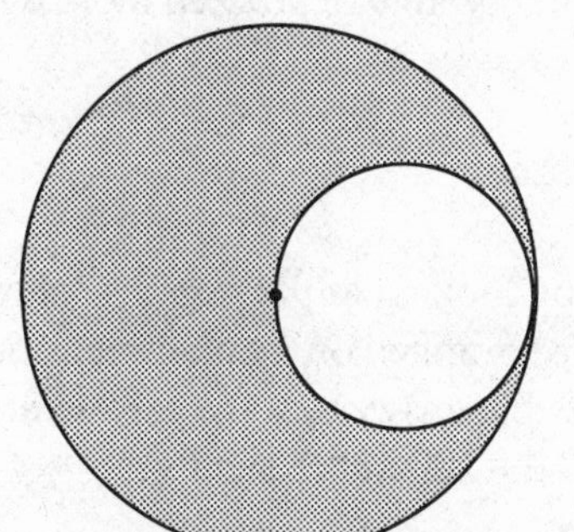

That will just be the area of the bigger circle minus the area of the smaller one. What information do you need to find the area of a circle? Do you have that information?

What would have happened if you had been given the following information?

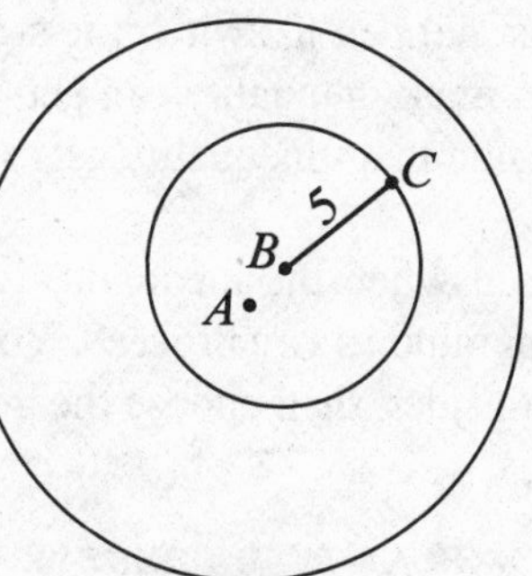

Would the answer be the same?

37. This problem asks you to find the equation of a line with a given slope and y-intercept. If you recall the slope-intercept form of the equation of a line, this problem is easy. (If you don't recall, refer to #34.)

Find the slope of the first line, the y-intercept of the second, and then put these together to get your answer.

38. Before beginning this problem, take a minute to sit back and decide exactly what is being asked for. Then you'll be able to proceed more directly toward the solution.

What is "$2x + 3 < 4x + 7$"?

It is an inequality in one variable. And, by looking at the response choices, you can see that this inequality's solution set will be graphed on a one-dimensional graph—a number line. Notice that, among the possible answers, some arrows are pointing to the left and some to the right. What does this difference signify?

When the arrows point to the right, numbers that are greater than a particular number are being indicated; when the arrows point to the left, numbers that are less than a particular number are being indicated. What else do you notice?

The inequality uses a "less than" sign. So, if the "greater than" arrow (pointing to the right) is to be correct, then something must happen to switch the sign around. This leads you to recall the cases when the sign in an inequality can get "switched." Do you remember under what conditions the sign in an inequality gets switched?

The direction of an inequality gets reversed when the inequality is multiplied (or divided) by a negative number. Keep this in mind as you proceed. You can solve this inequality by doing the same things to both sides; then choose the graph that shows the solution set.

39. Before beginning it would be a good idea to recall some basic facts about the slope of a line. Do you remember that the concept of the slope of a line refers to the slantedness of that line? There are different ways to find slope, depending on what information you have about the line in question.

This problem gives you the actual slope, and you are asked to find the missing coordinate in each ordered pair. In order to find c, you need to recall the relationship between points that lie on a given line and the slope of that line.

One way to conceptualize the slope of the line is to say that the slope of a line is defined as the ratio of the change in y-coordinates to the change in x-coordinates. To relate this concept to the problem at hand, we would say that the change in y is $c - (-c)$ and the change in x is $5 - 2$. (You could also say the change in y is $-c - c$ and the change in x is $2 - 5$.) The slope is the ratio of these two expressions.

Now you have two ways of writing the slope and you can construct an equation and solve for c.

40. If $I = Pr$, then, by substitution, you have $40 = 500r$. How do you solve for r?

What does it mean to express an interest rate as a percentage? A percentage is always a percentage **of something.** The interest rate is a fixed percentage **of what**?

Notice that some of the answer choices are closely related—they differ only in the placement of the decimal point. That might be a signal to be careful when moving the decimal to express the ratio as a percent.

41. There are several ways to do this one. You could find the equations for each of the four lines that form the square. (What do you know about the slopes of opposite sides of the square?) Once you have the equations of the four lines, how do you find the vertex of the square?

It might be helpful to draw a graph. Can you see a nice way to solve this problem by counting squares on the grid? How do you know which two points form a side? Why can't the line segment between (2,0) and (2,–4) be a side?

A square is just a special rhombus. Would either of these methods work if the problem had given three points on a rhombus? On a parallelogram? On a trapezoid? On a quadrilateral?

42. This is the basic type of exponent problem. Many people who miss this do so because they simplify $x^4 + x^4 + x^4$ to x^{12}. Just because 4 + 4 + 4 = 12, that doesn't mean that you should add whenever you see three 4's and a couple of plus signs. If you're not sure that a "rule" like this is true, try to find a counterexample. For example, try substituting $x = 1$ into $x^4 + x^4 + x^4 = x^{12}$. Since $x^4 = 1$ and $x^{12} = 1$, you have 1 + 1 + 1 = 1. Does 1 + 1 + 1 = 1? No. So you have a counterexample. (If you had tried $x = 0$, you wouldn't have found a counterexample.)

When do you add exponents? How can you properly simplify $x^4 + x^4 + x^4$? When do you subtract? A good technique is to try out some numbers in any "rule" that you aren't quite sure about. (Be careful in choosing 1 or 0 as your "tryout" numbers.) For example, what happens when you let x equal –2 in the problem and the answer choices?

43. In this problem, the correct answer to the division is not given, but it seems a pretty important quantity to work with. Let's give it a name so that we can talk about it. Let y be this correct result. So, $\frac{N}{7} = y$.

Since mistakenly dividing N by 8 yields a result of 12 less than y, that can be expressed $\frac{N}{8} = y - 12$.

Now there are two equations and two unknowns. How can they be combined to give one equation with only N as a variable?

You might prefer to do this problem without introducing the y, since you just get rid of it at the end. What you're probably doing is exactly the same as putting the y in and taking it back out, but doing all that in your head. That's great, but writing down more work can help if the problem turns out to be too complex to keep track of in your head.

---

44. The problem asks you to find the sum of the values of x that satisfy the equation $2x^2 - 4x - 6 = 0$. In order to answer the question, you need to find the solutions to this equation, and then find their sum.

It helps some people to be able to classify equations. Then the classification can be a cue to help remember the ways to solve the equation. This can be classified as a quadratic equation. How can you solve a quadratic equation?

> There are three main ways to solve a quadratic equation:
>
> 1. factoring
> 2. using the quadratic formula
> 3. completing the square

If the quadratic is easily factored, factoring may be the easiest method. Looking at the quadratic $2x^2 - 4x - 6$, you can see that it has a common factor of 2. This can be factored out of the trinomial.

$$2x^2 - 4x - 6 = 0$$

then $$2(x^2 - 2x - 3) = 0.$$

Since 2 is nonzero, you can divide both sides of the equation by 2.

So $$x^2 - 2x - 3 = 0.$$

This equation has the same solutions as the original equation.

Now, if $x^2 - 2x - 3$ factors, it will factor into the form $(x - m)(x - n)$, where you have to find the right numbers for m and n. Working backwards, $(x - m)(x - n) = x^2 - (m + n)x + mn$, so the product of your two numbers must be -3. How many ways can you get two integers m and n whose product is -3? Check to see if $(x - m)(x - n)$ is really $x^2 - 2x - 3$. If it isn't, you'll probably want to try the quadratic formula next.

Do you recall the quadratic formula? Most people just say: $\frac{-b \pm \sqrt{b^2 - 4ac}}{2a}$, but there's really a little more that you should remember.

Quadratic formula:

If $ax^2 + bx + c = 0$, then

$$x = \frac{-b \pm \sqrt{b^2 - 4ac}}{2a}.$$

Can you find the solutions this way? What are a, b, and c? You probably found that this equation did factor, though, so the quadratic equation isn't necessary. You have $(x - m)(x - n) = 0$.

How can a product be zero? The product is zero only when one of the factors is zero. So, $x = m$ or $x = n$. Be careful with your signs and you should have your answer.

45. What are you asked to do in this problem?

If you don't know any trigonometry at all, you might as well take a guess. But if you've learned just a little bit, you'll be able to do this problem. The plan for solving this problem will be to figure out what the value is for $\cos\frac{\pi}{3}$ and for $\sin\frac{\pi}{3}$, substitute those values into the expression, simplify, and choose the correct answer.

There's really no reasonable way to get the values for $\cos\frac{\pi}{3}$ and $\sin\frac{\pi}{3}$ without memorizing something. Perhaps you've worked with trigonometry just enough to know the values without actually sitting down to memorize them. Many people find it easier to remember a pattern for finding special trig values rather than memorizing the values themselves. Look for patterns in the following chart.

angle	sine	cosine
0	0	1
$\frac{\pi}{6}$	$\frac{1}{2}$	$\frac{\sqrt{3}}{2}$
$\frac{\pi}{4}$	$\frac{\sqrt{2}}{2}$	$\frac{\sqrt{2}}{2}$
$\frac{\pi}{3}$	$\frac{\sqrt{3}}{2}$	$\frac{1}{2}$
$\frac{\pi}{2}$	1	0

Here's one pattern:

If you write 0 as $\frac{\sqrt{0}}{2}$ and $\frac{1}{2}$ as $\frac{\sqrt{1}}{2}$ and 1 as $\frac{\sqrt{4}}{2}$, the pattern is $\frac{\sqrt{x}}{2}$, where x goes from 0 to 4. You may use other patterns to remember these special values—for example, the unit circle definition in terms of x- and y-coordinates. Use whatever pattern works best for you. You may even want to change $\frac{\pi}{3}$ back to degrees.

You can now substitute and simplify.

There's a tidier way to do this problem, though, that saves you the mess of simplification. This problem can be written as $\sin^2 x + \cos^2 x$ with the right choice of x. (You might recognize this from a trig identity.) Though you may think a problem never would be simpler with a variable instead of a number, this one is.

46. What does this problem ask for? Do you have a plan?

Stuck? Here's a case where trying specific numbers might help you get unstuck. What if you tried a "reverse" problem: If 17 student tickets were sold, what would the total revenue be? How many nonstudent tickets would have been sold if the total number of tickets sold was 35?

Now generalize. If you know that S represents the number of student tickets sold, what expression represents the number of nonstudent tickets sold? What expression represents the amount paid for the S student tickets? For the nonstudent tickets? For the total?

If you're still not getting one of the answers, try an alternate approach. How much did the class collect in ticket sales if $S = 17$? What should happen if you substitute $S = 17$ into the answer choices?

47. Let's step back and take a look at this problem. The problem asks when a product is positive. You can tell when a product is positive by knowing the signs of the two factors:

(positive) × (positive) = positive
(negative) × (negative) = positive
(positive) × (negative) = negative
(negative) × (positive) = negative

This means that the original inequality has the same solution as the logic statement below:

$$(3 - x) > 0 \text{ and } (x + 2) > 0 \text{ or } (3 - x) < 0 \text{ and } (x + 2) < 0$$

It may look like the problem's become more complex, but at least there's no product to worry about now. Can you solve this?

You can also use a number line to see where the signs of the two factors are the same. First, graph the points that make the product zero. The value 3 makes $(3 - x) = 0$ and -2 makes $(x + 2) = 0$. As we can see, the points -2 and 3 divide the number line into three intervals. Next, we check a point from each interval, substituting into each of the factors, to determine whether the factor is positive or negative in that interval. The sign of the product can now be determined from the signs of the factors.

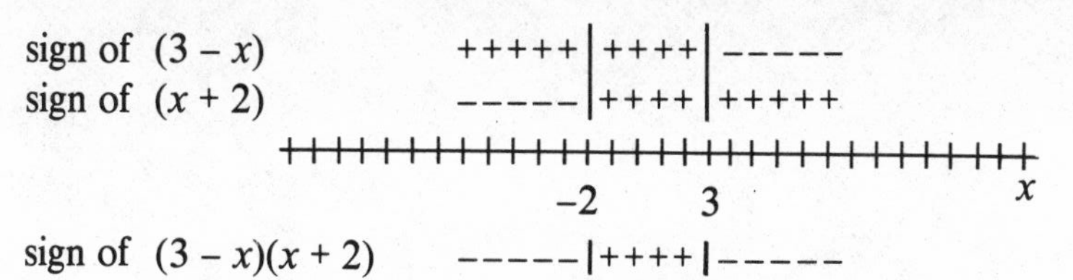

Now you can see where the product is positive.

48. If you're stuck, try writing the measures of $\angle A$ and $\angle C$ onto the figure. What kind of triangle is this?

> In a 30°-60°-90° triangle, if the side opposite the 30° angle has length x, then the hypotenuse opposite the 90° angle has length $2x$ and the side opposite the 60° angle has length $x\sqrt{3}$.

You need to find the ratio of the length of side $\overline{CB}$ to the length of side $\overline{AC}$, so decide which parts of the triangle these are. Since side $\overline{AC}$ is opposite the right angle, it is the hypotenuse and has length $2x$. Side $\overline{CB}$ is opposite the 60° angle, so it has length $x\sqrt{3}$. If you knew the value of x, you could find the ratio. Can you find the ratio without knowing the value of x?

---

49. If you know the cosine of an angle, you can always find the sine by using the most common of the trigonometric identities.

Remember: $\cos 45° = \frac{\sqrt{2}}{2}$ and $\cos 315° = \frac{\sqrt{2}}{2}$, but $\sin 45° = \frac{\sqrt{2}}{2}$ and $\sin 315° = -\frac{\sqrt{2}}{2}$. When is $\sin(x)$ positive and when is it negative? People often use a unit circle approach or imagine the graphs of the trig functions in order to keep these signs straight.

---

50. What does this problem ask you to do? Can you tell without looking at the form of the answer choices? You might guess that you're supposed to simplify, but you don't know for sure until you check the answer choices.

So which of the following should you do?

A. Cancel the $(x - y)$ in the numerator with one of the $(x - y)$'s in the denominator.
B. Cancel the $(x - y)$ in the numerator with both of the $(x - y)$'s in the denominator.
C. Multiply out the denominator, simplify, and then look at it to decide what to do next.
D. Factor $(x - y)$ from the denominator and cancel.
E. Use long division: $4(x - y) - x(x - y) \overline{)x - y}$
F. Use long division: $x - y \overline{)4(x - y) - x(x - y)}$

What's your plan? Which of these six plans would you try first? Which are incorrect? Does it help you to choose a plan when you see that all of the answer choices have a 1 in the numerator, so the $(x - y)$ must cancel out somehow?

Actually, several of the plans will work. One of the plans will get you an incorrect answer that's actually one of the answer choices, though. Which one?

Why does the problem say that $x < y < 4$? Just to keep the denominator from being zero. Since $x < y$ then $x - y \neq 0$ and since $x < 4$ then $4 - x \neq 0$.

51. If $\overline{AB}$ is 4 units long, how long is $\overline{AM}$? How long is $\overline{AD}$? Write these lengths on the figure. What's the angle at D? Now you can probably see a way to calculate the length of $\overline{AN}$. And once you have the lengths of all 4 sides of $AMCN$, you can find the perimeter.

52. What kind of information are you given? Two points and the slope of a line through those points. If you knew the coordinates of those two points, could you calculate the slope? If so, here's a fine time to try setting up an equation to solve. Just put t into the equation the same way you would use a number, then set the slope equal to -3 and solve for t. Check your answer by sketching a graph to see if the answer looks reasonable.

Another plan might be to find the equation of the line through $(1,-1)$ with slope -3. You could get this pretty quickly if you remember the point-slope form for the equation of a line. Then $(-1,t)$ must satisfy this equation, since the point's on the line.

Which of these methods do you like better?

53. If you didn't have a figure, it wouldn't be so easy to see that you're dealing with similar triangles. Did you see that? If not, can you see the similar triangles now? How will you know to look for them in the future?

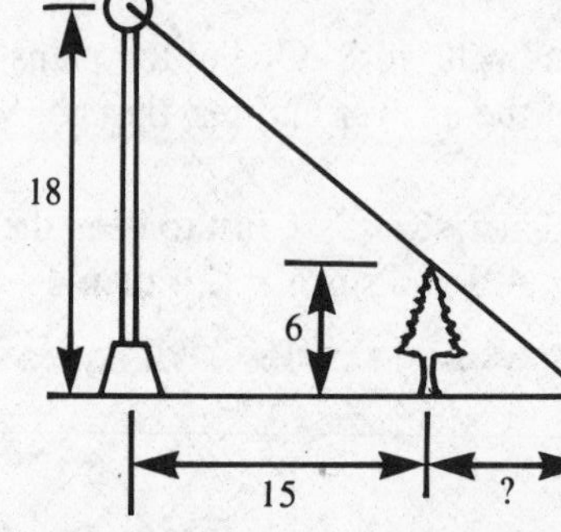

It's not clear how you should use these similar triangles, so you might try setting up all the possible proportions (there are three different ones, or six if you count turning the proportions upside down). It might help to add more labels to the figure—maybe labels for the vertices of the triangles. Can you list all three proportions? Then, choose the proportion to solve that has only one variable. (That variable may occur more than once.)

Do you need to use a variable? Does your answer make sense? That is, is your answer a reasonable one for the length of the shadow if all the other lengths are as given in the figure?

What's wrong with this proportion: $\frac{6}{18} = \frac{?}{15}$?

9

54. Here's a problem that looks pretty innocent, so why is it among the supposedly harder ones near the end of the test? Because many people follow rules without really thinking about what they're doing, they sometimes use the wrong rules. This problem illustrates one of the "classic mistakes."

$-2 < 3$, right? But what happens when you multiply both sides by -4? Is $8 < -12$? You have to remember to reverse the inequality when you multiply or divide by a ___?___ number. Do you remember hearing this? Now remember to think about what you're doing when you solve this inequality.

You can always check your answer by trying out a few numbers. If you think $x > -2$ solves this equation, try $x = -1$ to see if it works in the original equation. It should. Try $x = -3$. If it satisfies the original equation, your solution is wrong, since $x = -3$ isn't in the solution set $x > -2$.

55. Is there a base and its associated altitude where the lengths are given? Since three lengths are given, you can just check to see which could be for a base of the triangle and which could be for an altitude.

If you don't find any such pairs, maybe you can get at the answer indirectly. What areas **can** you find? Can you combine these areas to find the one you want?

56. This is an unusual type of question. You're not asked for the solution to the equation, just for a range that contains that solution. Is there a way to get the answer without actually solving the equation? Or should you just go ahead and find the solution and then see which interval it's in?

57. Do you know what *minor arc AB* means? If not, this problem will be difficult. Maybe you can get a clue from the answer choices. They all have π's in them. What kind of lengths on a circle with radius 6 would have π's in them? The circumference. Minor arc AB goes from A, downward along the circle, to B. (Major arc AB would go from A across the left side of the circle and back to B.)

So this problem is just asking you to find a fraction of the circumference of the circle. What's the entire circumference? What fraction of the circumference is contained in a 60° central angle?

58. What are the differences between the two lines? What kind of differences should you be looking for? Wouldn't differences in the **slopes** be the thing to look for, from what the problem gives?

The answer choices mainly ask whether something's positive, negative, or zero—although G is different. Can you estimate the slopes of these lines? Do you even know whether the slopes are positive, negative, or zero? Slope can be calculated as $\frac{y_2 - y_1}{x_2 - x_1}$ if you know two points on a line. Can you estimate two points on each line and use those to get estimated slopes?

Take all of this information and try to eliminate some of the answer choices. Can you find one that has to be correct? What argument would you use to convince someone that you're right?

59. What must you know in order to find the tangent of $\angle A$?

> In a right triangle, the tangent of $\angle A$ is defined as:
>
> $$\frac{\text{length of the side opposite } \angle A}{\text{length of the side adjacent to } \angle A}$$

By definition, then, the tangent of $\angle A$ is $\frac{BC}{AC}$, from ΔABC. Check to be sure this is really a right triangle; the definition doesn't apply unless it's a right triangle.

So, do you know the length of $\overline{BC}$ and $\overline{AC}$? How can you find the one you don't know? Can you find the sine or cosine of $\angle A$? Will this help?

60. Which of your techniques might apply here? You might recall information relating the slopes of perpendicular lines. You might choose to draw a picture. Is there anything special about the line $x = 2$?

This is the last question on the math test, so it's supposed to be hard, but you can probably solve this easily if you draw a nice graph.

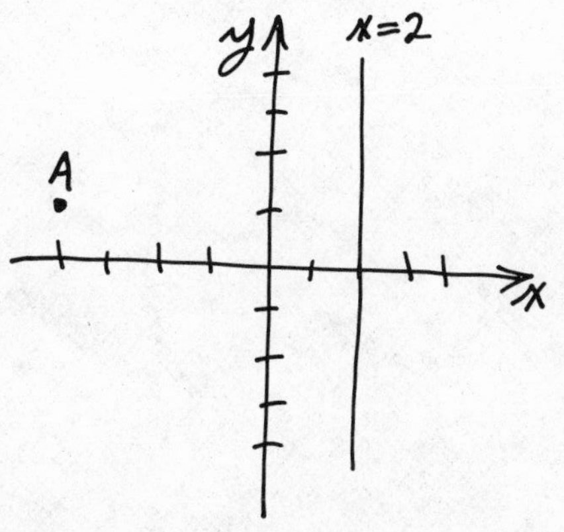

On the real test, if there were time left you'd be able to go back and work on any math problems that you skipped or wanted to recheck.

So, how did you do (not "how did you score")? Do you feel like you learned something by thinking about these problems? At least you should feel comfortable with the format of the test and know that there are lots of problems that you can solve. If you missed some, see what you can learn from those problems. It's likely that there will be problems similar to some of them on the version of the test that you take.

1. This question asks you to determine Julie's motivation for saying what she does. The motivation for the statement can best be understood in the context of the girls' relationship. As you're considering the best answer, you might think about what you know about Julie and Selina's relationship from the passage as a whole. Taken out of context, Julie's line of dialogue sounds a bit harsh. From the other information you're given about how the two girls interact, however, would you say it's logical to conclude that Julie is trying to **humiliate** Selina (D) or make her feel **guilty** (C)? Are there other clues in the passage that indicate the mood of the conversation? What does the word *importunings* in line 6 suggest about Julie's intentions?

We don't know where Selina's father goes at night. We know only that she's a bit touchy about the subject, from her dialogue in lines 31–32. Is there evidence in the passage that Julie either knows or doesn't know what Mr. Peake does after supper? Does anything in the passage support the idea that she's trying to find out (A)?

What is the main topic of conversation up to lines 31–32? There's quite a bit of talk about food. Can you find sections supporting the idea that Julie's rather blunt statement is aimed at persuading Selina to stay for supper (B)?

---

2. This question begins with the word *if.* Notice that it's not asking you **if** the difference between the meals at Mrs. Tebbitt's and at the Hempels' indicates a difference in status. You're being asked to **assume** there's a difference before you go on to identify what that difference is.

What are the meals like at Mrs. Tebbitt's? Which girl eats there? What are the meals like at the Hempels'? Which girl eats there? How would you characterize the difference between the two meals and, therefore, between the status of the girls who will be eating them?

Go back and look at the menus of the two meals, as they're revealed in the dialogue between Julie and Selina. Compare the number of items in each menu and the words used to describe them. Which meal sounds as if the food is more plentiful and more appetizing? Is that meal to be served to Selina or to Julie? Is it logical to assume that the better meal would be at the table of whichever girl has the higher financial status?

---

3. Again, as in the first question, you're asked to determine Julie's motive. As you did for question 1, think about the nature of the relationship between Julie and Selina as it's revealed in this passage as a whole. Question 1 asked you about Julie's motive in saying, "He leaves you right after supper. And you're alone." Thinking back to how you answered that question can help you answer this one, which focuses on the line just before Julie's remarks.

Julie's decision to pit steel against steel has a combative connotation. It may make you think of a sword fight, for instance. In the context of the girls' relationship, however, do you think it's logical to interpret *steel against steel* to mean that Julie wants to start a fight (B) or cut Selina down to size (A)? What other qualities do you associate with steel?

The author specifically mentions "the steel of Selina's decision" (lines 27–28). What does the word *steel* suggest about the nature of her decision? How final is it? Is there other information in the passage to contribute to your idea of how strong Selina's determination is? If Julie thinks in terms of the "steel" of Selina's decision, is it logical to infer that she musters her own steel to help Selina **make** a decision (C)? Has Selina made a decision? What is Julie's reaction to the decision? Is she trying to **persuade** Selina to change her decision (D)?

4. This question asks us to consider why Selina is groaning. A groan can mean a variety of things. How would you interpret the one in this context?

The question refers to Selina's "final" groan. To help interpret this groan, you may want to locate the reference to her earlier groans and notice how they're described. Is her final groan one of pain, as H suggests? We're told that she snaps the elastic band of her hat just before she groans, but is it this potentially painful action or the words she says immediately afterward that you would logically associate with the groan? Were her earlier groans related to the act of putting on her hat?

How is Mrs. Hempel's cooking portrayed in the passage? Would you agree with J that it sounds "really awful"? Remember the adjective used to describe Selina's first groans. Why would they be "greedy" groans if she knew the food was bad?

A groan can indicate pain, sorrow, or disgust—among other things. Can it also show regret or longing? What is the last thing Julie says before Selina utters a final groan? What is the first thing Selina says after groaning? Do you think she groans because desserts are forbidden her (G)? Does anything in the passage suggest that she is struggling with a diet or has a medical condition that would force her to avoid sweets? Does she groan because she wants the apple roll (F)? Looking at the reason for Selina's earlier greedy groans, could you conclude that this final one springs from the same feeling?

5. This requires careful reading—both of the question and the passage. Notice that you're asked when Julie **first** invited Selina to dinner. Think about the chronological order of the events in this passage. When does the "tragedy at the boarding house," mentioned in C, occur? Is it logical that Julie could have learned of it before inviting Selina?

From all the foods Julie lists, it certainly sounds as if there would be enough to go around if Selina joined the Hempels for dinner. Beware of making assumptions, though. Is it specifically stated in the passage that Julie's mother told her there would be enough for Selina (A)?

When does Julie hear what Selina will eat at the boarding house (B)? What is Julie's reaction? Is that the first time she tries to persuade Selina to come to supper?

When do you learn that Selina and Julie have spent the day together (D)? Is there any mention of supper invitations at that time? What does *importunings* (line 6) indicate?

Remember that the first invitation to supper isn't necessarily the first line of dialogue in which Julie urges Selina to stay. You need to concentrate on the first reference to the invitation and decide which event most closely precedes it.

6. What does the phrase *well beyond hurting* mean in this context? The phrase *heavy inert burden* can provide a clue. The word *inert* is particularly telling. Why might the burden be inert, or unmoving? Think about *well beyond hurting,* too. In this context, does *well* refer to health? Does it follow logically that something described as heavy and inert would be "so healthy it cannot be hurt" (G)? Or is *well* used to express a degree—to say that the burden is **far** beyond hurting?

Is there anything about the words *heavy* and *inert* that you can equate with *tough* (H)?

Is it accurate to say that the burden has been "severely damaged" (F)? Is that why it's being carried with "infinite care" (line 73)? Think about why something that's beyond feeling pain is being carried with infinite care. Is there anything ironic about that? Would something that has been severely damaged necessarily be incapable of feeling pain? What kind of state **would** make something incapable of feeling pain?

Is there evidence to support the idea that the burden is dead (J)? Study the final paragraph, not just lines 73–74. What do the words *still* (line 88) and *listlessly* (line 91) convey to you? What do the references to the feet, boots, and face suggest? What could the coat covering the face signify? Would a corpse be carried with "infinite care"?

7. It might be helpful to take another look at what follows *She knew* in line 81, as well as what precedes it. Pay particular attention to the last paragraph.

After answering question 6, you have a good idea of what the burden is that's being carried with infinite care. If you assume that a body is being carried into the boarding house, can you think of a reason why it should have such a strong effect on Selina? Who is the "he" she thinks about in the last sentence? From what you've read, who is the one man Selina knows well enough to observe that he was always "finicking" about his boots? If the word *finicking* isn't in your vocabulary, try not to let that throw you. Can you figure it out from the context? How might it relate to Selina's noticing the shininess of the boots? The crucial word in the last sentence, however, is *always.* Think about the length and intimacy of a relationship suggested by that word.

Where is there a reference to Mrs. Tebbitt in relation to the line *She knew?* What is Mrs. Tebbitt doing? Do you think her "shrill clamour" (lines 84–85) is directed at Selina? Why would she be angry with Selina (A)?

Does any information in the lines just before *She knew* suggest that Selina's father hated the boarding house (B)? Does anything earlier in the passage suggest that Selina might already know her father's feelings? Look at Selina's physical reactions to the sounds she's hearing and how they contribute to her sudden realization. Would the sounds, her reaction, and the suddenness of her revelation be appropriate if what she "knew" was that her father hated the boarding house?

Again, considering how the sounds she hears lead to her sudden knowledge, is there any evidence to suggest that Selina will never see Julie again (C)? In the last paragraph, do any details of the "burden" indicate that it might be Julie? Do any details suggest that it's Selina's father (D)? Remember to pay close attention to the corpse's physical characteristics—the heaviness, the boots—and to the implications of the phrase *he always.* Notice, too, that when Selina calls to her father, he hasn't yet come in (line 60). Is it possible that he's making his entrance at the end of the passage, as a "flat still burden"?

8. Be careful not to confuse Julie Hempel and Selina Peake. Try looking through the passage for references to Julie's home life. Scan the dialogue as well as the narrative portions.

In lines 14–17, which girl is talking about her mother and father (H)? Which girl says she'll be eating cold mutton and cabbage at Mrs. Tebbitt's (F)? Which girl is left alone every night after her father leaves—leading a reader to infer that she lives with him alone (G)? Does anything in the passage suggest that Julie lives with Selina (J)? Why does Julie put so much energy into persuading Selina to stay for supper if they live together? Look carefully at lines 57–60 for indications of where the girls' homes are in relation to each other. Who does "her second-floor room" (line 59) belong to?

9. Look back at the paragraph in which Selina sews her hat. Watch for a cause-and-effect order to the events and for information that either supports or contradicts the answer choices.

Why does Selina regard her hat with distaste (line 62)? What does she decide to do? What makes her change her mind about her original plan?

When Selina sews her hat, is she repairing something done "purposely" (A) or "accidentally" (B)? Does anything in the passage indicate that her hat doesn't fit (C)?

Notice Selina's opinion of the flowers currently on her hat. Could you surmise that she might want to add new flowers (D)? Does the passage **tell** you that's what she wants to do? Be careful about making assumptions—pick the best response based on evidence in the passage.

10. Go back and look at what the word *modish* describes. What else are you told about Selina's costume? What other adjectives does the author apply to it? Is being "modish" a desirable or undesirable characteristic?

Think about how Selina's clothing testifies to her father's setbacks (line 44). Don't jump to conclusions, though. Let the passage tell you how she looks. Two key words are *true* (line 44) and *but* (line 48). Notice the kind of details each word introduces. The words after *true* show the way in which her clothes **don't** reflect her father's misfortune. The words after *but* reveal the costume's flaw.

According to the passage, the modish dress was "bustled, and basqued, and flounced." Obviously, the style comes from an era before ours. We'd probably consider it "old-fashioned" (G), but is that what the author intends by calling it "modish"? In this context, if a dress is last season's style (lines 48–49), is it necessarily "old-fashioned"? Does the sentence sound logical if you substitute *old-fashioned* for *modish?*

Likewise, the bustle and flounces might conjure an image of a dress that's more likely to be "modest" (F) than provocative. But is that necessarily what *modish* means here—even if modesty **is** the mode? (Be careful not to be unduly influenced by the similarity in the spellings of *modish* and *modest.*)

Does anything in the passage suggest that Selina's costume is "cheap" (J)? Notice how her hat is described (lines 46–48). What is suggested by the author pointedly mentioning that the hat came from New York?

If you weigh the costume's positive qualities against the negative, what do you come up with?

True, the costume is:

- modish
- bustled
- basqued
- flounced
- topped off by a New York hat.

But:

- it was purchased **last spring.**

Could you interpret this to mean that the costume was "somewhat stylish" (H)? Is the sentence logical if you substitute that phrase for *modish?*

11. This item asks you to consider "electors' loyalties"; if electors are loyal to a presidential candidate (that is, pledged to vote for him or her), do the electors actually vote for that candidate when the electoral college meets? Notice the degrees of difference in responses A, B, and D. A deals with the idea that electors **must vote** for the candidate; B with the idea that there is **no guarantee** that electors will vote for the candidate; and D with the idea that electors **bolt** from their candidates and vote for someone else. Which response is most accurate, according to the passage? For C, did the 29 electors pledged to Jimmy Carter really vote for Ford? (Note the word *if* in line 18!)

12. The key to answering this question correctly is recognizing that the dates in each of the responses are found in the passage; your job is to locate the dates that correspond with "elections in which the **House of Representatives** had to resolve a tie in the electoral vote." What happened in elections on the dates 1976, 1800, 1824, 1876, and 1888? In which of those years were ties in the electoral college resolved by the House of Representatives?

13. The information needed to answer this item is located in the passage. You need to be aware that, in the passage, the term *swing vote* refers to a group of people whose votes can determine the outcome of an election. If *urban* means "relating to a city," then what is an "urban" state? In large urban states, where are the most important groups of voters? Where is the "swing vote" concentrated? For A, what is a suburb? Is it the same as a city? Rural areas (B) relate to the country. Are voters in large urban states concentrated in rural areas? For C, who are the most important voters? Are these voters of large urban states located in major cities? For D, many people feel interest groups are favored by the electoral college (lines 60–61), and one of those interest groups is big urban states. Are the most important groups of voters in these large urban states found in special interest groups? Is there an important distinction between what the passage refers to as "interest groups" (small states and big urban states) and "special interest groups" (voters throughout the nation who agree on particular issues)?

14. How can Congress eliminate the electoral college? The answer to this item can be found in the passage. What is the procedure Congress must follow to "abolish the electoral college" (line 58)? Would Congress need to enact a constitutional amendment (F), issue a statute (G), request that the president issue an order (H), or hold a referendum—that is, submit a measure to popular vote (J)?

15. What does the phrase "the electoral college will not reflect the popular vote" indicate?

There is a concern that—as happened in 1876 and 1888—candidates who do not win the popular vote will nevertheless be elected to the presidency by the electoral college. Find the lines that talk about this fear (lines 51–52). Which answer is most directly referred to in those lines?

For A, are special interest groups discussed in conjunction with when fears about the electoral college surface? For B, does the passage state that concerns surface about the electoral college and the popular vote almost **every time** an election is held? Or, for C, are concerns voiced when the popular vote is close? For D, in what context does the passage mention states with 4 to 14 electoral votes? Is this discussion related to concerns about the electoral college and the popular vote?

16. Note two key phrases in this question: *most likely believe* and *is contradicted by*. The question asks you to decide what the writer **would** believe (it asks you to think from his viewpoint) **based on** what he's told you in the passage. The phrase *is contradicted by* tells you that the best answer is the one that is **not** true about the electoral college system. As you read through the choices, what do you notice about F and H? What does each say about the importance of votes? Now refer to the passage and see what is said about the equality of votes. (Keep in mind that you're looking for the response that is "**contradicted** by the electoral college system": the one that is **not** true.) For G, think about how you would define the electoral college. If, indeed, the electoral college is a limited number of people choosing the nation's leaders, then this response is true. Is it the best answer here? For J, does the passage state that "electors face no legal penalty for switching candidates"? Is this response the best answer? Now, consider which responses you have ruled out because they are true. Which one is **not** true about the electoral college system?

17. This question first requires a careful reading of relevant lines in the passage to distinguish between what **did** happen in the 1976 election and what **might have** happened. Note who won the election and what his popular vote and electoral vote margins were. Now consider what might have happened in the election. What are two ways that Carter would not have become president, even though he had a popular vote plurality? Note the words *would have caused* in A. This question deals with what might have happened in the election. You need to determine if a change in electoral votes would have caused Carter to lose in the electoral college (and thus lose the election). For B, what **did** happen in the election? Did the electoral vote actually overturn the popular vote? For C, can you say that this election was close? Did the electoral college operate "properly" in this case? For D, when is an election decided in the House? Did this happen in 1976?

18. Read carefully the **entire** quotation that begins in line 77. Be sure, when choosing your answer, to consider **all** information stated in the passage. Remember, too, that you may choose more than one option. For option I, does the passage state that "large states have a net advantage"? For option II, are states with 4 to 14 electoral votes at a disadvantage? For option III, the inhabitants of which states are favored and those of which states are discriminated against? After you choose the option or options that are supported by the passage, then consider the responses. Is response F (option I only) the best answer? Or is response G (option II only) better? Would you say that options I and II are both accurate? If so, then you'll choose response H. Finally, you'll choose response J if you think that options I and III are both accurate.

19. For this question, you are looking for:

1. the author's claim that the electoral college is undemocratic and
2. the reason (from the passage) for his claim.

Does the author state somewhere in the passage that the electoral college is undemocratic? (The last sentence of the passage says this proposal "would be much more democratic." What does the rest of this last sentence say?)

Is A (certain voters are prevented from voting) supported by the passage? For B, does the passage say (possibly in other words) that there is a "winner-take-all provision" that causes votes for the losing candidate in each state to be "lost"? For C, when is the House of Representatives in control of the electoral college's choice of candidates?

If you eliminate A and C, how can you choose between B and D? For D, does the passage state that voters are more trustworthy than electors? What is stated about **electors** being considered more trustworthy than voters? Who held that view? Is there anything else in the passage that might justify D? In the seventh and eighth paragraphs, the author explains favoritism and bias in the electoral college. In these two paragraphs does the author claim that voters are more trustworthy than electors? The final sentence of the passage deals with direct popular election. Does this sentence support the idea that the author believes voters to be more trustworthy than electors? Does the writer talk about voter trustworthiness as a reason the electoral college is undemocratic? So which response is a better answer—B or D?

20. This item requires you to read **very** carefully! Notice that both the seventh and eighth paragraphs discuss states and groups that are favored by the electoral college system. You are asked to find which group is "most likely to be discriminated against." The last two sentences of the eighth paragraph (lines 80–84) specifically discuss this topic, using the same language as the question. But you must "translate" words from the passage in order to find the best response.

For F, is there a word in lines 80–84 that means "big city"? What are "central city and urban citizen-voters"? Once you have figured out the words, then decide if big city residents are indeed discriminated against. For G, does the passage state that suburban voters near large cities are discriminated against? (Don't **assume** that because big city residents are favored, suburban voters are discriminated against. What does the passage indicate?) For H, are "farmers" discussed in lines 80–84? What term would include "farmers"? Are farmers discriminated against? For J, does the passage mention "youth" and indicate that they are treated unequally by the electoral college system?

Note: The questions referring to Passage III will ask you to make comparisons or generalizations based on what you're told in this passage about four painters. It may be helpful if, right from the start, you notice that the authors have divided the painters into two pairs, based on their artistic philosophies. Consider taking a moment to identify each pair and the major Post-Impressionist attitude associated with it. You might even want to jot down that information for easy reference.

21. How were van Gogh and Gauguin alike? Find the paragraph that discusses their similar feelings about their work. Do any of the choices restate the words of the passage?

At first, it could appear to you that more than one of the responses would be a good choice. Notice that A, B, and D refer to emotions. For A, C, and D you need to look not only at what is said about van Gogh and Gauguin but also at what's implied about artists in general.

A broad, superficial generalization about any group of people—whether they're defined by physical qualities, profession, religion, or ethnic background—is in danger of being a stereotype. Before you settle on one of the responses, make sure it's not based on a stereotype or any other idea not stated in the passage. The answer you pick should be fully supported by information in the passage. Does the passage talk about the "emotionalism of most artists"? Does it talk about "most artists" at all? On that basis, which responses could you rule out?

22. Try not to let yourself be overwhelmed by all the combinations of names. Instead, think back to those pairs you identified earlier. If you see either pair of artists among the choices, that might be a good place to start. Look back at the passage for references to that pair. Is there information to support the choice's generalization about them?

Another approach might be to think about each characterization presented. For instance, after reading J, you might ask yourself: **Who** wanted to systematize optical color mixing? Refer to the passage for the answer. Is it Cézanne and van Gogh, as J proposes?

Take your time so that you can avoid hastily picking an answer that looks reasonable simply because **part** of the wording matches a reference in the passage.

23. Again, bear in mind the pairs of artists you've identified. As you read through the choices, notice that A, B, and C all speak in terms of pairs. D generalizes about all four artists.

Do Gauguin and Seurat form one of the pairs you've identified? According to the passage, are their works similar (A)? Can you locate a specific reference in the text to ancient and non-Western values and their relationship to European art? Are the works of Gauguin and Seurat a reaction against those values (C)?

Would you contrast Gauguin and van Gogh with Seurat and Cézanne as representing two different attitudes toward Impressionism (B)? Does the passage show that Gauguin and van Gogh share similarities? That Seurat and Cézanne share similarities? Although the passage is about Post-Impressionism, B mentions only Impressionism. Before you rule out B, make sure you've read the passage carefully, especially the first paragraph. What definition of Post-Impressionism are you given?

Considering the passage as a whole, would you say that its focus is on linking the four artists with a single aspect of Post-Impressionism (D)? Again, be sure you haven't read the first paragraph too quickly.

24. Rather than studying each choice individually, you might find it more efficient to first skim the passage for references to geometric aspects of painting. Then go back and check your findings against those choices.

Does the word *geometric* crop up with respect to an individual painter or a group of artists? Make sure you're aware of the style each artist is associated with. At the same time, be wary of generalizing about a group of artists based on the characteristics of one artist.

An alternative approach would be to consider what information you have about each of the four choices. Does the passage represent the Impressionists (F) as being interested in the geometric aspects of painting? (You may have to search carefully to find a reference to them that will give you a clue.) What attitude do the Expressionists (G) represent? Which Expressionists are discussed in the passage? Are they portrayed as being interested in geometric aspects of painting?

What information do you have about Gauguin's work (H)? About Cézanne's (J)? Is either painter linked with an interest in the geometric aspects of art?

25. Read the responses carefully and make sure you have a sense of what's being implied by the entire answer. Notice that each answer has two parts. First, there's a description of an artistic technique van Gogh might have used:

A. bold, simple shapes and brushwork
B. pure color and rhythmic movements
C. impressionistic techniques of textural surfaces
D. textural brushwork and color

The second part proposes what van Gogh wanted to depict:

A. the physical world
B. the outer world
C. reality
D. his emotions

You should pick the response in which **both** parts seem to be the most accurate.

Which group is van Gogh associated with throughout the essay? Is it the Expressionists or the Formalists? Does this provide you with any clues about what he was interested in depicting?

Scan the essay for references to van Gogh. What did he want his work to reflect? How is his technique described?

Remember to base your answer solely on information in the passage. You may have seen some of van Gogh's works in museums or textbooks, but you shouldn't let any visual images interfere with your analysis of what the authors of this passage are trying to convey.

26. This is another question for which the answers have two parts. Make sure you pick the one that best describes pointillism and correctly identifies who painted in that style.

Find the reference to *pointillism* in line 26. Can you locate the painter associated with it? Was it Cézanne (F)? Seurat (G, H)? Or both (J)?

Is there an explanation of *pointillism* that resembles any of the descriptions in the responses?

Look at F. Was pointillism an attempt to develop a "scientific" technique based on color optics? Where do you see a reference to color optics? Which artist is associated with it?

Does *pointillism* (notice that the name of the technique is "point-illism") refer to applying paint in tiny points or dots of color (G)? Which artist is mentioned as using this method?

Scan the passage for a possible reference to Seurat and the observation of nature. Remember, a response that makes an accurate statement isn't necessarily the best answer. It must also address the question of what *pointillism* refers to. Does the passage link observation of nature to the technique of pointillism (H)? Did Cézanne and Seurat try to use separate shades of color (J)? Did both artists work with pointillism?

27. There are two possible approaches to this question. One is to skim the passage for references to Cézanne and Seurat. If you glance ahead at the rest of the passage, you'll notice that this pair is the subject of all the questions from here to the end, so it might be to your advantage to take a moment now to refresh your memory. As you read, be aware of what generalizations are made about Seurat and Cézanne—as well as the similarities and differences in their work.

An alternative is to look for the techniques mentioned in the choices. Notice the artist or artists associated with them in the passage.

Where is there a reference to using "color for atmospheric effects" (A)? Who is associated with this technique, and in what way?

Can you locate any mention of "direct observation of nature" (B)? What about "planar surfaces" (C) and "loose brush strokes" (D)?

Remember, **both** Seurat and Cézanne must favor the technique for it to be the **best** answer.

28. What's the style of Post-Impressionism that Seurat and Cézanne are both associated with? Is it Formalism or Expressionism? As you did for the preceding question, you might search the passage for references to both artists and their similarities. Alternatively, look for references to the four concepts mentioned in the responses and try to identify the artist or artists associated with each. Who is linked with "formal aspects of painting" (F)? With "expressing inner feelings" (G)? With "Cubism" (H)? With "pointillism" (J)?

29. Take note of the word *implies* in this question. It's an indication that you won't find the answer spelled out in the passage. You'll have to synthesize the information you're given and come up with your own conclusion. Notice that each response has two parts. Make sure you agree with both parts of the one you pick. For instance, A makes two generalizations:

1. Cézanne and Seurat expressed inner emotions.
2. They both used demanding techniques.

Consider dealing with each generalization separately. Were Seurat and Cézanne working to express inner emotions? (Do you feel like an expert on these two by now?) *Express* is a key word. Were they Expressionists or Formalists?

What is meant by "demanding techniques"? Can you infer from the methods mentioned in this paragraph how difficult they were to use?

It's probably occurred to you that if you can rule out the first generalization, you don't have to spend time thinking about whether the second one is supported by the passage. In other words, an answer that's only **half** right is **all** wrong.

You could apply this process to the other responses. According to the seventh paragraph, can you conclude that Cézanne and Seurat "used color conventionally" **and** "had an equally lasting impact on painting" (B)? What evidence of their impact is presented in that paragraph?

From the seventh paragraph, would you infer that both artists "used unconventional methods" **and** that "Cézanne's technique was more popular with younger painters" than Seurat's (C)? Do you have a basis for concluding that their methods were unconventional? What does the paragraph say about "strokes of color" (D)? About the relative popularity of each artist's techniques?

30. By this time you probably feel as if Cézanne and Seurat are members of your family. You've spent so much time thinking about them that you can almost predict what kind of cereal they'd eat for breakfast and who they'd root for in the World Series. Think about their similarities one more time.

According to the passage, did they **both:**

- Reject the intuitive approach (F)? Or use it (J)? What does *intuitive* connote?
- Reject divisionism (G)? What's another name for divisionism? Who developed it? What motivated him?
- Apply paint in dots (H)?

Both is a key word. Cézanne and Seurat were both Formalists. Their styles, however, were not identical. You can't assume that a generalization about Cézanne's approach is automatically a valid generalization about Seurat's, and vice versa.

As you scan the passage, be alert for specific characteristics that are clearly associated with only one artist. Be cautious about attributing those characteristics to both men.

You'll have to use your powers of inference here. The best answer may not jump out at you, but it may be easy to eliminate some of the wrong ones fairly quickly if you recognize them as being too specific—that is, applicable to only one artist.

Even if science isn't your forte, you **can** do well on this part of the reading test. Don't let yourself be intimidated by technical words or scientific concepts that seem difficult to grasp. Concentrate only on what you need to know **to answer the questions.** Otherwise, as you read this passage, you run the risk of getting needlessly sidetracked by such fascinating but irrelevant concerns as:

How can a theory be **robust,** anyway? Isn't that the same as healthy?

Does microwave radiation float up into space from microwave ovens?

How can **plasma** generate electromagnetism? Isn't that the stuff my blood is made of?

Remember, all the information you need is in the passage or can be inferred from it. Don't spin your wheels over terms and concepts that aren't related to the questions.

31. Think about what's discussed in the passage as a whole. Skimming it for the word *question* or for telltale question marks won't help you decide on the best answer. Also beware of hastily settling on one of the responses simply because it repeats a phrase you recognize from a section of the passage. Find the exact reference in the passage and see if it is, in fact, an example of something that's being questioned. What does the passage say about electromagnetic fields (A)? About Alfvén's Nobel prize (B)? About positively charged ions (C)?

Consider the focus of the entire passage. What controversy or controversies do you see at its center? What viewpoints are being argued? You might look for words that will help you pinpoint conflicting attitudes. References to *critics* and *dissidents* can indicate an area of dispute. Can you identify any "basic astrophysical theories" (D) put forth in this passage? Are any theories being challenged?

Speaking of dissidents, this might be a good time to think about something that could trip you up as you work your way through these questions. Lines 62–63 identify two groups: the plasma dissidents and the red-shift dissidents. Notice that the plasma dissidents, as typified by Alfvén, disagree with the big-bang theory and support the plasma theory. The red-shift dissidents, such as Arp, disagree with the explanation for red shift suggested by the big-bang theory. So, you have this interesting juxtaposition:

The plasma dissidents are **for** plasma.

The red-shift dissidents are **against** red shift.

One group of dissidents is identified by the concept it **supports,** while the other is identified by the concept it's trying to **disprove.**

---

32. Notice that each response has two parts. First, you need to decide whether the passage is or isn't logically consistent, then pick the reason that best supports your decision.

As you read the second part of each response, be careful not to bring in your own preconceived ideas. The answer you pick should be substantiated by the passage. Be alert for stereotypes and other generalizations that aren't supported by the information you've read.

Make sure you've read the question carefully, too. Ask yourself whether it's appropriate to equate *persistent* criticism with *serious* criticism. What does *persistent* mean? What does *serious* imply?

Consider the alternatives to the big-bang theory discussed in the passage. From what you've read, can you tell how widely these theories have been accepted (F)? Take a moment to compare the second part of F and H. F says the big-bang alternatives aren't widely accepted; H says the alternative theories don't seriously challenge the big bang. Is there a significant difference between what those two statements imply? They seem to be making the same essential point, but notice that F uses it as an argument for why the passage **is** logically consistent—H uses the same statement to argue that the passage **isn't** logical.

G makes a statement about professional writers. Is the statement supported by information in the passage? Can you locate a reference to professional writers? Think about what this statement implies—that anything by a professional writer must be logically consistent. Does anything in the passage lead a reader to that conclusion?

Take a close look at J. Is it logical to say that persistent criticism **must** invalidate a theory? Does it matter who's doing the criticizing? Is criticizing the same thing as **disproving?**

Remember to cast a suspicious eye on terms that strike you as absolutes, or as particularly emphatic or judgmental (*always, never, every, none,* etc.). Such terms can hint at a broad generalization that's difficult to support. Consider the implications of **any** theory, **must** invalidate, **obviously,** and **invariably.**

---

33. You can go directly to the passage for the answer to this one. Look for references to the big-bang theory. Be sure not to confuse it with the alternative theories some scientists have proposed. Also, notice how the question is worded. You're being asked what the universe's expansion was a result of, **not** what it resulted in.

If the explanation of the big-bang theory still isn't clear to you after locating references to it, you might try searching the passage for references to the phenomena proposed by the various responses. For example, where is "cosmic plasma" (A) mentioned in this essay? Is it associated with the big-bang theory? Is it suggested as a cause of the universe's expansion? Does the passage mention cosmic objects outside the known galaxies (B)? Are these objects discussed as causes of the universe's expansion? Where, if at all, does the passage mention an increase in the occurrence of red shift (D)?

---

34. You might start by finding the section of the essay devoted to Alfvén's theories. Is he associated with the big-bang theory (F) or with its critics?

Read through the responses and think about what they have in common. Each includes a version of the word *expansion.* As you review Alfvén's theories, be aware of how he views the expansion of the universe. Is it governed by "unidentified forces" (J)? What does *unidentified* mean? Are any specific forces linked with expansion in this discussion of his theories? Does Alfvén draw a connection between expansion and "matter-antimatter annihilation" (G)? Remember, you don't need to **understand** matter-antimatter annihilation. That's not the question. Concentrate on the relationship mentioned in the passage between matter-antimatter annihilation and the universe's expansion. It's that relationship you should focus on, **not** on figuring out how matter and antimatter could possibly do each other in.

What does Alfvén propose about the rate of the universe's expansion? Can you find any references to his opinion about its speed of expansion (H)?

35. You might recall that red shift, as it relates to distance, is one of the astrophysical theories under fire in this passage. What exactly is red shift? Where is the first reference to this phenomenon? What does that reference say about it?

You've probably noticed that lines 8–11 seem to contain something as close to a definition of red shift as you'll find in this passage. However, it may take a little effort to "translate" it and find the answer choice that best corresponds to what it says.

As you scan the choices, what do you notice about how D differs from A, B, and C? Does red shift refer to a property of motion? Or of light?

What does *displacement* mean in line 8? If you're not sure from the context, look for other clues. Try breaking down the definition into parts. Red shifts:

- are displacements toward the red end of the spectrum
- are seen in light emanating from distant objects
- testify to the universe's continuing expansion

Think about a simpler way to express "toward the red end of the spectrum." Now take another look at the choices. Does anything you've just read suggest that red shift can be seen only with a red filter (D)? Is star motion the same thing as the expansion of the universe?

Does anything you've read allude to a star moving from one color phase to another (B)? Try not to be influenced by any prior exposure to astronomy you might have had. Stars **can** have different colors and phases, but is that phenomenon specifically discussed in this passage? Is it related to red shift?

A and C both propose basically the same thing: that red shift is a property of light reaching an observer. The difference between them is that A says the light moves **away from** the red end of the spectrum; C says the light moves **toward** it. Does anything in lines 8–11 suggest a direction for red shift? Is an observer mentioned? What does the word *seen* (line 9) imply?

If you were to pick one choice that came closest to summarizing or paraphrasing the information in lines 8–11, which would it be?

36. Look at the third paragraph and think about how electromagnetic forces are discussed in it. Also, read the responses carefully and see how the ideas they mention appear in the paragraph, with respect to electromagnetism.

Are electromagnetic forces linked with the shaping of galaxies (F)? Can you find a reference to shaping? How could you paraphrase the idea that something "caused this cosmic plasma to coalesce into galaxies" (lines 31–32)?

Locate the reference to filaments and positive ions (H). Are they components of electromagnetic forces? Is there evidence in this paragraph that cosmic plasma can—or can't—generate electromagnetic forces (J)? Does the passage indicate that electromagnetic forces can be shaped in distinctive ways (G)? Or does it say that plasma can be formed into distinctive shapes?

37. What's a quasar? Don't panic—**that's** not the question you have to answer. You're given a statement: Quasars are actually no more distant than galaxies. Go back and look at the eighth paragraph and at the paragraphs before and after it. Based on its context in the passage, would you classify the quoted statement as:

- a universally accepted fact (A)?
- an outdated theory proven false (B)?
- a recent theory proven false (C)?
- a disputed theory (D)?

Whose theory is it? Is there evidence to suggest that the statement is universally accepted? Does anything in the passage contradict that idea?

Is the statement part of a theory that's been proven false, as both B and C propose? The word *proven* is important. Think about what you've read. Make sure you don't confuse a lack of enthusiasm for a theory with the act of **proving** it false.

Is the theory being disputed (D)? Is its validity still being questioned?

Consider the other information in each choice as well. For instance, when was the Hubble relation discovered (C) relative to the quasar theory that's being discussed? Is the link between quasars and galaxies "obvious" (A) or merely "apparent" (D)?

38. Find the paragraphs that discuss the Hubble relation and Arp's feelings about it. Consider each response carefully—not only whether it makes an accurate statement, but also whether that statement represents Arp's reason for questioning the Hubble relation.

Do you agree with the statement in F? What bearing does it have on why Arp is challenging Hubble's theory? Is Arp an example of a plasma dissident who is also a red-shift dissident?

Can you find a reference to Arp's "observational evidence" (G)? (It might help to think about how you could paraphrase those words.) Do Arp's findings **conform** to the Hubble relation or contradict it?

How does Arp feel about the plasma approach? Does the Hubble relation contradict that approach (H)? Does Hubble's hypothesis about red shift conform to the plasma theory or to the big-bang theory (J)?

39. As you did for the preceding question, try to be aware not only of whether each response makes an accurate statement but also of whether that statement could justify the remark cited in the question.

It's also important to consider Eastman's comment (lines 49–51) in the context of both the paragraph in which it appears and the passage as a whole. What is at the heart of the revolution Eastman predicts? What new knowledge is he referring to?

Does the passage imply that the big-bang theory has become obsolete (A)? Where do you see a reference to the theory and its longevity? Where do you see a comparison between astrophysics and astronomy (C)? Does the passage support the generalization that astrophysics is the more speculative science?

Take a look at B and D. Is it true that more powerful plasma generators have been constructed? Are they the source of a possible revolution? How are they being used? Have laboratory experiments confirmed some of Alfvén's predictions? What are those predictions? What effect would it have on astrophysics if they were proven true?

40. This question requires you to combine reference and a certain amount of inference. Where do you see references to the relation between distance and red shift? What is the relation called? What assumption could you reasonably make about why it's called that?

If you're still not sure, try searching the passage for references to the scientists mentioned in the options. See if they're associated with red shift theories and, if so, how. Which one is most likely to be the originator of the theory that distance and red shift are related?

1. For which food choice does the storage period increase the most when the food is treated with gamma rays? What is the storage period for onions without and with irradiation? What is the increase in its storage time? What about for sun-dried Bombay duck? Semi-dried shrimp? Bananas? Which increase in storage period is greatest? Why is the term *absolute increase* used?

Be careful to notice that the storage period in one of the diagrams is expressed in weeks, while the other is in days. In order to make direct comparisons between each of the food items, you have to use the same unit of time, either days or weeks. (Use of the term *absolute increase* means the answer won't be expressed as a percentage.)

2. What are the storage properties of pomfret? Of the listed foods, which has the most similar storage properties?

This question presents a practical problem, because it might be nice to know what foods could be stored in similar conditions. Pomfret has very specific storage properties. It can be stored for 7 days without irradiation and for 20 days after being bombarded with a 100-kr dose, as long as it is refrigerated at a temperature between 0° C and 2° C. Which of the listed foods has nearly identical properties? Be sure that you make comparisons using the same measure of time (days or weeks).

3. Given a new food item and specific irradiation and storage conditions for it, can you predict its storage time by making a comparison with a similar kind of food for which you have data? What kind of food is a peach? What is the storage period for a similar kind of food subjected to similar irradiation and storage conditions?

Until you have real data to the contrary, you are often forced to make do with what you have. In this case, you have no data that says an irradiated peach stored at a temperature between 25° C and 35° C will last for a particular number of days. But can you predict how long it will last based on the storage properties of a similar kind of food subjected to similar conditions? A peach is a fruit. So are mangoes and bananas. The data for mangoes and bananas are similar. Is it reasonable to infer that data for a peach would also be similar?

4. After you have compared the data for vegetables and fruits, what conclusions can you reach about the relationship between irradiation and storage time?

What radiation dosage did onions and potatoes receive? What were their resulting storage periods? What were the dosage and storage periods for mangoes and bananas? How do these data compare? Do the graphs provide any information about **increasing** radiation to fruits? To vegetables?

It would be nice to know what kinds of storage differences there are between certain kinds of foods to see whether one kind might be more appropriate than another to treat in this way. In this case, it's a battle between fruits and vegetables. The data show that both vegetables were subjected to lower dosage than either kind of fruit. It's also clear that there's a great difference in storage periods. There is a clear winner here, at least as far as storage period and radiation dosage are concerned. What is that winner?

5. Which foods are you to put in a specific order? What is the basis for putting them in order?

Ordering is a common human activity. What you need to order here are some of the foods discussed in the passage (fruits, vegetables, and seafood that is unprepared in any way). You want to put first the one with the shortest storage period when untreated with gamma rays. The last one in your list should be the one that keeps longest without irradiation.

6. You're asked to find the approximate height at which a specific wavelength is completely absorbed, using information provided in a diagram. In the figure, at what height does a wavelength of 10^{-9} centimeters intersect the cosmic radiation absorption curve?

Wavelengths are shown along the horizontal axis at the bottom of the figure. If you read straight up the diagram from a wavelength of 10^{-9} centimeters until you hit the cosmic radiation curve, you then will be at the height, on the diagram, where this wavelength is shown to be completely absorbed in the atmosphere. Now read across from that point on the curve to the vertical axis at the left of the diagram.

What is that height (in kilometers)?

7. In which two subdivisions of the cosmic radiation spectrum (across the top of the figure) does the absorption curve correspond with the highest altitudes?

This question asks you to use the curve in the diagram to find two different types of cosmic radiation that are completely absorbed at the highest altitudes. (This also means you're looking for the two types that penetrate the atmosphere the least.) The diagram and passage indicate that cosmic radiation is present at altitudes above the curve. The high points of the curve represent the highest altitudes at which cosmic radiation is completely absorbed.

Which two types of cosmic radiation have specific wavelengths that are completely absorbed at the highest altitudes?

---

8. In order to measure fully a type of cosmic radiation, would you need to be able to record that type at all heights, at all wavelengths at which it exists, or both? Which types of radiation can a satellite fully measure? Which types can a rocket fully measure?

As shown in the figure, cosmic radiation is subdivided by wavelengths. A particular type of cosmic radiation is found in the range between two different wavelengths. In order to measure fully a type of cosmic radiation, you would need to be able to measure all of its wavelengths. As shown on the right side of the figure, a satellite can reach a height (shown at the left of the figure) considerably higher than a rocket can reach.

Which types of cosmic radiation have wavelengths that do not penetrate to the maximum altitude at which a rocket can be used and, therefore, can be measured only by a satellite?

---

9. In the context of this passage, what does the phrase *least absorbed* mean? Can you think of another way of saying that a type of radiation is least absorbed by Earth's atmosphere?

The possible answers actually help you figure out the meaning of the question. Since infrared and radio waves are not given as choices, the phrase *is least absorbed by* can be read equally well as *most penetrates.* In other words, the rays that penetrate the farthest are the ones that are least absorbed by Earth's atmosphere.

Which of the types of radiation come closest to Earth's surface? Do gamma (γ) rays (A) reach the ground? X rays (B)? How about visible radiation (C)? If you can't be sure from the diagram, notice that the curve representing penetration levels appears to be continuous (there are no breaks in it). Where is it on the left side of the band representing visible radiation? On the right side? If the curve is unbroken, where must it be in between? What does the word *visible* suggest? Finally, how far do ultraviolet (uv) rays (D) penetrate? Are any uv rays completely absorbed before they reach the ground?

10. What is the lowest altitude at which you could locate a radio receiver that could observe all radio wavelengths? What is the lowest altitude at which none of the radio wavelengths are completely absorbed?

This is a practical question with a clear goal. If you wanted to observe all wavelengths in the radio spectrum, you'd need to locate your receiver at an altitude at which all of those wavelengths are present. Do all radio wavelengths reach the ground, or are some of them completely absorbed at higher altitudes? How far up would you have to go to get above the point at which **any** radio wavelengths were completely absorbed?

11. One of the major points of this passage is that organisms are adapted to their environment to a greater or lesser extent and that adaptation can be used to tell you something about the conditions in past environments. Based on the associations between modern organisms and physical conditions found in Study 1 and the past biological associations found in Study 2, you can infer the past physical conditions that likely resulted in the deposition of Formation A.

First, consider Study 2. What fossil remains does it say are present in Formation A? Modern associations between organisms and environment are presented in Table 1. Table 1 shows the presence of particular living organisms in various environments. It shows three different categories each of salinity, water clarity, substrate firmness, and water depth. What categories contain the same organisms present in Formation A? Do any categories contain **all** of the same organisms? Keep in mind that not all organisms were tested for all environmental factors. Therefore, the presence of an organism in an environment may be more important than its absence in the data you're given to work with.

---

12. This question directs your attention to Study 1 and Table 1. Which environmental factors listed in Table 1 would affect an organism's ability to burrow into bottom sediments? What does *bottom* suggest? What does *burrow* suggest? What does an animal do when it **burrows into** something? Would it be easier for an animal to burrow into one kind of bottom sediment than another? According to Table 1, which aquatic organism is found in an environment where it would be easy to burrow into bottom sediment?

---

13. This question asks you to pick out a generalization or conclusion about aquatic organisms supported by all three of the studies in the passage.

For A, do all three studies support the conclusion that water clarity has little effect on the distribution of aquatic organisms? How about Study 1? Do all or most of the organisms listed in Table 1 appear in every category of water clarity—clear, mildly turbid, and muddy? If your answer is no, then Study 1 does not support the generalization in response A.

For B, do all three studies support the conclusion that some aquatic organisms are more tolerant of environmental variations than others? Again, how about Study 1? Are some types of organisms listed in more than one of the categories for each environmental factor? Are some listed in only one? Does this suggest that some organisms can adapt to a variety of environmental conditions while others can't? Does either of the other studies contradict this generalization? Does the first sentence of the passage support it?

For C, do all three studies support the conclusion that aquatic organisms generally require similar environments in order to survive? Do they all show that aquatic organisms generally require shallow, muddy, fresh water, for instance, as opposed to deep, clear, "normal marine" water?

For D, do all three studies support the conclusion that environmental conditions have little to do with their distribution? Do **any** of them support this conclusion?

14. Based on the presence of specific fossils in Study 2, can you infer the kind of water clarity in which Formations A, B, and C probably were deposited? Which graphic best represents that inference?

What fossils are present in Formations A, B, and C? Which water clarity condition do these particular fossils imply for each formation? Which graph shows this inference?

Formation A contains green algae, corals, and snails, which are all found in clear water. Formation B has barnacles, clams, oysters, and snails. Since barnacles were not tested for water clarity, the presence of those creatures doesn't help you to answer this question. The others are all found in mildly turbid water, which must be somewhere between clear and muddy conditions. Formation C contains snails, clams, and hyalosponges. Hyalosponges were not tested for water clarity, so you have to rely on the presence of clams and snails. Unfortunately, clams and snails are found together under more than one condition of water clarity—clear and mildly turbid. So you have a couple of possible answers to look for.

Which graph shows Formation A associated with clear water, Formation B associated with mildly turbid water, and Formation C associated with either clear or mildly turbid water?

---

15. What does it mean to be tolerant of variations in water clarity? The organism that is most tolerant of variations in water clarity would occur in the greatest number of varying conditions. According to Table 1, which organism is present in clear, mildly turbid, and muddy water conditions?

---

16. This question asks you to make a connection between the information you're given about Formation E in Study 3 and the information you're given about corals in Table 1. The word *no* makes the question a little tricky, so be careful.

After you reread the description of Formation E in Study 3 and look for corals in Table 1, consider each answer in turn. Ask yourself two questions: First, does it describe an environmental condition in which corals are **not** found today? If the answer is yes, then it might explain why **no** corals would have been found in the same condition in the past. Second, does it state a fact about Formation E that is **not** contradicted by the description of Formation E in Study 3? (It doesn't have to be confirmed by the description of Formation E; it just can't be contradicted by it.) If the answer is yes again, you've got your answer.

---

17. Using the data presented in Figure 1, what general conclusion can you reach about the decomposition of pats? How does the percent of original pat dry weight change for each group over the time frame of the experiment?

The graph shows that when the pats were first placed in the field, they were, of course, 100% there (they had not begun to decompose). At the end of each twenty-day interval, however, one particular group consistently had decomposed more than the other group. As shown on the graph, this group of pats retained less of its original pat dry weight composition than the other group.

Which group of pats decomposed faster than the other group?

---

18. Grass death is one very real result of this experiment. What do you need to look at in order to determine why that grass died?

With which group is grass death associated? How is this group different from the other group?

A lot of science involves looking at causes and effects. Many times you just have effects, and the causes are hard to figure out. In this case, the effect that you have is grass death, and you need to try to understand why the grass died. The obvious first clue that you have is the fact that grass associated with only one group of pats died. Grass around Group T pats died, and Group T pats were made up of feces full of antibiotics, whereas Group C pats were not. So what conclusion can you draw?

---

19. Based on several stated and implied associations, can you predict the future of a bacterial community and the insects that feed on it?

What role for bacteria is described in the passage? What role is described in the introduction of this question? What do Group T pats contain that would have an impact on bacteria? How would the introduction of this substance into the environment likely affect the local aquatic insect population?

You are given some new information: bacteria are food for aquatic insects, and bacteria help digest food in digestive tracts. From the passage, you also know that bacterial infection can occur in cattle, that those infections are treated with antibiotics, and that those antibiotics are then excreted in the feces of the treated cattle. Group T pats come from cattle treated with antibiotics. These facts should lead you to the conclusion that runoff from Group T pats flowing into a nearby stream would probably contain significant though diluted amounts of antibiotics. Table 1 shows the numerical presence of bacteria in Group C and Group T pats.

What is the effect of antibiotics on bacteria, and how would that affect the aquatic insect population?

20. What does the passage say is the purpose of Figure 1? What do the labels on Figure 1 say? Does Figure 1 show any relationship between soil bacteria and fecal decomposition (F)? Between earthworms and fecal decomposition (G)? Among soil bacteria, insects, and fecal decomposition (H)? How about antibiotics and fecal decomposition (J)?

21. What likely effect would a reduction in the level of antibiotic have on the results of the experiment? Would a reduction in the level of antibiotic increase or decrease the rate of bacterial survival? Do pats decompose faster or slower when there are more (or fewer) bacteria present?

This kind of question requires you to think about the possible consequences of changes in an experiment. There can be many reasons other than purely scientific ones to make a change. In this case, a practical reason would be that a lower level of antibiotic may cost less. But what are the trade-offs? Table 1 shows that bacteria are still present, though in much lower numbers, in Group T pats, which contain antibiotics. So, clearly, the original level of antibiotic is not completely effective in eliminating bacteria. What level of antibiotic would it take to eliminate the bacteria, if that's possible? Would you necessarily even want to eliminate all of the bacteria? It might be perfectly acceptable to find some middle ground in which the harmful effects of bacteria are kept under control and the helpful effects of bacteria are allowed to continue. After all, the passage does state that grass around Group C pats, which have significantly more bacteria than Group T pats, was lush and green.

In Figure 1, is it likely that a lower level of antibiotic would result in data that could be plotted above, on, or below the data for Group T pats?

22. Which organism shows the greatest change in numbers between Group C and Group T pats?

Table 1 shows the numbers of various organisms present in soil associated with both Group C and Group T pats. A general comparison between Group C and Group T for each organism will reveal which organism's numbers changed most. You probably won't need to add or subtract every pair of numbers to get the general idea here.

23. According to Hypothesis 2, why is Hypothesis 1 not likely to be entirely true? Does there appear to be sufficient energy? Is water in abundant supply? Is organic matter available? Has enough time passed for life to have appeared randomly from organic molecules?

This problem may be solved by systematically examining each of the possible answers in light of the discussion of Hypothesis 2. For each choice, reread Hypothesis 2 to determine if it is the lack of this ingredient that causes Hypothesis 1 to break down.

24. What are the main features of early cells described in Hypothesis 1? How could you diagram those features?

This question asks you to visualize a concept in pictures rather than express it in words. Early cells are discussed in the second paragraph of Hypothesis 1. Key points in this discussion are that

1. protein-coated droplets can form,
2. these droplets can absorb other organic molecules and divide,
3. early droplets probably formed in a "soup," and
4. some probably contained DNA.

Concepts or factors not talked about or described in Hypothesis 1 are irrelevant to an illustration of early cells according to that hypothesis.

Which diagram best illustrates the main points about early cells as discussed specifically in Hypothesis 1?

25. Of the processes listed, which, in a primitive form, is best associated with the phrase "some form of advantage"? What process best describes how protein-covered droplets **changed** into the cells that we know today?

Photosynthesis describes a reaction that takes place between light and plants. Does Hypothesis 1 mention anything about the interaction of light and plants, whether primitive or not? Diffusion represents movement from areas of high concentration to areas of low concentration, like scent from perfume spreading throughout a room. Are substances evenly distributed in the primitive environment of Hypothesis 1? Osmosis also involves the movement of substances so that some kind of equilibrium concentration is reached. Is the external "soup" of Hypothesis 1 the same as or different from the internal composition of the protein-coated droplets? Evolution involves change, which implies that differences exist. Is there some variation discussed between different protein-coated droplets that would provide one some form of advantage over another?

26. Hypothesis 2 presents an interesting problem for Hypothesis 1 to explain. What is the significance of L amino acids as explained by Hypothesis 2? Which of the arguments given most effectively reduces the significance of the idea presented in Hypothesis 2?

This question requires you to act like a defense lawyer. You're presented with what could be some pretty damaging evidence against your client, Hypothesis 1. How can you knock holes in this evidence or at least reduce its impact? You need to look for an effective argument that either provides contrary issues to think about (a diversion tactic) or overriding factors to consider.

Would the "fact" that clay crystals have structures that prevent D amino acids from attaching to them help Hypothesis 1 or 2? Would the idea that organisms containing L amino acids were better able to adapt to life in primitive oceans account for the presence of only L amino acids in modern organisms? Would the idea that cells containing D amino acids evolved faster than those containing L amino acids account for the fact that only L amino acids occur in modern organisms? Is it likely that of all the organisms studied by scientists, not one is known to have D amino acids?

27. Which biological process listed is most similar to the imperfect replication of clay crystals? What is implied by the replication of clay crystals? What does it mean when a clay crystal is imperfectly replicated? Which of the biological processes suggests the same kind of idea?

In this kind of question, you need to identify the important point behind the initial concept (in this case, imperfect replication of clay crystals) and then associate it with a list of possible similar concepts. The **replication** of clay crystals suggests that an object is being duplicated over and over again. **Imperfect** replication suggests that something has changed so that you are not getting exactly the same product as you did at first.

Which of the biological processes listed incorporates inadvertent or accidental change, as opposed to the same thing happening again and again without change?

28. Which possible discovery would help you convince someone else that Hypothesis 1 is correct or most likely? What facts are present in Hypothesis 1? What speculations are present in Hypothesis 1? Which of the possible discoveries agrees with one of the speculations in Hypothesis 1?

Hypotheses should not only explain facts but also lead to further predictions and expectations. If your hypothesis is sound (that is, it explains things well), then you should expect to make certain discoveries based on it. Hypothesis 1 incorporates data from many experiments, involving two major areas. The first paragraph talks about the Stanley Miller experiment in which organic molecules form spontaneously from a special "soup" when energy is applied. The second paragraph summarizes other experiments involving protein-coated droplets. Both groups of experiments lead to certain speculations about how life could have progressed from these beginnings.

Would the presence of bacteria in oceans specifically agree with any of these speculations? What about crystalline cell membranes? What about cells associated with clay deposits in the oceans? What about cells created from a solution of organic molecules?

29. The idea that clay crystals funnel solar energy to organic molecules leads to speculation in Hypothesis 2 about the possible evolutionary role of clay in photosynthesis. A particular discovery would provide supporting evidence for this argument. In what ways would clay and chloroplasts have to be similar in order to provide supporting evidence for an evolutionary role in photosynthesis?

This kind of question and its possible answers ask you to separate important features from nonessential aspects. You again want to make a supporting discovery. You are to assume that clay crystals actually have the ability to capture and transmit solar energy to the organic molecules attached to their surface. It can be inferred that chloroplasts capture and transmit solar energy to other areas within a plant cell. Therefore, the important similarities can be seen to revolve around the capture and transmission of solar energy.

Which of the possible discoveries focuses on similarities between how clay and chloroplasts capture solar energy?

30. Notice that you're given a statement of the law of conservation of mass at the beginning of the passage: the sum of the masses of the reactants is equal to the sum of the masses of the products. Assuming that there were no errors in measurement, how can you find the mass of the unknown product when you know the masses of the other substances?

What are the masses of the known substances in this experiment? Which are the reactants and which are the products?

The reactants in this case are potassium chromate (5 g) and lead(II) nitrate (10 g). They are in aqueous (water) solutions so that when they are poured together they will be able to react. One product of the reaction is a solid yellow precipitate (8.3 g) that forms at the bottom of the beaker. The sum of the masses of the reactants (5 g + 10 g = 15 g) should equal the sum of the masses of the products (8.3 g + ____ g = 15 g). Subtracting should give you the mass of the unknown substance.

31. You're asked here to think about a different reaction, one that yields gas as a product. Will the current laboratory setup be able to handle this new reaction and still yield results that demonstrate the law of conservation of mass?

If you heat the aqueous solution as you did for the first reaction to drive off the water, will the gaseous product be left behind in the beaker?

To verify the law of conservation of mass, you need to be able to accurately measure the masses of all reactants and all products. In the experimental reaction described in the passage, your products are all solids, so you only have to make sure that when you weigh the products, all you have are those products and nothing else—excess water, for example. However, if a gas is one of your products, you will need to make sure you have captured and measured all of it. Otherwise you are not fulfilling your goal of verifying the law of conservation of mass.

How can you measure a gas? Would the procedure described in the passage need to be modified to ensure that the mass of the gas is weighed?

32. Which of the statements is always true in any experiment that has the goal of verifying the law of conservation of mass?

Since the law of conservation of mass, if it is true, would be expected to apply to all chemical experiments, not just the ones designed to verify it, you're really looking for a general statement that is true of all chemical reactions. However, you only need to think carefully about the information presented here. Remember, you're looking for a statement that works for **all** experiments designed to verify the law of conservation of mass.

Would the total mass of the products subtracted from the total mass of the reactants **always** be expected to equal zero? Would a yellow precipitate **always** be expected to form? If water is produced by a reaction, should it **always** automatically be removed as a product? Do **all** chemical reactions take place in water?

33. Why would the total masses be different after the heating and cooling procedure of the experiment was repeated? Why is the beaker containing the yellow precipitate heated and cooled? How can you tell if you have achieved a constant mass in a beaker?

This question focuses on an important point in the experimental setup. You are trying to verify the law of conservation of mass. In order to do that, you need to accurately weigh the masses of the reactants and the products. From the passage, you know that hot or wet samples affect the measurement of mass. Therefore, when you measure the mass of a sample, that sample must be cool and thoroughly dried. Under those conditions, it will presumably be at a constant mass. You can really determine that it is at a constant mass only by repeating the heating and cooling procedures until you no longer get any significant change in the mass. At that point, complications resulting from excess moisture or hot air currents should have been eliminated.

Which of the answer choices best reflects what probably happened during the heating and cooling procedure?

34. This question presents a thinly disguised new situation, encouraging you to think about why it is necessary to heat and cool a product before you weigh it. The beaker and product are heated to drive off moisture and cooled to minimize the effects of heat-induced air currents, as stated in the passage. You can only tell if you have an accurate and constant mass by carrying out this procedure more than once. Which response tells what the chemist must do to obtain an accurate and constant product mass value?

---

35. The experimenter made an error: Some of the yellow stuff got into the wrong beaker. Would this invalidate the results of the experiment? What is the goal of the experiment? Because of the specific goal you're after, would this particular error make a difference?

This question presents an interesting practical problem likely to be faced by any scientist. Scientists are human, and humans make errors. But does a particular error affect what you are trying to find out? Sometimes this question is difficult to answer.

The goal of the experiment in this passage is to verify the law of conservation of mass. Therefore, the sum of the masses of the reactants must equal the sum of the masses of the products. The result of the particular error described in this question transfers some of one product (yellow precipitate) to the other product. The **sum** of the masses of the products in the beakers does not change, just the amount of mass in each beaker. If you have only one sixteen-ounce bottle of soft drink to pour into two glasses, does how you divide it change the fact that you still have only sixteen ounces?

---

36. Two types of chemical reactions are represented in Figures 1 and 2. How does this hypothetical third reaction compare to the two types of reactions? Can you make a general prediction about the outcome of the new reaction?

Which type of reaction is the hypothetical reaction most similar to, based on the reactants-products curve? What are the similarities between the types of reactions in Figures 1 and 2? What are the differences?

This question and its possible answers focus on how the fundamental concepts discussed in the passage can be visually displayed. The hypothetical reaction is similar to the one shown in Figure 2. Figures 1 and 2 each show the relative potential energy of the reactants and the products. However, in Figure 1 the relative potential energy of the products is higher than that of the reactants, while the reverse is true in Figure 2. Each type of reaction requires a certain amount of activation energy for the reaction to begin; the activation energy is much greater for the reaction in Figure 1 than that in Figure 2. A catalyst decreases the amount of energy required for the reaction to start; in Figure 1, the catalyst reduces the activation energy needed for the reaction to occur by only about an eighth, while in Figure 2, the activation energy is reduced by over half. The passage and the figures indicate that energy (net) is either absorbed or released over the full course of the reaction.

Do any of the reactions shown occur spontaneously, or do they require some input first? Would a net amount of energy be released or absorbed in the hypothetical reaction? Is a catalyst shown in the hypothetical reaction? Are exact times shown for any of the reactions in the passage?

---

37. As shown by the figures, how does a catalyst affect a reaction? How is the catalyst (---------) changing the curve in each of the figures? What specific type of energy is affected by the addition of the catalyst? How is this type of energy affected?

Catalysts are not discussed in the passage, but the presence of a catalyst is shown to have an effect on the reaction in each of the graphs. The catalyst lowers the curve in each of the reactions in Figures 1 and 2. This means that the reaction can start producing products at a lower potential energy than when the catalyst is not present. Each figure shows that the catalyst reduces the relative potential energy of the reaction profile in one specific area, the activation energy.

How is the activation energy affected by the catalyst?

---

38. Which of the factors shown in the figures allows you to conclude that a chemical reaction absorbs or releases energy? How is the amount of energy absorbed or released shown in Figures 1 and 2? What relationship does this representation of energy absorption or release have to the other factors in the figures?

The amount of energy absorbed or released in the reaction is shown in the figure as the interval (of relative potential energy) between the reactants level and the products level. If the products level is higher than the reactants level, net energy was absorbed in the reaction. If the reactants level is higher than the products level, net energy was released by the reaction.

Are exact amounts of reaction time shown for any of the reactions? Do you have information about whether a catalyst has a different function depending on whether energy is released or absorbed? Do the figures show the amount of product formed during a reaction?

39. What is the mathematical meaning of *difference,* and how do you apply it to the specific example in this question?

Essentially, this is a math equation written out in words, and all you have to do is complete the sentence. In order to calculate a difference, you subtract. If you want the difference between the height of the tallest person and the shortest person in a room, then you subtract the height of the shortest person from the height of the tallest one. If you want the difference between the potential energy of the reactants and that of the products, what would you subtract from what?

40. How does the net energy change in the reaction represented in Figure 2? In other words, is energy released or absorbed by the reaction? How is that change calculated? If numbers were added to the figure, how would you calculate the change?

This question uses different phrases to explore many of the same ideas that have been brought up in other questions. For instance, the change in net energy of a reaction is simply the amount of energy released or absorbed by a reaction. You've seen this before. You start with a certain amount of energy and end with a different amount, and that difference is the change in energy. For the reactions shown, this change is a net change, since energy is expended to get the reaction started in the first place. For example, you might imagine owning a store. You need to buy merchandise to stock your shelves. If you absorb more money from sales of that merchandise than you release by paying the bills for it, then you'll have a net profit.

What is the specific change in net energy (is energy absorbed or released) for the reaction in Figure 2? Would net energy result from the addition or subtraction of the potential energies of products and reactants?

1. A. A offers the best way to express what this sentence is asking. Have you ever: (a) found a ten-dollar bill? (b) discovered a great restaurant? The auxiliary verb *have* supports both *found* and *discovered.*

2. J. The first part of this sentence says, "There's a word for that kind of lucky accident." The colon signals the reader that the writer is going to supply the word: *serendipity.* The phrase "although not all accidents are lucky" isn't part of the word, obviously, nor does it modify the word. (For example: "There's a word for that kind of lucky accident: *serendipity,* which derives from the Persian.") No matter how it's worded, the writer's observation that not all accidents are lucky doesn't belong after the colon in this sentence. In fact, it's such a digression it doesn't fit in the passage at all.

3. B. The discovery of sugar substitutes is an example of the kind of serendipitous scientific discoveries mentioned in the first sentence of the paragraph. So, *for example* is the best way to begin the second sentence. *However* (A) sets the reader up for a contradiction ("Many scientific discoveries were the result of serendipity. **However,** the discovery of sugar substitutes wasn't one of them.") *Rather* (D) also suggests a contradiction. ("Many scientific discoveries weren't the result of systematic research. **Rather,** they were the result of serendipity.") *Thus* (C) implies more of a cause-and-effect relationship. ("Many scientific discoveries have been the result of serendipity. **Thus,** many scientists are deciding to abandon their research and simply hope for lucky accidents.")

4. G. F, H, and J are redundant because *currently, today,* and *now* all mean about the same thing, as they're being used here. It goes without saying—it **should** go, anyway—that something currently popular is popular **now.** Today. This very minute. Can something be currently popular last year? *Currently so popular* would be acceptable. So would *so popular now.* They're not among the choices, though, so G is best.

5. A. You could argue that a certain amount of luck is involved in much scientific research, even the most systematic, and that *lucky* isn't quite the same as *accidental.* However, A is still better than the other choices. Another example of an accidental discovery, like the anecdotes about penicillin and sugar substitutes, would strengthen the emphasis on accidental discoveries more than a list of parasites (B), an outline of the scientific method (C), or a description of laboratory procedures (D). C and D might be valid ways for the writer to contrast systematic research with lucky accidents or show certain points in laboratory procedures where accidents are particularly likely.

6. F. *Who* is a subject here. *Who* acted—namely, **benefited.**

Subject: The scientist **who** benefited from serendipity was Joseph Priestley.

Object: No matter **whom** serendipity benefits, it will never replace systematic research. (*Serendipity* does the acting here.)

Although it opts for *who* over *whom,* G is wrong because no comma is needed between *scientist* and *who.*

7. B. *The best* (A) and *best* (C) are superlatives, like *most,* but they're associated with the idea of quality. It might seem like a fine distinction. After all, whoever benefits "most" would also, it seems, benefit "best"—that is, would derive the best benefits.

But as the sentence is structured, the word *best* would modify not the benefits but the action of benefiting: the scientist who "benefited best." *The more* (D) is wrong because—assuming the writer wanted to compare Priestley directly to the other scientists—the best way to make a comparison here would be to simply use the word *more*: Priestley benefited **more** than all other scientists. *The more* is used to compare no more than two things. For example: Of soda water and pencil erasers, soda water is the more thirst-quenching. Or: The more I think about all this, the more my head hurts.

8. H. Neither F nor G clarifies that what began to bubble was the water, not Priestley. J creates a comma splice (there's a complete sentence on each side of the comma).

9. A. The adjective *good* is what's called for here. Water can't **taste** well any more than boots can **look** well. Water can't taste a thing, and boots are blind as a bat, so the adverb *well* is clearly ill advised. B is wrong because it creates a comma splice. A comma and a conjunction are needed to join these two complete sentences: "It tasted good. That's how Priestley discovered seltzer or soda water." By the way, we didn't want to muddy the waters (so to speak) by mentioning this earlier, but that mercurial *well*—not content with being an adverb and an adjective—can also turn up as a noun or a verb:

> The water welling up from the spring near the well made me instantly well; it had been chilled well, so it tasted good.

See? Things could be worse.

10. F. *Thus* (G) and *consequently* (H) suggest that Priestley's oil of vitriol discovery sprang directly from his carbon dioxide experiment. It's possible that dabbling in carbon dioxide led Priestley to fool around with oil of vitriol, but the passage doesn't indicate that. In fact, the passage suggests that Priestley's "idly" toying with carbon dioxide and his "trying to identify" oil of vitriol's characteristics were two entirely different activities. *This* (J) is wrong because it implies that the soda water discovery occurred during the oil of vitriol experiment. In fact, it's a different discovery that's being introduced. *This* would be acceptable—though not terrific—if the sentence ended with a colon instead of a period, signaling the reader that another serendipitous discovery was about to be revealed.

11. D. Paragraph 3 talks about two of Priestley's experiments and how he applied the results. You may not consider this exactly taking advantage of serendipitous occurrences (how much advantage did he take?—sure, he invented seltzer, but did he become president of Canada Dry?) and you might also argue that *several* sounds like more than two. Remember: An answer doesn't have to be perfect to be the **best** of those offered. Response A could follow a paragraph devoted to Priestley's long, painstaking seltzer research. However, it isn't logical to conclude from this paragraph, which talks about the accidental discoveries of seltzer and sulfur dioxide, that Priestley "finally" invented seltzer. The passage doesn't support the idea that Priestley didn't believe in cause and effect (B). It says only that he benefited from luck, not that he based his life on it. C is wrong, because we have no evidence that Priestley never used systematic methods.

12. G. The verb in the sentence must agree with *another,* which is singular, rather than with *discoveries,* which is plural. *Another* tells you that the writer is talking about only one discovery. If the phrase were "many of Priestley's accidental discoveries," a plural verb form like *have been* (F) or *are* (H) would have worked. J is wrong because *had been* is a verb tense for something that happened in the past but is now over ("Another of Priestley's discoveries *had been* useful to students until the outlawing of lead pencils"). *Has been* is the best way to show that the usefulness of the pencil eraser, which began in the past, continues.

13. D. Priestley "allowed the sap to harden," then rubbed **the sap** on paper. *Sap* is a singular noun, so it should be referred to by the singular pronoun *it.* If the writer wanted to talk about several saps (Priestley's hardworking but unlucky colleagues, for instance), the pronoun *them* would have been preferable.

14. J. All versions of the underlined phrase, no matter how they're worded, are redundant. They simply restate that the discoveries were accidental. Accidents are, by definition, things that people don't intend to make. There is no such thing as an intentional accident (except for accidentally destroying your algebra book by dropping it in the middle of the lake to see if it will float, which is a specialized case that we don't have time to get into here).

15. A. In an essay focusing on the role of serendipity in scientific research, it's logical to begin by telling a reader what serendipity is. The writer defines serendipity in Paragraph 1, then goes on to give examples. D's arrangement gives the examples, then the definition—a strategy that would be confusing in this essay. C's arrangement puts the definition in the middle, then further confuses a reader by separating the two paragraphs devoted to Priestley. B makes the mistake of introducing "another" of Priestley's discoveries before mentioning his first ones.

16. H. F and J are poor choices for several reasons. For one thing, as it's used here *prospect* itself refers to an act of anticipation ("The prospect of going bowling made him quiver from head to toe"). The writer is anticipating **watching** the tea ceremony, not anticipating **anticipating** watching it. G is wrong because the expression *champing at the bit* is a cliché, is too informal for the style of this essay, and calls up an image that doesn't fit with the subject of the essay. Besides, only a horse can **literally** champ at the bit; the rest of us must be satisfied with doing it figuratively.

17. B. *Who,* rather than *whom,* is called for here, because it's the subject of the clause "who was eighty years old." *Whom* can't act, so it can't precede the verb *was.*

C, which uses the pronoun *he,* is wrong because it creates a comma splice that merely strings together two ideas without relating them clearly. *He* would be acceptable if the writer wanted to have two sentences instead of one—perhaps to emphasize the tea master's age—"The teahouse had been built by the tea master himself. He was eighty years old."

18. J. Although at first glance this question looks like a who/whom problem, it turns out that the best answer doesn't include either one. G and H are wrong because they both repeat the word *with,* when there's no need to use the same preposition twice in this construction. It's like saying "the room in which I was in." F puts the words in an awkward order that could confuse a reader.

19. A. The difference in meaning between *accomplished* (A) and *practiced* (B) is sometimes insignificant. Both adjectives imply a certain level of expertise. What makes *accomplished* preferable here is how it works with *practitioners.* It sounds redundant to refer to "practiced practitioners." A practitioner is one who **practices** a specific profession or activity. In this sense, *practice* means "to engage in." As an adjective, *practiced* means "experienced," or "skilled." Saying "Practicing practitioners" would be like saying "they do what they do" or "they practice what they practice." If *practiced* doesn't work in this context, *well-practiced* (D) is even less effective. C is wrong because *accomplishing* means "bringing about," which doesn't fit the idea of the sentence. To call someone an "accomplished practitioner" is to pay a compliment, suggesting that the person is skilled at the activity—and that's the meaning that makes sense here.

20. H. *Own personal* (F) and *own individual* (J) are redundant. *Personal own* (G) is a peculiar way to order the words that isn't standard English. It's sufficient to simply say "his **own** hand." Calling it "his **own personal** hand" doesn't make it any more his. Yet expressions like F and J are used reasonably often, in the belief that they add emphasis—which they sometimes do. Caught up in enthusiasm, even a person of few words might say something like, "I personally made this double chocolate fudge torte for you myself, with my own two hands." Only a grump would take the baker to task for redundancy (sometimes it's wiser to simply shut up and eat). The tone of the passage about the tea master is formal and restrained, however, and embellishing "his own hand" doesn't add useful emphasis.

21. C. In Sentence 3, the phrase "it consisted of two rooms" refers to the teahouse. As the paragraph is structured now, the pronoun *it* seems to refer to the outer room. The writer doesn't intend to say that the outer room consists of two rooms, an outer one and an inner one, so A is wrong. Sentence 2, which talks about what takes place in the outer room, belongs immediately after Sentence 3, which first mentions that room. Sentence 2 would be a poor way to begin the paragraph (B), because a reader would learn about the outer room before being told about the teahouse in which it was located. D would be confusing because it inserts the sentence into a description of how tea was passed around the room. It would also confuse a reader by putting two sentences between the first and second references to the outer room.

22. G. *Solemnly* is an adverb that describes how the writer reached for the box. It doesn't describe how the accident happened (F and J). The writer could have chosen to "solemnly take it" or to "take it solemnly," but to "take solemnly it" (H) is awkward, confusing wording that isn't standard English.

23. D. If tea covered the writer's blue suit and the surrounding floor, we can infer that's where it was spilled. The clauses in A and B are acceptable standard English, but they aren't necessary in this sentence. C isn't standard English. It's unclear who or what the writer intends to describe as "having spilled": the tea? the floor? the writer?

24. J. Of the four choices, J offers the best way to state without ambiguity that the writer believes the laughter wasn't aimed at him. *I believe* is a parenthetical phrase that should be set off with commas because it occurs in the middle of another thought.

25. D. D offers the best way to express the contradiction the writer intends: that the laughter wasn't provoked entirely by his clumsiness, but rather by the tension of the solemn occasion. D is also the one option that creates an independent clause.

26. G. Of the choices offered, G is the best way to convey the writer's meaning that the tea master:

1. imparted to us knowledge of the tea ceremony;
2. offered an example of profound kindness.

F is unnatural and awkward-sounding ("to us also offered" rather than "offered to us"). So is J. It puts too many words between *imparted* and *to us* and also breaks up the phrase "knowledge of the tea ceremony." H ("imparted not only to us") suggests that the tea master imparted knowledge to others besides the Americans—something that might be true, but isn't specifically supported by the passage.

27. D. The writer is talking about consideration of "others"—other people—so no apostrophe is needed. It's unclear what *those* (A) is supposed to refer to. Only if the sentence mentioned something like the feelings of one other person (the other's feelings) or more than one person (others' feelings) would an apostrophe be needed.

28. G. It's redundant to say that polite consideration is "ritualized in the ritual" (F and H) or "traditionalized in the tradition" (J). *Ritualized* means "to be made into a ritual." It's overkill to refer to something as being made into a ritual in the ritual.

29. B. The use of *I* is appropriate because the essay is a personal account of one American's experience with the Japanese tea ceremony. There's no reason why **all** travel writing should be in the first person, as A suggests, any more than there's a reason why factual writing shouldn't be, as D suggests.

30. F. The plural form of *student* is called for here. The students themselves are the subject of this sentence, not something belonging to them, so the apostrophes in H and G are wrong. The comma in J is wrong because it unnecessarily separates the subject (*students*) and verb (*must have*) of this sentence.

31. C. Students can't get the card without swearing. Therefore, they "must" swear. *Should* (D) isn't strong enough. (If you're told you **should** clean your room before you go out, are you as likely to do it as if you're told you **must** clean your room?) *Would* (A) and *were to* (B) could be appropriate if the passage said that the ID card policy was a thing of the past (students **had to have** ID cards; they **would** swear before a librarian).

32. H. Sure, an argument sometimes livens things up, but that doesn't mean it's always suitable in an essay, as the pugnacious J asserts. The writer cites the American tradition of "majoring" only as a lead-in to the essay's main focus: an informative discussion of reading at the Bodleian Library in England. No argument against the American system is made or even implied by the essay as a whole, as G suggests (majoring is never even mentioned after the first sentence), nor would such an argument be a fitting ending to this essay about a major British library, as F recommends.

33. A. The sentence order is best as it is. C and D suggest beginning with a sentence stating that the Bodleian acquires new books "in this manner"—a phrase for which a reader has no point of reference except the preceding paragraph. It makes no sense for the writer to refer to the process of students' swearing before a librarian. B arranges the information about library acquisitions in a confusing order; if Sentence 4 immediately follows Sentence 1, the phrases *in addition* and *other books* have no point of reference.

34. J. G uses the wrong verb form. "On account of there **being** so many books" would be a better way to put this essentially cumbersome expression. F and H have no grammatical errors, but they're wordy (*because* would be better than either *due to the fact that* or *on account of the fact that*), and the bottom line is simply that these phrases are unnecessary. The underlined phrase should be omitted because *vast collection* says enough. It's implicit in F, G, and H that the writer is talking about a very large collection of books.

35. C. A colon is the best way to lead into what is basically a list of three buildings, accompanied by details describing each of them.

If you didn't turn the page and read what came after "The Old Library, which was," you might have picked A, thinking that a complete sentence was going to follow. (For example: The Old Library, which was finished in 1849, is one of the three landmarks.) But as it turns out, the phrase that follows has no subject and verb. Since it's not a complete sentence, the period suggested by A and B is wrong (B also puts an unnecessary comma between *Old* and *Library*).

36. J. Notice that you can't eliminate any of the optional answers on the basis of grammatical flaws. Each is an acceptable way to phrase an irrelevant sentence. The writer is discussing three of the buildings that make up the Bodleian Library and that are considered Oxford landmarks. The passage doesn't suggest that St. Paul's Cathedral is part of a library (it isn't), but the passage **does** state that the cathedral is in London, not Oxford. Mention of St. Paul's is irrelevant here, even if St. Paul's is a landmark that happens to have a dome like one of the Bodleian's buildings. Furthermore, removing the sentence makes the paragraph flow more smoothly: there is no interruption between the two references to the New Library.

37. D. A, B, and C are wrong because they all include the word *awaiting* or *awaits*—which merely repeats, without adding new information or emphasis, the idea already present in the phrase *waiting reader.*

In this passage, it happens that every time OMIT is one of your choices, it's the best one. This won't necessarily be the case in other passages, though, so you should avoid jumping to the conclusion that OMIT should automatically be chosen whenever it's an option.

38. F. J is inaccurate because, in fact, all the books being discussed **are** in the Bodleian—distributed among its seven different buildings. The ideas in H are poorly coordinated, and the phrase *pretty famous* is too informal for the tone of the passage. G would be a possible opening sentence for a paragraph about Radcliffe Camera, but its focus is too narrow to introduce a description of a group of buildings as well as the library's retrieval system. Also, the paragraph would sound choppy, since Radcliffe Camera is mentioned again later, as just one of many features of the Bodleian Library. Granted, F is not a terrific sentence. The expression *old and very old,* while accurate, sounds repetitious; and it's questionable whether being linked by "mechanics" is the same as being linked by a mechanical conveyor belt. Nevertheless, F most nearly meets the standards specified in the question, so it's the best choice available.

39. D. Students must read the Bodleian's books in one of its reading rooms **because** the Bodleian does not lend the books out. *Therefore* best expresses the relationship between the ideas that the Bodleian is not a lending library and that its patrons must do their reading on the premises. *Notwithstanding, contrarily,* and *on the other hand* would not provide a good transition between the clauses because they imply a contradictory, rather than cause-and-effect, relationship.

40. G. The ghosts of past students "are moving through the air and hovering over shoulders." The verb tense expressing the first action is consistent with that expressing the second action. Both are in the present progressive tense: "are moving" and "[are] hovering." Careful reading is crucial here. If you read too hastily, you could miss a phrase or syllable that could affect your choice. If you read *hover* for *hovering,* for instance, you might have picked F. If you skipped over the phrase *a sense that,* you might have picked H. J, like G, includes the best verb tense; however, breaking up the prepositional phrase *through the air* with a comma is unnecessary and confusing.

41. A. The comma between *shoulders* and *just* sets off the modifying phrase "just out of sight." C and D make the mistake of adding an apostrophe to *shoulders.* The word is neither a possessive nor a contraction here, so *shoulders* is the correct form. B is wrong because the comma would separate the adverb *just* from the phrase it modifies—*out of sight.*

42. J. Adding any form of the verb *occur* here creates a construction shift. "There are the sounds of current students" introduces a list of sound-producing activities. The best choice is another student action—chuckling.

43. B. Paragraph 2 does mention the types of material collected by the Bodleian, including books, pamphlets, and periodicals. Manuscripts would be a logical addition here. C is a poor choice because, although the Bodleian's vast collection is mentioned in Paragraph 3, the focus of the paragraph isn't on the contents of the collection but rather on some of the buildings that house it. A and D should be ruled out because of their inaccurate statements that (A) **all** important information should be mentioned in the first paragraph (in which case, the typical first paragraph could be pages long) and (D) new information should **always** go in a new paragraph. "New information" could warrant a paragraph of its own, or it could consist of only a sentence or phrase. The word *always* should put you on your guard in situations like this.

44. G. The noun or pronoun in the answer you select must agree with the plural noun in the first clause: *Americans.* Since *Americans* is plural, *the person* can be ruled out (D). Unless the writer is directly addressing the people of the United States ("My fellow Americans . . ."), *you* is also inappropriate. Only *they* (G) agrees with *Americans.*

45. D. The writer's mental image of fox hunting is different from the image most Americans have. *However* is the only choice to express that contrast.

46. H. F creates a sentence fragment out of "in the hill country of the southern United States," a phrase that tells where the writer came to know this form of fox hunting. A sentence fragment can be effective when it's appropriate to the style and tone of a piece of writing as a whole. In this passage, the tone is fairly formal and the overall style is to use complete sentences, so a fragment would be out of place. G is wrong because it breaks up the phrase *in the hill country* with a comma. J makes the same mistake, and compounds it by using a semicolon to link an independent clause with a prepositional phrase.

47. B. *Being different to* (C) is wrong because the preposition *to* isn't used with *different* in standard English. The idiom is either *different from* or *different than. It being different,* in A and D, while not exactly ungrammatical, is an awkward construction. Not only are A and D wordier and more cumbersome than B, but A also makes another mistake by inserting a comma. Separating *it being different* and *from the English version* makes an already clumsy phrase even harder to understand.

48. G. As it's written, this is a confusingly complicated sentence. There are two complete clauses here whose subject/ verb constructions are "the form of fox hunting I remember was" and "the main purpose of the hunt was." G is the only choice that makes them into two clear and separate sentences.

49. C. Two independent clauses make up this sentence, so a semicolon is the best way (of the choices available) to punctuate it. A and B are comma splices. D creates the redundant phrase *so therefore* (the words *so* and *therefore* mean about the same thing here).

50. J. The subject of the sentence is the plural noun *traditions,* not the singular *huntsman's horn,* so the verb should be the plural *were.*

51. D. The apostrophe indicates that the horns belong—or once belonged—to cows. In this context, the word *of* is another way of saying "belonging to," so the apostrophe after *cows* in B is unnecessary. It's also misleading: horns of cows' **what**? The apostrophe in A is wrong because it suggests that *horns* is the possessive. C is wrong because it omits the apostrophe altogether.

52. F. The parenthetical phrase *not just the leader* should be set off with commas. Without a comma (G), the sentence is confusing. It's also confusing to add a semicolon (H and J). A semicolon links two independent clauses and usually shouldn't be used more than once in a sentence—unless a writer is listing items that contain commas. (For example: The hunters came from as far away as Ponca City, Oklahoma; Tuba City, Arizona; and Cuba City, Wisconsin.)

53. B. The word chosen should provide the best way of referring to "**a hill-country hound's** owner's call." *Hound's* is possessive, so the pronoun that replaces it should be, too. We don't know if the hound is male or female, so *its*—the possessive form of *it*—is the best option to replace this singular noun. *It's* (D) is a contraction of *it is. It's* is not a possessive, and neither is *there* (A). *Their* (C) is a possessive pronoun, but it is plural and therefore doesn't agree with *hound,* which is singular.

54. J. *Lay* is the correct form of *lie* for this context. An intransitive verb is called for because a difference can't **lay** anything; it can only lie. *Lain* (H) is the past participle of *lie* and needs an auxiliary verb. (She **had lain** awake for hours, watching the bat swoop across the ceiling.) *Laid* (G) is the past tense of *lay.* (When the bat landed, she **laid** her unabridged dictionary on it.) Layed (F) incorrectly forms the past tense of *lay* by adding *-ed.* Remember: A difference can't lay anything. It can only lie.

55. C. The relationship between the modifier *eating choice leftovers* and the noun it modifies—namely whoever, or whatever, is doing the eating—is awkwardly expressed in A, B, and D. It can't be the porch or the hearth doing the eating; it's the hound. Only C expresses that relationship clearly.

56. H. The hounds' deeds **became** legends. The action is placed firmly in the past, just like the other actions described in the paragraph. *Had became,* with or without the unnecessary comma, is wrong because the past participle form is *become. Was becoming* (J) is a poor choice because the singular verb *was* doesn't agree with the plural noun *deeds* and because it isn't consistent with the past tense used throughout the paragraph.

57. D. It's the only choice that suggests starting the paragraph with Sentence 2—the best transition from the preceding paragraph about some of the differences between American and English fox hunting. Sentence 1 (A, B, C) is a poor transition because the observation that "American hunters prize their dogs more highly" has no point of reference. More highly than what? Or whom? The meaning is clear only if it follows Sentence 2, leading a reader to the conclusion that American hunters prize their dogs more highly than English hunters prize theirs.

58. H. Inclusion of these terms from fox hunting enlivens the writing. F is wrong because an essay doesn't have to be about speech patterns to use specialized language effectively. The expressions might call attention to themselves, as G suggests, but they aren't irrelevant. They pertain to the essay's topic: fox hunting. J is wrong because it poses the nonsensical premise that writers should use the vocabulary of fox hunting whenever possible—even, presumably, in essays about medieval feasts and Japanese tea ceremonies. Be wary of absolute terms like *whenever possible.*

59. D. All of the choices make statements that can be supported by information in various sections of the passage, but D is the only one that sums up the main points of the essay as a whole: that American fox hunting was unlike the British version and that the writer remembers it as a pleasant pastime.

60. G. The other choices are wordy and awkward. F and J create awkward shifts from *the word . . . evokes* to *there being.* It's redundant to repeat the words *images evoked,* as H suggests. G offers the best way to make the list of images clear and consistent. For most people, the word *vacation* evokes images:

- of mountains and beaches,
- [of] a small boat bobbing on a lake,
- [of] a hammock swaying in the shade of a tree.

61. B. The writer has quite a different notion of *vacation* than most people, so *however* is the best way to introduce that contrasting opinion. It's choosing the word, not the word order, that dominates this question. *Too* (A) implies that the writer agrees with most people. *Therefore* (C) implies that the opinions of others have shaped the writer's opinion. *Besides* (D) implies that the writer's opinion supports other people's opinion rather than contrasting with it.

62. G. A comma corresponding to the one preceding *anticipating* is the best way to set off the parenthetical expression "anticipating a restful two weeks at home free of ringing phones and impatient customers" from the independent clause that begins with "*overhaul syndrome.*" F and H cause confusion by inserting an unnecessary conjunction—*and* or *and so*—between that parenthetical phrase and the rest of the sentence. By changing *and* to *until,* J creates two sentence fragments—long ones, but fragments nonetheless.

63. B. Only B doesn't create a comma splice. A, C, and D all make the mistake of using a comma to join two independent clauses. In addition, C makes it unclear whether the writer's vacation began on Friday or on Saturday. Likewise, it's hard to tell whether *unfortunately* in D refers to the writer's vacation beginning on Friday or to the lawn mower breaking down on Saturday. We might make a logical assumption, of course, but it's the writer's job to make the sentence so clear and unambiguous that we don't have to.

64. H. No comma is needed. No items are being listed, no dependent clause is being joined to an independent one, nor is there a nonrestrictive clause that should be set off by commas. (For example: No amount of adjusting and coaxing, **including the promise of an oil change,** could induce the lawn mower to resurrect itself.)

65. B. B is the only choice to use the correct possessive of *it: its.* The usual way to form a possessive is with an apostrophe and an *s.* However, if you try that with *it,* you get *it's* (A and C): a contraction of *it is. Its'* is a word you won't find in the dictionary.

66. H. It's the only choice that offers the parallel verb phrases *who was expected* and *who arrived.* G and J both misuse *arriving,* which needs some form of *to be* as an auxiliary verb here.

67. A. The idiom is *house itself,* not *house by itself,* so D is a poor choice. The heart of the sentence is the subject/verb phrase *the house itself is begging for attention.* It shouldn't be broken up by a comma between *house* and *itself* (B) or between *itself* and *is* (C).

68. G. The idiom is to make comments **about**—or **on,** or **regarding**—a subject. J, which also proposes *about,* is wrong because it includes a semicolon, which would be appropriate here only if the clause beginning with *When* and ending with *about* were an independent clause.

It's important to notice that the idiom we've been talking about involves making comments on a topic. In other contexts, other prepositions work very well:

> The neighbors made comments **from** June until September.
>
> They made comments **for** the sole purpose of embarrassing me.
>
> They made comments **with** no regard whatsoever for my wounded feelings.

69. A. There isn't a big difference between "I know it's time" and "I know that it's time." Both are perfectly acceptable. What makes A the best answer here is punctuation, not wording. The commas inserted by B, C, and D confuse a reader by setting off *I know* or *I know that* from the rest of the sentence, as if it's a parenthetical comment by the writer. (For example: My house is a mess, **I know,** but I resent my neighbors' telling me so.) The writer is setting up a simple cause-and-effect relationship: **When** my neighbors complain, **(then) I know it's time** to get cracking.

70. F. The writer discusses **two** presentable elements of the house: the yard and the exterior. Therefore, the plural verb *are* is best. It's also in the present tense, appropriately. Note the use of the present tense in the preceding sentence: "neighbors **begin** . . . I **know it's** time." If you weren't reading carefully, and mistakenly thought that the subject was the singular noun *house* or *exterior of the house,* you might pick the singular verb *is* (H). At least you'd have the correct tense. *Was* (G) and *has been* (J) are both singular verb forms, but they're also in the past tense.

71. D. If the first part of this sentence included a subject/verb combination—"My two-week overhaul **is** at an end"—it could be linked to the second with *and,* as A suggests. Instead, the sentence begins with an absolute construction, which should be followed by just a comma, as D proposes. *So* (B) and *therefore* (C) are poor choices because they imply a cause-and-effect relationship between exhaustion and a two-week overhaul—a relationship that isn't inherently clear to a reader from the information in that sentence.

72. J. Only J corrects the problem of the misplaced modifier. The writer—not the desk chair—is modified by the phrase "Ignoring coworkers clamoring to see my vacation photos." (Of course, the desk chair is ignoring them, too, but a reader would take that for granted.) G is a double whammy. The desk chair is not only ignoring the clamoring coworkers, but it also takes a deep breath as it greets the writer's body.

73. C. There should be no commas in or around the restrictive modifier *where I can relax.* It's a restrictive modifier because without it the sentence wouldn't be logical: "What a relief to find a place before I need an overhaul myself." Does the writer mean **any** place? No. What's needed is a place "where I can relax." The idea of relaxation is vital to what the writer is saying about needing an overhaul.

74. H. By repeating the idea of an overhaul, the writer provides a conclusion that echoes the essay's beginning. It gives the essay symmetry and makes it rhetorically cohesive. F is wrong because although the writer claims to consider *overhaul* and *vacation* synonymous, it's clear that the statement is ironic and is intended to set up a humorous contrast; a reader isn't likely to confuse the two words. There's nothing to suggest a relationship between the concepts of work and an overhaul (G), nor does anything in the word *overhaul* pertain to the idea of something being **over** (J).

75. A. B is wrong because the essay talks at length about vacation stress but says nothing about how to avoid it. C is wrong because although the writer discusses various tasks related to household repairs and maintenance, the approach is personal rather than factual; it's not a how-to article on home improvements. And it's the **opposite** of a persuasive article on the benefits of staying home (D). If anything, it's indirectly a persuasive article about why a vacationer should flee as far as possible from the dirty windows, rampant crabgrass, and capricious appliances of home.

1. B.

Since $m(\angle S) = 40°$ and $m(\angle T) = 2 \cdot m(\angle S) = 80°$, and recalling that $m(\angle R) + m(\angle S) + m(\angle T) = 180°$,
then $m(\angle R) = 180° - (40° + 80°) = 180° - 120° = 60°$.

2. G.

$\frac{19}{12} \cdot \$133.20 = \$210.90$.

3. C.

Since \$72 represents the basic fine of \$15 plus an additional fine of \$57, then Sally was driving $\$57 \div \$3 = 19$ mph over the speed limit. She was charged for traveling at a rate of $55 + 19 = 74$ mph.

4. F.

Since $E = IR$, by substitution $12 = I \cdot 4$, and so $I = \frac{12}{4} = 3$.

5. A.

Since $\angle a \cong \angle b$ (vertical angles are congruent) and $\angle b \cong \angle d$ (alternate interior angles are congruent), then by the transitive property of congruence, $\angle a \cong \angle b \cong \angle d$.

6. K.

$20{,}000 + 3{,}400{,}000 = 3{,}420{,}000 = 3.42 \times 10^6$.

7. D.

$0.02\overline{)2.542} \longleftrightarrow 2\overline{)254.2}$

$$\begin{array}{r} 127.1 \\ 2\overline{)254.2} \\ \underline{2} \\ 5 \\ \underline{4} \\ 14 \\ \underline{14} \\ 2 \\ \underline{2} \\ 0 \end{array}$$

8. G.

$\frac{x^2 + 12x + 32}{x + 4}$ in factored form is $\frac{(x + 8)(x + 4)}{(x + 4)}$, which simplifies to $x + 8$, when $x \neq -4$.

9. B.

If $x = -2$, then $12 - x^2 + 1 = 12 - (-2)^2 + 1 = 12 - 4 + 1 = 8 + 1 = 9$.

10. J.

If the \$35 shirt is discounted by 20%, then the discount is 20% of \$35 = $\frac{1}{5}$ (\$35) = \$7. The purchase price is \$35 – \$7 = \$28. The sales tax is 5% of \$28 = $\frac{1}{20}$ (\$28) = \$1.40. Then, the total cost of the shirt is \$28 + \$1.40 = \$29.40.

11. D.

$x \leq 2$ means "x is less than or equal to 2" and will include values less than 2 as well as 2. The correct graph will consist of a closed circle at $x = 2$ and a heavy arrow extending left from there to represent the points where x is less than 2.

12. H.

$\frac{6a}{7b}$ is 2 times $\frac{3a}{7b}$. So if $\frac{3a}{7b} = \frac{1}{7}$, then $\frac{6a}{7b} = \frac{2}{7}$.

13. A.

ΔABC is a 3-4-5 right triangle, and then ΔBCD can be recognized as a 5-12-13 right triangle. (Or, the Pythagorean theorem will give $BC = \sqrt{3^2 + 4^2} = 5$ and then $CD = \sqrt{5^2 + 12^2} = 13$.)

14. K.

The formula for area of a rectangle is $A = lw$. If w represents the width, then $w + 3$ represents the length, so by substitution $w(w + 3) = 54$.

15. B.

We know that $d = st$ and, if $s = 30$ mph and $t = \frac{1}{2}$ hour, then, from the information about the 30-mph trip, $d = 30(\frac{1}{2}) = 15$ miles. So from the information about the 3-mph trip, $15 = 3t$, which means $t = 5$.

16. H.

If s represents the length, in feet, of a side of the new square garden, then, since the two areas are equal, $16 \cdot 9 = s^2$. So, $s = \pm\sqrt{16 \cdot 9}$. We also know that s cannot be negative, since it's a length, so $s = \sqrt{16 \cdot 9} = 4 \cdot 3 = 12$. It makes sense that s is between 9 and 16.

17. C.

The number of rooms rented is 80% of 225 = 180, and the total rent is (180 rooms) × ($50 a day per room) × (2 days) = $18,000.

18. H.

Since $\angle BCD$ measures 120°, then $\angle BCA$ measures $180° - 120° = 60°$. The measures of the 3 angles in the triangle must sum to 180°, so
$m(\angle B) = 180° - (60° + 30°) = 90°$.
(You could also use the exterior angle theorem to solve this problem.)

19. B.

Addition Method

$$\begin{array}{lcr} 2x + 5y = 20 & \text{multiply by 1} & 2x + 5y = 20 \\ & \Longrightarrow & \\ 6x - \frac{1}{2}y = 29 & \text{multiply by 10} & \underline{60x - 5y = 290} \\ & & 62x = 310 \\ & & x = 5 \end{array}$$

Substitution Method

$$6x - \tfrac{1}{2}y = 29 \longrightarrow y = 12x - 58$$

Substituting into the top equation

$$\begin{aligned} 2x + 5(12x - 58) &= 20 \\ 2x + 60x - 290 &= 20 \\ 62x &= 310 \\ x &= 5 \end{aligned}$$

By either method, if $x = 5$, then

$$\begin{aligned} 2(5) + 5y &= 20 \text{ (top equation)} \\ 5y &= 10 \\ y &= 2 \end{aligned}$$

Check: $2(5) + 5(2) = 10 + 10 = 20$ ✓

and $6(5) - \frac{1}{2}(2) = 30 - 1 = 29$ ✓

So (5,2) solves both equations.

20. H.

$$\tfrac{1}{2} + (\tfrac{2}{3} \div \tfrac{3}{4}) - (\tfrac{4}{1} \times \tfrac{1}{6})$$
$$= \tfrac{1}{2} + (\tfrac{2}{3} \times \tfrac{4}{3}) - (\tfrac{4}{6})$$
$$= \tfrac{1}{2} + (\tfrac{8}{9}) - (\tfrac{2}{3})$$

(Let's combine the $\frac{8}{9}$ and $-\frac{2}{3}$ first because the denominators are most alike.)

$$= \tfrac{1}{2} + (\tfrac{8}{9} - \tfrac{6}{9}) = \tfrac{1}{2} + \tfrac{2}{9}$$
$$= \tfrac{9}{18} + \tfrac{4}{18}$$
$$= \tfrac{13}{18}$$

21. E.

$$26y - (-10y) - 3y(-y + 3)$$
$$= 26y + 10y + 3y^2 - 9y$$
$$= 3y^2 + 27y$$

22. K.

The numerator is a difference of squares, and the denominator has a common factor of 2. So $\frac{a^2 - 4}{2a + 4} = \frac{(a + 2)(a - 2)}{2(a + 2)}$.

This simplifies to $\frac{a - 2}{2}$, as long as $a \neq -2$.

23. A.

If $x = -3$ is a solution to $x^2 - kx - 24 = 0$, then by substitution

$$(-3)^2 - k(-3) - 24 = 0$$
$$9 + 3k - 24 = 0$$
$$3k - 15 = 0$$
$$3k = 15$$
$$k = 5$$

24. J.

Since $\overline{BD}$ bisects $\angle ABC$, $m(\angle ABD) = m(\angle CBD) = 50°$. By the exterior angle theorem, $m(\angle BDC) = m(\angle ABD) + m(\angle BAC) = 50° + 30° = 80°$. You could also use ΔABC to find $m(\angle ACB) = 180° - (100° + 30°) = 50°$. Then ΔBCD has two 50° angles and $\angle BDC$ must measure 80° to complete the triangle. A third way to find $m(\angle BDC)$ involves finding $m(\angle ADB)$ and seeing that $\angle BDC$ is its supplement.

25. A.

If the length of the garden is to be between 20 and 25 yards, then two lengths of the garden would take up between 40 and 50 yards of fence. This would leave between 28 and 38 yards of fence to make two widths of the garden, meaning that one width could be between 14 and 19 yards. Algebraically, $2l + 2w = 78$ so $l = 39 - w$. Since $20 < l < 25$ then $20 < 39 - w < 25 \rightarrow -19 < -w < -14 \rightarrow 19 > w > 14$.

26. H.

I. $a > c$ and $b > 0$ combine to show that $a + b > c + 0 \rightarrow a + b > c$.

II. $a > c$ and $a > 0$ combine to give $a + a > c + 0 \rightarrow 2a > c$.

III. If $a = 3$ and $b = 4$, then $a + c > b$ becomes $3 + c > 4$.

From this, you can see that $c = 2$ makes the statement true and $c = 1$ makes the statement false. So III isn't always true.

27. C.

Using the Pythagorean theorem ($a^2 + b^2 = c^2$, where a and b are the lengths of the legs and c is the length of the hypotenuse) for ΔRST, $3^2 + 4^2 = c^2$, for which the only positive solution is $c = 5$. Thus, $\sin x$, which is $\left(\frac{\text{opposite}}{\text{hypotenuse}}\right) = \frac{4}{5}$.

9

28. J.

By cross-multiplying,

$$6x + 3x^2 = 4x^2 + 3x$$

Simplifying:
$$0 = x^2 - 3x$$
$$0 = x(x - 3)$$
$$x = 0 \text{ or } x - 3 = 0$$
$$x = 0 \text{ and } x = 3.$$

Check:
$$\frac{0}{2+0} \stackrel{?}{=} \frac{3(0)}{4(0)+3} \rightarrow \frac{0}{2} = \frac{0}{3} \checkmark$$
$$\frac{3}{2+3} \stackrel{?}{=} \frac{3(3)}{4(3)+3} \rightarrow \frac{3}{5} = \frac{9}{15} \checkmark$$

So the sum of the solutions is $0 + 3 = 3$.

29. A.

$-2|-3| - |-5| = -2(3) - (5) = -6 - 5 = -11.$

30. K.

Since $\overline{BE} \parallel \overline{CF}$ and $\overline{AD}$ is a transveral, alternate interior angles are congruent and $m(\angle EBC) = m(\angle FCD) = 50°$. Also since $BE = CE$, isosceles triangle BEC gives $m(\angle ECB) = m(\angle EBC) = 50°$. Since $m(\angle EBC) = 50°$ and $m(\angle ECB) = 50°$, then $m(\angle E) = 180° - (50° + 50°) = 80°$.

31. C.

$x^2 - 1 \leq 8$ becomes $x^2 - 9 \leq 0$, which in factored form is $(x - 3)(x + 3) \leq 0$. A product is negative in two cases: (I) the first factor is negative and the second is positive, or (II) the first factor positive and the second negative. Writing this algebraically (and including the case where the product is equal to zero) gives:

I		II
$x - 3 \leq 0$ and $x + 3 \geq 0$	or	$x - 3 \geq 0$ and $x + 3 \leq 0$
$x \leq 3$ and $x \geq -3$	or	$x \geq 3$ and $x \leq -3$
no solution	or	$-3 \leq x \leq 3$

9

32. G.

Using the Pythagorean theorem, $a^2 + b^2 = c^2$, where x is the length of one side of the square,

$$x^2 + x^2 = 10^2$$

or $$2x^2 = 100$$

and $$x^2 = 50$$

$$x = \pm\sqrt{50}$$

$$x = \pm 5\sqrt{2}.$$

Since the side of a square must be positive, $x = 5\sqrt{2}$ is the only solution.

33. D.

The general form of the equation of a circle is $(x - h)^2 + (y - k)^2 = r^2$, where (h,k) is the center and r is the radius. So by substitution $(x + 3)^2 + (y + 4)^2 = 36$ is the equation of this circle.

34. F.

To find the slope, take the given equation and solve for y to put it into slope-intercept form. The slope will be the coefficient of x. So

$$5x - 2y = 7$$

becomes $$-2y = -5x + 7$$

or $$y = \frac{5}{2}x + \frac{7}{-2}.$$

So the number representing the slope is the one in the place of m in $y = mx + b$ form:

$$y = \boxed{\frac{5}{2}}x - \frac{7}{2}.$$ The slope is $\frac{5}{2}$.

35. D.

If you were watching the intersection and writing down the number of people in each of the 100 cars, you'd have a list with 50 1's, 30 2's, 10 3's, and 10 4's. If you add up all of these 1's, 2's, 3's, and 4's, you'll get
$50 \cdot 1 + 30 \cdot 2 + 10 \cdot 3 + 10 \cdot 4 = 50 + 60 + 30 + 40 = 180$. Therefore, the average is $\frac{180}{100}$, or 1.8.

36. H.

If $AB = 5$, then the radius of the circle centered at B is 5. The radius of the larger circle has the same length as the diameter of the smaller circle, 10 units. If the smaller circle is removed from the larger circle, the difference in area will be the area of the larger circle ($\pi \cdot 10^2 = 100\pi$) minus the area of the smaller circle ($\pi \cdot 5^2 = 25\pi$), which equals 75π.

37. E.

If the line is to have the same slope as $y = 3x - 4$, then its slope is 3. If it is to have the same y-intercept as $x + y + 2 = 0$, which can be written as $y = -x - 2$, then its y-intercept is -2. So the line you want has equation $y = 3x - 2$.

38. G.

If $2x + 3 < 4x + 7$, then $-2x < 4$. Multiplying both sides by $-\frac{1}{2}$, you'll get $x > -2$. The correct graph will have an open circle at $x = -2$ and a ray extending from there to the right. Check this by trying, for example, $x = 0$ and seeing that it satisfies $2x + 3 < 4x + 7$.

39. E.

The slope of a line is the change in y divided by the change in x.

So $\quad \frac{4}{3} = \frac{c - (-c)}{5 - 2}$

or $\quad \frac{4}{3} = \frac{2c}{3}$

and $\quad 6c = 12$

making $\quad c = 2$.

9

40. H.

If $I = Pr$, then by substitution $40 = 500r$ and $r = 0.08$. You can also express .08 as $\frac{8}{100}$ or 8%.

41. B.

Drawing a graph is a great tool to use for this problem.

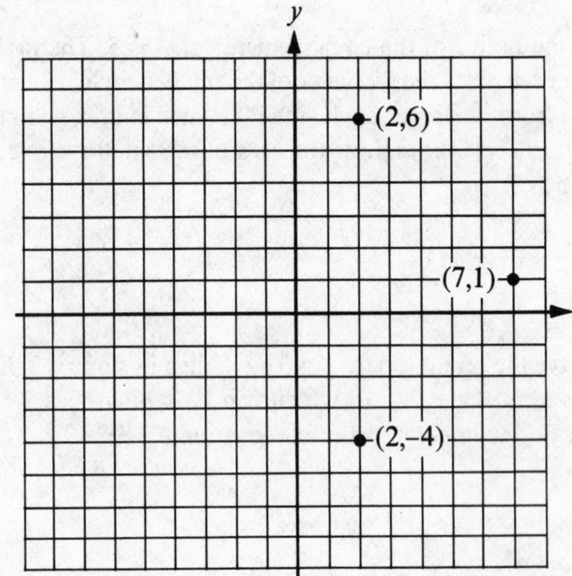

It looks like one side of the square will be the segment between (2,–4) and (7,1); the next side will be the segment between (7,1) and (2,6). Since the figure is a square, the sides must be perpendicular, so the slopes of these sides must multiply together to equal –1.

$$\left(\frac{-4-1}{2-7}\right)\cdot\left(\frac{1-6}{7-2}\right) = \frac{-5}{-5} \cdot \frac{-5}{5} = -1.$$ ✓

So the fourth vertex will be somewhere left of the other three points. Since opposite sides of a square are parallel and the same length, what's the pattern for getting from (7,1) to (2,6)? The pattern is up 5, left 5. Follow that pattern from (2,–4) and you'll end up at the fourth vertex. Up 5 from (2,–4) is (2,+1) and then left 5 will be (–3,+1).

You could also have noticed that diagonals of a square are the same length and are perpendicular. Since one diagonal is a vertical line segment, the other is horizontal, and both are 10 units long. So 10 units left of (7,1) is (–3,1). ✓

42. F.

$\frac{x^4 + x^4 + x^4}{x^2} = \frac{3x^4}{x^2} = 3x^{4-2} = 3x^2$.

Check: If $x = -2$, $x^2 = 4$ and $x^4 = 16$. $\frac{16 + 16 + 16}{4} = \frac{48}{4} = 12 = 3(4)$

43. E.

If y represents the correct answer, then $\frac{N}{7} = y$ and $\frac{N}{8} = y - 12$. To combine these and eliminate y, substitute the first into the second: $\frac{N}{8} = (\frac{N}{7}) - 12$. Looking at the answer choices, this is equivalent to $\frac{N}{8} + 12 = \frac{N}{7}$.

44. J.

$2(x^2 - 2x - 3) = 0$

$(x^2 - 2x - 3) = 0$

$(x - 3)(x + 1) = 0$

$x = 3$ or $x = -1$

The two solutions to the equation are 3 and –1, and their sum is 2.

Check: $2(3)^2 - 4(3) - 6 = 2 \cdot 9 - 12 - 6 = 18 - 12 - 6 = 0$ ✓

$2(-1)^2 - 4(-1) - 6 = 2 \cdot 1 + 4 - 6 = 2 + 4 - 6 = 0$ ✓

45. E.

$(\cos\frac{\pi}{3})(\cos\frac{\pi}{3}) + (\sin\frac{\pi}{3})(\sin\frac{\pi}{3}) = (\frac{1}{2})(\frac{1}{2}) + (\frac{\sqrt{3}}{2})(\frac{\sqrt{3}}{2}) = \frac{1}{4} + \frac{3}{4} = 1$. It would save a little time to view this as $\cos^2 x + \sin^2 x$, where $x = \frac{\pi}{3}$. A trig identity states that $\cos^2 x + \sin^2 x = 1$ for all values of x.

46. J.

Total dollars collected = (\$ from student tickets) + (\$ from nonstudent tickets) = $1(S) + 2(35 - S) = S + 70 - 2S = 70 - S$.

47. B.

The product is positive exactly when the factors have the same sign. That means you can "simplify" to:

$$[(3 - x) > 0 \text{ and } (x + 2) > 0] \quad \text{or} \quad [(3 - x) < 0 \text{ and } (x + 2) < 0]$$

$$[3 > x \text{ and } x > -2] \quad \text{or} \quad [3 < x \text{ and } x < -2]$$

$$[x < 3 \text{ and } x > -2] \quad \text{or} \quad [x > 3 \text{ and } x < -2]$$

$$[-2 < x < 3] \quad \text{or} \quad [0]$$

$$-2 < x < 3$$

48. H.

Since this is a 30°-60°-90° triangle, side $\overline{CB}$, which is the side opposite the 60° angle, has length $x\sqrt{3}$, and side $\overline{AC}$, which is the hypotenuse, has length $2x$, where x is the length of the side opposite the 30° angle. So $\frac{CB}{AC} = \frac{x\sqrt{3}}{2x} = \frac{\sqrt{3}}{2}$.

49. A.

$$\sin^2\theta + \cos^2\theta = 1$$

$$\sin^2\theta + \left(\frac{5}{13}\right)^2 = 1$$

$$\sin^2\theta = 1 - \frac{25}{169}$$

$$= \frac{144}{169}$$

$$\sin\theta = \pm\frac{12}{13}$$

Since $\sin\theta > 0$, for $0° < \theta < 180°$, $\sin\theta = \frac{12}{13}$.

50. F.

Given that $x \neq y$ and $x \neq 4$ (which are consequences of $x < y < 4$),

$$\frac{(x - y)}{4(x - y) - x(x - y)} = \frac{\cancel{(x - y)}}{(4 - x)\cancel{(x - y)}} = \frac{1}{(4 - x)}$$

51. D.

Each side of the square is 4 units long. Since $\overline{MA}$ and $\overline{NC}$ are formed by midpoints, each has length 2 units. Since $ABCD$ is a square, $\angle D$ is a right angle and ΔAND is a right triangle. Using the Pythagorean theorem to find the length of $\overline{AN}$, $4^2 + 2^2 = AN^2$ or $20 = AN^2$. Taking the positive square root (since AN represents a length), $AN = 2\sqrt{5}$; $\overline{MC}$ is the same length. The perimeter is
$2 + 2\sqrt{5} + 2 + 2\sqrt{5} = 4 + 4\sqrt{5}$.

52. J.

Since (1,–1) and (–1,t) are two points on a line that has slope –3,

$$-3 = m = \frac{y_2 - y_1}{x_2 - x_1} = \frac{t-(-1)}{-1-1} = \frac{t+1}{-2} = -\frac{t+1}{2}$$

That gives

$$-3 = -\frac{t+1}{2}$$
$$3 = \frac{t+1}{2}$$
$$6 = t + 1$$
$$5 = t$$

53. B.

The ratio of the height of the tree to the height of the streetlight is $\frac{1}{3}$. The ratio of the length of the shadow of the tree to the length of the segment from the base of the streetlight to the tip of the shadow must also be $\frac{1}{3}$. If s represents the length of the shadow, then

$$\frac{s}{15+s} = \frac{1}{3}$$
$$3s = 15 + s$$
$$2s = 15$$
$$s = 7.5$$

54. J.

I. $-4x + 5 > 2x + 17$ or II. $-4x + 5 > 2x + 17$

I.
$$5 > 6x + 17$$
$$-12 > 6x$$
$$-2 > x$$
$$x < -2$$

II.
$$-6x + 5 > 17$$
$$-6x > 12$$
$$x < \frac{12}{-6} \quad \text{(reversing the inequality)}$$
$$x < -2$$

55. C.

In ΔDGE, $\overline{DE}$ is the base and $\overline{GF}$ is the corresponding altitude. Therefore, the area of $\Delta DGE = \frac{1}{2}(12)(10) = 6(10) = 60$. Or you could find the area of ΔDFG as $\frac{1}{2}(12 + 7)(10) = 95$ and the area of ΔEFG as $\frac{1}{2}(7)(10) = 35$. So the area of ΔDGE is $95 - 35 = 60$.

56. J.

$$\frac{x-7}{4} = x - 10$$
$$x - 7 = 4(x - 10)$$
$$x - 7 = 4x - 40$$
$$-7 = 3x - 40$$
$$33 = 3x$$
$$11 = x$$

and 11 is between 10 and 12.

57. B.

$60°$ is $\frac{1}{6}$ of the $360°$ in a circle, so the answer is $(\frac{1}{6})(2\pi)(6) = 2\pi$.

58. K.

Line 1 has a positive slope, since it goes from lower to upper as it goes from left to right. Line 2 has negative slope. $m_1 > 0$ and $m_2 < 0$, so $m_1 \cdot m_2 < 0$.

9

59. A.

The tangent of $\angle A$ is $\frac{BC}{AC} = \frac{12}{AC}$, and $(AC)^2 = 13^2 - 12^2$, so $AC = 5$ (choose the positive root since it represents a distance). Then the tangent of $\angle A$ is $\frac{12}{5}$.

60. K.

$\overline{AB}$ must be horizontal, so the y-coordinate of B is 1. The midpoint of $\overline{AB}$ is (2,1), so, since (−4,1) is 6 units to the left of (2,1), B must be 6 units to the right of (2,1). That makes the x-coordinate equal to 8. The coordinates of point B are (8,1).

1. B. Julie is getting tough in an effort to persuade Selina to stay for supper. She begins with "importunings" in lines 6–7, proceeds to outline the menu in lines 14–17, reiterates "Why not stay?" in line 23, and finally decides to get tough—to try "steel against steel," as line 27 says—by bringing up the subject of Selina's father. For A, though Mr. Peake's comings and goings aren't explained to us and we as readers may well find ourselves wondering about them, there's no evidence given to support the idea that Julie was trying to worm that information out of Selina. The picture we get of the girls' relationship is one of warm friendship. There's no hint of any discord that would make Julie want to cause feelings of guilt (C) or humiliation (D) in Selina—though humiliation might very well be an unintended result of Selina's being forced to discuss her unfortunate father.

2. J. The question tells you that, in this context, food quality is related directly to status. Julie's elaborate dinner, including two side dishes and dessert, is a marked contrast to Selina's, described starkly as "cold mutton and cabbage." Therefore, it's reasonable to infer that Selina is poorer than Julie. Nothing in the passage suggests that Selina is wealthier than her father (F) or even that there's any difference in their status. Since Selina's still in school and lives with her father at the boarding house, we can assume she's not financially independent from him. In fact, line 44 shows that Selina's rather dated dress is a direct result of the downturn in her father's fortunes. As for Julie **once** having been wealthier than Selina (G), that would imply that she no longer is—something we know to be untrue. H is obviously incorrect if J is correct.

3. D. After deciding that Julie's get-tough speech in question 1 was merely a last-ditch effort to persuade her friend to stay for dinner, you should find it relatively easy to conclude that the line introducing Julie's speech should be interpreted in the same way. Nothing in the passage indicates that Julie feels anything but warmth and sympathy for Selina, so there's no support for the idea that she wants to start a fight (B) or cut her friend down to size (A). The "steel" of Selina's decision implies that her mind is made up—her resolve is as hard as steel—so it isn't logical to infer that she's in need of, much less open to, any help in changing her decision (C). Julie is only trying to change her tactics and be as firm as Selina; *steel against steel* is a metaphor for a battle of wills.

4. F. Julie's description of the rest of the dinner elicits "greedy groans" from Selina, who's firm in her conviction to dine on cold mutton and cabbage with her father. The groans show how much she regrets having to stick to her course of self-denial. The final groan is an acknowledgment of Julie's playing her ace in the hole: the delectable apple roll. The mention of dessert has certainly made many a dieter groan in the anguish of self-denial, too, but nothing in the passage suggests that dieting is the basis for Selina's decision (G). The earlier "greedy groans" would be inappropriate if Mrs. Hempel's cooking were "really awful" (J), and there's no basis for the conclusion that Selina hurt herself while donning her hat (H), especially since the first groans are associated with Julie's description of the Hempels' dinner, "dish for dish" (line 11).

5. D. Selina "had been spending the afternoon with Julie" (lines 3–4). The passage goes on to say that as Selina is getting ready to leave, she covers her ears to shut out "Julie's importunings that she stay to supper" (lines 6–7). Even if you're not certain what *importunings* means, you can probably figure out from the context—Julie's urgency (line 12), her eloquent food descriptions (lines 14–17)—that Julie is using all her powers of persuasion to coax Selina into staying. Therefore, we can pinpoint the first time Julie invited Selina as occurring in lines 6–7, after they've spent the afternoon together. That's not exactly the same as spending the day together, as D says, but it's still the best answer of the four. The first line of dialogue involving the dinner invitation is line 23, which does immediately follow Selina's grim recital of the Tebbitt menu (B). But we know that Julie has been "importuning" Selina to stay long before she's quoted directly. Since the incident at the boarding house happens after Selina has left Julie, it's impossible for Julie (unless she has clairvoyant powers we're not told about) to know about the tragedy before extending her invitation (C). And nowhere in the passage is there evidence of a conversation between Julie and her mother about whether there was "enough food for Selina" (A).

6. J. F is certainly **true**—anything dead has undoubtedly been severely damaged in one way or another—but that's not sufficient to cause a state of being "well beyond hurting." The burden clearly isn't healthy (G), because it's heavy, inert, and still. None of those qualities imply toughness, either, so H is a poor choice. If you had a shred of doubt—despite all the ominous description—about whether the burden was actually a corpse, you should have been convinced by the detail of the coat covering the face. You've probably seen movies and TV shows where a blanket or coat is used to cover the face of a person who has just died. The "infinite care" with which the burden is carried is another clue. It's somewhat ironic that the men are so careful with something that can't feel pain; it should be a clue that what they're feeling is something like respect or reverence, an emotion that could suggest they're affected by the presence of death.

7. D. From the reference to "he" in line 92, we can deduce that the corpse is male. From the information we're given—the magnitude of Selina's reaction and the fact that she knows this man well enough to know what he "always" did—it's likely that the body being carried in is her father's. A is a poor choice because Mrs. Tebbitt is shouting at the men bringing the body into the boarding house, not at Selina. Selina knew long before line 81 that her father hated the boarding house (B), because she tells Julie so in lines 37–38. There's no basis for assuming that she'll never see Julie again (C), especially since it's clear that Julie isn't the one who died.

8. H. Julie's dialogue in lines 14–16 refers to the meal of chickens brought to her father and cooked by her mother. It isn't logical that she'd have to persuade Selina to stay for supper if they lived together (J). Selina is the one who lives with her father alone (G), as references like lines 29–30 indicate—after he leaves, she's alone. There's no mother in the picture. The passage includes numerous references to the fact that they live in a boarding house run by Mrs. Tebbitt (F); "her [Selina's] second-floor room" (line 59) is just one of them.

9. A. If you're a very careful reader, you probably noticed that the hat isn't actually ripped. Selina removes only "a stitch or two" (line 63), sees the discolored spot underneath the flower, and decides to cover it up again. Nevertheless, the other three responses are even farther from the passage. Whether she rips stitches or the hat, she doesn't do it "accidentally" (B). Her intent was to take off the old faded flowers. Still, we can't assume that she wanted to add new ones (D). If she had wished to place **more** flowers on the hat, she need not have removed the old roses; if her intention had been to **replace** the old flowers with new ones, she wouldn't have sewn the old rose back into its place (lines 67–68). Nothing in the passage indicates that her hat didn't fit (C).

10. H. It's important not to let your own opinions about style and about what might constitute the outfit of someone who's down on her luck mislead you. Selina's elaborately fancy costume might very well strike you as "modest" (F) and "old-fashioned" (G), but that's not what *modish* means in this context. What's modish about the costume is that it's "bustled, and basqued, and flounced"; it's flawed by being last spring's model—therefore, it's only "somewhat stylish" (H). With all those flounces, feathers, and flowers, you might conclude that Selina's costume is a bit "flamboyant" (J). The fact that her hat came from New York, however, suggests that it wasn't cheap. You don't have to know where the incident takes place to pick up the prestige implied in the passage by owning a big-city hat.

11. B. There are two statements in the passage that support this response. Lines 15–17 state, "nothing guarantees that all electors chosen in November will vote as they are pledged in December." And lines 53–56 add, "electors in most states are not legally bound to vote for the candidate they are pledged to. In others, they face no legal penalty for bolting." So B is the closest in meaning to the statements in the passage. A is ruled out as clearly inaccurate. C is incorrect as well. The twenty-nine electors did **not** actually bolt from Carter to Ford. For D, although the possibility exists, there is nothing in the passage to suggest that many electors do, in fact, bolt from their candidates.

12. F. The fifth paragraph discusses two dates, 1800 and 1824, on which a tie in the electoral college had to be resolved in the House of Representatives. Note that in 1876 and 1888 presidents who had **not** won the popular vote were elected by the electoral college (these elections were not cases decided by the House of Representatives). The popular vote between the two presidential candidates was very close in 1976, but there wasn't a tie in the electoral college. Thus, responses G (1800 and **1876**), H (1800 and **1888**), and J (**1888** and **1976**) can be ruled out.

13. C. In "big urban states . . . the swing vote is usually concentrated in the major cities" (lines 69–71). Thus, the most important groups of voters are the "swing" voters in the major cities, who can change the outcome of an election. So A (suburbs) and B (rural areas) are ruled out. For D, the passage does state that big urban states are an important interest group. But the most important voters in large urban states are found **in cities,** not in special interest groups.

14. F. "Amending the Constitution" is the best answer. The passage states, "In almost every session of Congress an effort is made to abolish the electoral college **by constitutional amendment**" (lines 57–59). Therefore, the remaining responses are ruled out.

15. C. The best answer is: "To this day, every time there is a **close election,** such as that of 1976, there is fear that a candidate will win the electoral vote but not the popular vote" (lines 50–52). Thus, when the popular vote is close, concerns surface that the electoral college will not reflect the popular vote. A is ruled out because special interest groups are discussed only in the context of electoral college favoritism. B is ruled out because the statement is not specific about which elections raise concerns (almost every election vs. close elections). Candidates who win in states with 4 to 14 electoral votes (D) are mentioned in relation to biases in the electoral college; this discussion does not deal with the electoral college vote reflecting the popular vote.

16. F. The statement in F is contradicted by the electoral college system (so it is **not** true). Lines 24–29 state that the electoral college "influences the strategies employed by the major parties because, in effect, some votes . . . are more important to the outcome than others. This is true even though we usually think that in our system of 'one person, one vote,' all votes are equal." In other words, in the electoral college, all votes are **not** equal. All votes **do not** carry an equal amount of weight in deciding an election.

So F, which is not true, is the best answer. Notice that H is the opposite of F; the passage states that some votes are more important to an election's outcome than others. So even though the statement in H is true—in fact, **because** it is true—it is not the best answer to this question. Since G defines the electoral college and is true, it cannot be the correct choice.

17. A. The 1976 election is discussed in the first and second paragraphs. Note that Carter did become president in 1976. But there are two ways that Carter, who had the most popular votes, could have lost the electoral college vote to Ford (and thus Carter would not have become president): (1) if 5000 voters (in the popular vote) from Ohio and Hawaii had voted for Ford, this would have shifted the majority of **electoral** votes to Ford; or (2) if 29 electors pledged to Carter had instead voted for Ford, this also would have given Ford a majority of electoral votes. B is incorrect because Carter won the popular vote and the electoral college. C is incorrect because the electoral college did operate "properly" in the Carter election. D can be ruled out because only the elections of 1800 and 1824 were decided in the House.

18. H. Notice that **both** options I and II are accurate, according to the passage. Line 78 begins: "biases, which result in a net advantage to large states (option I), and a disadvantage to states with 4 to 14 electoral votes (option II)." Option III is inaccurate because inhabitants of the Midwest are described as being discriminated against (lines 82–83).

19. B. The best answer is: "votes for the losing candidate in each state are 'lost' because of the winner-take-all provision." Note that the last paragraph of the passage discusses direct popular election; the final sentence states that this proposal "would be much more **democratic** than our present system, in which all of a state's electoral votes go to the winner, even if he or she receives only one more popular vote than the loser." In other words, our present electoral college system is based on the "winner-take-all" idea, which, according to the author, is undemocratic.

Response A can be eliminated since it is not supported by the passage, and C is not true because the House of Representatives maintains control over the choice of the winning candidate only when there is a tie in the electoral college. For D, the author does not cite this statement to support his claim that the electoral college is undemocratic. In fact, the fourth paragraph states that the **founders** believed the **electors** were more trustworthy than the **voters.** The seventh and eighth paragraphs discuss favoritism and bias in the electoral college but do not give reasons for you to conclude that voters are more trustworthy than electors. D might appear to be supported by the final paragraph of the passage, but a careful reading shows that the author does not cite this as support for his claim.

20. H. The best answer is "farmers." Lines 80–84 state that the electoral college "discriminates against inhabitants of the Midwest, South, and Mountain States, as well as blacks and **rural residents.**" So you need to figure out that farmers are among the residents of rural areas and are discriminated against by the electoral college. For F, the passage indicates that big-city residents ("central city and urban citizen-voters") are **favored** by the electoral college. The passage doesn't deal with suburban voters (near large cities) or youth; thus, G and J are ruled out.

21. B. Lines 14–15 refer to the "inner thoughts and feelings" that Gauguin and van Gogh wanted to make visible. We might assume that they were emotional people, as D suggests, but the idea that **most** artists are highly emotional isn't supported by the passage. It's a stereotype. A also refers to the stereotypical emotionalism of most artists, while C projects a related generalization: that most artists are not rational and scientific.

22. F. Throughout this section, it may help to keep in mind the two major Post-Impressionist attitudes mentioned in the first paragraph and which artists espoused each of those attitudes:

Expressionistic—Gauguin and van Gogh

Formalistic—Seurat and Cézanne

Much of the passage compares the emotional intensity of Gauguin and van Gogh, as expressed by the bold colors and broad shapes they used, with the more structural, systematic approach favored by Seurat and Cézanne. F is the only response to mention one of the pairs, so you should have zeroed in on it first. Line 21 says that both Cézanne and Seurat were interested in achieving a "structured clarity of design." You might have been bothered by the discrepancy between *structured* in the passage and *structural* in the option, but a quick check of the other choices shows that F is clearly the best one. Cézanne and Seurat, not Gauguin and Cézanne (G), were interested in the structural or formal aspects of painting (lines 38–40). Gauguin and van Gogh, not van Gogh and Seurat (H), recorded inner feelings with broad, bold shapes (lines 13–17). Seurat, not Cézanne and van Gogh (J), systematized optical color mixing (line 22).

23. B. The first paragraph contains quite a bit of important information, including the two major attitudes alluded to in B: Expressionism (Gauguin and van Gogh) and Formalism (Cézanne and Seurat). Remember that Post-Impressionism encompassed several styles that were "various reactions to Impressionism" (line 7). The passage contrasts the reactions of Gauguin and van Gogh with those of Seurat and Cézanne. The four painters exemplify Post-Impressionist **attitudes** (line 11)—note the plural!—not a single aspect (D). A is wrong because Gauguin was an Expressionist, while Seurat was a Formalist. C doesn't make sense, because the point of lines 83–89 is that Gauguin felt European art **lacked** the strengths of ancient and non-Western culture; their values were **not** embodied in European art at that time.

24. J. Lines 56–57 cite Cézanne's concept of a "geometric substructure in nature and art"; lines 66–67 say that the houses and trees in his work approach "geometric planes." He represents the Formalist attitude among the Post-Impressionists. The Expressionists (G)—Gauguin (H) among them—were more interested in conveying emotion than in creating a formal structure. We can infer that the Impressionists (F) weren't concerned with geometric aspects because, according to lines 2–5, Impressionism was a style tending toward "fleeting impressions of light and color" rather than "solidity of form and composition."

25. D. Van Gogh strove to "express his emotions" (line 78) with "textural brushwork" (line 80) and "bold color contrasts" (lines 15–16). A, B, and C all describe aspects of van Gogh's techniques, but they propose that his main interest was depicting reality, or the physical (outer) world. If you've seen any of van Gogh's paintings, you might remember that he **did** in fact depict the physical world: flowers, fields, the night sky, his bedroom. But with their bright colors and distinct brush strokes, his paintings are not considered realistic. Van Gogh's passion was for expressing his inner world, his own personal interpretation of the outer world, as the passage makes plain in statements like this:

> With van Gogh, late nineteenth-century painting moved from an outer *impression* of what the eyes see to an inner *expression* of what the heart feels and the mind knows . . . (lines 71–74).

26. G. According to the fourth paragraph, Seurat developed the method of *pointillism* (he called it *divisionism*), by which he "applied his paint in tiny dots of color to achieve a richly colored surface through optical mixture" (lines 30–32). It was Seurat, not Cézanne (F), who set out to develop a "*scientific* technique" (line 27) based on "the principles of color optics" (line 29). According to lines 46–47, it's true that Seurat tried to base his work on the observation of nature (H). However, that statement addresses only his subject matter, not his specific technique. Both Seurat and Cézanne used "separate strokes of color" (lines 47–48), but separate **shades** of color (J) aren't mentioned. Also, if J were the best answer, it would mean that both Seurat and Cézanne embraced pointillism—a technique that the passage links specifically **only** with Seurat.

27. B. Response B is taken directly from lines 46–47. A is wrong because line 54 says that Cézanne's paintings "are free of atmospheric color effects." C and D should be ruled out because only Cézanne is associated with "planar surfaces" (line 49) and "looser (brush) strokes" (line 56).

28. F. Seurat and Cézanne were considered Formalists because they were "more interested in the structural or formal aspects of painting than in its ability to convey emotions" (lines 38–40). The Expressionists, including van Gogh and Gauguin, worked at "expressing inner feelings" (G). Cubism (H) was an outgrowth of Cézanne's work, while *pointillism* (J) was a name given to Seurat's style only.

29. C. First, Seurat and Cézanne used unconventional methods. Cézanne "did not use light and shadow in a conventional way" (lines 50–51). By the time we get to this point in the passage, we know that Seurat's methods were unconventional, too; after all, he departed from convention to develop his own technique: pointillism (lines 26–32). Second, although the passage doesn't say so outright, it implies that Cézanne's technique was more popular with young artists by emphasizing how **unpopular** Seurat's technique was (lines 54–56). A is wrong because the Expressionists—van Gogh and Gauguin—were the artists who expressed inner emotions; Cézanne and Seurat were Formalists. B is wrong because, as we've seen from lines 50–51, Cézanne **didn't** use color conventionally. D is wrong because Cézanne "carefully developed relationships between adjoining strokes of color" (lines 51–52)—he didn't **avoid** them.

30. F. We can interpret Seurat's attempts to "make the intuitive approach obsolete" (lines 27–28) as a rejection of that approach. The intuitive approach isn't explained, but we can infer an association between intuition and emotion—a trail that leads straight to the Expressionists, including Gauguin and van Gogh. We know that Cézanne, like Seurat, was more interested in form and structure than in emotion (lines 38–40) so we can guess that he, too, rejected the intuitive approach. At any rate, it's obvious that Seurat didn't **use** the intuitive approach, so J can be ruled out. *Divisionism* is Seurat's term for pointillism, the technique he developed—not **rejected** (G). H is wrong because Seurat is the only artist specifically named as having applied dots of paint (lines 30–32); Cézanne used "looser strokes" (line 56).

31. D. You won't find the phrase *basic astrophysical theories* in the passage. You have to read carefully and recognize that the big bang and the Hubble relation between red shift and distance are basic astrophysical theories being questioned by some scientists. The essay begins by summarizing the big-bang theory and alluding to how it's "resisted all serious challenges" (lines 13), then goes on to introduce two groups of challengers in the second paragraph. These groups are referred to as the *plasma dissidents* (line 25) and the *red-shift dissidents* (lines 62–63).

The "existence of electromagnetic fields" (A) isn't being challenged; Alfvén theorizes about the effects of electromagnetic forces on plasma (lines 37–41) to question the big-bang theory. No mention is made of any attempts to contest Alfvén's Nobel prize (B) or of the **dimensions** of positively charged ions (C). Positively charged ions are referred to only as a component of plasma (lines 28–29).

32. F. G and J are generalizations that aren't supported by information in the passage. G stereotypes professional writers, while J makes the sweeping statement that persistent criticism (never mind whether the critics are experts or crackpots) of **any** theory (political, mathematical, literary) invalidates it. F and H both propose that the alternative theories outlined in the passage don't seriously challenge the big bang. H, however, claims that the lack of serious challenge offered to the big-bang theory makes the passage illogical. What **is** illogical is to equate **persistent** criticism with **serious** criticism. *Persistent* is a way of discussing the frequency of criticism over time; *serious* refers to its quality—the expertise of the critics and how well they can support their criticism. According to the fifth and sixth paragraphs, some scientists are taking Alfvén's theories seriously, but only time—and research—will tell how seriously they challenge the big bang.

33. C. The big-bang theory got its name from the hypothesis that the universe began with a bang—a giant explosion (lines 2–3). Cosmic plasma (A) figures in the big-bang alternative theory put forth by plasma dissidents including Alfvén (lines 34–37). Red shift (D) is considered an **aftereffect** of the big bang and evidence of the universe's expansion. B's rather fuzzy statement about cosmic objects outside of the known galaxies isn't supported by any information in this passage, though it could very well turn up in Steven Spielberg's next movie.

34. G. Alfvén's view is put forth in lines 37–41. He theorizes that the expansion is influenced by energy he identifies as coming from matter-antimatter annihilation, not from mysterious, unidentifiable forces, as J suggests. F is wrong because Alfvén is mentioned as one of the "plasma dissidents" (line 25)—one of a group of scientists who dispute the big-bang theory. Alfvén believes the universe's expansion "is less dramatic than the big-bang theory proposes" (lines 37–38), not that it's "more rapid" (H).

35. C. The reason why the displacement of light testifies to the continuing expansion of the universe is not explained in the passage. However, you should have picked up on the idea that, whatever it is, light displacement happens "**toward** the red end of the spectrum" (lines 8–9), not **away** from it (A). The passage doesn't mention an observer, but the presence of an observer is implied by the word *seen.* There's no discussion of using a red filter (D) or of a star's color phases (B).

36. F. Alfvén's theory is that electromagnetic forces caused cosmic plasma to coalesce into galaxies (lines 30–33)—in other words, **shaped** them. Electromagnetic forces form **plasma** into distinctive shapes in the laboratory (lines 30–31); the forces don't take shape themselves (G). Filaments and positive ions are found in plasma (lines 27–29), not in electromagnetic forces (H). The second paragraph refers to plasma's ability to generate electromagnetic forces, which contradicts J.

37. D. This is Arp's theory, and it is disputed since he is one of the dissidents. Many "astronomers have dismissed Arp's observations as coincidences" (lines 88–89), so his theory about galaxies and quasars is hardly "a universally accepted fact" (A). The Hubble relation was formulated **before** Arp's theory; it is, in fact, what Arp's red shift research is aimed at proving false (lines 67–70), so B and C are wrong.

38. G. Arp's observational evidence ("he has observed many objects," line 74) doesn't conform to the Hubble relation. F is an accurate statement, based on lines 62–63, but it's not why Arp doubts Hubble. Arp himself is an example of a red-shift dissident who's **not** a plasma dissident (lines 64–65). In fact, you could think of him as a plasma dissident **dissident.** J is inaccurate because the Hubble relation, which links red shift with the notion of an expanding universe, does conform to the big-bang theory. Whether the Hubble relation conforms to the plasma approach or not, Arp doesn't—so H would be an illogical reason for him to doubt it.

39. B. Laboratory experiments have confirmed many of Alfvén's predictions (lines 46–49), which are attempts to refute the big-bang theory—a tenet of astrophysics for the past 20 years. Those experiments use new, more powerful plasma generators (D), but it's the predictions they help to validate—not the existence of the generators themselves—that could rock the foundation of astrophysics. The passage doesn't distinguish between astrophysics and astronomy, much less support sweeping generalizations about them, like the one in C. And, far from being obsolete (A), the big-bang theory "has resisted all serious challenges" (line 13).

40. J. The relation between distance and red shift is called the Hubble relation (lines 67–70). The passage doesn't actually state that Edwin Hubble originally proposed the relation, but we can infer it from the fact that the relation is named after him. It's clearly the best answer in any case because: Arp (H) is trying to **refute** the Hubble relation; Alfvén (F) is concerned with plasma, not red shift; while Peratt (G) is among the researchers working to corroborate Alfvén's theories.

1. B. The storage period for sun-dried Bombay duck increased from a little over 16 weeks (about 115 days) to over 2 years (more than 730 days) when it was irradiated. Onions (A) increased from 14 weeks (98 days) to 28 weeks (196 days). Semi-dried shrimp (C) increased from about 2.5 weeks (18 days) to about 17 weeks (118 days). Bananas (D) increased about 1 week (7 days).

2. J. Shrimp (as is) has storage properties almost identical to those of pomfret. Onions (F) last much longer whether irradiated or not. Cooked shrimp (G) lasts much longer after irradiation. Bananas (H) have completely different storage properties in all regards.

3. B. Based on similarities between the data for mangoes and bananas, which are also fruits, and assuming similar conditions applied to a peach, it is reasonable to predict that a peach would also last between 10 and 20 days.

4. F. The data show that the storage time for vegetables is greater, even at reduced dosage, than that for fruits. The data show that irradiation increases storage time and that, with or without irradiation, fruits rot more quickly than vegetables, so there is no evidence to suggest that the dosage causes fruits to rot more quickly (G). A conclusion involving multiple dosage amounts (H and J) is not supported.

5. D. Without irradiation, seafood (as is) keeps for just over 5 days, fruits for under 10 days, and vegetables for more than 10 weeks. Responses A, B, and C show different orderings.

6. G. The figure shows that cosmic radiation with a wavelength of 10^{-9} centimeters is completely absorbed by the atmosphere at a height of about 38 kilometers. Below this height, as in response F, radiation with a wavelength of 10^{-9} centimeters does not penetrate. Above this height, as in responses H and J, this particular cosmic radiation is not completely absorbed.

7. B. Ultraviolet radiation with a wavelength of about 10^{-5} centimeters and X rays at a wavelength of about $10^{-6.5}$ centimeters are completely absorbed at altitudes higher than any other type of cosmic radiation (greater than 100 kilometers). The highest altitude at which gamma (γ) rays (A), visible (C and D), radio (C), or infrared (D) radiation are completely absorbed is less than 100 kilometers.

8. F. According to the figure, a rocket would be unable to measure all of the wavelengths included in X rays and ultraviolet radiation, while a satellite could measure them. Both a satellite and a rocket **could** measure all wavelengths associated with infrared (G, H, and J), visible (H and J), and radio waves (J), ruling out those answer choices.

9. C. Of the choices, visible cosmic radiation is least absorbed by Earth's atmosphere, because all of its wavelengths reach the surface of Earth. Gamma (γ) rays (A), X rays (B), and ultraviolet radiation are all completely absorbed before they reach Earth's surface.

10. J. To observe the full radio spectrum of cosmic radiation, you would have to locate a receiver higher than about 40 kilometers, at which height radio wavelengths of approximately 10^{-2} centimeters are absorbed. Responses F, G, and H are all below the altitude at which the complete radio spectrum is present.

11. D. From the modern data available, Formation A could very well represent a shallow, clear ocean deposit, since corals and snails are both listed under these three categories (shallow, clear, and "normal marine"), and green algae is listed under two of them (shallow and clear). A freshwater lake deposit (A) is only supported by the presence of snails in Formation A and so would be a poor choice. A mudflat deposit (B) is not supported by the presence of anything. Corals, snails, and green algae support a clear water environment, not a muddy one (C), which would be supported by the presence of clams.

12. J. Clams are found in soft muddy environments, where it would be easy for them to burrow. Barnacles (F), oysters (G), and snails (H) were not tested for substrate firmness in Study 1, so there is no evidence to support the idea that they might burrow into the bottom sediments.

13. B. According to the data in the studies, some aquatic organisms occur in a greater number of different environments than others and so are probably more tolerant of environmental variation. Table 1 shows that water clarity (A) **does** have an effect on distribution. Study 1 shows that very different conditions can support aquatic organisms, contrary to C. Data from the studies suggest that environmental conditions have a lot to do with the distribution of aquatic organisms, not a little, as suggested by D.

14. F. Graph F shows the inference that Formation A was deposited in clear water and Formations B and C in mildly turbid water. Graphs G, H, and J are not as well supported because Graphs G and J suggest that Formation A was deposited in muddy water and Graph H suggests that Formation A was deposited in mildly turbid water and Formation C in muddy water.

15. C. In Study 1, clams are shown to occur in all tested water clarity conditions.

16. H. The presence of muddy water during the deposition of Formation E could account for the absence of corals in that formation, since corals are shown to live in clear water and not to tolerate muddy water. Study 1 shows that corals survive in normal marine (F), shallow (G) water, and on hard substrates (J), so the presence of these conditions is not a good reason to account for the absence of corals in Formation E.

17. B. The graph in Figure 1 shows that Group C pats decomposed faster than Group T pats. Response A draws exactly the opposite conclusion. The data presented in Figure 1 show clearly different trends for the two groups, so the pats did not decompose at the same rate (C). Group C decomposed rapidly, while Group T, contrary to response D, decomposed extremely slowly.

18. F. Because the grass that died was associated with Group T pats, which were full of antibiotics, one should examine the effects of antibiotics on grass to try to determine the cause of death. Responses G, H, and J involve substances that were not known to be a part of the experiment, and so, from the information available, there would be no reason to look at their effects.

19. A. Runoff from Group T pats likely contains significant amounts of antibiotics, which would reduce the population of bacteria as a source of food for aquatic insects. Table 1 shows that the number of bacteria is lower in Group T pats, which contain antibiotics, suggesting that antibiotics decrease the survival of bacteria, not increase it (B). The population density of aquatic insects would be expected to decrease in response to a decrease in the numbers of bacteria, not increase (C and D).

20. J. After 100 days, Group T pats had decomposed much less than Group C pats, suggesting that the presence of antibiotics in Group T pats reduces their rate of decomposition. Soil bacteria (F and H), earthworms (G), and insects (H) are not part of the data presentation in Figure 1, and it would therefore be inappropriate to include them in a conclusion based on that figure.

21. A. A lower level of antibiotic will likely result in greater pat decomposition because of an increase in bacterial survival. A decrease in bacterial survival (B and D) would probably result in less pat decomposition (C and D). The bacterial decrease is not likely to happen because of a lowering of antibiotic level, but rather from a raising of antibiotic level.

22. F. The number of bacteria was reduced from many thousands to a few hundred individuals. The numbers of fungi (G) and insects (H) were reduced much less. The number of earthworms (J) stayed about the same or increased a little bit.

23. D. According to Hypothesis 2, not enough time has passed for life to have appeared as described in Hypothesis 1. Hypothesis 2 agrees that organic molecules probably formed as suggested by Hypothesis 1. Therefore, there was enough energy (A) to form organic molecules (C) in the primitive ocean (B) "soup," but not enough time for them to randomly collide to create life as we know it.

24. G. Diagram G shows a protein-coated droplet incorporating DNA and other organic molecules within a "soup." These are all key factors of the discussion of early cells in Hypothesis 1. Diagrams F, H, and J all show amino acids as an important part of the diagram. Amino acids are not discussed in Hypothesis 1 and therefore do not illustrate that hypothesis.

25. D. The presence of DNA in protein-coated droplets likely provided those droplets with an evolutionary advantage over similar droplets without DNA. Photosynthesis (A) is not discussed or implied in Hypothesis 1. Presumably the presence of DNA in a protein-coated droplet would eventually lead to some kind of control of rates of diffusion (B) or osmosis (C).

26. G. If organisms containing L amino acids were somehow better able to adapt to life in the primitive oceans, that might explain why modern organisms have only L amino acids. Hypothesis 2 would then be unnecessary. Clay crystals with structures that prevent D amino acids from attaching (F) would provide additional support for Hypothesis 2. If cells with D amino acids evolved faster (H), that would not explain why only cells with L amino acids are present now and Hypothesis 1 would neither be supported nor defended. It seems highly unlikely that undiscovered organisms containing D amino acids exist (J), but even if they did, their presence alone (presumably rare) would not necessarily support or provide a reasonable defense for Hypothesis 1 to the disadvantage of Hypothesis 2.

27. B. Mutation results in an imperfect copy of the original DNA from one cell to another, with a resulting change in the new DNA code. Similarly, an imperfect copy of a clay crystal won't match the original crystal.

28. J. The discovery of cells created from a solution of organic molecules is predicted by Hypothesis 1. The presence of bacteria in the oceans (F) is irrelevant to Hypothesis 1. Cell membranes found to be crystalline in nature (G) might better support Hypothesis 2 because of its clay crystal association. Cells associated with clay deposits in the ocean (H) may be accounted for in many ways and so do not support either hypothesis.

29. C. Supporting evidence for the idea that clay was an early forerunner of chloroplasts would be a similarity in the way both absorb solar energy. The relationship of chloroplasts to protein droplets (A) has no bearing on a relationship with clay. Factors dealing with replication (B) do not deal with the specific evolutionary function relating clay and chloroplasts (capture of solar energy) in this question. Similarity of crystalline structure (D), again, has nothing to do with the function attributed to both clay and chloroplasts.

30. G. The mass of the unknown substance would have to be 6.7 grams in order for the sum of the masses of the products to equal the sum of the masses of the reactants (15 grams). Responses F, H, and J would make the sum of the masses of the products be equal to 13.3 grams (F), 16.6 grams (H), or 18.3 grams (J).

31. B. The procedure would need to be modified in order to make sure that all of the gaseous product was captured and weighed. Driving off the gas (A) would reduce the sum of the masses of the products by the amount of the mass of the gas. Gas does not have a "lack of mass" (C), so it **would** affect the goals of the experiment. In the experiment, water is heated and driven off so that the products can be weighed, contrary to D.

32. F. "The total mass of the products minus the total mass of the reactants equals zero" is just another way of stating the law of conservation of mass. A yellow precipitate is not always a product in a reaction (G). If water is a product of a reaction (H), its mass should be included in the total mass of the products. Not all chemical reactions have to take place in water (J).

33. A. The reason the total mass decreased from the first heating and cooling to the second is most likely that additional water was driven off as steam during the second heating. Lead(II) nitrate (B) is identified as one of the reactants, not a product, and the solution was filtered off. The beaker is heated then cooled so that air currents won't have an impact (C). Water, not lead(II) ions (D), would be driven off by heating.

34. H. In order to ensure that an accurate mass value for the product is obtained, the chemist should continue to reheat, cool, and weigh the beaker until a constant weight results. It is apparent from the situation that consecutive heating and cooling procedures are still driving off additional moisture, so obtaining an average (F) of the available information would do nothing to ensure a constant and accurate value. Values of 83.6 grams and 83.9 grams were obtained for the combined weight of the beaker and the product (G). It is uncertain whether 83.6 grams (J) represents an accurate and constant mass for the beaker and product unless additional heating, cooling, and weighing procedures are carried out.

35. A. The error described in this question does not affect the particular results that are sought, because the sum of the masses of the products would still equal the sum of the masses of the reactants. Further heating would eventually drive off all of the moisture, whether or not the yellow precipitate dissolved (B). At the completion of the experiment, water (C) is entirely removed so that an accurate weight for the products can be obtained. The liquid and precipitate represent products of the reaction. There is no evidence to suggest that they are still reacting (D), and even if they were, the final products should still conform to the law of conservation of mass.

36. G. The hypothetical reaction resembles the type of reaction shown in Figure 2, in which a net amount of energy is released by the reaction. The shape of the curve for the hypothetical reaction implies that activation energy is needed for the reaction to begin, so the reaction would not occur spontaneously (F). The energy levels of the hypothetical reaction are shown in the diagram. The reaction proceeded even though no catalyst (----) was present (H). There is no indication of the speed of any of the reactions in any of the figures, so response J would be inappropriate.

37. B. A catalyst lowers the activation energy required for a reaction to begin. The potential energy of the reactants (A) is not changed by the addition of a catalyst. A catalyst tends to speed up the reaction, not slow it down (C). A catalyst is not shown to alter the amount of product (D) or reactant in a reaction.

38. J. The relative potential energies of the reactants and products are used to differentiate whether a chemical reaction absorbs or releases energy. The amount of reaction time needed to form products from reactants (F) is unknown from the information provided, and it is unclear what, if anything, that would say about whether a chemical reaction releases or absorbs energy. An appropriate catalyst (G) would reduce the activation energy needed for a reaction to begin, regardless of whether the reaction absorbs or releases energy. The amount of product formed during the reaction (H) depends on the amount of reactants present in the beginning and says nothing about whether the reaction absorbs or releases energy.

39. C. The difference between the potential energy of the reactants and the potential energy of the products is obtained by subtracting one from the other. The difference between the lowest potential energy point and the highest potential energy point (A) incorporates the activation energy. The difference between the potential energy of the product and the lowest potential energy (LPE) point on the diagram (B) would be correct for Figure 1 in which energy is absorbed (LPE = reactants) but incorrect for Figure 2 in which energy is released (LPE = products). The difference between the potential energy of the reactant and a higher potential energy point (D) refers to the activation energy in Figure 1 and may refer to either the activation energy or the potential energy of the product in Figure 2; in either case this choice is inappropriate.

40. J. Figure 2 shows a reaction in which net energy is released. Net energy is calculated from the difference between the potential energies of the products and reactants. Figure 2 shows a reaction in which energy is released, not absorbed (F and G). Net energy is calculated by the subtraction, not the addition (H), of the potential energies of the products and the reactants.

9

SAMPLE TEST 2

YOUR SIGNATURE (do not print): ____________________

YOUR SOCIAL SECURITY NUMBER OR ACT ID NUMBER: ___-__-____

THE ACT ASSESSMENT

DIRECTIONS

This booklet contains tests in English, Mathematics, Reading, and Science Reasoning. These tests measure skills and abilities highly related to high school course work and success in college.

The questions in each test are numbered, and the suggested answers for each question are lettered. On the answer sheet, the rows of ovals are numbered to match the questions, and the ovals in each row are lettered to correspond to the suggested answers.

For each question, first decide which answer is best. Next, locate on the answer sheet the row of ovals numbered the same as the question. Then, locate the oval in that row lettered the same as your answer. Finally, blacken the oval completely. Use a soft lead pencil and make your marks heavy and black. *DO NOT USE A BALLPOINT PEN.*

If you change your mind about an answer, erase your first mark thoroughly before marking your new answer. For each question, make certain that you mark in the row of ovals with the same number as the question.

Your score on each test will be based only on the number of questions you answer correctly. You will NOT be penalized for guessing. *HENCE IT IS TO YOUR ADVANTAGE TO ANSWER EVERY QUESTION.*

You may work on each test ONLY when your test supervisor tells you to do so. If you finish a test before time is called for that test, you should use the time remaining to reconsider questions you are uncertain about in that test. You may NOT look back to a test on which time has already been called, and you may NOT go ahead to another test. To do so will disqualify you from the examination.

Lay your pencil down immediately when time is called at the end of each test. You may NOT for any reason blacken ovals for a test after time is called for that test. To do so will disqualify you from the examination.

Do not fold or tear the pages of your test booklet.

DO NOT OPEN THIS BOOKLET UNTIL TOLD TO DO SO.

ENGLISH TEST

45 Minutes—75 Questions

DIRECTIONS: In the five passages that follow, certain words and phrases are underlined and numbered. In the right-hand column, you will find alternatives for each underlined part. You are to choose the one that best expresses the idea, makes the statement appropriate for standard written English, or is worded most consistently with the style and tone of the passage as a whole. If you think the original version is best, choose "NO CHANGE."

You will also find questions about a section of the passage, or about the passage as a whole. These questions do not refer to an underlined portion of the passage, but rather are identified by a number or numbers in a box.

For each question, choose the alternative you consider best and blacken the corresponding oval on your answer sheet. Read each passage through once before you begin to answer the questions that accompany it. You cannot determine most answers without reading several sentences beyond the question. Be sure that you have read far enough ahead each time you choose an alternative.

Passage I

"The dog is our best friend" is a maxim that will set many heads wagging, yes, in agreement.[1] Its truth, however, may be open to question. A recent national poll indicated that the cat, not the dog, is the more popular pet.[2] Vexing as this idea may be to the pro-canine pack, ailurophiles (that is, cat lovers) have long subscribed to the notion of feline superiority. [3]

While it is true that dogs have been fetching slippers and retrieving sticks for millennia, but[4] cats have a history that shall have combined[5] usefulness with nobility. The cat has been employed by gainful employment[6] in humanity's relentless quest to control the rodent population. The cat has also been revered throughout history.

1. A. NO CHANGE
   B. wagging in agreement.
   C. wagging affirmatively in agreement.
   D. wagging, up and down, yes.

2. F. NO CHANGE
   G. most popular of the two pets.
   H. still more popular pet.
   J. popularest pet.

3. The writer most likely uses the expressions "wagging" and "pro-canine pack" in the above paragraph because they:
   A. are synonyms for commonly used expressions.
   B. convey images associated with dogs.
   C. convey images appropriate to public opinion polls.
   D. are expressions commonly used to convey irony.

4. F. NO CHANGE
   G. While it is true that dogs have been fetching slippers and retrieving sticks for millennia,
   H. However it is true that dogs have been fetching slippers and retrieving sticks for a millennia, thus
   J. It is true that dogs have been fetching slippers and retrieving sticks for millennia,

5. A. NO CHANGE
   B. had been combined
   C. would combine
   D. combines

6. F. NO CHANGE
   G. granted gainful employment
   H. granted gainful employment productivity
   J. granted gainful employment work

8939D

GO ON TO THE NEXT PAGE.

1 ■ ■ ■ ■ ■ ■ ■ ■ ■ 1

The Egyptians, for example, deified <u>it: and priestly</u>[7] decrees protected cats from mistreatment. After <u>death, dead</u>[8] cats were often honored with mummification and entombment.

In keeping with <u>the cats'</u>[9] aristocratic origins, the cat has inspired writers and artists. What would *Alice in Wonderland* be without the grinning Cheshire cat? How many children have delighted in the gallant deeds performed by the hero of *Puss in Boots?* And what canine can possibly compete with the infamous comic-strip character Garfield?

<u>While cats</u>[10] have many practical advantages, which clearly recommend them as ideal pets for millions. They require less maintenance <u>then dogs do.</u>[11] Whether in a high rise or a hayloft, cats adapt readily to their environments. A few simple amenities—food, a glowing hearth or a small patch of sun, and affection—are all a cat requires.

The cat was first domesticated in prehistoric times. Since then it has offered utility, intrigue, and, most important, companionship. Still, some die-hard dog lovers claim cats are antisocial, <u>to mistake</u>[12] dignity for indifference, composure for coolness. Yet cats continue to <u>aspire</u>[13] their way to the top of the pet popularity charts. So, apparently, more and more people are able to see the signs of friendship less in the crazed wagging of a tail <u>than in</u>[14] the quiet coiling in one's lap.

7. **A.** NO CHANGE
   B. it; and priestly,
   C. it, and priestly
   D. it and priestly,

8. **F.** NO CHANGE
   G. death, the dead
   H. death,
   J. life, the dead

9. **A.** NO CHANGE
   B. its
   C. it's
   D. their

10. **F.** NO CHANGE
    G. (Begin new paragraph) Cats
    H. (Begin new paragraph) Therefore, cats
    J. (Do NOT begin new paragraph) Therefore, cats

11. **A.** NO CHANGE
    B. then dogs.
    C. than dogs'.
    D. than dogs.

12. **F.** NO CHANGE
    G. mistaking
    H. that was mistaking
    J. who was mistaking

13. **A.** NO CHANGE
    B. lead
    C. clamor
    D. claw

14. **F.** NO CHANGE
    G. than has
    H. as in
    J. more than

GO ON TO THE NEXT PAGE.

Item 15 poses a question about Passage I as a whole.

15. Which of the following best describes the tone and purpose of this essay?

A. The tone is satiric; the purpose is to point out how some people overindulge their pets.
B. The tone is informal; the purpose is to entertain.
C. The tone is bitter; the purpose is to advocate cat superiority.
D. The tone is serious; the purpose is to present a strict logical argument on the superiority of cats.

Passage II

"Eavesdrop." "Snob." "Put a sock in it." [16]

Each <u>were</u> [17] a familiar expression to anyone my age. Yet while their meanings may be well known, their origins are buried deep in the past. Words or <u>phrases made up of words</u> [18] that were born with quite specific, literal meanings <u>can, as language evolves,</u> [19] come to have either new or enlarged meanings.

<u>Take for example,</u> [20] the word "eavesdrop." Originally "eavesdrip," referring to the water which drips from the eaves of a house, the term "eavesdrop" refers quite literally to the area beneath the eaves of a house. This area provides an excellent place for an outsider to overhear a conversation within a house without being seen. <u>And thus</u> [21] the expression "eavesdrop" gained its current meaning.

[1] Yet the origins of some words are not entirely clear. [2] Many dictionaries give a verdict of "origin unknown" to the word "snob," while some say it derives from a British dialect for shoemaker. [3] Another

16. The writer uses the preceding series of words and short phrases in quotation marks for the purpose of:

F. introducing the topic.
G. appealing to authority.
H. explaining the purpose.
J. employing complete sentences.

17. **A.** NO CHANGE
B. are
C. is
D. have been

18. **F.** NO CHANGE
G. verbiage
H. phrases
J. OMIT the underlined portion.

19. **A.** NO CHANGE
B. can as language evolves,
C. can as language evolves
D. can, as language evolves

20. **F.** NO CHANGE
G. Take, for example,
H. Take the example
J. Take, for example

21. **A.** NO CHANGE
B. Nevertheless
C. And so, then,
D. However

GO ON TO THE NEXT PAGE.

1 1

explanation of the expression says the word that[22] originated at Oxford University in England.

[4] At one time, registering freshmen,[23] were required to list their rank in social class. [5] Thus the word "snob" came to mean a commoner who would like to be associated with the upper classes. [6] Those in the lower classes were classified *sine nobilitate,* Latin for "without nobility." [7] The abbreviation of this term is "s.nob." [24]

Secondly,[25] if I were told to "put a sock in it," I'd know that I needed to make a lot less noise. This phrase dates back to the days of gramophones, the early record players whose sound came through there[26] large horns. Since these machines were not equipped with volume controls, which[27] would stuff socks in the horns to dampen the sound. Modern sound systems with carefully calibrated controls and headphones have eliminated the need for socks in the stereo, therefore[28] the expression meaning[29] "put a sock in it" still comes through loud and clear.

22. **F.** NO CHANGE
G. were
H. which
J. OMIT the underlined portion.

23. **A.** NO CHANGE
B. time registering, freshmen
C. time, registering freshmen
D. time registering freshmen,

24. For the sake of unity and coherence, Sentence 5 should be placed:
F. where it is now.
G. after Sentence 2.
H. after Sentence 3.
J. after Sentence 7.

25. **A.** NO CHANGE
B. Finally,
C. First,
D. Primarily,

26. **F.** NO CHANGE
G. it's
H. its'
J. their

27. **A.** NO CHANGE
B. the machines
C. they
D. listeners

28. **F.** NO CHANGE
G. thus,
H. quite the contrary,
J. but

29. **A.** NO CHANGE
B. expression of the meaning
C. meaning expression
D. meaning of the expression

Items 30 and 31 pose questions about Passage II as a whole.

30. The essay consists of four paragraphs. Which of the following is the best description of their relationship?
F. Example; explanation; definition; conclusion
G. Introduction; argument; example; call to action
H. Introduction; example; second example; third example
J. Definition; personal account; background information; conclusion

31. The essay focuses on these three particular words or phrases because they:
A. illustrate a variety of interesting word origins.
B. build to a story line.
C. share common linguistic roots.
D. went from having positive to negative connotations.

GO ON TO THE NEXT PAGE.

Passage III

By 1934, the Great Depression had crushed the economy of the United States. Jobs dried up <u>overnight,</u> [32] breadlines and soup kitchens were opened to feed the hungry. People by the thousands lost their homes <u>due to the fact that</u> [33] they could not pay their mortgages. The situation was very serious. When it was announced that work would soon begin on the Lincoln Tunnel to connect New York and New <u>Jersey, job applicants</u> [34] showed up in large numbers.

The engineers' <u>plans for building the tunnel</u> [35] called for digging from both banks of the Hudson at the same <u>time if</u> [36] all went according to plan, the two parts of the tunnel would meet in the middle of the river. The work was dirty, exhausting, and dangerous. Because of the high air pressure in the tunnel, the workers had to be physically fit: no one with any kind of disability could withstand the harsh <u>conditions, which were difficult to work in,</u> [37] of this workplace. <u>In addition to</u> [38] the hardships and <u>dangers, the men were</u> [39] hired to build the tunnel considered themselves lucky. They had jobs when few others did.

A year after the work started, the two parts of the tunnel, which had been inching toward each <u>other, they</u> [40] finally met. Two years after that, the Lincoln Tunnel was finished and opened to

32. **F.** NO CHANGE
G. overnight, and
H. overnight and,
J. overnight; and

33. **A.** NO CHANGE
B. the reason being that
C. for the reason that
D. because

34. **F.** NO CHANGE
G. Jersey; job applicants
H. Jersey, job applicants,
J. Jersey job applicants

35. **A.** NO CHANGE
B. plans, for building the tunnel
C. plans, for building the tunnel,
D. plans for building the tunnel,

36. **F.** NO CHANGE
G. time, if
H. time—if
J. time. If

37. **A.** NO CHANGE
B. conditions, which made the work tough,
C. conditions, which were hard on the workers
D. conditions

38. **F.** NO CHANGE
G. Regarding
H. Despite
J. Because of

39. **A.** NO CHANGE
B. dangers, the men
C. dangers; the men
D. dangers the men were

40. **F.** NO CHANGE
G. other they
H. other,
J. other

GO ON TO THE NEXT PAGE.

1 ■ ■ ■ ■ ■ ■ ■ ■ ■ 1

traffic. However, many people are afraid of tunnels.[41] Many of the men who had[42] worked on the tunnel were in the huge crowd of spectators on opening day. Exhausted but elated, the opening ceremony included a congratulatory speech by Babe Ruth.[43] Building the tunnel had taken hundreds of tons of concrete, steel,[44] and thousands of hours of backbreaking work. It had also taken the lives of eight men. The workers in the crowd that day had reason to feel grateful for and proud of the ambitious undertaking in which they had played as[45] vital a role.

41. **A.** NO CHANGE
    B. Many people, however, are afraid of tunnels.
    C. Many people are, however, afraid of tunnels.
    D. OMIT the underlined portion.

42. **F.** NO CHANGE
    G. whom had
    H. whom
    J. having

43. **A.** NO CHANGE
    B. they listened to a congratulatory speech by Babe Ruth.
    C. the tunnel was officially opened with a congratulatory speech by Babe Ruth.
    D. Babe Ruth's congratulatory speech marked the official opening of the tunnel.

44. **F.** NO CHANGE
    G. concrete and steel
    H. concrete, and steel,
    J. concrete, steel

45. **A.** NO CHANGE
    B. play so
    C. play as
    D. played so

Passage IV

My neighbor was already well into his eighties when I, at the ripe, old, age of thirty,[46] bought the house next door to his. In the seven remaining years of his life, we became as close as family. We were a bit of an odd couple, I suppose. At least, some people acted as if we were.

But I enjoyed this friendship. Like any other genuine friendship, this one was mutually gratifying. I helped Dr. Peterson with small chores[47] he provided me with a sense of life larger than my own. From him I learned history firsthand, as if it were.[48]

For instance, he fought in the Great War, which we now call World War I. He was a runner in France,

46. **F.** NO CHANGE
    G. thirty;
    H. thirty,
    J. the ripe old age, of thirty,

47. **A.** NO CHANGE
    B. chores, therefore
    C. chores: and
    D. chores;

48. **F.** NO CHANGE
    G. from the horse's mouth, and firsthand.
    H. straight from the horse's mouth, or source.
    J. firsthand.

GO ON TO THE NEXT PAGE.

carrying messages[49] from one group of soldiers to another. Once he was exposed briefly to gas. Slight exposure produced survivable respiratory illness, but inhaling the dreaded gas could lead to the slowest,[50] agonizing death.

The soldiers stoically bore the terror of the gas, so that[51] in camp they complained about smaller concerns, like the quality of their provisions. Coffee beans were often scarce, and chicory was substituted. Much[52] to the troops' disgust. In the morning as the men made their way to the mess tent, someone would ask, "Is it coffee?" Those already eating, would usually sing[53] back, "Chicory, chicory, chicory, chick!"

[1] Another of Dr. Petersons anecdotes[54] was a depressing story about the war's end. [2] The Armistice was to be signed an hour before noon on November 11, 1918. [3] On that day, both sides knew at 11:00 A.M., the war would be over.[55] [4] In the last hour, only an occasional shell was fired. [5] But at exactly 11:00 both sides shot off every remaining shell, senselessly killing and wounding many men in the final seconds of that war. [56]

Over the years, I came to value Dr. Peterson's friendship very highly. I have also made new friends, some of them less than half my age, and I have found that kind of friendship just as valuable. We lose something special if we associate only with people our own age.

49. **A.** NO CHANGE
B. delivering, by hand, messages, and war-related data
C. transporting documents and information by hand himself
D. delivering and transporting war-related documents

50. **F.** NO CHANGE
G. the most slowest,
H. a slow,
J. what was the slowest,

51. **A.** NO CHANGE
B. but
C. as
D. OMIT the underlined portion.

52. **F.** NO CHANGE
G. substituted much
H. substituted—much
J. substituted; much

53. **A.** NO CHANGE
B. eating, usually would sing
C. eating, usually sang
D. eating would usually sing

54. **F.** NO CHANGE
G. Peterson's anecdote's
H. Peterson's anecdotes
J. Petersons' anecdotes

55. **A.** NO CHANGE
B. the war at 11:00 A.M. would be over.
C. the war would be over. At 11:00 A.M.
D. the war would be over at 11:00 A.M.

56. For the sake of unity and coherence, Sentence 3 should be placed:
F. where it is now.
G. before Sentence 1.
H. after Sentence 1.
J. after Sentence 5.

GO ON TO THE NEXT PAGE.

Items 57–59 pose questions about Passage IV as a whole.

57. Which of the following sentences most effectively summarizes the conclusion drawn by the essay as a whole?

A. People can have good friends of all ages.
B. Many people were pointlessly killed in World War I.
C. History requires firsthand knowledge.
D. Friendship is an important thing.

58. Suppose that a newspaper editor had assigned the writer to describe the historical observance of Veterans Day. Does the essay successfully fulfill the assignment?

F. No, because the overall point of the essay is about friendship, not war veterans.
G. No, because the examples relate only to one veteran of one war.
H. Yes, because all the examples in the essay are actual experiences of a veteran of World War I.
J. Yes, because the essay mentions November 11, which is Veterans Day.

59. If the author of this essay wanted to reinforce her assertion that friendship with a younger person can be just as valuable as friendship with an older person, which of the following changes would be most useful to the reader?

A. Deleting some of the details of the older friend's stories
B. Offering an example of the rewards of the friendship with the younger person
C. Listing the ages of all the author's friends
D. Deleting the last sentence of the essay

Passage V

The following paragraphs may or may not be in the most logical order. Each paragraph is numbered in brackets, and item 74 will ask you to choose the sequence of paragraphs that will make the essay most logical.

[1]

For elegance, extravagance, and excess, nothing can surpass the fourteenth-century <u>feast seated</u> (60) on hard wooden benches in cold stone castles, with fires blazing merrily in the fireplaces behind them, knights and ladies were royally entertained by their host. They ate with <u>costly</u> (61) gold and silver spoons from plates made of hard bread, while trumpets blared and bagpipes squalled from the musicians' gallery above their heads. <u>Whenever</u> (62) harps, flutes, and recorders would produce sweeter music, soothing to the ears. Dancers might circle the floor, or jugglers might enter the hall,

60. **F.** NO CHANGE
G. feast, seated
H. feast. Seated
J. feast seated,

61. **A.** NO CHANGE
B. costly, and expensive,
C. costly—expensive—
D. costly and expensive

62. **F.** NO CHANGE
G. During which
H. Sometimes
J. There being times when

GO ON TO THE NEXT PAGE.

tossing everything from knives to goblets into the air. On occasion, animal trainers would show off their monkeys or command their little dogs to leap through hoops.

[2]

Not content[63] to have his performers provide all the entertainment, a clever host would have tricks of his own up his sleeve. You might, for example, furnish your[64] guests with an ingenious "puzzle jug," designed so that liquid that was poured into the spout would not remain in the jug but would circle around inside and exit that same spout. Until[65] perhaps a lord would slyly place into his guests' glasses the petals of a scarlet flower that, after a time, would change white wine into red.

[3]

Even more marvelous, however, were[66] some of the masterpieces from the kitchen, where they were cooked.[67] Servants might fill a cooked chicken with mercury; causing[68] the lifeless bird would dance before the eyes of the astonished guests at the table. Acting creatively, a culinary monster might be made[69] by attaching the head of one animal to the hindquarters[70] of another—a squirrel's head to a peacock's body, for example.

[4]

After an evening of revelry, the guests would leave their tables, laughing gaily. Satiated and

63. **A.** NO CHANGE
B. If he was
C. Because he was
D. He was not

64. **F.** NO CHANGE
G. They might, for example, furnish their
H. He might, for example, furnish his
J. One might, for example, furnish ones

65. **A.** NO CHANGE
B. Or
C. Unless
D. But

66. **F.** NO CHANGE
G. however, was
H. however; were
J. however were

67. **A.** NO CHANGE
B. kitchen, which is where they were cooked.
C. kitchen, the place they were cooked in.
D. kitchen.

68. **F.** NO CHANGE
G. mercury, causing
H. mercury; so that
J. mercury, so that

69. **A.** NO CHANGE
B. Acting creatively a culinary monster might be
C. Creative cooks might serve up a culinary monster
D. Creative cooks, might serve up a culinary monster

70. **F.** NO CHANGE
G. to the hindquarter's
H. to the hindquarters'
J. with the hindquarter's

GO ON TO THE NEXT PAGE.

sleepy, they would retire to their own castles with memory's of a fabulous feast—and [71] plans to reciprocate their host's hospitality with treats and surprises of their own. [72]

71. **A.** NO CHANGE
B. memories of a fabulous feast. And
C. memories of a fabulous feast and,
D. memories of a fabulous feast—and

72. Which of the following sentences would offer the best overall conclusion to Paragraph 4?

F. Everyone lived in castles in the fourteenth century.
G. Revelry made the guests laugh.
H. Though exhausting, medieval feasts were festive occasions for both guests and hosts.
J. Guests at medieval feasts made plans to reciprocate the hospitality of the host.

Items 73–75 pose questions about Passage V as a whole.

73. If the essay were revised to give readers a more detailed description of the lavish food served, the new sentences would most logically be incorporated into Paragraph:

A. 1, because it mentions eating.
B. 2, because it mentions drinking wine.
C. 3, because it describes masterpieces from the kitchen.
D. 4, because it describes the guests as being satiated.

74. Which of the following sequences of paragraphs will make the essay most logical?

F. NO CHANGE
G. 1, 3, 4, 2
H. 1, 4, 3, 2
J. 2, 1, 3, 4

75. Suppose the editor of a magazine for gourmet cooks had assigned the writer to describe the menu of a medieval feast. Does the essay successfully fulfill the assignment?

A. Yes, because the feast described is a fourteenth-century one.
B. No, because the essay describes music and entertainment.
C. No, because readers would want more information about the food served.
D. No, because the writer could not possibly have firsthand knowledge of the subject.

END OF TEST 1

STOP! DO NOT TURN THE PAGE UNTIL TOLD TO DO SO.

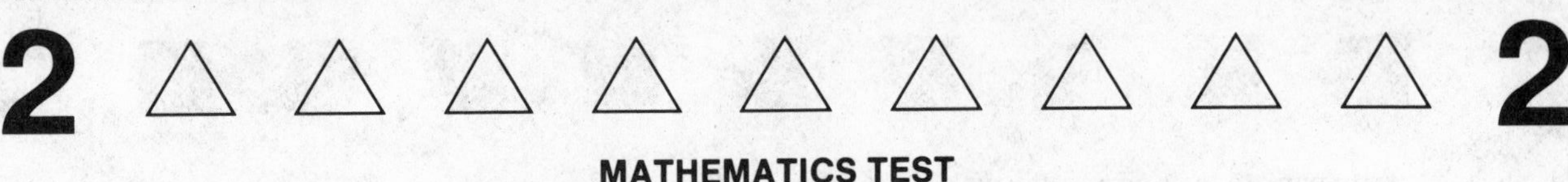

MATHEMATICS TEST

60 Minutes—60 Questions

DIRECTIONS: Solve each problem, choose the correct answer, and then blacken the corresponding oval on your answer sheet.

Do not linger over problems that take too much time. Solve as many as you can; then return to the others in the time you have left for this test.

Note: Unless otherwise stated, all of the following should be assumed.

1. Illustrative figures are NOT necessarily drawn to scale.
2. Geometric figures lie in a plane.
3. The word *line* indicates a straight line.
4. The word *average* indicates arithmetic mean.

DO YOUR FIGURING HERE.

1. Normal systolic blood pressure is sometimes approximated by using a person's age, in years, plus 100. Using this approximation, what is the difference between the systolic blood pressure of a 10-year-old and the systolic blood pressure of that same person at the age of 75 ?

A. 65
B. 85
C. 100
D. 105
E. 185

2. If $\left(\frac{3}{4} - \frac{2}{3}\right) + \left(\frac{1}{2} + \frac{1}{3}\right)$ is calculated and the answer reduced to simplest terms, what is the denominator of the resulting fraction?

F. 24
G. 12
H. 6
J. 4
K. 3

3. Adam tried to compute the average of his 7 test scores. He mistakenly divided the correct sum of all of his test scores by 6, which yields 84. What is Adam's correct average test score?

A. 70
B. 72
C. 84
D. 96
E. 98

8939D

GO ON TO THE NEXT PAGE.

READING TEST

35 Minutes—40 Questions

DIRECTIONS: There are four passages in this test. Each passage is followed by several questions. After reading a passage, choose the best answer to each question and blacken the corresponding oval on your answer sheet. You may refer to the passages as often as necessary.

Passage I

Most people still imagine that raindrops take on a teardrop shape when they fall. . . . Yet, for more than 80 years, scientists have known that falling water drops are flattened rather than elongated. This shape is the result of a delicate balancing act that involves the force of gravity, the liquid's surface tension and the pressure of air rushing past the drop.

More recent laboratory studies have revealed that the shape of a falling drop also depends on its size. Drizzle drops, those less than 0.5 millimeter across, are essentially spherical. In contrast, a drop more than 5 millimeters in diameter is distinctly flattened and may even begin to show a dimpled lower surface. This squat object resembles nothing so much as a hamburger bun.

Moreover, there is evidence that raindrops can take on other shapes and that they actually oscillate from one shape to another while they fall. . . . Kenneth V. Beard, a meteorologist, . . . has been studying the shape of raindrops for more than 10 years. Beard's colleague, atmospheric scientist David B. Johnson, joined the research project a few years ago to investigate the factors that cause raindrops to shake. . . .

The idea that raindrops oscillate was reinforced by measurements of raindrops frozen in photographs taken many years ago at several locations in Illinois. Researchers found a wide variation in the ratios of the raindrops' dimensions, hinting that the drops were caught at different stages during their oscillations.

Beard and Johnson suspect that these oscillations are the result of collisions between drops. Larger drops, as they fall, reach a higher terminal velocity or constant speed (when the air's drag balances the gravitational force on the drop) than smaller droplets. These large, speeding raindrops readily overtake smaller, slowly falling drizzle droplets.

A collision produces large oscillations in the newly coalesced drop, says Beard, or in the fragments created if the collision causes a breakup. "So it's important that you don't have just big raindrops all by themselves," he says. "You have to have a kind of drizzle drop, which happens in very intense showers where there is lots of mist.

"Calculations indicate that in heavy rainfall each raindrop experiences collisions with other raindrops every few seconds," Beard says. "If you've got small drops around, they'll get in the way of the large drops often enough to keep them oscillating." Last year, Johnson showed theoretically that a significant fraction of raindrops in heavy showers should be oscillating noticeably.

Wind tunnel studies, in which water drops are suspended in air streams, also show that these drops oscillate. Although here the oscillations are induced by turbulence rather than by collisions, the effects are similar to those observed in nature, says Beard. The frequency of the oscillations depends strongly on the size of the drops. Small water drops shake at a few hundred cycles per second; large ones oscillate at 20 cycles per second.

One puzzle, however, involves how a droplet "decides" whether it should oscillate in a vertical, horizontal or transverse mode. Drop collisions should excite vertical oscillations, says Beard. But why small drops prefer to oscillate vertically and large drops horizontally is a mystery. . . .

Beard is now planning an experiment that involves firing water drops of various sizes down a seven-story shaft to see what the natural modes of oscillation are and how they die out. It's not the way that a drop is excited initially so much as the air pressure and acceleration experienced by a drop that keep it oscillating in a certain way, Beard suggests. . . .

Another aspect that needs checking is how raindrop oscillations get started in the first place. Next summer, Johnson is coordinating a study in Hawaii that involves aircraft measurements to determine the size and number of raindrops in a typical shower. Johnson's theoretical calculations indicate that raindrops slightly smaller than a millimeter across contribute most to a drop's oscillations.

"There's a rather delicate size range there because if the small raindrops are too small, they don't impart enough energy when they hit a big raindrop," says Johnson. "This led us to look more closely at the size range of raindrops in nature."

GO ON TO THE NEXT PAGE.

3 3

"Another thing we want to look at in our experiment in Hawaii is to trace how drizzle drops come out of a cloud base," says Beard. "Do they come from the bursting apart of drops as they collide and rupture, or do they actually fall down on their own? They are the key to the source of the oscillations."

1. The first visual observation that raindrops oscillate came from:
   A. wind tunnel studies.
   B. photographs of falling raindrops.
   C. films of drops falling down a shaft.
   D. aircraft measurements.

2. As it is used in the passage, the word *turbulence* (line 54) means:
   F. heavy rainfall.
   G. rapid fall.
   H. spiraling motion.
   J. fluctuations in the movement of air.

3. Why is a five-millimeter raindrop falling in a light shower less likely to be constantly oscillating than one falling during a heavy downpour?
   A. It breaks apart more quickly.
   B. It experiences fewer collisions.
   C. It is too small to oscillate.
   D. It is too large to oscillate.

4. The main idea of the last paragraph of the passage is that:
   F. drizzle drops come out of a cloud base.
   G. drizzle drops must collide before they rupture.
   H. drizzle drops cause all raindrop oscillation.
   J. finding out how drizzle drops are created may help explain raindrop oscillation.

5. As it is used in the passage, the word *oscillate* means to:
   A. collide.
   B. accelerate.
   C. change shape.
   D. fall.

6. Beard's proposed shaft experiments would differ from the wind tunnel studies described in the passage in that:
   F. a variety of drop sizes could easily be studied.
   G. the drops would be moving downward, not suspended.
   H. the drops would be larger.
   J. drop oscillations could be measured and photographed.

7. If a raindrop is too tiny, it does not cause a large raindrop to oscillate after colliding with it because the tiny raindrop will:
   A. not coalesce with the larger drop.
   B. cause the breakup of the larger drop.
   C. not impart enough energy to the larger drop.
   D. oscillate too rapidly to affect the larger drop.

8. Compared to large raindrops, small raindrops fall:
   F. with less chance of collision.
   G. more slowly.
   H. more rapidly.
   J. in a more vertical path.

9. Which of the following best describes the oscillation of seven-millimeter water droplets in a wind tunnel?
   A. Vertical oscillations of 20 cycles per second
   B. Horizontal oscillations of 20 cycles per second
   C. Transverse oscillations of 100 cycles per second
   D. Horizontal oscillations of 200 cycles per second

10. Based on the information presented in the passage, which of the following is a hypothesis rather than a fact?
   F. Drizzle drops are formed primarily from the rupture of larger drops.
   G. A raindrop of eight millimeters in diameter would take on the shape of a hamburger bun as it falls.
   H. Drizzle drops are found in heavy downpours.
   J. Water droplets oscillate in vertical, horizontal, and transverse modes.

GO ON TO THE NEXT PAGE.

Passage II

Besides the neutral expression that she wore when she was alone, Mrs. Freeman had two others, forward and reverse, that she used for all her human dealings. Her forward expression was steady and driving like the advance of a heavy truck. Her eyes never swerved to left or right but turned as the story turned as if they followed a yellow line down the center of it. She seldom used the other expression because it was not often necessary for her to retract a statement, but when she did, her face came to a complete stop, there was an almost imperceptible movement of her black eyes, during which they seemed to be receding, and then the observer would see that Mrs. Freeman . . . was no longer there in spirit. As for getting anything across to her when this was the case, Mrs. Hopewell had given it up. She might talk her head off. Mrs. Freeman could never be brought to admit herself wrong on any point. She would stand there and if she could be brought to say anything, it was something like, "Well, I wouldn't of said it was and I wouldn't of said it wasn't," or letting her gaze range over the top kitchen shelf where there was an assortment of dusty bottles, she might remark, "I see you ain't ate many of them figs you put up last summer."

They carried on their most important business in the kitchen at breakfast. Every morning Mrs. Hopewell got up at seven o'clock and lit her gas heater and Joy's. Joy was her daughter, a large blonde girl who had an artificial leg. . . . Joy would get up while her mother was eating and lumber into the bathroom and slam the door, and before long, Mrs. Freeman would arrive at the back door. Joy would hear her mother call, "Come on in," and then they would talk for a while in low voices that were indistinguishable in the bathroom. By the time Joy came in, they had usually finished the weather report and were on one or the other of Mrs. Freeman's daughters, Glynese or Carramae. . . . Carramae, a blonde, was only fifteen but already married and pregnant. She could not keep anything on her stomach. Every morning Mrs. Freeman told Mrs. Hopewell how many times she had vomited since the last report.

Mrs. Hopewell liked to tell people that Glynese and Carramae were two of the finest girls she knew and that Mrs. Freeman was a *lady* and that she was never ashamed to take her anywhere or introduce her to anybody they might meet. Then she would tell how she had happened to hire the Freemans in the first place and how they were a godsend to her and how she had had them four years. The reason for her keeping them so long was that they were not trash. They were good country people. She had telephoned the man whose name they had given as a reference and he had told her that Mr. Freeman was a good farmer but that his wife was the nosiest woman ever to walk the earth. "She's got to be into everything," the man said. "If she don't get there before the dust settles, you can bet she's dead, that's all. She'll want to know all your business. I can stand him real good," he had said, "but me nor my wife neither could have stood that woman one more minute on this place." That had put Mrs. Hopewell off for a few days.

She had hired them in the end because there were no other applicants but she had made up her mind beforehand exactly how she would handle the woman. Since she was the type who had to be into everything, then, Mrs. Hopewell had decided, she would not only let her be into everything, she would *see to it* that she was into everything—she would give her the responsibility of everything, she would put her in charge. Mrs. Hopewell had no bad qualities of her own but she was able to use other people's in such a constructive way that she never felt the lack. She had hired the Freemans and she had kept them four years.

Nothing is perfect. This was one of Mrs. Hopewell's favorite sayings. Another was: that is life! And still another, the most important, was: well, other people have their opinions too. She would make these statements, usually at the table, in a tone of gentle insistence as if no one held them but her, and the large hulking Joy, whose constant outrage had obliterated every expression from her face, would stare just a little to the side of her, her eyes icy blue, with the look of someone who has achieved blindness by an act of will and means to keep it.

When Mrs. Hopewell said to Mrs. Freeman that life was like that, Mrs. Freeman would say, "I always said so myself." Nothing had been arrived at by anyone that had not first been arrived at by her.

11. When does Mrs. Freeman regularly arrive at the Hopewell residence?

A. Before Joy wakes up
B. At seven o'clock
C. While Mrs. Hopewell is lighting the heaters
D. While Joy is in the bathroom

12. Mrs. Hopewell hired the Freemans primarily because:

F. there were no other applicants.
G. Mr. Freeman would not ask for high wages.
H. Mrs. Hopewell had known the Freemans for years.
J. Mrs. Freeman is the nosiest woman on earth.

13. The Freemans' reference emphasized that:

A. although Mr. Freeman was tolerable, Mrs. Freeman was an unbearable busybody.
B. while Mr. Freeman was friendly, his wife was very unsociable.
C. while Mr. Freeman farmed, Mrs. Freeman allowed the dust to settle.
D. if his wife would leave him alone, Mr. Freeman could become a good farmer.

14. Based on the passage's description of Joy, her name can best be described as:

F. influential.
G. apt.
H. ironic.
J. suitable.

GO ON TO THE NEXT PAGE.

3 3

15. Joy most likely stares "to the side of" (line 83) Mrs. Hopewell because:

A. Joy is blind in one eye.
B. Mrs. Hopewell is not speaking to Joy.
C. Mrs. Freeman is present.
D. Joy wants to ignore her mother.

16. The main point of the first paragraph is that one of Mrs. Freeman's primary character traits is:

F. losing her temper without any provocation.
G. driving a truck steadily in forward or reverse.
H. pretending to be sociable.
J. refusing to admit herself wrong.

17. Based on the information in the passage, which of the following statements about the characters is a *fact* instead of an opinion?

A. Joy Hopewell's physical disability justifies her spiteful attitude.
B. The dusty bottles on Mrs. Hopewell's shelves indicate she is a lazy housekeeper.
C. Mrs. Hopewell's sayings are trite and unimaginative.
D. Mrs. Freeman makes daily remarks about her daughter's vomiting.

18. Which of the following statements accurately describe(s) Mrs. Hopewell's opinion of Mrs. Freeman?

I. Mrs. Freeman's bad qualities can be put to constructive use.
II. Mrs. Freeman's best quality is her willingness to compromise.
III. Since she is an employee, Mrs. Freeman is not entitled to have opinions of her own.

F. I only
G. II only
H. III only
J. I and III only

19. The passage as a whole suggests that Mrs. Freeman, Mrs. Hopewell, and Joy Hopewell all:

A. are perfectly satisfied with their lives.
B. remain together because of enormous mutual admiration.
C. frequently grate on one another's nerves.
D. are unopinionated people.

20. In their attitudes toward life, Mrs. Freeman, Mrs. Hopewell, and Joy Hopewell can best be described, respectively, as:

F. dogmatic, practical, and outraged.
G. flexible, pitiless, and stoic.
H. relentless, unconcerned, and charitable.
J. fatalistic, ruthless, and carefree.

GO ON TO THE NEXT PAGE.

3 3

Passage III

American plays of the early nineteenth century popularized two important native types: the Indian and the Yankee. The Indian was presented sympathetically, following the romantic tradition of the "noble savage," and provided strong roles for serious performers. The Indian had been introduced in American drama as early as 1766 in Robert Rogers's *Ponteach,* but Barker's *The Indian Princess* sketched the outline that was to be followed by others. The vogue for Indian dramas was given its major impetus by George Washington Parke Custis's (1781–1857) *The Indian Prophecy* (1827) and *Pocahontas* (1830). Between 1825 and 1860, more than fifty Indian plays were performed in the United States. . . . The type was dealt a serious blow by John Brougham's burlesque, *Po-ca-hon-tas* (1855), but not until after 1870 was the "noble savage" tradition abandoned.

The Yankee character was the province of the comic actor or "specialty" performer. Although the Yankee had appeared in many plays after his introduction in *The Contrast* (1787), the idea of making him the central character seems to have stemmed from Charles Mathews's *A Trip to America* (1824), a work satirizing various American types. . . . After 1825, the Yankee became a favorite character and a number of "specialists" appeared. The Yankee was the symbol of the American common man, simple and naive on the surface, but upholding democratic principles and despising pretense and sham. The first important actor of Yankee roles was James H. Hackett (1800–1871), who conceived the character Solomon Swap in *Jonathan in England* (1828), the first important Yankee play. . . . Hackett was succeeded by George Handel Hill (1809–1849), by 1832 considered the best of the Yankee specialists. In addition to monologues and skits, Hill performed full-length plays, such as J. S. Jones's *The Green Mountain Boy* (1833) and *The People's Lawyer* (1839). With Hill, the Yankee became more sympathetic and sentimental. Dan Marble (1810–1849) achieved fame after 1836 in the role of Sam Patch, a more generalized American type, while Joshua Silsbee (1813–1855) was the acknowledged master of Yankee roles after the deaths of Hill and Marble. Silsbee turned the type once more toward broad and eccentric humor. Of the later specialists, John E. Owens (1823–1886) was the most famous. Ultimately, the vogue for the Yankee, which reached its height between 1830 and 1850, is perhaps most important for its role in establishing a native American comedy.

The black, another important native type, also fell to specialists. The black may be found in American drama from the beginning as a faithful servant or comic caricature, but the popularity of the type dates from about 1828 when Thomas D. Rice (1808–1860) introduced his "Jim Crow" song and dance. Soon a major star, Rice spawned a host of imitators, most notably Barney Williams, Jack Diamond, Barney Burns, and Bob Farrell. . . .

Despite such caricatures, the black was able to make his own mark during the early nineteenth century. In 1821 the first known company of black actors in the United States was assembled in New York by James Brown, who presented occasional theatrical performances at the African Grove, an outdoor tea garden, and later at an indoor theatre. The repertory included *Richard III, Othello,* and other plays, and starred James Hewlett, a native of the West Indies. It also included the first known American play written by a black author, Brown's own *King Shotaway,* which dealt with an insurrection on the island of St. Vincent. Unfortunately, the company was plagued by white rowdies and perhaps because of these difficulties it fades from surviving records after 1823.

The African Company left one important legacy, however, for it seems to have provided Ira Aldridge (1807–1867) with his first acting experience. Unable to pursue a theatrical career in America, Aldridge went to London, where he made his debut in 1825; within a few years he was known throughout England as "the celebrated African Roscius." In 1852 he undertook his first European tour and aroused such enthusiastic response that he spent much of his time thereafter on the continent. Noted for his performances of Othello, Shylock, Macbeth, and Lear, he was decorated by the rulers of Prussia, Russia, and Saxe-Meiningen. He died while performing in Poland. By all indications, Aldridge was one of the great actors of his age, but racial barriers prevented him from ever exercising his mature power in the land of his birth.

21. According to the passage, the reason Ira Aldridge did not achieve professional success as an actor in America was that:

A. black characters appeared infrequently in American plays.
B. other performers, like Thomas D. Rice, were better actors.
C. the Shakespearean roles he played were not popular in America.
D. prejudices against black performers were common.

22. The popularity of Yankee roles in America influenced the development of:

F. a more realistic manner of acting in tragedies.
G. melodramas that imitated European successes.
H. roles suited for minority performers.
J. a particularly American style of comedy.

23. The passage implies that "Jim Crow" (line 55) was a:

A. partner of Thomas D. Rice.
B. faithful black servant character.
C. comic caricature of a black.
D. black actor.

GO ON TO THE NEXT PAGE.

3 3

24. According to the passage, Brown's African Company may have closed down because of:

F. harassment from prejudiced whites.
G. the departure of Ira Aldridge.
H. the scarcity of plays suitable for black performers.
J. the scarcity of suitable theater buildings.

25. The description of the Yankee character type as "naive" (line 27) indicates that he was NOT:

A. eccentric.
B. sophisticated.
C. likable.
D. serious.

26. Which of the following is implied by the last three paragraphs of the passage (lines 50–89)?

F. Black characters would have been more popular if they had been less stereotyped.
G. Black performers would have been more popular if they had performed in roles which were less stereotyped.
H. European audiences were more receptive to black performers than were American audiences.
J. European audiences were not receptive to plays involving American native types.

27. Which of the following statements about black character types is supported by the information in the third paragraph (lines 50–58)?

A. Realistic black characters first appeared in an American drama in 1828.
B. In early American drama, stereotypical black characters were popular.
C. By his depictions of black characters, Thomas D. Rice advocated racial equality in America.
D. American drama has never offered accurate depictions of black characters.

28. Compared to that of George Handel Hill, James H. Hackett's Yankee was:

F. more sympathetic.
G. less sentimental.
H. more important.
J. less generalized.

29. *Ponteach, The Indian Princess, The Indian Prophecy,* and *Pocahontas* were all plays which:

A. were written by Indian playwrights.
B. were performed by Indian actors.
C. promoted Indian causes.
D. included Indians as characters.

30. Brougham's play, *Po-ca-hon-tas,* affected the American vogue for Indian dramas in which of the following ways?

F. It provided a major impetus for Indian plays by introducing a new kind of Indian character.
G. It set the standard for Indian drama by being the best example of the type.
H. It encouraged a decline in interest in Indian drama by satirizing the conventional features of Indian plays.
J. It decreased interest in Indian drama by following the romantic tradition of the "noble savage."

GO ON TO THE NEXT PAGE.

Passage IV

Nurtured by propaganda and publicly proclaimed by all governments was the notion that the enemy was evil and that his defeat would create the foundation for a better world. This ideological and moralistic view made impossible a negotiated peace aimed at reestablishing a balance of power and restoring international collaboration. Each side was convinced that the war could end only with the complete defeat of the enemy, so that an entirely new world could be created. Each therefore attempted to present its aims in generalized idealistic terms showing that victory would serve the interest of all mankind. Formulation of such war aims was relatively easy for Great Britain, France, and their allies in the last two years of the conflict. The war was declared to be a struggle for a new world order based on the principles of democracy and national self-determination, its purpose succinctly summarized in the famous slogan "to make the world safe for democracy." As long as Russia with its authoritarian government was a member of the coalition against Germany, the assertion about fighting for democracy had a hollow sound. But after the overthrow of the tsar in March, 1917, the notion of a struggle between democracy and authoritarianism gained meaning, particularly since the overthrow coincided with the entrance into the war against Germany of the greatest democracy in the world, the United States. The fact that men and women of all classes contributed to the military effort gave force to the demand that they should have the right to decide the political fate of their country. Where before the First World War the demand for suffrage for women had been regarded as utopian and even ridiculous, and the request for women's suffrage had inspired a movement of some strength only in Great Britain, now this demand became more urgent and its justification was much more generally recognized. In Great Britain, Germany, and the United States, female suffrage was achieved soon after the war. In Italy and France its adversaries were able to delay giving women the vote until after the Second World War. But even there the final victory of female suffrage was never seriously in doubt.

It was difficult for Germany and its allies to place the war on a broad ideological level. The German Social Democratic party had been the largest and best organized of all socialist parties. Socialist approval of the money bills required for the financing of the war was the most striking and also the most surprising example of the abandonment of revolutionary internationalism by Social Democrats in favor of defense of the homeland. The German government gained the support of socialist and progressive forces without taking them into the government. Thus, during most of the war Germany continued to be ruled by the members of the conservative bureaucracy. Their innate resistance to liberal and democratic reforms was reinforced by the military, whose power now increased immensely. William II, who even in peacetime had failed to exercise steady leadership, did not dare to challenge the men of the hour. Thus the German military leaders . . . began to exert—if not in form, at least in fact—a military dictatorship. As allies of the Conservatives they resisted political reforms, and the tensions which had existed in peacetime reemerged during the last two years of the war, expressing themselves in a bitter struggle about war aims. In the early weeks of the war, when the German advance in France appeared irreversible, industrialists and their Conservative allies insisted that the results of the war must be acquisition of a secure foundation for German world hegemony. Germany ought to keep Belgium and the valuable French steel and coal mines of the Longwy-Briey Basins. Later in the war, when the Germans occupied broad territorial stretches in the east, demands arose to annex these agricultural areas so that the German food supply would be secured for all time. Until almost the final months of the war, leaders of heavy industry and Conservatives supported by the military under Ludendorff asserted the need to fight for total victory so that Germany could attain these expansionist goals. When a quick victory proved elusive, however, those who opposed such war aims—whether they considered them unrealistic or immoral—began to raise their voices. Annexationists were confronted by those who believed that peace ought to be concluded on the basis of the status quo and that every effort should be made to reach a peace of understanding.

From Felix Gilbert, *The End of the European Era: 1890 to the Present.*

31. According to the passage, why was the demand for women's suffrage generally recognized as justifiable during and after World War I?

A. Women had demonstrated their ability to contribute to the war effort.
B. The idealistic aim of making the world "safe for democracy" was written into the peace treaty.
C. Conservatives came to recognize the wisdom of liberal and democratic reforms.
D. The chief opponents of women's suffrage, the tsar and William II, were deposed.

32. The phrase "this ideological and moralistic view" (first paragraph) refers to the belief(s) that:

I. the enemy was evil.
II. propaganda was a tool used by the enemy.
III. a better world would result from the enemy's defeat.

F. II only
G. I and II only
H. I and III only
J. II and III only

33. The author asserts that until 1917 the slogan "to make the world safe for democracy" had a hollow sound because:

A. Russia had an authoritarian government until 1917.
B. the war became a struggle for national self-determination after 1917.
C. several nations were in coalition against Germany until 1917.
D. the new world order was already based on the principles of democracy before 1917.

GO ON TO THE NEXT PAGE.

34. World War I is labeled a total war because it required the efforts of the entire nation, not just the military, to fight it. Which of the following statements from the passage supports that view?

F. "Each side was convinced that the war could end only with the complete defeat of the enemy."
G. "Leaders of heavy industry and Conservatives supported by the military under Ludendorff asserted the need to fight for total victory."
H. "Men and women of all classes contributed to the military effort."
J. "The war was declared to be a struggle for a new world order."

35. The author implies that the reason William II did not exercise dictatorial control during World War I was that:

A. fundamentally, he was a weak leader.
B. the Social Democrats would not allow it.
C. the bureaucracy was too conservative to accept such control.
D. a majority of the people never wholeheartedly supported the war.

36. In which of the following ways does the passage support the theory that war causes social change?

F. It asserts that World War I was a major factor in women gaining the right to vote.
G. It demonstrates that World War I reestablished a balance of power and restored international collaboration.
H. It attributes the overthrow of the Russian tsar to World War I.
J. It links the rise of the German Social Democratic party to anti-annexationist sentiment in Germany.

37. According to the passage, the notion that the enemy was evil was proclaimed by:

I. Great Britain.
II. Germany.
III. the U.S.

A. I only
B. I and II only
C. I and III only
D. I, II, and III

38. The author suggests that the fundamental patriotism of the German Social Democrats compelled them to:

F. oppose the financing of the war.
G. keep socialist and progressive forces out of the government.
H. abandon revolution and accept internationalism.
J. act contrary to the principles of their ideology.

39. According to the passage, anti-annexationist sentiment was able to gain strength in Germany during the last two years of war because:

A. such sentiment was supported by the military under Ludendorff.
B. Germany had not yet been able to win the war.
C. the German Social Democrats took over the government.
D. leaders of heavy industry and Conservatives no longer supported the military.

40. Conservatives and the military effectively ruled Germany during World War I. The passage argues that because of this fact, the chief German war aim was to:

F. force the Social Democrats to abandon revolutionary internationalism.
G. overthrow the authoritarian tsarist regime in Russia.
H. annex valuable territory in Belgium, France, and the east.
J. transform Germany into a military dictatorship.

END OF TEST 3

STOP! DO NOT TURN THE PAGE UNTIL TOLD TO DO SO.

4 ○ ○ ○ ○ ○ ○ ○ ○ ○ 4

SCIENCE REASONING TEST

35 Minutes—40 Questions

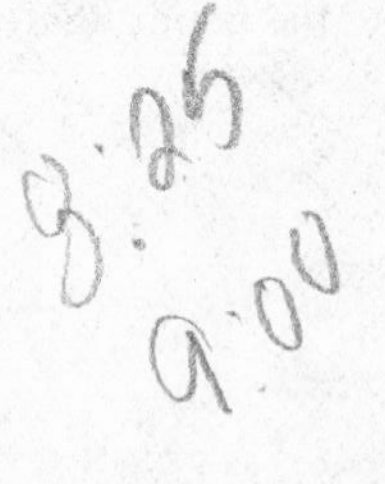

DIRECTIONS: There are seven passages in this test. Each passage is followed by several questions. After reading a passage, choose the best answer to each question and blacken the corresponding oval on your answer sheet. You may refer to the passages as often as necessary.

Passage I

A biologist investigated some of the environmental factors that could influence habitat selection in isopods, a kind of terrestrial arthropod. The following experiments were conducted at a constant temperature, and no isopod was tested more than once.

Experiment 1

Ten isopods were placed in each of 2 petri dishes, the bottoms of which were covered with paper towels. One-half of each towel was moistened with water, creating half-dry, half-damp chambers. The dishes were covered with petri dish lids. Dish 1 was placed in a darkened area and Dish 2 was placed in a lighted area. After 1 hour the location of the isopods was recorded (Table 1).

Table 1

	Dry side	Damp side
Dish 1 (in dark)	2	8
Dish 2 (in light)	0	10

Experiment 2

Ten isopods were placed in each of 2 petri dishes. One-half of the lid of each dish was covered by black opaque paper. Each dish was placed under a 25-watt fluorescent light, creating half-lighted, half-darkened chambers. After 1 hour the location of the isopods in each dish was recorded (Table 2).

Table 2

	Lighted side	Darkened side
Dish 1	0	10
Dish 2	3	7

Experiment 3

Ten isopods were placed in each of 2 petri dishes. Four different habitats were created in each dish—dry/lighted, dry/dark, damp/lighted, and damp/dark. After 1 hour the locations of the isopods were recorded (Table 3).

Table 3

	Dry/Lighted	Dry/Dark	Damp/Lighted	Damp/Dark
Dish 1	0	3	2	5
Dish 2	0	1	4	5

1. In nature, one reason why isopods might prefer darkened habitats is that such habitats:
   A. are likely to be moist.
   B. are likely to be warm.
   C. contain more green plants on which isopods could feed.
   D. have better air circulation, allowing for more efficient respiration.

2. On the basis of the experimental results, the best of the following explanations for the origin of this species of terrestrial isopods is that their ancestors:
   F. swam near the surface of freshwater lakes.
   G. lived on the surface of rocks.
   H. lived in the sand and mud of the bottom or shore of the ocean.
   J. lived on the sunlit surface of leaves.

3. Which of the following conclusions is supported by the results of Experiment 1 ?
   A. Isopods prefer damp habitats to dry habitats, regardless of lighting conditions.
   B. Isopods prefer dark habitats to lighted habitats, regardless of moisture conditions.
   C. Isopods show an equal preference for dry and damp habitats.
   D. Isopods show an equal preference for dark and lighted habitats.

GO ON TO THE NEXT PAGE.

4 ○ ○ ○ ○ ○ ○ ○ ○ ○ 4

4. Animals often follow behavior patterns they observe in other animals (social behavior). Which of the following changes in experimental design could be made to minimize this effect on habitat selection?

F. Use only animals of one sex in each test.
G. Use only sexually immature animals in each test.
H. Use only animals that have been raised in captivity.
J. Place each animal in a separate petri dish.

5. Some isopods are known to inhabit the desert. On the basis of the experimental results, which of the following locations will the isopods probably inhabit?

A. The surface of cactus stems
B. The surface of the desert sand
C. The top of desert rocks
D. Under desert rocks

6. In the 3 experiments, habitat preference was determined by recording the location of animals after 1 hour. Animals were often moving during the course of the experiment. The rate of selection of the habitat would be best measured by recording the location of the animals:

F. after 15 minutes.
G. after 30 minutes.
H. after 1 hour.
J. at 5-minute intervals for 1 hour.

GO ON TO THE NEXT PAGE.

4 ○ ○ ○ ○ ○ ○ ○ ○ ○ 4

Passage II

Oil, natural gas, and other hydrocarbons are generated by *thermal maturation* (heating and compressing) of *kerogen* (organic matter) contained in deeply buried "source rocks." The relative abundance of the various hydrocarbons that are generated depends on both the composition of the original kerogen and the degree of thermal maturation. Wood and other structured plant remains tend to yield coal and natural gas. Algae and other soft plant remains break down to form oils and waxes. During the process of hydrocarbon generation, kerogen undergoes a predictable series of color changes. By analyzing kerogen samples from a source rock, geologists can accurately determine whether it could have generated hydrocarbons.

Experiment 1

In a laboratory, geologists subjected kerogen to different temperatures and pressures for various lengths of time. They observed that as the kerogen underwent thermal maturation, it changed from light yellow to yellow, to orange, to brown, and finally to black. Based on those thermally induced color changes, a rating index of I (yellow) to V (black) was devised for thermal maturation of kerogen.

Experiment 2

Geologists in western Canada documented the relationship between kerogen alteration and the occurrence of significant hydrocarbon deposits. Areas where the kerogen maturation index was from I to III produced oil and gas. Areas rated IV produced only gas. Areas rated V seldom contained anything more than trace remains of hydrocarbons mixed with water and carbon dioxide. The geologists then related thermal maturation to depth of burial, and produced the following diagram for their area of study.

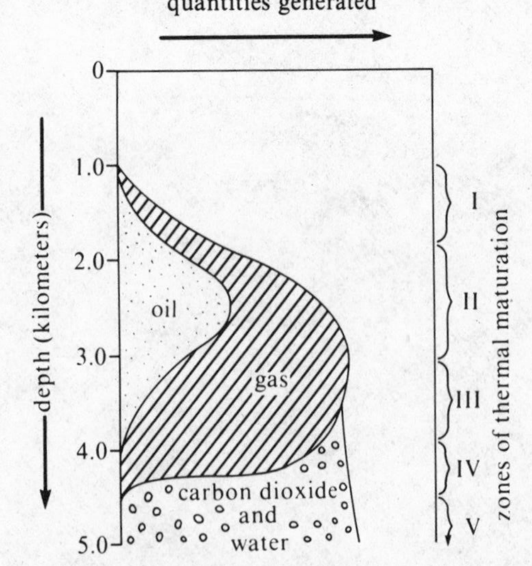

Diagram adapted from B. Tissot, et al., "Influences of Nature and Diagenesis of Organic Matter in Formation of Petroleum." ©1974 by The American Association of Petroleum Geologists.

7. At which of the following depths would a well drilled in the study area of Experiment 2 produce *only* carbon dioxide and water?

A. 0.5 kilometer
B. 2.0 kilometers
C. 3.0 kilometers
D. 4.7 kilometers

8. If a well drilled in the study area of Experiment 2 yielded kerogen samples with a thermal maturation index of III, at approximately what depth would the samples have been collected?

F. 1–2 kilometers
G. 2–3 kilometers
H. 3–4 kilometers
J. 4–5 kilometers

9. Which of the following diagrams best represents the relationship between kerogen color index and the degree of thermal maturation?

A.

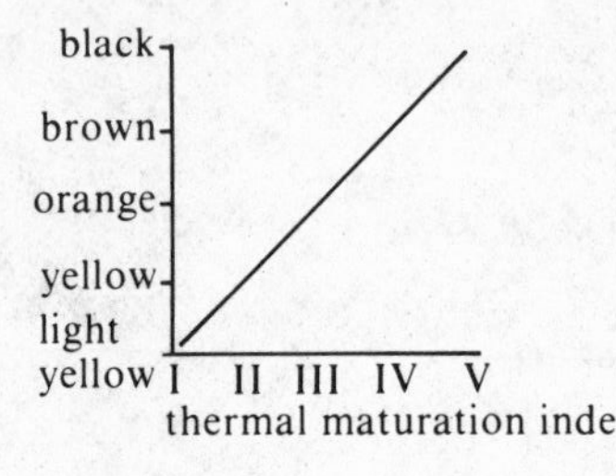

B.

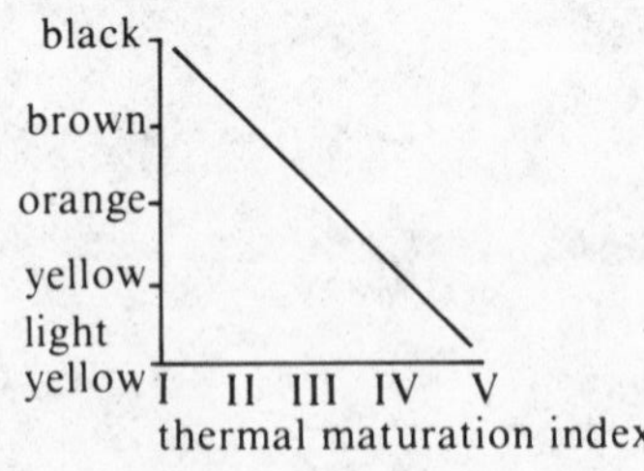

C.

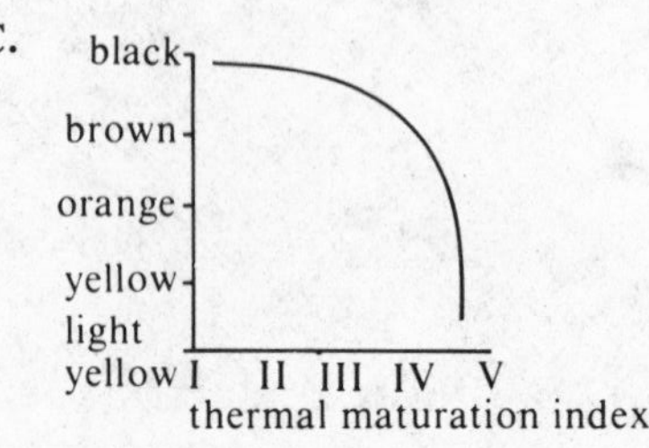

D.

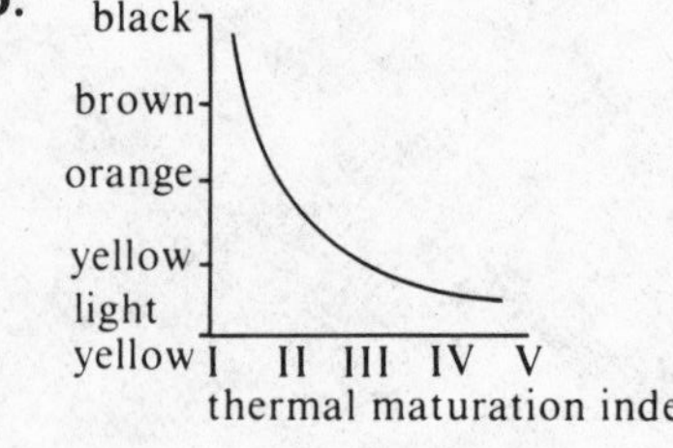

GO ON TO THE NEXT PAGE.

10. If a kerogen sample collected from the area studied in Experiment 2 was orange in color, which of the following substances would it probably produce?

I. Oil
II. Gas
III. Carbon dioxide
IV. Water

F. II only
G. III only
H. mainly I and II
J. mainly III and IV

11. Which of the following findings would NOT be consistent with the information provided about kerogen types and the generation of hydrocarbons?

A. Wood-derived kerogen produced gas.
B. Wood-derived kerogen produced oil.
C. Wood-derived kerogen produced coal.
D. Algal-derived kerogen produced waxes.

12. Which of the following aspects of the experiments allowed geologists to gather more information about the process of hydrocarbon generation in Experiment 1 than in Experiment 2 ?

F. In Experiment 1, geologists controlled more of the variables involved in kerogen maturation.
G. In Experiment 2, geologists measured the depths at which different hydrocarbons were found.
H. Experiment 2 failed to relate degree of thermal maturation to the quantity of hydrocarbons produced.
J. Experiment 2 failed to relate depth of burial to thermal maturation of kerogen.

GO ON TO THE NEXT PAGE.

4 ○ ○ ○ ○ ○ ○ ○ ○ ○ 4

Passage III

Four different species of animals were placed in environments at various temperatures. After 5 minutes at each temperature tested, the average number of breaths per minute (*respiratory rate*) was determined for each of the 4 animals while they remained at rest. Respiratory rate is often used as an indicator of cellular respiration or *metabolic rate* (a measure of oxygen consumption by the cells of the organism). The data from the experiment are shown in the following graph.

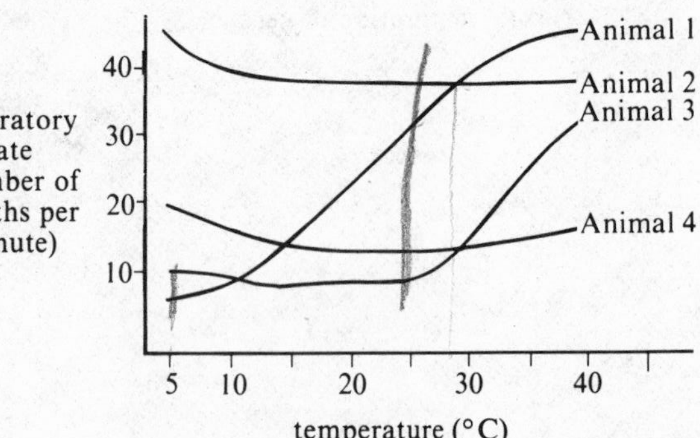

13. What is the relationship between respiratory rate and temperature for Animal 1 ?
    - **A.** Increases in temperature decrease the respiratory rate.
    - **B.** Increases in temperature increase the respiratory rate.
    - **C.** Increases in temperature have no effect on the respiratory rate.
    - **D.** Decreases in temperature increase the respiratory rate.

14. At which temperature did Animals 1 and 2 have the same respiratory rate?
    - **F.** 14° C
    - **G.** 29° C
    - **H.** 39° C
    - **J.** 40° C

15. Further measurements showed that Animal 4 used significantly more oxygen per minute than Animal 2. This would be consistent with the data from the graph if:
    - **A.** Animal 4 was significantly larger than Animal 2.
    - **B.** Animal 2 was significantly larger than Animal 4.
    - **C.** Animals 2 and 4 were the same weight.
    - **D.** Animal 4 was in the light and Animal 2 in the dark.

16. The utilization of food by the animals requires oxygen from respiration. According to the data in the graph, which of the animals would use less food at 5° C than they would at 25° C?
    - **F.** 1 only
    - **G.** 2 only
    - **H.** 4 only
    - **J.** 1 and 2 only

17. Cold-blooded (ectothermic) animals are unable to regulate their body temperature through the use of physiological mechanisms. Body processes are, therefore, directly linked to the ambient temperature. Based on the data in the graph, which of the animals might be hypothesized to be cold-blooded?
    - **A.** 1 only
    - **B.** 2 only
    - **C.** 3 only
    - **D.** 4 only

Passage IV

Neutrinos are particles produced inside stars by the process that fuses hydrogen into helium. Neutrinos move at the speed of light and pass easily through matter, rarely interacting with it. Enormous numbers of neutrinos, many of them produced in the Sun, pass through Earth each second. One of the few elements that reacts strongly with neutrinos is chlorine (Cl). Dr. Raymond Davis, Jr., built a neutrino detector at a depth of 4,850 feet in a gold mine. The detector is a closed, gas-tight tank containing 100,000 gallons of C_2Cl_4. When neutrinos interact with individual chlorine atoms, those atoms are converted to atoms of radioactive argon (Ar). From time to time, these argon atoms are collected and counted. The number of argon atoms collected is used to determine the rate at which argon atoms are produced in the tank. The tank was placed far underground so that the overlying rock would shield it from cosmic rays, which are also capable of producing argon from chlorine. Theoretical calculations of the rate of neutrino production in the Sun lead to the prediction that 1 argon atom per day should be created in the tank.

Experiment 1

The tank was set up as described above and several experimental runs were conducted. The results of two of the runs are given below:

Trial	Argon atoms/day
1	0.60 ±0.26
2	0.82 ±0.52

Experiment 2

The tank was submerged completely in a pool of water in order to shield the tank from locally produced particles capable of producing argon from chlorine. Some production rates obtained from shielded runs are given in the table below:

Trial	Argon atoms/day
1	0.11 ±0.36
2	0.21 ±0.20
3	1.19 ±0.40
4	0.40 ±0.40
5	0.25 ±0.38
6	0.17 ±0.23

GO ON TO THE NEXT PAGE.

4 ○ ○ ○ ○ ○ ○ ○ ○ ○ 4

18. During the next 5 billion years, the Sun will gradually become more luminous as it fuses hydrogen more rapidly. As the Sun's energy output increases, which of the following is most likely to happen to the argon production rate in experiments similar to those described in the passage?

F. It should gradually decline to zero.
G. It should gradually increase.
H. It should remain the same for about 2 billion years and then abruptly increase significantly.
J. It should decline for about 2 billion years and then increase for about 3 billion years.

19. Using 200,000 gallons of C_2Cl_4 instead of 100,000 gallons would most likely do which of the following to the rate at which argon atoms are produced in the tank by solar neutrinos?

A. Reduce the rate by approximately one-half
B. Increase the rate by approximately a factor of 4
C. Approximately double the rate
D. Reduce the rate by approximately a factor of 4

20. Which of the following procedures should Davis follow to obtain the most accurate value for the argon production rate?

F. Adding a known amount of argon to his experiment each day
G. Adding a known amount of water to his experiment each day
H. Carrying out a very great number of experimental trials and finding their average
J. Adding a new argon atom for every argon atom detected

21. To study the rate at which cosmic rays produce argon from chlorine, Davis would learn most by doing which of the following?

A. Setting up another detector on the surface of Earth
B. Surrounding the water jacket with lead
C. Placing radioactive materials near the present experiment
D. Reducing the amount of C_2Cl_4 in the experiment by half

22. Which of the following assumptions did Davis probably make in choosing C_2Cl_4 ?

F. Being in a compound does not significantly affect how chlorine atoms interact with the neutrinos.
G. Carbon atoms interact with neutrinos as much as chlorine atoms do.
H. Carbon atoms interact with neutrinos more than chlorine atoms do.
J. Chlorine atoms do not interact with neutrinos.

23. Do the results of the experiments support the theoretical prediction of the rate of neutrino production in the Sun?

A. Yes, because the measured Ar production rates for Experiment 2 correspond to the rate predicted from theory.
B. Yes, because the measured Ar production rates for Experiment 1 correspond to the rate predicted from theory.
C. No, because the measured Ar production rates for all trials are greater than the rate predicted from theory.
D. No, because the measured Ar production rates for Experiment 2 are less than the rate predicted from theory.

GO ON TO THE NEXT PAGE.

4 ○ ○ ○ ○ ○ ○ ○ ○ ○ 4

Passage V

The pedigree below shows individuals with inherited Characteristics X, Y, and Z. Each of these individuals has 1 gene form (allele) from each parent for each characteristic.

Dominant alleles (D) produce dominant characteristics; recessive alleles (d) produce recessive characteristics. Dominant alleles are expressed whenever present (DD, Dd), but recessives are expressed only when the dominant allele is absent (dd). Each parent with unlike alleles (Dd) has a 50% probability of passing either allele to each child.

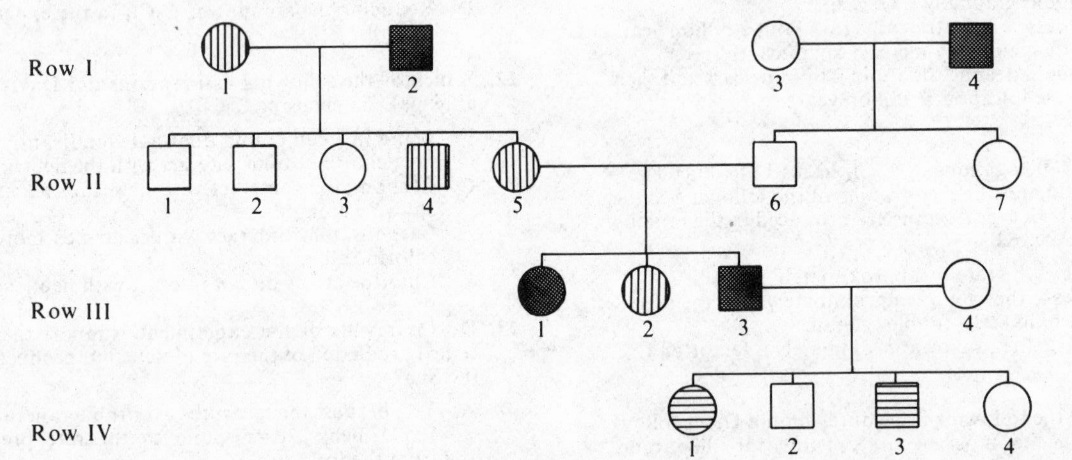

Key

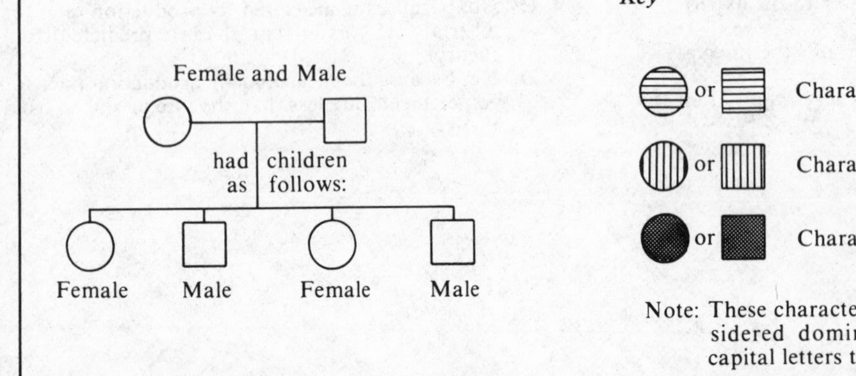

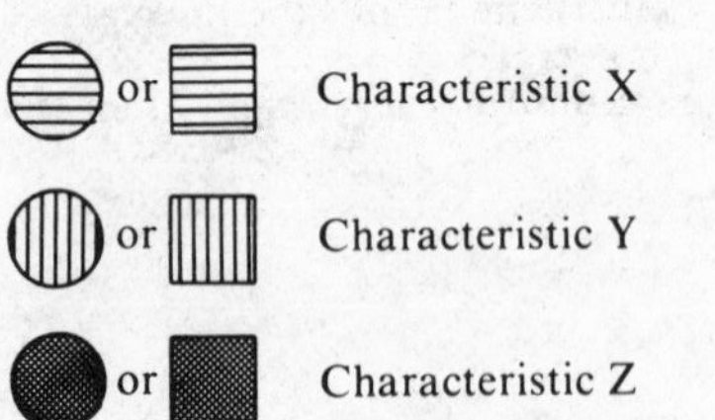

Note: These characteristics (X, Y, Z) should NOT be considered dominant simply because of the use of capital letters to name them.

24. In a family pedigree, all the individuals in one row represent:

F. brothers and sisters.
G. cousins.
H. married couples.
J. members of one generation.

25. Which of the following statements best explains the observation that Characteristic Y is seen in individuals in Rows I, II, and III ?

A. In order to have Characteristic Y, a person's children must have it.
B. Each individual with Characteristic Y has one parent who has it.
C. All individuals have a 75% probability of having Characteristic Y.
D. Characteristic Y is always due to a new dominant allele that develops commonly.

26. In which of the characteristics shown in this pedigree is dominance probable?

F. X only
G. Y only
H. Z only
J. X and Y only

27. Which of the following statements would best explain the observation that Characteristic X is seen only in individuals in Row IV ?

A. Characteristic X is a recessive characteristic.
B. Characteristic X is a dominant characteristic.
C. Expression of Characteristic X occurs only in children.
D. Expression of Characteristic X occurs only when neither of the person's parents has Characteristic X.

GO ON TO THE NEXT PAGE.

4 ○ ○ ○ ○ ○ ○ ○ ○ ○ 4

28. If Individual IV-1 marries a person who also has Characteristic X, what is the probability that any one of their children would have Characteristic X ?

F. 25%
G. 50%
H. 75%
J. 100%

GO ON TO THE NEXT PAGE.

4 ○ ○ ○ ○ ○ ○ ○ ○ ○ 4

Passage VI

Survival of a honeybee colony depends on hoarding food for use throughout the year. Survival of the colony also depends on finding new home sites. Biologists have suspected that certain worker bees, called scouts, search for nectar and for home sites. When scouts return to the hive, they report their discoveries to other workers, called foragers, by repeatedly performing a routine called the "waggle dance." The dance consists of the scout running up the honeycomb a few centimeters, wagging her abdomen from side to side, and emitting buzzing noises. She then returns to the starting point and repeats the wagging run multiple times. The foragers follow the scout, gaining information about the target. Different hypotheses exist about what type of information is provided by the dance.

Hypothesis 1

The dance provides information about the distance and the direction of the food or home site. Distance is indicated by the rate of the dance—the closer the target, the more cycles of the dance in a given time period. Direction is indicated by the angle of the waggle run on the vertical honeycomb, with the Sun serving as the reference point. For example, if the target is toward the Sun, the waggle run is straight up the honeycomb. If the target is 30° to the right of the Sun, the waggle dance is 30° to the right of straight up the honeycomb.

Hypothesis 2

The dance does not communicate the distance and direction. It is merely a ritual to alert the foragers about the availability of a new food source or home site. Contact with the scout allows foragers to detect distinctive odors of flowers or home sites located by the scout. Foragers then leave the hive and search for the objective by matching the target odor with the odor carried on the scout's body.

29. To accept Hypothesis 2, one must assume that:

A. bees have a poorly developed sense of sight.
B. all flower odors have at least 1 ingredient in common.
C. bees are not attracted to flowers more than $\frac{1}{2}$ mile from the hive.
D. odors of various flowers are distinctive to the senses of bees.

30. The waggle dance generally lasts only seconds to minutes. Occasionally, however, a scout will dance inside the hive for several hours continuously without seeing the Sun, and while doing so, alter the dance angle to conform with the Sun's changing position. This suggests that:

F. bees have an internal clock.
G. Hypothesis 1 should be discarded.
H. foragers can use the waggle dance only if the flowers have a distinctive odor.
J. scouts use other reference points in addition to the Sun.

31. In an attempt to confirm Hypothesis 2, investigators placed 2 scented feeding stations, A and B, as shown in the diagram below. Foragers visited these stations for several days. Then the scented food at A and B was replaced with unscented food, and another station with scented food, C, was established between A and B. Which of the following statements about the relationship between the experimental results and Hypothesis 2 is(are) correct?

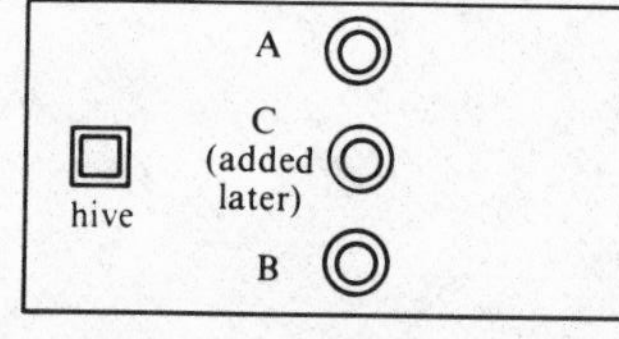

I. If most of the newly recruited foragers arrived at Station C, the experiment supports Hypothesis 2.
II. If most of the newly recruited foragers arrived at Stations A and B, the experiment supports Hypothesis 2.
III. If newly recruited foragers visited all 3 stations in equal numbers, the experiment fails to support Hypothesis 2.

A. I only
B. II only
C. III only
D. I and III only

32. During an experiment, food targets were placed at varying distances from a hive. Data were then collected to correlate scouts' rate of dance (cycles/15 secs) with distance to a target. Data were collected only on calm days, and all targets were placed in a straight line from the hive, on a flat stretch of land. A statistically significant variation was found in the dance rates among different scouts reporting targets that were an equal distance from the hive. Furthermore, there was no statistically significant variation in the dance rates of the same scout reporting targets at different distances from the hive. Which of the following explanations of these observations was(were) NOT investigated in this experiment?

I. Wind may confuse a scout about distance.
II. The dance rate does not predict distance from the food source.
III. Experienced scouts are more accurate than novice scouts in determining distance.

F. I only
G. II only
H. I and II only
J. I and III only

GO ON TO THE NEXT PAGE.

4 ○ ○ ○ ○ ○ ○ ○ ○ ○ 4

33. The 2 hypotheses are alike in that they both imply that bees:

I. have a symbolic language as the basis for communicating the location of a food source or new home site.
II. require precise information from the waggle dance itself to obtain information about food sites and home sites.
III. in a particular hive work together to form a functional hive.

A. I only
B. II only
C. III only
D. II and III only

34. Which of the following discoveries would most clearly favor Hypothesis 2 ?

F. Finding that foragers continue to collect food from the same target after the scouts have stopped advertising that particular location
G. Finding that bees locate a food source more easily if they must fly against the wind to reach it
H. Finding that bees locate a food source more easily if there is no wind
J. Finding that bees locate a food source more easily during periods of low relative humidity

35. Which of the following observations could be used to DISCOUNT Hypothesis 1 ?

I. When scouts are chemically intoxicated, they dance in a random pattern, yet the recruited foragers still find the target.
II. Different species of honeybees perform the dance at different rates to indicate distance.
III. When a dance is performed on a honeycomb placed on a horizontal rather than vertical plane, the same number of foragers locate the target.

A. I only
B. II only
C. III only
D. I and III only

GO ON TO THE NEXT PAGE.

4 ○ ○ ○ ○ ○ ○ ○ ○ 4

Passage VII

Electronegativity is a relative measure of the attraction that an atom has for electrons. The electronegativity values are useful in determining how electrons are shared when two atoms are bonded together, since the values can be different for each element. Figure 1 shows the electronegativity values of elements of the first 5 periods of the periodic table (to atomic number 53). The elements in each period (except the first, which contains only hydrogen) are connected by a line.

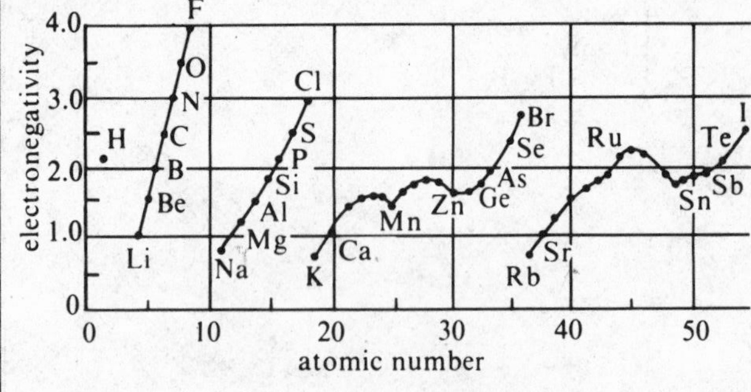

Figure 1

If two atoms are bonded together and the electronegativities are the same, then the electrons are shared equally, and the bond is referred to as *nonpolar covalent.* When atoms of different electronegativities bond, the electrons are not shared equally. This unequal sharing of electrons is referred to as bond polarity. These bonds may be categorized either as *polar covalent* or as *ionic.* In ionic bonds, the electrons are completely transferred to one of the atoms. Figure 2 shows the relation of the electronegativity difference between bonding atoms to the polarity of a bond (percent ionic character).

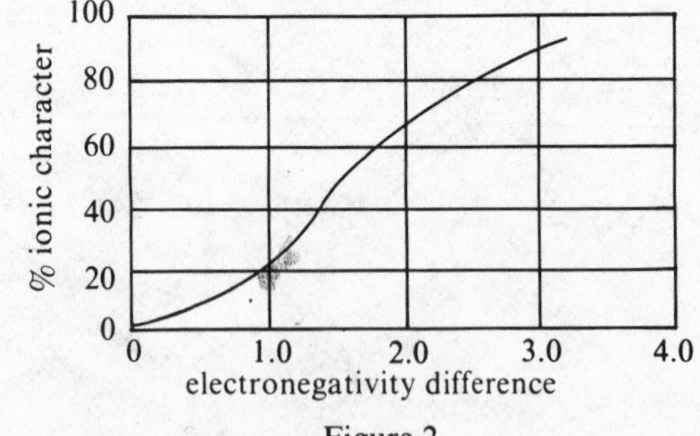

Figure 2

36. A bond between atoms having an electronegativity difference of 1.0 could be formed with which of the following pairs of atoms?

F. S and Cl
G. Mn and Br
H. C and N
J. N and F

37. Generally speaking, the lower the electronegativity, the more metallic the element. The three *most* metallic elements shown in Figure 1 are:

A. Ca, Na, K.
B. Li, Na, K.
C. Na, K, Rb.
D. F, O, N.

38. A pictorial representation of the continuum of bonding types is obtained by considering the distribution of bonding electrons about the nuclei in a diatomic molecule as a function of an increasing difference in the electron-attracting ability of the two nuclei. Which of the following diagrams best depicts the distribution of electrons in a *highly polar* covalent bond?

F.

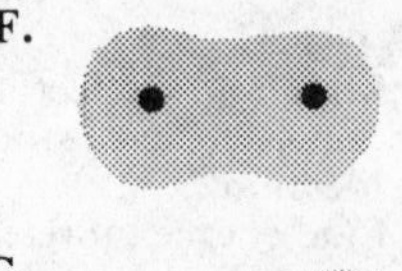

G.

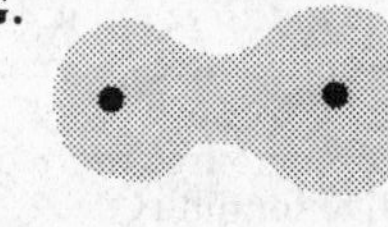

H.

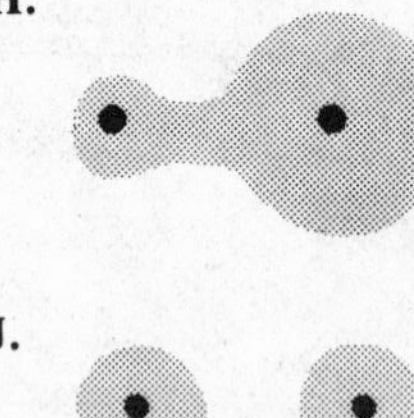

J.

39. Which of the following bonds is considered to have more than 60% ionic character?

A. Na–F
B. Mg–S
C. N–Cl
D. Te–I

40. Which of the following is the correct order of increasing ionic character for bonds between these pairs of elements: C–Br, C–I, C–O, C–N ?

F. C–Br < C–I < C–N < C–O
G. C–I < C–Br < C–O < C–N
H. C–I < C–Br < C–N < C–O
J. C–N < C–I < C–Br < C–O

END OF TEST 4

STOP! DO NOT RETURN TO ANY OTHER TEST.

1. As you read each possible version of the first sentence of Passage I, ask yourself if there are any unneeded words. Is the writing redundant—that is, does it restate an idea unnecessarily? For example, it's redundant to say, "I cheerfully cried happy tears of joy." There are times when you might want to restate an idea as a way of emphasizing it—but would that kind of repetition be useful in the first sentence of Passage I?

In the original sentence, the writer mentions heads "wagging, yes, in agreement." In our culture, do people normally wag their heads **no** in agreement? Is the *yes* necessary? Similarly, C mentions "wagging affirmatively in agreement." Could anyone wag **negatively** in agreement? What is the difference between *affirmatively* and *in agreement* here? Are they both necessary? See how the sentence sounds if you omit *in agreement.* How does it sound if you omit *affirmatively* instead? Does each version make sense by itself, or does the writer need both expressions to convey the idea?

D includes a description of the head-wagging motion: up and down. Is this a helpful addition to the essay? Does it clarify the writer's meaning, or is it redundant? How would D sound if you read it out loud? (Learning to "hear" writing, even without reading aloud, can be very helpful.) What is the effect of using commas to break up the phrase? Does it sound smooth, or choppy?

The main idea of this sentence is that many people agree with the maxim "The dog is our best friend." One way a person can show agreement is to nod—or wag—his or her head. Each response links the idea of head-wagging and agreement, but only one of them expresses the idea concisely.

---

2. According to the writer, do cats or dogs have higher popularity as pets? How do you usually make comparisons between two things or groups?

F and G focus on the choice between *most* and *more.* How do you decide between them? It's important to notice that the writer is comparing only two groups: cats and dogs. How is that different from comparing three or more things or groups? When should you say "most"? When should you say "more"?

H adds the word *still* to the original sentence. How does that affect the meaning? The phrase "**still** more popular," which means "**even** more popular," suggests three things are being compared. Is that the case here?

How would J sound if you read it aloud? Would it sound like a real word?

---

3. As you were reading the first paragraph, what did the words *wagging* and *pack* make you think of? The writer uses them to describe human behavior. Can the words have other meanings, too?

Response A suggests that *wagging* and *pro-canine pack* are synonyms for other expressions. A synonym means about the same thing as another word or expression—for instance, *love* and *adore* are synonyms. You can undoubtedly think of several synonyms for *wagging* and *pack*. The question, though, is why the writer chooses those particular words. Why not *nodding* and *crowd,* for example?

B proposes that the two expressions convey images associated with dogs. Do the words *wagging* and *pack* remind you of dogs? Why would the writer want to include them in a paragraph about the popularity of dogs? Do they add to a reader's understanding or enjoyment of the subject?

As you read C, consider whether the expressions we've been discussing sound as if they're associated with public opinion polls. Do poll results usually refer to the opinions of a "pack" of people? Do you think the writer would have used these expressions if the essay had been about public opinion polls?

Are *pack* and *wagging* commonly used expressions of irony, as D suggests? Do you think the writer uses these particular words just to be ironic?

4. The sentence this question is based on combines two ideas. First, dogs have been performing useful tasks for a long time. Second, cats are not only useful but have a noble history to boot (not to be confused with *Puss in Boots,* which comes up later in the passage). Which response joins these ideas most clearly?

At a glance, it's hard to tell the difference between such long responses. How would they sound if you read them aloud? What do you notice about each version? Are there extra words? Missing words? Is the meaning clear? Confusing?

Look at the original sentence. As in all of the choices, the two basic ideas here are separated by a comma. What are the words that begin each idea? Focus on those words and how they work together. Simplify the sentence in your mind. Essentially, it says, "**While** dogs have been fetching and retrieving for millennia, **but** cats have a useful and noble history." Does the sentence flow logically from the first idea to the second? Do *while* and *but* work together? Do they contradict each other?

Read the sentence without the word *but,* and you have the essence of the version in G. How does this version sound? Is the meaning clear? Is the flow logical?

Repeat this simplifying process with response H, and ask yourself the same question. Do *however* and *thus* link the two ideas clearly and logically? *Thus*—like *so* and *therefore*—implies cause and effect. Is this what the writer intends?

Now simplify J. Is this new sentence clear and logical? Does it read like two related thoughts, or two thoughts that just happen to appear side by side?

5. The writer says that cats have historically been both useful and noble. Which is the most appropriate verb tense for this part of the sentence?

Notice that the four choices are forms of present, past, and future tenses. Starting with "cats have a history that," read the sentence through. Try each of the choices. How does each verb tense affect the meaning of the sentence?

Do *shall have combined* (A) and *would combine* (C) imply that the action has already happened? Or that it hasn't happened yet? What does *had been combined* (B) imply? Does it make sense to say "history had been combined"? D offers the choice "combines." How clearly does it express the idea of the sentence?

6. The point of this sentence is that the cat has been given a job—namely, controlling the rodent population. The writer calls this job "gainful employment," though it's doubtful the cat gets much gain besides being permitted to eat the captured rodent. At any rate, all of your choices include those two words. What are the differences?

According to F, the cat is employed by whom—or what? Does it make sense to talk about anyone—even a cat—being "employed by employment"?

If "gainful employment" is the aspect of feline history the writer wants to emphasize, what's the clearest way, among the choices offered, to get that point across? Considering that *employment* means "job," does J's reference to "employment work" sound logical? H mentions "employment productivity." Is productivity something that can be granted?

7. Which punctuation has some function in this sentence, and which is just a drag on the flow of ideas?

Read each choice aloud, or to yourself, pausing slightly for each punctuation mark. As you read B and D, what is the effect of pausing between *priestly* and *decrees?* As you read C, what is the effect of pausing between *it* and *and?* Does one of these choices make it easier to separate the sentence into two clear ideas?

The colon in A and semicolon in B offer other ways to separate the two ideas. Remember that a colon usually signals the reader that additional, clarifying information follows: examples, details, a definition, or even an emphatic restatement of the sentence's main idea. A semicolon usually signals equivalence; the two parts of the sentence are each capable of standing alone but are connected with a semicolon because they're closely related. You could think of a semicolon as halfway between a comma and a period. It's like putting on the brakes in a car. A comma taps the brakes, a semicolon brings the car to a rolling stop, and a period stops the car completely.

8. Does anything in F and G strike you as redundant? After death, could a cat be anything but dead? Is it helpful to the reader to be reminded that death follows life, as J states? Which is the one expression that doesn't include irrelevant or redundant information?

9. As you read this sentence, think about what the underlined phrase refers to. What other part of the sentence should it agree with?

The writer is talking about the aristocratic origins of the cat. Is *the cat* singular—an "it," as B and C imply—or plural, as in A and D?

Look again at B and C. Most possessive words require an apostrophe. Is that the case with the pronoun *it?*

10. There are two things to consider here. First, does it make sense to begin a new paragraph? Second, what is the most logical way to begin the sentence?

In the passage, the preceding paragraph gives examples of how cats have inspired artists and writers. Does the section beginning "While cats" continue to discuss this topic, or does it introduce a new one—which would, therefore, call for a new paragraph?

H and J suggest starting this sentence with *therefore.* Like *thus* and *so, therefore* implies a cause-and-effect relationship. Does anything in the preceding paragraph support the conclusion that "therefore, cats have many practical advantages"?

While, in F, is often used to make a contrast or a contradiction. (Remember question 4?) Used this way, it means something like "although." For example: "While it's very sunny today, it isn't exactly hot." Does the sentence in the passage include that kind of contrast or contradiction?

G offers the option of starting the sentence simply with "Cats." Does the resulting sentence make more sense than the ones formed by the other choices?

11. The first thing you probably noticed about this question is the choice between *then* and *than.* The sentence compares the maintenance required by cats to the maintenance required by dogs. Which word is used for comparisons: *then* or *than?*

Also notice that in C, there is an apostrophe after *dogs,* indicating a possessive. Does the sentence discuss anything belonging to dogs?

12. Who, or what, is making mistakes about what cats mean by their behavior?

What is the subject of the sentence? Is it singular or plural? Whichever it is, the answer shouldn't conflict with it. Does this help you eliminate any of the choices?

One way to test your answer is to rearrange the sentence. For instance: "Still, some die-hard dog lovers, **to mistake** dignity for indifference, . . . claim cats are antisocial." Is this what the writer means to say?

13. Which response offers the best word to describe cats' method of getting to the top of pet popularity charts?

What does *aspire* mean in A? Can you get to the top simply by aspiring—or do you have to perform some action?

Look at *lead* in B. The writer argues that cats lead dogs in popularity. However, is that the same as cats leading their own way, as B implies? Does it even make sense? Would you say, "I'm leading my way to a better job"?

What does *clamor* mean in C? Is it logical to suggest that cats are getting to the top by making a loud noise?

Finally, D offers the word *claw.* What kind of action does that verb suggest? Does it have any other associations that might make it particularly appropriate here?

14. What is being compared to what in this sentence? And what is the most effective way to coordinate the terms of the comparison? The sentence coils around a bit, so be careful.

Try paring the sentence down to essentials: "people" (subject) "are able to see" (verb) "signs" (object). **Where** or **in what** do they see the signs? "**Less in** wagging ___?___ ___?___ coiling."

If paring down that way doesn't help, try another angle. (You're editing the sentence now, not the cat lover who wrote it.) Do you want to say "less. . .than," "less. . .as," or "less. . .more"?

15. Imagine yourself as the writer of the essay (a harder job for dog lovers than for ailurophiles). Considering all the decisions you've made about such things as which words to use and what to emphasize, how would you describe the whole essay? As you study the choices offered, you might spot more than one that seem to describe the purpose **or** the tone. Look for the response that best describes both the purpose **and** the tone.

The passage's first paragraph relates that cat lovers have long subscribed to the notion of feline superiority, and the essay goes on to support that premise. C and D pinpoint that as the essay's purpose, but what do they say about its tone? Does the writer sound bitter to you? How serious is the tone? Is the writer's argument strictly logical? For instance, the writer believes cats are superior but supports that statement mainly by discussing how popular they are, which isn't necessarily the same thing.

A says the tone is satiric. B says it's informal. You might concede that the tone has elements of both. But what about the essay's purpose? Does the writer talk about people who spoil their pets? Or pets that don't spoil? (Reread the paragraph about mummification.) Is the purpose more informative, or entertaining?

16. Imagine that you've just sat down to write an essay about three familiar expressions and where they came from. You think your first inspiration is a good one—you write down three good examples, put quotation marks around them, and decide to go on from there. Now, what was your purpose in taking that approach? (And what will be the purpose of a reader who's reading what you've just written?)

As you go through the choices here, think about whether the statements they make are true. What is the topic of this essay? Do these words and phrases provide an introduction to it (F)? Do they appeal to authority (G)? Do they explain anything (H) by themselves? Are they actually complete sentences (J)?

Note that it's virtually impossible to answer this question sensibly without reading through the whole passage first. Note, too, that you have to read the question carefully. (The question is not, as a hasty reading might suggest: What is the purpose of using the words **in** quotation marks as opposed to **without** them?)

17. What is the subject of the sentence? Is it singular or plural? Does it require a singular or plural verb?

18. How does the underlined section—"phrases made up of words"—sound to you? How do you define *phrase?* If you think of a phrase as a group of related words, is it economical writing to refer to "phrases made up of words"?

G and H offer two shorter expressions. What does *verbiage* mean? Think back to your definition of *phrase.* Does either *phrase* or *verbiage* seem to fit here better than the underlined expression?

Suppose you take out the underlined section, as J suggests. Does what's left of the sentence make sense? Pay particular attention to the word *or.* What does it refer to?

---

19. You've probably noticed that your four choices here differ only in their use of commas. If you're not sure which one is best, try reading the sentence through each of the different ways, pausing at the commas. Properly placed, commas should help clarify the meaning of this long and rather complex sentence.

Response A uses commas to separate the phrase "as language evolves." Do the commas make the sentence clear and easy to understand?

Is the meaning clear without a pause between *can* and *as* (B)? Without a pause between *evolves* and *come* (D)? Without any pauses at all (C)?

---

20. The preceding question involved proper comma placement and parenthetical phrases. This question also deals with commas. Is there a parenthetical phrase here as well? Try out the various choices by reading them through, pausing at the commas. H substitutes *the* for *for.* When you read the sentence that way, what does it say? Does it make sense?

---

21. The writer has just explained how the expression "eavesdrop" was coined. Which of the responses best leads the reader smoothly into the concluding sentence of the paragraph? Since the writer demonstrates that "eavesdrop" evolved in a reasonably logical way, you should be able to eliminate responses that imply contradictions. Is the point that "eavesdrop" gained its current meaning **as a result of** people overhearing conversations beneath a house's eaves, rather than **in spite of** it?

Should the answer suggest a cause-and-effect relationship between the first three sentences of the paragraph and the last sentence? An example of such a word would be *therefore.* Do you see any similar words or phrases among the choices given?

Thus (A) and *so* (C) mean approximately the same thing. What is the effect of adding *then* to C?

---

22. How does this sentence explain the origin of the word "snob"? It says "the word ___?___ originated at Oxford." Which of the answer choices creates an explanation that reads as a complete thought?

It might help to read the sentence through, imagining that there's a colon after *says.* Think about what would follow that colon. How would you make it sound like a complete thought? As it's written, is the thought complete? Does *that* make sense where it is?

H offers the choice of substituting *which.* Is the point of this question to decide when you should use *which* instead of *that?* The main thing to ask yourself is: Does either one sound right here? Does either one make the meaning of the sentence clear?

What happens if you substitute *were,* as G proposes? *Were* is a verb. How does that affect what the writer is trying to say?

---

23. Once again, all the responses offer the same choice of words. They differ only in their use of commas. As you read this sentence, what do you think the punctuation should clarify? Which phrase needs to be set off by a comma, or commas, to make the meaning of the sentence clear?

Try reading the sentences through, pausing at each comma. How does it sound to pause before and after *registering freshmen* (A)? To pause only **after** *registering freshmen* (D)? B separates the phrase "At one time registering," while C separates only "At one time." How do those two alterations affect the meaning? Is the writer explaining **when** these freshmen were registering, or that they were all registering at one time?

24. One important decision you make in writing, or in editing what you've written, is the order in which to present your ideas. This question asks if Sentence 5 is where it belongs, or if it would be more effective somewhere else in the paragraph.

What is this paragraph about? As it's structured now, does it give a clear, easy-to-follow explanation of the origin of "snob"? Would a reader be confused at any point in the explanation? Is there any place where you feel the writer might have included some information out of order?

Remember that *thus,* as discussed in question 21, is a word that signifies cause and effect. With that in mind, look at each choice and think about which one best prepares a reader for the conclusion implied by *thus.*

For instance, Sentence 2 (G) suggests that "snob" derives from a word for *shoemaker.* Granted, a shoemaker would be considered a commoner. You might even assume that the shoemaker aspires to nobility. But does it necessarily follow that a snob is a commoner who would like to be associated with the upper classes? Has the writer supported this conclusion?

Test all the choices this way until you find the most logical one.

25. Is this a math question masquerading as an English question? That's what you might think when you notice that two of your choices are *first* and *secondly.* But are you being asked to do arithmetic—or to choose the best way to start this paragraph?

At the beginning of this essay, the writer presents three expressions, then systematically explains how they originated. Is "put a sock in it" the *second* expression to be explained, as *secondly* in A might indicate? It doesn't take a pocket calculator to figure out that it isn't the first, as implied by C.

If we give the writer the benefit of the doubt and assume that he or she can count to three as well as we can, we need to consider if *first* and *secondly* might have other meanings that would be appropriate here.

What else could *secondly* mean? Could it signal the reader that the writer is about to add information related to what's been stated in the preceding paragraph (for instance, another possible origin of the word "snob")? Is this, in fact, the case?

What else could *first* mean? Is the writer saying, "If I were told to put a sock in it, the **first** thing I'd know is that I needed to make a lot less noise"? If that's true, can you find a **second** thing in the passage?

Primarily (D) suggests that a warning to make less noise would be the main message—but not the only one—if the writer were told to put a sock in it. Does the paragraph support that idea? Are other messages mentioned?

How does *finally* (B) work here? Is it the writer's gasp of relief—"At last! Finally!"—or is it a way of introducing the **final** explanation in the series of three?

26. The important thing here is to zero in on what the underlined word refers to. Read the sentence carefully. Is the writer explaining **where** the sound came through: namely, **there?** If so, how do the large horns fit in?

Or is the writer saying something about who the horns belong to? Who **do** those horns belong to—the early record players, or their sound? One way to figure it out is to try both expressions in place of the underlined one:

> early record players whose sound came through **the early record players'** large horns
>
> or
>
> early record players whose sound came through **the sound's** large horns.

Even if you've never seen one of those gramophones, does it seem possible for a **sound** to have large horns?

Now that you've pinpointed whose large horns they are, what kind of possessive pronoun do you need: singular or plural? Does the underlined word allude to an "it" or a "they"?

---

27. Who, or what, did the stuffing?

Could "which"—referring to "volume controls"—do the stuffing (A)?

If these machines weren't sophisticated enough to have volume controls, is it likely that they could stuff socks in their horns (B), even if they wanted to? (Remember, this is a test, not an episode of "Star Trek.")

Who would a reader assume *they* refers to (C)? Does the writer supply enough information for a reader to make an assumption?

The passage hasn't mentioned listeners before, which might lead you to dismiss D at first. Still, compared to the other options, does it seem logical that "listeners" would, in fact, be the designated sock-stuffers?

---

28. A comma breaks this sentence into two ideas. How would you summarize them? Here's one possibility:

1. Modern sound systems have eliminated the need for socks in the stereo.
2. The expression "put a sock in it" is still understandable.

Does idea #2 follow as a logical consequence of #1—or in spite of #1? When you think of the best way to connect these ideas, consider whether they tend to support or contradict each other.

What kind of relationship between these ideas is implied by *therefore* (F) and *thus* (G)? (Substitute the word *so,* if that helps.) Do you agree with the implication? Is it logical?

What do *quite the contrary* (H) and *but* (J) imply about the relationship between the two statements? Although H and J are both expressions that suggest a contradiction, are they interchangeable here? Try them both in the sentence. Does one make the writer's meaning come through "loud and clear"?

29. What is it that "comes through loud and clear"? Keep in mind that the question is asking you to distinguish between an expression (the words) and its meaning (the sense of the words).

Look at A, B, and D and think about the different choices they offer. Think about the phrase "put a sock in it." What does it mean in this passage? Can you think of other ways to say that meaning? Is the phrase itself an expression? Or a meaning?

C mentions a "meaning expression." What exactly is a "meaning expression"? Does the phrase "meaning expression" mean anything?

30. What is the "blueprint" of this essay? How is it "constructed"? As you scan the choices for the one that best describes the essay's structure, be alert for choices that you can rule out because one element in the series is clearly inappropriate. You wouldn't pick a response as the correct one simply because one of its elements is correct, but it's logical to reject a response as incorrect if one part of it is wrong.

For instance, G characterizes the last paragraph as a call to action—in other words, a message urging the reader to think or act in a particular way. That's how many advertisements and political speeches end. Is there a call to action in the fourth paragraph? If you decide there isn't, it doesn't matter if the other three elements are on target or not.

Does the writer give a personal account in the second paragraph, as J says?

Look at F. Does the passage begin with an example? Does the last paragraph contain a conclusion? But look at H. Does the passage have an introductory paragraph? Are the following three paragraphs each devoted to an example?

Be sure to read all the answer choices before you pick the one you think is best. Don't be misled by options that sound possible because they're partially correct.

31. Besides thinking about why the writer might have picked these three words or phrases, as you go through the optional answers, ask yourself how accurate each one is.

Does the essay, as A says, illustrate a variety of word origins that are interesting? *Interesting* might be too enthusiastic an adjective. Nevertheless, read on and see if any of the other options is better.

Does the essay build to a story line (B)? The passage has a structure—a beginning, middle, and end—but so does a newspaper editorial. Does this essay tell a story?

Do the three words have common linguistic roots (C), according to the information you're given in the passage? Does the writer say, for instance, that they **all** derive from Latin?

Do **all** the words have negative connotations? This answer isn't so obvious. "Snob" definitely has a negative connotation. Eavesdropping, like snobbery, is an undesirable character trait. And "put a sock in it" can sound very negative if someone says it while you're recounting highlights of your summer vacation on a mink farm in East Mudflap. However, can you say that all three **original** meanings were **positive?** Is the original meaning of "snob"—without nobility—particularly positive? Is there anything positive **or** negative about eaves?

32. What are the two main ideas in this compound sentence? What is the best way to link them in one sentence?

You can break this sentence down into two parts:

1. Jobs dried up overnight.
2. Breadlines and soup kitchens were opened to feed the hungry.

Can each statement stand alone? Does each make sense as a separate sentence? Even if they **are** independent clauses, making two shorter sentences out of one long one isn't among the options you're given here. The writer wants to join the two clauses in a single sentence. Which response offers the best way to do it?

Three of your choices add the conjunction *and.* In a situation like this, should *and* have a comma before it (G)? After it (H)? If you're in doubt, try the familiar (by now) method of reading the sentence through, pausing at the comma. Which version makes the sentence easier to understand? J includes a semicolon. A semicolon creates a bigger break than a comma, but not as big as a period. Is the combination of a semicolon and *and* appropriate here?

33. Why, according to the passage, did people by the thousands lose their homes? They could not pay their mortgages. What is the best way for the writer to convey the relationship between these two events clearly and economically?

More than one of the choices might look good to you. None of them appear to have glaring errors. But does one of them strike you as more precise, more to the point, than the others?

For stylistic or rhetorical reasons, there are times when it's acceptable—even desirable—to say "four score and seven years" when what you mean is "eighty-seven." In general, however, if several expressions have the same meaning—and if you are not Abraham Lincoln—it's best to pick the one that's most concise, unless you're striving for some special effect.

---

34. What is the main action in the sentence? "Job applicants showed up," right? **When** did they show up? Try dividing the sentence this way:

1. When it was announced that work would soon begin on the Lincoln Tunnel to connect New York and New Jersey.
2. Job applicants showed up in large numbers.

Does part 1 make a complete sentence by itself? Does part 2? Only if you can answer "yes" to both questions is G your best choice. Two independent clauses can be joined by a semicolon or by a comma and a conjunction; they can also be broken into two separate sentences.

Responses F and H propose linking the two parts with a comma. H adds a comma after the phrase *job applicants.* Why would the writer want to separate that phrase from the rest of the sentence with commas? Does it seem appropriate here?

By now, your brain may be clogged with commas and semicolons. If so, then J, which has none of those annoying little marks, might look very appealing. But how does the sentence sound if you read it without **any** pauses? Are there places where a reader could get confused?

---

35. Does this underlined phrase need a comma or two to make its meaning clear in this sentence? Or is the punctuation all right as it is?

In questions 32 and 34 we discussed two of the ways in which commas can be used: with a conjunction to separate two independent clauses, and without a conjunction to separate a dependent and an independent clause. Are you being asked to look at a different use for commas here?

Certain phrases containing parenthetical information—details that aren't necessary to the basic meaning of the sentence—are called nonrestrictive. They should be set off with commas (or with dashes or parentheses). On the other hand, restrictive phrases—which contain essential information—should not.

Restrictive: The new restaurant **in the shopping mall** serves great enchiladas.

Nonrestrictive: The new restaurant, **which is in the shopping mall where I bought my rubber armadillo,** serves great enchiladas.

It's sometimes hard to decide whether information is or isn't essential, particularly if you happen to be in the market for a rubber armadillo yourself.

Look at the phrase "for building the tunnel." Is the information essential to what the writer wants to convey? Or is it more of an aside—parenthetical information? Does it need to be separated from the rest of the sentence by a pair of commas (C)?

Looking at the sentence as a whole (it might also be helpful to look ahead to the next question about this sentence), is there any other reason why commas might be appropriate here (B and D)?

36. Here, the writer has penned a sentence that's almost as long as the Lincoln Tunnel. The question is: Should it be one sentence, or two?

Long sentences aren't necessarily wrong, provided they're not actually two sentences masquerading as one. Read the sentence as it is (F). Is it clear? Is there any point where a reader might have trouble following the writer's train of thought?

If you think the sentence is unclear, try the alternatives: adding a comma, a dash, or a period.

A comma can be used to divide a dependent clause from an independent one. It can separate two independent clauses if it precedes a conjunction. Without a conjunction, you'd have a comma splice. Look at the two clauses that would be formed by adding a comma (G). Is one dependent upon the other? Or could each be a complete sentence by itself? If each is an independent clause, what punctuation is called for? Would a period (J) be better? A dash (H)?

A dash doesn't usually separate complete sentences although, informally, you might write to a friend: "I was so upset—I was out of my mind!" It can add emphasis by setting off information within a sentence:

> Workers would dig the tunnel—if all went according to plan—from both banks of the Hudson at the same time.

Notice how the "iffiness" of the project is further emphasized if that information appears near the end of the sentence:

> Workers would dig from both banks of the Hudson at the same time—if all went according to plan.

Is using one dash the best way to punctuate the sentence in the passage?

37. Is this sentence correct as it stands? Is there a better way to express the underlined phrase? Does "which were difficult to work in" explain or help describe the phrase it follows—namely, *harsh conditions?*

Does a reader get a more vivid picture of the harsh conditions after reading that they were difficult to work in (A), made the work tough (B), or were hard on the workers (C)? In past questions, you've explored the different ways to punctuate essential and nonessential information. Certain nonessential, or parenthetical, information should be set off in commas. However, there's a difference between nonessential information and information that's simply redundant. Redundant information doesn't belong in commas. It belongs on the cutting room floor (D). What kind of information is being presented in these choices?

38. Is this another case where breaking the sentence down into its basic ideas can help you pick the best linking word? What are the two main ideas?

One way to express them is:

1. There were hardships and dangers in building the tunnel.
2. The men who were hired considered themselves lucky.

Did the men consider themselves lucky **because of** the dangers (J)? Or **despite** them (H)? What does *regarding* (G) mean here? What does *in addition* (F) mean here? Do those expressions imply that the men perceived the dangers and hardships as a drawback—or as an added attraction? How do you think they felt about work that, according to the passage, was "dirty, exhausting, and dangerous"?

39. This question asks two things:

1. Does this sentence need the word *were?*
2. How should this sentence be punctuated?

If you can answer the first question, you'll narrow your options down to two.

What is the action of this sentence? How is that action related to the statement that the men "were hired" to build the tunnel? Read the sentence with and without the word *were.* Which way is clearer?

Next, try dividing the sentence this way:

1. Despite the hardships and dangers.
2. The men hired to build the tunnel considered themselves lucky.

Do you use a semicolon to separate a prepositional phrase from the clause it modifies? Be sure to pick the response that not only includes the best punctuation, but also reflects your decision about the word *were.*

40. Like question 39, this one has two parts. Solving one part rules out two of your options, and you're halfway home. The two parts are:

- Should there be a comma after *other?*
- Is the word *they* necessary?

What kind of expression is "which had been inching toward each other"? (If you need to refresh your memory, take another look at the explanation for question 35.) What is the best way to punctuate this?

Next, think about the word *they.* Does it belong in this sentence? Suppose you were to take out the words "which had been inching toward each other" and the commas enclosing them. What do you have left? Read that sentence with and without the word *they.* Which version is clearer?

41. Read the sentences just before and after the underlined one. Does the paragraph flow more logically with the underlined sentence, or without it? Does the topic—fear of tunnels—fit with what's being discussed in the rest of the paragraph? Is the topic effectively placed in the paragraph, or does it seem awkward and irrelevant? Does moving the word *however* help?

If you glance at A, B, and C, you'll notice that they differ **only** in the placement of *however.* Does it matter where that word appears if the sentence itself is out of place?

If the writer wanted to make this paragraph as clear and concise as possible, would it be better to find the best place for the word *however*—or to make sure that each sentence contributes to the paragraph's meaning?

42. More than 350 years ago, the poet John Donne cautioned, "And therefore never send to know for whom the bell tolls." Nowadays, we're far more likely to ask, "Who's that bell tolling for, anyway?" Most of us would rather try to play "Flight of the Bumblebee" on a xylophone than tackle the problem of when to use *whom* instead of *who.*

We would note that in this question, F offers *who.* We would note that G and H offer *whom.* We would probably scratch our heads, nibble our pencils and discover that J suggests we chuck **both** of those nasty pronouns. Our eyes would light up. We would shout, "AHA!" We would mark J and go on to the next question. However, we would never be sure that we had made the right choice.

It's becoming more and more acceptable to use *who* instead of *whom,* particularly in questions: "**Who** is that bell tolling for?" Yet *who* and *whom* aren't interchangeable. The basic rule is: *Who* is the subject pronoun; *whom* is the object pronoun.

A subject pronoun can act. An object pronoun can't—it can only be the receiver of an action. Some examples:

> **Who** rang the bell? The person **who** rang it is gone. (**Whom** can't ring.)
>
> John Donne, **who** wrote the poem, is dead. (**Whom** can't write a poem. Can't die, either.)
>
> Donne was a poet by **whom** many poems were written. (**Who** can't be the object of the preposition *by.* We'd do better, by the way, to say "Donne was a poet **who** wrote many poems.")

To return to the question: can a "whom" work on a tunnel (G and H)? Can a "who" (F)? Does your head ache?

If you pick *having* (J), is the meaning of the sentence clear without adding any punctuation?

And therefore never send to know for whom the Lincoln Tunnel was dug. All we can tell you is: the bell tolls for this discussion.

43. What was "exhausted but elated"? Does it make sense to think of a **what** as exhausted but elated? So, **who** does this phrase describe? Who would logically be "exhausted but elated" (besides someone who had just successfully differentiated between *who* and *whom*)?

As you scan the responses, ask yourself: Could "the opening ceremony" be exhausted but elated (A)? Could "they" (B)? Who does the pronoun *they* refer to? Could "the tunnel" (C) or "Babe Ruth's congratulatory speech" (D) be exhausted but elated?

44. The writer lists some of the elements that went into building the Lincoln Tunnel: concrete, steel, and backbreaking work. The important thing to note is that these **three** items are modified by **two** descriptive phrases: "hundreds of tons of" and "thousands of hours of."

One decision you need to make, then, is whether the expression is clearer and more effective with a series of three items or a pair of related items.

If you try reading the responses through, pausing at each comma, which one is most effective at conveying the meaning in a way that's clear, graceful, and unambiguous?

---

45. Here it is at last: the light at the end of the tunnel. The Lincoln Tunnel, that is.

This final question asks you to make two choices: between *play* and *played* and between *so* and *as.*

The word *had,* just before the underlined phrase, will determine your first choice. What tense is *play?* What tense is *played?* Try both with *had.* Which one better conveys the idea of an action that occurred in the past?

This should have eliminated two of your four choices. Next, concentrate on the choice between *so* and *as.* What's the difference between playing "as vital a role" in something and playing "so vital a role"? Does either word imply a comparison when it's used that way? In this sentence, is the writer comparing the workers' role to any other?

---

46. Is there anything wrong, in principle, with the adjectives the writer uses to refer to the age of thirty? No doubt she intends to be ironic, given that her neighbor, in his eighties, is considerably "riper" and older. (This irony might be lost on **you,** however, if you happen to be a decade or more shy of the advanced age of thirty yourself.)

Even if you feel that this ironic aside fits the tone of the passage as a whole, it's the best choice only if it's punctuated correctly in one of the responses. Look at F and J. If necessary, read both aloud, pausing at each comma. Does either one strike you as a clear, concise way to punctuate this expression?

G and H eliminate any sort of commentary on the age of thirty. Try reading them aloud in the sentence. Does the writer's basic meaning still come through? Does either option offer an acceptable way to punctuate the sentence? Keep in mind that a semicolon should only separate two **independent** clauses—parts of a sentence that could stand on their own. Would the semicolon, as it's placed in G, do this?

How would the comma in H affect the sentence? Is it appropriate that the phrase *at thirty* be set off with commas? To test this, treat the commas like parentheses and remove the phrase. Does the sentence still make sense?

---

47. As you study this sentence, you should be able to find two different actions taking place. Which option best expresses the relationship between those actions?

You can divide the sentence this way:

1. I helped Dr. Peterson with small chores.
2. He provided me with a sense of life larger than my own.

Response A presents this sentence with no break between the two actions. Could this be confusing to a reader? Do you think the sentence would be easier to understand with some kind of pause in it?

B links the actions with a comma and the word *therefore.* What does *therefore* imply here? Is the writer trying to say that she was provided with a sense of life larger than her own as a direct result of doing small chores for her neighbor?

What type of relationship does a colon indicate? Is it the best way to join these two actions, as it's used in C? Is the *and* after it appropriate?

What kind of clauses can be joined by a semicolon? Would the semicolon in D join two of them?

---

48. Which response best describes how the writer learned history from Dr. Peterson?

F says the writer learned it "firsthand, as if it were." Read the underlined words carefully. Do they form a complete sentence? "As if" **what** were . . . **what?**

G and H suggest that she learned it "from the horse's mouth." We can be relatively sure that Dr. Peterson wasn't a horse (although we're told he was some kind of "runner" in France) because, with the exception of Mr. Ed, horses don't tell stories. What does the phrase mean here?

G adds *firsthand* to it, while H adds *straight* and *source.* What do those words mean? Would you consider them—in this case—helpful clarifications to a reader, or are they redundant?

J suggests simply *firsthand.* Is that single word clear enough? Do any of the other responses offer information that adds to a reader's understanding of the writer's history lessons?

49. The underlined phrase tells a reader a little bit about being a runner in World War I. That is, A tells a little. B, C, and D tell a **lot.** Or do they? They're all much longer than A. But does the added verbiage give a reader a more complete picture of a runner's job? Do any of the responses contain unnecessary words? Are they written clearly and concisely?

Look at "messages, and war-related data" in B, "by hand himself" in C, and "delivering and transporting" in D. What's similar about these phrases?

Take C, for instance. If Dr. Peterson delivered messages "by hand," could they have been delivered by anyone **but** himself? Does the writer need both expressions? Do any of the other options basically say the same thing twice?

A is short and sweet. Granted, it leaves you wondering about the nature of these messages. They might have been documents, as D suggests, or communiqués about the enemy's position, or even urgent memos about the coffee bean situation back in camp. You might consider *carrying messages* pithy and not completely satisfactory. But do the longer answers give you more information? And do they do it without cluttering the sentence with redundancies?

50. Here's an appealing subject: agonizing death. Let's spend as little time as possible agonizing over the answer, shall we?

Notice that you don't have the opportunity to tinker with the adjective *agonizing.* Therefore, make sure the expression you pick sounds appropriate with it.

F, G, and J include the word *slowest.* What kind of adjective is *slowest*—positive, comparative, or superlative? What does it mean? Does the word *most* in G make the meaning more emphatic, or is it redundant?

Does *slowest* agree in **degree** with the adjective *agonizing?* For instance, we say "sadder but wiser," not "sad but wisest."

---

51. The problem here is: What's the best way to link the two main ideas of this sentence and show the relationship between them? What are those ideas? Does one follow as a logical consequence of the other? Are they expressed in two independent clauses, or is only one independent? These are all factors to consider when looking at your options.

Think of the writer's two main points in this sentence:

1. The soldiers stoically bore the terror of the gas.
2. In camp they complained about smaller concerns, like the quality of their provisions.

Why does the writer combine these points in one sentence? The gist of the sentence is: The soldiers didn't complain about the gas; they did gripe about the little stuff. Is it logical to say they were stoic about the gas "so that" they weren't stoic about coffee beans, as A suggests? Were the soldiers purposely holding back their emotions on the battlefield so they could vent them in the mess tent?

Consider the implications of *but* (B) and *as* (C). Does either one express the bearing one part of the sentence has on the other?

Suppose you scrap the conjunctions and join the two actions only with a comma (D). A comma without a conjunction shouldn't join two independent clauses, because that creates a comma splice. How would you classify the two clauses in this sentence?

---

52. You may never have drunk coffee made with chicory and, therefore, may not understand the soldiers' strong aversion to it. Some people like chicory's strong, bitter flavor, but it's something of an acquired taste. As you read the passage, in place of chicory try substituting a food item from your own personal blacklist: liver, brussels sprouts, iguanas, etc. Get the picture?

F, H, and J suggest setting two elements of the sentence apart:

1. Coffee beans were often scarce, and chicory was substituted.
2. Much to the troops' disgust.

Are these both independent clauses? If so, they can be separated by a period (F) or, if they're very closely related, a semicolon (J). If only one is independent, a comma or a dash (H) could be used. What effect would a dash add to the sentence?

G proposes omitting punctuation altogether. Without any pause after *substituted,* would the resulting sentence be confusing to a reader?

53. Before you get too involved in conundrums like which sounds better, *would usually sing* or *usually would sing,* take a moment to note the biggest difference in the four choices. A, B, and C put a comma after *eating.* D doesn't. It makes sense to try D first, because if the sentence doesn't need a comma, then it doesn't matter which verb combinations A, B, and C offer.

So ask yourself: Who did the singing? The answer: Those already eating. Be careful not to separate this subject from its verb with unnecessary punctuation.

54. This question deals with possessives. The writer is about to relate another anecdote from the vast memory bank of Dr. Peterson, the human time machine. What kind of punctuation shows the possessive relationship? Is the writer referring to something belonging to Dr. Peterson? To something belonging to one of his anecdotes? Is the possessive noun singular or plural?

55. What are the implications of placing the phrase *at 11:00 A.M.* at the various points proposed by the responses? Think about what the writer is saying. Look for the choice that says it most clearly and unambiguously.

Is the writer suggesting that both sides "**knew** at 11:00 A.M." (A)? That there was a "**war** at 11:00 A.M.," which would end (B)? That the war would "**be over** at 11:00 A.M." (D)? Can *at 11:00 A.M.* stand alone as a complete sentence (C)?

---

56. In this paragraph, the writer is chronicling a chain of events that took place on the day World War I ended. What is the best way to order the sentences so that a reader forms a clear picture of what happened, as well as **when** it happened?

A key phrase in Sentence 3 refers to specific information elsewhere in the paragraph and therefore dictates where the sentence would most logically be placed.

Look at the introductory phrase *on that day.* In Sentence 3's present location (F), can a reader tell exactly which day is being referred to? Would it be clearer if Sentence 3 began this paragraph (G)? Or ended it (J)? What if it came right before the sentence that includes *November 11, 1918* (H)?

---

57. Focus on the phrase *as a whole* in this question. You might decide that one or more of the optional answers could reflect opinions expressed by the writer in this essay. Yet, as you read each one, ask yourself whether it's truly the theme of this essay—the writer's reason for putting pen to paper (or hands to keyboard) in the first place.

Where does the writer allude to the idea that "people can have good friends of all ages" (A)? Does the placement of this statement in the essay seem to signify that the writer wants to give it any special emphasis?

Where in the essay does a reader learn that "many people were pointlessly killed in World War I" (B)? What does the placement of that information suggest? How many times is the pointless killing mentioned? What does that suggest?

The writer says she learned history firsthand. A reader might infer that the writer thinks it's a good way to learn, maybe even better than reading a history textbook. But is she necessarily saying that the **only** way to learn history is through firsthand knowledge? Is that idea feasible?

Friendship is, of course, "an important thing" (D). Certainly the writer valued her friendship with Dr. Peterson. She also mentions other friends. If friendship alone is the theme of the passage, how do you interpret the fact that the writer brings up the issue of age at the beginning of the essay as well as at the end?

58. Does this essay actually describe "the historical **observance** of Veterans Day"? What does that phrase mean? Is the historical observance discussed in the passage, or is it only a bit of historical background? How much of the essay is devoted to November 11, the day we now observe as Veterans Day? Where in the passage is Veterans Day mentioned?

In addition, look back at your answer to question 57. Does that answer fit with the idea that this essay focuses on describing Veterans Day observances?

One or more of the responses could be at least partly right. H, for instance, says the examples are all experiences of a World War I veteran. However, does it follow that the essay is necessarily a description of Veterans Day observances?

59. How does the writer support her assertion that friendship with an **older** person is valuable? Could she use the same method to illustrate the rewards of friendship with a younger person (B)?

If the writer shortened some of Dr. Peterson's stories (A), could **that** add to a reader's understanding?

What about listing her friends' ages (C)? What does a catalog of ages say about the value of these friendships? It could show that the writer values friends of all ages, but could it show us why they're valuable?

Look at the last sentence of the essay. Would the writer's point about young friends be strengthened by cutting this sentence (D)? Does this sentence in any way contradict the writer's assertion about young friends? Would deleting it give a reader a clearer picture of why young friends are worthwhile?

60. Feast your eyes on this lengthy sentence. Is there anything confusing about it, as written, that could be clarified by better punctuation?

Read the sentence as it is (F). Is it clear and easy to understand? Is there any point at which a reader might be confused? As you read this sentence, do you think the writer did a good job of organizing the ideas and information? Could the writer be trying to fit too much into a single sentence?

How does a comma after *seated* (J) affect the meaning of this sentence? What about placing a comma after *feast* (G)? Remember that a comma shouldn't separate two independent clauses unless a conjunction follows the comma. Do you see an independent clause—that is, a complete sentence—on one side of the comma? On both? What punctuation marks can be used if both clauses are independent?

61. Is the question here one of punctuation—or of choosing the right word?

B, C, and D propose adding the word *expensive* to the sentence. How would you define *costly?* How would you define *expensive?* Is a silver spoon worth more if it's costly **and** expensive, rather than merely costly (A)? Does the word *expensive* add to a reader's understanding of what the spoons were like?

62. Here you're offered four different ways to begin this sentence about fourteenth-century dinner music. Think not only about what these words mean, but also about what kind of sentence they produce.

The sentence before the one in question tells us that "trumpets blared and bagpipes squalled." Is it logical that the next sentence would talk about the sweeter music produced **during** this squalling and blaring (G)? Also, with the phrase *during which* at the beginning, would this be a complete sentence?

Look at the other choices in the same way. Do they make sense? Do they form complete sentences?

63. The writer says that "a clever host would have tricks of his own." Ask yourself why. Would it be "**because** he was content" to leave all the entertainment to his hired performers (C)? Is that a logical way to express the relationship between those two parts of the sentence? Would a host have tricks up his sleeve "**if** he was content" to leave everything to the jugglers and animal trainers (B)?

A and D suggest something quite different: that tricks would be performed by a host who was "**not** content" to let the performers do it all. Was he or wasn't he? Which sounds more logical to you?

D adds another wrinkle—beginning the sentence with the words *he was.* How does that change the first part of the sentence? Is it an independent or a dependent clause? What kind of clause is the second part of the sentence? Does the comma after *entertainment* fit with D? What kind of clause is the first one if it begins simply with *not* (A)? Again, is the comma after *entertainment* appropriate?

64. This question asks you to choose the best pronoun: *you, they, he,* or *one.* What is the noun this pronoun is intended to replace?

The first sentence in the paragraph says that a clever host would have tricks up his sleeve. The next sentence shares one example of what this host might do. What is the subject of the first sentence? What is the subject of the second? Which choice would make the second sentence most consistent with the first?

Try substituting *the host* for the first pronoun in each set offered by the options. In addition, pay attention to both pronouns in each optional answer: you/your (F), they/their (G), he/his (H), one/ones (J). The possessive form should agree with the first pronoun, and it should be spelled and punctuated correctly.

65. This question continues to explore what passed for clever tricks back in the fourteenth century. They may not strike you as quite as witty and uproarious as the party tricks of the twentieth century, but before modern science came up with such innovations as whoopee cushions, people just had to do the best they could with what was available.

Likewise, you have to do the best you can with what's available in these choices. Which word offers the best way to begin this sentence? It should provide a logical transition from the previous sentence. Naturally, it should also help form a sentence that's logical and complete in itself.

What does the word *until* (A) suggest about the relationship between the two sentences? Do you think it reflects the relationship accurately? Is the resulting sentence logical and complete? Apply the same tests to *or* (B), *unless* (C), and *but* (D).

66. What is the appropriate verb to use in the sentence—the singular *was* or the plural *were?* What sort of punctuation, if any, should follow *however?*

One approach is to look at the elements of the sentence in a different order. What does the phrase "even more marvelous" describe? Does the verb have to agree with a singular or a plural noun? Focus on the phrase "some of the masterpieces." What if you place it at the beginning of the sentence? Which sounds better: some of the masterpieces **was** more marvelous or **were** more marvelous?

What sort of punctuation should be used when a parenthetical word like *however* interrupts a sentence? Read the sentence with and without the comma after *however.* Which way makes the sentence clearer? Look at the semicolon in H. What kind of constructions can be separated by a semicolon?

67. Is this sentence better with or without one of the expressions suggested to modify *the kitchen?* What do A, B, and C say about the kitchen? Is the information different in each response, or is it simply arranged differently? What would be lost if the writer decided not to use any of these modifying expressions? Would the sentence be confusing without the information that the kitchen was where the cooking took place? What would a reader expect to take place in the kitchen, if not cooking?

68. Which is better here: a semicolon or a comma? What kind of clauses are on either side of the punctuation mark in this sentence? Can both of them stand alone as complete sentences, or only one? When should a semicolon be used between clauses? Is this one of those situations?

Now, like it or not, you have to focus on that dancing dead chicken. Read the second clause of the sentence and see which sounds better with *would dance: causing* or *so that.* The clever host really did show his guests a good time, didn't he?

69. As you read this sentence, is there anything that makes you stop and do a double take? Do you think the writer means to suggest that a culinary monster could act creatively? Who, in fact, **is** acting creatively? Who's making the monster? (No, Dr. Frankenstein is **not** one of your choices.)

C and D refer to creative cooks. Based on the passage, is it logical to infer that creative cooks are the ones making monsters? How does the phrase *creative cooks* function in this sentence? Does it need a comma after it? Is the sentence clearer with or without a pause between *creative cooks* and *might serve up?*

---

70. Does this Frankenstein's monster of the kitchen remind you of anything—a headline in the *National Enquirer,* perhaps? Back then there was no *National Enquirer,* not even a *People* magazine, so people were sometimes forced to bizarre extremes to provide their own entertainment. Count your blessings.

Anyway, this question is really asking two things:

1. Should *hindquarters* have an apostrophe?
2. Which is better: attached **to** or attached **with?**

An apostrophe can make a word either a contraction or a possessive. What does the apostrophe signify in G, H, and J? Does the sentence discuss anything that the hindquarters possess? Does the word end in *s* because it's possessive? Or because it's a plural noun?

Is the head attached **with** (J) or **to** (F, G, H) the rest of the body?

Note: If you should decide that the answer to the first part of the question is "no," then the question of *to* vs. *with* becomes immaterial. Only F offers *hindquarters* without an apostrophe.

---

71. Which word is better here: *memory's* or *memories?* Should this be one sentence or two?

What does an apostrophe do to a word? Is the possessive form of *memory* appropriate here? Is the writer talking about something belonging to a memory? Is a contraction appropriate here? Is the writer saying that "memory is" something? If the writer is talking about more than one memory, how should the plural form of *memory* be spelled?

What is the best way to punctuate this sentence, or sentences? Could this sentence be broken in two? B begins a new sentence with the word *and.* Is this new sentence complete? Is anything missing from it?

How does the sentence sound with a pause between *and* and *plans* (C)? With a pause between *feast* and *and* (A and D)? Does the added emphasis of a dash seem appropriate here?

72. The sentence you're being asked to choose carries special weight because it's the last sentence not only of Paragraph 4 but of the entire passage. Think about what a good concluding sentence should do. Ideally, it ties together the ideas that have been discussed and sums up the writer's main point. It shouldn't focus only on one minor element or introduce a new topic.

As you read the choices, think about whether each one provides a logical, accurate summary. Does it mention ideas that have been discussed at some length in the essay? Does it make a statement that is supported by what the writer has said earlier in the passage? Is it an effective way to leave a reader with one final impression of what the writer has been trying to show about fourteenth-century feasts?

73. As you read the choices, consider not only whether the paragraphs cited **mention** food, but whether food is actually the **focus.** Does this essay currently include any descriptions of food? Would those descriptions lead naturally into more details?

Is eating mentioned in Paragraph 1, as A says? Is it the main topic of the paragraph? Is there a phrase or sentence that would flow logically into examples of what people were eating? Is there such a phrase or sentence in Paragraph 3 (C)? Does the main topic of Paragraph 3 lend itself to descriptions of food?

Wine often accompanies a festive meal, but is it the most effective lead-in here to a detailed description of food, as B suggests? Is wine mentioned more as part of the meal—or the entertainment?

In Paragraph 4, the writer tells us that guests left a feast feeling satiated—presumably from all the food they'd just eaten. But is that paragraph, as D proposes, the best place to go into detail about what satiated them? Would those details fit with what's being discussed in the rest of the paragraph?

74. When you think about the best sequence of paragraphs for this essay, you might want to quickly review the essay as a whole, looking for paragraphs that appear to be out of place or transitions that seem confusing. Does the essay have an introduction and a conclusion? Does the writer make smooth transitions from topic to topic and from paragraph to paragraph? Is there any kind of chronological order that should be maintained?

Even if you feel the essay is acceptable as it is, make sure that one of the other choices wouldn't make it even better. Both G and H propose ending the essay with Paragraph 2. Would it make an effective concluding paragraph? Would the rest of the passage have a logical order? If Paragraph 3 followed 4, as H suggests, what would the phrase *even more marvelous* at the beginning of Paragraph 3 refer to?

Would Paragraph 2 provide a good introduction to the essay, as J suggests? When would a reader learn that the events were taking place at a fourteenth-century feast?

75. Put on your editorial hat again and get out your blue pencil. Does this writer get a paycheck—or a rejection slip?

How much of this essay is about food? How many specific foods are mentioned? Does the essay contain anything like a menu or a complete list of food and drink?

The feast described might be "a fourteenth-century one," as A says, but is that fact alone sufficient to make it interesting to readers of a gourmet magazine? (The writer also talks about grafting a squirrel's head onto a peacock's body, but does that necessarily make the essay interesting to taxidermists?)

B, C, and D claim that this essay doesn't fulfill the assignment. Each offers a different reason why. Is the essay unsuccessful because it "describes music and entertainment" (B)? Does it describe **only** music and entertainment? Would those descriptions necessarily be inappropriate as part of an essay on medieval menus? Is the piece unsuccessful because the writer didn't personally live in the fourteenth century and attend one of the feasts (D)? Is the editor likely to find a writer who did? Is the essay's main flaw, from a gourmet reader's point of view, too little specific information about what was served at a feast (C)?

1. What are you given? You're given a formula, in words, for approximating the normal systolic blood pressure of a person. What are you asked to find? You're asked to use the formula to find the difference between a person's normal systolic blood pressure at age 10 and at age 75.

You could write down a formula for the approximated systolic blood pressure (call it N_A) for a person of age A. This would just be a translation of the first sentence from the problem, and it's a fine way to work this problem. Then, using your formula, you can figure out N_{75} and N_{10} and find their difference.

But you might not want to be this formal, since you can probably figure out what the approximation is for a 10-year-old without actually writing down the formula. What do you have to do to the 10 to get the approximate blood pressure? If you can answer that, you've got the formula in your head. So figure out the two blood pressures. Now what?

---

2. **Step 1:** What do you have to do before you can add or subtract fractions with different denominators? Recall:

> To add or subtract fractions with different denominators, first find a common denominator for the fractions; then rewrite each fraction as an equivalent fraction with that common denominator. The least common denominator (LCD) is usually the best choice for a common denominator, since that keeps the numbers as small as possible, which usually makes the numbers easier to work with.

What's the LCD of $\frac{3}{4}$, $\frac{2}{3}$, $\frac{1}{2}$, and $\frac{1}{3}$? It's the least common multiple of 4, 3, and 2. Since 4 is a multiple of 2, the least common multiple of 4 and 2 is 4, and the least common multiple of 4 and 3 is 12. So the least common multiple of 4, 3, and 2 is 12.

Step 2: How do you express $\frac{3}{4}$, $\frac{2}{3}$, $\frac{1}{2}$, and $\frac{1}{3}$ as equivalent fractions, each with a denominator of 12? You multiply each fraction by whatever "name" for 1 will give you 12 in the denominator. (Note: 1 has an infinite number of "names"—$\frac{2}{2}$, $\frac{3}{3}$, $\frac{4}{4}$, and so on.) For $\frac{3}{4}$, the name in this case is $\frac{3}{3}$; for $\frac{2}{3}$ and $\frac{1}{3}$, it's $\frac{4}{4}$. What name for 1 should be multiplied by $\frac{1}{2}$ to give a fraction in twelfths? If all the fractions have denominators of 12, won't that be the answer to the whole question? If you're not **sure,** you'd better keep going.

Step 3: How do you add and subtract fractions with the same denominator? Recall:

> To add or subtract fractions with the same denominator, add or subtract their numerators and place the sum or difference over the common denominator.

Don't forget to reduce your answer to lowest terms, and then use this to answer the question.

You might see a way to simplify your work a bit. Look at the original fractions: $\frac{3}{4}$, $\frac{2}{3}$, $\frac{1}{2}$, and $\frac{1}{3}$. You don't have to add them left to right—additions can be done in any order. Which two of these would be easiest to add first? How can you finish from here?

If you were sure at Step 2 that 12 would be the answer, try the same numbers but add them all instead of subtracting the $\frac{2}{3}$. What's your answer now? Why does it change?

3. This is an "average" problem, so recall:

$$\text{Average} = \frac{\text{sum of values}}{\text{number of values}}$$

In this case, the "values" are Adam's test scores. You're given the number of values, 7, but you're not given the sum of the values. So to find Adam's correct average, you first have to find the sum of his 7 test scores.

Before you do that, think for a second about the sort of answer you should expect. If Adam divided the sum of his 7 test scores by 6 instead of 7, would he end up with a higher average than he should have or a lower one? Or could 84 be correct? Thinking about questions like these helps you understand the problem, but it also would help you on a multiple choice test because you could now eliminate at least 3 of the 5 answer choices.

All right, how can you find the sum of Adam's 7 test scores? By "undoing" what Adam did. The problem says he mistakenly divided the correct sum of his 7 test scores by 6 and came up with an answer of 84. If you let S stand for the unknown sum, then Adam's equation looked like this:

$$\frac{S}{6} = 84$$

Can you solve this equation for S? Of course. Once you've done that, just use it to find the correct average.

4. You're asked to find the measure of an angle, and you're given the measure of another angle. Now you have to find some way to relate these two angle measures. What's the connection between $\angle APD$ and $\angle PCD$?

It's possible that there's extra information given in this problem that you don't need to use. Do you think so? Does the fact that there's a circle seem unnecessary? If you just had a triangle with a 120° angle, could you draw $\overline{AB}$ at two different angles?

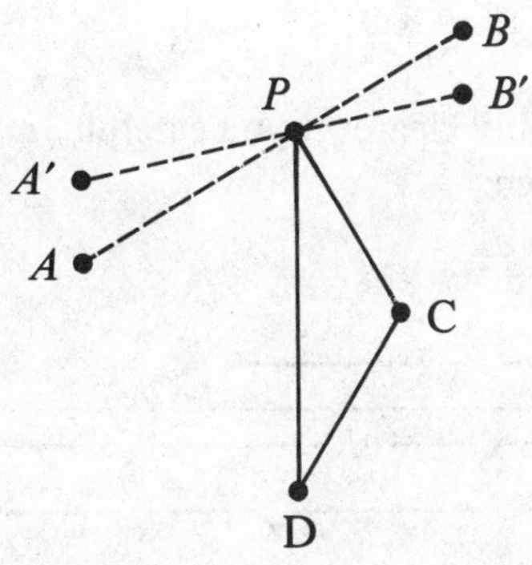

It looks like the circle is important. Is it important that $\overline{AB}$ is **tangent** to the circle? Does it matter that C is the **center** of the circle? Any of these conditions that are important should lead to a mathematical relation that helps "connect" the two angles we're working with.

Is there an "angle connection" having to do with tangents to a circle? Which lines are perpendicular? Now if you could find the measure of $\angle CPD$, you'd have it. You know what the measure of $\angle CPD$ and $\angle CDP$ add up to, right? (All three angle measures in a triangle add to 180°, and you know one of them is 120°). You could hope that each of these was 30°, but couldn't one be 40° and the other 20°? Or 35° and 25°?

You need to find one more relation to finish the connection. What's special about this triangle? Can all triangles be put inside a circle this way? Can you describe the sides of the triangle in circle vocabulary? Arc, chord, radius, diameter, . . . ?

Once you've found that last connection, you have to put it all together. This is getting pretty complicated, isn't it? Here's where having a good way to write down your thoughts can come in handy. Having things written down really helps when they get complicated, and you need to practice this to become good at it.

When you're looking back at your solution, does your answer choice **look** correct? (Does the figure look approximately to scale?) If you'd had to guess from just the figure, which of the answer choices would be reasonable?

5. This question is perfectly straightforward. You do have to know what the $\sqrt{}$ signs means, and you have to do operations in the indicated order, but there is no trick or any "easy" way to do this problem.

So where do people go wrong? What's the difference between the expression given, $\sqrt{16+9}$, and the expression $\sqrt{16}+\sqrt{9}$? The mistake of thinking that these two are equal is one college professors hate, so be careful to understand how square roots work with addition.

6. Here, things are probably clearer if you carefully mark up the figure with the information you're given:

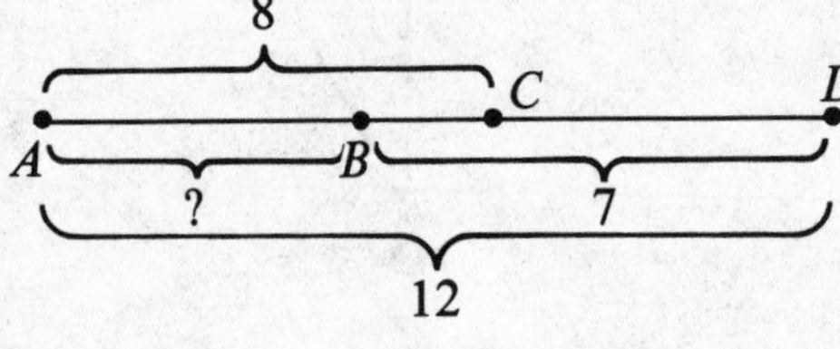

Remember, length is never negative.

Have you seen a problem like this before? The typical way to start is to find the length of the middle piece, $\overline{BC}$. You'd use the relation $AC + BD = AD + BC$. It's important that you understand this relation geometrically; you shouldn't memorize the equation but rather the logic behind the equation. What would happen if you put $\overline{AC}$ end to end with $\overline{BD}$? You'd get a piece as long as $\overline{AD}$ plus some more.

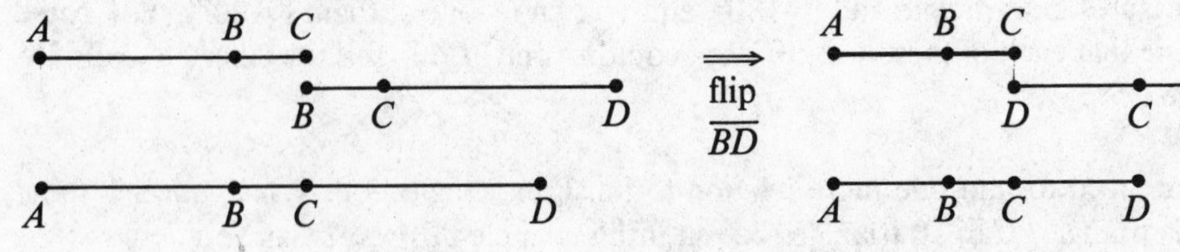

Once you have the length of $\overline{BC}$, can you find the length of $\overline{AB}$?

There's another way to solve this problem. It's much simpler, so you might be disadvantaged, in a sense, by knowing that the "typical" thing to do first is to find the length of $\overline{BC}$. There's extra information given in this problem. What is it? On the test, you wouldn't want to be fooling around trying to find a second way to do a problem you've already done, but here it might be instructive. Which length isn't needed? Will you notice that next time?

7. When two parallel lines are cut by a transversal, eight angles are formed. These angles have names, and if you can remember the names, great. You can just remember this:

> When two parallel lines are cut by a transversal, the eight angles formed can be divided into two groups of four congruent angles. Also, any angle in one group is supplementary to any of the angles in the other group (that is, the two measures add to 180°).

Your eyes will tell you which angles belong to which group if you look at the picture in this problem. Are $\angle x$ and $\angle y$ congruent or supplementary?

---

8. You could solve this problem in more than one way. If you think geometrically, think of absolute value as representing distance. $|a - b|$ represents the distance between a and b. So $|4 - 3|$ is the distance between 4 and 3 and $|3 - 4|$ is the distance between 3 and 4. Aren't these distances the same? If you want to think algebraically, start by performing the operations inside the absolute value bars.

$$|x| = \begin{cases} x \text{ if } x \geq 0 \\ -x \text{ if } x \leq 0 \end{cases}$$

You can think of taking the absolute value as just dropping the minus sign from negative numbers. This isn't quite good enough for working with variables, though.

What's $|-x|$? If $x = 1$, then $|-x| = x$.

But, if $x = -1$, then $|-x| = -x$.

---

9. If you're given a value for x and you're asked to evaluate an expression like $2x^2 - 3x - 4$, what do you do first? You substitute the given value for x in the expression, right? So if $x = -2$, then

$$2x^2 - 3x - 4 = 2(-2)^2 - 3(-2) - 4$$

All right, to complete the evaluation, you have to perform several operations. Which do you do first? Recall:

> When performing a sequence of mathematical operations, follow this order:
>
> (1) Perform any operation within grouping symbols first. (Grouping symbols include parentheses, brackets, absolute value bars, fraction bars, and radicals.)
> (2) Raise any number with an exponent to the designated power.
> (3) Multiply and divide in order from left to right.
> (4) Add and subtract in order from left to right.

In this problem, you have two sets of parentheses. Are there any operations within them to perform? No. So the first thing you have to do is raise –2 to the second power. How do you do that? You multiply –2 by itself. Recall:

> Negative × negative = positive.

So $(-2)(-2) = 4$.

Now, multiply in order from left to right. Recall:

> Positive × positive = positive.
> Positive × negative = negative.

So $2(4) = 8$ and $3(-2) = -6$.

Finally, subtract in order from left to right. Recall:

> To subtract a negative number, add its opposite.

So $-(-6) = +6$. The rest is easy.

10. Start by labeling the figure so that it's a complete picture of everything you're given and everything you're asked to find: $m\angle a = 70°$, $m\angle b = 50°$, $m\angle c = ?$

Now, take a look at the figure. If it's drawn to scale, you can tell just by looking at $\angle c$ that only two answers are reasonable. Is the figure drawn to scale? Well, $\angle b$ looks more like a 45° angle than a 50° angle, but $\angle a$ probably measures 70°. So even though the figure may not be drawn exactly to scale, it's close enough to confirm the conclusion that three answers are unreasonable.

All right, which of the two reasonable answers is correct? If you're careful not to confuse the two transversals, you can use the same principle as used for question 7. Can you write down enough of your work to keep it all straight?

There are several other ways to solve this problem, too. What do you see in the middle of the figure? A triangle, right? Do you notice any relationship between angles *a*, *b*, and *c* and the three interior angles of the triangle? Of course! They form three pairs of vertical angles. What do you know about vertical angles?

> Vertical angles (the nonadjacent, or opposite, angles formed when two lines intersect) are equal in measure.

So two of the interior angles of the triangle measure 70° and 50°, respectively. What well-known theorem from plane geometry can you use to find the measure of the third interior angle?

11. What are you asked to find? You're asked to find a general formula for Stacey's average speed. Many people will automatically recall $D = rt$ (Distance = rate × time). If your memory works that way, fine, but you should still really **understand** this formula—not just how to use it, but also where it came from.

When you're reading, you can't just figure out what all the words mean individually and then put those pieces together. If it were that easy, we could teach computers to read. Real comprehension has to take into account the whole context. Still, the individual words should give you some clues to the meaning, and thinking about the individual words will often help you to see what kind of mathematical relations are appropriate.

You're asked to find kilometers per minute. *Kilometer* is a measure of distance and *minute* is a measure of time. What does *per* mean? It tells you that there's a ratio. Just from looking at the words in the problem, you can deduce that the relation you want will follow the pattern

$$\text{Average speed} = \frac{\text{kilometers}}{\text{minutes}}$$

Now you can replace the words in this pattern with numbers and variables, and you'll have a general formula.

First, the easy part: How many minutes does Stacey run? Is her running time going to change? Replace the word *minutes* with the number of minutes she's going to run.

Now the rest: How many kilometers does Stacey run? She usually runs 10 kilometers, but she wants to increase that by s kilometers. What does the word *increase* tell you? So what's Stacey's new distance? Just replace the word *kilometers* with the expression for distance and you've got an answer. Perhaps you'll have to change its form to make it look like one of the answer choices.

12. You probably understand that you're supposed to find an equation that looks like: $x =$ (something that might have a's but won't have x's), where this solution equation is equivalent to the one you're given in the problem.

What does that mean in terms of numbers? If you had a value for x and a value for a that made the equation $2x + 3 = 2a + 4$ true, then those two values should make your solution equation true, too. Can you find numbers that make the original equation true?

You could, of course, try one of these pairs of numbers in each of the answer choices to see which of those are true. And, if you could eliminate four choices as false, you'd be left with what must be the correct answer. But this strategy would take quite a bit of time, and there's no guarantee you'd be able to eliminate four choices, is there? Still, it's good to keep this method in mind, as this shows the underlying relation of what *solution* really means.

What's left is algebra. You want to manipulate the original equation into a form x = something, and you want to do it in such a way that you always have an equivalent equation at each step of the way. Since there's only one x in the original equation, you really just need to simplify the left side down to x, but you have to keep changing the right side, too, to keep the equations equivalent.

If you can imagine enough in your head to do this all in one step, that's great, but you still might want to write it down as several steps, just to be able to check over your ideas. (Isn't it often true that when you write down your ideas, you find things weren't quite as clear as you'd thought?)

Algebra says that you can do whatever you want to an equation if you do the same thing to both sides and you'll end up with an equivalent equation. (Actually, this is oversimplified, but the idea's a good one to remember.) What would you like to do to the $2x + 3$ to change it?

There are several possibilities, but two would make the "best" choice here, meaning that they'd give the most efficient path toward the solution. What are they?

One general method of getting x by itself in this situation is analogous to undressing. Think of the 2 and the 3 as some clothes that have been put on the x. First someone multiplied the x by 2, **then** added 3. If you had socks and shoes on, how would you take them off? Shoes **first** and then the socks—in the opposite order that you put them on, right? Do the same here. What would you have to do to get rid of the 3? Be sure to do that to both sides. Now get rid of the 2. What's left?

Check by finding a pair of numbers, x and a, that satisfies this equation. They should also satisfy the original.

Could you solve this by dividing both sides by 2 as the first step?

13. If you knew what d was, you could tell in an instant whether 6,d47 was larger than 6,437, right? There are only ten choices for the digit d, of course, namely 0–9. You can probably get pretty close by looking at the hundreds' digit in 6,437. You know from looking here that if $d = 5$ then 6,d47 is greater, since the thousands' digit is the same and the hundreds' digit is greater. Similarly, you also know that if $d = 3$ then 6,d47 will be less than 6,437. So the correct answer must be either 3, 4, or 5. Which is it?

---

14. You could even work this problem in your head: If flood insurance costs \$.40 per \$100 in value, how much does it cost per \$1,000 in value? Since $\$1{,}000 = \$100 \times 10$, and $\$4 = \$.40 \times 10$, this insurance costs \$4 per \$1,000 in value.

Now, how much does it cost for \$40,000 in value? Do the same kind of operation.

If you wanted to write down your work, what mathematical concepts might be appropriate? (There's more than one appropriate concept.)

---

15. When you're stuck on a problem like this, try to figure out what you know. Mark that information on the figure and try to see relations. For example, angle measures in a triangle add to 180°, or vertical angles have the same measure.

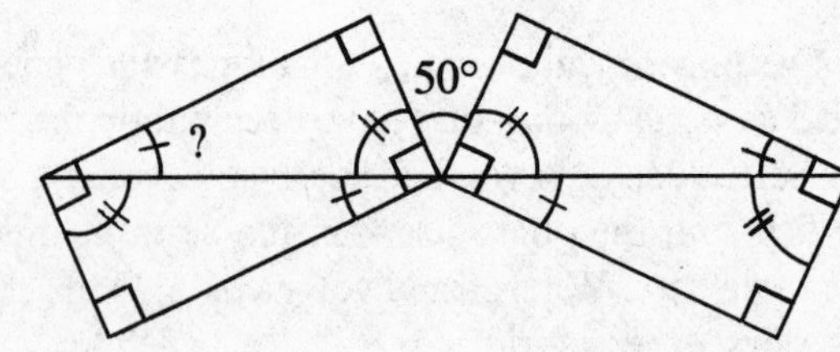

The figure above shows what you get after seeing the symmetry of the figure. Symmetry is a powerful tool, and you should try to capitalize on any symmetry that you see. Now do you see how to work this problem?

If you draw a blank when you're taking the real test, you can at least decide whether the figure is drawn to scale and take your best guess. Make a note in your test booklet so you can come back to the problem if you have time.

---

16. This is a "which of the following" question, and when you're confronted with a "which of the following" math question, always look at the answer choices first—before you try to do anything else. They may not tell you exactly how to proceed, but they should at least tell you how much you have to do. Here it's clear from the answer choices, which are all statements about x, that you're going to have to solve the given inequality for x.

How do you solve an inequality like this? You solve it almost exactly the same way you solve an equality (that is, an equation). The only difference is that if you choose to multiply or divide both sides by a negative number, you have to reverse the direction of the inequality sign (from a "less than" sign to a "greater than" sign, or vice versa).

All right, what should you do first? Well, one subgoal is to get all of the x terms on one side of the inequality and all of the non-x terms on the other side. But the parentheses make it difficult to do this, so first separate the x terms from the non-x terms by multiplying (that is, by using the distributive property); then collect like terms. Now can you see how to proceed?

---

17. This problem, like the last one, is a "which of the following" question, so look at the answer choices first to see if they provide a clue as to how you should proceed. It's probably good to realize that you aren't asked to find **all** of the divisors of 180, just to know which set contains some of those divisors and no extra numbers.

What strategy do you want to try first? Should you write out all the divisors of 180 and then see which set qualifies? How many divisors are there? Do you have a good systematic way of listing all divisors of a number? Some problem might ask for all the divisors, even though this one doesn't, so you might want to know how.

What does it mean for an integer to be a divisor of 180? If you divide 180 by that integer and get an integer quotient, then it's a divisor. So why not just try dividing 180 by 15, then by 30, and so on? If you ever find a number that doesn't work, you can eliminate that set as an answer choice. You could also eliminate any other set that contains that nondivisor. Can you see a good way to keep track of the ones you've tried? Maybe you'll want to circle all the ones you know are divisors and cross out the ones you know aren't divisors. Then you won't have to check numbers twice, such as the 30s in responses A and D.

---

18. People often get confused when they have to subtract negative numbers. Which signs are you supposed to change, and which don't you change? You'll probably notice that more than one of these problems test your use of signs, so you probably want to take the time to understand what a negative number really means and how you can work with negative numbers through addition, subtraction, multiplication, division, and even exponentiation.

Here, you're supposed to subtract one polynomial from another polynomial. Subtracting something is the same as adding its negative. But what is the negative of a polynomial? You can think of it as the original multiplied by –1, or as the original with **all** the signs changed. If you weren't sure, what property could you use to check? You probably know that the negative of 7 is –7. What relation is there? If you add 7 and –7, what do you get? Now think about the negative of $2x^5 - 3x^4 + 3x^2 - 4$.

$$\begin{array}{r} 2x^5 - 3x^4 + 0x^3 + 3x^2 - 4 \\ + \ -2x^5 + 3x^4 - 0x^3 - 3x^2 + 4 \\ \hline 0x^5 + 0x^4 + 0x^3 + 0x^2 + 0 \end{array} \quad \checkmark$$

Finish the problem by adding the first polynomial to the negative of the second.

19. Here's one that's a little different from your usual problem. To solve it, you're going to have to figure out what to do with those $\sqrt[k]{\ }$. How can you deal with them? Would you be more comfortable if it were a square root ($k = 2$)? There are only five values listed in the answer choices. Maybe you want to try out all five values to see which makes the statement true, but there's probably a better way.

One of the general techniques in mathematics (and in many other fields, too) is to simplify by "undoing" the part that causes the complications. Generally, you can undo something by doing its opposite. The opposite of adding 3 is adding –3; the opposite of multiplying by 3 is multiplying by $\frac{1}{3}$. What's the opposite of taking the kth root?

If you had $x = \sqrt{4}$, you could square both sides to eliminate the square root. You'd get $x^2 = (\sqrt{4}\ )^2 = 4$. But it's not a square root, it's a kth root. What would you have to do to both sides?

The right side is a product. You're going to have to take this product to a power, so how do you do that? Try $(yz)^3$. Taking something to a power is just multiplying it by itself that many times so $(yz)^3 = yz\ yz\ yz = yyyzzz = y^3z^3$.

If you just tried to memorize $(yz)^n = y^nz^n$, you might do okay, but you'll probably remember it longer and understand it better if you see the reason why it works.

Are these enough tools to help you solve the problem?

You could also change the roots to fractional powers. That may give a more elegant-looking solution, but it's all really the same.

20. What are you asked to find? You're asked to find the equation for the width of a floor. What are you given? You're given four pieces of information:

1. The floor is rectangular.
2. The area of the floor is 165 square feet.
3. The length of the floor is 4 feet longer than the width.
4. The floor is w feet wide.

To find an equation, you first have to find a mathematical relationship. Do you know of a relationship between some of the quantities discussed in this problem: the length, width, and area of a rectangle? Once you've thought of a relation, write it down. Then try to find ways to express that relation where the only variable is w. When you do that, you'll have an answer. Choose the answer choice that's equivalent to your answer.

21. This looks like a pretty simple geometric figure. For most of the simple geometric figures there's a formula for computing area, right? What's the formula for this one? You might not even care—there are ways to do this without having to know the specialized formula. You can divide this shape into even simpler shapes and use some formulas that are more basic.

But having the correct formula at your fingertips might help you get the answer to this problem a little faster than an alternate technique. One system for remembering the right formula is to:

1. Remember the formulas as associated with a specific geometric figure (for example, remember that the area of a triangle is $A = \frac{1}{2}bh$).
2. Classify the figures you need to know the area of. Then the name of the figure can be your cue to remembering the right formula.

What kind of figure is this?

Name	Reminder	Area
Quadrilateral	four-sided figure	No specific formula
Parallelogram	opposite sides parallel	$A = bh$
Rectangle	4 right angles	$A = bh$
Triangle	three-sided figure	$A = \frac{1}{2}bh$
Circle	(no reminder needed)	$A = \pi r^2$
Trapezoid	2 of the 4 sides are parallel	$A = \frac{1}{2}(b_1 + b_2)h$
Rhombus	parallelogram with 4 congruent sides	$A = bh$ or $A = \frac{1}{2}d_1d_2$
Square	rectangle with 4 congruent sides	$A = s^2$

If you're going to use this method, you'll have to be able to recall a formula by name. You probably don't have to sit down and memorize all these formulas—you probably know a bunch of them already.

For this problem, you could get by with knowing just the formula for a rectangle, though you'd have to be very creative. Knowing the formulas for a trapezoid, triangle, and circle would get you a long way. Can you see how to divide this figure into trapezoids, triangles, and/or circles so that you can find the area of each piece?

22. This problem would be a lot simpler if you knew what N was, so why not pretend that you do? Can you think of a "nice" number that will give you a remainder of 3 when you divide it by 7? Well, if you divide 7 by 7, you'll get no remainder, so if you divide $7 + 3 = 10$ by 7, you'll get a remainder of 3, right? So pretend that N is 10. Now, if N is 10, what's $(N + 5)$? And if you divide $(N + 5)$ by 7, what's your remainder?

Do you think that the remainder is always going to be the same, no matter which such N you pick? You could try a few more. What's another N that leaves a remainder of 3 when divided by 7?

You still don't **know** that the remainder will be the same for any N, but the answer choices tell you this information. If there was some N that gave a different remainder, then one of the answer choices would have to be something like:

- There is more than one possible remainder.

  or

- Cannot be determined from the given information.

So you're safe in testing just one case here.

---

23. This problem asks you to find the average of three binomials. How do you find the average of three binomials? The same way you find the average of any three numbers. You add them together and divide the sum by 3.

9

24. This problem gives you some information about a group of 50 people that has been divided in two different ways—by sex (some are men and some are women) and by voter registration (some are registered and some aren't). One simple way to organize this information so that you can see how it's all related is to make a table or a Venn diagram:

	Registered	Unregistered	Total
Men			
Women			
Total			

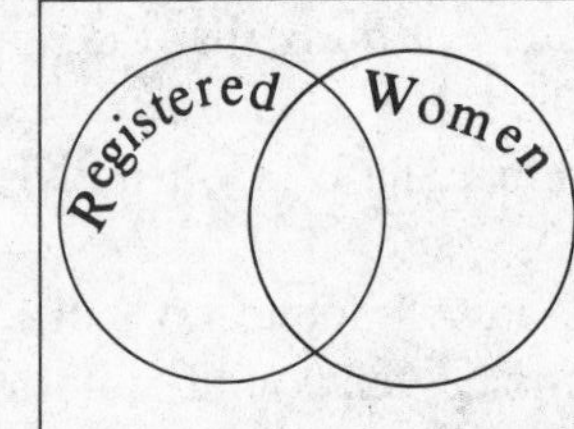

Now, see if you can fit the information into these formats. There were 50 people in this survey. Where does the 50 go? What about the 38 registered to vote? The 5 women not registered to vote? The 30 men surveyed?

Can you figure out the missing quantities? Does that let you answer the question?

25. What are you given? You're given an equation in two variables, x and c. What are you asked to find? You're asked to find the value of c. Do the answer choices tell you anything about that value? Yes. They tell you that the answer is a constant, not some algebraic expression with the variable x in it. And what does that tell you? It tells you that if you solve the equation for c, somehow the x's will all disappear.

Now, if you want to solve the equation for c, what's your goal? Your goal is to get all the terms with c in them on one side of the equation and all the terms with x in them on the other side of the equation. Which terms have c in them? Well, you can pick out the c term on the right side, but before you can pick out the c terms on the left, you first have to multiply the two binomials on that side. How do you multiply two binomials?

To multiply two binomials, you can use the FOIL method:

1. **F** stands for First, so multiply the first terms of the two binomials: $(3x)(2x) = 6x^2$.
2. **O** stands for Outer, so multiply the outer terms of the two binomials: $(3x)(c) = 3xc$.
3. **I** stands for Inner, so multiply the inner terms of the two binomials: $(-7)(2x) = -14x$.
4. **L** stands for Last, so multiply the last terms of the two binomials: $(-7)(c) = -7c$.

Now what?

26. Can you find the number of solutions without actually finding the solutions and counting? You probably could, but it might be trickier than actually solving. You'll have to decide. There are some equations where it's easier to tell the number of real solutions than to actually find them—for example, a quadratic equation. You can tell the number of real solutions to a quadratic equation by looking at the discriminant; that is easier, in general, than actually solving the equation.

Maybe you can think about related equations. How many solutions does $|y| = 9$ have? How about $2x + 5 = -9$? If you choose to solve the equation and count, you should probably have a routine method for solving absolute value equations. Here are a couple, but you might have your own. Having a routine for solving these basic problems will let you use your thinking time for the more important things.

Geometric: The distance between $2x$ and -5 is 9 units. Try using a number line to find where $2x$ would have to be.

Algebraic: If $|y| = a$, then $y = a$ or $-y = a$. Find out what y and a are and substitute.

---

27. For this, you have to know what $\sin\theta$ means. If you don't, you may as well take a random guess and go on to the next problem. You might mark this one to come back to, in case you remember more as you progress on the test. Maybe one of the later problems will help remind you.

If you do remember how to find $\sin\theta$ in a right triangle, you still might be having some trouble because the figure doesn't look like the one you remember. Try looking at the figure from different directions. You won't always be given a triangle in standard orientation.

Why can you eliminate responses C, D, and E? What do you know about the range of values for $\sin\theta$?

---

28. What strategy do you think will work here? That depends upon how you think of "slope." If you know lots of ways of thinking of slope, you'll have several different strategies, and you can pick the one that looks easiest.

$\text{slope} = \frac{\text{rise}}{\text{run}}$	You can graph the line and get the slope from the graph.
$\text{slope} = \frac{y_2 - y_1}{x_2 - x_1}$	You can find two points on the line and then use the formula.
slope = m in the form $y = mx + b$	You can put the equation into slope-intercept form and pick out m.

---

29. Did you draw a picture of this situation? If not, draw it here.

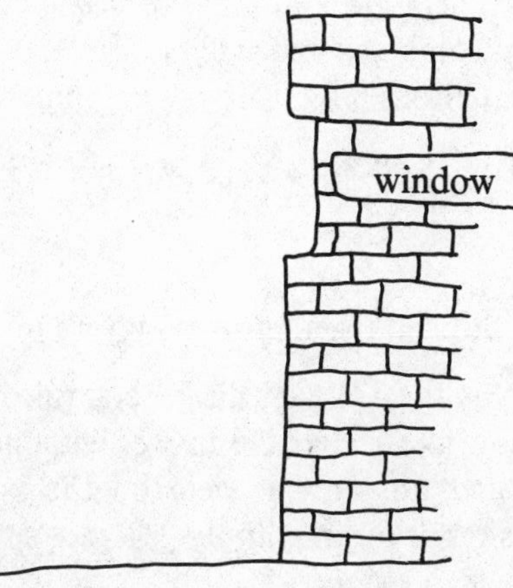

What kind of geometric figure is present here? It's not just a triangle, it's a special kind of triangle. You know the lengths of two of the sides, so what's the length of the third side?

30. This problem looks messy, but there's really nothing too complicated about it—you just have to be careful to do things in steps, not all at once. How can you divide this into steps? There are a number of ways. One guiding principle in simplifying expressions is to combine **similar** things. Here, one set of similar things is the x's. (The exponents just tell you how many x's are multiplied together.) Another set of similar things is the y's. If you view $\frac{2x^5y^{-2}}{x^2y^{-3}}$ as $2\left(\frac{x^5}{x^2}\right)\left(\frac{y^{-2}}{y^{-3}}\right)$, you can work on each piece separately.

Think of $\frac{x^5}{x^2}$ as five x's multiplied together over two x's multiplied together on the bottom. How can you simplify that? What's the general rule involving the exponents that would have told you how to calculate the answer without having had to imagine how many were on top and how many were on the bottom and how many cancelled? You can use this result to simplify the y's.

Problems with exponents, like this one, are generally pretty straightforward, but lots of people have a tough time. The mistakes come mainly from jumping to conclusions without really thinking about what you're doing. For example, $x^3 + x^2 = x^5$. Your brain's so good at matching patterns that it sees a 3 and a 2 with a plus sign and immediately knows that $3 + 2 = 5$. That's great, but you have to be careful. The problem wasn't simply $3 + 2$—there were some x's in there, too. What if $x = 1$? Then $x^3 = 1$, $x^2 = 1$, and $x^5 = 1$. Does $1 + 1 = 1$? You should know the rules of exponents really well or make sure to check out all the conclusions you come up with. If you have an organized way to write down your work, you'll have an easier time checking things out.

31. Probably the quickest way to solve this problem is to use the formula for finding the distance between two points in a plane. (That distance is the length of the line segment connecting the two points.) But let's suppose that you don't remember that formula. Can you solve the problem anyway? Certainly. Here's how.

If it helps, start by sketching a coordinate plane, plotting the two points, and connecting them:

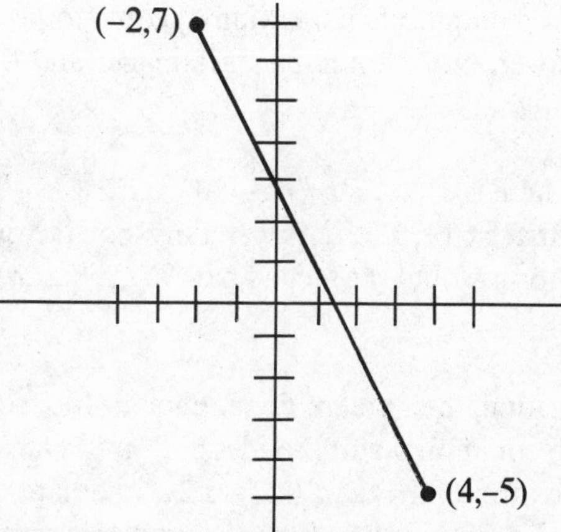

Now, this sketch will help you estimate the distance, but it won't allow you to figure it out exactly. You have to see that sketching in two additional line segments will give a right triangle with the line segment you've already drawn as the hypotenuse.

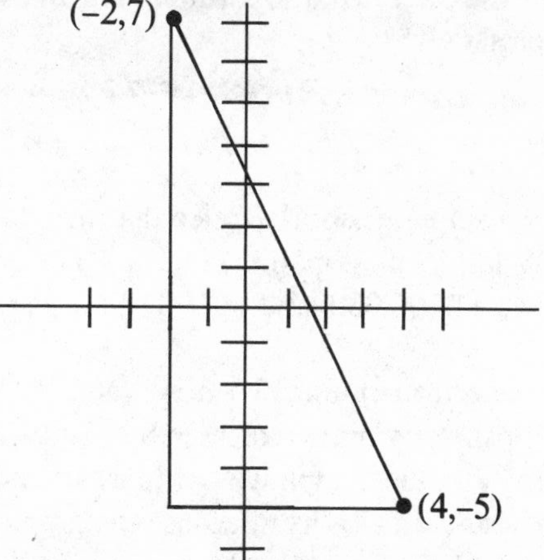

You know a formula that will allow you to figure out the length of the hypotenuse of a right triangle. That's the Pythagorean theorem. What you've done here is to derive the distance formula. It's really the same mathematical relationship as the Pythagorean theorem.

32. To find the complete factorization of this polynomial, you have to find other polynomials that, when multiplied together, will give $6a + a^2 - 5a^3$ **and** those other polynomial factors should not be factorable. It's like putting a number into prime factored form.

When you're putting a number into prime factored form, you start checking with the easy prime numbers, like 2 and 3, before you worry about the bigger ones. When dealing with polynomials, look for the simplest ones first—the ones with only one term. That is, look for common factors. Many people forget this step. They should still get the right answer, but the numbers are bigger and they'll have to do more complex tasks.

The common factor here is a. So, $6a + a^2 - 5a^3 = a(6 + a - 5a^2)$. Is this a complete factorization? The first factor, the a, is certainly not factorable. What about the $(6 + a - 5a^2)$? What form would the factors have? $(\_\_ + \_\_a)(\_\_ - \_\_a)$ where you fill in the numbers.

If you find a factorization, then you're done. Each of the factors will be linear, and linear factors with no common factor (besides ± 1) aren't factorable. If you can't find a factorization of the form $(\_\_ + \_\_a)(\_\_ - \_\_a)$, perhaps $(6 + a - 5a^2)$ is already completely factored. You can deduce from the answer choices that this isn't the case. And, from the form of the answers, you should have found a factorization. Go back and check your work. Maybe you missed a possibility.

In general, to show whether or not a quadratic expression such as $(6 + a - 5a^2)$ is factorable, you could use the quadratic formula, but from the answer choices, you can see that's not necessary here.

33. This is really a slope question. Notice that there are two points marked on the graph. What do these points tell you? They tell you that in 1983 the company's earnings were $100,000, and in 1987 they were $200,000.

What can you conclude from these two observations? Well, obviously you can conclude that the company's earnings increased by $100,000 over that 4-year period. Can you also conclude that the company's earnings are increasing at a constant rate of $100,000 every 4 years? Yes. Why? Because the graph is a straight line, and the slope of a straight line is the same everywhere along the line.

Now, if the company's earnings are increasing steadily at a rate of $100,000 every 4 years, at what rate are they increasing each year? And, if the company earned $200,000 in 1987, what are its expected earnings for 1990?

34. If *ABCD* is a square, what do you know about it? You know that all its sides are the same length, 6 units. What else do you know about it? You know that all four of its interior angles are right angles.

If $\angle ADC$ is a right angle and points *C*, *D*, and *E* all lie on the same straight line (which is what *collinear* means), what do you know about $\angle ADE$? It's a right angle, too. So what can you conclude about ΔADE? It's a 45°-45°-90° triangle, also known as an isosceles right triangle.

Do you remember the pattern that tells you how the sides of a 45°-45°-90° triangle are related in length? If so, you can use this to find out how long $\overline{EA}$ is. If not, first recall that an isosceles triangle has two congruent sides. Then use the Pythagorean theorem.

35. Here's another triangle that you should recognize—the 30°-60°-90° triangle. If you remember the pattern that tells you how the sides of this "nice" triangle are related, you know how long $\overline{TV}$ is. (You might also remember this pattern through sines and cosines; both are ways of expressing the same triangle relationships.)

36. Just from the form of this equation, you might be able to tell which of the choices applies. If you're not sure, you could always graph the equation and see. Your graph needn't be very accurate or complete—just enough to allow you to decide which of the five choices it is.

To graph this equation, start with a table of values. Choose "nice" values of x.

x	$y = x^2 - 12$
0	−12
1	−11
2	−8
3	−3
4	+4
5	+13

What about negative values of x? Do you see the symmetry? Now plot these points. Which choice is correct? (Do you remember what an ellipse looks like? A parabola?)

It's quite a bit of work to draw the graph. How else could you approach this? It's possible to look at the form of the equation—how many variables, their powers, the coefficients, etc.—to tell what the graph will be. Unless you've had to use that information lately, you may not remember all the conditions. Still, perhaps you can see a relation between this equation and some other equation that you're familiar with.

$y = x^2 - 12$ is closely related to $y = x^2$. What's the relation? What shape is the graph of $y = x^2$?

37. Draw a picture of the triangle:

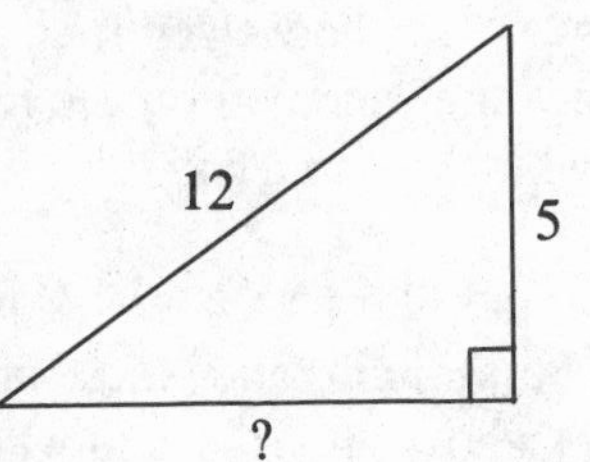

Now be careful! If you learned the 5-12-13 right triangle pattern, don't fall into the trap of thinking this triangle fits the pattern. It doesn't. Can you see why? The hypotenuse of the 5-12-13 right triangle is 13; the hypotenuse of this triangle is 12.

The 5-12-13 pattern is of some help, though. As you remember, it's a "nice" pattern because the sides of the triangle are all whole numbers. If there were a 5-*n*-12 pattern, you'd probably know it, so chances are the length of the missing side of this triangle is **not** a whole number—which means that choice B is probably the correct answer. Use the Pythagorean theorem to see how long the side is.

38. To find the area of a triangle, what do you need to know? You need to know the length of both the base and the height. Are you given either of these lengths? No. So you have to figure them out from the coordinates of the three points in the figure.

The height is easy. Its endpoints are both on the *y*-axis, so its length is just the vertical distance from O to A. The base is a little more difficult. You can see that the endpoints of the base are both on the *x*-axis, which means that the *y*-coordinate of B, like the *y*-coordinate of O, is zero. So the length of the base is just the difference between the *x*-coordinates of O and B. Since B is on the *x*-axis, one of its coordinates is zero. Does B have coordinates of the form $(0,k)$ or $(k,0)$?

Since you have two points on $\overline{AB}$, you ought to be able to find its equation. Then, from the equation, you could find the point where it crosses the *x*-axis. That's B.

You could also use slopes. The slope of the line through A and B is the same as that through $(0,2)$ and $(2,1)$. Using this relation, you'll get an equation that you can solve for k.

39. How do you find the solutions to a quadratic equation? Well, you can try to guess what they are, but unless you're a very good guesser, you're better off using one of the three standard methods: factoring, completing the square, or using the quadratic formula. Since the trinomial on the left side of this equation is fairly simple, factoring seems the best tool to try first.

How do you factor a trinomial like $x^2 - x - 6$? You look for two numbers whose sum is -1 (the coefficient of the x term) and whose product is -6 (the constant term). Do you know two numbers whose sum is -1 and whose product is -6? Certainly, -3 and 2. So one factor of $x^2 - x - 6$ is $(x - 3)$ and the other factor is $(x + 2)$. Check this to be sure.

Now, you know that $(x - 3)(x + 2) = x^2 - x - 6$ and, from the equation in the problem, you know that $x^2 - x - 6 = 0$. So by applying the transitive property of equality, you can conclude that $(x - 3)(x + 2) = 0$.

How does this conclusion help? Well, you know from the zero property of multiplication that if the product of two numbers is zero, at least one of the numbers must be zero. So $x - 3 = 0$ or $x + 2 = 0$ (or both). Just solve these two very simple equations for x, and you've got the two solutions to the equation. The set that includes both of these solutions is the answer to the question.

40. This question is described in words and is abstract, but if you simplify it, it's not difficult. First of all, what are you asked to find? You're asked to find an algebraic expression that represents the total income from sales on one day at a shoe store. What are you given? You're given the price per pair of shoes at the store and the number of pairs sold by each of four clerks and the manager on the day in question.

All right, let's try to simplify the problem. First let's suppose that only one person was working, instead of five, and that each pair of shoes in the store cost 10 dollars, instead of P dollars. If it was a slow day and that person sold only 2 pairs of shoes all day long, how would you figure out the store's total income for the day? You'd multiply \$10 by 2 and get \$20, right?

Now let's suppose that two people were working. If it was another slow day, and one sold only 2 pairs of shoes and the other sold only 3, how would you figure out the store's total income for the day? You'd add 2 and 3, multiply the sum by \$10, and get \$50, right?

So to find the store's total income on any given day, what do you have to do? You have to add up all the pairs sold by all the people working at the store and multiply the sum by the price per pair.

Let's get back to the problem now. There were five people working at the store on the day in question. How many pairs of shoes did each one sell? Al sold w, Betty sold x, Charles sold y, Dawn sold z, and Ellen sold "as many pairs as Al and Betty combined." How many pairs did Ellen sell?

Just add these five "numbers" up and multiply the sum by P, the price per pair. That's your answer. (You may have to simplify to see which of the answer choices matches your answer.)

41. You're looking for the slope and y-intercept of a line. Though there are lots of ways to do this, putting the equation into slope-intercept form and reading off the appropriate coefficients is probably the most efficient method. Do you remember the slope-intercept form? If not, you'll have to use another method to get the answer.

42. You're asked to find the average weight of 25 students, and you're given the average weight of the 10 male students and the average weight of the 15 female students.

Now, before you do any computing, what do you expect the average weight to be? Do you expect it to be as low as 105, which is one of the answer choices? No, it can't possibly be 105—or 145, for that matter. It has to be somewhere between these two numbers. Should it be closer to 105 or 145? It should be closer to 105, since 15 of the 25 students weigh an average of 105, while only 10 weigh an average of 145. And what does this mean? It means that the average weight must be less than 125, which is midway between 105 and 145.

Notice that you've narrowed the possible answers down to two. As you remember, to figure out the average weight of 25 people, you have to add up all their weights and divide that sum by 25. How can you add up their weights if you don't know what they are? You can't actually add them up; however, you **can** find the sum of the weights of the males and the sum of the weights of the females the same way you found the sum of Adam's test scores for problem 3. Then all you have to do is add these two sums together and you've got the sum of the weights of all 25 students.

If the average weight of the 10 males is 145, what's the sum of their weights? Think about how averages are figured. And then finish the problem.

43. Slope again. So, you should put the equation into slope-intercept form and read off the coefficient of *x*, right? Since there is no equation, you'll have to think of another characterization of slope.

Does it matter which point you call (x_1,y_1) or (x_2,y_2)? No. Just be consistent. Don't call one (x_1,y_2) and the other one (x_2,y_1). If you do, you'll change the sign of the slope, and the sign of the slope is very important. It tells you whether the line is rising or falling. (This mistake would also cause you to get the wrong answer.)

A line with a positive slope rises from left to right.

A line with a negative slope falls from left to right.

From the picture, you can see that the slope of the line in this problem is positive. And when you're calculating the slope, remember: The change in *y* goes on top. If you put the change in *x* on top, you'll get a wrong answer that is one of the answer choices.

44. This problem is loaded with information that you don't need, so before you begin, ask yourself some questions.

First, what are you asked to find? You're asked to find the cosine of $\angle D$. What do you know about $\angle D$?

Now can you do it?

---

45. You've probably talked about solving quadratic inequalities in your math classes; almost all algebra books cover this topic. Basically, you get a zero onto the right of the inequality, factor, and use the properties you know about when a product is positive (that is, greater than zero). You'll end up with a statement with *and* and *or* that you can simplify. It's not hard—you just have to write down your work and proceed step by step.

But it does get a bit messy. If you don't have a good system for writing down the solution steps, you might want to practice (before the real test). What could you do if you didn't think you could solve this inequality this way?

What would happen if you found a value of x less than zero where $x^2 > x$ was false? You've eliminated three answer choices—A, C, and E. Can you find such a value of x?

Look at the answer choices and try to find a value of x that would eliminate one of them. If you choose the values carefully, this can be a pretty efficient method for eliminating some answers on a multiple-choice test. You might not always be able to eliminate all four of the incorrect choices, as you could if you remembered how to solve a quadratic inequality, but approaching the problem this way will allow you to show more of what you really know.

---

46. This question looks a little like the last one, but it's not that close. You're asked to do something different. Here, drawing a graph is a great way to start. You may have to do some algebra later, but first use the graph to plan what needs to be done.

---

47. By now you know that there are at least two possible ways to try when you want to find the length of one side of a right triangle if you know the lengths of the other two sides. One way is to recognize a pattern. The other way is to use the Pythagorean theorem.

Does the triangle in this question fit any of the patterns you recognize? Well, it certainly doesn't fit the 3-4-5, the 5-12-13, or the 8-15-17 pattern. And since the two legs are different lengths, it doesn't fit the 45°-45°-90° pattern, either. Does it fit the 30°-60°-90° triangle pattern? No. Since one side is twice as long as another, it looks like it might, but it doesn't. In the 30°-60°-90° triangle, it's the hypotenuse that's twice as long as the shortest side. In this triangle, it's the second leg that's twice as long.

So try the Pythagorean theorem.

48. From the form of the answer choices, you know that $x^2 + 5kx + 4k^2$ will factor. And, if you think about how the factors would have to look to multiply together and give this result, you'll see that the product has to look like $(x + \_k)(x + \_k)$, where you have to find the numbers to fill in the blanks. You also know that the product of the numbers in the blanks is 4. So try out your possibilities, solve the equation, and check your answers.

What other ways could you do this? You could check all ten roots to see which worked. This plan would probably get you the right answer if you did the substitutions correctly. Take care not to make mistakes, as these are fairly complex substitutions.

You could also think about the "reverse" problem. If you knew the roots, what would the equation look like? Could you reconstruct one equation for each of the five answer choices and see which one gives $x^2 + 5kx + 4k^2$?

All three of these methods take about the same amount of work. The first method is the only one that doesn't rely too heavily on having this kind of a multiple-choice question. What would you have done if the question had asked for the difference of the roots?

49. What are you asked to find? You're asked to find the length of the hypotenuse of the triangle. You're given the area of a right triangle and the length of one leg.

Is there a mathematical relation involving any two of these: area, leg, hypotenuse? All three? You might start by drawing a rough sketch of the triangle, so that you can "see" how to use the information you're given to find the length of the hypotenuse of the triangle:

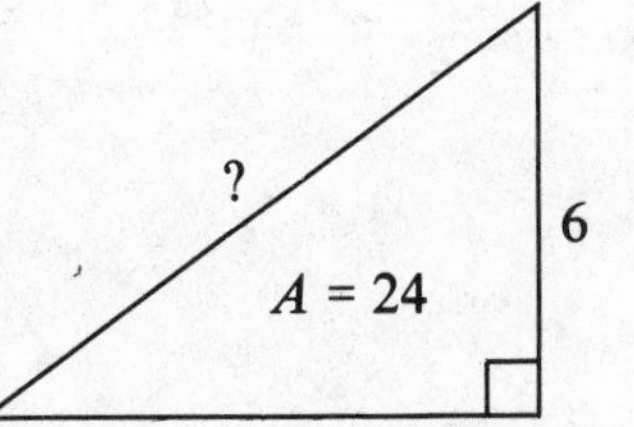

You might think about what quantities are **missing** from this problem. This is a pretty simple picture. The problem talked about two sides and the area of a triangle. What's left? Think about any relations involving this new quantity and you can probably find a couple of relations that connect what you're given to what you want to know.

Can you explain what you did? That's a good test of whether you really understand what you did.

50. If the figure is a square, what is the line from home plate to second base? It's the diagonal of the square. Go ahead and draw the diagonal in.

Now what do you have? Since the angles at first and third are right angles, and since the diagonal bisects the angles at home and second, you have two 45°-45°-90° triangles, right? What do you know about the sides of a 45°-45°-90° triangle?

51. One of the answer choices to this problem is the slope of the line through (1,–1) and (4,5). But that's not what you're asked to find. Maybe finding this slope would be helpful, but don't start calculating until you've thought about it. Is there a relation between the slope of a line and the slope of a perpendicular line? Do you know what that relation is? Only if you answer "yes" to both of those questions will it do you any good to calculate the slope of the line through (1,–1) and (4,5). Well, maybe it would let you eliminate an answer if you're **sure** that a line can't have the same slope as a line perpendicular to it.

So, how else might you approach this? How about a graph?

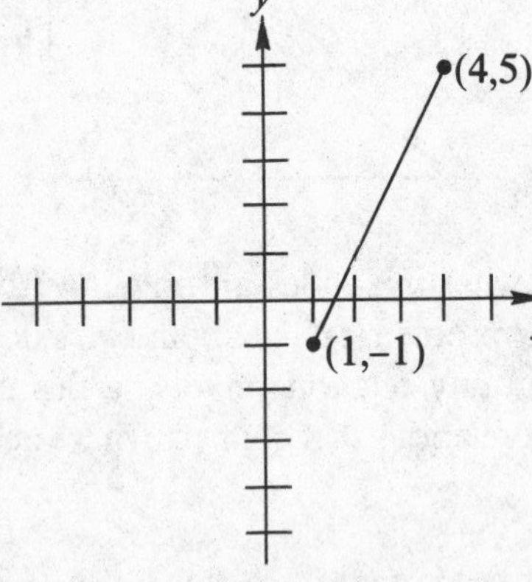

Now draw on a perpendicular, maybe one through (1,–1), just so you know a point on the line. Do you see anything yet? Is the slope of this perpendicular line going to be positive or negative? Just with this information you can eliminate some answers.

Try drawing in grid lines and looking for a connection between the slopes (that is, rise and run) of the two lines. If you're still stuck and your graph is accurate enough, you might be able to guess correctly from among the two or three choices left.

52. You'll have to remember what $\cos\theta$ means in a right triangle (or else $\sec\theta$, which is what the problem is really asking for). Maybe the answer choices will give you a little clue. Do you have to know the length of the third side of the triangle? Do you have to know the area of the triangle?

53. Have you noticed that the problems seem to be getting a little more complex? Not many people can look at this one and know immediately what to do. When you find a problem where you're not sure what to do, you can give your problem-solving method a real test. Have you seen any problems like this before?

Did you label the 10- and 30-unit distances on the figure? Did you mark the right angle that's at A? Did you mark the length you're trying to find? What things **could** you find if you saw that they'd be helpful? Don't calculate them until you decide on your strategy.

What strategies do you know for working with triangles? Trigonometry, the Pythagorean theorem, similar triangles, the formula for area—do any of these seem appropriate here? If you're not sure, **try** some of these tools to see where they'll get you. Keep thinking about what you're trying to accomplish—if you think you're "going off on a tangent," stop and rethink your solution. Can you make an educated guess from the figure? This one isn't drawn to scale.

54. After the last problem, this one looks easy. The similarity is all set up and waiting for you. Perhaps this is hard for some people because there's a little extra information given. Did you spot that? Just set up your proportions carefully for **corresponding** sides and you should be able to get this one pretty quickly. Remember to check your answer. Should x be more than 3, or less?

55. Would you have any trouble answering this question if you knew what *x*, *b*, and *y* were? No. So just pretend that you do and think about what happens.

Suppose that you go to the store one day and pay 20¢ for 2 apples. If both are the same price, how do you figure out the cost of each apple? You divide 20¢ by 2, of course, and you get 10¢. So your arithmetic looks like this:

$$\frac{20¢}{2} = 10¢$$

Now suppose that you want to go back to the store the next day and buy 3 apples, but you're not sure if you have enough money. How do you figure out how much the 3 apples will cost altogether? You multiply the cost of each apple by 3, of course, and you get 30¢. Today's arithmetic looks like this: 3(10¢) = 30¢. But you can also write today's cost using yesterday's information as:

$$3\left(\frac{20¢}{2}\right) = 30¢$$

The left side is the pattern you need for finding a general formula for the cost of *y* apples. Can you see how to use it? Look for the letter in the problem that corresponds to each number in your pattern.

After you have your own general formula, think about it. Does it make sense? What part of it represents the price per apple? Then check a few examples. Try your 20¢-for-2-apples example in the general formula. What if you wanted to buy 10 apples that were 5 for $1?

56. If you haven't had much trig, you might be tempted to skip this question. Don't. It's really quite simple.

The key to understanding it is the first sentence. What does the first sentence say? It says that the sine curve in the figure repeats itself every 16 seconds. Why is this information important? It's important because it tells you that if you started at 0 and drew a trillion cycles of the curve, every complete 16-second cycle would look **exactly** like the first one.

All right, now let's take a closer look at the problem. What are you asked to find? You're asked to find the height of the curve at 46 seconds. What do you have to do first? You have to figure out where the complete 16-second cycle that includes 46 seconds begins and ends. Then you have to find the point on the first 16-second cycle that corresponds to the 46-second point.

The only real trigonometry in this question is the idea that sine curves repeat themselves.

57. When is an algebraic fraction, otherwise known as a rational expression, undefined?

A rational expression is undefined when its denominator is zero.

Does this make sense? Of course. A rational expression, like any other fraction, is just one way of writing a division problem. Imagine trying to divide a number into zero parts. Or, equivalently, how many parts of size zero would it take to be equal to your number? Even if your number is zero, there's no single right answer. So, yes, it makes sense that a rational expression should be undefined when its denominator is zero.

How do you figure out when the denominator of a rational expression is zero? You set the denominator equal to zero and solve the resulting equation. You've solved equations like this before. There were even some on this test. A quadratic equation usually has two solutions. Once you've found the solutions, find which one's an answer choice.

You could also try substitution to see which answer choice makes the denominator zero, but that technique won't even work for all multiple-choice questions, let alone a problem where you don't have answer choices.

58. You're asked here to do some algebraic simplifying on this fraction. What ways do you use to simplify a fraction when it's just numbers? Division or cancelling factors. Do either of these work here?

If all else fails, you could try substituting in some numbers for x. Be careful to pick numbers less than -3, as the problem says. Perhaps you can eliminate some solutions that way.

59. If you remember the standard form for the equation of an ellipse, this problem's pretty straightforward. You still have to think about what a "major axis of length 10 on the y-axis" means, but you can probably figure that out even if you don't remember the specific equation. Does the format of the answer choices give you a reminder of the equation?

Can you draw a graph of this ellipse? That might be a big help. It will also make you think about major axis, intercepts, and center.

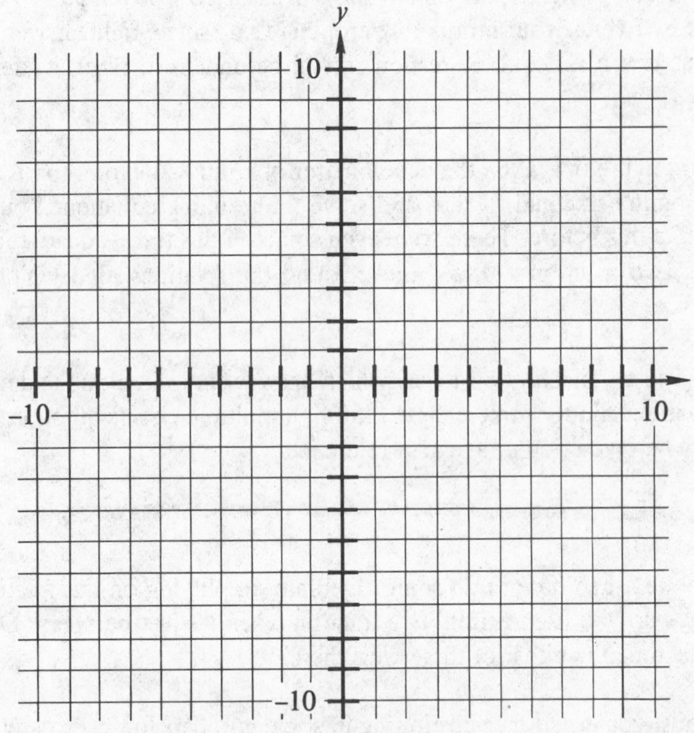

From this graph, you probably know the coordinates of at least four points on the graph. Can you use these coordinates to eliminate any of the answer choices? It's a time-consuming strategy, but one that might help if you don't know the standard equation for an ellipse.

60. What do the equations of two lines have to do with the coordinates of point A? If you don't see that right away, maybe a diagram will help. You could actually plot the two lines, but that would take a bit of time. How much can you get from a general picture?

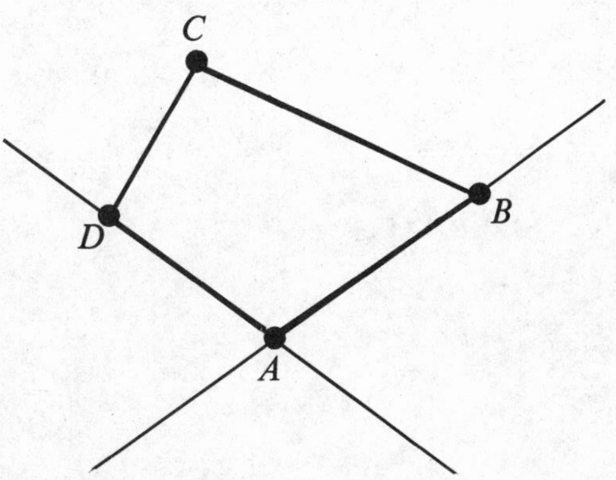

What's special about point A and the two lines?

You could probably graph these two lines more precisely and then you might even be able to take a guess at the coordinates of A, but some of the answer choices are pretty close together. You might not be able to tell them apart on your graph.

What methods do you know for finding the point of intersection exactly?

1. The item asks for "the first visual observation." Where does the passage first tell when researchers saw raindrops? The fourth paragraph (lines 23–28) discusses measurement of raindrops. How did researchers discover that there was variation in the raindrops' dimensions? How were the raindrops stopped in time? What clue did this variation give to the stages of raindrops? Remember that you are looking for the "first visual observation that raindrops oscillate." For each response, find the paragraph that relates: A (lines 51–59), B (lines 23–28), C (lines 66–72), D (lines 73–80). Which of these actually mentions "visual evidence"? Which occurs first?

2. If you do not know the meaning of the word *turbulence,* the sentence containing the word does not help to define it. However, what words in the preceding sentence (lines 51–53) offer clues to help you arrive at the right answer? What do *air streams* and *wind tunnel* signal?

The movement of air is indicated, and that's one of the three factors mentioned that influence the shape of a water drop (lines 4–7). Do responses F and G—which refer to the actions of water drops, not air movement—make sense when substituted for *turbulence* in the sentence?

Of the remaining choices, J refers specifically to air movement, while H can be applied to the movement of the air **or** the water drop. What is the difference between the **spiraling motion** of wind and the **fluctuation** of wind?

You might find it helpful to think of the **spiraling motion** of the air in a tornado (continuous movement around a pole or axis) and the **fluctuations** of the gusts of wind that hit you on a blustery day. Which of these fits more closely with the sense of *turbulence* in the passage?

3. Note that the question deals with a five-millimeter raindrop and with the variables of light rain versus heavy rain and frequency of oscillation. We're told that a five-millimeter raindrop will be less likely to constantly oscillate in light rain than in heavy rain. Why? What causes raindrops to oscillate? Beard says it is important for which sizes of raindrops to be together at the same time (lines 38–42)? In heavy rainfall, when you have big raindrops (5 millimeter) and drizzle drops (less than 0.5 millimeter), what happens to the raindrops? "If you've got small drops around," what do they do (lines 45–47)? What did Johnson show theoretically in heavy rain showers? So if collisions between raindrops happen frequently in a heavy rain, what happens in a light rain?

Is there any part of the passage that discusses the breaking apart of raindrops (A)? Does the passage discuss the relative speed of the breakup? What is the relationship between size and oscillation (C, D)? Do five-millimeter drops oscillate?

4. Be sure the statement you pick is the one that best represents the last paragraph. A statement might be true without necessarily expressing that paragraph's main idea. Also, take your time. Don't hastily pick an option simply because it repeats a phrase word-for-word from the passage.

Take another look at the last paragraph. How would **you** summarize it? Do you see a statement among the answer choices that sounds like your summary?

According to the paragraph, what is known about drizzle drops? Do they come out of a cloud base (F)? What does the paragraph say about how they come out? Is it true that drizzle drops must collide before they rupture (G)? Is that the focus of the last paragraph?

What connection is drawn between drizzle drops and **all** raindrop oscillation (H)? Do drizzle drops **cause** all oscillation? Is **causing** the same as being "the key to the source of the oscillations" (line 91)?

Does the paragraph focus on how drizzle drops might be created and their possible impact on scientists' knowledge of oscillation (J)? Can you find references to the **creation** of drizzle drops? Look for terms that connote creation; you may have to do a little "translating."

5. Oscillation is, of course, a key concept in understanding what this passage is all about. Even if you're familiar with the word *oscillate,* try not to bring that outside knowledge to the question. The word is used here in a sense that may differ slightly from the definition you have in mind. Focus on the information you learn about oscillation from the passage.

What does the passage as a whole discuss about the nature of raindrops? You might skim the text for references to oscillation. Look for places where *oscillate* might be paraphrased. Think about whether each response comes close to being synonymous with *oscillate* in this context, or whether it mentions something that's only **related** to oscillation.

Try picking a sentence that contains the word *oscillate* or *oscillation.* Substitute each of the optional answers in turn. Which one sounds most logical? For example, try "there is evidence that raindrops can take on other shapes and that they actually **oscillate** from one shape to another . . . " (lines 15–17). Does it make sense to substitute collide (A), accelerate (B), change shape (C), or fall (D) for *oscillate*?

---

6. Find the section of the passage that discusses wind tunnel studies, then the section on shaft experiments. Do they differ in:

- the effects each one studies?
- the characteristics of the raindrops?
- the procedures involved?

As you survey each response, consider whether any information in the passage supports it. Try to avoid speculating on what the differences might be; look for **evidence** before you make your choice.

Does any information suggest how a variety of drop sizes might be studied more easily in a shaft than in a wind tunnel (F)? Is it possible to study drops of various size in only one of the experiments, or both? Is there evidence that larger drops would be studied in a shaft (H)? Are there characteristics of the shaft experiment that imply it would be more conducive than the wind tunnel to measuring and photographing oscillations (J)?

Look at the description of the shaft compared to the wind tunnel. How would the drops move through each one? Would they be suspended in the wind tunnel but moving downward through the shaft (G)?

---

7. Where do you see references to the relation between raindrops' size and oscillation? Between size and how raindrops behave when they collide? Can you find information about what happens when a large raindrop collides with a tiny one?

This is an instance where a little "translation" could be called for on your part. The question refers to a raindrop that's "too tiny," but you might think about words that mean the same as *tiny.* Also, keep in mind words that mean *collide.*

An alternative is to try going through the responses, then scanning the passage for references to the ideas they mention. Where in the passage can you locate a discussion of:

- how drops coalesce (A)?
- what causes drops to break up (B)?
- how collisions are related to energy (C)?
- the effects of rapid oscillation (D)?

8. Where can you find a comparison between the way large and small raindrops fall? Are there sections of the passage devoted to the characteristics of large drops? Of small drops?

As you scan the passage, pay particular attention to the concepts mentioned in the possible answers. Do you see references to falling slowly (G) or rapidly (H)? What do terms like *velocity* and *speed* (lines 31–32) suggest?

Where in the passage is the collision of small drops (F) discussed? Is there a statement about the **chances** of collision? What kind of raindrops are needed in order for collisions to occur? Where is the path of small raindrops mentioned (J)? What kind of motion is described in terms of being vertical?

Look for clear, unambiguous observations that contrast large and small raindrops with respect to their speed, direction, and chances of collision.

9. You need to think about two characteristics of raindrops: the direction in which they oscillate (vertical, horizontal, or transverse) and how fast they oscillate (20, 100, or 200 cycles per second).

According to the passage, what kind of drops tend to oscillate slowly? More rapidly? What kind of drops are associated with horizontal oscillations? With vertical? With transverse?

First, it would probably be helpful to determine whether a seven-millimeter droplet would be considered large or small. Don't panic if you can't find a reference to droplets of that exact size. Concentrate on the sizes that **are** mentioned and on what you're told about their characteristics. How would you label a seven-millimeter drop in light of the information you have about other specific sizes?

Naturally, all raindrops look relatively small to us. But to a scientist, how small is a small raindrop? You might try looking for another word for small raindrops that's often used in this passage. Look for mention of a specific dimension. At what point is a drop considered to be **large**?

Once you decide whether a seven-millimeter drop is classified as large or small, look for characteristics associated with that size. This involves synthesizing information from several different sections of the passage, so read carefully. Make sure **both** parts of the response you pick up are applicable.

10. Take a moment to think about the difference between a hypothesis and a fact. Which one is an opinion or a theory? Which one has been proven to be true? You might also think about what you've read in the passage in terms of what scientists **know** about raindrops, what they **theorize,** and what they're still trying to find out.

As you study each possible answer, you need to decide whether it's supported by evidence in the passage or whether it's a matter of speculation.

When you're trying to classify G as fact or hypothesis, don't be thrown when you notice that eight-millimeter droplets aren't mentioned in the passage. Remember the process you went through to answer question 9. Base your decision on what you know about the sizes that **are** specifically cited.

F and H involve drizzle drops. Keep in mind that drizzle drops are sometimes referred to as small drops. Skim the passage for references to what's been learned about these drops and what's merely been theorized about them.

What do scientists know about how drops oscillate (J)?

Passage II

The focus in this passage from a story by Flannery O'Connor is on the characters and their relationships with one another. The three women have interacted every day for the past four years. How is each woman described? What positive qualities does she have and what does she lack? What is the relationship among Mrs. Hopewell, Joy, and Mrs. Freeman? When and how did this relationship begin? How do they interact with one another? How would you describe their life together?

11. Think about the sequence of events in the passage. The morning's events are presented in chronological order (by time). If you do not recall when Mrs. Freeman regularly arrives at the Hopewell residence, see if the information is stated directly in the passage. Find the place where Mrs. Freeman arrives at the back door. Her arrival coincides with another event that is mentioned earlier in the paragraph. When does she arrive in relation to the other event? Is Joy asleep (A) or is she in the bathroom (D)? Who gets up first at the Hopewells'? At what time? What does she do after she arises? Does Mrs. Freeman arrive at seven o'clock (B) or while Mrs. Hopewell lights the heaters (C)? Which event begins just before and continues while Mrs. Freeman arrives? Where is Joy when Mrs. Freeman arrives?

12. In order to answer this question, try to determine if the information is stated in the passage or if you need to figure out the answer on your own (**based** on the information). A discussion of how Mrs. Hopewell happened to hire the Freemans begins in line 47. Keep reading. Find the place where it tells **why** she hired them. Is that reason the same as one of the responses?

For G, do you know from the passage that Mr. Freeman would not ask for higher wages? What information in the passage relates to H, that Mrs. Hopewell had known the Freemans for years? When did she first meet them? Did she hire them because she knew them? For J, does the man who provides the reference say that Mrs. Freeman is nosy? What does he mean? Is that a positive reason for Mrs. Hopewell to hire her?

13. Here you are asked to characterize Mr. and Mrs. Freeman in terms of what the reference says about them. You may want to look back at the passage to find the comments made by the man "whose name they had given as a reference" (lines 52–61). How does the reference get along with Mr. and Mrs. Freeman? Why? Notice that the wording of the responses is not identical to that of the passage. Which response best conveys the reference's impression of the Freemans?

In A, what does it mean to be "tolerable"? **Is** Mr. Freeman tolerable? What is a "busybody"? Could you describe Mrs. Freeman as "an unbearable busybody"? The word *although* signals a contrast. Is there a contrast between Mr. and Mrs. Freeman that is supported by the passage? For B, is Mr. Freeman "friendly"? Is Mrs. Freeman "unsociable"? Can you find evidence in the passage?

What is Mr. Freeman's job (C)? Does Mrs. Freeman allow the dust to settle? Find the place where the reference says, "If she don't get there before the dust settles, you can bet she's dead, that's all" (lines 56–58). What is the reference saying about Mrs. Freeman? "Before the dust settles" is an expression that means what? Does it mean that Mrs. Freeman is a poor housekeeper? Does she do nothing? Does it mean that because she is "into everything," she is always around when things happen? The reference says that if she isn't there, "you can bet she's dead, that's all." Does this exaggeration mean that the only reason she would not be involved would be because she had died? Is this statement consistent with his view that she is a person consumed with knowing all about other people? Now go back to the original question. Response C asks you to decide if Mrs. Freeman "allowed the dust to settle." The last part of D states that Mr. Freeman "could become a good farmer." What do you know already about Mr. Freeman? What do the words *could become* suggest about this response?

14. The basis for this item is the author's description of Joy. Notice that O'Connor uses few words, yet conveys a vivid impression of the large blonde girl with an artificial leg. Which words in the passage refer to Joy's emotions? How does she express her feelings? What is "constant outrage" (line 81)? Why does she always feel angry and resentful? Why has she "obliterated" (wiped off) any facial expression (lines 81–82)? Keep in mind your impression of Joy while you think about her name. What does *joy* mean? Is this a word you would use to describe the girl in this passage? Is it a suitable (J) or an apt or fitting (G) name for her? For F, does either the word *joy* or the name *Joy* suggest the quality of exerting influence or power? Consider H, "ironic." Based on the passage, does Joy express joy, happiness, or delight? How might she behave if her personality **did** reflect her name? What is the term for the idea that her name doesn't fit her personality and, in fact, is the opposite? When something (in this case, a character's personality) is the opposite of what we expect, what do we call this literary technique?

15. The word *because* is a cue to look for the **reason** that Joy stares "to the side of" Mrs. Hopewell. *Most likely* indicates that the reason will not be stated directly in the passage. Try to picture Joy, with no expression on her face, staring "to the side of" Mrs. Hopewell. What do you know about Joy? What has made her face expressionless? If Joy has "the look of someone who has **achieved** blindness by an **act of will** and **means** to keep it," is her blindness physical (A)? What does the phrase "her eyes icy blue" (line 83) reveal? Are Joy's eyes warm and expressive? What aspect of blindness does the author want to convey? What is an "act of will"? Which words emphasize her determination? What is the effect when Joy stares "a little to the side" and appears to be blind? Does she invite communication with other people? What does she achieve by not looking at her mother? Is there something Joy does not want to see or deal with?

Where are Mrs. Hopewell and Joy when Mrs. Hopewell makes her statements (B)? Who is Mrs. Hopewell talking to? Does anything in the passage indicate that Mrs. Freeman's presence causes Joy to stare to the side of her mother (C)? Consider, for D, the communication between Mrs. Hopewell and her daughter, who stares with icy blue eyes and does not look directly at her mother. If Mrs. Hopewell talks but Joy tries not to see her, what might Joy be avoiding?

16. The question asks for the main point of the first paragraph, which deals with Mrs. Freeman's character traits. How would you describe Mrs. Freeman? In the first paragraph, the author uses a metaphor to portray Mrs. Freeman. (A metaphor uses one thing—in this case, a truck—in place of another—here, Mrs. Freeman—to suggest a comparison between them.) In the same way that a truck has three gears, so Mrs. Freeman has three facial expressions: neutral, forward, and reverse. Notice that these expressions also state the way she relates to other people. What is Mrs. Freeman's "forward expression"? Here the author directly compares (using a simile) some quality of Mrs. Freeman's expression as being **like** a truck (lines 4–5). What is that quality? Which is her most prevalent way of dealing with people—this unswerving aggression or her "reverse expression"? Why is it "not often necessary for [Mrs. Freeman] to retract a statement" (lines 8–9)? How does Mrs. Freeman react when she does have to change something she said? What is it that Mrs. Hopewell has given up on? Even if Mrs. Hopewell talks and talks, how does Mrs. Freeman respond? If Mrs. Freeman does say something, she either changes the subject or says what?

For F, does Mrs. Freeman lose her temper? Instead, how *does* she respond? Does Mrs. Freeman really drive a truck (G)? For H, does the first paragraph tell whether or not Mrs. Freeman is sociable? Does she **pretend** she is sociable? Is "refusing to admit herself wrong" one of Mrs. Freeman's character traits (J)? Is there evidence in the passage to support this response?

17. This item requires that you distinguish between fact and opinion.

> Remember that a fact can be tested; it states what exists or what happens. An opinion often is a judgment or belief that describes a quality about someone or something, using language that is not neutral.

Which response is a fact—simply a report of a happening in the passage?

In A, the word *justifies* signals what? Could someone say that her disability does **not** justify her attitude? Can it be demonstrated from the passage that her physical disability does or does not justify her attitude? For B, the passage states that there are dusty bottles on Mrs. Hopewell's top kitchen shelf (lines 21–22), so this part of the sentence is fact. Do the dusty bottles indicate that she is a "lazy housekeeper"? If your answer is yes, is this fact or your opinion? Is there a word in B that indicates a judgment about Mrs. Hopewell? In C, which words indicate disapproval of Mrs. Hopewell's sayings? Does C, then, state an opinion? For D, can you find a place in the passage where Mrs. Freeman makes daily remarks about her daughter's vomiting? Are there words in D that indicate a judgment or belief, or does this response restate a sentence in the passage?

18. In order to choose the best response, you need to determine Mrs. Hopewell's opinion of Mrs. Freeman. Then look for a response that either is similar in meaning to one or more sentences in the passage or is a general idea of Mrs. Hopewell's opinion. Mrs. Hopewell's views of Mrs. Freeman are expressed in several places in the passage. Which idea is most like one of the responses? Note that you are asked if a single sentence (I, II, or III) is accurate, or whether sentences I **and** III both describe Mrs. Hopewell's opinion of Mrs. Freeman.

Response F deals with Mrs. Freeman's bad qualities. Can you find a place in the passage that corresponds? How does Mrs. Hopewell use other people's bad qualities? [If you think that I is the best answer, remember that you need to consider III also, so you can choose between F (I only) and J (I and III).] For G (II only), is Mrs. Freeman willing to compromise? What do you know about her from the first paragraph? Does she ever "swerve" or retract a statement or admit herself wrong? For III, does Mrs. Hopewell believe that because Mrs. Freeman is an employee, she is not entitled to have opinions of her own? In the passage, Mrs. Hopewell's favorite and most important saying is about other people's opinions. What is Mrs. Hopewell's saying? Is there evidence in the passage to indicate that this saying does not apply to Mrs. Freeman, too? [If you think that III is the best answer, remember that you need to consider I also, so you can choose between H (III only) and J (I **and** III.)]

19. For this question, you need to consider what the three women have in common. The word *suggests* is a clue that you must make an inference, based on the passage. *All* indicates that the task is to decide if each response is an accurate statement about **all three** women. If the response is not correct for one of the women, then you can rule out that response.

For A, are Mrs. Freeman, Mrs. Hopewell, and Joy Hopewell all satisfied with their lives? Are there words in the passage that tell you Joy is not content? For B, do you have clues that Joy may not admire her mother? Would you describe the relationship between Mrs. Freeman and Mrs. Hopewell as based on "enormous mutual admiration" or something else? What does "to grate on one another's nerves" mean (C)? What places in the passage describe how Mrs. Freeman, Mrs. Hopewell, and Joy interact? What do you know about each woman that might make her difficult to be around? Are there suggestions that the women irritate one another? For D, how do you know, from the first paragraph, that Mrs. Freeman **is** opinionated? How would you describe Mrs. Hopewell, based on her sayings? What do you know about Joy that would cause you to think that she is opinionated? So are all three women unopinionated?

20. Consider the three women's attitudes toward life. The word *respectively* indicates that you need to pay attention to the order of the women's names and the order of the descriptive words. The first word in each response (*dogmatic, flexible, relentless,* and *fatalistic*) applies to Mrs. Freeman, the second word (*practical, pitiless, unconcerned,* and *ruthless*) to Mrs. Hopewell, and the third word (*outraged, stoic, charitable,* and *carefree*) to Joy. In the best response, all three words will be accurate.

If you do not know the meaning of each descriptive word, try to find a word in the response that you know is accurate for one of the women, and consider this response as a possible best answer. Another strategy is to rule out an entire response if you can find a word that is **not** accurate for one of the women, because all three words in the response **must** be accurate.

For example, for F, assume you do not know what *dogmatic* means. Go on and decide if you would describe Mrs. Hopewell as "practical." Think about her "sayings" and how she deals with hiring the Freemans. Is Joy "outraged"? We know that this word is used to describe her in the passage. So even if you're not sure of *dogmatic,* F is a good possibility. Now consider G. Perhaps you do not know the word *stoic* for Joy. Still, could you say that Mrs. Freeman is "flexible" (changeable)? We know she is unswerving. So this knowledge rules out G, because all three words must be accurate and Mrs. Freeman is **not** flexible. In H, is Mrs. Freeman "relentless"? To "relent" means to back down, so "relentless" means she doesn't back down. Yes, she is relentless—she is unswerving and won't admit she's wrong. So H **could** be another possibility. But is Mrs. Hopewell "unconcerned"? In the passage, she appears concerned about Mrs. Freeman's daughter, for example, and about turning people's faults to advantages. Maybe you believe that there's not enough evidence in the passage, though. Now think about whether you could describe Joy as "charitable" (sympathetic and generous). We know she is expressionless and does not want to communicate with other people, so she does not appear to be "charitable." So even though Mrs. Freeman is "relentless" and you have a question about Mrs. Hopewell, Joy is definitely **not** "charitable"; thus H is not the best answer. Remember that F is still a possibility, and go on to J. Is Mrs. Freeman "fatalistic" (always seeing the worst)? Is Mrs. Hopewell "ruthless" (pitiless) and Joy "carefree" (lighthearted)? We can say, based on the passage, that Mrs. Hopewell is **not** ruthless and Joy is **not** carefree, so this rules out J. We have eliminated responses G, H, and J. Go back to F and see if you can describe Mrs. Freeman as "dogmatic" (stubborn). We already have decided that, yes, Mrs. Hopewell is practical and Joy is outraged.

21. Find the place in the passage that discusses Ira Aldridge. Watch for words (not identical to those in the question) that tell about his "professional success as an actor in America." Notice that "exercising his mature power" (line 88) means about the same as "professional success as an actor" and America is the "land of his birth." What prevented Aldridge's success? What are racial barriers?

Response A is a possibility because you might infer that black characters appeared infrequently in American plays and this might be because of a racial barrier. But the idea that black characters actually appeared **frequently** in American plays could be inferred from the third paragraph of the passage. Also consider whether A offers the reason that Aldridge did not achieve success in America. Did the racial barriers exist for **characters** or **actors**? For B, does the passage state that Thomas D. Rice (and others) were better actors than Aldridge? Is there evidence in the passage that Aldridge's Shakespearean roles were not popular in America (C)? In D, do the words "prejudices against black performers" mean the same as "racial barriers" (against actors)?

22. Find the place in the passage where Yankee roles are discussed. Notice that the words you'll need to find in the passage to determine the best answer are different from those in the question. Which words in the passage mean "the **popularity** of Yankee roles"? Which words mean that the Yankee roles influenced development?

For F, does the passage discuss the idea that Yankee roles influenced tragedies—in particular, realism in acting? Were there Yankee tragedies? For G, did Yankee roles lead to the development of melodramas? Did they imitate successful European melodramas? For H, is there evidence in the passage that the Yankee character influenced the roles for black or other minority performers? Does the passage establish a tie or tradition between the Yankee characters and minority performers? For J, did the Yankee character (role) help to develop an American style of comedy? What does the last sentence in the second paragraph state about the Yankee? Does "the vogue for the Yankee" mean the same as "the popularity of Yankee roles"? Does "most important for its role in establishing" mean the same as "influenced the development of"? Is a "native American comedy" the same as a "particularly American style of comedy"?

23. In this question, the word *implies* signals that the answer is not stated directly in the passage. Be sure to read the entire sentence, and, in this case, at least the two sentences that follow it. Also ask yourself why "Jim Crow" is enclosed in quotation marks.

For A, is "Jim Crow" a partner of Thomas D. Rice or does Rice do his own song and dance? For B, the "faithful black servant" is discussed in the passage as a type in American drama from its beginning. Would a servant be likely to do a song and dance? (If so, response B might be a possibility.) Notice, for C, that the "comic caricature" has been a native type in American drama from the beginning. What does *caricature* refer to later in the passage? How can you decide between responses B and C? Does the sentence that begins "Despite such caricatures" (line 59) help refer you to C? For D, what actors besides Rice are mentioned? Is "Jim Crow" one of them?

24. Begin by locating the paragraph in the passage that tells about the company of black actors (the fourth paragraph). (Note that the name of the company—the African Company—is not mentioned until the following paragraph.) Find the lines that tell why the company may have "closed down." The word *unfortunately* signals bad luck. What happened? What are "white rowdies"? Also, notice the next words: "perhaps because of these difficulties." What has caused the company to fade from surviving records? Which response is most like "plagued by white rowdies"?

F includes the word *whites,* which also appears in the passage. What is harassment? For G, when did Aldridge make his debut in London? Was it before or after the end of the acting company? It might be possible to infer that if there was discrimination against the black company, the actors might not be able to find suitable plays (H) or suitable theater buildings (J). But read the fourth paragraph carefully. Is either of these ideas suggested by the passage?

25. The wording of this question indicates that you need to look for the opposite (antonym) of *naive.* Line 27 supplies a context for the word *naive:* "The Yankee was the symbol of the American common man, simple and naive on the surface." The passage adds that a simple, common man was one "despising pretense and sham." The question asks you to decide what he is **not**—in other words, the **opposite** of *naive.*

Is the best answer A (eccentric: odd, a deviation from the norm) or B (sophisticated: worldly wise)? Or is the opposite of *naive* C (likable) or D (serious)?

---

26. What is the focus of the last three paragraphs of the passage? What is indirectly stated about blacks in American drama? Which response agrees with information in the passage?

Note the distinction between **characters** (F) and **performers** (G). Does the passage imply that characters were stereotyped? If so, would these characters have been more popular if they had been more individual and original? For G, were the roles stereotyped? Does the passage suggest that this quality affected the performers' popularity? For H, note that European audiences are mentioned in the discussion of Aldridge. How did European audiences respond to him? Compare this reaction to the way Aldridge was received by American audiences. For J, what does the passage state about the black as an American native type? If the black is an American native type, can you say that European audiences were not receptive to plays involving American native types? Notice that response J is almost the opposite of H. Which response do you choose as the best answer?

---

27. For this item, consider what the third paragraph is about and decide, based on the passage, which statement can be made. Note certain key words in each of the responses.

For A, in this paragraph are the characters **realistic** (true to life)? For B, are the characters **stereotypical**? (A stereotype is an oversimplified idea—one that fails to recognize individual differences.) What black characters appeared in American drama? Were they types—mostly all alike? Were they popular? For C, does the paragraph discuss the idea that Rice supported racial equality and showed this view through his depiction of black characters? Note that D deals with the depiction or representation of black characters. Can you say, based on the third paragraph, that American drama has **never** offered accurate depictions? Does it make sense to say that American drama has never depicted black **characters** accurately? Instead, do the characters depict black people?

---

28. This question asks you to compare the portrayal of the Yankee by Hill and Hackett; you must also be sure you don't confuse the two actors. Find the paragraph that describes both Hackett and Hill. Who is discussed first? What words in the passage then describe Hill's Yankee? Now read the question carefully. You have information about Hill, and in order to answer the question, you need to compare Hackett to him. Key words are *more* and *less.* If Hill was _____, then Hackett was _____.

For F, who was more sympathetic, Hill or Hackett? (Remember that for the response, you are describing **Hackett's** Yankee.) For G, was Hackett or Hill more sentimental? For H, was Hackett's Yankee more important than Hill's? Which actor was considered "the best of the Yankee specialists" (lines 34–35)? For J, is either Hill or Hackett discussed in terms of a "generalized" Yankee type?

---

29. Locate the four play titles. What does the passage say about each? Also read lines 3–5. What does it mean to "present" the Indians? What is a "strong role"? Is the **Indian** the playwright (A); the actor (B); or the character (D)? Do the plays support Indian concerns or causes (C)?

---

30. The term *American vogue* refers to the sentence in line 9, "The **vogue** for Indian dramas. . . ." Note that this was a time when Indian dramas were popular: more than fifty Indian plays were performed. Find the place in the passage where *Po-ca-hon-tas* is discussed. (Don't confuse this with *Pocahontas!*) What is a burlesque? If you don't know, there are some words in the sentence that may help you to find the best answer anyway: "dealt a serious blow" and "tradition abandoned." What happened in 1855 to Indian plays? After 1870, what became of the "noble savage" tradition? Now consider the responses.

For F, the last part of the statement is accurate, but even if you say that *Po-ca-hon-tas* introduced a new kind of Indian character (a burlesque or humorous exaggeration of the old character), can you say this play was a driving force (major impetus) for new Indian plays? Instead, what happened to Indian drama? For G, did *Po-ca-hon-tas* set the standard for Indian drama? Was the play the best example of the type (Indian drama)? What happened to this type of drama as a result of the burlesque? For H, did *Po-ca-hon-tas* satirize (ridicule) Indian plays? Thus, did it "encourage a decline in interest"? Keep this response as a possibility as you read the next response. The first part of J is accurate—interest was decreased—but did *Po-ca-hon-tas* **follow** the romantic tradition of the "noble savage"? What happened to this tradition of the "noble savage" after *Po-ca-hon-tas* was performed? Which response is **completely** true based on the passage?

---

31. For this question, you'll want to find the place in the passage where women's suffrage (the right to vote) is discussed. What happened during the war to make the demand for women's suffrage more urgent and justified? What action by women of all classes gave force to the idea that they should vote?

For A, how did women contribute to the war effort? Did this justify their demand for suffrage? Response B deals with the motto "to make the world safe for democracy." Was this motto written into the peace treaty? Does this slogan justify the demand for women's suffrage? Suffrage may be considered a democratic reform (C). Are views of the Conservatives discussed in connection with suffrage in this part of the passage? In D, were the tsar and William II the chief opponents of women's suffrage? Was William II deposed?

---

32. This item requires careful reading and a caution that more than one of the options may be partially correct. Find the phrase "this ideological and moralistic view" in the first paragraph. The key word *this* indicates that the view is defined in the preceding sentence. What is "the notion" discussed in the first sentence of the passage? The word *and* in that sentence suggests there is more than one part to the idea.

Is option I—"the enemy was evil"—part of the "notion" of the first sentence? Is this the only part of the answer? For option II, what is said about propaganda? What was "nurtured by propaganda"? Did all governments use propaganda or only the enemy? For option III, the word *and* in the passage signals another part to the idea that "the enemy was evil." Does option III restate this additional part? The item asks which belief(s) are referred to by the phrase "this ideological and moralistic view." Which options are part of the view or "notion" stated in the passage? Which response includes the entire idea?

33. What is a hollow sound? How can a slogan have a hollow sound? In the question, the word *because* signals that you are looking for a reason. Find the slogan in the first paragraph. Why does this slogan ring empty or not true until 1917? Notice that to understand the answer, you need to line up the countries that fought on each side in the war and to figure out what *authoritarian* means.

Russia was one of the Allies and was fighting against Germany. What kind of a government did Russia have? Why was it not democratic? What happened in 1917? After that what kind of a government did Russia have? Why was the slogan more accurate after the overthrow of the tsar? Which response best expresses these ideas?

For A, did Russia have an authoritarian government until 1917? Did the fact that Russia had this kind of government cause the slogan to be lacking in truth? What happened in Russia in 1917? Did it change Russia's government to be more democratic and thus support the slogan? For B, was the war a struggle for national self-determination? When (in relation to 1917) was this idea declared? We know (for C) that several nations were in coalition against Germany. The date of 1917 is significant for two events; is one of them that the coalition against Germany ended in 1917? For D, the passage states that the war was declared to be a struggle for a new world order based "on the principles of democracy." But what was the reason that the slogan had a "hollow sound"? Why could every nation **not** be said to be based on the principles of democracy?

34. This item offers an idea about World War I and asks for facts from the passage to support the idea. Notice that each response is a quotation found in the passage. Your job is to decide which statement backs up the view that the war was a "total war because it required the efforts of the entire nation, not just the military, to fight it." Key words are "the efforts of the entire **nation.**" Which response deals with the idea that everyone in the country aided in the war effort?

F does contain the word *complete* in regard to the "complete defeat of the enemy." What part of the war does this response stress? Does this response relate to the efforts of the entire nation? G mentions which two groups? Are they the entire nation? For H, what did men and women of all classes do? What image is conveyed by the words "men and women of all classes"? J is a quotation about "a struggle for a new world order." Does this statement stress effort by a nation? Does it explain who was involved in the struggle?

35. Consider William II, leader of Germany. You are asked to make a general statement about him based on facts in the passage. Several of the responses sound correct because they refer to ideas and groups of people discussed in the passage. But don't lose sight of your objective, the **reason** that William II did not exercise dictatorial control. Keep in mind that the author doesn't state the idea directly. What is said in the second paragraph about William II's leadership during peacetime? (Note the word *even* for emphasis.) Was his leadership stronger during the war?

Now consider the responses. For A, could you say that, in essence, William II was a weak leader? How did he behave in peacetime? Was he different in war? Is A a good possibility? For B, what did the Social Democrats do in the war? Were they part of the government? Were they the reason that William II did not lead during the war? The passage states that the Conservative bureaucracy ruled Germany during the war (C). But was the conservative nature of the bureaucracy **the reason** that William II was not a strong leader? In D, does the passage reinforce the statement that "a majority of people never wholeheartedly supported the war"? Is this the reason that William II did not exercise dictatorial control?

36. "War causes social change." You are asked to find evidence in the passage to support this theory. First, what is "social change"? How does the passage support this idea that differences in society result from war? Which response is evidence or proof of the idea? As you read each response, ask yourself two questions: Can this idea be found in the passage? If so, does this idea provide evidence to support the theory that "war causes social change"?

For F, does the passage assert that World War I was a major factor in women's gaining the right to vote? The last half of the first paragraph discusses suffrage for women. If the passage does assert the relationship between the war and women's gaining the right to vote, is this sentence, then, evidence for the theory that war causes social change? Did the war cause women to gain the right to vote? Is women's suffrage an example of social change? Has war made society different? For G, does the passage demonstrate that the war "reestablished a balance of power and restored international collaboration"? Instead, what does the second sentence indicate happened? So is this idea found in the passage? If not, can it be used as evidence for the theory? The overthrow of the Russian tsar (H) is discussed in the first paragraph. The question is whether or not the war **caused** the overthrow of the tsar. (The fact that the tsar was overthrown could be considered social change, but this response is accurate only if the tsar's downfall was a direct result of the war.)

For J, the German Social Democratic party is discussed in the first part of the second paragraph. The last part of the paragraph deals with the conflict between expansionists and anti-annexationists. In the passage, is there any link between the rise of the German Social Democratic party and anti-annexationist sentiment? If there is no evidence for this link, then this idea cannot be used here to support the theory that "war causes social change."

37. Who is referred to here as "the enemy"? Be careful not to let your knowledge and biases about the United States' involvement in the war interfere with a close, careful reading of the passage. Think about the idea that each side has an enemy to defeat and propaganda is a way to announce a country's strengths while discrediting its enemy.

Who, according to the passage, proclaimed that the enemy was evil? Who are "all governments"? Did only one government declare that the enemy was evil? Think about who the enemy was, according to Great Britain. Germany was also in the war. Is Germany part of "all governments"? Did Germany proclaim, too, that the enemy was evil? For option III, the passage discusses when the U.S. entered the war against Germany. Who fought with and against the U.S.? Is the U.S. part of "all governments"? Now consider which response most accurately reflects the statement in the passage. Which countries proclaimed that the enemy was evil? Great Britain only (A)? Great Britain and Germany (B)? Great Britain and the U.S. (C)? Or Great Britain, Germany and the U.S. (D)?

38. Here you're asked to determine, based on information in the passage, what the patriotism of the German Socialist Democrats forced this political party to do. Read carefully the part of the passage that deals with the German Social Democrats and then "translate" those words into one of the responses. The German Social Democratic Party is referred to as a socialist political party.

For F, did the German Social Democrats **oppose** the financing of the war? The phrase "Socialist approval of the money bills required for the financing of the war" indicates what about this party's position? For G, who kept the socialist and progressive forces out of the government? Is the German Social Democratic party a socialist force? Read carefully the sentence about the abandonment of revolutionary internationalism. Does it offer the same idea as in H? For J, what were the beliefs of the German Social Democratic party? Note in the passage the key words *internationalism* (across national boundaries) and *homeland* (German only). If the German Social Democrats believed in revolutionary internationalism, what did they approve by their vote to finance the war? Why did they act in opposition to their beliefs? Is this an act "contrary to the principles of their ideology"?

39. This item states that, according to the passage, anti-annexationist sentiment was able to gain strength in Germany during the last two years of the war. Note the key word *because.* What caused this increase in strength? Find the part of the passage that discusses annexation of areas by Germany. In order to understand the passage, picture two groups: one supports expansion of Germany by taking over valuable territory belonging to other countries (annexation); the other group is anti-annexation—it favors immediate peace within existing boundaries. Where does the passage tell that those who opposed annexation began to gain strength? At what point in the war did anti-annexationists speak out?

For A, what did the military under Ludendorff support? Were Ludendorff and the military expansionists (annexationists) or anti-annexationists? For B, what words in the passage indicate that Germany had not been able to win the war? What happened "when a quick victory proved elusive"? The annexationists, who were fighting for total victory, were confronted by what group? So does B give the reason that anti-annexationist sentiment gained strength in the last two years of the war? For C, did the German Social Democrats take over the government? Is there a connection between the German Social Democrats and the rise of the anti-annexationists? For D, did the leaders of heavy industry and Conservatives no longer support the military? Is D true? (Remember which side the industrialists and Conservatives were on. Were they anti-annexationists?)

40. This question states a fact from the passage (during World War I, Germany was effectively ruled by conservatives and the military) and asks you to draw a conclusion based on that fact. Because of this fact, what was the **chief German war aim**? What was the purpose for fighting the war? (Consider, for a moment, that if a different group had ruled Germany, the war aim might have been different.) Now reread, if necessary, the part about German rule by the Conservatives and military. In considering the responses, your job is to determine which response relates directly to the Conservative and military groups and is the most important reason these groups were fighting the war.

For F, it is true that the Social Democrats abandoned their revolutionary internationalism in defense of the homeland. Was this position forced on them by the Conservatives and military? Was this change in the Social Democrat ideology the chief German war aim? For G, find the discussion of the overthrow of the tsar in March of 1917. Does the passage state that Germany caused the overthrow of the tsar? Was this the aim of the war? For H, were the Conservatives and military fighting the war in order to annex valuable territory in other countries? The last part of the passage explains that these two groups had expansionist goals. What were these goals? What was the war aim of the leaders of heavy industry, Conservatives, and the military? Could H be the best answer? But consider J. At first glance, this response might appear to be a possible choice. We know that, according to the passage, Germany was ruled by the conservative bureaucracy, which was reinforced by the powerful military. When the military leaders exerted their power, what happened? What is a dictatorship? Does a dictator gain power in a country by a struggle within that country or by a war effort against other countries? So was the dictatorship in Germany a chief war aim or a **means** to attain that aim? Now, which response offers the best statement of the chief reason that the German Conservatives and military were fighting the war?

1. On the basis of the information presented in the passage, what general conclusion can you draw about the environmental conditions that isopods prefer? What did the biologist investigate about isopods? Which environmental factors were studied? In each dish of the experiments, what was varied? What was held constant? Toward which condition or combination of conditions did the isopods seem to move? What conditions would you look for, if you wanted to find an isopod?

When trying to draw conclusions from a lot of information, you need to understand what question you are trying to answer and determine whether you have the right information to answer that question. In this case, you want to figure out why isopods might prefer the dark. The information you need to answer that question is in the form of tables showing the results of three different experiments. All of the results refer to a preference for a degree of moisture and/or light. Which condition did the isopods prefer in Experiment 1? In Experiment 2? In which of the four variable conditions of Experiment 3 (light, darkness, dryness, dampness) did the isopods most often locate?

2. Your job here is to figure out, on the basis of the preferences shown by the particular type of terrestrial isopod in the experiments, what kind of lifestyle habits in an ancestor would most likely have led to development of the bugs in the dishes. What combination of factors did the isopods in the experiments prefer? Which of the possible explanations most clearly reflects these conditions?

This question implies that changes in organisms happen and that you can reasonably infer a probable cause for the progression of these changes to the present. In this case, it is reasonable to assume that the ancestor of the terrestrial isopod being investigated had preferences similar to those of the present isopod. Are you given any information to the contrary, for instance that radical changes in preference have occurred in the past? If not, can you use the given data to make a reasonable choice?

3. The results of Experiment 1 lead to a specific conclusion, which you are asked to identify. In Experiment 1, which factor was varied in a dish? What remained the same in a dish? Given a choice in a dish, did the isopods show a preference?

Basically, Experiment 1 involves two experiments. In Dish 1, the isopods were given alternative locations in the dark; in Dish 2, the alternatives were in the light. Given the choice, the isopods apparently did have a preference, which is the result you want to identify.

4. What factors might affect how an animal follows patterns it observes in other animals? Might any of the changes proposed by the responses make any difference in the social behavior of isopods? Which change is most likely to minimize social behavior?

To have confidence in results and conclusions, it's important to keep as many experimental conditions as possible the same. Only the variable under investigation should change. Think about the possible changes given and decide whether each would have an impact on the ability of isopods to follow behavior patterns observed in other isopods.

5. One popular idea of the desert is that it is hot, dry, sandy, and the sun is forever beating down. However, many conditions are present in the desert, and a variety of animals and plants have adapted to some of those conditions and thrive there. Knowing the experimental preferences of isopods and recognizing that those preferences apparently vary a bit, which of the desert habitats listed do you think isopods are most likely to prefer?

6. You're asked to pick the best circumstances for measuring a **rate,** in this case the rate of habitat selection. What is a rate? Have any rates been calculated in the experiments?

A rate is a measurement of the amount of some action over a specific period of time. Examples of rates would include velocity, which is the amount of distance traveled per unit of time, and birth rate, which is the number of babies born per year. In this question, you want to pick the best choice for measuring the rate of habitat selection. In all of the experiments, the biologist recorded the habitat selection of each isopod after one hour. The question states that animals were often moving during the course of the experiment. From the results in the tables, can you tell how long it took each isopod to move to the habitat in which it was found after one hour, how many habitats the isopods visited during the course of the hour, or even if the habitat they were found in was their final choice? Which of the possible choices would yield data to give you the best idea of rate of selection?

7. Geologists in western Canada produced a single diagram to display the overlapping relationships they inferred among several factors involved in the search for hydrocarbons. One of these relationships is between the substances produced from a well and the depth those substances come from, which is the focus of this question.

Given a diagram with more than two axes, how do you read the data from it? Once you have figured out what the diagram is trying to show, how do you use this information to answer the question?

Scientists often create complex diagrams to visually display and simplify a lot of data and a number of ideas. In this particular diagram, three different axes convey information. The vertical axis on the left presents depth, in kilometers; depth increases downward, as the arrow shows. The arrow on the horizontal axis at the top indicates that quantities (of oil, gas, and carbon dioxide and water) increase from left to right.

Note that there are no units associated with these quantities, which means here that the amounts of substances generated are in relative terms as opposed to actual amounts. This means that, of the total quantities generated, a varying proportion of each substance is produced at different depths. For instance, if you drew a line from left to right at a depth of 2.5 kilometers until it just began to enter the blank region, you would find that your line was about 1 inch long. A little over $\frac{1}{2}$ inch of the line is in the oil region. These estimated lengths suggest that a little more than half of the total quantity generated at that depth is oil. If you looked at a different level, the total quantities generated and the particular proportion of each substance making up that total would likely be different. At this point, can you see what you need to answer this question? Since the vertical axis at the right deals with zones of thermal maturation, do you need to refer to it to answer the question?

As you move from left to right and top to bottom on the diagram, at which depths do you find only carbon dioxide and water?

8. What association can you make between depth and thermal maturation index?

This is another read-the-diagram question. You're guided directly to the diagram in Experiment 2 by the first words of the question. The diagram shows depth on the left vertical axis and zones of thermal maturation on the right vertical axis. The braces (}) and associated Roman numerals identify intervals of depth in which the thermal maturation is at a certain level (associated with a particular color). If you read from the top and bottom of a particular brace, over to the left side of the diagram, you can find the upper and lower depths for a zone with a particular thermal maturation index.

Which upper and lower depths are associated with a thermal maturation index of III?

---

9. How is kerogen color related to thermal maturation index?

This question asks you to visualize the relationship on a two-variable graph (as you can see from the answer choices you're given).

Thermal maturation index (I – V) is associated with a particular color of kerogen, which is a result of different temperatures and pressures. The order of color change is from light yellow through black, which is associated with a thermal maturation index of V. The best graph to picture this association should have a line in which any point directly above a given thermal maturation index also lies across from the corresponding kerogen color.

---

10. What thermal maturation index is associated with orange kerogen? According to the diagram, what kinds of substances are generated in thermal maturation index zone III? What is generated the most, next most, and least?

This is a practical kind of question (if you're in the energy business) in which you need to come up with the most likely answer based on the limited information you have. Experiment 1 associates orange kerogen color with a thermal maturation index of III. The diagram for Experiment 2 shows the kinds of substances generated and their relative quantities at various depths and rates of thermal maturation in an area of western Canada.

What would a well drilled in this area at the depth of zone III probably produce, based on the information you have in the diagram?

9

11. Keep in mind that the correct response to this question is the statement that's **not** consistent with the given information. Of the several statements about hydrocarbon generation given, which do you need to eliminate to get to the correct answer? According to the passage, is wood-derived kerogen a source for gas? Is wood-derived kerogen a source for oil? Is wood-derived kerogen a source for coal? Is algal-derived kerogen a source for waxes?

Which of the possible answers is **not** true?

12. Why does Experiment 1 yield more information about the process of hydrocarbon generation than Experiment 2 does? According to the passage, how are hydrocarbons generated? In Experiment 1, how did geologists investigate the process of hydrocarbon generation? In Experiment 2, what exactly did the geologists do to investigate the process of hydrocarbon generation?

This question focuses on the differences between Experiment 1 and Experiment 2. Experiment 1 is an actual experiment designed to investigate the effects of temperature and pressure on the generation of hydrocarbons from kerogen. Temperature and/or pressure were applied for varying lengths of time to simulate different conditions in the subsurface. These factors were seen to have an effect on the color of kerogen, the source for hydrocarbons.

Experiment 2 might better be described as a "Data Analysis." In a sense, the experiment had already been conducted by nature. Geologists in western Canada just brought together a lot of interesting data accumulated over many years from a long list of producing wells. The diagram that they drew up simplifies these data into a readily accessible format, which may be used in further exploration projects. However, it doesn't really say anything directly about how hydrocarbons are generated. You can infer that pressure and temperature change with depth on the diagram, but there is no direct data, like that which was produced in Experiment 1, to say specifically how these quantities were generated.

13. How can you use the information in the graph showing the relationship between respiration rate and various temperatures to conclude what that relationship is for Animal 1? What particular environmental factor (independent variable) is controlled and varied in the experiment? What response (dependent variable) is recorded as a result of a change in the independent variable?

In this case, the relationship between temperature and respiratory rate is displayed as a line for each of four different animal species. Each line can be thought of as a series of connected points. Each point stands for a particular temperature that is associated with a specific respiratory rate. For instance, at a temperature of 5° C (read straight up from the bottom of the graph), Animal 3 has a respiratory rate of about 10 breaths per minute (read straight over from the left side of the graph). At 15° C, its rate is about 8. At 25° C, about 9. At 35° C, about 25. This specific series of examples covers most of the temperature range over which Animal 3 was tested and suggests that its respiratory rate was fairly stable for most of the lower temperatures, but was much higher above a certain temperature. A quick visual examination of the line for Animal 3 confirms this, since the line is flat for certain temperatures and noticeably higher for others.

What was Animal 1's respiratory rate at a specific temperature? How did its rate differ over a range of temperatures? What does the line for Animal 1 look like on the graph, and what does that represent about the relationship you are after?

14. Is there a point at which Animals 1 and 2 have the same respiratory rate at a single temperature? What does the line for each animal in the graph stand for? What does a particular point on one of the lines mean? Where would a point on the line for Animal 1 be the same as a point on the line for Animal 2?

Lines in the graph cross each other at several points. When two lines intersect, they share a common point. In this particular graph, sharing a common point means having the same respiratory rate associated with the particular temperature that exists at that point. For instance, where the lines for Animal 1 and Animal 3 cross, the temperature is about 11° C and both animals take about 9 breaths per minute.

What is happening at the intersection of the line for Animal 1 and Animal 2?

15. In light of new information comparing the data for Animals 2 and 4, can you arrive at a reasonable conclusion about a relative relationship between them?

What new information is provided? In the graph, what does the line for Animal 4 look like? For Animal 2? How do the shape and position of both of these lines compare? How might you account for this comparison between the two lines?

You are handed a statement that says Animal 4 used more oxygen per minute than Animal 2. The graph enables you to make further general comparisons between these animals. The lines for both animals are relatively flat and slightly higher at the low-temperature end. The lines seem to be similar as the temperature increases. In addition, one line is always higher than another. From the graph, it appears that Animal 2 always takes more breaths in a minute than Animal 4, yet Animal 4 uses significantly more oxygen per minute. Taken together, these comparisons suggest that Animal 4 inhales a much larger volume of oxygen per breath than Animal 2.

What does this conclusion imply about a further comparison between Animals 2 and 4?

16. How is respiratory rate related to oxygen in the passage? How is utilization of food related to oxygen? Given a specific relationship between amount of food used and degree of temperature, which animal fits the data?

This question strings together a series of ideas that build up a picture of one of the animals in the passage. First, you are given a general statement that animals need oxygen to use food. The question itself states that one of the animals uses less food at a certain low temperature and more food at a certain higher temperature. It may now be apparent what the answer is from the information in the graph, but see if you can follow the thread of reasoning. At this point, you have a particular temperature-food (T–F) relationship and a general food-oxygen (F–O) association. The passage indicates that respiratory rate is sometimes used to suggest oxygen use by cells in an organism—an oxygen-respiratory rate (O–R) parallel. Therefore, to complete the circle of relationships (T–F, F–O, O–R, ?), make the connection, and answer the question, you need a specific respiratory rate-temperature (R–T) relationship for an animal. Which animal has a lower respiratory rate (associated with lower oxygen use and lower food use) at 5° C than at 25° C?

17. Can you see through all the technical terms to identify the animal that fits the pattern? What characterizes cold-blooded animals, as opposed to warm-blooded animals? What effect does external temperature have on a cold-blooded animal as opposed to a warm-blooded animal? In the passage, what body process is related to temperature? For which animal does this body process appear to be directly linked to a change in the temperature?

Technical terms used in a question (like *ectothermic,* which is a valid synonym for cold-blooded) may confuse you. Don't worry unnecessarily about unfamiliar words, particularly ones for which alternative phrases are available.

The question states that body processes for cold-blooded animals are directly linked to temperature. Therefore, a change in temperature will result in a similar change in the body function, in this case, breathing.

Which animal shows a change in respiratory rate that is related to a similar change in temperature?

18. Based on information in the passage, what trend in the argon production rate should accompany the increasing fusion of hydrogen by the Sun over the next five million years? At current activity levels in the Sun, how many argon atoms per day are produced in the tank? What is the relationship between argon atoms produced per day and neutrinos? How many neutrinos pass through Earth each second and how many interact with chlorine? How are neutrinos produced? If the Sun fuses more hydrogen, what effect will this have on the number of neutrinos produced?

This kind of question asks you to piece together a lot of relationships in order to make a general prediction—in this case, one that you may be able to get an idea about from the way the question is phrased. Well into the future, the Sun is expected to be more luminous as a result of more rapid fusion than that of the present. From the passage, you are told that fusion produces neutrinos. If you increase the rate of fusion, you would expect to create more neutrinos and, therefore, the supply of neutrinos penetrating the experimental tank. How would this affect the chances for neutrinos to interact with chlorine and produce argon?

19. If you change important initial conditions of an experiment, you will probably change the outcome in some way. How is the experimental setup being changed? Of what importance is the liquid in the experiment? What effect would this change be likely to have on the rate of production of argon atoms?

Neutrinos rarely interact with anything, but one of the elements they tend to interact with strongly is chlorine. If you increase the opportunity for interaction in some way, in this case by doubling the amount of C_2Cl_4 in the tank, you will probably increase the rate of interaction. An increase in the rate of neutrino interaction with chlorine atoms will lead to an increase in the rate of production of argon atoms.

By what proportion is this rate increased? Are there grounds for any other rate proportion change in the passage?

20. Scientists want to produce results that are as accurate as possible. Which of the actions listed will help most with ensuring accuracy?

What is accuracy? Why might results be different on different days or for different trials? What is the meaning of, for example, 0.21 ± 0.20?

This question gets at a fundamental concern in science. How accurate is your data? Accuracy is the extent to which your experimental measurement agrees with the "real value" of the quantity you are measuring. Of course, if you knew the "real value," you wouldn't need to measure it. The only way of determining the "real value" is through experimental measurement and the careful control of as many factors as possible. You need to reduce possible errors, which can cause results to vary, to a minimum.

The result of Experiment 2, Trial 2, is that 0.21 ± 0.20 argon atoms per day are created in the tank. From the passage you know that from time to time during a trial, argon atoms are collected and counted. This count is used to calculate the rate of argon atoms produced per day. The result of any single trial represents an average of many rates and its associated statistical variation, the plus-minus factor. So the result of Experiment 2, Trial 2, can be translated as: There is a very good chance that the "real value" for the rate of argon atoms produced per day lies between 0.01 and 0.41, the average being 0.21.

When you average numbers, the effect of extreme values is reduced. The more numbers you average, the lower the impact of unusual values, which might be a result of introduced errors or special circumstances, on the measurement of the "real value." For example, suppose you run two experiments in which you measure the weight of dirt in your tennis shoes. The experiments are identical in every way, except that in the first one you make 10 measurements of the amount of dirt, while in the second experiment you make 100 measurements. Which experiment will give you the more accurate result? The average of 100 measurements should be closer to the real weight of dirt than the average of only 10 measurements.

With this in mind, which procedure would be most likely to result in the most accurate value for the argon production rate?

9

21. This kind of change in experimental setups is common as scientists try to isolate effects. Davis has an idea of what neutrinos can do to chlorine. Now if he adds in cosmic rays by changing the experiment, he would expect to see additional argon atoms produced, perhaps a fractional increase, perhaps much more.

What is the effect of cosmic rays on chlorine? How was this effect neutralized in the initial experiments? What would be a simple way to restore this effect?

---

22. According to the passage, which elements react strongly with neutrinos? Why would Davis choose C_2Cl_4 to be the substance in the tank?

Decisions are based on assumptions, whether those assumptions are explicitly recognized or not. Some assumptions are more important than others. In this case, you are to pick the one that seems to matter most in the context of the passage.

Which of the listed assumptions did Davis probably have in mind when he decided to use C_2Cl_4 in this experiment?

---

23. One step in the process of gathering information is to evaluate ideas and hypotheses in light of new data in order to get a better idea of how things work. In this case, you're asked to evaluate a theoretical prediction and choose an answer that best supports that evaluation.

According to the passage, what is the theoretical prediction for the rate of neutrino production in the Sun? Do the data from the experiments support this prediction? How do you decide this?

You are **not** given the theoretical calculations for the rate of neutrino production in the Sun. However, as in many situations, there is an indirect and practical way to get at the question. The theoretical calculations lead to a particular prediction, which you can evaluate from the data in the experiments. One argon atom per day should be created in the tank. Look at the results for each trial in the experiment. Does the prediction fall within the range shown for the result of each trial? Well, some do and some don't. It is hard to come to any conclusion regarding Experiment 1, since there are only two trials and one encompasses the prediction while the other does not. However, Experiment 2 with its additional shielding provides clearer results.

What evidence can you find in the data to support, or fail to support, the predicted rate of neutrino production?

---

24. Which of the listed terms applies to **all** of the circles and squares in any row? What relationship exists between any pair of individuals in a row? Does this relationship hold for all other possible pairs in the row? Does it hold for all pairs in all rows?

This question, which deals with the diagram showing parent-offspring relationships (family pedigree) within an extended family, doesn't mention a specific row. So you need to be able to generalize your answer to all rows. Any listed relationship that doesn't work all of the time should be eliminated.

Which relationship works all of the time?

---

25. In what rows does Characteristic Y occur? What is the best reason available for why it occurs in those rows?

What is the relationship among individuals with Characteristic Y in Rows I, II, and III? Why isn't Characteristic Y seen in Row IV? Would all individuals have the same specific chance of having any one characteristic? From the passage and diagram, what does it mean to have an inherited characteristic?

This question raises several fundamental points about what ideas are represented by a family pedigree. Individuals that have a blood relationship with each other may display a specific characteristic—in this case Characteristic Y—that is handed down from generation to generation (inherited) or that skips generations. Not all children of a person showing Characteristic Y have that characteristic, but individuals showing Characteristic Y have parents with it. Characteristic Y is inherited, but not all of the time. If an individual has the characteristic, the chance that it will be passed on depends on how it is expressed in that individual (DD, Dd, or dd), as well as whether and how the characteristic is expressed in the mate (DD, Dd, dd, or something completely different). Because of this, chances are that the probability of passing on the characteristic will vary from mating pair to mating pair.

---

26. How can you infer dominance from the information available? Where is Characteristic X seen? Does it occur in many rows? Is there evidence that it is seen from generation to generation? What about Characteristic Y and Characteristic Z?

All individuals carrying a dominant allele show that dominant characteristic. All individuals with dominant characteristics have at least one parent who also shows the dominant characteristic. If a characteristic appears in offspring of parents who don't have it, then the characteristic can't be dominant.

Does X, Y, or Z show probable dominance?

27. Based on the information in the passage and the relationships shown by the pedigree in the diagram, which statement best explains the observation about Characteristic X? How is a recessive characteristic produced? Does it have to be or can it be expressed in parents of children who have it? How is a dominant characteristic produced? Does it have to be or can it be expressed in parents of children who have it?

This question is a further exploration of the relationship between dominant and recessive characteristics. Characteristic X is seen only in Row IV. A dominant characteristic would be seen in at least one parent of an offspring who had that characteristic. A recessive characteristic may or may not be seen in a parent of an offspring with that characteristic. Table 1 shows possible combinations of dominant (D) and recessive (d) alleles in which a recessive characteristic is seen or not seen.

Table 1

Baby	Mom	Dad
dd (seen)	Dd (not seen)	Dd (not seen)
dd (seen)	Dd (not seen)	dd (seen)
dd (seen)	dd (seen)	Dd (not seen)

28. Once you determine whether Characteristic X is dominant or recessive, can you figure out the likelihood that offspring of two people showing Characteristic X will have that characteristic? Is Characteristic X dominant or recessive? How would you express the pair of alleles (dd? DD? Dd?) making up Characteristic X for Female IV-1? What is the chance that Female IV-1 will pass on to children a dominant allele? A recessive allele? What about her mate with the Characteristic X? What reproductive future can you predict for a woman with an apparently rare characteristic (it occurs only in Row IV) and a man with the same characteristic?

Characteristic X does not appear in the parents of Female IV-1, so it is apparently not a dominant characteristic. The passage tells you that a recessive characteristic is seen only when dominant alleles are absent. Therefore, recessive Characteristic X in Female IV-1 can be expressed as (dd). There is a 100% probability that she will pass on a (d) to an offspring. The same holds true for her mate. Is there any chance that one of their offspring will **not** show Characteristic X?

29. What ideas do Hypothesis 1 and Hypothesis 2 have in common? How do they differ? Which of the listed assumptions must be true if we are to accept Hypothesis 2?

A fundamental basis for any theory is to recognize important assumptions underlying that theory and to be able to justify them in a reasonable way. Conflicting viewpoints can emerge from an agreed-upon base idea when additional information is brought to bear upon the issue. In this case, both hypotheses start from the idea that scouts dance to signal that food or a home site has been found. Hypothesis 1 maintains that the waggle dance informs foragers of the **distance** and **direction** of the food or home site.

According to Hypothesis 2, how are foragers supposed to be able to locate food or a home site? Which of the listed characteristics of bees and/or flower odors must be assumed if Hypothesis 2 correctly explains how bees locate a particular food or home site?

30. This question provides a few additional bits of information to help you draw a general conclusion. How long can a waggle dance last? What is the significance of the dance angle in either hypothesis? Without seeing the Sun, how could the bee determine its position after several hours?

Apparently a scout can dance for several hours and change the angle of the dance to agree with the position of the unseen Sun. You might ask yourself whether knowing the position of the Sun is a very unusual thing. Where is the Sun when you wake up in the morning? Where is it when you eat lunch? Where is it when you eat dinner? What about meals on cloudy days? Where would it be between meals? Can you think of other animals—like pets, fish in streams, or a bird outside your window—that seem to do things at the same time every day? Don't many animals apparently know when it is time to do something without the benefit of clocks or watches, or direct sunlight?

Which conclusion best accounts for the bees' knowledge of the Sun's position when they're unable to see it?

31. What would have to happen in the experiment to support Hypothesis 2?

What is the key idea in Hypothesis 2 about how foragers locate food or home sites? How is this tested? About how many foragers would you expect to go to Stations A and B before Station C was established? How about after Station C was established? Which statement(s) agree(s) with your expectations?

While it's nice to be able to test conflicting viewpoints, it's often difficult to design an experiment that could provide support for one idea **and** provide evidence against another. In this case, the experiment tests Hypothesis 2 while being neutral about Hypothesis 1.

Hypothesis 2 deals with odor. Before Station C was added, you would expect that most foragers would follow the scent to both Station A and Station B. (Note that all stations are designed to be the same distance from the hive, so that distance should not play a determining role.) Later, after Station C was added, and unscented food was placed at Stations A and B, you would expect most newly recruited foragers to follow the scent to Station C, according to Hypothesis 2.

What would you expect to happen if Hypothesis 2 is not supported?

When experimental results do not support a hypothesis, they can either contradict it or be inconclusive. A hypothesis can still be true and not be supported if, for instance, an uncontrolled or unperceived factor complicates the situation.

Without having any results available, which of the statements might correctly express the relationship between Hypothesis 2 and the results of this experiment?

32. Another experiment has been designed to test specific parts of this controversy. What is being tested, and what is **not** being tested? What is being varied in the experiment? What is expected to change, at least according to Hypothesis 1, as a result of variations in this factor? Are there other factors that do not vary? What are the results of the experiment? What is the question you are asked to answer, and how do the results help you answer it?

The long introduction to this question provides specific and valuable information that you need to answer the question.

Distance is varied in the experiment. Hypothesis 1 claims that the waggle dance provides distance information through the specific rate at which the scout dances. A different rate would mean a different distance. Things that are not being varied—and therefore are not being investigated in this experiment—are wind, direction of food source, and variation in the land surface elevation. The data of this experiment can support as valid only those conclusions that refer to what has been investigated. Other unperceived factors may influence the results of the experiment; you can speculate about what those factors might be, but you would need to subsequently test their validity.

What is being directly investigated and what is excluded from the investigation?

33. Of the implications listed, which fit(s) both hypotheses? Do both hypotheses suggest that a symbolic language (the waggle dance) communicates the location of food or a home site? Do both hypotheses suggest that bees use exact information from the waggle dance to locate food or a home site? Do both hypotheses suggest that honeybees work together to get food or find a home?

This kind of question focuses on the common basis from which conflicting viewpoints diverge. In this case, both hypotheses recognize that the waggle dance occurs and that it alerts foragers to food or a new home site somewhere outside the hive. However, the hypotheses diverge at the exact nature of the information provided by bees doing the waggle dance.

Which statement(s) about bees is(are) implied by **both** hypotheses?

34. Given what you know about the differences between Hypotheses 1 and 2, which of the listed discoveries would clearly favor Hypothesis 2?

Why might foragers continue to collect food from a source target after scouts have stopped advertising that location? How would flying against the wind affect Hypotheses 1 and 2, considering their differing explanations of how the bees know where to go? What does relative humidity have to do with anything mentioned in the passage?

The major emphasis of Hypothesis 2 is that distinctive odors, as opposed to information derived from the waggle dance, enable foragers to locate a food source or home site. Which discoveries involve the relationship between honeybees and odors? Which one suggests that conditions favorable to the detection of odors make it easier for bees to locate a food source?

35. Which of the observations presented make you question the validity of Hypothesis 1? According to Hypothesis 1, what are the key points about the dance? Would scouts dancing in a random pattern convey specific distance and direction information? Would the observation that different honeybee species perform the dance at different rates (communicate in a slightly different language) to indicate different distances mean that different species would be unable to locate their target? How would a change in orientation of the honeycomb in the hive affect the subsequent departure of honeybees from the hive?

For this "negative" question, you need to identify observations that could be used to show that key points of a hypothesis are wrong. The important points of Hypothesis 1 are that distance is indicated by how often the dance is performed in a given period of time and that direction is shown by the angle (from vertical) at which the dance is performed on the vertical honeycomb. Different dance rates correspond to different distances. Different angles from the fixed orientation of the honeycomb communicate different directions.

Which observation(s) involve(s) a change in the dance without a corresponding expected change in results and, therefore, discount(s) Hypothesis 1?

36. In this graph-reading question, what specific relationship (or difference) between two atoms are you supposed to look for? The correct answer requires a pair of elements whose electronegativity values are known to you. Which figure meets both of these requirements? Which pair of atoms best fits the specific condition you're looking for?

You're looking for an electronegativity difference of 1.0 between a listed pair of atoms. Both figures show electronegativity differences. In Figure 2, it's "spelled out" for you as the horizontal axis. In Figure 1, you have to do the subtracting yourself. Only Figure 1 has a combination of both elements and electronegativities, which is what you need to answer the question. Using the list of possible answers and subtracting electronegativities between the pairs of atoms shown, which pair has an electronegativity difference of about 1.0?

37. What is the general relationship between electronegativity and metallic elements? How could the question be phrased in terms of electronegativity instead of metallic elements?

The question relates a specific concept (metallic) with comparatively low electronegativities and asks you to find the extreme examples of this relationship (the lowest electronegativities). Figure 1 shows the electronegativity values of several elements. Which of the elements listed there have the lowest electronegativities? Which group of listed elements includes the three with the lowest electronegativities?

38. There is a long introduction to this question. If you skip the introduction for the time being and go straight to the question, what does it ask? You're trying to picture a **highly polar covalent** bond. Look for types of bonds in the passage. Compare the sharing of bonding electrons that takes place in a **nonpolar** covalent bond with that of a **polar** covalent bond. In which type of bond are electrons shared **unequally**? The introduction to the question tells you that you can represent differences in the types of bonds between two atoms by visualizing differences in electronegativities, that is, in the electron-attracting abilities of their nuclei.

In the style in which the possible responses are shown (dots stand for nuclei; shading represents electron pathways), which choice represents a highly polar covalent bond?

39. Beginning with a particular attribute of a bond between two atoms (60% ionic character), can you figure out associated relationships to arrive at the appropriate pair of bonding elements? In Figure 2, what electronegativity difference is associated with 60% ionic character? Which of the pairs of atoms listed as possible answers would have a bond with an electronegativity difference higher than that associated with 60% ionic character?

For this question, you need to make a connection between the relationship shown in Figure 2 and the electronegativity values given for particular elements in Figure 1. Electronegativity difference of about 1.8 in Figure 2 corresponds to about what percent ionic character? According to Figure 1, which of the four pairs of elements listed as bonds has an electronegativity difference greater than 1.8 (and thus, a bond of more than 60% ionic character)?

40. What are you asked to arrange in a sequence? What characteristic will you use to put the items in a specific order? What specific order is asked for?

Anything can be put in order. You just need specific guidelines to do it. In this particular case, you want to arrange pairs of elements by percent ionic character, from lowest to highest. The complication is that in order to get the percent ionic character of a pair of elements from the data in the passage, you have to figure out the electronegativity difference between those elements. Once you get the electronegativity difference from Figure 1, you can apply it to Figure 2 to get the percent ionic character for that specific pair. When you have the percent ionic character for all four pairs, you can place them in order from lowest to highest.

Can you see a simpler way to approach this problem, one that might save time? As shown in Figure 2, percent ionic character increases as electronegativity difference increases. So if you use Figure 1 to determine the differences in electronegativity for the pairs of elements and order them on that basis, the order should be the same as if you were basing it on ionic character, shouldn't it?

1. B. The original version of the sentence is redundant. If heads are wagging in agreement, the *yes* is unnecessary. Heads don't wag **no** in agreement in our culture. Likewise, the phrase "affirmatively in agreement" is redundant in C. Both words convey the same idea. D describes the wagging motion unnecessarily, and is choppy and awkward besides.

2. F. When you compare only two items, *more*—not *most*—is the preferred word. However, if the passage discussed three or more types of pets—for instance, dogs, cats, and boa constrictors—the writer would be correct in saying that cats are the most popular of the three. H suggests that the dog is more popular than some other pet and the cat is **even** more popular than the dog. J is ungrammatical. Besides, even if there were such a word as *popularest* to mean "most popular," it wouldn't be a logical conclusion to the sentence. The writer says only that cats are **more** popular than dogs. For all we know, tropical fish or iguanas might be the most popular pet of all.

3. B. *Wagging* and *pro-canine pack* conjure up canine images that emphasize the dog/cat pet competition discussed in the paragraph, which is probably why the writer uses them. The expressions are synonymous with other expressions, as A suggests, but the writer could have chosen others, such as *nodding* and *crowd,* that aren't associated with dogs; *wagging* and *pro-canine pack* are not used **because** they have synonyms, nor are their synonyms "commonly used expressions." C and D are wrong because the expressions don't convey images appropriate to public opinion polls, nor are they commonly used to convey irony.

4. G. In F, *while* and *but* are a losing team—you can have one or the other, but not both. H is wrong because *however* is illogical and the word *thus* implies, also illogically, that cats have a history of usefulness and nobility **because** dogs have been useful for millennia. J links two long, independent clauses with a comma, creating a comma splice and blurring the logical connection between the two complete thoughts in those clauses.

5. D. The phrases "shall have combined" in A and "would combine" in C imply something that hasn't happened yet. They are inappropriate here because the history referred to—the history of cats—has already occurred. B uses a past tense—"had been combined"—but it changes the sentence from active voice to passive voice. That doesn't work for two reasons: it sounds as if this history of cats has somehow been acted upon; and the direct object *usefulness* no longer receives the action of the verb *combined.*

6. G. "Gainful employment," a fancy term for "work," fits with the essay's praise of cats and its droll tone. Response F is redundant—"employed by employment"? So is J—*employment* is the same as *work.* H is wrong because productivity isn't something that can be granted.

7. C. In a compound sentence, it's usually desirable to put a comma before the conjunction—in this case *and*—that joins the two thoughts. The colon after *it* in A would be appropriate if the writer deleted *and,* then introduced examples of how Egyptians deified the cat: "The Egyptians, for example, deified it: they even built shrines and temples honoring the cat." The semicolon can be an effective way to link related thoughts; the semicolon in B, for example, is entirely acceptable. The comma after *priestly,* however, prevents B from being the best answer. In both B and D, the comma between *priestly* and *decrees* is useless; it creates an unnecessary pause between a noun and the adjective that modifies it.

8. H. F and G are redundant because they talk about dead cats after death. A dead cat **before** death would be a live cat. J needlessly includes the idea that death comes after life.

9. B. B is the only response that agrees with the singular noun *cat.* A and D—*cats'* and *their*—include plurals. C is wrong because although the cat is an "it," the possessive doesn't contain an apostrophe. *It's* is the contraction of *it is.*

10. G. Since a new topic—care and maintenance of cats—is being introduced, J can be ruled out because it advises against starting a new paragraph. *While* in response F sets up the reader for a contradiction that doesn't come. *While* also turns the whole sentence into a dependent clause—that is, it's no longer a complete sentence. *Therefore* in H and J implies that the preceding paragraph leads to the conclusion that cats have many practical advantages. On the contrary, the preceding paragraph discusses cats in art, not in the world of practicality. The new paragraph on cats being practical doesn't follow as a consequence from the preceding paragraph on cats in art, so *therefore* doesn't work.

11. D. *Than,* not *then,* is used in expressions of comparison. C also uses *than,* but the apostrophe after *dogs* is a mistake because it unnecessarily makes the word a possessive.

12. G. *Mistaking* introduces a phrase modifying *dog lovers. To mistake* in F doesn't work because it implies that the dog lovers claim cats are antisocial "in order to" or "so as to" mistake dignity for indifference. H and J do not result in successful sentences because *that was* and *who was* (both singular) cannot refer to *dog lovers* (a plural), because they make a needless shift to past tense, and because they are very confusing (What is **that**? Who is **who**?).

13. D. Aspiration alone (A) isn't enough to get you to the top. Neither is clamor (C). In fact, if you're a cat, clamor can make you very unpopular, especially late at night. If you're not reading carefully, *lead* in B might seem like a possibility. However, though cats might lead **the** way to the top, they can't lead **their** way there. *Claw* is preferable because it not only suggests a strong action, but is also a word associated with cats. This type of wordplay is consistent with the style of the first paragraph of this passage, in which the writer used canine references such as *pack* and *wagging.*

14. F. F is the best way to discuss a quality seen **less in** one thing **than in** another. The key phrase is *less than,* though the writer has split the two words and you must read carefully to coordinate them. In G, *than has* doesn't work because the sentence is set up so that "people see signs **in**" wagging and coiling; changing *in* to *has* breaks that pattern. H includes the word *in,* but *as* fails to set up the comparison, and *as in* confusingly suggests that the quiet coiling is a form of crazed wagging. *More than* (J) breaks the sentence's pattern and contradicts the *less* earlier in the sentence.

15. B. A is partly true—the essay does have its satiric moments—but the essay barely touches on how people overindulge their pets: to the ancient Egyptians, respectful treatment of dead cats doesn't really sound like "overindulgence." C and D are correct in mentioning the essay's focus on cat superiority; but the tone is not bitter, and the approach is loose and lighthearted rather than serious and strictly logical.

16. F. F best describes the writer's purpose in beginning the essay by introducing the three expressions—examples of words or phrases that have acquired new meanings over time—to be discussed in the course of the passage. It isn't clear how this approach might appeal to authority (G) or explain the purpose (H), since the words themselves aren't explained until later in the essay. The words and phrases are merely words and phrases, not complete sentences (J).

17. C. C offers the only singular verb—*is*—and so is the only option that agrees with the singular pronoun *each,* which here refers to "each one" of the three expressions singly—"a familiar expression."

18. H. Since a phrase by definition is a group of related words, F is redundant. Would you talk about "a group of words made up of words"? Similarly, *verbiage* in G refers to the manner of expressing oneself in words; this choice is also redundant. J leaves no alternative to *words* to follow the word *or,* so the sentence is incomplete.

19. A. The phrase "as language evolves" needs to be set off by commas because it is a parenthetical phrase. Imagine that the commas are parentheses. See how the sentence makes sense even with that phrase, in effect, removed?

20. G. G is the answer because parenthetical phrases like *for example* should be set off with commas. H, which substitutes *the* for *for,* creates a sentence that doesn't express a complete thought. H would have been acceptable, though a bit clumsier than G, with the addition of the word *of*: Take the example **of** the word "eavesdrop."

21. A. Most of us seldom use a word as formal-sounding as *thus.* Nevertheless, it's the best of the four choices here for conveying the cause-and-effect relationship described. C has the right idea, but *then* is redundant with *and so.* B and D wrongly suggest a contradictory relationship between the last sentence and the rest of the paragraph, as if "eavesdrop" got its current meaning **despite** its original association with dripping eaves.

22. J. J is the answer because it's the only response that conveys the complete idea of what the other explanation says: the word originated at Oxford. If you add *that* (F) or *which* (H), you're creating an incomplete sentence that leads the reader to expect more information. For example: "Another explanation says the word **that** originated at Oxford has nothing to do with shoemakers." It's also inappropriate to add the plural verb *were,* as in G. *Were originated* doesn't agree with the singular noun *word.*

23. C. The writer tells you that registering freshmen were required to list their social rank. When were they required to do this? "At one time," the writer says. This is the only phrase that needs to be set off by a comma; it is a parenthetical phrase that adds information about when the main action in the sentence occurred.

24. J. It's the only possible answer that sums up the premise of the paragraph **after** the reader has been given all the necessary supporting information. F, G, and H tell us what "snob" has come to mean before the writer has even explained its literal meaning: an abbreviation for the Latin term *sine nobilitate.*

25. B. B is the best answer because it conveys the idea that this is the final of three examples showing how different expressions originated. D suggests that making less noise is the primary message behind "put a sock in it," but it's meaningless to talk about a primary message unless lesser ones are mentioned, too. *First* (C) is wrong for a similar reason: the writer never explains what a second meaning of the phrase might be. *Secondly* (A) implies either that "put a sock in it" is the second example (we've already ruled that out) or that the writer is giving us some additional information; in fact, a new expression is being introduced, not supplementary details describing "snob."

26. J. J is the answer because the underlined phrase refers to early record players—a plural noun that requires a plural possessive pronoun (*their*). Its homonym, *there* (F), isn't possessive. It can refer to a place, but the writer is **not** saying, "The sound came through **there.**" And, even if the sentence discussed a **single** early record player and **its** large horn, neither G nor H gives the correct possessive form of the singular *it—it's* is the contraction of *it is,* while *its'* simply doesn't exist. The possessive *its,* like *hers,* has no apostrophe. Could *it* have a *plural* possessive form? No, because if you have more than one "it"—whether it's a gramophone or a compact disc player—then you have a "they."

27. D. A is an incomplete sentence that consists of two dependent clauses: one beginning with *since,* the other with *which.* B is wrong because machines can't stuff themselves, no matter how much we sometimes might wish they would. *They,* in C, is vague; who are "they"—the machines or the people listening to them? We've already dismissed the machines as a nonsensical possibility (in this context, anyway), and we can't assume the writer is referring to listeners, because no listeners have been mentioned yet in the passage.

28. J. J—the conjunction *but*—is the best answer. *Therefore* (F) and *thus* (G) imply that "put a sock in it" is understandable today **because** stereos are no longer sock-stuffed. That's illogical. Actually, the expression is still understandable **in spite of** modern audio technology. "Quite the contrary," in H, doesn't fit because it's too direct a contradiction; it's like saying "just the opposite." The two parts of this sentence don't completely contradict each other, as the two parts in the following example do: "Modern sound systems should have eliminated the need for socks in the stereo; quite the contrary, socks are still routinely stuffed in the best speakers." As you can see, since the phrase isn't a conjunction, it also requires different punctuation.

29. D. "Put a sock in it" is an expression meaning "quiet down." The writer is asserting that this meaning still comes through loud and clear. The phrase itself is not a meaning, as B proposes; it's an expression. It's confusing to talk about an expression of another expression, as A does. In any case, the writer is emphasizing that the concept "still comes through"—not that the words can be clearly heard. And the "meaning expression" in C isn't terribly meaningful here. It might be interpreted as a reference to a facial expression full of meaning—a significant glance, for example. In any case, it doesn't belong in a discussion of verbal expressions and their meanings.

30. H. H best sums up the essay's structure. After an introductory paragraph, the next three paragraphs are each devoted to an example of a word or term whose meaning has changed. The fourth paragraph doesn't really offer a conclusion, as F and J suggest; it simply includes a concluding sentence that summarizes the point of that paragraph. And the essay doesn't end with a call to action, so G is wrong.

31. A. The essay is designed to present an assortment—the writer apparently hopes an interesting one—of word origins. D might seem like a possibility because you can interpret all the examples as having negative connotations; however, the original meanings weren't all positive. The essay's introductory paragraph announces the writer's premise that as language evolves, words can come to have new or enlarged meanings; but that's not the same as saying that words change from having positive connotations to having negative ones. B is wrong because there is no story line. C is wrong because the words don't share common linguistic roots, according to the essay. "Eavesdrop" and "put a sock in it" come from modern English, while "snob" derives from Latin.

32. G. As this compound sentence is written (F), it's a comma splice. The best way to join the two independent clauses is with a conjunction (in this case *and*) preceded by a comma—not **followed** by one (H). A semicolon **could** replace the comma in F, but you wouldn't use *and* with a semicolon, as J suggests, because the first clause is so short and because there's no other internal punctuation in the sentence.

33. D. In a straightforward descriptive essay like this, it's better to use one clear word than four or five fuzzy ones. There is nothing grammatically wrong with A; in fact, it's a commonly heard expression. It is, however, wordy and imprecise. So are B and C.

34. F. The part of the sentence beginning with "When it was announced" is a dependent adverbial clause. It's adverbial because it tells **when** the job applicants showed up. It's dependent because it doesn't express a complete thought without the second part of the sentence. Because it's a long clause, it needs a comma to link it clearly to the independent clause that follows it. G is wrong because a semicolon should not be used to link a dependent clause to an independent clause. H is wrong because the comma after *job applicants* confusingly separates the subject *applicants* from its verb, *showed up.* Eliminating punctuation altogether, as J proposes, makes this long sentence too confusing.

35. A. No other punctuation is called for because the underlined phrase is restrictive—that is, it's essential to the meaning of the sentence. Only nonrestrictive phrases—those containing information without which the sentence would still make sense—need to be set off with commas. The two commas in C would be correct if, for instance, the sentence said: "The engineers' plans, which had been drawn up some time before, called for. . . ."

36. J. F is a run-on sentence; in other words, two independent sentences have been fused to form one long, confusing, and rather breathless sentence. G is wrong because it would create a comma splice, joining two independent clauses. H, which uses a dash, might be appropriate in very informal writing but doesn't seem to serve any purpose here. In addition, H is confusing because it's not clear whether "if all went according to plan" refers to "digging . . . at the same time" or "would meet in the middle." Using a period, as in J, eliminates any confusion.

37. D. A, B, and C simply tell a reader that the harsh conditions were, respectively, difficult, tough, and hard. To the careful reader, this hardly comes as news. The passage has already mentioned that the work was dirty, dangerous, exhausting, and took place under high air pressure. None of the choices add anything useful to a reader's body of knowledge.

38. H. It's the only choice expressing that the men felt lucky **even though** their new jobs were fraught with dangers and hardships. F, G, and J wrongly imply that the dangers somehow made the job more attractive to these men. Even if it were logical, *in addition to* (A) would be awkward here. It sounds as if the hardships and dangers considered themselves lucky, and so did the men.

39. B. The phrase "hired to build the tunnel" is a restrictive phrase that tells which men considered themselves lucky. The verb *were* is out of place in the sentence because the clause already has a verb—*considered.* The best punctuation here is a comma after *dangers.* The sentence consists of a phrase introducing an independent clause, and a comma is the preferred punctuation.

40. H. "Which had been inching toward each other" belongs in commas.

41. D. You could spend a lot of time spinning your wheels over the best position for the word *however.* A, B, and C are all grammatically acceptable, but your best move is to get rid of the entire sentence. The writer's observation that many people are afraid of tunnels has nothing to do with the preceding sentence about when the Lincoln Tunnel was finished, or with the following sentence about opening day. The paragraph has a more logical flow without it.

42. F. J might seem like an attractive way out of the who/whom dilemma, but adding *having* to this sentence creates a phrase that would need to be set off by commas: "Many of the men, having worked on the tunnel, were in the huge crowd. . . ." That expression fails to define **which** men gathered—those who had worked on the tunnel. *Whom* is an object, not a subject, so it can't take an action; "whom" can't have worked on the tunnel, as G and H suggest.

43. B. *They* refers to the men who had worked on the tunnel, mentioned in the preceding sentence. As the sentence is written (A), it includes what's called a dangling modifier. The modifying phrase—in this case, "exhausted but elated"—is not immediately followed or preceded by the element the writer intended it to describe. Inanimate objects, such as an opening ceremony (A) or a tunnel (C), are incapable of feeling anything, except in certain Stephen King novels. If the passage included the information that Babe Ruth had come to the ceremony from Yankee Stadium, fresh from slugging a game-winning home run, we'd speculate that he could conceivably have been "exhausted but elated." His congratulatory speech (D), however, could not have been.

44. G. G offers the most effective way for the writer to express this idea. Response G makes it clear that the writer is talking about "hundreds of tons of" materials (concrete and steel) and "thousands of hours of" manpower (backbreaking work).

J is wrong because the writer has placed just two items in the materials list, and a comma would be needed only if there were three or more items in that list: "hundreds of tons of concrete, steel, and rocks."

H is wrong because, although it correctly inserts *and* between concrete and steel, the comma before *and* creates too big a separation.

F may seem to be an attractive option. It is, after all, perfectly possible to read the sentence as written: "building the tunnel had taken hundreds of tons of concrete, [some] steel, and thousands of hours of backbreaking work," with three loosely related items in one series. G is preferable, however, because it eliminates the ambiguity of how much steel was required, making it clear "hundreds of tons" is intended to modify both steel and concrete. In addition to being clearer, G, by separating the items into two parallel series of similarly modified groups—materials and labor—conveys the information in a way that is stylistically more graceful.

45. D. B and C can be eliminated because they include the present tense of *play* instead of the past participle. The form of *play* must work with the auxiliary verb *had,* so *had play* is not a possibility. A is wrong because the word *as* here suggests to the reader that the writer is making a comparison—for example: "**as** vital a role **as** the engineers played"—which isn't the case.

46. H. It encloses the parenthetical descriptive phrase *at thirty* in commas. In an informal essay, it would be perfectly acceptable for the writer to speak ironically of herself "at the ripe old age of thirty," compared to her octogenarian neighbor. Neither F nor J, however, includes the correct punctuation for this phrase. G is incorrect because a semicolon should only separate two **independent** clauses. A semicolon after *thirty* wouldn't do this.

47. D. The semicolon divides the sentence into two independent clauses. A is a run-on sentence. C follows the colon with an unnecessary *and.* Finally, while a trade-off did go on between the writer and the doctor—small chores for war stories—the word *therefore* in B implies a much stronger cause-and-effect relationship. Dr. Peterson might well have said, "After you finish weeding my tomatoes, I'll tell you more about tear gas," but that's hardly the kind of formal transaction *therefore* suggests. If the writer insisted upon linking parts 1 and 2 of this sentence with an adverb, *likewise* would be a better one than *therefore.*

48. J. The underlined portion following the comma in F sounds like the beginning of a thought that goes uncompleted. The phrase "as it were" is sometimes used in the same way as "so to speak." The phrase "as **if** it were" doesn't complete a thought. The writer learned history "as if it were" what? Basket weaving? G and H are redundant because they restate what's implied by the phrase "from the horse's mouth." The term refers to getting information firsthand, or straight from the source.

49. A. *War-related data* in B adds nothing to a reader's knowledge, and B is awkwardly structured besides. C and D are redundant. We assume a runner would carry messages "by hand himself." Who else's hand would he use? In D, *delivering* and *transporting* mean virtually the same thing, as used here.

50. H. *Slowest* is a superlative. All by itself, it means "the most slow." It doesn't make sense to describe something as the **most** most slow, as G does. Furthermore, if a superlative comes before another adjective, it's generally best to make that adjective superlative, too. To make F or J correct, you'd need to say: "the slowest, **most** agonizing death." Sometimes, for effect, a person might violate this rule and say something like, "Our date at the landfill site last Friday was the best bad time I ever had." But that's another story and not, as far as we know, one of Dr. Peterson's.

51. B. Neither A nor C expresses the incongruity of the soldiers being so stoic about the terror of the gas, yet so outspoken about the relatively minor shortcomings of camp conditions. D creates a comma splice by using only a comma to join two independent clauses.

52. H. The dash emphasizes that the soldiers were strongly anti-chicory (**much** to their **disgust**). A comma would be a good alternative, but it's not among the choices. At first it might look reasonable to put a period after *substituted* (F). After all, there's a complete sentence on one side of it—but not, as it turns out, on the other. "Much to the troops' disgust" is not an independent clause, which is why the semicolon in J won't work, either. If you take G's advice and avoid punctuation here altogether, the resulting sentence is confusing—much to a reader's disgust.

53. D. It's the only option that doesn't place an unwanted comma between the subject and verb. Except for the confusing comma, the verb phrases proposed by A, B, and C are all acceptable.

54. H. The possessive form of the singular proper noun *Peterson* is *Peterson's.* It doesn't matter how many anecdotes there are. If Peterson is the one telling them, then they are "Peterson's anecdotes." Only if, for instance, the doctor and his wife were telling stories would the writer refer to "the Petersons' anecdotes." The writer isn't talking about anything belonging to an anecdote (for example: "Dr. Peterson's anecdote's main character was a Sherman tank"), so G is wrong.

55. D. It's the clearest, most logical way for the writer to say that the war would end at 11:00 A.M. A reader **might** deduce that from B, after discarding the notion that the writer was talking about the end of some war that habitually occurred at 11:00 A.M., but it's a much clumsier way to organize the sentence. Likewise, a reader looking at A might infer that the writer means to say, "both sides knew that at 11:00 A.M., the war would be over." It's still not as clear as D. Finally, the phrase *at 11:00 A.M.* isn't an independent clause, so it shouldn't stand alone as a complete sentence (C).

(We saw in question 16 that sentence fragments are sometimes treated as if they were complete sentences. Here, though, that strategy doesn't work. A sentence fragment would make it unclear **what** happened at 11:00 A.M.—the knowing or the ending.)

56. F. F is the answer because it places *on that day* right after the day being referred to—November 11, 1918. If Sentence 3 began the paragraph (G), a reader might think *on that day* referred to a day mentioned in the previous paragraph—perhaps one on which some anti-chicory demonstrations occurred. Placing the sentence right **before** where the date is mentioned (H) doesn't clarify things one bit. At the end of the paragraph (J), it would be clear to the reader exactly which day the writer was talking about, but it's not the most logical place to introduce the information that both sides had known the war would end at 11:00 A.M.

57. A. In fact, the essay suggests not only that it's possible to have friends of all ages, but also that it's desirable to have such friendships. In the introductory paragraphs, the writer refers to the age difference between herself and Dr. Peterson. The last paragraph mentions her young friends. The very last sentence, which carries extra weight because it's usually the thought the writer wants to leave the reader with, reiterates the importance of having friends of all ages.

B is true, as illustrated by the doctor's anecdote about the senseless shooting just before the Armistice was signed. However, that information doesn't dominate the essay and isn't even mentioned in the essay's conclusion, so we can hardly interpret it as the point of the essay, any more than we can say that the point is the superiority of coffee over chicory. The writer hints that it's good to learn history firsthand, but nowhere in the passage does she even insinuate that it's the **only** way. Besides, it's a pretty preposterous premise, if you stop to think about it. The writer happened to meet someone who remembered World War I. Where would she find someone old enough to give firsthand knowledge of, say, the Revolutionary War?

58. F. The answer has to be "No." The newspaper editor would reassign the muddled writer to the obituary desk. The essay **doesn't** describe the historical observance of Veterans Day, which would be a history of how the day has been observed, but rather provides some historical background about events that happened on the day we now observe as Veterans Day—a phrase that doesn't even appear in the passage, by the way. G also says "No," but F is better. It doesn't matter how many veterans the examples relate to. The essay simply doesn't talk about the observance of Veterans Day. The answer to question 57 is another hint. If the conclusion drawn by the essay as a whole is that people can have good friends of all ages, it's unlikely that the same essay would be a description of Veterans Day. H and J are correct only in that the experiences recounted are those of a World War I veteran and November 11 is mentioned. They are, however, wrong in suggesting that the essay describes the day's observance.

59. B. A list of friends' ages (C) doesn't say anything about the value of young friends; it only shows, if anything, that the writer values them. Deleting the last sentence (D) would weaken the assertion, not reinforce it, because it would eliminate fully **half** of the sentences alluding to friendships with younger people. If the writer had to strictly limit the length of her essay, she might be forced to condense Dr. Peterson's stories (A) to make room for one about a younger friend. Simply condensing the doctor's stories without adding a new one, though, wouldn't do anything but make the essay shorter.

60. H. The original version of this sentence (F) is a run-on: one long sentence that should be two. F also suggests, ridiculously, that the feast itself is seated on benches. G creates a comma splice by joining two independent clauses with a comma. J sounds as if the writer is saying "nothing can surpass the fourteenth-century feast seated" (as opposed, perhaps, to the fourteenth-century feast **standing**?). The period in H separates the introductory sentence about the extravagance of the fourteenth-century feast from the supporting sentence that gives details of the feast itself.

61. A. Regardless of the punctuation used, the sentence is better without the word *expensive. Costly* and *expensive* are synonyms, so it's redundant to use them together. If the writer wanted to emphasize the spoons' value, a better way would be to change the degree of costliness—perhaps calling the spoons "priceless" or "extremely costly." Another way might be to add descriptive details. Were the spoons "jewel-encrusted," for instance? One thing is clear: restatement isn't effective here. A person who is destitute and impoverished is no worse off than one who's simply destitute.

62. H. It's the only option that makes the sentence a **complete** sentence.

63. A. The clever host would plan his own tricks because he was **not** content to leave all the entertainment to his performers. D expresses the same idea, but it changes the first part of the sentence to an independent clause—and that makes the comma after *entertainment* wrong because it creates a comma splice. It's also confusing to introduce the pronoun *he* **before** *clever host.*

64. H. More than any of the other options, H makes the subject of the sentence consistent with the preceding one. If that first sentence talked about clever **hosts,** G would be preferable. *You* and *one* aren't patently unacceptable here, but they're not as clear and consistent as *he*; and the following sentence refers to "a lord," not "you" or "one." J is wrong in any case because it's missing an apostrophe in the possessive *one's.*

65. B. *Until* (A) and *unless* (C) make the sentence incomplete. They also form a misleading connection with the preceding sentence about the puzzle jug. It doesn't make sense to say that the liquid in the jug would circle around and exit the same spout "unless"—or "until"—a lord put red petals in someone's drink. *But* (D) also implies a contradiction between the sentences. *Or* is the best way to introduce another example of medieval mischief-making.

66. F. The plural phrase "some of the masterpieces" requires a plural verb—*were.* The parenthetical word *however* should be set off in commas. H is wrong because it uses a semicolon to separate an introductory adverbial phrase from the verb it modifies.

67. D. Similar to question 61, the problem here is one of redundancy. The writer doesn't need to describe silver spoons as both costly **and** expensive—or to explain that the kitchen was where the masterpieces were cooked. Everyone knows what a kitchen is for. A modifying phrase should add information, not simply restate it.

68. J. *So that* is more fitting than *causing* here because of the verb phrase *would dance.* "**Causing** the bird **to dance**" would be correct; "**causing** the bird **would dance**" is not. And a comma, not a semicolon, should separate the dependent clause from the independent one.

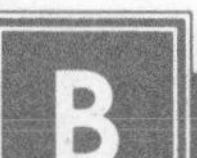

69. C. A and B serve up that dreaded grammatical monster—a misplaced modifier. The modifying phrase *acting creatively* is best followed immediately by what it's supposed to describe. It's the cooks, not the culinary monster, who are the creative ones. C and D both say that, but D inserts an inappropriate comma between the subject—*creative cooks*—and verb—*might serve up.*

70. F. *Hindquarters* is a plural noun. The *s* at the end has nothing to do with possession. If the writer wanted to talk about "the hindquarters' skin," an apostrophe after the *s* (as in H) would be appropriate—but never before the *s* (as in G and J). Furthermore, the correct preposition is *to,* not *with.* The head could be attached **to** the hindquarters **with** Elmer's glue, but that's a horse (or squirrel) of a different color.

71. D. *Memories* is the plural of *memory,* and the best punctuation is a dash. The writer could use a comma instead, but it would have to come before the conjunction *and,* not after it, as C suggests. B would be correct only if the clause beginning with *and* began with a subject-verb construction like "and they would make plans." As it's written, though, it can't stand alone as a complete sentence.

72. H. The entire passage has shown how medieval feasts were enjoyable both for hosts—who could play tricks and supervise the creation of culinary monsters—and for their guests, the beneficiaries of all this planning and hard work. The last paragraph describes the departing guests as "satiated and sleepy," so it seems reasonable to describe medieval feasts as exhausting. Yet they were so much fun that, according to the writer, the guests looked forward to being hosts themselves.

F is wrong because, although the passage suggests that guests and hosts alike tended to live in castles, it's illogical to assume that everyone did. Furthermore, the passage isn't **about** living in castles; it's about feasts. G is wrong because, although the writer says that the guests would leave laughing after an evening of revelry, the laughter was only one element of what made these feasts such unforgettable events. J, like G, is true in itself, but it doesn't provide a summary. It merely restates the second half of the preceding sentence in the paragraph.

73. C. Paragraph 3 already describes some of the food—if a squirrel-headed peacock is truly food—so it would be the best place to include more details. It's fair to say that the topic of this paragraph **is** masterpieces from the kitchen, so a few examples of those masterpieces would be appropriate. Paragraph 1 mentions eating, as A says, but entertainment—**not** eating—is the main topic. As B says, Paragraph 2 mentions drinking wine, but descriptions of the puzzle jug and the scarlet petal trick aren't the best lead-in for a discussion of the food. D isn't a good choice because the guests are satiated **after** the feast is over. It would be more effective to elaborate on the food before it's eaten and show how the guests came to be satiated. Furthermore, the main topic of the last paragraph isn't food, but rather the guests' mood after a feast.

74. F. It sets the scene—a fourteenth-century castle—in the very first paragraph, then leads the reader chronologically through the components of a typical feast of that time. The phrase "not content to have his performers provide all the entertainment," which begins Paragraph 2, should immediately follow a section of the essay that mentions the performers' tricks—a tip-off that options G and H aren't good choices. J could confuse a reader by failing to introduce the essay's time or setting until the second paragraph. Although the writer doesn't describe a feast step-by-step, there is a loose chronological order to this essay. The paragraph about the guests leaving and making plans to host their own feasts works best at the end of the passage **after** the writer has adequately shown why the feast was as "fabulous" as the last sentence claims.

75. C. If you told the writer "no sale," good for you. The essay doesn't come close to providing a menu or cataloging the food and drink that satiated medieval guests. The writer gives few specifics other than that guests drank wine (white or dyed red) and occasionally used their silver forks to spear a dancing chicken. Although B and D also give thumbs-down to the essay, C is the response that best zeroes in on its biggest problem: not enough information about the food. Some incidental description of the music and entertainment could enhance an article about medieval feasts—provided the focus was on food—so B is out. D is out because an article doesn't have to be written from firsthand experience to be valid.

1. A.

This person's systolic blood pressure at age 10 is approximated as 10 + 100 = 110; at age 75 it is 75 + 100 = 175. So the difference is

$$(75 + 100) - (10 + 100) = 75 - 10 = 65.$$

2. G.

$\left(\frac{3}{4} - \frac{2}{3}\right) + \left(\frac{1}{2} + \frac{1}{3}\right) = \left(\frac{9}{12} - \frac{8}{12}\right) + \left(\frac{6}{12} + \frac{4}{12}\right) = \frac{1}{12} + \frac{10}{12} = \frac{11}{12}$. Alternately, by regrouping, $\left(-\frac{2}{3} + \frac{1}{3}\right) + \left(\frac{3}{4} + \frac{1}{2}\right) = -\frac{1}{3} + \left(\frac{3}{4} + \frac{2}{4}\right) = -\frac{1}{3} + \frac{5}{4} = -\frac{4}{12} + \frac{15}{12} = \frac{11}{12}$. This is in lowest terms, and the denominator is 12.

3. B.

Let S represent the correct sum of Adam's 7 test scores. First find S:

$$\frac{S}{6} = 84$$

$$S = 84 \cdot 6 = 504$$

Then compute Adam's average correctly by dividing S by 7:

$$\text{Average} = \frac{S}{7} = \frac{504}{7} = 72$$

4. H.

The measure of $\angle APD$ is connected with the known 120° measure of $\angle PCD$ through $\angle CPD$ and $\angle CDP$. Because the triangle is inside the circle in this particular way, it's isosceles. (Two sides are radii of the circle, so they're the same length.) So $m\angle CPD = \frac{1}{2}(180° - 120°) = 30°$. Since $\overline{AB}$ is tangent to the circle at P, then $m\angle APC = 90°$. That leaves $m\angle APD = m\angle APC - m\angle CPD = 90° - 30° = 60°$.

5. A.

$\sqrt{16+9} = \sqrt{25} = 5.$

6. K.

$AB = AD - BD = 12 - 7 = 5$.

7. E.

The measure of $\angle x$ is 40° and that of $\angle y$ is 140°, so the sum of the measures of $\angle x$ and $\angle y$ is 180°.

8. J.

$$\frac{|4-3|}{|3-4|} = \frac{|1|}{|-1|} = \frac{1}{1} = 1$$

9. E.

Just substitute −2 for x in the expression $2x^2 - 3x - 4$ and compute the value:

$$2(-2)^2 - 3(-2) - 4 = 2(4) - (-6) - 4 = 8 + 6 - 4 = 10$$

10. F.

Lines L, N, and O form a triangle. The interior angles of the triangle and angles a, b, and c form three pairs of vertical angles. Because vertical angles are equal in measure and since the sum of the measures of the interior angles of a triangle is 180°, it follows that $m\angle a + m\angle b + m\angle c = 180°$. The measures of angles a and b are given as 70° and 50°, respectively. Therefore, $m\angle c = 180° - (70° + 50°) = 60°$.

11. D.

Speed = $\frac{\text{kilometers}}{\text{minutes}}$ [or rate = $\frac{\text{distance}}{\text{time}}$]. Then substitute: Stacey's new distance is 10 kilometers increased by s kilometers, or $(10 + s)$ kilometers; her new time is the same as her old time, 50 minutes. So a general expression for her new average rate of speed in kilometers per minute is $\frac{10+s}{50}$.

9

12. F.

$2x + 3 = 2a + 4$	To get rid of the 3, subtract 3 from both sides.
$2x = 2a + 1$	To get rid of the 2, divide both sides by 2.
$x = \frac{2a+1}{2}$	

13. B.

If $d = 4$, then $6,\underline{4}47 > 6,437$ and this is the smallest value, because if $d = 3$, then $6,\underline{3}47 < 6,437$.

14. J.

If insurance costs \$.40 per \$100 in value, then (multiplying by 10) it costs \$4 per \$1,000 in value, and (multiplying by 40) \$160 per \$40,000 in value. Essentially, you've been finding equivalent ratios. If you'd rather, you could have set up a proportion.

$$\frac{\$.40}{\$100} = \frac{\text{cost}}{\$40,000} \Longrightarrow \text{cost} = \frac{(.4)(40,0\not{0}\not{0})}{1\not{0}\not{0}} = (.4)400 = (4)(40) = 160$$

So the cost of insuring the house is \$160.

15. C.

Take advantage of the symmetry of this situation. The two rectangles are congruent; that makes all four triangles congruent, too. You can assign labels to make the angles easier to describe.

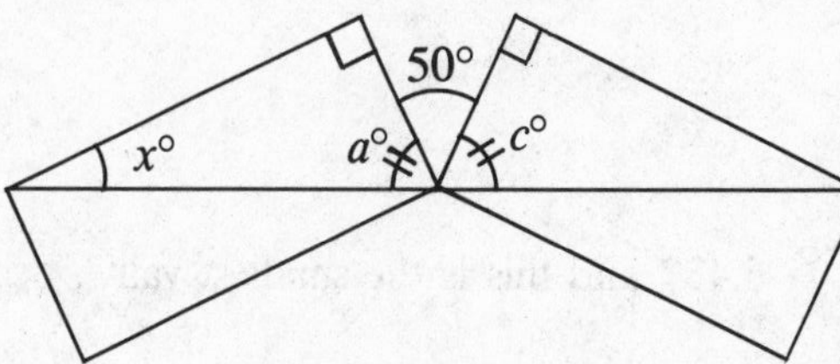

$a + 50 + c = 180$ (since these three angles form a straight angle)

and $a = c$ from the symmetry

so $a + 50 + a = 180$

$2a = 130$

$a = 65$

Now $x + a + 90 = 180$ (since these three angles are in a triangle)

so $x + 65 + 90 = 180$

$x + 65 = 90$

$x = 25$

So the measure you're asked to find is 25°. (Is it a coincidence that this is half of the 50° angle from the problem?)

16. J.

$4(3x - 1) < 7x + 2(x + 4)$	Multiply as indicated.
$12x - 4 < 7x + 2x + 8$	Combine like terms.
$12x - 4 < 9x + 8$	Subtract $9x$ from and add 4 to both sides.
$3x < 12$	Divide both sides by 3.
$x < 4$	

9

17. E.

$$\begin{aligned}
\mathbf{2} \cdot 90 &= 180 \\
\mathbf{3} \cdot 60 &= 180 \\
\mathbf{5} \cdot 36 &= 180 \\
\mathbf{6} \cdot 30 &= 180 \\
\mathbf{15} \cdot 12 &= 180 \\
\mathbf{45} \cdot 4 &= 180
\end{aligned}$$

and $180 \div \mathbf{50} = \frac{18}{5}$ eliminates A

$180 \div \mathbf{24} = \frac{15}{2}$ eliminates B

$180 \div \mathbf{40} = \frac{9}{2}$ eliminates C

$180 \div \mathbf{120} = \frac{3}{2}$ eliminates D

18. G.

It's appropriate to think of subtraction as adding the negative, so subtracting $(2x^5 - 3x^4 + 3x^2 - 4)$ is the same as adding $(-2x^5 + 3x^4 - 3x^2 + 4)$. Now add. Be careful to combine only like terms.

$$\begin{array}{rrrrr}
8x^5 & + 0x^4 & + (-1x^3) + & 3x^2 & + 4 \\
+ (-2x^5) & + 3x^4 & + \quad 0x^3 & + (-3x^2) & + 4 \\
\hline
6x^5 & + 3x^4 & + (-1x^3) + & 0x^2 & + 8
\end{array}$$

The result is $6x^5 + 3x^4 - x^3 + 8$.

19. C.

$$\sqrt[k]{54} = 3\sqrt[k]{2}$$

$$\frac{\sqrt[k]{54}}{\sqrt[k]{2}} = 3$$

$$\sqrt[k]{\frac{54}{2}} = 3$$

$$\sqrt[k]{27} = 3$$

and since $\sqrt[3]{27} = 3$

$$k = 3$$

or

$$54^{\frac{1}{k}} = 3 \cdot 2^{\frac{1}{k}}$$

$$(54^{\frac{1}{k}})^k = (3 \cdot 2^{\frac{1}{k}})^k$$

$$54^{\frac{k}{k}} = 3^k \cdot 2^{\frac{k}{k}}$$

$$54 = 3^k \cdot 2$$

$$27 = 3^k$$

and since $3 \cdot 3 \cdot 3 = 27$

$$k = 3$$

Check: $\sqrt[3]{54} = \sqrt[3]{3^3 \cdot 2} = \sqrt[3]{3^3} \cdot \sqrt[3]{2} = 3\sqrt[3]{2}$

20. H.

The width of the rectangular floor is w feet, the length is 4 feet longer, or $w + 4$ feet, and the area is 165 square feet. Because the area is the product of the width and the length, an equation for finding the width of the floor is $w(w + 4) = 165$.

21. C.

Sides $\overline{AB}$ and $\overline{CD}$ are parallel because of the two right angles at A and D, so figure $ABCD$ is a trapezoid. The area of a trapezoid is given by $A = \frac{1}{2}(b_1 + b_2)h$, where b_1 and b_2 are the lengths of the two parallel sides and h is the distance between those parallel sides. So the area is

$$\frac{1}{2}(23 + 18)12 = (23 + 18)6 = 41 \cdot 6 = 246 \text{ square units}$$

Alternately (if you don't want to bother remembering this formula), you can divide a trapezoid into a triangle and a rectangle.

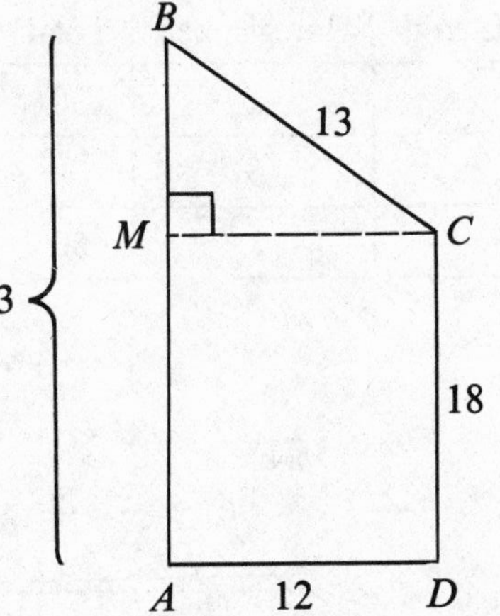

Here ΔBMC is a right triangle. $BM = AB - AM = 23 - 18 = 5$, so the area of ΔBMC is $\frac{1}{2}(5)12 = 5 \cdot 6 = 30$.

The area of rectangle $AMCD$ is $12 \cdot 18 = 216$, and that makes the area of the trapezoid equal to $216 + 30 = 246$ square units.

22. F.

When N is divided by 7, the remainder is 3, so $N = 7n + 3$, where n is an unknown integer. Now, $N + 5 = (7n + 3) + 5 = 7n + 8 = 7n + 7 + 1$. When you divide this by 7, the remainder is 1.

23. A.

To find the average of the three expressions, just add them (by combining like terms) and divide the sum by 3:

$$\frac{(3n+6)+(2n-4)+(4n-5)}{3} = \frac{9n-3}{3} = \frac{9n}{3} - \frac{3}{3} = 3n - 1$$

24. K.

You might use a table or Venn diagram to keep track of your work on a problem like this.

	Registered	Unregistered	Total
Men	x	d	30
Women	b	5	a
Total	38	c	50

$a = 50 - 30 = 20$ $\quad$ $c = 50 - 38 = 12$

$b = a - 5 = 20 - 5 = 15$ $\quad$ or $\quad$ $d = c - 5 = 12 - 5 = 7$

$x = 38 - b = 38 - 15 = 23$ $\quad$ $x = 30 - d = 30 - 7 = 23$

and a Venn diagram would be

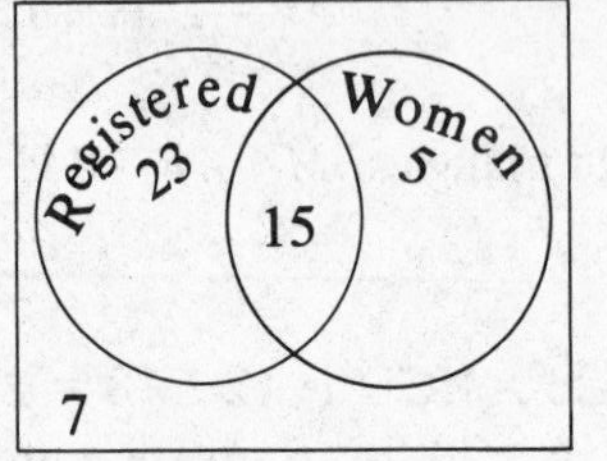

25. C.

$(3x-7)(2x+c) = 6x^2 + x - 7c$	Multiply as indicated.
$6x^2 + 3xc - 14x - 7c = 6x^2 + x - 7c$	Subtract $6x^2$ from both sides.
$3xc - 14x - 7c = x - 7c$	Add $14x$ and $7c$ to both sides.
$3xc = 15x$	Divide both sides by $3x$.
$c = 5$	if $x \neq 0$.

Because this has to be true for all x, as given in the problem, $c = 5$ must work for $x = 0$, too.

26. H.

Geometric solution: This equation translates into a statement about distances on the real number line. The distance between $2x$ and -5 is 9 units.

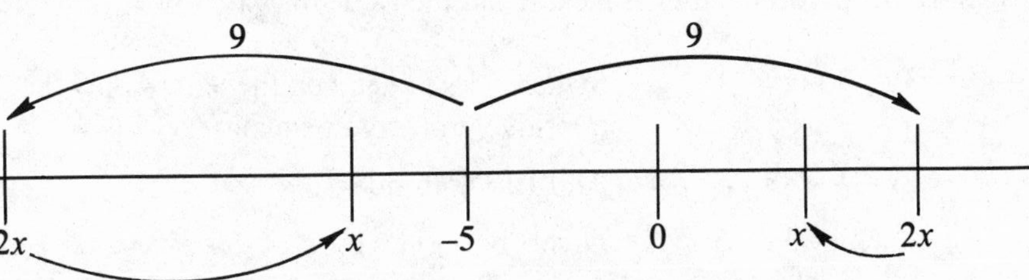

You can go either right or left by 9 units from -5 to get to $2x$. Then x is just $\frac{1}{2}$ of $2x$, so it's halfway to zero. Because one of these values of x is positive and one is negative, there are two different solutions.

You could find them as

$$\frac{-5-9}{2} = \frac{-14}{2} = -7 \quad \text{and} \quad \frac{-5+9}{2} = \frac{4}{2} = 2$$

Algebraic solution: A definition of absolute value states that $|y| = a$ is equivalent to the logic statement $y = a$ or $-y = a$. So, we can substitute $2x + 5$ for y and 9 for a to get $|2x + 5| = 9$ is equivalent to $2x + 5 = 9$ or $2x + 5 = -9$.

$2x + 5$ is a nonconstant linear polynomial, so each of the equations $2x + 5 = 9$ and $2x + 5 = -9$ has exactly one solution. The two solutions can't be the same, since a consequence would be that $9 = -9$. So, there are two different solutions.

You could find them as

$$\begin{aligned} 2x + 5 &= 9 & & & 2x + 5 &= -9 \\ 2x &= 4 & &\text{or} & 2x &= -14 \\ x &= 2 & & & x &= -7 \end{aligned}$$

27. A.

The sine of θ is the ratio of the length of the side opposite θ, which is 3, to the length of the hypotenuse, which is 5. So $\sin\theta = \frac{3}{5}$.

9

28. H.

The slope-intercept form of a linear equation is $y = mx + b$, where m is the slope and b is the y-intercept. You can find the slope of your line by putting its equation into slope-intercept form and then picking out the value for m.

$3x + 4 = 2y - 1$	Switch sides to get y on the left. (Apply the transitive property of equality.)
$2y - 1 = 3x + 4$	Add 1 to both sides.
$2y = 3x + 5$	Divide both sides by 2.
$y = \frac{3}{2}x + \frac{5}{2}$	

The slope is $\frac{3}{2}$, the coefficient of x.

29. C.

The ladder, the ground, and the house form a right triangle. The hypotenuse of the triangle is the length of the ladder, 17 feet. The base of the triangle is the distance from the foot of the ladder to the house, 8 feet. And you're asked to find the height of the triangle. A right triangle with a hypotenuse of 17 and a base of 8 fits the 8-15-17 pattern, so the height of the triangle is 15 feet. Or, by the Pythagorean theorem, the window ledge is

$$\sqrt{17^2 - 8^2} = \sqrt{(17-8)(17+8)} = \sqrt{9 \times 25} = 3 \times 5 = 15 \text{ feet above the ground.}$$

30. F.

$$\frac{2x^5y^{-2}}{x^2y^{-3}} = 2\left(\frac{x^5}{x^2}\right)\left(\frac{y^{-2}}{y^{-3}}\right) = 2x^{(5-2)}y^{[(-2)-(-3)]} = 2x^3y$$

31. D.

$$
\begin{aligned}
d &= \sqrt{(x_2 - x_1)^2 + (y_2 - y_1)^2} \\
&= \sqrt{[4 - (-2)]^2 + [(-5) - 7]^2} \\
&= \sqrt{(6)^2 + (-12)^2} \\
&= \sqrt{(6)^2 + (12)^2} \\
&= \sqrt{6^2 + (6 \cdot 2)^2} \\
&= \sqrt{(6^2 \cdot 1) + (6^2 \cdot 4)} \\
&= \sqrt{6^2 (1 + 4)} \\
&= \sqrt{6^2 \cdot 5} \\
&= 6\sqrt{5}
\end{aligned}
$$

32. K.

$6a + a^2 - 5a^3$ can be factored into $a(6 + a - 5a^2)$ and then into $a(6 - 5a)(1 + a)$.

33. C.

The slope of the line in the graph tells you that the earnings of the company are increasing at a rate of \$100,000 every 4 years, which is equivalent to \$25,000 a year. The earnings were \$200,000 in 1987, so 3 years later, in 1990, they should be \$200,000 + 3(\$25,000) = \$275,000.

34. G.

Because C, D, and E are collinear and $ABCD$ is a square, $\angle EDA$ is a right angle and ΔEDA is a right triangle. A right triangle with an angle of 45° is an isosceles right triangle. One of the two equal sides of the triangle is a side of square $ABCD$, so it has a length of 6 units. Thus, by the pattern for a 45°-45°-90° right triangle, the hypotenuse of the triangle has a length of $6\sqrt{2}$.

35. B.

ΔTUV is a 30°-60°-90° triangle, so if $\overline{TU}$, the hypotenuse, is 12 units long, then $\overline{UV}$, the side opposite the 30° angle, is half as long, or 6 units, and $\overline{TV}$, the side opposite the 60° angle, has a length of $6\sqrt{3}$ units.

36. H.

$y = x^2$ is the classic parabola, and $y = x^2 - 12$ is this same parabola translated down by 12 units.

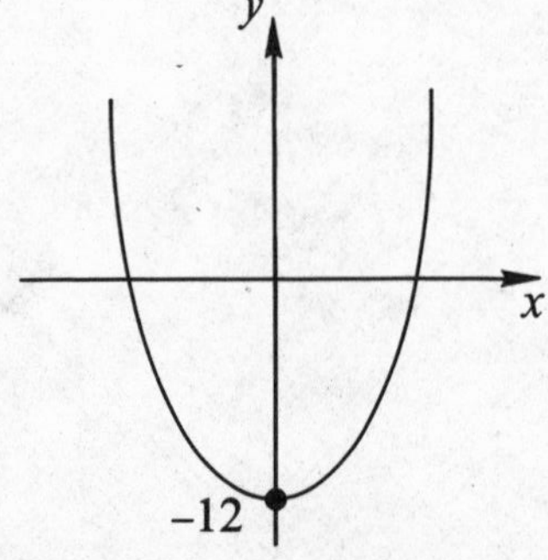

In terms of the form of the equation, for equations of the form $ax^2 + bx + cy^2 + dy + e = 0$, the graph is:

- a circle if $a = c \neq 0$
- an ellipse if $ac > 0$
- a parabola if either $a = 0$ or $c = 0$ but not both
- a straight line if a and c are zero and either b or d is not zero
- two rays forming a "V" might come from an absolute value equation, but wouldn't come from one in the form $ax^2 + bx + cy^2 + dy + e = 0$
- a hyperbola if $ac < 0$

These classifications include the "degenerate" cases, too. For example, the graph of an equation of the form $x^2 + y^2 = 0$ is just 1 point: (0,0). It gets classified as a degenerate circle or degenerate ellipse.

37. B.

By the Pythagorean theorem:

$$a^2 + b^2 = c^2$$
$$5^2 + x^2 = 12^2$$
$$25 + x^2 = 144$$
$$x^2 = 119$$
$$x^2 = \pm\sqrt{119}$$

and because x represents a length, the only actual answer is that the other side is $\sqrt{119}$ inches long.

38. F.

This figure is a triangle, and to find the area of a triangle using $A = \frac{1}{2}bh$, you need to find b and h. Because this is a right triangle with the right angle at O, the length of $\overline{OA}$ is h and the length of $\overline{OB}$ is b.

The length of $\overline{OA}$ is $2 - 0 = 2$. To find the length of $\overline{OB}$, first find the coordinates of B.

The slope of $\overline{AB}$ is $\frac{1-2}{2-0} = -\frac{1}{2}$

The coordinates of B are $(x,0)$ because it's on the x-axis. You can calculate the slope of the line through A and B as

$$\frac{0-2}{x-0} = -\frac{2}{x}$$

But these are the same line, so

$$-\frac{2}{x} = -\frac{1}{2} \Longrightarrow 4 = x$$

Now $b = 4 - 0 = 4$ and $A = \frac{1}{2}(2)(4) = 4$

39. A.

$$x^2 - x - 6 = 0$$

$$(x-3)(x+2) = 0$$

$$x - 3 = 0 \quad \text{or} \quad x + 2 = 0$$

$$x = 3 \qquad\qquad x = -2$$

Both of these are in set A.

40. J.

The total income from shoe sales is the total number of pairs sold times the price per pair. The four clerks sold $w + x + y + z$ pairs; the manager sold $w + x$ pairs. So the total number of pairs sold is $2w + 2x + y + z$. The price per pair is P dollars. So the store's total income from shoe sales is $P(2w + 2x + y + z)$ dollars.

41. E.

The slope-intercept form of a linear equation is $y = mx + b$, where m is the slope and b is the y-intercept. To put the equation in this form, solve it for y:

$5x + 3y = 15$	Subtract $5x$ from both sides.
$3y = -5x + 15$	Divide both sides by 3.
$y = -\frac{5}{3}x + 5$	
$y = mx + b$	

The slope, m, is $-\frac{5}{3}$; the y-intercept, b, is 5.

42. H.

The average weight of all 25 students is the total weight of the students divided by 25 (the number of students). The average weight of the 10 male students is 145, so their total weight is $10 \times 145 = 1{,}450$. The average weight of the 15 female students is 105, so their total weight is $15 \times 105 = 1{,}575$. Thus the total weight of all 25 students is $1{,}450 + 1{,}575 = 3{,}025$, and the average weight is $3{,}025 \div 25 = 121$.

Cancellation might help the calculations:

$$\frac{\overset{2}{\cancel{10}}(\overset{29}{\cancel{145}}) + \overset{3}{\cancel{15}}(\overset{21}{\cancel{105}})}{\underset{1}{\cancel{\underset{5}{\cancel{25}}}}} = 2 \cdot 29 + 3 \cdot 21$$
$$= 58 + 63 = 121$$

43. D.

$$m = \frac{y_2 - y_1}{x_2 - x_1} = \frac{0 - 3}{-4 - 0} = \frac{-3}{-4} = \frac{3}{4}$$

44. G.

All that's essential in this problem is that $\angle D$ is a 30° angle. The cosine of 30° is $\frac{\sqrt{3}}{2}$. You might refer back to the 30°-60°-90° triangle pattern to get this value. If you don't want to have to memorize all the sines and cosines, this is a good way to get sines and cosines when you need them.

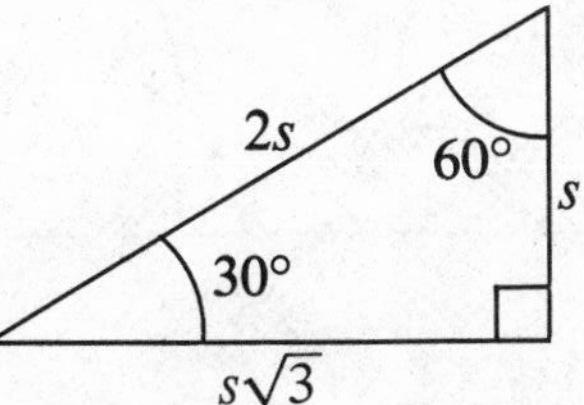

The cosine of the 30° angle in this pattern is the ratio of the length of the side adjacent to the angle (that's $s\sqrt{3}$) to the length of the hypotenuse of the triangle (that's $2s$). No matter what s is, the value of this ratio is $\frac{\sqrt{3}}{2}$.

45. A.

$x^2 > x$	Subtract x from both sides.
$x^2 - x > 0$	Factor the left side.
$x(x - 1) > 0$	

Now recall: If the product of two numbers is greater than 0 (that is, it's positive), then either both numbers are positive or both numbers are negative. So $x^2 > x$ is equivalent to:

$[x > 0$ and $x - 1 > 0]$	or	$[x < 0$ and $x - 1 < 0]$
$[x > 0$ and $x > 1]$		$[x < 0$ and $x < 1]$

The statement $[x > 0$ **and** $x > 1]$ is true if and only if (iff) $x > 1$. The statement $[x < 0$ **and** $x < 1]$ is true iff $x < 0$. Now our original inequality, $x^2 > x$, is reduced to $[x > 1$ or $x < 0]$, and that is an answer choice. Check this by trying some numbers, say $0, \pm\frac{1}{2}, \pm 1, \pm 5$.

9

46. J.

Drawing a quick graph will get you started on this problem. $y = x^2 + x = x(x + 1)$ is zero when $x = 0$ or $x = -1$.

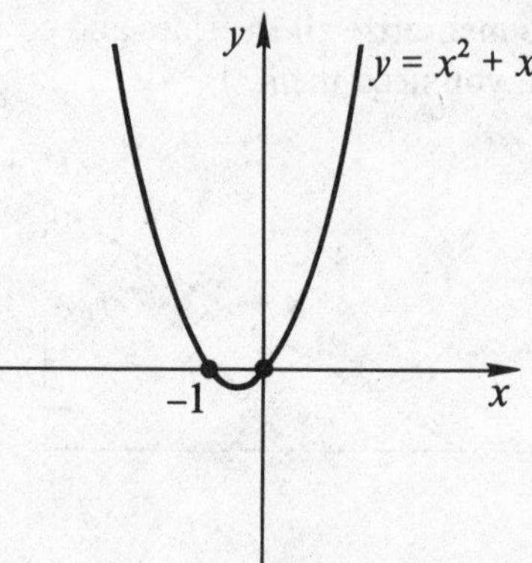

If y is **equal** to $x^2 + x$ for those points **on** the parabola, then y is **less than or equal** to $x^2 + x$ for points **on or below** the parabola—the y-coordinate gets smaller as you go down.

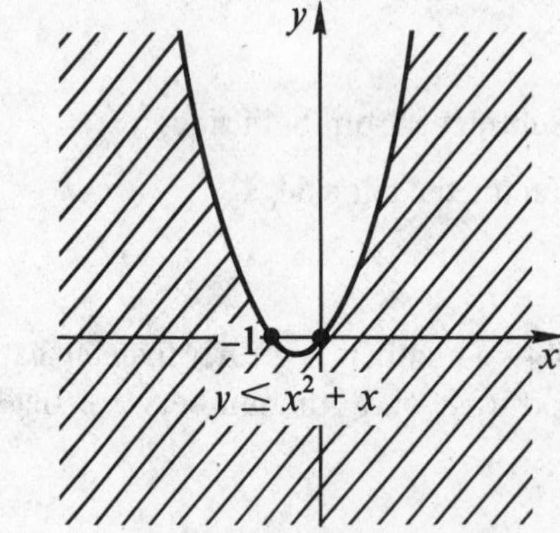

$-2 \leq x \leq 3$ looks like this:

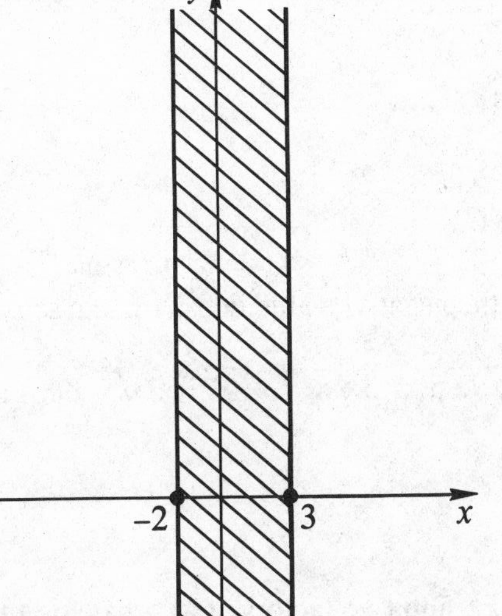

And, putting it all together:

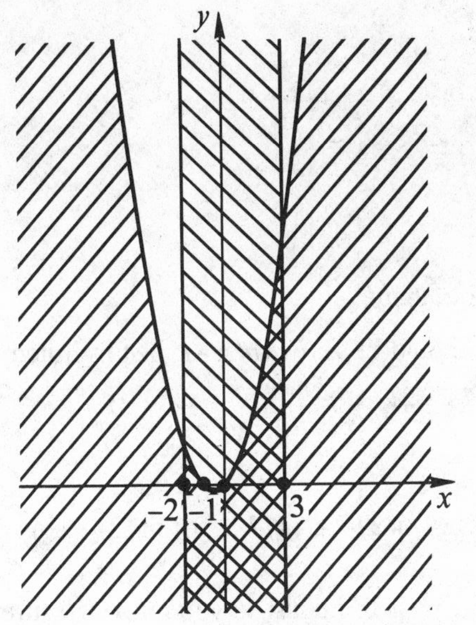

(You could draw this on one graph; the graphs are separated here to show the steps.)

Now, where is the y-value greatest in this shaded region? Where the parabola crosses $x = 3$. And the y-coordinate at the point is calculated from $y = x^2 + x$ as $3^2 + 3 = 9 + 3 = 12$.

47. B.

By the Pythagorean theorem:

$$AB^2 + BC^2 = AC^2$$
$$3^2 + 6^2 = AC^2$$
$$9 + 36 = AC^2$$
$$45 = AC^2$$

So $AC = \pm\sqrt{45}$, and the negative value doesn't make sense for the length of a side.

Then $AC = \sqrt{45} = \sqrt{9 \cdot 5} = 3\sqrt{5}$, so $\overline{AC}$ is $3\sqrt{5}$ units long.

48. G.

To factor $x^2 + 5kx + 4k^2$, find two factors of $4k^2$ that add up to $5k$. Those factors are $1k$ (or k) and $4k$. Therefore:

$$x^2 + 5kx + 4k^2 = 0$$
$$(x + k)(x + 4k) = 0$$

$x + k = 0$ or $x + 4k = 0$

$x = -k$ or $x = -4k$

Then check these:

If $-k$ is a solution, then

$x^2 + 5kx + 4k^2$ should be zero when $-k$ is substituted for x.

$$(-k)^2 + 5k(-k) + 4k^2 = k^2 - 5k^2 + 4k^2 = 0$$ ✓

And for $-4k$

$$(-4k)^2 + 5k(-4k) + 4k^2 = 16k^2 - 20k^2 + 4k^2 = 0$$ ✓

The information that $k > 0$ is there just so you know for sure that the other answers are wrong. What would happen if $k = 0$? The correct answer would still be G, even if you weren't told that $k > 0$.

49. E.

In a right triangle, one leg is the base and the other leg is the height. So, given the area of a right triangle and the length of one leg, you can find the length of the second leg by using the formula for the area of a triangle:

$$A = \frac{1}{2}bh$$

$$24 = \frac{1}{2}(6)h$$

$$24 = 3h$$

$$8 = h$$

A right triangle with legs of 6 and 8 is exactly twice as big on each side as a 3-4-5 right triangle. Therefore, its hypotenuse has a length of twice 5, which is 10, meters.

50. H.

There's a 45°-45°-90° triangle in this problem.

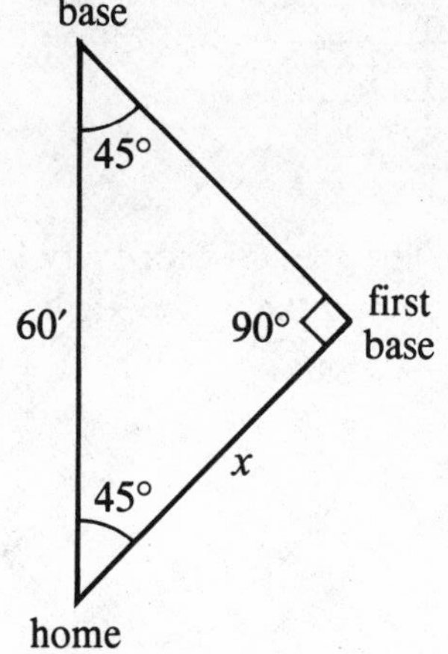

typical 45°-45°-90° triangle

45°
$\sqrt{2}$
1
45°
1

So, by similar triangles, $\frac{x}{60} = \frac{1}{\sqrt{2}} \Longrightarrow x = \frac{60}{\sqrt{2}} = \frac{60\sqrt{2}}{\sqrt{2}\sqrt{2}} = \frac{60\sqrt{2}}{2} = 30\sqrt{2}$

51. B.

If two lines in the (x,y) coordinate plane are perpendicular, their slopes are negative reciprocals of each other. So first find the slope of the given line:

$$m = \frac{y_2 - y_1}{x_2 - x_1} = \frac{5 - (-1)}{4 - 1} = \frac{6}{3} = 2$$

And the perpendicular line's slope is the negative reciprocal, or $-\frac{1}{2}$.

You can see this negative reciprocal relation from the graph.

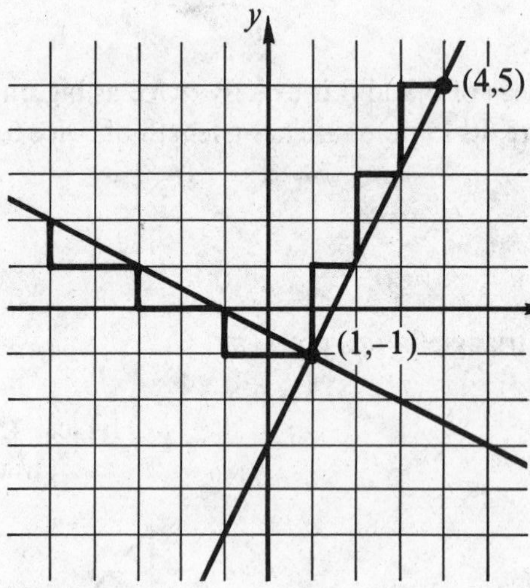

Do you see that the slope of the given line is 2? The line goes up 2 for every 1 that it goes right. The perpendicular line goes down 1 for every 2 that it goes right. And its slope is $\frac{-1}{2} = -\frac{1}{2}$.

52. J.

By definition:

$$\cos\theta = \frac{\text{length of side adjacent to } \theta}{\text{length of hypotenuse}}$$

The length of the side adjacent to θ is given as 5. To find the length of the hypotenuse, use the Pythagorean theorem:

$$a^2 + b^2 = c^2$$

$$4^2 + 5^2 = c^2$$

$$16 + 25 = c^2$$

$$41 = c^2$$

$$\sqrt{41} = c$$ (choose the positive root, since it represents a distance)

So $\cos\theta = \frac{5}{\sqrt{41}}$ and its reciprocal, $\frac{1}{\cos\theta} = \frac{\sqrt{41}}{5}$.

53. C.

Two triangles, $\triangle BAD$ and $\triangle BAC$, are right triangles with $\angle B$ in common, so (by angle-angle-angle similarity) they are similar triangles.

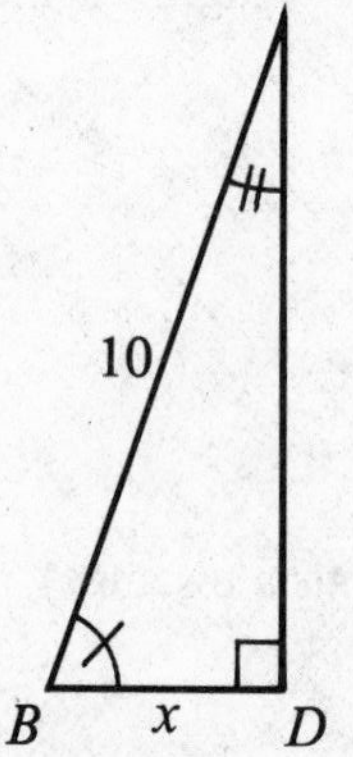

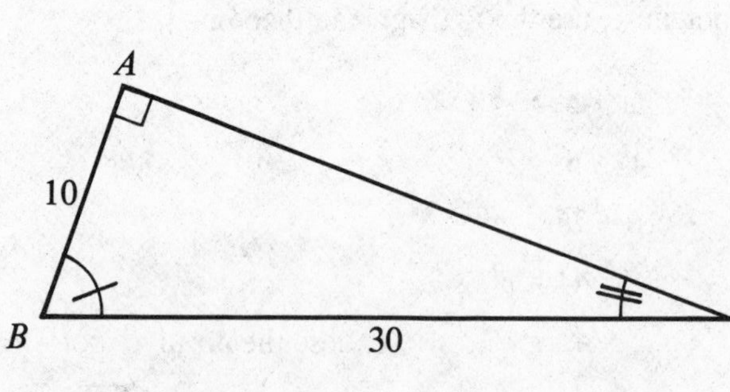

Because the lengths of corresponding sides of similar triangles are proportional,

$$\frac{BD}{AB} = \frac{AB}{BC} \Longrightarrow \frac{x}{10} = \frac{10}{30} \Longrightarrow x = \frac{10}{3}$$

You could also solve this by using the Pythagorean theorem twice, letting y represent the length of $\overline{AD}$ and then solving the system of equations.

54. H.

The lengths of corresponding sides of two similar triangles are proportional. Hence:

$\frac{DE}{AB} = \frac{EF}{BC}$ Set up the proportion and substitute.

$\frac{x}{5} = \frac{3}{4}$ Multiply both sides by 5.

$x = \frac{15}{4}$

55. E.

If x apples cost b cents, then each apple costs $\frac{b}{x}$ cents. At that price, y apples will cost $y\left(\frac{b}{x}\right) = \frac{by}{x}$ cents.

56. J.

Because the curve repeats every 16 seconds, you just have to determine what part of this cycle corresponds to the 46-second point. The zero point corresponds to 16 seconds, 32 seconds, 48 seconds, ... Then, you could draw another graph of the interval from 32 to 48 seconds (or just mark them in on this graph).

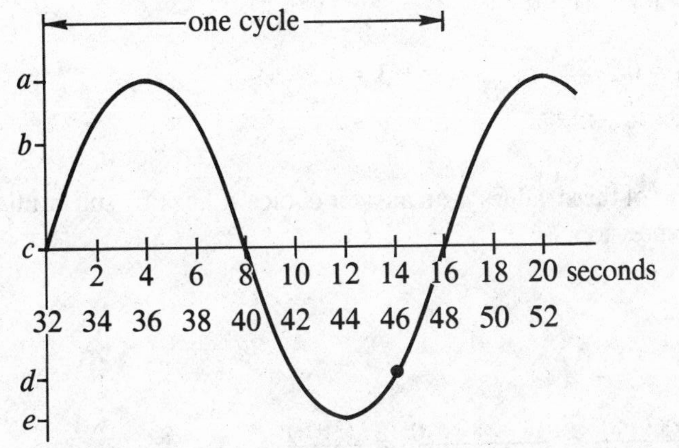

So 46 seconds corresponds to 14 seconds, which has height *d*.

You could have looked at the remainder when 46 was divided by 16, too.

57. A.

A rational expression is undefined when its denominator has a value of 0. Thus, when

$$2x^2 + 5x - 3 = 0$$

$$(2x - 1)(x + 3) = 0$$

$$2x - 1 = 0 \quad \text{or} \quad x + 3 = 0$$

$$x = \frac{1}{2} \qquad\qquad x = -3$$

And the second of these values is an answer choice. Check by substituting $x = -3$ into the rational expression.

58. K.

$$\frac{9 - x^2}{x - 3} = \frac{(3 - x)(3 + x)}{x - 3} = \frac{(3 - x)(3 + x)}{-1(3 - x)} = \frac{(3 + x)}{-1} = -3 - x = -x - 3$$

Or, by division:

$$x - 3\overline{)9 - x^2} \iff \begin{array}{r} -x - 3 \\ x - 3\overline{)-x^2 + 0x + 9} \\ \underline{-x^2 + 3x} \\ -3x + 9 \\ \underline{-3x + 9} \\ 0 \end{array}$$

What about the $x < -3$ part? If $x = +3$, none of the answer choices would be correct. The original fraction is undefined, but choice K has the value –6.

59. D.

The standard form for an ellipse with axes parallel to the coordinate axes is $\frac{(x-h)^2}{a^2} + \frac{(y-k)^2}{b^2} = 1$, where (h,k) are the coordinates of the center, $2a$ is the length of the ellipse's horizontal axis, and $2b$ is the length of the ellipse's vertical axis.

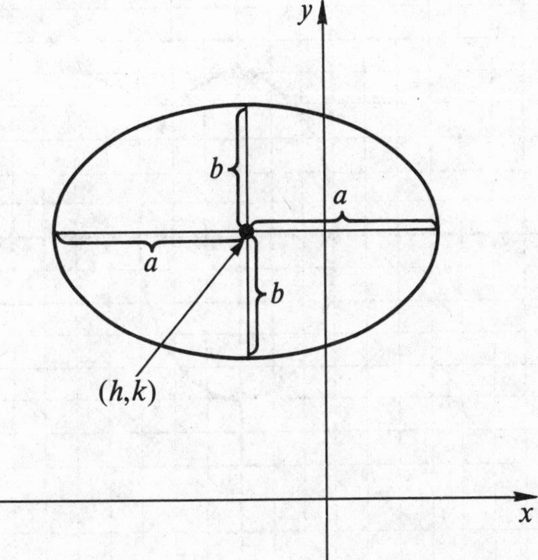

The problem gives enough information to determine that $h = 0$ and $k = 0$, because the center is at (0,0); $a = 3$, because the x-intercepts are at ± 3; and $b = 5$, because the major axis lies on the y-axis and is 10 units long. So, the equation is

$$\frac{x^2}{3^2} + \frac{y^2}{5^2} = 1 \Longrightarrow \frac{x^2}{9} + \frac{y^2}{25} = 1.$$

And here's a graph of the ellipse.

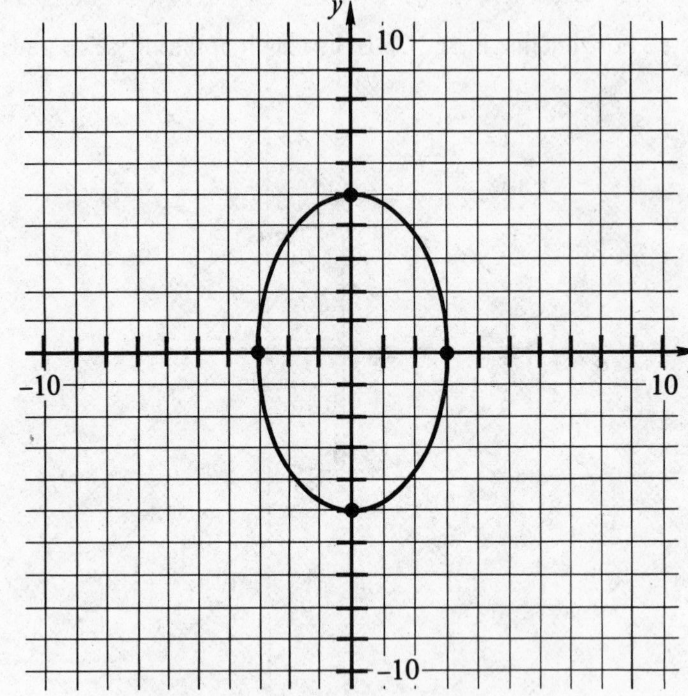

60. K.

Point A is just the intersection of $\overline{AB}$ and $\overline{AD}$. There are lots of ways of finding the intersection. Here are two ways:

Addition:

$6x - 4y = 8$	no change $\Longrightarrow$	$6x - 4y = 8$
$2x - 3y = 4$	multiply by -3	$-6x + 9y = -12$
		$0x + 5y = -4$
		or $y = -\frac{4}{5}$

Now continue this method after step II.

Substitution:

If $6x - 4y = 8$, then $6x = 8 + 4y \Longrightarrow x = \frac{8+4y}{6} = \frac{4+2y}{3}$

And substituting this into $2x - 3y = 4$ gives $2\left(\frac{4+2y}{3}\right) - 3y = 4$

$\Longrightarrow 2(4 + 2y) - 9y = 12 \Longrightarrow 8 + 4y - 9y = 12$

$\Longrightarrow 8 - 5y = 12 \Longrightarrow -5y = 4 \Longrightarrow y = -\frac{4}{5}$

And once you've found y, you can find x.

If $y = -\frac{4}{5}$, then $2x - 3\left(-\frac{4}{5}\right) = 4$

$$2x + \frac{12}{5} = 4$$

$$2x = 4 - \frac{12}{5}$$

$$x = 2 - \frac{6}{5} = \frac{10}{5} - \frac{6}{5} = \frac{4}{5}$$

So the coordinates of A should be $\left(\frac{4}{5}, -\frac{4}{5}\right)$

As a check, substitute $\left(\frac{4}{5}, -\frac{4}{5}\right)$ into each equation

$6x - 4y = 6\left(\frac{4}{5}\right) - 4\left(-\frac{4}{5}\right) = 6\left(\frac{4}{5}\right) + 4\left(\frac{4}{5}\right) = \overset{2}{\cancel{10}}\left(\frac{4}{\underset{1}{\cancel{5}}}\right) = 8$ ✓

$2x - 3y = 2\left(\frac{4}{5}\right) - 3\left(-\frac{4}{5}\right) = 2\left(\frac{4}{5}\right) + 3\left(\frac{4}{5}\right) = 5\left(\frac{4}{5}\right) = 4$ ✓

9

1. B. B is the best answer since the item asks for the **first** visual observation that raindrops oscillate. The fourth paragraph states, "The idea that raindrops oscillate was reinforced by measurement of raindrops frozen in **photographs** taken many years ago at several locations in Illinois." So the visual observation was made through photographs. Response A (wind tunnel studies) does not say whether visual observation was part of those studies or when the studies were conducted. The experiments described in C and D have not yet occurred: "Beard is now planning an experiment," and "Next summer, Johnson is coordinating a study in Hawaii. . . ."

2. J. In this passage, *turbulence* means "fluctuations in the movement of air." The terms *air streams* and *wind tunnel* in lines 51–53 help to define turbulence. F (heavy rainfall) is ruled out because the passage states that water drops are suspended in air streams in the wind tunnel. There is no basis for choosing G (rapid fall) or H (spiraling motion).

3. B. Lines 43–45 state that in **heavy rainfall** the raindrops collide every few seconds. The small drops (less than 0.5 mm) keep the large ones (5 mm) oscillating. Thus, you can infer the opposite—that in a light rainfall, the raindrops **do not collide as often** and are not constantly oscillating. A is ruled out because even though the passage states that a collision between raindrops may create fragments in a breakup, there is no information that the breakup occurs more quickly in heavy rain. C and D deal with the size of the raindrop. The size of the raindrop has an effect on the frequency at which the raindrop oscillates and the plane in which it oscillates, not on whether it will oscillate (lines 55–65).

4. J. The main idea is that scientists believe that studying the creation of drizzle drops—where they **come from** (line 88)—will provide information about raindrop oscillation in general. In this paragraph, Beard speculates about whether drizzle drops are created by collision or start out as drizzle when they fall from the cloud. Drizzle drops are seen as "the key to the source of the oscillations" (lines 90–91), which isn't the same as **being** the source (H). It's true, as F says, that drizzle drops come out of a cloud base (lines 87–88), but the focus of this paragraph is on the implications suggested by how they do so. Drops do collide and rupture (line 89), but the paragraph doesn't concentrate on a discussion of whether they **must** collide before they rupture (G).

5. C. C is the answer—proving that an answer doesn't have to be **perfect** to be **best.** In this context, a better synonym for *oscillate*—which can mean either "to fluctuate" or "to vibrate"—would be *shake.* In fact, if you're a careful reader, you may have noticed the reference in line 22 as well as the way the two words are used interchangeably in lines 57–59. This motion—call it shaking or call it oscillation—causes raindrops to change shapes (lines 15–17). So "change shape" (C) is the best answer—mainly because the other choices are even poorer. Response A is wrong because *collide* means "to bump into"; collisions are **causes** of oscillation, not oscillation itself (lines 36–38). Raindrops oscillate **while** they fall (lines 15–17), so D is wrong. *Accelerate* (B) means "to move faster"; acceleration is mentioned as having a possible effect on oscillation (lines 69–72) but it is not the same as oscillation.

6. G. In wind tunnel studies, drops are suspended (lines 51–52), but they would be fired downward in the shaft experiments (lines 66–69). A variety of drop sizes can be studied both in the wind tunnel (small and large drops are mentioned in lines 63–65) and in the shaft (line 67); there's no basis for concluding that in the shaft they'd be larger (H) or easier to study (F). The only specific mention of photographing and measuring drops (J) is in the fourth paragraph; nothing in the passage implies that photographing and measuring could be done in a shaft but not in a wind tunnel.

7. C. You have to paraphrase *tiny* into "small" and *collide* into "hit" to find the best response. If raindrops are too small, they don't impart enough energy when they hit a big raindrop (lines 82–83); therefore, they **can't** cause the breakup of the larger drops (B). It's true that smaller drops oscillate faster than large ones (lines 57–59), but it's their smallness—not their rate of oscillation—that keeps them from affecting larger drops (D). The sixth paragraph is the only place where coalescing drops are discussed; there's no basis for concluding that a tiny drop and a large one wouldn't coalesce (A).

8. G. Larger drops fall faster and "readily overtake smaller, slowly falling drizzle droplets" (lines 34–35), so H is wrong. Smaller drops tend to **oscillate** vertically (line 64), but they don't necessarily **fall** more vertically (J) than large ones. The sixth and seventh paragraphs explain that collisions don't occur without small drops falling among the large ones; there's no basis for concluding that small raindrops fall with less chance of collision (F).

9. B. A seven-millimeter droplet is considered large. Small drops, or drizzle drops, are less than 0.5 millimeter across (line 10). A drop more than five millimeters across is mentioned **in contrast** (lines 11–12) to the small drops, so we can infer that a drop of that size is considered large. The seven-millimeter drop in this question is even larger. According to the passage, large drops oscillate at **20 cycles per second** (lines 58–59) and tend to oscillate **horizontally** (lines 64–65). Small drops oscillate **vertically** (line 64), at **a few hundred cycles per second** (lines 57–58).

10. F. F is a hypothesis. Meterologist Beard says scientists **don't know** whether drizzle drops are formed when large drops collide and rupture, or if they actually fall from the cloud base as drizzle (lines 88–90). G is a fact—we're told that a drop more than five millimeters across "resembles nothing so much as a hamburger bun" (line 14), so that's how an eight-millimeter drop would appear. (Just think—when people say it's raining cats and dogs, little do they know it's really raining hamburger buns!) H is a fact because according to the passage, a drizzle drop "happens in very intense showers" (line 41), which is another way of describing a heavy downpour. J is a fact, according to lines 60–65. Scientists have identified three modes of oscillation, though why certain drops prefer certain modes is still unknown.

11. D. Mrs. Freeman arrives while Joy is in the bathroom. "Joy would get up . . . and lumber into the bathroom . . . and before long, Mrs. Freeman would arrive at the back door." So Mrs. Freeman does not arrive **before** Joy wakes up (A). The passage states that Mrs. Hopewell gets up at seven o'clock and lights the heaters, but this is **before** Mrs. Freeman arrives. So B and C are ruled out, also.

12. F. F is the best answer because the passage states, "She had hired them in the end because there were no other applicants." There is no evidence in the passage for G. While it is true that Mrs. Hopewell had known the Freemans "for years" (H), she had known them only for the four years **after** she hired them. If she had known them for years **before** she hired them, she probably would not have telephoned references. In J, the reference said that Mrs. Freeman was the "nosiest woman ever to walk the earth." This is a negative quality and not a reason to employ her.

13. A. The reference states, "I can stand him real good," which means that Mr. Freeman is "tolerable" to him. This contrasts with Mrs. Freeman, who is nosy: "She'll want to know all your business," reports the reference. So she is a busybody: "she's got to be into everything." Is she an "unbearable busybody"? Probably so, because neither the reference nor his wife "could have stood that woman one more minute on this place." This passage does not support B; it does not tell whether or not Mr. Freeman is friendly or Mrs. Freeman is unsociable. She is probably very social since she is "into everything." For C, it is true that Mr. Freeman is a farmer. But the passage indicates that Mrs. Freeman doesn't let the dust settle: she makes sure she is around when things are happening so she can know other people's business. The reference states that the only reason she wouldn't be there would be because she had died. For D, line 54 states that Mr. Freeman is already a good farmer, so he doesn't need to **become** one.

14. H. Joy's "constant outrage had obliterated every expression from her face" (lines 81–82). She is not a happy person; she is constantly resentful and angry, and this emotion has left her expressionless. Thus, her name *Joy* does not fit the person described in the passage. Joy's personality is the opposite of what we would expect from her name. When an actual situation is the opposite of an expected result, we label it *ironic.* G and J both mean "appropriate" or "fitting." We know from the passage that Joy's personality does not fit her name. For F, the passage does not indicate that Joy is influential; neither does the word *joy* suggest power or influence.

15. D. It is "most likely" that Joy stares "to the side of" her mother because she does not want to see her mother—she wants to ignore her. This idea is reinforced by the image of a resentful, determined Joy, whose icy blue eyes and expressionless face convey that she is blind. Joy is not physically blind, but here she does not want to look directly at her mother, and therefore can try to disregard or avoid what she chooses. Response A doesn't work because we know that Joy's blindness is not physical. There is no evidence in the passage that the reason for Joy's behavior is that Mrs. Hopewell is not speaking to Joy (B) or that Mrs. Freeman is present (C). What's more, the fact that Joy's outrage is constant (line 81) suggests that the cause of that outrage is larger than either of these considerations.

16. J. The paragraph states that "Mrs. Freeman could never be brought to admit herself wrong on any point" (lines 16–17). Mrs. Freeman rarely uses this "reverse" expression "because it was not often necessary for her to retract a statement" (lines 8–9). The paragraph tells how she responds when it does become necessary (she was "no longer there in spirit"). Then, if she does speak, instead of admitting herself wrong, she is noncommittal or changes the subject.

G is wrong because Mrs. Freeman doesn't really drive a truck (her facial expressions are compared to the gears of a truck). F and H are ruled out because Mrs. Freeman does not lose her temper (with or without provocation), nor does she pretend to be sociable (her sociability is not mentioned in the paragraph).

17. D. D is the best statement of fact. It can be tested against information in the passage; in neutral terms, it restates a happening described in lines 40–42: "Every morning Mrs. Freeman told Mrs. Hopewell how many times she had vomited since the last report."

In A, the key word *justifies* is a judgment or an opinion because a reader could come to the opposite conclusion, based on the passage. According to the passage, it is a fact that Mrs. Hopewell had dusty bottles on her top kitchen shelf (B), but the word *lazy* indicates a judgment about Mrs. Hopewell; so B is not entirely factual. In C, *trite* and *unimaginative* express negative opinions about Mrs. Hopewell's sayings.

18. F. Option I (only) most accurately describes Mrs. Hopewell's opinion of Mrs. Freeman. Lines 70–73 state, "Mrs. Hopewell had no bad qualities of her own but she was able to use other people's in such a constructive way that she never felt the lack." The previous sentences in the passage explain how Mrs. Hopewell decided that since Mrs. Freeman "was the type who had to be into everything," she would turn the bad into good by putting Mrs. Freeman in charge. Since we know that I is accurate, consider III at this point to determine if it is also accurate (J includes both I and III). Note that Mrs. Hopewell's favorite and most important saying is: "well, other people have their opinions too" (lines 77–78). There is no evidence in the passage to indicate that this saying does not apply to Mrs. Freeman. So we can rule out III, which then eliminates responses H and J. For II (G), we know from the first paragraph that one of Mrs. Freeman's qualities is her **un**willingness to compromise. She is "steady and driving" and never swerves; she seldom retracts a statement and could never be brought to admit herself wrong.

19. C. To "grate on one another's nerves" means to irritate or annoy one another. Several sentences contain information about how the women interact; based on the passage, you must infer that there is conflict among the three women. A scene that strongly suggests the three women "grate on one another's nerves" is the one in which Joy sits at the table with Mrs. Freeman and Mrs. Hopewell while Mrs. Hopewell makes her statements.

In addition, for the other responses, there is at least one exception that prevents each statement from applying to **all three** women. For A, we know that Joy is not content with her life; thus, all three women are **not** perfectly satisfied. For B, we can infer that Joy does not admire her mother. In addition, the relationship between Mrs. Hopewell and Mrs. Freeman might be described at best as one of tolerance, rather than "enormous mutual admiration." For D, Mrs. Freeman is described in the first paragraph as unyielding. Mrs. Hopewell's opinions are couched in her "favorite sayings." Thus, D does not apply to all three women.

20. F. From the passage, we can describe Mrs. Freeman as "dogmatic" (stubborn: she will not admit herself wrong), Mrs. Hopewell as "practical" (realistic: she turns other people's faults into advantages), and Joy as "outraged" (she is described in line 81 as being in a state of "constant outrage"). In G, we know that Mrs. Freeman is **not** flexible. (Mrs. Hopewell is not pitiless and Joy is not stoic, either.) For H, even though Mrs. Freeman is relentless, Mrs. Hopewell is not unconcerned and Joy is not charitable. J is ruled out because (even if there is not enough evidence to decide whether Mrs. Freeman is "fatalistic") Mrs. Hopewell is not ruthless and Joy is certainly not carefree.

21. D. The passage states, "but racial barriers prevented him from ever exercising his mature power in the land of his birth" (lines 87–89). In other words, he did not achieve professional success as an **actor** in America because prejudices against black performers (racial barriers) were common. Although A might imply a "racial barrier," the issue is not the frequency of black **characters,** but whether Aldridge, who was a black actor, was allowed on stage to perform. There is no evidence in the passage to support B or C.

22. J. The best answer is J—"a particularly American style of comedy." The second paragraph ends with this statement: "Ultimately, the vogue for the Yankee . . . is perhaps most important for its role in establishing a native American comedy." *Vogue* means popularity, and *native* means that it was a particularly American style. For F, the passage discusses Yankee roles for comic actors or specialty performers, but does not deal with influence on tragedies. Neither, for G, is there mention of an influence that Yankee roles had on melodramas. For H, there is no evidence in the passage that Yankee roles influenced roles for black or other minority performers. Black roles are discussed after Yankee roles, but no tie is stated.

23. C. The quotation marks enclosing "Jim Crow" indicate that he is a character in American drama, not a real person. The passage states that the black is a "faithful servant or comic caricature" (lines 52–53). The following sentence discusses "Jim Crow" doing song and dance; the next phrase, "despite such caricatures," suggests that Jim Crow is a caricature or a comic imitation. Thus, he is not a faithful servant (B). Since "Jim Crow" was a character, not a person, he could not be an actor (D) or an actor's partner (A).

24. F. Brown's African Company may have closed down because of "harassment (annoyance) from prejudiced whites." F is the best answer because the passage states that the company was "plagued by white rowdies and perhaps because of these difficulties it fades from surviving records after 1823" (lines 71–73). Notice that the company was not mentioned after 1823, and Aldridge made his debut in London in 1825. Thus, Aldridge's departure (G) could not be a reason for the end of the company. The passage does not support either scarcity of suitable plays (H) or scarcity of suitable theater buildings (J).

25. B. The best answer is B, that the Yankee was **not** sophisticated. He was not worldly; he was a simple, common man, "despising pretense and sham."

26. H. Aldridge is discussed as receiving "enthusiastic response" in Europe and was decorated by rulers of several countries. The last sentence indicates that Aldridge was not well received by **American** audiences because he was black. Line 71 also refers to the company of black actors, which was "plagued by white rowdies." For F, even if you assume that black characters **were** stereotypes, the passage implies that the characters were very popular. They had "a host of imitators" (line 56). For G, again assuming that the roles were stereotypes, there is no evidence that it would have been possible for the performers to be more popular. J deals with "American native types." Note that the passage considers the black an American "native type" (line 50). European audiences **were** receptive to Aldridge, particularly his performances of Shakespeare. Thus, if blacks are "American native types," J could not be accurate.

27. B. In early American drama, stereotypical (overworked, trite, unoriginal) characters were popular. The passage discusses the "faithful servant," the "comic caricature," and the "Jim Crow" song and dance, which was created by Rice and imitated by other actors. Response A treats **realistic** black characters. The characters discussed in the third paragraph are not realistic or true to life. For C, the passage does not discuss Rice's views on racial equality; nor does it say that he promoted his views through his characters. For D, you cannot say, based on the third paragraph, that American drama has **never** offered accurate depictions, because there is not enough information.

28. G. The passage states, "With Hill, the Yankee became more sympathetic and sentimental" (lines 38–39). So if Hill was "more sympathetic" and "more sentimental," then **Hackett** was **less** sentimental. F is ruled out because it was Hill who was more sympathetic. For H, Hackett was "the first important actor of Yankee roles" but Hill was "considered the **best** of the Yankee specialists." For J, Hackett and Hill are not discussed in terms of a "generalized" Yankee character. It was Dan Marble who was "a more generalized American type."

29. D. Response D (included Indians as characters) is the best answer. It is the Indian characters who are common to the four plays. Lines 3–5 state, "The Indian was presented sympathetically, following the romantic tradition of the 'noble savage,' and provided strong roles for serious performers." In other words, Indian characters were presented in American plays; these characters provided strong roles for performers. The passage doesn't state that the playwrights were Indian (A) or that the actors were Indian (B). For C (Indian causes), the passage does state that the Indian was "presented sympathetically," but this was a character in the **romantic tradition** of the "noble savage." The passage doesn't detail any beliefs held by the Indians or indicate that any causes were promoted in the plays.

30. H. The passage states, "The type was dealt a serious blow by John Brougham's burlesque, *Po-ca-hon-tas* (1855), but not until after 1870 was the 'noble savage' tradition abandoned" (lines 14–17). So *Po-ca-hon-tas* (not *Pocahontas*), a burlesque or comic play, satirized "conventional features" of Indian plays. For F, *Po-ca-hon-tas* did not provide impetus, but instead aided the decline of Indian plays. For G, the passage indicates that the play *Po-ca-hon-tas,* instead of being the "best example of the type," actually was a satire of the "noble savage" type and led to its abandonment. Part of J is true: *Po-ca-hon-tas* decreased interest in Indian drama, but it did not **follow** the romantic tradition of the "noble savage." Instead, the play made fun of this Indian character in American drama.

31. A. The best choice is A, "Women had demonstrated their ability to contribute to the war effort." The first paragraph states, "The fact that men and women of all classes contributed to the military effort gave force to the demand that they should have the right to decide the political fate of their country." Their decision would be made by voting. The rest of the paragraph tells how this contribution by women to the war made the demand for suffrage "more urgent and its justification was much more generally recognized." For B, the passage does not state that the motto was written into the peace treaty; neither does this sentence explain why the demand for women's suffrage was recognized as justifiable. In C, suffrage can be considered a democratic reform, but the passage does not discuss the Conservatives in relation to women's suffrage. For D, the passage does not state that the tsar and William II were the chief opponents of women's suffrage. Also, there is no information in the passage to indicate William II was deposed.

32. H. The "belief" is expressed by both options I and III. The phrase "this ideological and moralistic view" refers to the preceding sentence. The view or "notion" is that:

1. "the enemy was evil" and
2. "his defeat would create the foundation for a better world."

So the best answer includes both options I and III. Option II is incorrect because the passage indicates that propaganda was used by **all** governments; therefore, those choices that include II (F, G, and J) are incorrect.

33. A. The first paragraph states, "As long as Russia with its authoritarian government was a member of the coalition against Germany, the assertion about fighting for democracy had a hollow sound. But after the overthrow of the tsar in March, 1917, the notion of a struggle . . . gained meaning." In other words, the slogan was not entirely accurate until 1917, when the authoritarian government of Russia was overthrown. Then all of the Allies had democratic governments. B can be ruled out because the war was a struggle for a new world order based on "national self-determination" **before** 1917. C is not accurate because the coalition against Germany did not end in 1917 but actually became stronger because the United States entered the war. D is a true statement, based on the passage, but does not answer the question of why the slogan had "a hollow sound" until 1917.

34. H. The quotation from the passage that best supports the view is H. "Men and women of all classes" conveys the idea of the entire nation's efforts, and the rest of the quotation states that these men and women "contributed to the military effort." F stresses the end of the war and the defeat of the enemy but doesn't mention the efforts of the entire nation. G includes only two groups involved in the war effort: leaders of heavy industry and Conservatives; these two groups are not the entire nation. J discusses a struggle for a new world order, but the response emphasizes the **world** effort (not the effort of a nation as is required by the question) and does not specify **who** was involved in the struggle.

35. A. The second paragraph states, "William II, who even in peacetime had failed to exercise steady leadership, did not dare to challenge the men of the hour." So you know that William II was not powerful in peacetime and that he didn't dare challenge the military leaders during the war. Therefore, you can reason in general terms that he was a "weak leader."

The remaining responses (B, C, and D) are based on ideas discussed in the passage but not connected to William II. The Social Democrats of B are discussed as being important to the leaders in power, but they were not part of the government. It was the Conservative bureaucracy that ruled Germany along with the military dictatorship. But the problem was not that the bureaucracy was too conservative (C); it was that William was weak and the military was powerful. The passage doesn't state or imply (D) that "a majority of the people never wholeheartedly supported the war"; this idea is not the reason for William's lack of dictatorial control.

36. F. It is the only response that is true, according to the passage; also it is evidence for the theory that "war causes social change."

The first paragraph begins a discussion of the idea that World War I was a major factor in women's gaining the right to vote. Women's suffrage is an example of social change (where some aspect of society is altered); World War I caused this change in women's voting rights. For G, note that the second sentence in the passage states that this "view made **impossible** a negotiated peace aimed at reestablishing a balance of power and restoring international collaboration." Therefore, the response is not accurate and cannot support the theory. The passage does discuss the overthrow of the tsar during World War I (H), but not enough information is given to assert that the war **caused** the overthrow of the tsar. So this sentence is not accurate and thus cannot support the theory. There is nothing in the passage on which to base J: the rise of the German Social Democratic party is not linked to anti-annexationist sentiment in Germany. So J is not true and cannot be used to support the theory that war causes social change.

37. D. In the passage, the first sentence states that the notion the enemy was evil was "nurtured by propaganda and publicly proclaimed by **all governments.**" In addition, the third sentence states that, "Each side was convinced that the war could end only with the complete defeat of the enemy." In World War I, Germany considered Great Britain and the U.S. the enemy; to Great Britain and the U.S., Germany was the enemy. D includes option I (Great Britain), option II (Germany), and option III (the U.S.). The notion that the enemy was evil was proclaimed by all three countries; therefore, the correct response must include all three.

38. J. The fundamental patriotism of the German Social Democratic party compelled them to act contrary to the principles of their ideology. The passage states, "Socialist approval of the money bills required for the financing of the war was the most striking and also the most surprising example of the **abandonment of revolutionary internationalism** by Social Democrats **in favor of defense of the homeland.**" In other words, the Social Democrats gave up their goal of internationalism in order to defend their homeland of Germany. This patriotic move was in opposition to their ideology. For F, "Socialist approval of the money bills required for the financing of the war" indicates that the German Social Democrats **approved** the financing of the war. So F is incorrect. It was the **government** that kept socialist and progressive forces out of the government (G) but still gained their support. The German Social Democratic party **is** a socialist force, so G is illogical. For H, the passage states that the socialists **abandoned revolutionary internationalism** in favor of defense of the homeland, so H is ruled out.

39. B. "When a quick victory proved elusive, however, those who opposed such war aims . . . began to raise their voices. Annexationists were confronted by those who believed that peace ought to be concluded on the basis of the status quo. . . ." In other words, there were two opposing views during the war. On one side were leaders of heavy industry and Conservatives supported by the military under Ludendorff who believed in total victory to attain expansionist goals. On the other side were the anti-annexationists who, when they realized that Germany was not winning the war, spoke out to end the war. Note that A is inaccurate. The military under Ludendorff supported total victory to attain expansionist goals; thus, their goal was annexation, not **anti**-annexation. Response C is also inaccurate: the Social Democrats didn't take control of the government, nor was this a reason for the rise of anti-annexationist sentiment. For D, the passage states that the leaders of heavy industry and Conservatives were supported **by** the military under Ludendorff. So this response is inaccurate because it is not the reason for the anti-annexationist strength.

40. H. You are asked to draw a conclusion (about the chief German war aim) based on the stated fact that Conservatives and the military effectively ruled Germany during the war. The last part of the passage discusses how the Conservatives, military, and others had as their goal the annexation of valuable territory belonging to other countries. In particular, land in France, Belgium, and the east is mentioned: "Until almost the final months of the war, leaders of heavy industry and Conservatives supported by the military under Ludendorff asserted the need to fight for total victory so that Germany could attain **these expansionist goals.**"

For F, while it is true that the Social Democrats abandoned revolutionary internationalism, this position was not forced on the group by the Conservatives and military. ("The German government gained the support of socialist and progressive forces without taking them into the government.") So, the Social Democrats' view was not the chief German war aim. G can be ruled out because the passage does not support the idea that Germany caused the overthrow of the authoritarian tsarist regime in Russia. The overthrow was not related to German war aims. At first glance, J might be a possible best answer. The second paragraph states that the German military became powerful during the war and "began to exert—if not in form, at least in fact—a military dictatorship." But this dictatorship was not the chief war aim; it was a means to attain power in the government in order to achieve the war aim of annexing territory.

1. A. The experimental results suggest that most isopods prefer to live in a dark, damp place. All experiments took place at a constant temperature (which is not known) so you have no information to conclude B. Green plants need light, and nothing is mentioned about what isopods eat, so C would be a poor choice. You again have no information from the passage in order to arrive at D as a conclusion, even if it were true.

2. H. A home in the sand and mud of the bottom or shore of the ocean would be damp and relatively dark. A freshwater lake (F) would certainly be moist enough, but it would be too light near its surface. G (the surface of a rock) doesn't provide you with enough information to evaluate the degree of moisture or light present. The sunlit surface of leaves (J) is clearly too light.

3. A. Given a choice, isopods prefer damp conditions. Isopods were given a choice of moisture conditions in Experiment 1, not lighting conditions as in B and D. The results of Experiment 1 show that isopods have a marked preference for damp conditions, unlike the equal preferences stated in C.

4. J. Isolating each isopod would neutralize the influence of social behavior. The other choices do not involve isolation. Using isopods of one sex (F) might result in limiting your conclusions to characteristics of one sex. Using only sexually immature isopods (G) might bias your conclusions toward pre-adults. Using only isopods raised in captivity (H) might not reflect the preferences of wild isopods.

5. D. It is dark under desert rocks, which appears to be one of the primary concerns of an isopod when there is a lack of water. The other choices (A, B, and C) involve the surface of objects in the desert, where there are likely to be light and dry conditions at least some of the time. This combination of factors is not preferred by any of the isopods in the experiments.

6. J. Recording information at five-minute intervals would give you more opportunities to determine what is happening and when it is occurring. The other responses (F, G, and H) involve more widely spaced periods of time, so you could miss changes that occur in shorter intervals. Habitat locations are apparently also recorded only once in F, G, and H, so you wouldn't get an idea of developments over a period of time.

7. D. On the diagram, 4.7 kilometers falls within the depth interval at which you find only carbon dioxide and water being produced. At a depth of 0.5 kilometers (A), the diagram does not show that anything is being generated or produced. At a depth of 2.0 kilometers (B), oil and gas are generated and produced. At a depth of 3.0 kilometers (C), again oil and gas are generated and produced.

8. H. A sample with a thermal maturation index of III would have been collected from a depth between 3 and 4 kilometers. A depth between 1 and 2 kilometers (F) would have yielded a sample with a thermal maturation index of I or II. A depth between 2 and 3 kilometers (G) would have yielded a sample with a thermal maturation index of II. A depth between 4 and 5 kilometers (J) would have yielded a sample with a thermal maturation index of IV or V.

9. A. Diagram A shows the kerogen color and thermal maturation index determined in Experiment 1 (light yellow = I; yellow = II; orange = III; brown = IV; black = V). Diagram B shows exactly the opposite association. Diagram C suggests that black indicates a thermal maturation index of I, II, or III, brown indicates IV, and orange, yellow, and light yellow indicate V. According to Diagram D, black indicates a thermal maturation index of I, brown and orange indicate II, yellow indicates III and IV, and light yellow indicates V.

10. H. An orange kerogen sample indicates thermal maturation index zone III. Based on the previous studies in western Canada, this zone generates relatively large quantities of gas, lesser amounts of oil, and a small amount of carbon dioxide and water. Therefore, a well penetrating such a source rock would probably produce mainly gas and oil. Substances other than just gas (F) or carbon dioxide (G) would most likely be produced. You would have to have really bad luck for the well to produce mainly carbon dioxide and water (J).

11. B. Wood-derived kerogen tends to be a source of gas (A) and coal (C), not oil. Algal-derived kerogen tends to be a source of waxes (D) and oil. So only B is **not** consistent with the information.

12. F. In Experiment 1, geologists investigated the process of hydrocarbon generation by controlling the temperature, pressure, and length of time kerogen was submitted to these conditions. Experiment 2 documented at what depths hydrocarbons and other substances were found in western Canada (G), but not how they got there. Responses H and J are simply false statements about what the diagram in Experiment 2 is or is not showing, and they say nothing about how hydrocarbon generation occurs.

13. B. The line for Animal 1 shows that an increase in temperature always leads to an increase in respiratory rate for this animal. Unlike the other animals, Animal 1 never shows a decrease in respiratory rate with an increase in temperature (A). There is always a change in respiratory rate associated with a change in temperature for Animal 1, contrary to C. Decreases in temperature never lead to an increase in respiratory rate for Animal 1 (D), unlike the other animals.

14. G. Animals 1 and 2 both breathe about 38 times per minute at a temperature of 29° C. Animal 1 and **Animal 4** have similar respiratory rates at a temperature of 14° C (F). All lines seem to end at about 39° C (H), where the respiratory rate for each animal is different. The highest labeled temperature is 40° C (J), but no line extends that far.

15. A. Animal 4 uses significantly more oxygen per minute than Animal 2, yet Animal 2 breathes about twice as much as Animal 4. This implies that Animal 4 is significantly larger than Animal 2, since it takes in more oxygen per breath. Response B offers exactly the opposite conclusion. Significant **differences** are discussed above, which doesn't seem to be a good reason to conclude that Animals 2 and 4 weigh the **same** (C). Since all of the animals were tested under the same conditions, response D makes no sense.

16. F. Respiratory rate is sometimes used to suggest the amount of oxygen used by cells in an organism. Oxygen is necessary for an animal to use food. The respiratory rate line for Animal 1 suggests that it uses less oxygen and therefore probably less food at 5° C than at 25° C. Animals 2, 3, and 4 have higher respiratory rates at 5° C than at 25° C, which rules out responses G, H, and J.

17. A. Animal 1 has a body process that changes in a similar way with a change in temperature, and therefore fits the cold-blooded pattern. Animals 2, 3, and 4 (B, C, and D) have respiratory rates that decline or remain steady over a significant part of the temperature range shown. This suggests that their respiratory rates are not directly linked to external temperature, although temperature could very well be a complicating factor.

18. G. A gradual increase in the rate of fusion would lead to the gradual production of more neutrinos and gradually increasing chances of interaction with chlorine to produce argon. A gradual decline (F) would be an opposite conclusion. Responses H and J involve trends that reverse course and are not necessarily gradual.

19. C. If twice as many gallons of C_2Cl_4 were used, the rate of argon production would likely increase and be approximately twice what it was before, due to the presence of twice as much chlorine. There would be more opportunities for interaction, not less (A and D). From what is stated in the passage, a rate increase by about a factor of 4 (B) would imply **more** than doubling the initial amount of chlorine available.

20. H. Davis should carry out many trials and calculate averages to obtain an accurate and stable value. Adding a known amount of argon each day (F) would inflate the amount of argon collected and might be a good test if you suspected that there was some kind of leak in the system. Adding water (G) would dilute the C_2Cl_4. Adding one argon atom for every argon atom produced (J) would double the amount of argon.

21. A. The passage states that the tank was placed far underground to neutralize the effect of cosmic rays. This effect could be studied simply by not shielding the tank. Davis would learn most about the influence of cosmic rays on argon production from chlorine by setting up a detector exposed to cosmic rays on the surface of Earth. Surrounding the water jacket with lead (B) would further shield the tank from cosmic rays. Placing radioactive materials nearby (C) would test the effect of those radioactive materials on the C_2Cl_4. Reducing the amount of C_2Cl_4 (D) doesn't help cosmic rays get to the tank.

22. F. Since enormous numbers of neutrinos pass through Earth each second and few of them interact with matter of any kind, and since the rate that is being measured is the amount of argon produced from chlorine per day, Davis probably assumed among other things that being in a compound wouldn't significantly affect how chlorine atoms interact with neutrinos. Whether carbon atoms interact with neutrinos (G and H) is irrelevant, because of the specific rate being measured and the large quantity of neutrinos available. Chlorine atoms do interact with neutrinos, contrary to J.

23. D. The results from Experiment 2 appear to be less than the theoretical prediction of one argon atom produced per day. Trial 3 is much higher than the other trials and probably reflects an unknown event or error of some kind. Range results from five of six trials in Experiment 2 fall below the theoretical prediction (A). Experiment 1 has results close to the theoretical prediction, but likely reflects additional argon production by non-neutrinos (B). Response C is directly contradicted by the data.

24. J. All members of one row represent one generation. All members in Row IV represent brothers and sisters (F) of each other, but this relationship cannot be applied to all the other rows. No pairs of individuals are shown to be cousins (G) in any row. Rows II, III, and IV have individuals that are not shown to be married to each other (H).

25. B. Individuals with Characteristic Y inherited it from a parent. Not all children of parents with Characteristic Y have that characteristic (A). Probabilities of having Characteristic Y in offspring (C) vary from mating pair to mating pair. The pedigree shows how Characteristic Y has been inherited from generation to generation; there is no evidence, and it is highly unlikely, that Characteristic Y would spring commonly from a new allele (D), whether dominant or not.

26. G. Characteristic Y is seen in offspring of parents with Characteristic Y and therefore may result from a dominant allele. Parents of individuals with Characterisic X (responses F and J) do not show Characteristic X; therefore, there is no evidence to show that that characteristic is dominant. Characteristic Z (response H) skips a generation and so is not dominant.

27. A. Characteristic X is seen only in Row IV because it is probably a recessive characteristic. Characteristic X is not seen in parents of individuals having it, so the characteristic is not dominant (B). Everyone has biological parents (we are all children), and there is no evidence to suggest that Characteristic X mysteriously disappears at some point; therefore, response C is inappropriate. It is entirely possible that an individual with Characteristic X could have children with Characteristic X, so response D is incorrect.

28. J. Characteristic X is a recessive characteristic—that is, it is only seen in the absence of a dominant allele. Therefore, offspring of a female (xx) and male (xx) with Characteristic X have a 100% chance of showing Characteristic X. No other combinations (F, G, and H) are possible.

29. D. Hypothesis 2 maintains that honeybees use distinctive odors to locate food or home sites. This idea requires that bees be able to tell the difference among odors in order to find particular food or home sites. Smell rather than sight (A) is the particular emphasis of Hypothesis 2. Differences in odors instead of similarities (B) are supposed to be what allows a bee to locate a particular food or home site. The effect of distance (C) is not specifically mentioned as a part of Hypothesis 2 and would not eliminate the attractiveness of flowers for bees anyway.

30. F. Honeybees are apparently a fine judge of the passage of time and can be said to have an internal clock. The new information seems to add support to Hypothesis 1 rather than suggest that it be discarded (G). Hypothesis 1 provides an alternative use for the waggle dance, contrary to H. Scouts may use other unknown reference points in addition to the Sun (J), but the new information refers to the Sun and no other hypothetical reference point.

31. D. If most newly recruited foragers went to Station C, the experiment would support the emphasis on odor in Hypothesis 2 (option I). If newly recruited foragers visited all three stations, Hypothesis 2 might still be true even though it isn't supported (option III). An unperceived complicating factor, such as the social behavior of following another forager, might account for the discrepancy. If most newly recruited foragers still went to Stations A and B after Station C was established, then the experiment would not support Hypothesis 2—but would it tend to strongly disagree with it?

32. J. The effect of distance on the dance rate of scouts is being investigated (option II). Therefore, explanations involving other factors (not being investigated) make up the correct answer. The experiment was performed on calm days, so that wind would not be a complicating factor (option I). Experience of scouts was not accounted for in any way in the experiment, so explanations involving it (option III) are pure speculation.

33. C. Both hypotheses imply that honeybees work together to find food and new home sites, and therefore have a functional hive (option III). While both agree that the waggle dance implies that food or a new home site has been found, only Hypothesis 1 claims that the dance communicates where they are to be found (options I and II).

34. G. Honeybees that fly into the wind will collide with odors sooner or in a more robust state of smell and therefore will be able to locate food or a home site more easily. Finding that foragers continue to collect food from the same target after scouts have stopped advertising the location (F) says nothing about the method by which the scouts originally advertised the location. A lack of wind (H) would not clearly affect either hypothesis. The effects of relative humidity (J) are not discussed in the passage, and it is unclear what those effects would be.

35. D. A random dance pattern (option I) would not be expected to inform foragers of a specific target, according to Hypothesis 1. A change in the fixed orientation of the honeycomb (option III) would be expected to confuse, at least temporarily, the foragers' geographic orientation outside of the hive (sort of like being told the directions to a house beginning from a particular spot, but then starting out for that house from a different spot), so that not all would be able to find the target. A dance rate corresponding to a particular distance can differ among different species of honeybees (option II). The important thing is that for a particular species, different dance rates correspond to different particular distances.

36. J. Nitrogen (N) has an electronegativity of about 3.0, which is about 1 less than fluorine (F). The difference between chlorine (Cl) and sulfur (S) is about 0.5 (3.0 – 2.5). The difference between bromine (Br) and manganese (Mn) is about 1.2 (2.7 – 1.5). The difference between nitrogen (N) and carbon (C) is about 0.5 (3.0 – 2.5).

37. C. Sodium (Na), potassium (K), and rubidium (Rb) have the three lowest electronegativities (all less than 1.00) and are therefore the most metallic. Calcium (Ca) has a higher electronegativity than rubidium (response A). Lithium (Li), while the lowest in its line, has a higher electronegativity than rubidium (response B). Fluorine (F), oxygen (O), and nitrogen (N) have the highest electronegativities, so they may be thought of as the least metallic.

38. H. Diagram H represents the highly unequal sharing of electrons between atoms with a high electronegativity difference. Diagram F shows a nonpolar covalent bond. Diagram G represents a covalent bond that is less polar than the one shown in H. Diagram J displays an ionic bond.

39. A. An electronegativity difference of about 1.8 in Figure 2 corresponds to a 60% ionic character. Sodium (Na) and fluorine (F) have an electronegativity difference of about 3.2, which corresponds to a percent ionic character greater than 60 (about 90%). Magnesium (Mg) and sulfur (S) differ by about 1.3, which corresponds to about 30% ionic character (response B). Nitrogen (N) and chlorine (Cl) differ by very little, suggesting their bond reflects almost no ionic character (response C). Tellurium (Te) and iodine (I) differ by about 0.5, suggesting about 10% ionic character (response D).

40. H. Here's a way of showing the pairs of elements, their approximate electronegativity differences, and associated percent ionic character. The order of increasing percent ionic character is C—I < C—Br < C—N < C—O.

Bonding pair	Electronegativity difference	% ionic character
C—Br	0.3	5
C—I	0.1	2
C—O	1.0	22
C—N	0.5	10

9

SCORING YOUR PRACTICE TESTS

HOW TO SCORE THE PRACTICE TESTS

In this section you'll find scoring keys and score conversion tables. Follow the instructions below and on the following pages to score the practice tests and review your performance.

RAW SCORES

The number of questions you answered correctly on each test and in each subscore area is your *raw score.* To compute your raw scores, check your answers with the scoring keys on the following pages. Count the number of correct answers for each of the four tests and seven subscore areas, and enter the numbers in the blanks provided on those pages. These numbers are your raw scores on the tests and subscore areas.

Because there are many forms of the ACT, each containing different questions, some forms will be slightly easier (and some slightly harder) than others. A raw score of 57 on one form of the English Test, for example, may be about as difficult to earn as a raw score of 60 on another form of that test.

SCALE SCORES

To adjust for the small differences that occur between different forms of the ACT, the raw scores for tests and subscore areas are converted into *scale scores.* Scale scores are printed on the reports sent to you and your college and scholarship choices.

When your raw scores are converted into scale scores, it becomes possible to compare your scores with those of examinees who completed different test forms. For example, a scale score of 26 on the English Test has the same meaning regardless of the form of the ACT on which it is based.

To determine the scale scores corresponding to your raw scores on the practice test in Section 6 or the two sample tests in Section 9, use the score conversion table that applies to the specific test. In each case, the first table shows the raw-to-scale-score conversions for the total tests, and the second table shows the raw-to-scale-score conversions for the subscore areas. Because each form of the ACT Assessment is unique, each form has somewhat different conversion tables. Consequently, these tables provide only approximations of the raw-score-to-scale-score conversions that would apply if a different form of the ACT Assessment were taken. By the way, the scale scores obtained from the practice tests would not be expected to match precisely the scale scores received from a national administration of the ACT Assessment.

SCORING KEYS FOR THE ACT PRACTICE TEST (IN SECTION 6)

Use the scoring key for each test to score your answer sheet for the practice test. Mark a "1" in the blank for each item you answered correctly. Add up the numbers in each subscore area and enter the total number correct for each subscore area in the blanks provided. Also enter the total number correct for each test in the blanks provided. The total number correct for each test is the sum of the number correct in each subscore area.

ENGLISH—SCORING KEY

	Key	Subscore Area* UM	Subscore Area* RH		Key	Subscore Area* UM	Subscore Area* RH		Key	Subscore Area* UM	Subscore Area* RH
1.	D	____		26.	J	____		51.	D	____	
2.	F		____	27.	C	____		52.	J	____	
3.	A	____		28.	H		____	53.	B	____	
4.	H		____	29.	D		____	54.	J		____
5.	B		____	30.	J		____	55.	B		____
6.	J		____	31.	A		____	56.	H		____
7.	C	____		32.	J		____	57.	C	____	
8.	F	____		33.	B		____	58.	F	____	
9.	A		____	34.	J		____	59.	A		____
10.	H	____		35.	D	____		60.	G		____
11.	B		____	36.	J		____	61.	A		____
12.	G	____		37.	D		____	62.	F	____	
13.	D		____	38.	G	____		63.	A		____
14.	H	____		39.	C	____		64.	F	____	
15.	D	____		40.	H	____		65.	C	____	
16.	F	____		41.	D		____	66.	J		____
17.	B	____		42.	J	____		67.	A	____	
18.	F	____		43.	D	____		68.	J		____
19.	D	____		44.	G		____	69.	C	____	
20.	G	____		45.	B		____	70.	J	____	
21.	B	____		46.	H		____	71.	B		____
22.	F		____	47.	C	____		72.	J	____	
23.	B	____		48.	J	____		73.	C	____	
24.	J		____	49.	A		____	74.	G		____
25.	C	____		50.	H	____		75.	B		____

Number Correct (Raw Score) for:

Usage/Mechanics (UM) Subscore Area	____ (40)
Rhetorical Skills (RH) Subscore Area	____ (35)
Total Number Correct for English Test (UM + RH)	____ (75)

* UM = Usage/Mechanics
RH = Rhetorical Skills

MATHEMATICS—SCORING KEY

	Key	Subscore Area* EA	AG	GT
1.	E			____
2.	K	____		
3.	A	____		
4.	K	____		
5.	C	____		
6.	K		____	
7.	C			____
8.	J	____		
9.	D	____		
10.	K	____		
11.	D	____		
12.	J		____	
13.	D			____
14.	K	____		
15.	A	____		
16.	G	____		
17.	C			____
18.	G			____
19.	E	____		
20.	F	____		
21.	B		____	
22.	G	____		
23.	D			____
24.	H	____		
25.	B		____	
26.	G		____	
27.	B		____	
28.	F		____	
29.	E	____		
30.	J			____

	Key	Subscore Area* EA	AG	GT
31.	C			____
32.	J			____
33.	C			____
34.	F	____		
35.	B	____		
36.	G		____	
37.	D		____	
38.	J	____		
39.	B			____
40.	H	____		
41.	D		____	
42.	J		____	
43.	A		____	
44.	H	____		
45.	E			____
46.	F		____	
47.	C		____	
48.	G			____
49.	D		____	
50.	G			____
51.	D		____	
52.	K	____		
53.	A			____
54.	F		____	
55.	C			____
56.	J			____
57.	E	____		
58.	J	____		
59.	E			____
60.	K		____	

Number Correct (Raw Score) for:

Pre-Alg./Elem. Alg. (EA) Subscore Area	____ (24)
Inter. Alg./Coor. Geo. (AG) Subscore Area	____ (18)
Plane Geo./Trig. (GT) Subscore Area	____ (18)
Total Number Correct for Math Test (EA + AG + GT)	____ (60)

* EA = Pre-Algebra/Elementary Algebra
AG = Intermediate Algebra/Coordinate Geometry
GT = Plane Geometry/Trigonometry

9

READING—SCORING KEY

	Key	Subscore Area* SS	AL		Key	Subscore Area* SS	AL		Key	Subscore Area* SS	AL
1.	A		____	15.	C	____		29.	D		____
2.	J		____	16.	G	____		30.	J		____
3.	C		____	17.	B	____		31.	B	____	
4.	J		____	18.	G	____		32.	F	____	
5.	C		____	19.	D	____		33.	B	____	
6.	F		____	20.	H	____		34.	F	____	
7.	D		____	21.	B		____	35.	D	____	
8.	F		____	22.	J		____	36.	J	____	
9.	A		____	23.	D		____	37.	D	____	
10.	H		____	24.	F		____	38.	H	____	
11.	B	____		25.	A		____	39.	B	____	
12.	H	____		26.	G		____	40.	J	____	
13.	B	____		27.	C		____				
14.	J	____		28.	F		____				

Number Correct (Raw Score) for:

Social Studies/Sciences (SS) Subscore Area ____ (20)

Arts/Literature (AL) Subscore Area ____ (20)

Total Number Correct for Reading Test (SS + AL) ____ (40)

* SS = Social Studies/Sciences
AL = Arts/Literature

SCIENCE REASONING—SCORING KEY

	Key			Key			Key	
1.	D	____	15.	D	____	29.	C	____
2.	F	____	16.	F	____	30.	G	____
3.	A	____	17.	D	____	31.	A	____
4.	G	____	18.	G	____	32.	H	____
5.	C	____	19.	C	____	33.	A	____
6.	G	____	20.	F	____	34.	J	____
7.	C	____	21.	B	____	35.	B	____
8.	J	____	22.	F	____	36.	H	____
9.	B	____	23.	C	____	37.	B	____
10.	F	____	24.	J	____	38.	G	____
11.	B	____	25.	D	____	39.	A	____
12.	J	____	26.	G	____	40.	F	____
13.	B	____	27.	A	____			
14.	F	____	28.	J	____			

Number Correct (Raw Score) for:

Total Number Correct for Science Reasoning Test ____ (40)

PROCEDURES USED TO OBTAIN SCALE SCORES FROM RAW SCORES

On each of the four tests, the total number of correct responses yields a raw score. Use the table below to convert your raw scores to scale scores. For each of the four tests, locate and circle your raw score or the range of raw scores that includes it in the table below. Then, read across to either outside column of the table and circle the scale score that corresponds to that raw score. As you determine your scale scores, enter them in the blanks provided on the right. The highest possible scale score for each test is 36. The lowest possible scale score for any of the four tests is 1.

Next, compute the Composite score by averaging the four scale scores. To do this, add your four scale scores and divide the sum by 4. If the resulting number ends in a fraction, round it off to the nearest whole number. (Round down any fraction less than one-half; round up any fraction that is one-half or more.) Enter this number in the blank. This is your Composite score. The highest possible Composite score is 36. The lowest possible Composite score is 1.

ACT Test	**Your Scale Score**
English	________
Mathematics	________
Reading	________
Science Reasoning	________
Sum of scores	________
Composite score (sum ÷ 4)	________

Now turn the page and use the table to convert raw scores on the subscore areas to scale subscores.

	Raw Scores				
Scale Score	**Test 1** English	**Test 2** Mathematics	**Test 3** Reading	**Test 4** Science Reasoning	**Scale Score**
36	75	60	37-40	40	36
35	74	59	36	39	35
34	-	58	35	38	34
33	73	57	34	37	33
32	71-72	56	33	36	32
31	70	54-55	32	35	31
30	68-69	51-53	-	34	30
29	67	49-50	31	33	29
28	65-66	46-48	30	32	28
27	63-64	43-45	29	31	27
26	60-62	41-42	28	30	26
25	58-59	38-40	26-27	29	25
24	56-57	35-37	25	28	24
23	54-55	33-34	24	26-27	23
22	51-53	30-32	23	25	22
21	49-50	27-29	22	23-24	21
20	46-48	25-26	21	22	20
19	44-45	23-24	20	20-21	19
18	41-43	20-22	18-19	18-19	18
17	38-40	18-19	17	16-17	17
16	36-37	15-17	16	15	16
15	32-35	13-14	15	13-14	15
14	29-31	11-12	14	11-12	14
13	26-28	9-10	13	10	13
12	23-25	8	11-12	8-9	12
11	20-22	6-7	10	7	11
10	17-19	5	9	6	10
9	14-16	4	8	5	9
8	12-13	-	7	4	8
7	10-11	3	6	3	7
6	8-9	2	5	2	6
5	6-7	-	4	-	5
4	4-5	-	3	-	4
3	3	1	2	1	3
2	2	-	1	-	2
1	0-1	0	0	0	1

PROCEDURES USED TO OBTAIN SCALE SUBSCORES FROM RAW SCORES

For each of the seven subscore areas, the total number of correct responses yields a raw score. Use the table below to convert your raw scores to scale subscores. For each of the seven subscore areas, locate and circle either the raw score or the range of raw scores that includes it in the table below. Then, read across to either outside column of the table and circle the scale subscore that corresponds to that raw score. As you determine your scale subscores, enter them in the blanks provided on the right. The highest possible scale subscore is 18. The lowest possible scale subscore is 1.

ACT Test	Your Scale Subscore
English	
Usage/Mechanics	________
Rhetorical Skills	________
Mathematics	
Pre-Algebra/Elem. Algebra	________
Inter. Algebra/Coord. Geometry	________
Plane Geometry/Trigonometry	________
Reading	
Social Studies/Sciences	________
Arts/Literature	________

Scale Subscore	Raw Scores							Scale Subscore
	Test 1 English		Test 2 Mathematics			Test 3 Reading		
	Usage/ Mechanics	Rhetorical Skills	Pre-Alegbra/ Elem. Algebra	Inter. Algebra/ Coord. Geometry	Plane Geometry/ Trigonometry	Social Studies/ Sciences	Arts/ Literature	
18	39-40	35	23-24	18	18	18-20	18-20	18
17	38	34	22	17	17	17	17	17
16	37	32-33	21	16	16	16	16	16
15	35-36	31	19-20	15	14-15	15	15	15
14	33-34	29-30	18	13-14	13	14	-	14
13	31-32	27-28	16-17	11-12	11-12	13	14	13
12	29-30	25-26	15	9-10	9-10	12	13	12
11	27-28	23-24	13-14	8	8	11	12	11
10	25-26	20-22	11-12	6-7	7	10	11	10
9	22-24	18-19	9-10	5	5-6	8-9	10	9
8	20-21	15-17	8	3-4	4	7	9	8
7	17-19	13-14	6-7	-	3	6	8	7
6	15-16	10-12	5	2	-	5	7	6
5	12-14	8-9	3-4	-	2	4	6	5
4	9-11	6-7	2	1	-	-	5	4
3	7-8	4-5	-	-	1	3	4	3
2	5-6	3	1	-	-	2	3	2
1	0-4	0-2	0	0	0	0-1	0-2	1

SCORING KEYS FOR ACT SAMPLE TEST 1 (IN SECTION 9)

Use the scoring key for each test to score your answer sheet for the practice test. Mark a "1" in the blank for each item you answered correctly. Add up the numbers in each subscore area and enter the total number correct for each subscore area in the blanks provided. Also enter the total number correct for each test in the blanks provided. The total number correct for each test is the sum of the number correct in each subscore area.

ENGLISH—SCORING KEY

	Key	Subscore Area* UM	RH		Key	Subscore Area* UM	RH		Key	Subscore Area* UM	RH
1.	A	___		26.	G	___		51.	D	___	
2.	J		___	27.	D	___		52.	F	___	
3.	B		___	28.	G		___	53.	B	___	
4.	G		___	29.	B		___	54.	J	___	
5.	A		___	30.	F	___		55.	C		___
6.	F	___		31.	C	___		56.	H	___	
7.	B	___		32.	H		___	57.	D		___
8.	H	___		33.	A		___	58.	H		___
9.	A	___		34.	J		___	59.	D		___
10.	F		___	35.	C	___		60.	G		___
11.	D		___	36.	J		___	61.	B		___
12.	G	___		37.	D		___	62.	G	___	
13.	D	___		38.	F		___	63.	B	___	
14.	J		___	39.	D		___	64.	H	___	
15.	A		___	40.	G	___		65.	B	___	
16.	H		___	41.	A	___		66.	H		___
17.	B	___		42.	J	___		67.	A	___	
18.	J	___		43.	B		___	68.	G	___	
19.	A		___	44.	G	___		69.	A	___	
20.	H		___	45.	D		___	70.	F	___	
21.	C		___	46.	H	___		71.	D	___	
22.	G	___		47.	B		___	72.	J	___	
23.	D	___		48.	G	___		73.	C	___	
24.	J		___	49.	C	___		74.	H		___
25.	D		___	50.	J	___		75.	A		___

Number Correct (Raw Score) for:

Usage/Mechanics (UM) Subscore Area	___ (40)
Rhetorical Skills (RH) Subscore Area	___ (35)
Total Number Correct for English Test (UM + RH)	___ (75)

* UM = Usage/Mechanics
RH = Rhetorical Skills

MATHEMATICS—SCORING KEY

	Key	Subscore Area* EA	AG	GT		Key	Subscore Area* EA	AG	GT
1.	B			____	31.	C		____	
2.	G	____			32.	G			____
3.	C	____			33.	D		____	
4.	F	____			34.	F		____	
5.	A			____	35.	D	____		
6.	K	____			36.	H			____
7.	D	____			37.	E		____	
8.	G		____		38.	G		____	
9.	B	____			39.	E		____	
10.	J	____			40.	H	____		
11.	D		____		41.	B		____	
12.	H	____			42.	F		____	
13.	A			____	43.	E	____		
14.	K	____			44.	J	____		
15.	B	____			45.	E			____
16.	H			____	46.	J	____		
17.	C	____			47.	B		____	
18.	H			____	48.	H			____
19.	B		____		49.	A			____
20.	H	____			50.	F	____		
21.	E	____			51.	D			____
22.	K		____		52.	J		____	
23.	A	____			53.	B			____
24.	J			____	54.	J		____	
25.	A	____			55.	C			____
26.	H	____			56.	J	____		
27.	C			____	57.	B			____
28.	J		____		58.	K		____	
29.	A	____			59.	A			____
30.	K			____	60.	K		____	

Number Correct (Raw Score) for:

Pre-Alg./Elem. Alg. (EA) Subscore Area	____ (24)
Inter. Alg./Coor. Geo. (AG) Subscore Area	____ (18)
Plane Geo./Trig. (GT) Subscore Area	____ (18)
Total Number Correct for Math Test (EA + AG + GT)	____ (60)

* EA = Pre-Algebra/Elementary Algebra
AG = Intermediate Algebra/Coordinate Geometry
GT = Plane Geometry/Trigonometry

READING—SCORING KEY

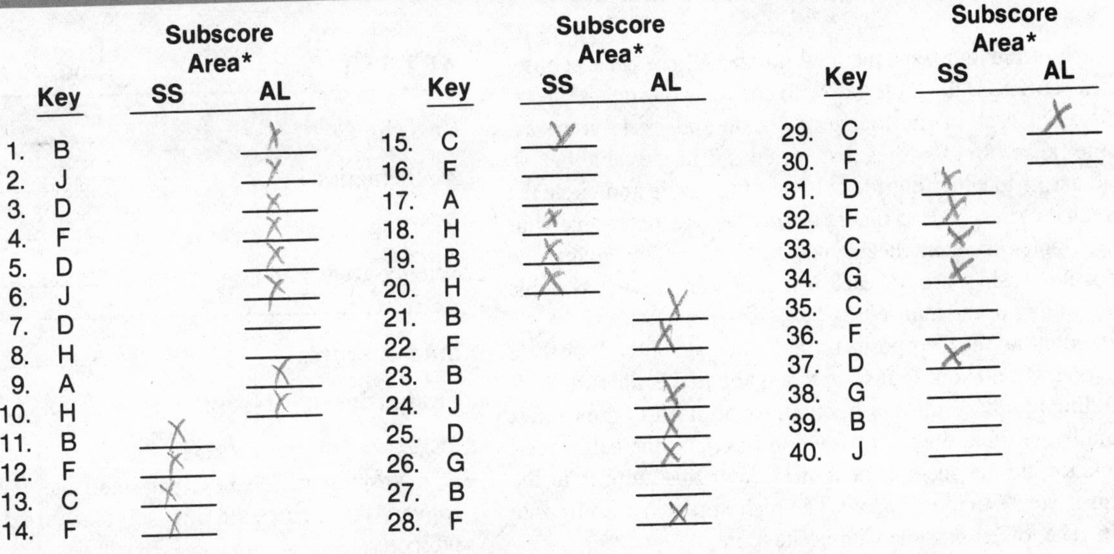

	Key	Subscore Area* SS	AL		Key	Subscore Area* SS	AL		Key	Subscore Area* SS	AL
1.	B		____	15.	C	____		29.	C		____
2.	J		____	16.	F	____		30.	F		____
3.	D		____	17.	A	____		31.	D	____	
4.	F		____	18.	H	____		32.	F	____	
5.	D		____	19.	B	____		33.	C	____	
6.	J		____	20.	H	____		34.	G	____	
7.	D		____	21.	B		____	35.	C	____	
8.	H		____	22.	F		____	36.	F	____	
9.	A		____	23.	B		____	37.	D	____	
10.	H		____	24.	J		____	38.	G	____	
11.	B	____		25.	D		____	39.	B	____	
12.	F	____		26.	G		____	40.	J	____	
13.	C	____		27.	B		____				
14.	F	____		28.	F		____				

Number Correct (Raw Score) for:

Social Studies/Sciences (SS) Subscore Area ____ (20)

Arts/Literature (AL) Subscore Area ____ (20)

Total Number Correct for Reading Test (SS + AL) ____ (40)

* SS = Social Studies/Sciences
AL = Arts/Literature

SCIENCE REASONING—SCORING KEY

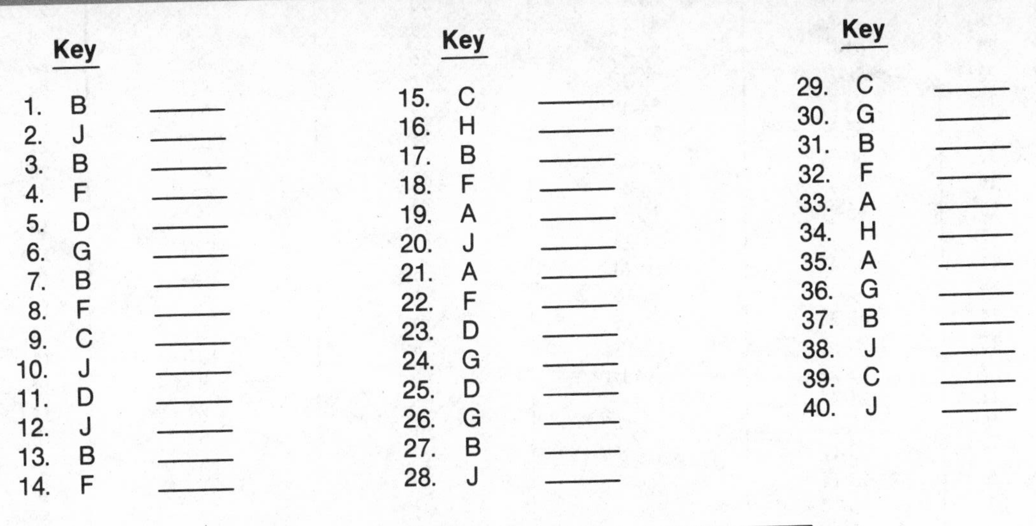

	Key			Key			Key	
1.	B	____	15.	C	____	29.	C	____
2.	J	____	16.	H	____	30.	G	____
3.	B	____	17.	B	____	31.	B	____
4.	F	____	18.	F	____	32.	F	____
5.	D	____	19.	A	____	33.	A	____
6.	G	____	20.	J	____	34.	H	____
7.	B	____	21.	A	____	35.	A	____
8.	F	____	22.	F	____	36.	G	____
9.	C	____	23.	D	____	37.	B	____
10.	J	____	24.	G	____	38.	J	____
11.	D	____	25.	D	____	39.	C	____
12.	J	____	26.	G	____	40.	J	____
13.	B	____	27.	B	____			
14.	F	____	28.	J	____			

Number Correct (Raw Score) for:

Total Number Correct for Science Reasoning Test ____ (40)

PROCEDURES USED TO OBTAIN SCALE SCORES FROM RAW SCORES—SAMPLE TEST 1

On each of the four tests, the total number of correct responses yields a raw score. Use the table below to convert your raw scores to scale scores. For each of the four tests, locate and circle your raw score or the range of raw scores that includes it in the table below. Then, read across to either outside column of the table and circle the scale score that corresponds to that raw score. As you determine your scale scores, enter them in the blanks provided on the right. The highest possible scale score for each test is 36. The lowest possible scale score for any of the four tests is 1.

Next, compute the Composite score by averaging the four scale scores. To do this, add your four scale scores and divide the sum by 4. If the resulting number ends in a fraction, round it off to the nearest whole number. (Round down any fraction less than one-half; round up any fraction that is one-half or more.) Enter this number in the blank. This is your Composite score. The highest possible Composite score is 36. The lowest possible Composite score is 1.

ACT Test	Your Scale Score
English	______
Mathematics	______
Reading	______
Science Reasoning	______
Sum of scores	______
Composite score (sum ÷ 4)	______

Now go to the next page and use the table to convert raw scores on the subscore areas to scale subscores.

Scale Score	Raw Scores				Scale Score
	Test 1 English	Test 2 Mathematics	Test 3 Reading	Test 4 Science Reasoning	
36	75	60	39-40	40	**36**
35	-	-	38	39	**35**
34	74	59	37	38	**34**
33	-	58	36	37	**33**
32	73	57	35	36	**32**
31	72	55-56	34	35	**31**
30	71	53-54	33	34	**30**
29	70	51-52	32	33	**29**
28	68-69	48-50	31	32	**28**
27	67	46-47	-	30-31	**27**
26	65-66	43-45	30	29	**26**
25	63-64	41-42	29	27-28	**25**
24	61-62	38-40	28	26	**24**
23	58-60	36-37	26-27	24-25	**23**
22	56-57	34-35	25	23	**22**
21	53-55	31-33	24	21-22	**21**
20	50-52	29-30	23	20	**20**
19	48-49	26-28	21-22	18-19	**19**
18	45-47	24-25	20	17	**18**
17	42-44	21-23	19	15-16	**17**
16	39-41	19-20	17-18	14	**16**
15	36-38	16-18	16	12-13	**15**
14	32-35	14-15	15	11	**14**
13	28-31	12-13	13-14	9-10	**13**
12	25-27	9-11	12	8	**12**
11	21-24	8	11	7	**11**
10	18-20	6-7	10	6	**10**
9	15-17	5	9	5	**9**
8	13-14	4	8	4	**8**
7	10-12	-	6-7	3	**7**
6	8-9	3	5	2	**6**
5	6-7	-	-	-	**5**
4	5	2	4	-	**4**
3	3-4	1	3	1	**3**
2	2	-	2	-	**2**
1	0-1	-	0-1	-	**1**

PROCEDURES USED TO OBTAIN SCALE SUBSCORES FROM RAW SCORES SAMPLE TEST 1

For each of the seven subscore areas, the total number of correct responses yields a raw score. Use the table below to convert your raw scores to scale subscores. For each of the seven subscore areas, locate and circle either the raw score or the range of raw scores that includes it in the table below. Then, read across to either outside column of the table and circle the scale subscore that corresponds to that raw score. As you determine your scale subscores, enter them in the blanks provided on the right. The highest possible scale subscore is 18. The lowest possible scale subscore is 1.

ACT Test	Your Scale Subscore
English	
Usage/Mechanics	________
Rhetorical Skills	________
Mathematics	
Pre-Algebra/Elem. Algebra	________
Inter. Algebra/Coord. Geometry	________
Plane Geometry/Trigonometry	________
Reading	
Social Studies/Sciences	________
Arts/Literature	________

Scale Subscore	Raw Scores							Scale Subscore
	Test 1 English		Test 2 Mathematics			Test 3 Reading		
	Usage/ Mechanics	Rhetorical Skills	Pre-Algebra/ Elem. Algebra	Inter. Algebra/ Coord. Geometry	Plane Geometry/ Trigonometry	Social Studies/ Sciences	Arts/ Literature	
18	40	35	24	18	18	19-20	19-20	**18**
17	38-39	-	23	17	-	18	18	**17**
16	37	34	22	16	17	17	-	**16**
15	36	33	20-21	15	16	16	17	**15**
14	34-35	32	19	13-14	14-15	15	16	**14**
13	32-33	31	17-18	12	12-13	14	15	**13**
12	30-31	29-30	16	10-11	11	13	14	**12**
11	27-29	27-28	14-15	8-9	9-10	12	12-13	**11**
10	25-26	24-26	13	7	8	11	11	**10**
9	23-24	21-23	11-12	5-6	6-7	9-10	10	**9**
8	20-22	18-20	9-10	4	5	8	9	**8**
7	18-19	15-17	8	3	4	7	8	**7**
6	15-17	12-14	6-7	-	-	6	7	**6**
5	12-14	9-11	5	2	3	5	6	**5**
4	9-11	7-8	3-4	-	2	4	5	**4**
3	7-8	5-6	2	1	-	3	4	**3**
2	5-6	3-4	1	-	1	2	3	**2**
1	0-4	0-2	-	-	-	0-1	0-2	**1**

SCORING KEYS FOR ACT SAMPLE TEST 2 (IN SECTION 9)

Use the scoring key for each test to score your answer sheet for the practice test. Mark a "1" in the blank for each item you answered correctly. Add up the numbers in each subscore area and enter the total number correct for each subscore area in the blanks provided. Also enter the total number correct for each test in the blanks provided. The total number correct for each test is the sum of the number correct in each subscore area.

ENGLISH—SCORING KEY

	Key	Subscore Area* UM	Subscore Area* RH		Key	Subscore Area* UM	Subscore Area* RH		Key	Subscore Area* UM	Subscore Area* RH
1.	B		____	26.	J	____		51.	B	____	
2.	F	____		27.	D		____	52.	H	____	
3.	B		____	28.	J		____	53.	D	____	
4.	G		____	29.	D	____		54.	H	____	
5.	D	____		30.	H		____	55.	D	____	
6.	G		____	31.	A		____	56.	F		____
7.	C	____		32.	G	____		57.	A		____
8.	H		____	33.	D		____	58.	F		____
9.	B	____		34.	F	____		59.	B		____
10.	G		____	35.	A	____		60.	H	____	
11.	D		____	36.	J	____		61.	A		____
12.	G	____		37.	D		____	62.	H	____	
13.	D		____	38.	H		____	63.	A	____	
14.	F	____		39.	B	____		64.	H	____	
15.	B		____	40.	H	____		65.	B		____
16.	F		____	41.	D		____	66.	F	____	
17.	C	____		42.	F	____		67.	D		____
18.	H		____	43.	B	____		68.	J	____	
19.	A	____		44.	G	____		69.	C	____	
20.	G	____		45.	D	____		70.	F	____	
21.	A		____	46.	H	____		71.	D	____	
22.	J	____		47.	D	____		72.	H		____
23.	C	____		48.	J		____	73.	C		____
24.	J		____	49.	A		____	74.	F		____
25.	B		____	50.	H	____		75.	C		____

Number Correct (Raw Score) for:

Usage/Mechanics (UM) Subscore Area	____ (40)
Rhetorical Skills (RH) Subscore Area	____ (35)
Total Number Correct for English Test (UM + RH)	____ (75)

* UM = Usage/Mechanics
RH = Rhetorical Skills

MATHEMATICS—SCORING KEY

	Key	EA	AG	GT		Key	EA	AG	GT
			Subscore Area*					Subscore Area*	
1.	A	____			31.	D		____	
2.	G	____			32.	K	____		
3.	B	____			33.	C		____	
4.	H			____	34.	G			____
5.	A	____			35.	B			____
6.	K	____			36.	H		____	
7.	E			____	37.	B			____
8.	J	____			38.	F		____	
9.	E	____			39.	A	____		
10.	F			____	40.	J	____		
11.	D	____			41.	E		____	
12.	F	____			42.	H	____		
13.	B		____		43.	D		____	
14.	J	____			44.	G			____
15.	C			____	45.	A		____	
16.	J		____		46.	J		____	
17.	E	____			47.	B			____
18.	G	____			48.	G	____		
19.	C		____		49.	E			____
20.	H	____			50.	H			____
21.	C			____	51.	B		____	
22.	F	____			52.	J			____
23.	A	____			53.	C			____
24.	K	____			54.	H			____
25.	C	____			55.	E	____		
26.	H		____		56.	J			____
27.	A			____	57.	A		____	
28.	H		____		58.	K	____		
29.	C			____	59.	D		____	
30.	F		____		60.	K		____	

Number Correct (Raw Score) for:

Pre-Alg./Elem. Alg. (EA) Subscore Area	____ (24)
Inter. Alg./Coor. Geo. (AG) Subscore Area	____ (18)
Plane Geo./Trig. (GT) Subscore Area	____ (18)
Total Number Correct for Math Test (EA + AG + GT)	____ (60)

* EA = Pre-Algebra/Elementary Algebra
AG = Intermediate Algebra/Coordinate Geometry
GT = Plane Geometry/Trigonometry

9

READING—SCORING KEY

	Key	Subscore Area* SS	AL		Key	Subscore Area* SS	AL		Key	Subscore Area* SS	AL
1.	B	____		15.	D		____	29.	D		____
2.	J	____		16.	J		____	30.	H		____
3.	B	____		17.	D		____	31.	A	____	
4.	J	____		18.	F		____	32.	H	____	
5.	C	____		19.	C		____	33.	A	____	
6.	G	____		20.	F		____	34.	H	____	
7.	C	____		21.	D		____	35.	A	____	
8.	G	____		22.	J		____	36.	F	____	
9.	B	____		23.	C		____	37.	D	____	
10.	F	____		24.	F		____	38.	J	____	
11.	D		____	25.	B		____	39.	B	____	
12.	F		____	26.	H		____	40.	H	____	
13.	A		____	27.	B		____				
14.	H		____	28.	G		____				

Number Correct (Raw Score) for:

Social Studies/Sciences (SS) Subscore Area ____ (20)

Arts/Literature (AL) Subscore Area ____ (20)

Total Number Correct for Reading Test (SS + AL) ____ (40)

* SS = Social Studies/Sciences
AL = Arts/Literature

SCIENCE REASONING—SCORING KEY

	Key			Key			Key	
1.	A	____	15.	A	____	29.	D	____
2.	H	____	16.	F	____	30.	F	____
3.	A	____	17.	A	____	31.	D	____
4.	J	____	18.	G	____	32.	J	____
5.	D	____	19.	C	____	33.	C	____
6.	J	____	20.	H	____	34.	G	____
7.	D	____	21.	A	____	35.	D	____
8.	H	____	22.	F	____	36.	J	____
9.	A	____	23.	D	____	37.	C	____
10.	H	____	24.	J	____	38.	H	____
11.	B	____	25.	B	____	39.	A	____
12.	F	____	26.	G	____	40.	H	____
13.	B	____	27.	A	____			
14.	G	____	28.	J	____			

Number Correct (Raw Score) for:

Total Number Correct for Science Reasoning Test 28 (40)

12

3̶4̶6̶
−12
28

PROCEDURES USED TO OBTAIN SCALE SCORES FROM RAW SCORES—SAMPLE TEST 2

On each of the four tests, the total number of correct responses yields a raw score. Use the table below to convert your raw scores to scale scores. For each of the four tests, locate and circle your raw score or the range of raw scores that includes it in the table below. Then, read across to either outside column of the table and circle the scale score that corresponds to that raw score. As you determine your scale scores, enter them in the blanks provided on the right. The highest possible scale score for each test is 36. The lowest possible scale score for any of the four tests is 1.

Next, compute the Composite score by averaging the four scale scores. To do this, add your four scale scores and divide the sum by 4. If the resulting number ends in a fraction, round it off to the nearest whole number. (Round down any fraction less than one-half; round up any fraction that is one-half or more.) Enter this number in the blank. This is your Composite score. The highest possible Composite score is 36. The lowest possible Composite score is 1.

ACT Test	**Your Scale Score**
English	28
Mathematics	26
Reading	
Science Reasoning	25
Sum of scores	
Composite score (sum ÷ 4)	

Now turn the page and use the table to convert raw scores on the subscore areas to scale subscores.

Scale Score	Raw Scores: Test 1 English	Raw Scores: Test 2 Mathematics	Raw Scores: Test 3 Reading	Raw Scores: Test 4 Science Reasoning	Scale Score
36	75	60	38-40	40	36
35	74	59	37	39	35
34	73	-	36	38	34
33	72	58	35	37	33
32	71	56-57	34	36	32
31	70	55	-	35	31
30	69	53-54	33	34	30
29	67-68	51-52	32	33	29
28	65-66	49-50	31	32	28
27	64	46-48	30	31	27
26	62-63	44-45	29	29-30	26
25	60-61	42-43	28	28	25
24	57-59	39-41	27	27	24
23	55-56	36-38	26	25-26	23
22	52-54	34-35	25	24	22
21	49-51	31-33	23-24	23	21
20	47-48	28-30	22	21-22	20
19	44-46	25-27	21	19-20	19
18	41-43	23-24	20	18	18
17	38-40	20-22	19	16-17	17
16	35-37	18-19	17-18	15	16
15	32-34	15-17	16	13-14	15
14	29-31	13-14	15	11-12	14
13	25-28	11-12	13-14	10	13
12	22-24	9-10	12	9	12
11	20-21	7-8	11	7-8	11
10	17-19	6	9-10	6	10
9	14-16	5	8	5	9
8	12-13	4	7	4	8
7	10-11	-	6	3	7
6	8-9	3	5	2	6
5	6-7	2	4	-	5
4	4-5	-	3	-	4
3	3	1	2	1	3
2	2	-	1	-	2
1	0-1	-	-	-	1

PROCEDURES USED TO OBTAIN SCALE SUBSCORES FROM RAW SCORES SAMPLE TEST 2

For each of the seven subscore areas, the total number of correct responses yields a raw score. Use the table below to convert your raw scores to scale subscores. For each of the seven subscore areas, locate and circle either the raw score or the range of raw scores that includes it in the table below. Then, read across to either outside column of the table and circle the scale subscore that corresponds to that raw score. As you determine your scale subscores, enter them in the blanks provided on the right. The highest possible scale subscore is 18. The lowest possible scale subscore is 1.

ACT Test	Your Scale Subscore
English	
Usage/Mechanics	________
Rhetorical Skills	________
Mathematics	
Pre-Algebra/Elem. Algebra	________
Inter. Algebra/Coord. Geometry	________
Plane Geometry/Trigonometry	________
Reading	
Social Studies/Sciences	________
Arts/Literature	________

	Raw Score							
	Test 1 English		Test 2 Mathematics			Test 3 Reading		
Scale Subscore	Usage/ Mechanics	Rhetorical Skills	Pre-Algebra/ Elem. Algebra	Inter.Algebra/ Coord. Geometry	Plane Geom./ Trigonometry	Social Studies/ Sciences	Arts/ Literature	Scale Subscore
18	39-40	35	23-24	18	18	19-20	19-20	18
17	38	34	22	17	-	17-18	18	17
16	36-37	33	21	16	17	16	17	16
15	34-35	32	20	15	16	15	16	15
14	32-33	31	19	13-14	15	14	15	14
13	30-31	29-30	17-18	12	13-14	13	-	13
12	28-29	27-28	16	10-11	11-12	12	14	12
11	25-27	25-26	14-15	9	9-10	11	13	11
10	23-24	22-24	13	7-8	7-8	10	12	10
9	21-22	19-21	11-12	5-6	5-6	9	11	9
8	18-20	17-18	9-10	4	4	8	10	8
7	16-17	14-16	8	3	3	7	9	7
6	13-15	11-13	6-7	-	-	6	8	6
5	11-12	8-10	5	2	2	5	6-7	5
4	9-10	6-7	3-4	-	-	4	5	4
3	7-8	4-5	2	1	-	3	-	3
2	5-6	3	1	-	1	2	3-4	2
1	0-4	0-2	-	-	-	0-1	0-2	1

ACT Assessment *Sample Answer Sheet*

SIDE 1

You may wish to remove this sample answer sheet from the book to use in a practice test session.

A NAME, ADDRESS, AND TELEPHONE

Last Name | First Name | MI (Middle Initial)

House Number and Street

City | State | ZIP Code

Area Code / Number

ACT

P.O. BOX 168, IOWA CITY, IOWA 52243

MATCHING INFORMATION

Enter the information in blocks B, C, and D, EXACTLY as it appears on your test center admission ticket, even if any part of this information is missing or incorrect. Blacken the corresponding ovals. Leave block E blank unless you are given special instructions.

B FIRST FIVE LETTERS OF LAST NAME

C SOCIAL SECURITY NUMBER (OR ACT ID NUMBER)

D DATE OF BIRTH

Month | Day | Year

Jan. Feb. Mar. Apr. May Jun. July Aug. Sep. Oct. Nov. Dec.

E

If the information on your test center admission ticket is complete and correct, put down your pencil and wait for further instructions.

If any corrections are necessary, complete ONLY those blocks below for which the information on your test center admission ticket is INCOMPLETE or INCORRECT. Leave the other blocks blank.

F NAME CORRECTION

Last Name | First Name | MI

G SOCIAL SECURITY NUMBER CORRECTION

H DATE OF BIRTH CORRECTION

Month | Day | Year

Jan. Feb. Mar. Apr. May Jun. July Aug. Sep. Oct. Nov. Dec.

I HIGH SCHOOL CODE CORRECTION

SIDE 2

BOOKLET NUMBER

1	1	1	1	1	1
2	2	2	2	2	2
3	3	3	3	3	3
4	4	4	4	4	4
5	5	5	5	5	5
6	6	6	6	6	6
7	7	7	7	7	7
8	8	8	8	8	8
9	9	9	9	9	9
0	0	0	0	0	0

FORM

BE SURE TO BLACKEN THE CORRECT FORM OVAL.

○ 8939B

TEST 1

1 A B C D
2 F G H J
3 A B C D
4 F G H J
5 A B C D
6 F G H J
7 A B C D
8 F G H J
9 A B C D
10 F G H J
11 A B C D
12 F G H J
13 A B C D
14 F G H J
15 A B C D
16 F G H J
17 A B C D
18 F G H J
19 A B C D
20 F G H J
21 A B C D
22 F G H J
23 A B C D
24 F G H J
25 A B C D
26 F G H J
27 A B C D
28 F G H J
29 A B C D
30 F G H J
31 A B C D
32 F G H J
33 A B C D
34 F G H J
35 A B C D
36 F G H J
37 A B C D
38 F G H J
39 A B C D
40 F G H J
41 A B C D
42 F G H J
43 A B C D
44 F G H J
45 A B C D
46 F G H J
47 A B C D
48 F G H J
49 A B C D
50 F G H J
51 A B C D
52 F G H J
53 A B C D
54 F G H J
55 A B C D
56 F G H J
57 A B C D
58 F G H J
59 A B C D
60 F G H J
61 A B C D
62 F G H J
63 A B C D
64 F G H J
65 A B C D
66 F G H J
67 A B C D
68 F G H J
69 A B C D
70 F G H J
71 A B C D
72 F G H J
73 A B C D
74 F G H J
75 A B C D

TEST 2

1 A B C D E
2 F G H J K
3 A B C D E
4 F G H J K
5 A B C D E
6 F G H J K
7 A B C D E
8 F G H J K
9 A B C D E
10 F G H J K
11 A B C D E
12 F G H J K
13 A B C D E
14 F G H J K
15 A B C D E
16 F G H J K
17 A B C D E
18 F G H J K
19 A B C D E
20 F G H J K
21 A B C D E
22 F G H J K
23 A B C D E
24 F G H J K
25 A B C D E
26 F G H J K
27 A B C D E
28 F G H J K
29 A B C D E
30 F G H J K
31 A B C D E
32 F G H J K
33 A B C D E
34 F G H J K
35 A B C D E
36 F G H J K
37 A B C D E
38 F G H J K
39 A B C D E
40 F G H J K
41 A B C D E
42 F G H J K
43 A B C D E
44 F G H J K
45 A B C D E
46 F G H J K
47 A B C D E
48 F G H J K
49 A B C D E
50 F G H J K
51 A B C D E
52 F G H J K
53 A B C D E
54 F G H J K
55 A B C D E
56 F G H J K
57 A B C D E
58 F G H J K
59 A B C D E
60 F G H J K

TEST 3

1 A B C D
2 F G H J
3 A B C D
4 F G H J
5 A B C D
6 F G H J
7 A B C D
8 F G H J
9 A B C D
10 F G H J
11 A B C D
12 F G H J
13 A B C D
14 F G H J
15 A B C D
16 F G H J
17 A B C D
18 F G H J
19 A B C D
20 F G H J
21 A B C D
22 F G H J
23 A B C D
24 F G H J
25 A B C D
26 F G H J
27 A B C D
28 F G H J
29 A B C D
30 F G H J
31 A B C D
32 F G H J
33 A B C D
34 F G H J
35 A B C D
36 F G H J
37 A B C D
38 F G H J
39 A B C D
40 F G H J

TEST 4

1 A B C D
2 F G H J
3 A B C D
4 F G H J
5 A B C D
6 F G H J
7 A B C D
8 F G H J
9 A B C D
10 F G H J
11 A B C D
12 F G H J
13 A B C D
14 F G H J
15 A B C D
16 F G H J
17 A B C D
18 F G H J
19 A B C D
20 F G H J
21 A B C D
22 F G H J
23 A B C D
24 F G H J
25 A B C D
26 F G H J
27 A B C D
28 F G H J
29 A B C D
30 F G H J
31 A B C D
32 F G H J
33 A B C D
34 F G H J
35 A B C D
36 F G H J
37 A B C D
38 F G H J
39 A B C D
40 F G H J

I hereby certify that I have truthfully identified myself on this form. I understand that the consequences of falsifying my identity include cancellation of my scores.

Your Signature ______________________

Today's Date ______________________

SIDE 1

A **NAME, ADDRESS, AND TELEPHONE**

Last Name First Name MI (Middle Initial)

House Number and Street

City State ZIP Code

/

Area Code Number

ACT

P.O. BOX 168, IOWA CITY, IOWA 52243

MATCHING INFORMATION

Enter the information in blocks B, C, and D, EXACTLY as it appears on your test center admission ticket, even if any part of this information is missing or incorrect. Blacken the corresponding ovals. Leave block E blank unless you are given special instructions.

B **FIRST FIVE LETTERS OF LAST NAME**

C **SOCIAL SECURITY NUMBER (OR ACT ID NUMBER)**

D **DATE OF BIRTH**

Month Day Year

Jan. Feb. Mar. Apr. May Jun. July Aug. Sep. Oct. Nov. Dec.

E

If the information on your test center admission ticket is complete and correct, put down your pencil and wait for further instructions.

If any corrections are necessary, complete ONLY those blocks below for which the information on your test center admission ticket is INCOMPLETE or INCORRECT. Leave the other blocks blank.

F **NAME CORRECTION**

Last Name First Name MI

G **SOCIAL SECURITY NUMBER CORRECTION**

H **DATE OF BIRTH CORRECTION**

Month Day Year

Jan. Feb. Mar. Apr. May Jun. July Aug. Sep. Oct. Nov. Dec.

I **HIGH SCHOOL CODE CORRECTION**

You may wish to remove this sample answer sheet from the book to use in a practice test session.

SIDE 2

BOOKLET NUMBER

1	1	1	1	1	1
2	2	2	2	2	2
3	3	3	3	3	3
4	4	4	4	4	4
5	5	5	5	5	5
6	6	6	6	6	6
7	7	7	7	7	7
8	8	8	8	8	8
9	9	9	9	9	9
0	0	0	0	0	0

FORM

BE SURE TO BLACKEN THE CORRECT FORM OVAL.

○ 8939B

TEST 1

	10 FGHJ	20 FGHJ	30 FGHJ	40 FGHJ	50 FGHJ	60 FGHJ	70 FGHJ
1 ABCD	11 ABCD	21 ABCD	31 ABCD	41 ABCD	51 ABCD	61 ABCD	71 ABCD
2 FGHJ	12 FGHJ	22 FGHJ	32 FGHJ	42 FGHJ	52 FGHJ	62 FGHJ	72 FGHJ
3 ABCD	13 ABCD	23 ABCD	33 ABCD	43 ABCD	53 ABCD	63 ABCD	73 ABCD
4 FGHJ	14 FGHJ	24 FGHJ	34 FGHJ	44 FGHJ	54 FGHJ	64 FGHJ	74 FGHJ
5 ABCD	15 ABCD	25 ABCD	35 ABCD	45 ABCD	55 ABCD	65 ABCD	75 ABCD
6 FGHJ	16 FGHJ	26 FGHJ	36 FGHJ	46 FGHJ	56 FGHJ	66 FGHJ	
7 ABCD	17 ABCD	27 ABCD	37 ABCD	47 ABCD	57 ABCD	67 ABCD	
8 FGHJ	18 FGHJ	28 FGHJ	38 FGHJ	48 FGHJ	58 FGHJ	68 FGHJ	
9 ABCD	19 ABCD	29 ABCD	39 ABCD	49 ABCD	59 ABCD	69 ABCD	

TEST 2

	8 FGHJK	16 FGHJK	24 FGHJK	32 FGHJK	40 FGHJK	48 FGHJK	56 FGHJK
1 ABCDE	9 ABCDE	17 ABCDE	25 ABCDE	33 ABCDE	41 ABCDE	49 ABCDE	57 ABCDE
2 FGHJK	10 FGHJK	18 FGHJK	26 FGHJK	34 FGHJK	42 FGHJK	50 FGHJK	58 FGHJK
3 ABCDE	11 ABCDE	19 ABCDE	27 ABCDE	35 ABCDE	43 ABCDE	51 ABCDE	59 ABCDE
4 FGHJK	12 FGHJK	20 FGHJK	28 FGHJK	36 FGHJK	44 FGHJK	52 FGHJK	60 FGHJK
5 ABCDE	13 ABCDE	21 ABCDE	29 ABCDE	37 ABCDE	45 ABCDE	53 ABCDE	
6 FGHJK	14 FGHJK	22 FGHJK	30 FGHJK	38 FGHJK	46 FGHJK	54 FGHJK	
7 ABCDE	15 ABCDE	23 ABCDE	31 ABCDE	39 ABCDE	47 ABCDE	55 ABCDE	

TEST 3

	6 FGHJ	12 FGHJ	18 FGHJ	24 FGHJ	30 FGHJ	36 FGHJ
1 ABCD	7 ABCD	13 ABCD	19 ABCD	25 ABCD	31 ABCD	37 ABCD
2 FGHJ	8 FGHJ	14 FGHJ	20 FGHJ	26 FGHJ	32 FGHJ	38 FGHJ
3 ABCD	9 ABCD	15 ABCD	21 ABCD	27 ABCD	33 ABCD	39 ABCD
4 FGHJ	10 FGHJ	16 FGHJ	22 FGHJ	28 FGHJ	34 FGHJ	40 FGHJ
5 ABCD	11 ABCD	17 ABCD	23 ABCD	29 ABCD	35 ABCD	

TEST 4

	6 FGHJ	12 FGHJ	18 FGHJ	24 FGHJ	30 FGHJ	36 FGHJ
1 ABCD	7 ABCD	13 ABCD	19 ABCD	25 ABCD	31 ABCD	37 ABCD
2 FGHJ	8 FGHJ	14 FGHJ	20 FGHJ	26 FGHJ	32 FGHJ	38 FGHJ
3 ABCD	9 ABCD	15 ABCD	21 ABCD	27 ABCD	33 ABCD	39 ABCD
4 FGHJ	10 FGHJ	16 FGHJ	22 FGHJ	28 FGHJ	34 FGHJ	40 FGHJ
5 ABCD	11 ABCD	17 ABCD	23 ABCD	29 ABCD	35 ABCD	

I hereby certify that I have truthfully identified myself on this form. I understand that the consequences of falsifying my identity include cancellation of my scores.

Your Signature ______________________

Today's Date ______________________

ACT Assessment Sample Answer Sheet

SIDE 1

A NAME, ADDRESS, AND TELEPHONE

Last Name First Name MI (Middle Initial)

House Number and Street

City State ZIP Code

Area Code / Number

ACT

P.O. BOX 168, IOWA CITY, IOWA 52243

MATCHING INFORMATION

Enter the information in blocks B, C, and D, EXACTLY as it appears on your test center admission ticket, even if any part of this information is missing or incorrect. Blacken the corresponding ovals. Leave block E blank unless you are given special instructions.

B FIRST FIVE LETTERS OF LAST NAME

C SOCIAL SECURITY NUMBER (OR ACT ID NUMBER)

D DATE OF BIRTH

Month Day Year

Jan. Feb. Mar. Apr. May Jun. July Aug. Sep. Oct. Nov. Dec.

E

If the information on your test center admission ticket is complete and correct, put down your pencil and wait for further instructions.

If any corrections are necessary, complete ONLY those blocks below for which the information on your test center admission ticket is INCOMPLETE or INCORRECT Leave the other blocks blank.

F NAME CORRECTION

Last Name First Name MI

G SOCIAL SECURITY NUMBER CORRECTION

H DATE OF BIRTH CORRECTION

Month Day Year

Jan. Feb. Mar. Apr. May Jun. July Aug. Sep. Oct. Nov. Dec.

I HIGH SCHOOL CODE CORRECTION

You may wish to remove this sample answer sheet from the book to use in a practice test session.

SIDE 2

BOOKLET NUMBER

1	1	1	1	1	1
2	2	2	2	2	2
3	3	3	3	3	3
4	4	4	4	4	4
5	5	5	5	5	5
6	6	6	6	6	6
7	7	7	7	7	7
8	8	8	8	8	8
9	9	9	9	9	9
0	0	0	0	0	0

FORM

BE SURE TO BLACKEN THE CORRECT FORM OVAL.

○ 8939B

TEST 1

1 A B C D
2 F G H J
3 A B C D
4 F G H J
5 A B C D
6 F G H J
7 A B C D
8 F G H J
9 A B C D
10 F G H J
11 A B C D
12 F G H J
13 A B C D
14 F G H J
15 A B C D
16 F G H J
17 A B C D
18 F G H J
19 A B C D
20 F G H J
21 A B C D
22 F G H J
23 A B C D
24 F G H J
25 A B C D
26 F G H J
27 A B C D
28 F G H J
29 A B C D
30 F G H J
31 A B C D
32 F G H J
33 A B C D
34 F G H J
35 A B C D
36 F G H J
37 A B C D
38 F G H J
39 A B C D
40 F G H J
41 A B C D
42 F G H J
43 A B C D
44 F G H J
45 A B C D
46 F G H J
47 A B C D
48 F G H J
49 A B C D
50 F G H J
51 A B C D
52 F G H J
53 A B C D
54 F G H J
55 A B C D
56 F G H J
57 A B C D
58 F G H J
59 A B C D
60 F G H J
61 A B C D
62 F G H J
63 A B C D
64 F G H J
65 A B C D
66 F G H J
67 A B C D
68 F G H J
69 A B C D
70 F G H J
71 A B C D
72 F G H J
73 A B C D
74 F G H J
75 A B C D

TEST 2

1 A B C D E
2 F G H J K
3 A B C D E
4 F G H J K
5 A B C D E
6 F G H J K
7 A B C D E
8 F G H J K
9 A B C D E
10 F G H J K
11 A B C D E
12 F G H J K
13 A B C D E
14 F G H J K
15 A B C D E
16 F G H J K
17 A B C D E
18 F G H J K
19 A B C D E
20 F G H J K
21 A B C D E
22 F G H J K
23 A B C D E
24 F G H J K
25 A B C D E
26 F G H J K
27 A B C D E
28 F G H J K
29 A B C D E
30 F G H J K
31 A B C D E
32 F G H J K
33 A B C D E
34 F G H J K
35 A B C D E
36 F G H J K
37 A B C D E
38 F G H J K
39 A B C D E
40 F G H J K
41 A B C D E
42 F G H J K
43 A B C D E
44 F G H J K
45 A B C D E
46 F G H J K
47 A B C D E
48 F G H J K
49 A B C D E
50 F G H J K
51 A B C D E
52 F G H J K
53 A B C D E
54 F G H J K
55 A B C D E
56 F G H J K
57 A B C D E
58 F G H J K
59 A B C D E
60 F G H J K

TEST 3

1 A B C D
2 F G H J
3 A B C D
4 F G H J
5 A B C D
6 F G H J
7 A B C D
8 F G H J
9 A B C D
10 F G H J
11 A B C D
12 F G H J
13 A B C D
14 F G H J
15 A B C D
16 F G H J
17 A B C D
18 F G H J
19 A B C D
20 F G H J
21 A B C D
22 F G H J
23 A B C D
24 F G H J
25 A B C D
26 F G H J
27 A B C D
28 F G H J
29 A B C D
30 F G H J
31 A B C D
32 F G H J
33 A B C D
34 F G H J
35 A B C D
36 F G H J
37 A B C D
38 F G H J
39 A B C D
40 F G H J

TEST 4

1 A B C D
2 F G H J
3 A B C D
4 F G H J
5 A B C D
6 F G H J
7 A B C D
8 F G H J
9 A B C D
10 F G H J
11 A B C D
12 F G H J
13 A B C D
14 F G H J
15 A B C D
16 F G H J
17 A B C D
18 F G H J
19 A B C D
20 F G H J
21 A B C D
22 F G H J
23 A B C D
24 F G H J
25 A B C D
26 F G H J
27 A B C D
28 F G H J
29 A B C D
30 F G H J
31 A B C D
32 F G H J
33 A B C D
34 F G H J
35 A B C D
36 F G H J
37 A B C D
38 F G H J
39 A B C D
40 F G H J

I hereby certify that I have truthfully identified myself on this form. I understand that the consequences of falsifying my identity include cancellation of my scores.

Your Signature

Today's Date

ACT Assessment Sample Answer Sheet

SIDE 1

You may wish to remove this sample answer sheet from the book to use in a practice test session.

A NAME, ADDRESS, AND TELEPHONE

Last Name | First Name | MI (Middle Initial)

House Number and Street

City | State | ZIP Code

Area Code / Number

ACT

P.O. BOX 168, IOWA CITY, IOWA 52243

MATCHING INFORMATION

Enter the information in blocks B, C, and D, EXACTLY as it appears on your test center admission ticket, even if any part of this information is missing or incorrect. Blacken the corresponding ovals. Leave block E blank unless you are given special instructions.

B FIRST FIVE LETTERS OF LAST NAME

C SOCIAL SECURITY NUMBER (OR ACT ID NUMBER)

D DATE OF BIRTH

Month | Day | Year

Jan. Feb. Mar. Apr. May Jun. July Aug. Sep. Oct. Nov. Dec.

E

If the information on your test center admission ticket is complete and correct, put down your pencil and wait for further instructions.

If any corrections are necessary, complete ONLY those blocks below for which the information on your test center admission ticket is INCOMPLETE or INCORRECT. Leave the other blocks blank.

F NAME CORRECTION

Last Name | First Name | MI

G SOCIAL SECURITY NUMBER CORRECTION

H DATE OF BIRTH CORRECTION

Month | Day | Year

Jan. Feb. Mar. Apr. May Jun. July Aug. Sep. Oct. Nov. Dec.

I HIGH SCHOOL CODE CORRECTION

SIDE 2

BOOKLET NUMBER

1	1	1	1	1	1
2	2	2	2	2	2
3	3	3	3	3	3
4	4	4	4	4	4
5	5	5	5	5	5
6	6	6	6	6	6
7	7	7	7	7	7
8	8	8	8	8	8
9	9	9	9	9	9
0	0	0	0	0	0

FORM

BE SURE TO BLACKEN THE CORRECT FORM OVAL.

○ 8939B

TEST 1	10 F G H J	20 F G H J	30 F G H J	40 F G H J	50 F G H J	60 F G H J	70 F G H J
1 A B C D	11 A B C D	21 A B C D	31 A B C D	41 A B C D	51 A B C D	61 A B C D	71 A B C D
2 F G H J	12 F G H J	22 F G H J	32 F G H J	42 F G H J	52 F G H J	62 F G H J	72 F G H J
3 A B C D	13 A B C D	23 A B C D	33 A B C D	43 A B C D	53 A B C D	63 A B C D	73 A B C D
4 F G H J	14 F G H J	24 F G H J	34 F G H J	44 F G H J	54 F G H J	64 F G H J	74 F G H J
5 A B C D	15 A B C D	25 A B C D	35 A B C D	45 A B C D	55 A B C D	65 A B C D	75 A B C D
6 F G H J	16 F G H J	26 F G H J	36 F G H J	46 F G H J	56 F G H J	66 F G H J	
7 A B C D	17 A B C D	27 A B C D	37 A B C D	47 A B C D	57 A B C D	67 A B C D	
8 F G H J	18 F G H J	28 F G H J	38 F G H J	48 F G H J	58 F G H J	68 F G H J	
9 A B C D	19 A B C D	29 A B C D	39 A B C D	49 A B C D	59 A B C D	69 A B C D	

TEST 2	8 F G H J K	16 F G H J K	24 F G H J K	32 F G H J K	40 F G H J K	48 F G H J K	56 F G H J K
1 A B C D E	9 A B C D E	17 A B C D E	25 A B C D E	33 A B C D E	41 A B C D E	49 A B C D E	57 A B C D E
2 F G H J K	10 F G H J K	18 F G H J K	26 F G H J K	34 F G H J K	42 F G H J K	50 F G H J K	58 F G H J K
3 A B C D E	11 A B C D E	19 A B C D E	27 A B C D E	35 A B C D E	43 A B C D E	51 A B C D E	59 A B C D E
4 F G H J K	12 F G H J K	20 F G H J K	28 F G H J K	36 F G H J K	44 F G H J K	52 F G H J K	60 F G H J K
5 A B C D E	13 A B C D E	21 A B C D E	29 A B C D E	37 A B C D E	45 A B C D E	53 A B C D E	
6 F G H J K	14 F G H J K	22 F G H J K	30 F G H J K	38 F G H J K	46 F G H J K	54 F G H J K	
7 A B C D E	15 A B C D E	23 A B C D E	31 A B C D E	39 A B C D E	47 A B C D E	55 A B C D E	

TEST 3	6 F G H J	12 F G H J	18 F G H J	24 F G H J	30 F G H J	36 F G H J
1 A B C D	7 A B C D	13 A B C D	19 A B C D	25 A B C D	31 A B C D	37 A B C D
2 F G H J	8 F G H J	14 F G H J	20 F G H J	26 F G H J	32 F G H J	38 F G H J
3 A B C D	9 A B C D	15 A B C D	21 A B C D	27 A B C D	33 A B C D	39 A B C D
4 F G H J	10 F G H J	16 F G H J	22 F G H J	28 F G H J	34 F G H J	40 F G H J
5 A B C D	11 A B C D	17 A B C D	23 A B C D	29 A B C D	35 A B C D	

TEST 4	6 F G H J	12 F G H J	18 F G H J	24 F G H J	30 F G H J	36 F G H J
1 A B C D	7 A B C D	13 A B C D	19 A B C D	25 A B C D	31 A B C D	37 A B C D
2 F G H J	8 F G H J	14 F G H J	20 F G H J	26 F G H J	32 F G H J	38 F G H J
3 A B C D	9 A B C D	15 A B C D	21 A B C D	27 A B C D	33 A B C D	39 A B C D
4 F G H J	10 F G H J	16 F G H J	22 F G H J	28 F G H J	34 F G H J	40 F G H J
5 A B C D	11 A B C D	17 A B C D	23 A B C D	29 A B C D	35 A B C D	

I hereby certify that I have truthfully identified myself on this form. I understand that the consequences of falsifying my identity include cancellation of my scores.

Your Signature

Today's Date

SIDE 1

A NAME, ADDRESS, AND TELEPHONE

Last Name | First Name | MI (Middle Initial)

House Number and Street

City | State | ZIP Code

Area Code / Number

ACT

P.O. BOX 168, IOWA CITY, IOWA 52243

MATCHING INFORMATION

Enter the information in blocks B, C, and D, EXACTLY as it appears on your test center admission ticket, even if any part of this information is missing or incorrect. Blacken the corresponding ovals. Leave block E blank unless you are given special instructions.

B FIRST FIVE LETTERS OF LAST NAME

C SOCIAL SECURITY NUMBER (OR ACT ID NUMBER)

D DATE OF BIRTH

Month | Day | Year

Jan. Feb. Mar. Apr. May Jun. July Aug. Sep. Oct. Nov. Dec.

E

If the information on your test center admission ticket is complete and correct, put down your pencil and wait for further instructions.

If any corrections are necessary, complete ONLY those blocks below for which the information on your test center admission ticket is INCOMPLETE or INCORRECT. Leave the other blocks blank.

F NAME CORRECTION

Last Name | First Name | MI

G SOCIAL SECURITY NUMBER CORRECTION

H DATE OF BIRTH CORRECTION

Month | Day | Year

Jan. Feb. Mar. Apr. May Jun. July Aug. Sep. Oct. Nov. Dec.

I HIGH SCHOOL CODE CORRECTION

You may wish to remove this sample answer sheet from the book to use in a practice test session.

SIDE 2

BOOKLET NUMBER

1	1	1	1	1	1
2	2	2	2	2	2
3	3	3	3	3	3
4	4	4	4	4	4
5	5	5	5	5	5
6	6	6	6	6	6
7	7	7	7	7	7
8	8	8	8	8	8
9	9	9	9	9	9
0	0	0	0	0	0

FORM

BE SURE TO BLACKEN THE CORRECT FORM OVAL.

◯ 8939B

TEST 1

	10 F G H J	20 F G H J	30 F G H J	40 F G H J	50 F G H J	60 F G H J	70 F G H J
1 A B C D	11 A B C D	21 A B C D	31 A B C D	41 A B C D	51 A B C D	61 A B C D	71 A B C D
2 F G H J	12 F G H J	22 F G H J	32 F G H J	42 F G H J	52 F G H J	62 F G H J	72 F G H J
3 A B C D	13 A B C D	23 A B C D	33 A B C D	43 A B C D	53 A B C D	63 A B C D	73 A B C D
4 F G H J	14 F G H J	24 F G H J	34 F G H J	44 F G H J	54 F G H J	64 F G H J	74 F G H J
5 A B C D	15 A B C D	25 A B C D	35 A B C D	45 A B C D	55 A B C D	65 A B C D	75 A B C D
6 F G H J	16 F G H J	26 F G H J	36 F G H J	46 F G H J	56 F G H J	66 F G H J	
7 A B C D	17 A B C D	27 A B C D	37 A B C D	47 A B C D	57 A B C D	67 A B C D	
8 F G H J	18 F G H J	28 F G H J	38 F G H J	48 F G H J	58 F G H J	68 F G H J	
9 A B C D	19 A B C D	29 A B C D	39 A B C D	49 A B C D	59 A B C D	69 A B C D	

TEST 2

	8 F G H J K	16 F G H J K	24 F G H J K	32 F G H J K	40 F G H J K	48 F G H J K	56 F G H J K
1 A B C D E	9 A B C D E	17 A B C D E	25 A B C D E	33 A B C D E	41 A B C D E	49 A B C D E	57 A B C D E
2 F G H J K	10 F G H J K	18 F G H J K	26 F G H J K	34 F G H J K	42 F G H J K	50 F G H J K	58 F G H J K
3 A B C D E	11 A B C D E	19 A B C D E	27 A B C D E	35 A B C D E	43 A B C D E	51 A B C D E	59 A B C D E
4 F G H J K	12 F G H J K	20 F G H J K	28 F G H J K	36 F G H J K	44 F G H J K	52 F G H J K	60 F G H J K
5 A B C D E	13 A B C D E	21 A B C D E	29 A B C D E	37 A B C D E	45 A B C D E	53 A B C D E	
6 F G H J K	14 F G H J K	22 F G H J K	30 F G H J K	38 F G H J K	46 F G H J K	54 F G H J K	
7 A B C D E	15 A B C D E	23 A B C D E	31 A B C D E	39 A B C D E	47 A B C D E	55 A B C D E	

TEST 3

	6 F G H J	12 F G H J	18 F G H J	24 F G H J	30 F G H J	36 F G H J
1 A B C D	7 A B C D	13 A B C D	19 A B C D	25 A B C D	31 A B C D	37 A B C D
2 F G H J	8 F G H J	14 F G H J	20 F G H J	26 F G H J	32 F G H J	38 F G H J
3 A B C D	9 A B C D	15 A B C D	21 A B C D	27 A B C D	33 A B C D	39 A B C D
4 F G H J	10 F G H J	16 F G H J	22 F G H J	28 F G H J	34 F G H J	40 F G H J
5 A B C D	11 A B C D	17 A B C D	23 A B C D	29 A B C D	35 A B C D	

TEST 4

	6 F G H J	12 F G H J	18 F G H J	24 F G H J	30 F G H J	36 F G H J
1 A B C D	7 A B C D	13 A B C D	19 A B C D	25 A B C D	31 A B C D	37 A B C D
2 F G H J	8 F G H J	14 F G H J	20 F G H J	26 F G H J	32 F G H J	38 F G H J
3 A B C D	9 A B C D	15 A B C D	21 A B C D	27 A B C D	33 A B C D	39 A B C D
4 F G H J	10 F G H J	16 F G H J	22 F G H J	28 F G H J	34 F G H J	40 F G H J
5 A B C D	11 A B C D	17 A B C D	23 A B C D	29 A B C D	35 A B C D	

I hereby certify that I have truthfully identified myself on this form. I understand that the consequences of falsifying my identity include cancellation of my scores.

Your Signature

Today's Date